Egyptian Sepulchres And Syrian Shrines: Including A Visit To Palmyra...

Emily Anne Beaufort Smythe Strangford (viscountess)

EGYPTIAN SEPULCHRES

AND

SYRIAN SHRINES.

O

EGYPTIAN SEPULCHRES

AND

SYRIAN SHRINES,

INCLUDING

A VISIT TO PALMYRA.

By EMILY A. BEAUFORT
(VISCOUNTESS STRANGFORD),
AUTHOR OF 'THE EASTERN SHORES OF THE ADRIATIC.'

NEW EDITION.

London:
MACMILLAN AND CO.
1874.

LONDON.
PRINTED BY WILLIAM CLOWES AND SONS,
STAMFORD STREET AND CHARING CROSS.

TO

R. E. B.

MY FRIEND AND SISTER,

WHO SHARED IN EVERY SCENE DESCRIBED IN THESE PAGES,

AND WITH WHOSE KIND ASSISTANCE THEY WERE WRITTEN,

THIS BOOK

IS AFFECTIONATELY DEDICATED.

PREFACE.

CIRCUMSTANCES having rendered change of scene and climate imperatively necessary for my sister and myself, we hastily determined, at the close of the year 1858, to leave England for Egypt, believing that we should there find an endless store of deeply interesting subjects for thought and study, unfatiguing travelling, and no society : our hopes of the two former were more than realised, but solitude it is less certain to obtain on the now fashionable and crowded Nile. I had no presumptuous intention of writing an account of our travels over such well-trodden ground, but, when I found that our long residence in the mountains of the Lebanon and at Jerusalem, as well as the unusual visit we had made to Palmyra, had given us opportunities of observation that did not fall to the lot of every traveller in those countries, I could not but wish to share our experiences with the public. Since that, the horrible Syrian war having fixed the attention of England for some time upon that unfortunate country, I have been glad to add my small offering towards appeasing the general desire for further information.

It is impossible for any one who has no personal experience of it, to understand the physical difficulties and impediments under which one's journals, and notes, are written amidst the fatigues of such travelling : and mine have had the further disadvantage of being re-written in a foreign land, without books or help of any kind. My work is, therefore, only a faithful, unornamented record of what we saw and heard ; the scholar will learn nothing by it save a few facts which I have recorded in hopes of his drawing those deductions from them of which I am myself incapable. I have, in fact, written chiefly for those who, compelled to stay at home, like to draw their chairs to the cheerful coal-fire, to shut out the grey sky and dripping rain of England, and to follow in fancy the footsteps of those who have enjoyed the realities of travel. I not only love to share my pleasure, but I earnestly trust that many may be incited to similar enterprise, by my showing them with what ease and security ladies may travel, even alone, in those countries which have been frequently supposed to be open only to strong and energetic men. In this hope I have endeavoured to supply them with some practical information as to routes, points of interest, and other details gathered from our own experience.

The chapter on Thebes may be useful to those travellers who cannot afford time enough to study the subject for themselves in deeper and more important works. That on ancient Jerusalem contains notices of some facts and recent discoveries which bear on the topography of the ancient City,—for which I am indebted to an able and intelligent gentleman, Signor Pierotti, Captain of Engineers in the Sardinian army, who is now Architect to the Pasha of Jerusalem,—an office which has afforded him several opportunities of studying ancient remains accidentally brought to light; the results of this study, on which he has been engaged for six years, will be found in his admirable plan of Jerusalem, published in Paris,—a small and rough sketch of which I have given upon the map that accompanies this book.

I have endeavoured to give the names of places in phonetic spelling, or, at least, in spelling more in accordance with the habits of English ears and lips than the now often-adopted rule laid down by Sir William Jones,—as experience has proved to me how very rarely names so written are pronounced by travellers with even an approximation to the Arabic; and, therefore, in the hope of making my book practically useful to them, I have preferred this to attempting to follow the other, perhaps more accurate, but, as I have found, generally unsuccessful plan.

VALENCIA, *April* 1861.

CONTENTS.

EGYPTIAN SEPULCHRES

AND

SYRIAN SHRINES.

EGYPTIAN SEPULCHRES

AND

SYRIAN SHRINES.

———◦◦◦———

CHAPTER I.

FOG AND SUNSHINE.

A DENSE wet fog, varying from every shade of yellow to brown, lasting with few intermissions for about three weeks, and ten days of heavy frost, during which, however, there were some rare glimpses of the sun, which enabled us to distinguish at a hundred yards off the skeletons of that black species of tree peculiar to Hyde Park,—such was our preparation for a draught of warm, delicious air, heavily laden with the scent of orange-blossoms which, seven days after we left London, stole in at our cabin window as we dropped anchor in Valetta Harbour, at one o'clock on the morning of the 1st of December, 1858. A few hours more and we were basking in the hot sun under the orange-trees, thankful for *limonade à la neige*, and forgetting the black bricks of London among the magnificent marbles of the church of the Knights Hospitallers of St. John of Jerusalem, and in the enjoyment of the kindness and hospitality of cordial friends at Malta. Still a few days more of the same cloudless blue sky and unruffled sea, and we landed on the dirty quay of Alexandria on the 10th of December. A boat and a janissary had been considerately sent to deliver us from the crowd of loud-voiced Indian passengers, and to gratify our impatience to tread the soil of old Egypt, though we only exchanged one scene of noisy confusion for another, as we were greeted by a mass of screaming Arabs, in and out of the water, each tumbling and fighting in order to gain possession of one member of the party, for the benefit of his donkey, vehicle, or hotel; and glad enough we were to mount into the carriage prepared by our stout,

B

grave, silver-sticked janissary, and to settle into a good hotel in the Grande Place. Here we found it nearly impossible to do anything but look out of the window at the motley crowd, which filled that baking hot, sandy place, with men of every colour of skin and garment that the most vivid imagination could conceive. Arabs of every tribe in Africa, from Morocco to Egypt, and from Abyssinia and Dongola to the Delta; Syrians, Turks, Greeks, and Italians; dozens of open carriages in every degree of shabbiness, driven by black Nubians in their white gowns, called *sudeyree*, with some bright-coloured stuff wound round the head for a turban, thrashing their fiery black horses; strings of tall, dust-coloured camels, slowly carrying their burdens of stones, winding round corners, while every one waits for the file to pass, or pushing their long necks over the heads of the passers-by; hundreds of donkeys, each with a horrid-looking goat-skin filled with water on his back, the four legs sticking up into the air, with an uncomfortable dead-alive look; more donkeys still, each carrying a snow-white oval-shaped balloon, with a huge flapping canary-coloured leather boot at each side—these are women, as you may know by the unceasing, shrill, screaming chatter which comes from under the white garment (called an *eezâr*), to which the donkey-driver never seems to pay the slightest attention;—Turks, Greeks, and Egyptian gentlemen, in various degrees of semi-costume, but all agreeing in the invariable red tarboosh, mounted on fine but small horses, sometimes richly caparisoned; and lastly, handsome European carriages, always preceded by a running saïs (who is really necessary to clear a path through the crowd), dressed in graceful white robes, with red or dark blue silk sashes, and sometimes a long stick—the carriages containing ladies dressed in the newest French fashion, or in black silk *hābarahs*, with white muslin veils across the face, leaving nothing to be seen but large sparkling black eyes painted with kohhl. As Arabs always appear to be in a violent passion when they speak, and they are endless talkers, it is not possible to describe the noise that rose to our windows from the Place, nor how harsh, shrill, and intensely guttural the various languages of Africa and Turkey sounded to our English ears.

The noise without seemed to us pretty well balanced by the confusion we immediately fell into within; ladies travelling alone were certainly a legitimate prey to the hosts (I use the word advisedly) of dragomans, old and young, experienced and inexperienced, from the master of eight or ten languages to the stammerer in all but one; natives of every country within three thousand miles, and of every degree of intelligence or stupidity, who obtruded themselves on our notice, at all hours of the day, walking into our *salon*, or, not finding us there, coming straight into our bedroom without knocking; as well as cooks and waiters, each with his packet of dirty, thumbed, faded, torn letters of recommendation, which each entreated us to read on the spot at once,—all these creatures besieging us one after another, all day and every day during the whole time we remained in Alexandria.

We found several kind, though new, friends in Alexandria, and were induced by their advice to change our plans and to take a boat at once, instead of waiting till we reached Cairo, which is by far the pleasantest plan; but we had fixed our minds upon securing a dragoman of whom we had heard much in England, Achmet Adgwa, and he would not separate himself from his own boat, or leave Alexandria until it was let to some one else; for the latter contingency we could not of course wait, and we therefore put an end to the hopes of all our besiegers and closed with him, after inspecting every boat on the Măh'moudieh Canal over and over again, until we were too glad to be obliged to decide finally. And a beautiful boat our *dahabieh* was; from first to last we thought her the best and most comfortable boat on the Nile, and only two were larger. She had six cabins: first a saloon, fifteen feet by twelve, containing two divans, fitted with presses underneath them along each side, two book-cases, and a large table; four sleeping cabins, large enough for comfortable washing apparatus; and a good-sized back cabin, which we used as a store-room, and a sitting-room for our maid. We had nine windows at each side of the dahabieh, with glass, green wooden shutters, and curtains; and plenty of shelves, cupboards, and drawers enough to house everything. We saw other dahabiehs, the interior of which were prettier and more tastefully fitted up than ours, but none were more comfortable, bright, and airy. In front of our saloon, on the lower deck, were two seats, and the table for the servants' dinner, and an enormous *goolleh* (a jar of porous clay used for filtering, from which the water was always deliciously fresh) enclosed in a lattice-work of wood prettily painted. On the upper deck we had a comfortable sofa on each side, and the raised skylight of the saloon made a table; there was, however, room for half-a-dozen tables besides. Beyond the mast, which is placed quite in the bow of the boat, the mysteries of cooking are conducted over a small stove, the sailors preparing their own food at a queer little fire made at one side of the mast, which, about twenty-four feet high itself, supported a lateen yard, 163 feet in length, slung on in a curiously clumsy manner, but which slewed about in the prettiest curves in a high wind. Our great sail was the largest on the river, and I never wearied of watching its graceful motions. There was a small sail on the little mast at the stern, and a platform over the stern cabin, where the sailors performed their ablutions at sunrise and sunset. The dahabiehs on the Nile are all very gaily painted, and have fanciful names, which some keep from year to year; ours we chose to change, and, after much consideration, we had the words *Wandering Maiden* painted on her sides—a name the appropriateness of which we found afforded much amusement among our fellow-travellers. We hoisted the British ensign at the stern; and a white fleur-de-lis on a dark blue ground floated from the end of the long yard, together with a very long streamer of red and white depending to the water, the best distinguishing mark at a long distance. This naming of their boat is an important affair among Nile travellers, and serves sometimes to bring out the odd fancies of people rather amusingly; some names have become hackneyed into cockneyism on the Nile, but certainly the "Ibis" or "Lotus" seems more appropriate as a name for such a nineteenth-century affair as a dahabieh, than one raked up from the ashes of a dead Pharaoh. The white bird that still flies over the Nile is a living, though degenerate, descendant of the sacred Ibis of ancient days, and the flower is said still to grow there: and we thought these names prettier than that of one gaily-painted boat we met floating down the river called *Sesortasen III.*! It was truly puzzling to imagine what that long-buried hero had to do with the blood-red banner of the Cross, or the French motto that floated from his (mast-) head.

Our crew consisted of the Reïs, or captain, the Mestâhmel, or steersman, fourteen sailors, and their cook-boy; besides which our dragoman had his own servant, a boy called 'Ali; and these, with our cook, our own maid, and German man-servant, made a complement of twenty-three persons on board the *Wandering Maiden.*

Two or three days were occupied in filling her with the stores required over and above what we had brought from Malta, and in getting the canteen, &c., in order; but we were rather glad of the delay, which enabled us to see the lions of Alexandria—the quays, the two harbours, Cleopatra's Needle (as it is absurdly called), and her fallen sister, and the various gates of the city, one or two of which are picturesque. Then we had several pleasant drives along the acacia-shaded roads all round Alexandria. Very pleasant they are, the trees forming a cool, green barrier on each side between the road and the sandy desert; and along the bank of the Mâh'moudïeh Canal, by the pretty villas of the European merchants, each with its luxuriant garden, throwing clusters and tangles of magnificent gorgeous-coloured creepers over the walls, such masses of scarlet poinsettias and convolvuli of all colours, with blossoms of four and five inches in diameter, so delightful and strange to English eyes. Here and there one comes to a small stone terrace built on the edge of the water, and shaded with bella-sombra or acacia trees; these are *kiosks*, where people come out from the city to lounge away the afternoons, smoking and drinking coffee or sherbet. One or two huge palaces are also to be seen, which presented no beauty externally; but we afterwards visited the Räs-e-teen Palace, belonging to Saïd Pasha, and built by Muhammed 'Ali, which stands on the north-east side of the principal harbour, that is, on the Island of Pharos, which is connected with the shore by the ancient causeway called the Heptastadium. The rooms are furnished with divans and ornamental tables of great delicacy and richness, but all entirely European, except some fine species of gold and silver damask on the Viceroy's couches, the *chefs-d'œuvre* of Constantinopolitan looms. The best thing in the palace are the parquet floors, which are of various woods inlaid with ivory and mother-of-pearl, exquisitely done, and different in each room; the palace is also worth visiting for the sake of the fine view from the balcony of the old harbour, Eunostus.

Another day we drove along the shady, sandy roads to see the Pillar erected in honour of the Emperor Diocletian, probably on his taking possession of the city of Alexandria, A.D. 296, which is vulgarly called Pompey's Pillar; and in returning we passed through an encampment of Bedoueen tents, which certainly did not realise any idea I had formed of them. " Black as the tents of Kedar" they were indeed, but far from "comely;" oblongs and squares of the darkest brown and black skins of rudely-tanned leather, with flat tops, and only from two-and-a-half to three feet high. Men and women, wild, dirty-looking, half-naked Arabs, were crawling in and out from under the tents, gathering up their dirtier rags, or attending to about a thousand black donkeys, goats, and sheep, which were standing in the encampment.

Sunday afforded us the opportunity of service in the very handsome English Church which the Alexandrians have lately erected, a privilege all the more valuable, as many a week was to elapse before we should enter another church; it is prettily built of white and pinkish stone, adorned with arcades and pilasters, and a semicircular apse. In the afternoon every road and street seemed filled with promenaders; but French fashion predominates, to the destruction of all orientalism or picturesqueness.

At last our preparations were completed, and we took up our abode on board the *Wandering Maiden*; one day more was allowed to elapse, on account of the Wednesday, a day of ill-luck, on which the sailors refused to commence a voyage; but on Thursday the 16th, at daylight, we started before a good breeze down the Mäh'-moudïeh Canal. About five P.M. we passed through the lock at Atfeh, and were at last floating on the bosom of the grand old Nile! I shall never forget that evening, when we slipped out of the long, narrow, high-banked canal on to the wide, swiftly-flowing, smooth river,—the low, flat banks made it seem even wider than it was, almost like a sea, and the setting sun gilded the mud-houses of the tarboosh-making town of Fouah opposite, brightening the palm-trees towering above the villages, and tipping the graceful white lateen sails of a score of khandjehs and little boats going down to Rosetta. We stayed on deck till it was quite dark, enjoying the new scene, and our last, for a long time, of fine weather; one or two tremendous downpours in Alexandria had warned us of what our fate might be, and from that evening, for eleven successive days, we had constant storms of rain and wind, the rain threatening to drown us as it leaked through deck, door, and window, and the wind making us pitch and roll until we were nearly sea-sick. Once, when looking at the magnificently blue sky in Alexandria, so new to English eyes, I made some remark to a gentleman residing there on its beauty: " Ah," he said, " you have not learned yet to *loathe* this cloudless sky! We have not had one drop of rain here since the middle of last February, and you cannot understand how one wearies, mind and body, of the changeless expanse, longing for the ever-varying clouds we think so beautiful, because we so seldom see them, and because they bring us so much refreshment and vigour." We had enough of them now, however; so much so that to some people our voyage to Cairo might have been tiresome, but to us it was not so. We were glad to rest after the long journey from England, and we had books in plenty; our boat dried in the first rays of sunshine, and sometimes, when the wind forced us to lie thumping on a bank, we managed to find a sheltered walk in the country, making acquaintance with castor-oil and gum-arabic trees, cotton-plants, and the ever-graceful palm-groves. Sometimes we examined the *shadoofs** and *sakiyehs*,† both on the banks of the river and in the fields, or we ventured into the tents and mud-huts of the

---

* The shadoof is the very simple machine used for lifting the water of the Nile up to the height of the bank: a man, almost naked and with his head uncovered, holds a long pole balanced horizontally on a perpendicular stick, with a palm leaf or wooden basket at one end and a weight at the other end; he dips the basket into the river and then throws it up expertly, making it empty itself into a hole or trough, cut to receive it, above his head. If the

fellaheen (from sing. *fellāh*), from whence we never failed to bring away many lively and unpleasant *souvenirs*. The men seemed to have nothing to do but to stand lounging about, leaving all the work of house and field to the women, whom we always found busy; they were lively and good-natured, though not by any means attractive in person or deportment. They wear but one garment, a long, dark-blue gown or chemise, thrown round the body in an untidy fashion, exposing generally the legs, always the arms, and sometimes the neck, but drawn over the head, and across the face, when any one is near. Their unkempt locks are thrown back and roughly plaited, their eyelids are painted black with kohl, and their grinning white teeth are set off with stripes or circles on the chin and forehead of blue tattooing. A large silver ring stuck through one nostril, earrings, a dirty silver bracelet or two on each arm, and generally one on each ankle, complete their costume, which is as ugly as it is scanty. I do not think I saw two women in Egypt, out of Cairo, whose appearance did not more or less disgust me. When we went near their huts they always invited us in, and generally insisted on shaking hands with us, laughing all the time, and expressing their wonder at our riches—the only reason they could devise for our putting on so many clothes one over another: and sometimes they would offer us their dhourra bread, or milk, or show us how they were grinding corn, between flat round stones, or making cheese by leaving the milk to drain through mats made of plaited palm-leaves; always asking about how they do the same things in the Howadji's country.

It is certainly a much less expensive plan to go from Alexandria at once by railroad to Cairo, and there engage your boat; since though you *may* reach Cairo in four days' sail, you may also occupy fourteen, as we did, and we heard of persons having been twenty-one days on the way! But at the same time you have the advantage of knowing your boat, and finding out her deficiencies before you come to the last place where you can buy stores, or get anything

---

bank is high, another or two more men stand above him with repetitions of the same contrivance.

† The sakiyeh is a huge wheel with earthen jars fixed all round it, which fill as they pass through the river, and empty themselves into a trough as they reach the top. It is turned by a couple of oxen, who pace round and round to the screeching, groaning music of the ungreased crank. This creak of the sakiyeh, with the eternal melancholy song of the shadoof men, half wail, half screech, is the true *sound of Egypt:* no hour nor half-hour passes without hearing one or the other, and the very name of the country brings the echo of it as distinctly into one's ears as the remembrance of the yellow sand, or of the broad river, floats before one's eyes.

altered or improved   and you have also some amusement and
pleasure in your voyage, while the line of rail is wholly uninteresting and ugly.   I contrived to find something for a sketch every
day, and doubtless there would have been plenty more subjects to
be found with better luck than the unusually bad weather we had.
For a sportsman I should think the boat much pleasanter than the
land journey ; as game is immensely more plentiful in the Delta
than above Cairo, and much less wild.   The sandbanks are covered
with thousands of wild geese and ducks, and there are wild boars
to be hunted in several localities.   If, however, people are likely to
weary of a long quiet voyage, it is better to go by railway, and
have the dahabieh sent up to Cairo to meet them, stipulating that
it *must* arrive within a certain number of days.   The dahabiehs are
decidedly better and nicer at Alexandria than at Cairo, but also
proportionably dearer.

At this time we were slowly tracking against head-winds; and at
Kefr-el-Aesh, where the railway crosses the Nile, the wind increased
so much that we were moored two whole days on the east bank.
On the second day, when we had lost all patience, and, in spite of
our dragoman's remonstrances, were going to insist on making an
attempt to shoot the opening left in the bridge now building for the
railway, an unexpected ally came to hand: the superintendent of
the station, Ismael Yousry Bey,—may his shadow never be less !—
arrived in a well-rowed boat alongside, saying, that on hearing there
were English ladies on board, he had come to see if we stood in
need of any assistance.   He assured us that it was quite impossible
to shoot the bridge, unless by the chance of an exactly favourable
wind.   "But," said he, "you English people always want to eat
dinner together on your Christmas-day, and you must be in Cairo
for that,— I will give you two hundred men to *pull* you through, if
you like it."   Of course we gladly accepted so obliging an offer, and
while his men went off with his orders, the Effendi sat chatting
in very good English with us, sipping his coffee and smoking his
shibouque.   He told us he had been educated at King's College,
London, and afterwards lived a year or two in Kent, and that the
English had been so kind to him, and made him so happy, that it
was an especial pleasure to have an opportunity of assisting any
English person who came to his country.

His pleasure was, however, frustrated; for, just as the men
were all ready, the wind, which had been unsteadily veering about
for the last hour or two, suddenly settled into the precisely right
point, and blew us through the opening with the Effendi on board,
and the two hundred workmen standing ready to assist on the

bridge, who, however, gesticulated, screamed, and shouted quite as much as if they had really been doing the business themselves.

Our good friend sent us in the evening some excellent milk and turkeys; on one of which, in consequence of the still unkind and cruel winds, we made our Christmas dinner, moored under a palm grove in the hot sun, the turkey stuffed with pistachio nuts and dates, and a " plum-pudding " of biscuit, citron, and dried apricots.

Two days afterwards, as I was watching the rich hues of the setting sun upon the sands and trees, I saw two small triangles, distinct and hard, on the western horizon, which my heart suddenly leaped up to greet: there were the Pyramids at last! I saw them many times afterwards, in various ways and at various times of day, but they never impressed me more than on that evening, painted in the exquisite lilac hues of sunset, yet golden-tipped, over the straight, flat green bank of the river, far away over line after line of sand—far away, standing sharp and clear against a background of coloured clouds.

CHAPTER II.

REAL LIFE IN DAY-DREAMS.

WE landed on the west bank, before we reached Boulak, on the morning of the 29th of December, scrambling over a forest of dirty boats to make our first essay upon the Arab saddles and Cairo donkeys: the latter are most excellent of their kind, as lively as they are small. The saddles are not uncomfortable; they are simply cushions mounted high on the donkey's back, with a round hump across them in front, and they are generally made of gay red leather, while the saddle-cloth is worked in colours with bands of cowrie-shells sewn on in strips: a charm, enclosed in a triangular silver box, is hung round the animal's neck.

Our road, which lay along a high causeway shaded with fine trees, brought us into the Esbeykiyeh, at the Shoobra corner, close to Shepheard's Hotel (where we entered the name and distinguishing flag of our boat in the Nile Howadji's book), and then went on to the English Consulate, and into the Turkish bazaars to buy sugar, sweetmeats, &c., which we wanted in the dahabieh.

Shall I here confess the truth? that my first view of Cairo absolutely disappointed me! During our second visit, when I came to know it better, I learned its full beauty and interest; and now I constantly wish that I could return there to gratify the unsatisfied feeling of not having had enough of its charms. One reads the result of every traveller's enthusiasm after he has had time to enjoy it and to think about it, and one's expectations thus become too highly exalted :—whatever it arose from, I certainly was just at first disappointed with the poorness and raggedness and want of solidity in the houses of Cairo. The gay wares in the wooden shops of the bazaars are bright enough, but the shops themselves are of rough, unpainted boards, uneven in size and height, and covered in from the sun with only ragged old palm-leaf mats, torn bits of carpet, and broken planks, "rags of rotten wood," which give one a feeling of squalor, not incompatible with its picturesqueness, perhaps all the more *mesquin* from its contrast with the variegated hues, like a brilliant flower-garden, of the crowd below. Then the contrast is continued between these wooden and mud-built houses and the beautiful public fountains; the water, enclosed in circular walls, roofed over with a sort of dome, flows into brazen mouth-pieces placed in compartments of exquisitely carved stone-work, divided by pilasters of coloured marbles with gilt capitals, and bordered with Arabic inscriptions in gilt letters, recounting the names of the benevolent Pashas who built them. Almost always in the courts of the mosque there are fountains open to the air; these are surrounded by a marble trough, with a wooden roof supported by pillars, very gaily painted, but tattered, torn, and dirty, under which the Moslems perform their ablution of face, hands, and feet all day long. Nor do the mosques strike one at first as handsome on the exterior; the high flat walls are unrelieved by window, column, or any architectural ornament, save one invariable line of cornice along the top of the wall, formed of simple pendentives of three bricks in the upper row, two bricks in the second, and one brick below these; simple as it sounds, its effect is very pretty, and even rich-looking. The mosque walls are always coloured in horizontal stripes of red or brown paint, roughly daubed along the courses of the stone, and the lively and handsome effect produced by it is wonderful.

The Esbeykiyeh is a very large irregular-shaped "*Place*," planted with a pleasantly-thick wood of orange, acacia, and many other trees, intersected with walks, and dotted round with wooden kiosks for the enjoyment of coffee, lemonade, and narghiles. The houses round the broad road might have made the Esbeykiyeh handsomer than most European *Places*, had any two of these buildings uniformity in height, colour, or kind; but they are so different, and mostly so shabby in exterior, that one loses all idea of the Esbeykiyeh being the Grande Place of a great city. Shepheard's Hotel and one of the Pasha's palaces occupy nearly all one side, but they are both of them ugly and common-looking buildings.

But whatever may be its shortcomings, when one's brains have become a little accustomed to the din, bustle, and noise of the streets, Cairo is essentially beautiful and charming; it seems as if one could never weary of the endless, ever-changing sights and sounds of the multitude who throng its ways (street is too western a term for them); a thousand times brighter and gayer than the

Grande Place at Alexandria, which seems tame after a single street
of Cairo.

Let us stand aside for ten minutes, while this fine old fellow with
a snow white beard, white and gold turban, a purple silk robe, and
dark red trousers, lays down his long shibouque, and weighs out
for us an oke of delicate rose-leaf *confiture* (having first held out
a little *dig* of two or three kinds on the end of his finger, for us
to taste!) and watch the crowd pushing by our donkey.   This
bazaar is for groceries, and the shops are heaped with loaves of
sugar of every hue except white, and palm-leaf baskets of dates,
dry and fresh, nuts of all kinds, spices, roasted Indian corn, figs,
olives, and innumerable sorts of dry sugar-stuff, pink, brown,
yellow, and white, in sticks and lumps, which the Arabs are
always eating; they are thoroughly nasty to our taste.   Every
shop is tenanted by a figure, rolled up cross-legged on the counter
in party-coloured robes and white turban, smoking and chatting
(or screaming rather) to their fellow shopmen; while the donkey-
boys in their dirty, ragged blue cotton shirts, and other idlers, sit
down to rest on the edge of the booth, and join in the conversation
right merrily.   The way is quite full, and the beggars demanding
" Baksheesh, howadji, baksheesh, ya sitt! " push by you as they go;
while every second minute a ragged Arab jingles his brazen cups,
and offers you fresh water out of a black goat-skin which he carries
under his arm, or a sherbet-seller bends down before you, while
the brass jar at his side spouts forth a stream of sweetened water or
lemonade into a cup, for which you pay two or three parás, if you
wish to taste its sickly sweetness.   A blind man is sure to stumble
over you, and a dozen women, entirely enveloped in white wrappers,
with a couple of holes for their eyes, stop to peep up under your
hat or to feel the texture of your dress, while you are intent upon
inspecting that Bey or this Effendi going by on a fine chestnut
horse, with a saddle-cloth splendid in gold embroidery, himself in
bright-coloured silks, satin, and cloth, smoking his long pipe as
he goes,—or this Turk of high degree, on a tall white donkey,
with bit and bridle made of strings of gold cord, hung thickly
with heavy gold sequins, and saddle of cherry-coloured velvet
embroidered in gold and pearls.   You are bending forward to
look at the jewels on his sword-sheath, when you suddenly see a
camel's ugly nose just over your own, and you start back while he
lazily pushes on, flattening you to the wall with his huge burden of
green fodder, or stones, or bales of calico.   In another minute half
a dozen men, carrying on their shoulders a deal box, daubed over
with red paint, saunter by, chanting a discordant song, and your

donkey-boy looks up with a grin, and says, "Dead man in there;" and you turn away to decline a quantity of sweetmeats in smoking hot pastry hastily thrust up to your mouth by a boy in rags, trying not to seem to see or hear the score of brown hands thrust out on whichever side you move your face, while the owners scream out "Baksheesh! baksheesh!" till you are glad to move on, though every third person assails you with the same wearying word as you pass.

We stayed in the bazaars till we were perfectly bewildered, and were glad to go back to our dahabieh, which had in the meantime moved to the palm-grove opposite Cairo, leaving the rest of our shopping to be accomplished on the following day, when we made acquaintance with a lady and gentleman who kindly offered to "keep company" with our boat, as we were strangers, and they were spending their fifth winter on the Nile. We moved on a little way the last day of the old year, stopping at sunset opposite the Island of Rhoda, and looking back at a view that few things of the kind can surpass. The vast city, studded with graceful domes and still more beautiful minarets, rises up loftily from the flat monotonous desert, partly placed on and partly backed by the bold white Mohkuttum cliffs, while at a little higher elevation the Mosque and Tomb of Muhammed 'Ali, with its white alabaster walls, dark blue roofs, and delicately-slight minarets, stands like a watchman guarding the city; in the foreground the river-bank is lined with large palaces, some white and some red, adorned with graceful arcades and handsome balconies, each with its own garden and orange-grove, meeting the gardens of Old Cairo and Rhoda. The forest of boats of every size and form, with brightly-painted masts, red and blue awnings, flags, and streamers, form a gay fringe to the wide grey river. On the other side, far away over the fields of green crops, and the wide expanse of desert-sand, the Pyramids raise their grave, calm, solemn forms, cutting sharply against the cloudless sky, clothed in strangely-beautiful sunset colours of violet and gold, all too gorgeous for any paint-box to depict.

We were joined the next morning by two dahabiehs; on the following day we overtook a third; while a fourth joined us two days after. The five boats made quite a pretty little fleet; and during the ten days that ensued of slow tracking, we found plenty of amusement in efforts and stratagems to outstrip each other; this, however, is against all ideas of propriety among the crew, and our Reïs invariably apologised to the other Reïses at sunset if we had gained any advantage over their boats during the day; which was rather exasperating to our feelings when we were chuckling over the accomplishment of a quarter of a mile beyond our neighbours. It is amazing how these great dahabiehs do get on in the tracking; although they go aground twelve times in a day, yet they absolutely float on in safety, when the men are walking all round them with the water reaching only just above their ankles; and sometimes so close to the banks, that one may touch the trees from the decks. They carry no ballast, in order to keep them light, and they require a directly fair wind to sail tolerably. We thought ourselves singularly unlucky in the strong head-winds, which blew perseveringly for ten successive days after we left Cairo, fearing that any long detention below Thebes would render our reaching the Second Cataract impossible under our three months' contract for the dahabieh. Our own boat was very heavy in tracking, though she outsailed all the others, and we were naturally anxious to benefit all we could by her virtues. Delicious as this Egyptian life was, we could not bear to think of being disappointed of seeing Nubia; and so we fretted from day to day about our progress, very unnecessarily as it turned out, and were not a little annoyed at our being obliged to put in at Beni Souef for provisions, while the rest of the little fleet took another passage for the sake of a short cut; but a favourable breeze sprang up in the night; we sped on, and in the morning could only just distinguish some of the red and white streamers of our disappointed companions behind us. The *Florence*, however, caught us up the next night, and we sailed on gallantly, with the pleasant little excitement of racing each other and enjoying the scenery of long low mountains of rugged shapes, at some distance from the river—blue and purple by day, pink and golden in the evenings—under the ever-cloudless sky. We passed Minyeh, with its pretty minarets and gardens—it is one of the prettiest towns on the Nile,—and reached Siout on the 15th of January.

Siout is chiefly remarkable for its many miles of roads, lifted up above the reach of the inundations by wide causeways; they are shaded by trees, and give one a fine idea of what can be effected by persevering labour. Beyond the town, the life in whose good bazaars is thoroughly amusing, are the catacombs of the ancient Lycopolis, the City of Wolves; they are very extensive, excavated in the side of the Libyan mountains, with high vaulted roofs, and the walls covered with figures and hieroglyphics, which are, however so much faded and defaced as to be nearly indecipherable; one vault is still pretty, with gold stars thickly painted on a bright blue ground. They are worth a visit, from their size and as the traveller's introduction to hieroglyphics; but perhaps the labour of mounting is best repaid by the very fine view seen from the entrance to the largest catacomb, called the *Stabl Antar* by the natives. The town, with its twenty-six minarets, stands in a rich plain of meadow, intersected with canals, and shaded with lofty trees; as far as the eye can reach, north and south, it is all the same bright and beautiful green, but on the east it is bounded by the broad Nile; while beyond that is the yellow desert to the foot of the Arabian mountains, fading away in the blue distance.

We rode back through a pretty Mooslim cemetery; each tomb, arched over in stone or stucco, and shaped like a huge bolster, stood in its own plantation of acacia-trees, and frequently a fountain, for the benefit of weary passengers, is added to the little building; most of the handsomer tombs being walled in and roofed over. The wind was blowing a gale, and the sun was very hot, so hot that we were right glad to get back to our shady cabin, although during the night before and the night after the thermometer showed some slight frost! The mornings, indeed, till an hour or two after sunrise, were always very cold and fresh until quite the end of the month; but the cold is never disagreeable, even when the thermometer is alarmingly near 32°. Travellers, however, should always be provided with warm clothing, although after half an hour of sunshine one forgets one has ever been chilly.

My idea of the Nile before I came to Egypt had been one of flat, shallow banks, and a palm-tree or a mud-hut here and there, such as it is in the Delta: I was therefore most agreeably surprised with the beauty and variety of the banks after Siout, which I, for one, never wearied of watching. On one side or the other there are *always* hills at no great distance from the river-bank; sometimes the Libyan chain, in various tones of grey, shading into lilacs and purples at sunset, advanced on the western shore, or receded into delicate blue distance; more often the Arabian hills mounted up in cliffs, sometimes very boldly and grandly from the water, leaving only a strip of castor-oil plants or a narrow track for passengers. And their colour was always so charming: a peculiar rosy yellow, more nearly resembling—if I may be allowed to use a very unpoetical simile—fresh Cheshire cheese than anything else I know—a colour that forms the prettiest contrast to the fresh cool greens of the banks, and to the glorious gentian-blue sky; it darkens in the strongly-marked lines of stratification, and in the abrupt, rugged ravines, into indescribably-rich shades of yellow brown. These cliffs are dotted all over with caves cut out of old by the monks of the Thebaid. Though I thought them beautiful on first landing in Egypt, I came to love the graceful palm-trees more and more every day; singly or in groves, they are always lovely and elegant, and even the most matter-of-fact mind could scarcely help indulging, I think, in a day-dream of fairy-land delights while reposing in the pleasant shade of a grove of fine palms waving in the cool sunset breeze.

Then the villages, though entirely built of mud, are not ugly when seen from the river, for the Nile mud is of a brown yellow, which glows in the sunshine, and looks rich in the shade; and the flat-roofed houses are often topped with white stones in a way that makes them appear something like fortifications from a distance. Each village has scores of tall dovecots, the mud walls of which are striped with whitewash, and thatched with Indian corn-stalks; they are quaint and almost pretty objects, while the minarets are always more or less elegant. These and the palm or acacia-groves, with the endless variety of picturesque groups in bright-coloured costumes, white turbans, and long pipes, form a constant succession of dissolving views passing into one another, with some fresh and interesting, though always changing, charm as one glides slowly by.

A complete change, indeed, from all European commonplace is this river-life—more especially in the proximity of those around one which is so strange and new at first;—it is not as on board ship, where the confusion of loud and inharmonious voices only gives one a sense of discomfort and isolation; here the voices are close to one, by day and by night, separated by only a thin plank or a glass from one's ear, yet are neither inharmonious nor disturbing. Then the faces are not merely individually strangers, but of an unaccustomed kind; while the scenery changes all the accustomed current of one's ideas with the many new interests and new sights on each side, leaving scarcely a trace of the every-day thoughts that have been one's companions for years past. You scarcely realise *what* you were and *where* only three or four weeks previously, until the silent darkness of night, hiding the engrossing sights of the present, enables you to think back into the past; even then the water ripples, gently murmuring, past your pillow—Mooslim prayers are heard in whispers on the other side of a plank, within a few inches of your ear—Arab snores come from un-English noses—jackals bark, shriek, and howl on the shore,—and one starts up to peer out of the window, so strangely close to one's face, whence one sees wild-looking Arabs crouching round a crackling fire of dhourra-sticks, and the glorious clear moon shining through palm-trees, unlike anything one has ever seen before but in the fairy-land of a bright dream.

As we every day improved our Arabic by a few more words, we soon began to try to string them together into sentences; these we bestowed chiefly on our Reïs, Abou Nour by name, and less they invariably afforded him the greatest delight and amusement. Our Reïs, who was as good as he was handsome—unlike nearly all the other Reïses, whom we saw sitting smoking or sleeping all day long, and only giving an occasional order with slow and solemn gravity, seldom *doing* anything themselves—was up and about from daylight to dark, and all night too if we were sailing, seldom taking more than an hour's sleep, and even then having one ear open for every sound of difficulty in the management of the vessel. And what he did he did with an active energy very different from the sailors, who seemed only to move each muscle as little as they could possibly help; while Abou Nour flew about here and there and everywhere, scrambling like a cat up and down the rigging, and dashing into the water, clothes, turban and all, pushing the dahabieh from the shore or shoals, guiding the little felucca with the towing-rope, which he often held in his teeth while his hands were employed in rowing or dragging the vessel athwart the stream by his own powerful strength, always with the same merry laugh and happy face, and a joke or an affectionate slap for each one of his sailors, who seemed to be as fond of him as soldiers are of a successful general. Sometimes he assembled them in a group, and gave them a solemn lecture or a scolding with uplifted hands. Then when an hour of quiet sailing came, with no sudden turns of the river, and a tolerably deep channel, they would collect on deck at the stern, lying or lounging round him while he laid aside his pipe, and with the eloquent gestures of the Arab, recounted to them some adventure, or told them a long story which elicited rapturous applause; and sometimes we used to laugh too, his face was so infectiously merry, and the changes of his voice so expressive. But their greatest delight of all was when I sketched his portrait, or that of one of the sailors. How eagerly they came to see it, and then how merrily they laughed over the grinning brown faces and white turbans on the paper, telling me approvingly it was " taïb keteer," or " quīyis " (very good and pretty), and then each one begging to be drawn too. Sir G. Wilkinson says " that no modern Egyptians, of any rank, can understand pictures;" but our experience everywhere was of the liveliest interest in all we showed them: our Reïs would point out immediately which of my portraits was most like, and would catch at the accident in the dress or attitude for the sake of which I had taken them; while of the passing dahabiehs or kandjehs which I sketched almost daily, he was always ready to point out any want of proportion, or to detect what ropes I had omitted, or how the sails had been changed when she had passed too quickly for me to seize them accurately. A friend afterwards

c

photographed him for us; but Abu Nour had specially prepared himself in his gala attire—a very handsome one it was, of Damascus silks and embroidery—and he was grievously disappointed at finding his rich dress metamorphosed into one dull grey colour: even the gilt frame did not reconcile him to the shadowy picture, and whenever he saw it afterwards he always signified to me how much he preferred my rough coloured sketches. He sat like a statue to have it done, only rolling his eyes in a way that made them come out *no how* in the photograph; and when it was finished he was allowed, as a reward, to put his head under the curtain of the photographing instrument: I was standing in focus at the time, and it was worth anything to see his face of astonishment and hear his " Mashallah! Wullah!" when he saw me standing upside down! He was too intelligent to think it magic, but I am sure he made many a long story about it afterwards. How much I wish I had still my sketch of him, in his beautiful white and coloured silk vest, his long khaftan of rich brown satin bound with black braid, his white turban embroidered in yellow silk, and over all the wide blue cotton shirt, which was his badge of Reïs-hood. He was physician-general also to the sailors, and bound up their scratches or gave them their physic, whenever any little accident took place, as tenderly as a nurse (though, to be sure, the Arabs have barbarous remedies for their maladies—such as dipping a cut finger into boiling oil, and setting fire to gunpowder on a wound); and we always saw him go to comfort any of them when they were in trouble, giving them affectionate squeezes or shakes, or long consolatory conversations.

Achmet told us that the Reïs was under a vow of virtue, which bound him to abstain from all lies or dishonesty, or from using bad words; to have but one wife, and to take no notice of any other woman, &c., &c.; and that he had kept it most religiously, punishing himself by two or three days of rigid fasting and abstinence from smoking (a terrible privation to an Egyptian), if he had failed by any shortcoming: and no one could be more steadily exact in the performance of his prayers, five times every day, during which, except occasionally in the telling of his beads, which is only a rapid repetition of the name of Allah, he seemed to be absorbed in the most earnest devotion. Some people object to this and call it fanatic, but we felt it far more satisfactory and pleasant to have the services of a conscientious man, acting steadily up to his own light, even though that light were darkness.

Our pleasant course was now varied for two days with sandstorms, which, to use the mildest expression, are very particularly disagreeable. We moored for one afternoon, because we could not see 300 yards before us; but the wind lulling at sunset, we sailed on slowly by the light of a magnificent full moon (such moonlight as one has in Egypt!) until we neared "*the* mountain," of which the Nile sailors have so much terror, Jebel-ez-Zaïd; it is a very wicked mountain, of sudden blasts and gusts that make one's sails seem bewitched, and which baffle the most expert of crews. Gliding on smoothly with the wind behind us, it was startling to be suddenly met by a violent blast ahead, and the great lateen sail in an instant reversed with a shock that sent one's books spinning off the tables; but we held on steadily, the Reïs calling up every sailor, and himself taking up a perilous situation on the long yard, where no one else would venture; while Achmet stood watching and counting the minutes between the blasts, and, as each one came whizzing past, saying his prayers with a very remarkable rapidity, and calling on the Sheikh-ez-Zaïd, the Mooslim saint to whom the mountain is dedicated, to assist us out of the difficulty. Achmet counselled mooring, but we insisted upon trying to proceed, until, finding that in four hours we had not made a yard, we gave it up at midnight, remaining on deck, however, for the amusement of watching the five dahabiehs of our little fleet, which we had not seen for two days, and two or three native boats, come sailing smoothly up in the bright moonlight, unconscious of what was awaiting them, and calling out to us to know "what we were stopping for," while, one after another, each was seized by the blast, and taken aback, and we heard the exclamations of astonishment and wrath proceeding from them. Early the next morning we left them all behind, passing pretty Negâdeh in a sandstorm that filled eyes, mouth, and nose with unpleasant pertinacity, descending upon one suddenly, like a December fog in London, obscuring everything in a thick brown cloud, penetrating everywhere. We came into Luxsor on Friday morning, the 21st, but—alas for our racing triumphs!—the *second*, by one hour, in the little fleet, for the *Selima* had passed us in the night, and we had only the consolation of hearing that the three other boats were "nowhere." We had been ten days doing the seventy-seven miles between Cairo and Beni-Souef, chiefly tracking, and now we had sailed the three hundred and seventy-eight miles between Beni-Souef and Thebes in only ten more.

We expected great delight in our first view of Luxsor and Thebes; but the river was already too low, and Karnak must be seen in detail first to be appreciated at a distance; nor could the Sitting Colossi of the plain be seen at all. We had determined to follow Sir G. Wilkinson's advice of seeing the temples of Nubia before examining Karnak, and accordingly devoted ourselves to the bundle of letters

we found awaiting our arrival; but an invitation to join a party
going to see Karnak by the light of a full moon, such as we then
had, was not to be resisted, and we started at 8.30, six of us, on donkeys, attended by sailors and donkey-boys *ad libitum* to guard us
from jackals, and headed by the obliging Consular Agent Mustapha.
The more fortunate chance would be to have a fine moonlight view
after becoming well-acquainted with the plan of the ruins; but even
under the disadvantage of seeing what we did not properly understand, it was a scene that impressed itself upon the mind for ever : the
deep black shadows concealing much of the brokenness and decay,
and the splendid light illuminating, with a sort of tender glory, the
massive columns, immense pylons, and slender obelisks.   By this
light it was only and altogether beautiful and lovely ; but one needs
the sunshine and blue sky to bring out the stupendous proportions
of these unrivalled ruins.   Perhaps few spots on earth could be
more solemnly beautiful than the centre aisle in the Great Hall,
with the six gigantic columns between the sixty-one attendant
columns on either side, the moonlight piercing through the open
clerestory of delicate tracery against the dark sky, turning the
obelisk, ninety-two feet high, at one end of the aisle, into a silver
needle, rising with a stern grace against the ruined temple behind
it ; and at the other end illuminating a single column, standing
alone in the centre of a vast square, between giant pylons and huge
walls, with its capital complete, its shaft uninjured, seeming almost
livingly sorrowful in its loneliness.

The howling of the jackals gave a wild dreariness to the scene,
but we very unwillingly remounted our donkeys and turned back
towards Luxsor, through the avenue of sphinxes, which, broken and
defaced into almost shapeless masses by daylight, became impres-
sively grand by moonlight.   What must have been the magnificence of Karnak when all these splendid avenues of sphinxes were
still perfect in their mighty limbs, leading up to the still more
magnificent walls !

At midnight we glided smoothly on, feeling on the morrow glad
to rest after even that slight view of Karnak, and glad to fall back
into the quite sameness of Nile-life: a sweet calm monotony it
is, but yet a monotony of pleasant little changes—dream-like
and hazy—a waking day-dream without the sudden kaleidoscope
changes of a sleeping dream.   From day to day, from night to night,
you sail calmly on, watching the golden and rosy-tinted mountains
advancing or receding on either side, offering indeed but little
variety of form, yet of colours so lovely that I think no Egyptian
travellers say half enough about them; watching the same brown

villages with their minarets and dovecots, and their luxuriant acacia-groves; the same ever-varying yet ever-graceful palms; the same picturesque Arab boats, with their burdens of dates, cotton, or donkeys; the same wide, smooth, rapid river, dark brown in one's hand, yet blue in the distance—a deep grey blue,—contrasting finely with the invariably bright and cloudless sky, broken only by the flocks of birds, which, hour after hour, rise whirling and wheel-ing in the air in gracefully-curving lines—vultures, flying singly at intervals like minute-guns—millions of wild geese and ducks—hoopoes, hopping about on the banks, with their handsome brown coroneted heads — zikzags, with their pretty black and white plumage—the snow-white ibis, like a winged star, dazzling in the sunshine—more rarely, rosy lines of lovely flamingoes, worth coming a long way to see: and from first to last the tiny black and white "Solomon's bird," with its yellow cheeks—the robin of the Nile—hopping about the deck, picking up crumbs from one's hand, and saying all manner of pleasant things with its little graceful nods.

Dreamy, too, is the Nile-life, because we see then with our real eyes the scenes we have all thought of till we fancy we have already seen them; now in flesh and blood, yet dreamily still, they stand before us—Joseph talking to his brethren in the field, or the sons of Jacob journeying with their asses and their sacks of provender to buy corn in Egypt; Boaz sitting at the gate, and saying, "Ho, such a one! turn aside, sit down here!" the two women grinding at one mill, and the unmuzzled ox treading out the corn; Rebekah carry-ing her pitcher on her head, or "letting it down upon her hand" to give drink to the wayfarer; Rachel coming out at even to water the flock; and the blessed Virgin Mother sitting on the ass, holding the young child in her lap, while Joseph, staff in hand, leads them on.

No one seeking much excitement, or any exercise beyond walking, should come to the Nile; for it is altogether calm and dreamy. You look on at life ever moving before your eyes—you hear ceaseless sounds of men on the banks, women washing at the river's edge, melancholy Arab songs droned out, donkeys continually braying, and the hoarse scream of the wild geese over your head; but you yourself lie dreamily and silently on your divan, and see it all pass by like pictures in a diorama. And yet you never feel shut up or inactive, for you know you are moving on and on: everything changes around you each hour, and all the while your mind wanders away—now to the far south before you, where you fancy you must come at last to the younger days of the great river you have been passing up so long; then back to the tideless sea into which you saw him pouring weeks ago—now among the nineteenth century of travellers like yourself; then back to the countless generations in the almost infinite history of Egypt. And so you look up at the everlasting hills on each side of you, that stood there, already old and timeworn, before the faintest light dawned on historic truths, or even poetic fables, that your furthest-seeking perspicacity can discover,—and you are so weary with the long search that you only care to lie still and think.

Then slowly sinks the sun, and evening closes in with a delicious fresh sweetness, which you must cross the Mediterranean to feel. The boat is generally moored early to the bank, where the sailors light a fire of Indian-corn-stalks, and immediately fall asleep in every imaginable and unimaginable attitude around it, or in heaps on the deck; voices of prayer come from the next village, until all is hushed but the howling and whining of dogs and jackals, and generally half-a-dozen frogs holding an evening gossip in stentorian ¡ croaks. A few hours after you hear the Reïs' beads pattering on the deck as he kneels at his prayers, and with the first rosy glow on the beautiful starry sky all the crew are up and the sails are hoisted, and the flags stream behind you; or the men jump ashore, and your pretty boat goes lazily thumping along the bank as the file of sailors pull her slowly on, only stopping to make a rush at some neighbouring sugar-canes, which they greedily devour all the day after, or to buy the more important " leben " (milk) for your own breakfast.

Perhaps the sound *most* peculiar to Egypt, rivalling even the groans of the sākiyah and the shadoof, because it is so often close to your ear, is the " Hay-a-lee-sāh! Hay-a-lee-sāh!"—the emphasis on the last or last but one syllable according as the action of the moment is quick or slow—sung by the sailors in chorus: a sound which I shall always consider, however rough in itself, as some of the sweetest music I have ever heard. I never got a satisfactory explanation of the words: our dragoman told us that Leesa was a daughter of the Prophet whose aid they invoked; but I have reason to believe this was nonsense. Sometimes, but seldom, they called on other saints—usually only in some locality especially dedicated to a dead saint whose wely was in the neighbourhood, or to some Fakir or hermit living there—and sometimes of an evening the sailors would sing a long descriptive song, the translations of which were always very vague indeed. It is pleasant to have a good singing crew, but they are generally engaged for Pashas' private boats; and if your own is a very small boat you are apt to wish a crocodile stuck in their throats before they have half done a long song; but if you keep their singing within bounds it is sweet and harmonious, and an agreeable break upon the monotony of the downward drifting.

We met with but one instance of dishonesty on the Nile among the sailors: we left our things lying about all day, both in the cabins and on the deck; we dropped small coins on the floor; we were out whole days, leaving the Reïs in charge—though any of the cabins might be entered by the windows unseen from the others—and we never missed so much as a pin: every single thing was picked up and restored with a simple straightforwardness that showed it was their natural habit. I heard the same from every one else on the Nile: your dragoman may eat up your stores—the rats may abscond with your dearest treasures, and the mice may breakfast on your new English gloves; but with the sailors you are perfectly safe.

We reached Esneh in twenty-four hours after leaving Luxsor, the only incident of the day being an ineffectual effort to capture a crocodile; but the wary monster, though lying asleep on the spit of a sandbank at least half a mile long, wakened at the first step of a man on the other end, and after one or two yawns and stretches waddled down into the water.

The bank at Esneh was very gay and crowded. The costumes of the Ghawazee, or dancing-girls, who are very numerous here, are generally a bright cherry-coloured silk robe, quite long, only just showing a pair of loose pink gauze shintyān below, their heads covered thickly with gold coins strung together into a kind of cap, and a white gauze veil thrown over all. They wear quantities of gold coin-necklaces and other ornaments, but we never saw a single really pretty face among them; some seemed to be only eight or ten years old.

We had here the good fortune of meeting Mr. Harris, the Egyptian antiquary, and his amiable daughter; they were so kind as to accompany us to the temple, and to read some of the hieroglyphics to us. The portico of this temple has been excavated, leaving the rubbish as a wall of its own height beside it, so that you descend into it from the level of its capitals. Though comparatively modern, having been built in the times of Tiberius and Trajan, it is well worth seeing for its massive elegance (an expression which can only be realised in Egyptian architecture) and for the harmonious symmetry of its proportions; it is pleasanter, too, to study than most of the temples, as it is walled off from the town, and you can sit enjoying your sketch in perfect silence and solitude: the stone of which it is built is of a rich yellow-brown, that tells well in a picture. We afterwards walked in the orange-groves of the Kashef's (or governor's) palace, the Kashef himself paying a visit to our dahabieh; he made himself as agreeable as any one can do through the medium of an interpreter, even though Achmet was a first-rate translator, and gave us a good deal of information more interesting than that in the conversation between the Pasha and " The Member for Mudcombe," famous in Eōthean annals. He descanted largely upon a map of Egypt, quite proud of being able to point out each place, though he could not, of course, read the names, and he criticised my sketches as freely as a drawing-master. He afterwards sent his daughter to see us, but we were unfortunately on shore when she came; and he was much disappointed at her not being able to see the novel, and to him incomprehensible, sight of a *hareem belonging to nobody* travelling in blissful liberty by itself on the Nile.

Our crew had a *soirée* in the evening, and entertained us with deafening music and dancing; the latter, which consists only of placing the body in awkward attitudes, bending backwards, and balancing upon bent knees, is as ungraceful as possible; and we were thankful when they were pleased to desist from the noisy darabooka (drum), clapping of hands, coffee and pipes, with which they amused themselves till ten o'clock: we sailed on an hour afterwards, determining to allow no more balls in our dahabieh. The mountains became more varied in form as they changed into the sandstones of Jebel Silsilis and the cliff on which Koom Ombos stands so finely; but darkness came upon us, and we saw no more till we reached Assouân at ten P.M. on the 26th of January, forty-two days after leaving Alexandria.

CHAPTER III.

WITHIN THE TROPIC.

> " Oh, mighty Jove!
> Forgive this monstrous love for a barbarian
> That knows not of Olympus!"

OUR eyes opened the next morning on a gay and pretty scene: instead of the yellow hills and smooth sandbanks of Egypt strange black, shining rocks popped up in the very middle of the stream— an old Saracenic wall or fortification stretched down to the river's edge on the north, as if to shut out Egypt from our sight, while in the narrow channel between the east side and the green island of Elephantine four dahabiehs besides our own were moored, with the Pasha's steamer, which had towed up Lord Dufferin's boats. The high sandy bank was shaded with palm-trees and covered with gaily-saddled donkeys, riding-camels, tame ostriches, and crowds of Nubians offering spears, daggers, bows and arrows, pieces of ivory and sandal-wood, ostrich-feathers and eggs, silver bracelets, clay cups and vases, savage-looking necklaces and head-dresses of shells, strips of rhinoceros and hippopotamus-hide, leopard skins, mats, and baskets of dates, all for sale.

It was tempting to linger among them, but we had business to settle: besides which a ride, our first ride in the desert, was more tempting still. Achmet had been to see the Sheikh of the Cataract, and learned that he was already engaged to take three boats up before our turn would come, and he stoutly refused to take up any dahabieh as large as the *Wandering Maiden* in less than two days; we might therefore expect to be detained five days at least before we reached the other side of the Cataract; and in returning we knew very well that she would be, proportionably to her weight, slower in descending the river. So we determined to see if any boat was to be had above the Cataract, and accordingly started early in the morning for Mahatta—a desert ride of an hour and a half. But what a different desert from one's nursery imaginations! The flat expanse of yellow sand had no place here—two or three hundred yards of white sand strewed with white stones, with banks of stones and lumps of granite piled up loosely on each side, as if " put away " by giants playing at bricks and suddenly called home to supper,— strange, fantastic shapes, sometimes like cairns, sometimes like walls, chiefly white, and yet shading into delicate hues of lilac and pale grey, with now and then a dash of purple. Solemn and stern it looked, seeming to close down upon one's heart with an almost tangible pressure as we journeyed on, we the only living things in the whole way, except one hyena, and some black and white vultures slowly sailing to and fro, some keeping watch while others picked at the bones of a dead camel, which it required no vulturine organ to scent at a good distance. A wely of some sheikh was the only sign of man, save the remains of an ancient wall or dyke, built by the Romans, some say, or by an Egyptian queen in the days long gone by. After leaving Assouân the road commences with a cemetery of the most ancient converts to Muhammedanism, with very small stone slabs, bearing inscriptions in Cufic writing—a pretty, elegant character. Many travellers have sought to carry away one of these slabs, but the people of Assouân will in no wise consent to part with them, even for the handsomest of baksheeshes.

The village of Mahatta looked more tropical than any we had as yet passed : it was neat and flourishing, every cottage having its enclosure of dôm-palms and its heap of gathered dates for sale or winter consumption; it was swarming with coffee-coloured children, destitute of any clothing save a leathern girdle or a shell necklace. Achmet fought a way for us through the crowd, and we descended to inspect an Arab boat, climbing over slippery, perilous rocks afterwards to the bank opposite Philæ, where two of the Reïses of the Cataract (there are eight of them) followed to make a bargain for its hire. In two minutes a cane divan was placed under a huge shady sycamore, two or three carpets or mats laid on the divan for us, and then the bargaining began. The two Reïses were perfectly black, with the woolly hair, negro nose, and turned-out lips characteristic of Nubia; each wore only a white cotton shirt tied round the throat, without sleeves, floating out in the wind from their tall black figures, polished and shining with castor-oil: very fine they looked as they stood gesticulating with Achmet. In about twenty minutes coffee was brought to us, and when the Reïs received the empty finjans from our hands he made a salaam, and Achmet said, " He says, Now you have drunk his coffee, you have *stepped upon his back,* so he must let you have the boat for the price you say;" upon which the other Reïs opened the bosom of his dirty gown, and poured out a quantity of dates into our laps, along with a platter of roasted Indian-corn, of which we duly ate before the bargain was concluded by shaking of hands and fresh salaams.

We ended that day with a row in the felucca near the foot of the Cataract, to enjoy the indescribable sight of that confusion of rocks, thrown about as if by hand, piled up and smoothed by the rushing water, shining and lustrous as coal and marble; the only two colours, the jet black basalt and the red porphyry, ornamented here and there with the vivid green of the little sont (mimosa) trees.

The desert looked strangely gay the next morning as we followed the same route from Assouân to Mahatta, for all the occupants of the six dahabiehs, then moored together, were on the same route, as well as four camels loaded with the furniture and provisions for our kandjeh,—beds, basins, baths, and baskets, all piled up in confusion on the swaggering camels, while, hanging out over the top of one of them, a great wooden sofa, painted green, went wagging ludicrously along. Our friends bade us adieu with a ringing cheer on the beautiful banks of Philæ—ever-lovely Philæ—and we sailed gaily on at 2 P.M. into Nubia, with eight of our own sailors under a Nubian Reïs. Our new boat looked hopelessly unpromising and dirty, but we determined to make the best of it; and having made her look as nice as her old boards would permit, we gave ourselves up to watching the lovely scenes through which we were passing.

It is Egypt no longer, but something wholly different: the river seems to run more rapidly in its much narrower channel, and is of a deeper, clearer grey; the rocky hills rise more abruptly on both sides, leaving on each bank only a narrow strip, but a few yards wide in many places, sometimes not even that, gay and bright with the vivid green of young lupins; then a fringe of palms, dôm-palms, or castor-oil-trees, a yard or two wide, and the dark red rock rises immediately behind them, or the sand of the desert closes upon the green, as if sternly saying, "Thus far, and no farther!" And thus it is throughout Nubia: scarcely anywhere does the cultivated land extend a quarter of a mile in width, and often the rocks tumble down in heaps into the water. Scarcely a village is to be seen, and but very few of the people, only occasionally one or two working singly among the lupins; a silence, almost deathly, reigns throughout the land, and the whole country seems, by a subversion of ideas, to consist of the river only—a snake-like kingdom of blue water set in green and yellow enamels. The boats with their singing crews are all gone; the birds have stayed behind in Egypt; there are no villages for the jackals to howl in; and the only sound that breaks upon the listening ear is that of the creaking säkiyahs and shadoofs at intervals.

And yet such is the beauty of the scene that Nubia is not melancholy; and so delicious is the air that breathing seems in itself a pleasure. The balmiest European summer's evening is raw and cold in comparison with the perfection of those Nubian nights; scarcely even cool, yet with nothing of the oppressive heat of the day, the evening air moves round one with a soft, sweet freshness as it bathes every sense at once in a dreamy but not languid feeling of pleasure, and charms sight, taste, touch, and hearing with equal enjoyment. We afterwards found two or three mornings about sunrise quite cool; but during our stay in Nubia the nights were always the same, bringing, as Eliot Warburton expresses it, a sort of conviction that existence is a blessed thing.

Not however that Nubian existence by day is particularly inviting: very black and very oily is the Berberi, and your olfactory organs shrink from the wind that blows from him to you; wild and fierce are the men, noisy and naked the women, and, in contrast to the resplendent varnish of their skins, unpolished is their manner. One girl tried to snatch rudely from my hand a dôm-palm-nut I had gathered, while her companion threw handfuls of sand at us; but we were taking a long walk, with only the protection of one sailor, and had we gathered as much of their slender provision as its equivalent in England the British peasant would probably have expressed his disgust quite as significantly, and perhaps more disagreeably.

One more word of our nights in Nubia. When we entered our boat at Mahatta we found her reeking wet throughout the inside: "She's been sunk all night, ma'am, to clear out the vermin," was the explanation we received; and relying on Sir G. Wilkinson's assurance of the purity of Nubia, we thought only of rats, and said no more about it. That night we slept in peace; the sunshine of the following day, however, dried up the whole boat into its normal condition; but, in the bliss of ignorance, we retired to rest, when, after a few minutes' slumber, I awoke with a kind of impression that the imps of Sheiten had got hold of me. Oh horror! Inside and outside of my mosquito curtains files of bugs were promenading all over me, and when, with more than usual contortions I had struggled out of my Levinge's bag, I saw on beds, walls, ceiling, and floor only bugs—bugs—bugs! In Syria you can buy tiny little scraps of the Koran, folded up in highly-ornamented silver, or gaily-worked leather bags, which are worn round the neck as infallible preservatives against bugs; I thought of importing them to England, but I remembered they could not be expected to guard any but Islamite bodies.

After that night we slept on deck; and much pleasanter it was, with the glorious stars for our roof, than in the stuffy cabin and cupboard, which was all our kandjeh afforded us. And indeed it was well worth while to sleep *à la belle étoile*, to have full opportunity of seeing the beautiful Southern Cross, denied to European eyes. We used to lie awake between two and four o'clock each morning for the pleasure of looking at the lovely constellation— such a mysterious emblem of Nature's holiness, it always seemed as if the heavens came closer to one's heart in wearing the simple but well-known symbol of our Faith, and that these lovely stars visibly glorified the material image of the only path on earth that leads to a sure home amongst those starry hosts of heaven. It is a strange sensation, but an absolute fact, that the stars in Nubia seem really and tangibly nearer to you than in Europe: not that the sky seems nearer, for, on the contrary, it is lifted up to an infinitude far above what we ever see in the cloudy skies of northern latitudes; but that the stars themselves seem to hang lower down, to *lean out* of heaven towards man, shining on him with the glowing radiance that one fancies should bring home to the heart a living testimony of the inconceivably glorious heaven above them.

Thus much of the sky over Nubia; of the land itself the produce is almost entirely confined to two vegetables, the palm and the castor-oil; it is one long, almost unbroken palm-grove from end to end. The palm-trees are all numbered, registered, and taxed; their fruit is the chief, almost the only food of the Nubians; they have nothing besides this but the beans, whose flowers perfume the air at this season. The dates are sent down largely into Egypt, for no one eats an Egyptian date in Cairo or Alexandria if he can get a Nubian date; and the trade has increased by the dates brought in the caravans from Sennaar, which are much prized in the more northern latitudes. The second product of Nubia is the castor-oil, of which an immense quantity is consumed, externally, by the Nubian; the woolly hair of both sexes is soaked and matted into a stiff paste with the oil, and their bodies are rubbed over with it till they become polished and shiny. The oil keeps the skin from blistering or burning in the hot sun, which is the more necessary from their wearing no clothes; it likewise protects them from the attacks of mosquitos and other insects. The plant is extremely pretty, with the fruit and flower on the same branch, like the cotton-tree, which bears the pretty yellow blossom along with the silky, white cotton tufts of the dry open pod both at once. The castor-oil is red-stalked and of large, deeply-cut leaves—the young ones dark crimson-brown and purple, the old ones a bright green; the berries, like small chestnuts, of two shades of green, and the flowers white. I have heard of red and white flowers on the same tree, but we never saw them. The ugly, stunted-looking dôm-palm every one knows by pictures, with its strange fan-shaped leaves, and its fruit, large, dark red, deformed-looking apples.

On nearing Korosko the colouring of the scenery changes marvellously; the river winds so much as to appear frequently like a succession of lakes, enclosed by hills or mountains which have all become of a dark deep purple, sometimes quite black, while the sand which creeps up their sides and over the plains beyond them is no longer white, or even yellow, but a full rich apricot colour. About Korosko and Ibreem the mountains are singularly beautiful, and still more strange; their dark purple tints and the bright-coloured sands contrasting finely with the luxuriant palm and the green beans, while the mountains themselves begin to assume the fantastic shapes which give to the whole land, more especially about Abou Simbil, such a weird and bewitched appearance. The idea irresistibly suggests itself that the country has been lately burned, and each hill roasted; it seems as if nothing but a general conflagration could have given such a resemblance to over-baked pies, which the flame-coloured sand around them increases. One felt that there *must* be a legend of some such thing, and accordingly we were soon told how Surya, the Regent of the Sun, descended on the country one morning to say his prayers, when the waters dried up immediately, the mountains took fire, and the inhabitants were roasted to death. Ibreem—a lovely subject for a sketch—is a lofty perpendicular bluff, with curious old caves cut in the face, and crowned with a castle, now in ruins, which must have been of great strength and size.

We reached Wady Halfeh only four days after leaving Mahatta, so that we had not exchanged boats for nothing; 220 miles in four days, one of which had been lost in tracking against a westerly wind, was not bad. It blew violently at Wady Halfeh—invariably the case there, it is said : the place looks wind-worn and desolate; however it was lively enough that evening, for a caravan from Dōngola and Sennaar had just arrived, and the shore was covered with camels, and bales of elephants' teeth, bags of gum-arabic and ostrich-feathers; and we were pestered with people offering us the veriest rubbish for sale, as " Antika, antika ! " even common bits of stone from the beach. One boy offered us an English halfpenny, and another some broken morsels of glass ; but better still, when a man, a few days after, picking up a button before the eyes of a gentleman from whose coat it had dropped off, and holding it up to him, cried out, " Antika ! baksheesh, ya Howadji ! "

There were no donkeys or any kind of ridable beast to be had at the village, so we mounted very early the following morning on rough baggage-camels belonging to the caravan, in order to reach the Hill of Abouseer; we had no saddles or riding arrangements beyond a carpet and a mat thrown loosely over the beast's back, and how we stuck on is still a marvel to me; but we firmly declined, after a momentary trial, all invitations to trot. After becoming a little accustomed to the discomfort of the situation, I liked the springy long step and even swing of the camel: it seemed in harmony with the scene around one. A marvellous scene indeed it was: an arid desert of apparently endless sand, both white and deep yellow, with rocks breaking through of pale green, red, yellow, white, and purple; sometimes pieces shone sparkling in the sun of so pure and clear an amethyst colour that one quite started to tread over the seeming precious stone. About half-way we came to a solitary sheikh's tomb in ruins: no other sign of habitation met our view during the whole five hours of the ride, not a man, nor a camel, nor even a gazelle or a jerboa; all was utter silence and space under the bluest of cloudless skies and the rays of a scorching sun.

In another hour we had climbed up the back of the famous Hill of Abouseer, whose face is a perpendicular cliff three hundred feet high, rising directly from the northern end of the second Cataract, or Batn-el-Hajar,* as the Arabs call it. Many a fair land and many a mountain panorama have I since seen, but never has any view made more impression on me than that wondrous, though scarcely beautiful scene. The rock stands almost isolated, yet with hills and heights on the west side, and an immense plain to the south and east, which of course makes it seem more lofty than it is; and standing alone on its summit, I thought of that " exceeding high mountain " whence " all the kingdoms of the earth and the glory thereof" were surveyed. But how different a view was this ! Kingdoms, indeed, there had been in the land laid out before me with hundreds of temples, and palaces, and pyramids, but of the glory of these there is now nought but ruin and desolation; " their memorial " even has almost " perished with them," and the scene is one of the

* Core of the rock.

wildness of Nature only.   Far, far away to the south and south-west
rose the mountains of Dŏngola and Kordofân, grey and blue in the
distance; between us and them the great river wound through
thousands of low black rocks, shining black like coals, and extending nearly twenty miles, a mazy archipelago, but all jumbled into
an indistinguishable mass—the black tinted here and there with
shrubs of tamarisk.   As the river came within a few miles of our
hill it dashed and foamed into wider channels of white frothy
waters, which joined themselves into a smooth swift river, and,
passing the base of Abouseer, flowed on past Wady Halfeh on its
northern course.   On each side of these miles of black cataract
spread the, flat yellow desert, carrying on the eye westwards to
the mountains of Dŏngola, and eastwards to the far-away Arabian
range, clothed in the loveliest hues of exquisite pale mauve, half
hidden in a dreamy kind of mist.

We gazed and gazed, feeling as if we could never have enough;
like prisoners from the window of their gaol looking with longing
eyes over the far " sweet south " we so ardently desired to explore,
and over probably the most tropical scene in all the world that our
eyes will ever behold.   Turning back is often sad, but it never
seemed so *triste*, or such starving work before, as when we set our
faces northward to regain the boat—almost like a hungry wayfarer
passing a baker's shop and turning away his head from the food he
longs for and cannot have.   But before we retraced our steps there
was something to do, to accomplish which I had armed myself
with a hammer and chisel, not knowing in the least how to use them,
but resolved to leave our names among the pilgrims who had rested
on that narrow ledge of rock before us.   A mighty company of
names are gathered there, and a feeling of something awful came
over one in the sight of the hundreds recorded on that unchanging
stone—abiding there still like tangible shadows of those who carved
them when in health and vigour, yet of whom so many have now
already passed away !   For only a few years—twenty at most—has
that ancient river been open to travellers, yet already, like the
Volume of the Great Book, that rock, the record of those who spent
but one short hour of their brief existence there, is crowded with
the names of the dead !   Of those we had personally known by
far the greater number were gone into that land whence none
return; and it was with a feeling of sad pleasure that we placed
our names among them—thus making a sort of re-union in matter
as well as in thought—a silent, half-living companionship.   The
sun was scorchingly hot, and, never having been a schoolboy, I
found the stone-carving a very hard task, and was heartily glad

when I had accomplished it. Then we went slowly back to the kandjeh, with our heads wrapped in thick Scotch plaids to guard us from the midday rays, to which we were not accustomed on shore.

The real wealth of the glorious old Nile is derived from its lowest affluent, called the Black Nile—a river that rises in Abyssinia, near the town of Gondar, and pours into the great Nile just above Berber. The inundation owes its value to the greasy black mud suspended in the waters of this branch; and it is doubted by some persons whether the annual inundation would even take place were the Nile robbed of the mass of water that comes down the Black Nile. There might be a very large rise annually, but the water would subside without leaving that peculiar sediment which makes the soil of Egypt so fruitful. It was from knowing this that propositions were occasionally made by the enemies of Egypt in olden times of cutting off this branch, by turning its waters, before they left Abyssinia, into the Red Sea, and thereby reducing Egypt to a desert, or at least a very poor land; and on this account the Abyssinians were reported, in an ancient tradition, to have the power of reducing Egypt to utter and irreparable ruin.

This thick, greasy-feeling mud is thought to act beneficially upon other substances besides land: it is largely exported, dried in cakes, to all the hareems of Turkey; and the mud, re-softened in water, is laid on the skins of the fair ones of Damascus, Constantinople, and the beauties of Circassia and Georgia, to give whiteness and lustre to their complexions. Certainly the water of the Nile has the most charming influence on the skin, especially during its thickest flow. When we ascended the Nile the water was of a deep rich brown, which had cleared before we returned to Cairo into a clear grey. It is the most delicious water in the world for drinking, even when very thick; you have but to let it stand an hour or so in a clay goolleh, and the most refreshing sweet water runs off, as agreeable to the taste as it is beneficial to the health.

The following evening we anchored close to Abou Simbil, in the prettiest reach of the river, where it was enclosed like a lake between ranges of purple hills, then dressed in sunset hues of lilac and gold. These hills are most curious from their fantastic shapes, besides hundreds of others which rise suddenly from the flat, flame-coloured sand, like huge round haycocks with steeply sloping sides. We toiled up the steep bank of sand very early the next morning, as it is only the newly-risen sun which can penetrate at all into the depths of that world-famous Temple of Abou Simbil, or Ibsamboul, as it is sometimes called.

D

Everybody is familiar with the interesting account of its resurrection from under the sand by the spade of Belzoni—that lesson of noble perseverance grandly rewarded; and since that time the temple has been too often and too well described by able pens for me to use my feeble one in portraying its wonders; nor indeed can I hope here or elsewhere to do more than to render in some degree the impression made upon our own minds, rather than to give the actual description of the magnificent ruins of Egypt in themselves.

Our entrance into the rock-temple is in no wise likely to be forgotten by us; the sand has now closed up the doorway (which was quite open a few years ago *) within eleven or twelve inches from the top, so that it would be impossible to enter it if the sand were level, instead of being, as it is, on a steep slope. We divested ourselves of hats, &c., for the heat inside is intense, and we were puzzling over what was to happen next, when Achmet suddenly disappeared, shouting back directions to us from the depths inside the hole, in obedience to which we laid ourselves, one by one, flat on our faces, inserting our heels into the aperture, when, being instantly seized on, a few vigorous pulls drew us each safely through! Such a ludicrously unpleasant operation that I could not help opening my mouth to laugh, thereby receiving half a pound of sand down my throat. Still more intensely ludicrous did it seem when, half an hour afterwards, we, being still inside, saw a gentleman undergo the same process—the feet first filling up the hole, and then the body coming thundering down the steep sand-slope into the darkness and silence within.

After this very unusual exercise we required a little rest, and Achmet left us for half an hour, that our eyes might become accustomed to the darkness within; and we were thankful enough to be alone, for very soon the light which pours through the little opening enabled us to distinguish the features of that far-famed hall, which sinks deeper and deeper into the heart the longer you behold it. Four colossal figures stand at each side of the middle aisle as pillars dividing off the narrow and dark recesses behind them; all the light there is falls on these eight figures of Rameses, now become Osiris, imbued with his almost superhuman strength, and majesty and divine calmness—the swathed legs and the unearthly repose of the face bespeaking the God of Death, as the crook and the knotted scourge portray the God of Judgment. There

* The temple was cleared out, by order of the Pasha, for the visit of Lord Haddo; but since then the villagers have thrown the sand in again out of pure mischief.

is little in accordance with our modern ideas of beauty in his features, yet the mind is more impressed with admiration—an admiration that almost oppresses one—at the majestic, passionless purity and perfect peace of that countenance than at the most exquisite Grecian model of all that is most beautiful in man. Something *more* is here, more than mere symbolism, and far beyond mere human beauty, however perfect—something that speaks to the mind with an eight-fold voice as clearly as the grave. The sweet mouth and the powerful arms crossed calmly on the breast, clasping the divine emblems, speak to the eye of the gazer something which tells of the rest obtained, not by inaction, but by conquest—something that whispers almost irresistibly to the mind, "When He giveth quietness, who then can make trouble?" A quietness, a repose that is indeed almost unearthly, for it comes from far away; he is dead, but speaking from beyond the earthly life he has quitted: it is not only that he has passed through Death, but that Death is no more to him; he is now living —living again, but in silence, not in action, but in the life of thought which is eternal—he is gone, not into Death, but through Death into the Silent Land—the land of the great departed; and from that land, through the long silence between us and him, through the deep darkness of intervening ages of idolatry and ignorance, there seemed to come softly to our living ears the spiritual echoes of those voices, for long ages silent upon earth, yet whose praises are still ringing through eternity in adoration of the one same God Almighty—the same then as now to the pure in heart—even to them and to us as children of the same eternal and ever-present Father. Through the long past ages these have stood there, and for long ages to come they will still stand there, silently singing their solemn, sweet chant, ever and ever the same, from those crossed arms and those serene, passion-stilled countenances, and those restful lips—" Children and brothers, your burden is heavy, your cares many; but be of good courage—strive, struggle, fight your way on—conquer through all, and attain this calm, this peace, this rest, forgetting all the trials, sorrows, struggles of life in eternity."

> " ' Daughter,' they softly said, ' peace to thine heart !
> We too, yes, daughter, have been as thou art :
> Hope-lifted, doubt-depressed, seeing in part,
> Tried, troubled, tempted, sustained as thou art.
> *Our* God is *thy* God; what He willeth is best;
> Trust Him as we trusted :—then—rest as we rest ! ' "

Besides this hall there are fourteen chambers in the temple, all

perfectly dark, of course, though before the sand had choked up
the entrance the four small figures which sit, as on an altar, at
the farthermost end of the adytum, facing the door, must have
been dimly illumined by the rays of the' rising sun (the temple
faces the east); and they must themselves have appeared to look
with their stony eyes along the whole length of the temple, and
across the sacred ever-flowing Nile, to the unchanging purple
mountains beyond his green banks. If the sacred hawk, the emblem
of the Sun, to whom the temple is dedicated, was kept at the feet
of these four statues, as some suppose, it must have been worse
than the " penalties of royalty " to him to be worshipped in the
dark enclosure instead of enjoying blessed liberty on the hills he
could just descry without.

On the walls of the outer hall are represented the historic deeds
and conquests of the great Rameses : the other chambers are also
sculptured all over; but the pictures are so blackened with smoke
as to be very difficult to decipher, and the heat and suffocation in
the inner rooms are so intense that it became impossible to examine
half of them—strong lungs and head are absolutely necessary for a
real examination of Abou Simbil in its present state. It was with
much vexation that we turned to hurry out, but one was forced to
retain strength enough in one's faint and semi-suffocated condition
for the exit—head foremost—through the same little hole: an
operation still more disagreeable than the entrance.

We lay down in the shadow of the rock to rest and breathe,
and to feast our eyes quietly and thoroughly on the four colossal
figures of the façade : three only are quite uncovered by the sand,
and one of these has been destroyed to the waist, while of the
fourth only the face is visible. These enormous figures—they are
sixty-six feet in height without the pedestals—are of the great
Rameses II., seated on his throne; his posture, the hands on the
knees, signifying his rest after his many conquests—viz. those
portrayed within the temple. These figures are as striking as the
Osirides in the interior, but even more beautiful in face: the
countenance is as grand, and perhaps more human, and it has an
expression of majestic sweetness in the mouth and of triumph in
the nose which gives conviction to the mind that they are portraits.
Till I saw those figures I never could believe that features of such
gigantic size could express such *grace* and benevolence so sweetly
and grandly mingled; but here in reality one felt in one's heart
that Rameses—the glory of ancient Egypt's many glories, and the
terror of the then-known world—must have reigned over a people
who loved him, as well as over slaves who feared him.

Then we turned to the mountains, now deep in violet shades against the Eastern sky, which we had seen from the inside of the temple, feeling that these at least had been beyond the power of man to change; but in truth they seemed to have come within reach of a hand's grasp, as it were, across the almost immeasurable gulf between us and the thousands of centuries when these figures were fashioned by men's hands. Strange to feel how Nature came close home to one's heart as man faded away into dim distance; how the

"sweet and potent voice"—

from

"within the soul itself" *

answered back the whisper from Nature's grandest works, and the inward life of Man and of Nature met together in the same God-given thought; strange to recognise the links of that immortal chain which bound up the spiritual life of Nature with the thoughts of those whose works of the Past were living still in the Present, in those old Egyptians and in the children of the new West,— children of the same Father, with thoughts alike eternal in both.

The small but tastefully-built Temple of Amada was the next at which we stopped; it is situated on the western bank, and commands a remarkably pretty landscape, and is in itself more picturesque than most of the ruins of Egypt: the sculptures are lively and interesting, and in some places very fresh; but the little temple is more than half buried in the sand. The next day a very high wind kept us moored to the bank—the only day on which we had imperfect weather in Nubia; but we found amusement in watching the brown children and girls who came down with butter and dates for sale: they were very shy, and screamed frightfully if ever we went near enough to pretend to touch them; but at any reasonably safe distance they would stand for an hour, even the tiniest of them, shouting "Baksheesh, baksheesh!" We went on in the night, but the wind continued to blow, and our old tub of a boat rolled so much that—I grieve to say—we were both sea-sick.

Koofideena (or Maharrāka) occupied us the next morning: an unfinished temple, looking still as if fresh from the hands of the builders, with its half-carved capitals, yet now in ruins. It is very pretty, and worth seeing, though almost without sculptures, and not to be compared with the noble ruin of Dakkeh, which we explored in the afternoon. Here there is a fine view from the summit of the great pylon, I believe, but such a splendid mirage spread all

* Coleridge.

around us during our stay that we never rightly distinguished
between the truth and the pretty fable: the temple itself is one of
the most interesting. Then came Garf Hosseyn—a coarse travestie
of Abou Simbil, nearly passing the "one step" from the sublime
to the ridiculous. The clumsy giants who are fast crumbling away
here bear little resemblance to the majestic figures in the other,
reminding one only of the monsters of ancient India. In the
beauty and dignity of Abou Simbil one almost forgets that from such
conceptions man could degenerate into the darkness of idolatry—for
there the spiritual life only is represented, which was afterwards
clouded over by error and materialism; but in Garf Hosseyn the
degradation of heathenism is brought before one. In the one you
feel instinctively that what is before you is the human representation
of what is divine—imperfect, perhaps mistaken, as from the hands
of men "seeing through a glass darkly;" yet with the aspirations
of a heart "desiring a better country" expressed in it: whereas
in the other the form is brutalised into the expression of something lower than human, and gigantically hideous; but what re-
finement should be expected in a temple dedicated to the rude
Vulcan? The whole place is swarming with bats, and is very
disagreeable to explore. The proportions of the temple, which is
hewn from the living rock, are very grand, and there has been a
fine portico: it is nobly placed too, and the landscape from it is very
green and lovely; as indeed were the views throughout this day's
voyage. We saw Dendour and Kalabshee—the latter a magnificent
ruin, but being only of the date of Augustus, it is too modern to
claim as much attention as its size would otherwise command, and
the hieroglyphics are miserable. Besides being imposing it is also
curious from its excessive ruin—it looks really as if it had been
chopped up, and it is only by very active scrambling that one can
see it at all.

But the gem of all the hieroglyphics of Nubia is to be found
within a mile of Kalabshee, beautifully situated on a cliff commanding a long reach of the river and its bright green banks,—this is
the rock-hewn grotto-temple of Beit-el-Wely. It is very small, consisting of only an adytum and a hall, supported on two columns;
the sides are filled with representations of the victories of Rameses
II. over the Cushites (Ethiopians) and the Shori. In many places
the paint is fresh as ever, the pupils of the eyes of Rameses still
preserving their sharply-defined blackness, and the pattern of red
and blue embroidery on his robes still bright and clear; the piece
washed by Miss Martineau is cleaner than most of the rest, and is
of course pointed out by every dragoman. Outside the temple the

two sides of the area or court are covered with small, but most lifeful figures—on the one side Rameses is represented in the act of conquering the Ethiopians, with portraits of all the offerings presented to him by the newly-subdued people; on the other the great king is seen besieging the fortified city of the Shori, who make a determined resistance. The conqueror is also represented engaging in single combat with a chief of the Shori, and afterwards sitting on his throne receiving a group of prisoners, conducted by his son; the figures are certainly most living and spirited, but they scarcely equal the highly-imagined description given of them by some travellers.

One night more of delicious fresh warm air—though at Kalabshee we had left the Tropic of Cancer—and on the evening of the next day, by the glorious starlight, we drifted swiftly and noiselessly down the narrow stream, between the dark high cliffs which charmed us still more in returning than when ascending the river, and anchored by the shore of beautiful Philæ. Our tent was already pitched on the sand, and we thankfully enjoyed such a night's sleep as we had not once had in our carnivorous kandjeh.

CHAPTER IV.

CATARACT AND FLAME.

WHO can describe Philæ? and what good would even pages upon pages of writing do to the minds of our readers? they could only produce confusion, since Philæ is made up of apparently incongruous elements, each beautiful in itself, though combining badly enough in description, but in reality melting into one harmonious whole—stern and wild, yet soft and lovely; grand in feature, yet exquisite in detail; calm and silent in its deep repose, yet surrounded with life and sound; the vast white of the desert and the deep grey of the river—the glowing purple of the mountains and the vivid green of the palm-trees—the lustrous black of the weird rocks in the water and the fiery orange and red of the infernal-looking rocks on the shore—the blue and pink granite and the red and purple porphyry—the creamy yellow of the ancient ruins, so grand and beautiful, yet so arid and unpicturesque, and the dry, cracked, and crumbling mud-huts around and all over them :—these are the various opposing features which combine into the one unique and perfect Philæ—of all spots in Egypt and Nubia the one to which, perhaps, one looks back with the most love and tenderness.

Much of its magnificently-planned temple was still unfinished when all was left to silence and ruin: what would it have been in its complete beauty! What must it have been even in its incomplete magnificence, when the pagan priests of old sang their hymns of worship along its sacred shore! Isis and Osiris, with their son Horus, the type of youthful beauty, was the Triad worshipped here (Egyptian worship was always in triads), and the interior of the great temple is filled with their "domestic annals;" but the earthly history of Osiris did not end here, for the oath which has dreamily thrilled through our minds, so ancient is history to us, was a modern error among the Egyptians, and "He who sleeps in Philæ" was really believed by them to have been buried temporarily in Abydos.

The temple and the buildings connected with it must have once entirely covered the island, which was nearly surrounded by a quay of smooth stone-work; only a portion of this remains, and the chief parts of the temple are now connected only by piles of broken stones. Nothing, however, can lessen the grandeur of the enormous pylons and pyramidal towers in the centre; of all the rest the effect is sadly spoiled, to our minds, by the perverse irregularity and un-symmetrical arrangement of all Egyptian architecture, which is no-where shown more broadly—I had almost said rudely,—than at Philæ. There are two splendid colonnades of pillars, commencing from a wall of rock rising at the southern end of the island; but only a few of the pillars can be seen in true perspective, as the line of each colonnade is almost unaccountably crooked, following with unnecessary closeness the shore of the island. Many of the columns too are unfinished, with uncarved capitals, the grace and elegance of the first score making one doubly regret the vacancy of the others. After this and a whole heap of ruins, among which lie the broken limbs of a gigantic lion, you enter between enormous towers through one court into another: every side of the second square is different from the other three; one of them is occupied by a corridor of richly-ornamented pillars, while on the opposite side is the small but beautiful temple dedicated to Horus. Beyond this is the gem of Philæ, "the ten-columned court," as it is called, of the great temple. These columns are still quite perfect, and are almost the only ones in Egypt where the colours *are really* as fresh and bright as they must have been two thousand years ago—unlike the descrip-tions of enthusiastic tourists; their capitals are of the most vivid blue and green, picked out with red, crimson, and orange; the roof is bright blue, with golden stars; and the winged orb typifying the Sun, is here more elaborately portrayed than usual. Then comes the adytum and several other chambers, all in darkness—thick dark-ness, the abode of bats and dismal odours—yet whose walls still hold vivid pictures, in spite of dirt and decay, of the birth and education of Horus, who stands between Isis, horned and sun-crowned, and Osiris with the crown and mitre. There are inner chambers, staircases still unbroken, passages innumerable, and some smaller temples; one among them on the western side was dedicated to the God of the Nile, and is full of pretty water-plants, lotus and papyrus, neatly and well sculptured. The colossal sculptures on the pylons, &c., are very coarse and ill done, unlike the really ancient hieroglyphics, this temple having been built by Ptolemy Epiphanes and Ptolemy Physcon, and begun about 200 B.C. Turning to the east side of the island, there is one beautiful and very graceful building : a quadrangle of columns, rising from a wall of only a few feet high, support an architrave, and again a cornice raised some feet above that; there is no roof, and the pillars and walls are, with the exception of a single winged Sun, quite unsculptured. The intention of the building in its unfinished condition is somewhat incomprehensible, but it is singularly elegant and pretty, in spite of the efforts of the vulgar to deface its beauty by the scribbling of their own paltry names on its walls.

On the west of Philæ there is a small island called Biggeh, one huge heap of black and purple rocks, thrown and piled upon each other in the most wild and fantastic confusion. To the top of this we climbed in the afternoon—not a very easy or pleasant task, but worth achieving, as without seeing Philæ from its summit it is hardly possible to understand the plan of the ruins through the thick crust of overlying mud-huts (built, it is said, by the ancient Christians); or to see how beautifully the great temple was placed in the centre of the river, which is here like a large oval lake, closed at the southern end by the lovely mountains, clad in soft Nubian colours. The river comes gliding from them to your feet, and flowing by in a rapid deep current, hastens over the wild black rocks, past all the bewitched-looking piled-up islands into the north-west corner of the picture, from whence the distant roar of the cataracts, borne upon the breeze, murmurs up occasionally into your ear. Behind you it is all black, burnt-up rock, like the outpourings from a furnace—mountains of slag, with patches of flame-coloured Nubian sand; at your feet lies Philæ, slumbering in calm beauty; and beyond that the broad white pathway through the desert to Assouân.

We were soon surrounded by the black islanders and a number of little children, entirely naked, except a girdle of leathern fringe round the loins. One lovely little girl, with properly oiled and plaited hair, made great friends with us, insisting upon giving the support of her six-year old hand to help even the gentlemen of our party to descend the rocks, or pointing out the way with her round, slender arms; nor would she quit us for a moment till we rowed away, leaving her graceful little figure poised on a pinnacle of rock, waving farewells with her little hands, and crying, " Ma es salâmé! ma es salâmé!"* Nor did she once ask for baksheesh—a very remarkable exception in Egypt.

* " Good bye! Good bye!" More literally, " Go in peace!"

We devoted the next day to sketching in the beautiful ten-columned court—a strange day for Philæ, for it rained unceasingly, small fine rain, such as they said had not been seen there for twenty-two years, and the dark purple mountains and wild black rocks looked more eerie, and sad too, than ever, in the lowering un-Egyptian sky. A sandstorm came on in the evening, filling our tent to about eight inches' depth of sand in the course of an hour; and the sun rose on the morrow in a lurid heavy glare, soon shaded by rain, in which, however, we took leave of our dirty kandjeh, and sailed over to Mahatta in the boat of some friends, who had kindly invited us into their dahabieh for the shooting of the Cataract; we were very anxious to enjoy that experience instead of riding again across the desert to join our *Wandering Maiden.* We had no sooner reached Mahatta than a furious thunderstorm broke forth, the lightning playing round the rocks, and the thunder pealing in thickening echoes, that seemed to gather up and give back the sound in hundred-fold majesty. The Arabs declared they would not pass the Cataract in such "weather of Satan," but after a couple of hours it passed off, and a cold sunshine having come out, we shipped about thirty Arabs, and the eight rowers took their places at the oars, tightening their turbans, and turning up their sleeves as though their work was to be done in earnest. We settled ourselves on the deck, admonished that the safety of the boat would be risked should we move hand or foot during the passage of the dangerous parts; and the Arabs squatted round, packing themselves tightly in the prow and on the upper deck, and carefully balancing the boat. At first they all talked marvellously fast, but the voices lulled as we neared the Cataract; and, in something less than half an hour, silence fell on all save the rowers, who, for once keeping good time with their oars, kept singing their "Hayalee-sah!" vigorously—the Reïs of the Cataract standing on the upper deck (a grand old white-bearded Nubian he was), shouting short, deep-toned words of command to the helmsman and to the Reïs of the dahabieh, who stood in the prow with a stout pole ready for action. Every face was turned to the narrow passage between the noble black rocks down which we were to pass—every eye was fixed and eager—and here and there a hand was raised or the fingers tightened in a clasp, as if in mute appeal to the spirits of the rushing waters to bear us down gently and safely. On we went, swiftly and smoothly gliding through the labyrinth of rocks, which seemed to fly past, scarcely a yard's distance on either side of us—swifter and swifter in the rushing, boiling mass, till the dahabieh seemed to bend for a brief second, poised in mid air over the edge, then, with one swinging bound, down she leaped into the white whirling foam at the bottom, spun half round in the eddy, sped away beyond the strength of the rowers in a sideways plunge—and the Cataract was passed! The Arabs all joined in a shout of triumph, and the Reïs of the Cataract had just time to snatch the turban from the head of the dragoman (his invariable perquisite from the owner of every boat which has safely passed the Cataract under his guidance), into whose white lips the blood had just time to return, when a reeling shudder seized the vessel from stem to stern; she gave a sort of stagger in the water, and bounded off from a pointed rock, which had knocked a tolerably large hole in her bow. No great harm was done, however, we passed another smaller descent a few minutes after in safety, and soon moored in a little cove, for the double purpose of getting rid of our host of Arabs and to put the vessel in order, as all the chairs, divans, spare spars, &c., had been built up *en masse* in the stern to balance the boat more perfectly. It was then just one hour since we had left Mahatta.

Three hours after we found ourselves comfortably reinstated in our pretty *Wandering Maiden*, which seemed a perfect palace after the miserable Nubian barge; and we spent the remainder of the day in walking over that much bepraised island of Elephantine, whose beauties, if it ever had any, are now hidden under heaps of broken pottery of marvellous depth. There is nothing else but the ruins of one small gateway, and a few palms. The view, however, from the southern end of the Nile, studded with black islets, with green and purple banks, is very pretty. It was more interesting to ride out once again into the desert, winding among the beautiful pink, white, and yellow rocks to the quarry, where the marks of man's work still linger in a sort of ancient freshness on the half-carved obelisk which lies unfinished and unremoved from the rock, whence so many thousands of blocks have been cut and conveyed down the Nile, to build up the unperishing memorials of " a people terrible from their beginning, and formerly a nation extending its limits, a victorious people, whose land is washed down by rivers!"

A heavy wind detained us within a few miles of Assouän for two days, the bumping of the boat against the waves being very unpleasant. On the third day we made a long row in the little felucca to the beautiful ruin of Koom Ombos, one of the finest in Egypt. An enormous wall, raised on an artificial substruction, and pierced with a lofty gateway in the centre, towers above the river; a grand hall once stood there, it is said, but it is entirely ruined, and fallen into heaps of broken stone. The temple itself, built in honour of two divinities—the God of the Temple hawk-headed, and that of

Ombos crocodile-headed,—is half buried in the sand; and the *two* sanctuaries, an arrangement peculiar to Koom Ombos, have almost disappeared; but what remains of the fine lofty portico is remarkably beautiful. The capitals of the huge but not clumsy pillars are richly and most elegantly carved; the sculptures are well done and easily decipherable, and the painting on the roof is still bright and fresh. It is the more interesting from being in some places unfinished, the squares, drawn for the convenience of the copying artist, being yet clearly visible. As the portico is almost perfect, within and without, it is a good example of the smaller Egyptian temples; and the finish of the carving is the more easily examined from the overlying sand raising one half way up the pillars. Yet how well this beautiful temple would repay clearing, and how easily it might be done!

It was now midday, and the sun was very hot. We waited hopelessly long, as it seemed to us, for our boat, and scarcely knew where to look for her; for, far away, winding from beneath our feet, the Nile glided into a misty haze, which seemed only to end in sand'; then, coming back from the dim horizon eastwards, came a long reach of the river, bending round towards us, and back again to the south. The banks were shaded with rich palm-trees, and we fancied we could distinguish sails upon the blue-grey water. We sat looking, and upbraiding ourselves for not having observed how much our course must have wound round in the early morning, when river and banks began to tremble; the sand seemed to rise in a faint hot haze, and on changing our point of view by a few yards in height, the whole panorama dissolved away into " the devil's water," as the Arabs call the mirage of the desert.

We spent the following morning, the 16th of February, in examining the very ancient rock-hewn grotto of Hajr Silsilis on the eastern side of the river, with its most interesting and life-like sculptures; and afterwards had a scrambling walk over some of the gigantic quarries on the same bank. We hoped to have reached Edfou by daylight, but the sun sank, and a glorious moon arose before we moored at the bank about six o'clock. A boat belonging to the Mr. Jacksons came up at the same time, and we agreed to visit the temple by moonlight in one party, in consequence of Sir G. Wilkinson's warning to travellers that the natives of Edfou are apt to be troublesome, and sometimes to molest one impertinently. We determined to be extra prudent, and desired our dragoman to select six of the sailors, provided with stout sticks, to accompany us, headed by Achmet himself and our man-servant; and, alas! we carefully took off our watches and rings, and the few trinkets and little valuables we cared for most, and put them by in our cabins, as we thought in safety. Then we sallied forth *en masse* without hats, for it was a very sultry, stifling night, and had a pleasant walk over the fields for about three-quarters of an hour before we reached the magnificent temple. It has gigantic pylons, and a huge square, with an interior peristyle of thirty-two columns; then comes a splendid portico of lofty and richly-carved pillars, which looked mysteriously beautiful in the strong lights from the torches, and the deep black conflicting shadows thrown by the bright moonbeams; then we mounted on the roof, in order to survey the wide extent of the temple, and looked down on the great courts, into which burning wood was thrown to show us, though dimly, their depth and width. The view thence, too, in the calm clear moonlight, was serenely pretty; from the lofty platform on which we stood we looked over the village, which lay in a hollow below us, over a mile or so of field between us and the river bank, and then across the river, shining in silver lustre, to the dark dim mountains on the other side. The bank was much too high to admit of our seeing the dahabiehs, but we remarked to each other that the sailors had lit a more than usually large fire on the bank, by the light of which our flags were gaily illuminated; but in another minute that seemingly trifling idea was forgotten. We lingered a little in the temple, and then walked quickly through the village, stopping only to observe a circle of derwishes performing a *zikr*, or sacred dance; about twenty of them joined hand in hand, jerking their bodies forward with a short sudden start as fast as possible, violently nodding the head with every movement, first over one shoulder, then over the other, uttering with each jerk a loud harsh grunt, exactly like a London paviour, only that instead of being expressed with slow stolidity this sound was flung out with passionate excitement. Achmet, however, begged us not to loiter watching them, as the Edfou people are very fanatical, and might take umbrage at Frank inspection; so we went slowly on through the fields, enjoying the quiet silence of the hot night, and the bright moonbeams playing on the picturesque figures of the sailors accompanying us. Alas, this pleasant half-hour was but the calm before the storm! We were within but a few yards of the bank when the sailors in front made some loud exclamations, and rushed up the steep slope—Achmet and all of us ran forward . . . . . and looked down . . . . . on what had been our beautiful boat—our little home—now a *mass of flame!* roaring and crackling with terrible, long-to-be-remembered noise,—the devouring tongues of flame licking round the sides of the vessel—hissing in sudden quenchings upon the water—running in fine darting lines up the ropes—clinging round the masts—and over all the gay flag and the red and white streamer flying out in the fierce draught, redder and prettier than ever, in a sort of demoniac dance of triumph at their own illumination, till a higher and still higher tongue of flame leaped up and shrivelled them into black nothingness! It is easy to describe it even now, for I have but to close my eyes, and the whole thing, living and horrible in its reality, comes only too vividly before me, burnt into my memory. The dragoman of the other boat, the *Tayr-el-Nil*, and a few of our sailors, now that we were at hand to see them, now and then threw a basinful of water upon the flames; the others stood passively looking on, only exclaiming " Mash-allah, Mash-allah!" except 'Ali, the sailors' cook-boy, who was crying bitterly. Not a single thing had been thrown from the interior of the boat, except the sailors' bread and their bundles of clothes; nothing of ours had they attempted to save, but, on the contrary, they had held back our maid by force when, with the courage of an Englishwoman, she attempted to rush into the burning vessel to secure my sister's desk, which was in the outer cabin, containing money and some valuables. Within a quarter of an hour after our return the masts had disappeared, and the flames sank down with sullen satiety into the hull, where alone there was anything left to consume; and we stood upon that bank absolutely bereft of everything—without home, food, clothes, or money, among a strange and savage people, three thousand miles away from home, and at some five hundred miles from the nearest spot where any of our wants could be supplied, with no means of getting there, apparently without friends or help! Who could describe the forlornness of such a position, or the overwhelming feelings that rushed over our sinking hearts! Such circumstances must be experienced to be understood; and were I to try to tell of even a part of our immediate loneliness or the dim vista of future difficulties and dangers, it would but appear exaggerated to those who have not gone through something of the kind. God alone knows what it was to us.

But in this hour of direst need help and friends were—God be thanked!—close at hand. The Mr. Jacksons, whose boat had arrived at the same time as our own at Edfou, insisted on our coming at once on board their dahabieh, and immediately, with the most generous kindness, devoted the whole of the inner cabins to the use of ourselves and our maid, and placed their stock of clothes, linen, stores, and all other necessaries at our disposal. With these, and other kind gifts received from several of the boats we afterwards encountered, and which were always pressed upon us with the most

delicate liberality, we managed to get through the seven weeks that
elapsed before we reached Cairo, not quite in rags, and in some
degree of comfort; although of course the want of constant change
of clothes is a great privation in a hot country, and necessarily there
were scores of things wanting which not even the kindest ingenuity
could supply from an outfit originally furnished only for the wants
of two gentlemen. It is needless to say how it distressed us to feel
to what discomfort our intrusion must have reduced our kind hosts,
excluding them from the principal part of the boat, and marring all
their own snug arrangements by the occupation of five persons
in a dahabieh only adapted for two. But from Edfou to Cairo no
one effort was ever spared by them to make us forget our own losses,
or to assure us that their comfort and convenience were not only
willingly but gladly sacrificed to ours.

No fellow Christians under the circumstances could have refused
to give us an asylum, but the manner in which the hospitality
was rendered made all the difference in the world to us; and,
anomalous as our position could not help being, it was a good
deal to be assured that we were not looked upon as intruders,
but were really welcome. We had hoped to have found at Thebes
a boat of some kind, in which we could have descended the river
to Cairo, with some of our sailors and our own dragoman; but
there was not even an Arab kandjeh to be had, and our friends
foresaw that we might find ourselves very unpleasantly situated
had the dragoman taken the opportunity of our separation from
Europeans to demand promissory notes of payment for his boat.
We thought our man-servant was sufficient protection against this,
but they decided that it was better we should not risk it. Failing
this we felt sure there would be some large dahabieh at Thebes,
with ladies on board, willing to make a spare cabin for us, but no
such offer came; one young lady lent us all she could spare of the
clothes we so much needed, and Mrs. Hood, who was still at Thebes,
shared with us everything she possessed with the most unselfish
kindness. But from the boats then at Luxsor no other lady broke
through the formalities of lacking an " introduction " to English-
women in distress; and we found our country*men* far more generous
and thoughtful for us than our country*women* ; all their little stores
of handkerchiefs, brushes and combs, needles and threads, &c., &c.,
were brought out and pressed upon us, and one gentleman even
sent us shawls and green veils.

There was one very large dahabieh with a small party on board,
which came down the river to Luxsor while we were there; they
offered nothing of their own accord, but in our utter distress for

some of the common necessaries that gentlemen could not supply, we ventured to send our maid on board to ask for some materials requisite for making up the clothes we had contrived out of Arab cotton: the reply to this, our first essay in the art of begging, was the gift of *one hook and eye!* We sought for nothing more from that boat.

In contrast to this another lady, who was at Assouān when the news of our misfortune reached her, immediately prepared with her own hands every article of clothing she could possibly spare, packed them up together, and kept them ready, in hourly hopes of overtaking us, or of finding some quicker means of sending them to us. Unfortunately their dahabieh was detained by the same winds that detained us, and it was not till her arrival in Cairo, a week later than ours, that we knew of, or could profit by, her true hearty kindness.

It was not at first that we fully realised how great our loss had been. Our penniless condition, forced to accept the hospitality, however kindly bestowed, of our companions and friends, was painful enough; so was the heavy loss in money, clothes, &c., and the necessity of replacing the latter at prices three times their value in Cairo. But besides this we had a really valuable stock of books on board, and—still more valuable to us, because irreplaceable—all our journals, notes, and our little collections of antiquities bought at various places, all our drawings and sketches, and, alas! many a dearly-loved little treasure of past days, which neither time nor money can ever replace. Not then, nor for very long afterwards, did we really know the length and depth of our losses— losses which we still feel sometimes sadly enough.

The cause of the fire was briefly this: our maid, who had been left in the boat, went out, as she usually did in the evenings, to walk for a few minutes on the bank. She had been ironing till dark in the stern cabin, and had hung up a quantity of clothes on lines across it; on leaving it she omitted to lock the door behind her, and 'Ali, the sailors' cook-boy, seized the opportunity of going in, with a light in his hand, to steal money out of the man-servant's coat, which was hanging up inside, or perhaps to pilfer the store-bags of nuts, raisins, &c., which were there also. We learned afterwards that he had stolen money twice before from the servants, but Achmet had always entreated that we might not be informed of this, saying that 'Ali (for whom, as well as all the sailors, he was answerable) must be caught in the very act of stealing. He was strictly forbidden to enter the cabins at all, but unhappily the fatal opportunity was now afforded him while the Reïs was at his prayers and the few sailors left on board were performing their evening

E

ablutions: the draught from the open window probably blew the hanging clothes into his candle, and seeing the flames all round him, he rushed out screaming, " What will become of me! I am undone, undone! I have set fire to the ship!" and in another minute the flames burst out of the windows.   These words of 'Ali's were translated *at the very moment* by Mr. Jackson's dragoman to our maid as she stood on the bank. Achmet afterwards denied all this when he got to Cairo, and gave out several stories, each one differing from the other, to account for the disaster. 'Ali, who was a bad specimen of the lowest Egyptian people, with a cunning, dishonest countenance, was taken up three times for stealing before we left Cairo, and we knew ourselves that neither Achmet nor 'Ali were very particular as to truth.

Our dragoman and man-servant both sat up all night to watch by the burned boat, and to keep off the villagers; and with the first dawn another dahabieh (the *Titania*) came up; two of the gentlemen in her joined our friends in superintending the digging through, and the careful sifting of the ashes from the inside of the boat. A party of Arab boys was organised for this dirty work, who laboured intelligently and industriously enough throughout the day, only stopping occasionally over the irresistible temptation of a roasted potato or broiled fig as they turned them up, or a pot of marmalade, into which they plunged their dirty fingers to suck off the jam, with great glee, ashes and all. A few sovereigns and some melted metal were recovered, fused into a shapeless mass, and the works of my watch, of which the case was found, curiously enough, at some distance from the works. A small box of silver ornaments, tightly packed in cotton wool, which had preserved them in perfect freshness, were the only other things found—a melancholy mockery to us, in want of all necessaries, was their silvery brightness shining in the ashes, so prettily useless. Complete and fierce had been the fire, and rapid too—for the dry, sun-heated boat burned like paper; but a good deal might have been saved in the first few minutes had any one of sense been at hand; and the sailors would probably have worked well and usefully if properly directed.

We had not either heart or head enough to revisit the Temple of Edfou, nor indeed had we much leisure for anything but trying to repair our losses as far as we could, by adapting the various contributions we had received to our use. The boat, which looked like a long green coffin with its painted hull just showing above the water, all black and charred within, and the words " Wandering Maiden" still visible on the outside, preceded us down the river, carrying our dragoman and sailors; the owner of the

Titania had kindly given a passage to our man-servant, for there was not a spare inch in the *Tayr-el-Nil*; and we stopped at Esneh only long enough to make a report of our loss to the worthy Kashef, or governor of the district, and to obtain a quantity of miserable Arab calico, after a long weary bargaining in the bazaar. At El-Kab we also made a halt, and rode to the rock-tombs, but we were so much worn out and stupefied that I can recall nothing about them beyond the general impression that they were well worth seeing.

Early in the morning of Sunday the 20th we reached Luxsor, where we had the comfort of attending the Church service, read by two clergymen at Mustapha's home, to a congregation of nearly forty English persons. There were, I think, ten dahabiehs at Luxsor on that day, and it required some little courage to face that congregation, even in the wilds of Egypt, in our destitute condition; this was indeed fully attested by our soiled dresses, half-burnt shawls, and old shooting-caps—a most useful contribution to our wardrobes, given to us by one of the gentlemen we had met, and which we had covered with muslin, to give them a somewhat more *lady-like* appearance. Alas! our nice large shady hats had been burnt, and only those who have been in a country of hot sun can imagine how much we missed them afterwards. Nor had I even a pair of boots or shoes,—I had gone out that evening, for it was very hot, in a pair of linen slippers, and I had nothing else but these to walk in over the sands, stones, and rocks of Egypt all the seven weeks that elapsed between the fire and our reaching Cairo.

CHAPTER V.

ETERNAL THOUGHT IN IMPERISHABLE STONE.

A BIRD skimming through the smoky sky of London, perching on this steeple or on that, here and there peering into a window, or picking a few crumbs in one street or in another, would have an endless tale of wonder to relate to the mate he left at home in his country nest; but the town-bred sparrow would not have much respect for the accuracy with which he described even the external architecture of the immense city—and of all that was " underneath the eaves," what would he know? Just as much as a traveller, lingering his longest possible on the green plain of Thebes, may fancy he knows of even the ruins of that ancient City whose stones and walls lie in desolate heaps upon the arid ground, whose statues and obelisks are now shapeless masses, and whose history is looked upon, but not read, by eyes that are unwillingly blinded by ignorance. The devotion of a long life is but sufficient for the understanding of a very little of what has gone before, while much labour, much thought, and much study is indispensable for the comprehension of even the broken materials that lie there still. For only this latter object we had endeavoured to prepare ourselves with some months of careful study—although neither expecting, nor even hoping to have attained much; but the unfortunate disaster described in my last chapter cleared everything but its own troubles out of our heads, and produced such a numbing ffect upon our minds and memories, that when, four days after, we began to examine the ruins of Thebes, we found it difficult enough to command our thoughts, and next to impossible to recall our memories of previous readings: present discomforts and small anxieties and awkwardnesses are sad obstacles to thought and study. A graver loss, both in itself and because they would have more than replaced our faded memories, was the loss of all our books, and the notes we had made in preparation for seeing the realities themselves, as well as various useful maps, plans, &c., with which we had been amply provided. From the want of books it was hard, more than hard, to profit even by what we saw; we were too much dispirited to recommence journals, &c., and we had no strength to spare for sketches of any kind, even had we had any materials. The shadowy memory of a bird's-eye view is, therefore, all I have to offer to my readers; such as it is, I must let it go, trusting only, as I do for every other page I have written, that it may succeed in presenting some faint picture of the reality to the minds of those who stay at home, and, what is much more important, that it may induce others to go and see for themselves.

Ancient Thebes stretched across the whole plain which we now see at each side of the River Nile; but the principal part of the city was on the east bank, and only the royal palaces and temples were placed on the western side, which was otherwise occupied by the tombs of the dead. The city was never enclosed by walls, and the "hundred gates" sung of by Homer are supposed to have alluded to the portals of a hundred temples, if indeed it was anything beyond a figure of speech. Thebes is believed to have been a great city even before the invasion of that hated race of Shepherds who ruled the country for several hundred years; but about 1500 years before Christ the Theban kings expelled the Shepherds, and their city then became the capital of all Egypt, both Upper and Lower, and continued to be so for a thousand years; this thousand years contains all that is most brilliant and glorious in the most ancient history of the world. The removal of the throne to Saïs in Lower Egypt caused the decline of Thebes, and the invasion of Cambyses, the Persian conqueror, in B.C. 525, threw her into ruins, the last magnificence of which were crumbled into their present condition by the siege of Ptolemy Lathyrus, in B.C. 116, when the Thebans had revolted from the yoke of the Romans. It is with the thousand years of the glory of Thebes that we have to do in the examination of the ruins that now lie upon the verdant plain; would we could rebuild in our minds even a dream of their former splendour!

The enormous quantity of mud—the source of all the riches of Egypt—brought down every year by the river gradually raises its bed; the water consequently extends slowly but surely over the plain, and leaves behind it a certain amount of soil. So, like the sand gathering round the feet of the Desert Temples, the green herbs wave higher and higher round the ruins of Thebes, and thus, year by year, the two great Colossi seem to be sinking gradually down among the young grasses of the plain. These two, sitting, like the Sphinx, wrapped in the silent mystery of unnumbered years, are the first objects that attract the view from the deck of one's dahabieh: scarcely changing in the varying light of morning and evening, they are always, and from every point, the same—grand, calm, and almost sublime—their very ruin making them more mysteriously fine, in contrast to the perfect tranquillity of repose— not idleness, but the rest earned by long labour—expressed in their impressive figures. One's first and last impressions of Thebes are hung upon those two broken but noble statues. Both represent Amunoph III.* (the predecessor by a thousand years of Rameses the Great), whose virtues and greatness are thus emphasised, as is always the case in Egypt, by reduplication and superhuman size. Behind them a stone causeway, of which the two Colossi were the outer sentinels, stretched back for eleven hundred feet, with pairs of statues and sphinxes at every few steps, up to the palace-temple of the same Amunoph; scarcely anything now remains of it. The Colossus that was anciently so famous for the sweet sounds emitted at morning was destroyed to the waist, it is said, by the barbarian Cambyses†: it has been rudely built up since with roughly-hewn stones. The sounds are supposed to have been caused by a man, hidden in the huge lap of the statue, striking a hammer upon a stone which stills lies there, and which rings like the sarcophagus of Suphis, and many other Egyptian stones. As the whole of this Libyan bank of the river was dedicated peculiarly to Athor, the Aphrodite of the Egyptians and the "president of the west," the Colossus, who surveyed the plain, could do no less than greet with a harmonious salutation the first rays of that sun who was to sink at evening into the arms of his divine mistress. Standing as it were underneath his knees are the figures of Amunoph's wife and mother, sculptured on the throne, as at Abou Simbil; the wife also reappears between his feet; while on the throne the god Nilus is represented holding some of the plants that then grew in his bosom far away, but which he now annually leaves around the feet of the statue— like flowers laid upon a grave.

---

* Other opinions are that the one covered with Greek inscriptions is that of Amunoph, but that the second represents his Prime-Minister, whose magnificent tomb is shown in the Valley of the Dead: it contains two very grand sitting figures of himself and his wife, besides some exquisite bas-reliefs of hieroglyphics. His name is said to have been *Shammar;* the Arabs call the colossi *Dammar* and *Shammar,* and also *Salamât,* salutations—an evident allusion to the musical sounds so famous in tradition.

† Strabo says it was destroyed by an earthquake—the one seems as probable as the other.

The great palace-temple of Rameses II. is the first ruin visited on this western bank; it has been commonly called the Memnonium, from a confusion caused by the title of Mi-Ammoun belonging to Rameses the Great, but it is more rightly called the Rameseum. The expression *palace-temple* does not, at least in this instance, mean that the king and his court resided in the temple, but only that rooms were attached to it where the king may have retired in the intervals of his own devotions, or after receiving the offerings of his people; and he may also have held his receptions in the grand courts or halls of assembly of the Temple. The Rameseum was called by Diodorus the " tomb of Osimandyas " (Rameses); but it is not quite this, for the dead king's actual tomb * was in the mountain side, towards the setting sun, and this temple is consecrated only to his memory; here, therefore, as in a few other temples, there is no sanctuary or adytum appropriated to the image of a particular god. The Pyramids had each of them a small temple on their eastern side, consecrated to the dead who lay beneath them; and the Rameseum bears the same relation to the mountain tomb of the king as the memorial temple bore to the Pyramid.

The Rameseum is one of the finest and most complete of all these ruins; the noble pylons are still standing, with a good deal of the first and second courts, including the fine interior peristyle of the latter, which once contained eight Osiride pillars and two splendid statues (the head of one of which is now in the British Museum); besides these there is nearly all the beautiful hypostyle hall, which, though small in comparison to that of Karnak, is very fine. The sculptures here are more than commonly interesting: they are boldly and well executed, chiefly of battle-scenes, some of them densely crowded with figures, but every figure is left perfectly clear and distinct. They illustrate the different modes of warfare, the varieties of kingdoms and peoples overcome by the great conqueror, with the king returning thanks to the gods for their assistance, while his deeds are noted down by Thoth. Here Rameses is given by the gods the sword and the sceptre—the one for his enemies and the other for his people, while the goodness of the king's character, which has rendered him the favoured son of the gods, is indicated by the stream of " pure life" poured upon his head by them. So vivid is the interest raised in one's mind by these graphically-por-trayed historic scenes, that one turns with double curiosity to the mysteriously-shattered colossal statue of the hero of all the incidents graven there lying close by, unquestionably a real, true portrait; it is about the same size as those of the pair sitting on the plain,

* No. 7.

but cut in a finer stone. It is difficult to conceive how such a block
was transported here, carved or uncarved, from Assouân, for it is
nearly as large and heavy as the famous stone still lying in the
quarry at Baalbek; but this huge mass once wore the same noble
and beautiful features as the giant faces at Abou Simbil, and those
of the fallen hero lying in the mud at Mitrahenny (Memphis).

Then comes at Gourneh the beautiful old temple of the great
warrior Sethi, or Osirei I., completed by his son Rameses II.—
perhaps the most venerable looking of all the Theban ruins; it has
a sad and melancholy air about it, but the sculptures are very
interesting. There are two pylons, one beyond the other, from each
of which an avenue of sphinxes led to the temple, where a corridor
of very elegant columns bears the dedication of the temple to
Amoun-Ra, the king of the gods, by Rameses II., who appears afterwards, introduced by his father Osirei to the gods: among them his
grandfather Rameses I. is standing, bearing the insignia of Osiris, as
a dead king now with or absorbed into Osiris. This temple lies to
the north of the plain. Far away at the southern extremity is
the magnificent pile of buildings now called Medeenet Habou, the
palace and temple of Rameses III., who reigned about a hundred
years later than Rameses the Great. This is probably the largest
ruin in Egypt. There is here a temple with all the usual pylons,
courts, sanctuary, &c.; and then another mass of towers, pavilions,
courts, halls, and pylons, in one immense heap of confused ruin.
The sculptures here, retaining the most vivid freshness of colour,
are perhaps, on the whole, the most varied and interesting to be
met with. Many pages would be required to give even a faint idea
of their subjects; one open court alone, with an interior peristyle,
123 feet by 133, is completely surrounded with battle and other
scenes depicted in the liveliest manner possible. Every column also
is painted in beautiful patterns, and, although these columns are
but three diameters in height, the *tout ensemble* is one of the grandest
things in ancient art. At Medeenet Habou everything connected
with the king may be seen and studied together: his leisure hours
and his amusements in his court at home, his state processions
abroad, are closely detailed in the walls of this palace, while on
those of the towers and huge areas are all his noble deeds and his
religious ceremonials and duties. Unfortunately within the latter
the Copts made their cathedral, and the houses of their village
filled up the surrounding ruins: much, therefore, has been sadly
spoiled and intentionally mutilated, though they happily preserved
many of the sculptures in their original brightness by concealing
them under a plaster of mud. One cannot help fancying what

grand cathedrals these beautiful hypæthral courts must have made, however incongruous the mixture of the past and the present.

Here Rameses III. dedicates all these buildings to his great father the god Amoun-Ra, who calls him his "friend," and, in company with other gods, presents him with the scythe wherewith to conquer and cut off all his enemies. The warrior-king is then seen fighting his battles, after which he returns in triumph, leading, or rather dragging, his enemies by their hair, to show them to the gods, to whom also he makes rich thank-offerings, gratefully receiving their praises: his conquests have been innumerable, and his god-given virtues are nearly as many; his new subjects assure him that he "reigns like a mighty sun in Egypt,"—that his "courage is like that of the griffin—our breath is thine, as well as our lives, which are for ever in thy power," —while he declares that he has but obeyed the command of Amoun-Ra, and conquered by the might of his god-given strength. The coronation of the king is also seen, and, while he offers incense to the protecting gods, carrier-pigeons announce his greatness in all the four quarters of the world. The king also gains a great victory at sea, assisting his fleet of finely-drawn ships by manœuvres on shore: to this fresh conquest he declares himself inspired by the spirit of Amoun-Ra, who has thus "laid the whole world at his feet."

Not far from the ruins of the royal palaces of Medeenet Habou the remains of an artificially-made lake are distinctly discerned, like that at Memphis: across this lake the corpses of the king and of all the nobles of the city were ferried with grand processions of boats, before they were drawn on sledges along the dreary valley, opening in the mountain range at whose feet we stand, to their "eternal habitations." We will delay speaking of them till we have glanced over the rest of the city of Thebes.

Luxsor, being now a market town of some small dignity, has clustered its miserable houses within and without the once beautiful ruins of its temple, and it is almost impossible to see them with any very intelligible understanding of their plan: one can only perceive that it is a fine and picturesque ruin. One beautiful obelisk (sister to that in Paris), still marks the site of the once proud city; it is the oldest and most interesting of all the obelisks in Egypt, for it bears the name of Sesortasen the Great, of the twelfth dynasty—the king in whose reign the wonderful tombs of Beni-Hassan were hewn and painted—and perhaps it stood there before Moses refused to be called the son of Pharaoh's daughter—perhaps even before Joseph was brought into the land of Egypt by the Bedouin! Yet the characters engraved upon its sides are as clear now as they were five or six thousand years ago, and one may well be excused for the fancy that the stone is as imperishable as the idea conveyed on it. These two obelisks commenced an avenue of *twelve hundred* giant ram-headed sphinxes, which led from Luxsor to the pylon of the first temple of Karnak, each standing on a pedestal; hundreds of these have been destroyed, but many, headless and broken, still border the empty path down which the long and gorgeous procession of priests, clad in panther skins, passed daily, carrying the ram-prowed barge containing the shrine of the god in whose honour the festival of the day was held, and before whom burning incense was borne. Several of these Sphinxes are at Turin, very many at St. Petersburg, some in Berlin, and one or two in England. Another avenue of Sphinxes led from the front of this temple to the bank of the river, overlooking Gourneh, and a third led in a southerly direction towards Luxsor.

The first temple reached at Karnak is a very complete and fine one, approached by another sphinx avenue; but one cannot linger here in one's impatience to see the grand temple itself, a few minutes farther on. Two giant pylons open into a large court, with columns on two sides, and an aisle of columns up the centre, leading into the famous hypostyle hall, which Fergusson calls "the greatest of man's architectural works;" the centre aisle is formed of twelve columns, sixty-two feet high, the largest, if not the tallest columns in the world, with sixty-one smaller columns on each side of them. A beautiful clerestory runs along the top of each first row of the lower columns, and may have supported a stone roof over the middle aisle, as in the Rameseum: the rest was probably hypæthral— some suppose it to have been covered in with hangings either of stuffs or of palm-leaf matting, but as ample shade must have been found beneath the very closely-placed columns, even had it been hypæthral one cannot help hoping that the blue sky was open to the worshippers within—so beautiful is the effect of the sunlight and the shade of the columns falling athwart the apparently innumerable pillars. This is the place to see what a complete tapestry the hieroglyphics formed, for here not an inch of wall or column is left uncovered with closely-sculptured figures, once all brilliantly coloured—as complete a covering for the stone as the marble inlay of a Damascene house, or the brocade pattern of a modern house-paper. Strange to say, *every column* has the same set repeated in rings all round it. But though so subordinate a feature, their sameness probably adds to the feeling of infinite space, as the eye is not attracted by any change of object, and therefore wanders on indefinitely among the mighty forest of 6420 square yards. Behind this and the slender rose-granite obelisks, happily still erect, is the fine *hall* and adytum of this Temple; then comes, within the same outer enclosure, the palace of Thothmes III., where the hall is supported by alternate rows of square and round pillars with reversed capitals. In one of the many chambers behind this the valuable list of the sixty predecessors of Thothmes was found sculptured which is now in Paris. Deeply interesting are the splendid sculptures that cover the great walls throughout this pile of buildings, portraying the history of a thousand conquests,—among them that of the land of Palestine, with its name of *Canaan* and *Yooda Melchi*—the Judah kingdom, conquered by Shishak or Sheshonk in 971 B.C.

Numbers of other ruins of great interest lie scattered around this great temple, in strange but picturesque variety, among palm-groves and verdant fields; and it is pleasant to wander from one to the other, and rest one's mind, oppressed with the stupendous ideas generated by these ruins, so sublimely expressed in the stone and pictured in the sculptures, while listening to the evening breeze among the palms, and the melancholy chaunt of the fellāh, and watching the flocks of exquisite tiny paroquets, with emerald green plumage and crimson bills, flitting about in the sweet air. And it is right to linger, for this is truly one of the grandest scenes that earth can show. Athens, with all the delicate refinements of comparatively modern days, stands smiling like a white dove pluming herself on the summit of her noble rock, a pæan of war still echoing round her white statues—Palmyra, far away in the silence and soltitude of Nature's wildest splendour, sings lowly to herself the sad elegy of her own dead glory; but Karnak, with no natural beauty save the ever-cloudless sky and the delicious air over the green palm-groves and yellow sand, closes down upon the mind with a grand and almost awful solemnity; and the feeling comes home, that while in the others the chivalry and poetry of life were solidified in stone, you have here the expression of man's deepest religion. I have often thought since that Athens told of the bright and hopeful ardour of the busy morning, Palmyra of the lovely tenderness of evening, and Karnak of the calm and holy night, in yet closer communion with all beyond this world.

Let us now go down over the fields, through the groups of trees to the river bank, and after crossing the wide grey stream, land on the western side, thread the green paths between the fields of waving dhourra till we reach the low mountain range at the back of the plain : here, turning a little to the right, we enter a narrow defile which the Arabs call the Biban-el-Moluk, or Valley of the Kings; it ought rather to be called the Valley of the *Shadow* of Death, for the *reality* of death is farther on. The winding ravine is an absolute desert of loose stones, with steep rocky sides, broken, jagged, and crumbling, of bright yellow and orange cliffs, with here and there a blackened, burnt-up summit: it is not high enough to be very grand, but is it utterly and intensely desolate and dreary, solitary and silent—not a bird nor a moving insect is to be seen— not a sound of any kind heard; almost always painfully hot and glaring, it forms a fit passage to the Land of Death beyond.

After a ride of about an hour the valley opens to a somewhat greater width. Here every rock and hill-side is honeycombed with excavations, receding back to the extent of from two to four hundred feet—chamber succeeds to chamber, passage to passage. Nearly all slope downwards as they recede; some have staircases cut down to much lower levels, as if to sink the body of the deceased lower and lower under the crust of the mountain, but the reason was probably to avoid faults in the rock. The larger chambers are supported on pillars left in the excavation, but smoothed over for the reception of hieroglyphics; some have divans round a few of the chambers: the sarcophagus rarely remains; in some it was buried in a pit, and carefully covered over.

The tombs in this valley appear to have been entirely devoted to kings and royal personages, whose bodies were probably concealed in secret passages, lest avarice should lead to the plunder of the tomb, and the sacred person of the king be discovered. The Egyptians considered that the body might at some time be reclaimed, and they regarded what had once contained the divine spark of any man as sacred; it was therefore carefully embalmed and laid by with some of his regal ornaments, a list of his possessions, and a roll of prayers written on papyrus. This set of tombs are all of the Theban kings of the XIXth and XXth dynasties: sometimes a king of later days has taken the place of one of his predecessors, when his name is seen to be marked in a different style to the rest of the sculptures. Near Medeenet Habou is a small valley containing the tombs of the queens; while beyond those of the kings are the tombs of priests and rich men, in a place called the Valley of Assaseef. It is believed that among these tombs some were excavated and ornamented with sculptures appropriate to the solemn place—with the lessons for the living drawn from the life of the dead, and the hopes and fears of the future; blanks were left for the names and peculiar titles or biography of the individual who afterwards bought the tomb, which were filled up at the time of his death; some remain still unfilled, and some tombs are supposed never to have been occupied save by the bodies of the modern dead, thrust in in after times. The roofs of these tombs are generally lined with crude brick, and covered with stucco, as are the walls on which the hieroglyphics are painted. Over the portal of each is painted the great red disk of the sun, signifying that the soul of the deceased is gone down into the darkness with him, and after traversing the shades, will ultimately rise up with him again. Near the entrance the scarabæus (the emblem of the resurrection) and the crocodile (the emblem of darkness) are figured; while *beyond* the sarcophagus is seen the young Horus, son of Osiris, the Divine Man, who yet more emphatically signifies the resurrection.

It is impossible to give an idea of the immense variety of the sculptures which tapestry the walls of these tombs, and happily it is unnecessary to do so, as so many excellent descriptions are already published of them: suffice it to say that they illustrate every trade, profession, manufacture, occupation, and custom of the ancient Egyptians, besides the religious and royal ceremonials, and the minutest details of the burying of the kings and the nobles: the tombs of private individuals are still more generally interesting.*

The chief thought made present to one's mind in examining the temples and palaces of the Egyptian kings is their (natural) pride in the extension and glory of their conquests: the next is the perception of how invariably every triumph and every blessing was acknowledged as bestowed by the supreme God, the Father and Giver of all good. At every moment throughout his life we find the king honouring, reverencing, and, perhaps, propitiating the gods, to whom he daily pays his grateful homage, and to whom he offers up his prayers for virtue and life, as well as his thanksgivings for the throne and power they have conferred upon him. In death he is portrayed in still closer communion with the gods: the short and varied term of earthly life appears over, and the spirit, parted from the body, commences a new and still more important existence. The entrance to this new life is attended by the most rigorous difficulties, but for the overcoming of these he has

---

* The tombs best worth seeing among those of the kings are Nos. 17, 11, 6, 14, and 9; the magnificent tomb of the priest Petumunap, in the Valley of Assaseef; that of King Amoun Toonh; Nos. 5, 16, 17, 31, 34, and 35, of those at Goorneh Murraee; and another among these latter, inhabited by a family of Arabs, and very difficult to crawl into, containing the most varied and lively representations of all kinds of hunting.

been preparing throughout his earthly careér. And truly to us this pictured Life in Death seems almost more comprehensible than that which has come before; here there are but few signs of ruin and destruction—we know that all have equally passed away, but the Life after Death seems nearer to us now than the Life before Death,—the idea of the grave and of judgment is closer akin to our minds than the old-world customs of the past; and Death becomes a link binding us into one brotherhood, almost more living than Life.

The awfulness of the future judgment began with the ancient Egyptians even upon earth;[*] a type of it was enacted over the dead body after being carried across the lake for burial. Forty-two judges examined the testimony given of the candidate's innocence or transgression in each of the forty-two sins most common to man; if the dead man was proved to have been of an immoral character, whether king, priest, or peasant, he was refused burial.[†] The mummy is everywhere entitled " the habitation of Osiris :" it is carried to the tomb in his boat, his symbols precede and follow it in procession, and the high-priest offers incense to it. The soul was supposed to sleep during the forty days of embalming; it then revived again, and accompanied the body to the tomb, where it received liberation. In the 'Book of the Dead' (the Turin copy) Isis and Nepthys are thus addressed :—" Oh ye liberators of the souls of them that are built into a house of Osiris " (that is, made into a mummy), "liberate the soul of M——— whom ye have made into a house of Osiris : he sees as ye see, he hears as ye hear, stands as ye stand, sits as ye sit." The soul is then directed to pay adoration to Ra, the rising sun, and Athom, the setting sun. In the illustrations that occur here in this papyrus the soul[‡] is seen entering the bark of the sun in the twelfth hour of the day; the disk of the sun is seen passing the portals of the west, which are opened by male and female guardians; then the orb of day is seen to have entered into the cave, where he is received into the arms of Athom, his human impersonation, while eight apes shriek forth the impurities of the soul that accompanies him; after this the soul is again seen, arrived in the world of spirits underground, adoring the souls of his deceased ancestors, and offering them incense and libations. Afterwards the adventures of the soul in Hades are

[*] Champollion. Martineau's 'Eastern Travel,' p. 194.

[†] Osburn, ' Mon. Hist.,' vol. i. p. 427.

[‡] The soul is portrayed under the symbol of a bird, usually the white ibis : it was natural to think "these beautiful white, silent, ghost-like birds, standing motionless and pensive on the sand-flats, might be the souls of the departed waiting the completion of the funeral ceremonies."—*Osburn.*

described : they consist of transmigrations into the forms of many divinities, all of them of the family of Osiris, who is styled "son of the sun," "the lord of the cave of Amenti," &c.; the disembodied spirit still navigating a river, which represents the nocturnal path of the sun. It at length reached the grand hall of the judge of the dead, where his heart is tried in the balance (upon which a cyno-cephalus, the emblem of Thoth, the scribe who has recorded his good and evil deeds, is sitting) by Anubis and Horus against the feathers (the emblem of truth and justice), and the sentence is pronounced by Thmee, the goddess of justice, in the presence of Osiris, enthroned and holding the emblems of supreme judgment, the crosier and the scourge. The dead were instructed to make deprecations to the divinities presiding there—to the assessors who wear the feathers of truth and justice, and also to the forty-two avengers (represented in the tombs with various heads), who sat with knives ready to inflict torments on those that failed at the balance; thus he says, "I have neither done any sin nor omitted any duty to any man; I have committed no uncleanness; I have not prevaricated at the seat of justice," &c., &c.* If the soul is found really wanting, it is seen sent away in the form of a black or white dog, driven by the servants of Typhon down steeply-sloping paths, descending in a Dantesque manner deeper and deeper, according to his guilt. If the soul was found worthy of acceptation the goddesses Hathor and Nutpe, deputed by Amoun-Ra, the Creator of the world, poured over him the water of eternal purity and life, and he was believed thenceforth to be reunited, if not absorbed, into the spirit of Osiris,—to have become a part of Osiris; and in all future offerings made to the god the soul is remembered as dwelling in Osiris, and therefore partaking of the gifts offered to him. At some future time, long after the judgment, three thousand years according to Greek tradition, the justified soul returned to the earth and resuscitated the body; but after many cycles the final doom was probably to rest with Osiris, the divine lord of spirits and of the spirit-world, in whose person they arrived at the indescribable happiness of the presence of Amoun-Ra, the "hidden one," the lord of heaven, from whom he had emanated.

In the Egyptian religion every principle was embodied in some recognised type, under which form it was worshipped as partaking of the divine nature: thus the generation of life—the most important, and, to their naturally reverent minds, consequently the most sacred fact in creation, a fact *in* this world but not *of* it, a

* Translated by Osburn.

mystery utterly incomprehensible, and therefore to be the more venerated—was worshipped in the persons of several gods and goddesses, such as Khem,* the chief god of generation, Kneph,† Maut, Pasht, Neith, Hathor, Isis, and many others; for each and every god and goddess had a share, as it were, in the divine power. The vulture, the cat, the lion, the cow, and others, each and all were supposed to typify some divine attribute, and were therefore considered sacred as *types,* not gods in themselves. They were to the Egyptians the less perfect manifestations of the things typified, partaking of the same one divine nature, and thus truly divine in themselves; yet it was only that peculiar attribute found in each which united them to divinity, or had a divine origin; just as the life which animated them must have been divinely given. Thus the crocodile was sometimes worshipped as the type of strength; but he was usually consecrated to Typhon as one of the types of evil things, such as darkness. It is somewhat hopeless now to determine the reasons why the sacred animals were made respectively typical of certain principles, as they occasionally represented contrary ones: the ignorance of natural history at that time may sometimes account for the choice.

There were also deities of each nome or division of the land, and local deities in great variety; but there are signs of the united empire under the great dynasties, in these deities having each other's attributes, while, as Herodotus tells us, Osiris was universally worshipped. The principle of Triads seems to pervade every form of the worship, and is a subject well worthy of study. It is difficult to ascertain the precise idea of the Father, Mother, and Child, but the Triad-principle runs through all mythology, and, together with the worship of a God-Man, dying in his strife with Evil, and rising triumphant as the Judge of the Dead, is one of the remarkable evidences that God has been speaking to Man everywhere, and in every age: to some minds, at least, such coincidences appear very strong evidence of truth.

The worship of the king is another instance of the worship of the divine attribute: he was deputed by the gods in heaven to rule on earth for them; he was divinely appointed and divinely assisted; a portion of the divine essence dwelt in the king *as king,* and was so completely a *part* of the god from whom it came, and so separate

---

* In the 18th dynasty Khem was erased in the hieroglyphic names, and Amoun-Ra (generator) substituted: Amoun-Ra was not worshipped earlier.

† Kneph is most frequently seen standing in the boat which Horus steers; he is the vivifying *spirit* of God, "brooding over the face of the waters." The serpent is stretched above him, and the ram is peculiarly sacred to him.

from the king's human nature, that he could offer worship—not to himself, but—to the divinity in him; although, of course, this divine essence can only be materially pictured by the temporary habitation of his own human body, holding or wearing divine symbols. For this reason the king bore the title of " the son of the sun"—a title which has been roughly rendered in our Bible as "Pharaoh"—*Ph* being the article *the*—*Ra*, the sun. The king was high-priest, and the princes were necessarily of the priestly order, while the queens were priestesses to the goddesses. Joseph and Moses, from their distinguished positions, must have been priests; and taking what St. Stephen says of Moses, that " he was learned in all the wisdom of the Egyptians,"* with the fact that Joseph married Asenath, daughter of Pet-ph-Ra, priest of On,† we may infer that they were both initiated into the mysteries of Osiris, On being one of the principal places of the worship of Osiris.

The Egyptians found a spiritual meaning in everything natural, and inculcated this with the deep religious poetry of their grave, calm minds: thus Osiris, the Father Nile, and Isis, the Mother Earth of Egypt, were brother and sister as well as husband and wife; their life, they taught, is one of perfect, divinely-given happiness (because perfectly pure and holy), until Evil or Typhon —that is all the noxious powers of Nature, sterility, darkness, and scorching heat—arrives and murders Osiris, who descends into the nether world, while the earth remains widowed under the dominion of Typhon—that is, dry, burnt-up, and sterile. Horus, the son of Osiris and Isis, the fruit grown upon the earth after the annual inundation of the river, grows up into manly strength, struggles with Evil, and, overcoming him, spreads fertility and blessing once more upon the soil; Horus is therefore entitled " the great deliverer, the support of the world," and is invested with the signs of power and life: his face is as the hawk's, he wears the royal head-dress, and holds the *anch*, the sign of pure life, in his hand.

To mention, for the assistance of travellers, a very few of the chief and most frequently-repeated figures, we may speak of: Amoun-Ra, the creator, distinguished by the red disk of the sun, winged, and the feathers of truth and justice on his head: he is the great god of Thebes, the capital of Egypt, which was probably one of the reasons for his being the chief god of all; many others take his name as a prefix. As the name meant *hidden*, he would in his own character express one of the highest religious Ideas, and other divinities would be merged in him, so that, amidst the endless com- plexities of this idolatrous system, we have a glimpse at times of

* Acts vii. 22.   † Gen. xli. 45.

F

the Truth of the Divine Unity underlying all. The hawk, signifying omnivision, and the scarabæus, chiefly typical of creation and of the world, were sacred to Amoun-Ra: the complete ball of mud with which the latter surrounds its egg, and which it fashions and rolls away so ingeniously, might well suggest creation; and they seem to have had a fancy about all the beetles being males. It was also distinctly a type of the resurrection, and with this meaning its images were bound in a hundred ways upon every corpse, and painted upon every coffin as the pledge and token of a future life. Still more strongly, and by a beautiful figure, the scarabæus is seen,* as it were, leaning out of heaven, and helping the mummy over the difficulties of the entrance, the body being thus included in the resurrection.

PASHT (corresponding to the goddess Diana) was the " mother of the gods," and had the vulture sacred to her as the emblem of maternity, because she was supposed to feed her young with her own blood: this was changed in later times to the pelican. But Pasht in the tombs is the goddess of fire, and presides over punishments; she is seen standing over souls enveloped in flames, with the sword of vengeance in her hand, and spitting fire upon them: she has a cat's head usually, but sometimes that of a lioness.

OSIRIS is known by the scourge of punishment for the wicked, and the crosier of acceptance for the righteous. The crosier is often seen held out by the kings to supplicants, just as Ahasuerus held it out to Esther.† He is called the "manifester of good, the lord of life, the lord of spirits," &c.; his legs are swathed, to represent the repose of one who has passed through death.

ISIS (whose face is, like that of Osiris, always full of sweetness and dignity) has the sun's disk, as the mother of the earth; and in the character of Athor, the horns of the cow on her head, as the provider of nourishment (milk) for all the world. She is continually represented with the attributes of other goddesses; but as the great goddess, "the mother of the child" (Horus), she is distinguished by the throne as her head-dress, which is one of the hieroglyphs in the name of Osiris: in fact her name is written similarly to his, but with the female sign, the egg; she has often the vulture as a head-dress, with the asp, and sometimes water-plants, as "the bride of the Nile." She corresponds, when in the Amenti, to Proserpine, but usually her character is that of Ceres.

NEITH is goddess both of wisdom and of war: she wears the crown of Lower Egypt, and sometimes holds a bow and arrows, but

---

* In the Harper's or Bruce's tomb.
† Esther iv. 11.

more frequently a sceptre of flowers; while her face is green, signifying the verdure of the fruitful earth. Her great temple was at Saïs, and over the portal was this remarkable inscription: " I am all that was, is, and shall be,—I proceed from myself,—none have lifted the veil that covers me." The great mysteries of the burial of Osiris were performed on the lake at Saïs by torchlight, with those of Neith as Isis,—whence, says, Herodotus, came the Greek Eleusinian mysteries, and the ' Thesmophoria.'

NUTPE—wife of Seb, and mother of the gods—the heaven or firmament: this is the divine origin of Osiris, from the primæval Mother, the ineffable Darkness, and Time, his father. The figure of Nutpe within the sarcophagus means that the soul is become as Osiris. In one tomb,* she surrounds the whole ceiling of a chamber like a winding river, giving birth at one side to the Sun, the form of Day, who is led away by a group of gods along a path which grows shallower till it reaches a lake on the other side, through which he passes, and thence in solitude and darkness returns to the side whence he commenced his course.

SEB corresponds to Saturn as Chronos, Time. An inscription reads: " Saturn, youngest of all the Gods, is my father,—I am Osiris; " so the Divine children of Seb constitute the *third order* of gods; for there were three of these orders: 1. the eight Great Gods, (according to Herodotus), Amoun, Kheph, &c.; 2. Ra, and his family; 3. the Osiride.

SET† represents Evil: he is brother of Osiris, and the son of Time; he and Horus are sometimes seen pouring the anointing oil over the king. Horus embraces him, and Set gives him weapons of war; the king also offers to and propitiates the destroyer Set, that he may be induced to favour the king, and make him his instrument.

One of the most interesting subjects of all in these tombs, both for examination and thought, is that of the Serpent, which meets the eye at every step, and evidently speaks a language of deep meaning, that one longs to hear and understand: it is one, however, about which, I believe, little is as yet known. These animals form the most conspicuous and important feature in every representation of a mystery, or of an unearthly ceremonial: frequently drawn as in nature, and as frequently with human heads, male or female; sometimes with many heads, with human legs, some turned one way, some another; occasionally with lion's paws; sometimes with a head at each end of the body, and some growing along the back, or ranges of mummies supported on it; sometimes—and these are

* No. 9.

† Possibly from this name comes the Arabic *Sheitán*, the devil or Satan.

always grand, giant serpents—they have vulture's wings, and bear a sun's disk. They are seen in battle with the gods, and in the end, overcome by them, they lie wounded and bound. Sometimes there are long rows of them, each one enwreathing a headless human body, forming grotesquely-shaped rings; they are painted of all colours, beautifully striped, mottled, or scaled; they are also seen lotus-crowned, with human legs, as the symbol of Kneph, the good spirit, the paternal and spirit-giving deity. In some tombs the Serpent commences at the entrance, and winds in countless folds throughout the whole tomb to the very end : sometimes he swallows his own tail, forming a circle—the symbol of eternity. One can only say that they *usually* represent Evil, and perhaps more peculiarly Moral Evil than the god Set does. Coleridge takes the Serpent as symbolising the understanding; and in some cases this may be the sense : "Now the serpent was more subtle than any beast of the field."

But with the most accurate knowledge of the meaning of the hieroglyphics, the scholar still gropes in the dark respecting their less tangible translation; little more than has been already read historically from the walls of temple and tomb will probably ever be educed by the mere hieroglyphist. The old Greeks—rude, untutored infants in the days of Egypt's glory—drew from her the first sparks of that fire which they afterwards refined and beautified into models for all the world. From the days when the little band of Egyptians left the mouth of the Nile to plant a new kingdom on the fair shores of Greece, down to the thirteen years that Plato studied at Heliopolis, every Grecian superstructure will be found to have its foundation in the Egyptian faith; and perhaps it is only by the light of those who taught the deepest and highest philosophy of the Greek school that the parent principles can be solved.[*] The very gods bear all the same attributes and functions : Zeus is but Amoun-Ra, keeping, indeed, his Egyptian name; Seb turned into Chronos; Phthah into Hephæstos; Pasht into Artemis; Thoth into Hermes; while Athor, the lovely lady of the West, the Morning-Star, became the queen of beauty, Aphrodite. True, the Greeks threw a poetic veil over them, and re-created them, as it were, with a new and fresh beauty, which made them peculiarly their own; yet not the less is every deep and holy idea of the Grecian mythology essentially and originally Egyptian.

The Temple of Denderah should be seen in ascending the Nile, as it loses all interest of detail after the temples and tombs of

[*] Doubtless the Greeks owed much also to the Phœnicians; but it is impossible to say how much the Phœnicians owed to the Egyptians.

Thebes, the hieroglyphics testifying their modern age by their poorness of outline and bad arrangement; its nearly perfect preservation, however, renders it a good explanation, in its plan and general construction, for the more ruined but more interesting temples farther on. The great square court succeeding the pylons usual in the larger temples is here wanting, but the magnificent portico makes up for the loss. This portico, leading to the fine hall and lofty adytum within, and which has scarcely even a chip on the stone, is supported by twenty-four grand columns with square capitals, to which the colossal face of Athor is affixed on each side; very sweet and dignified is the head, however singular the adaptation of a small pylon which is inserted below the abacus as her headdress; the whole front is richly covered with hieroglyphics. There are a number of other buildings near this, much ruined; one is a temple of the class that Champollion calls "mammeisi," where the child of Athor is supposed to be born: this is Ehu, the young god of day or light, born of Ra, the sun, and Athor, the morning-star. This temple is covered with representations of Typhon, the god of darkness, with whom Ra is in continual combat, and to whom the birth of a child is a fresh disaster. Outside the wall of the large temple is a portrait of the famous Cleopatra; she has a fat, chubby face, and is not very much prettier than the lion-headed gurgoyles which surround the roof, as grotesque in form as any mediæval monsters.

For the study of hieroglyphics there is no place, after Thebes, to be compared to Abydos; and in descending the Nile the difference in them, to the eyes that have looked on Kalabshee, Philæ, and Denderah, is very glaring; there is a neatness and precision here, an evident meaning vigorously expressed, even to those who cannot read them, which strikes the most cursory glance; while in some of the late Ptolemaic temples they seem only pictures stuck on as ornament. They are here conveyed, too, by a fine medium, the walls of the now ruined sanctuary and chambers being lined with slabs of alabaster and finished with all the princely richness and fine execution of Rameses the Great. I remember three most living figures, larger than life, sculptured on one wall with something like chain mail over the head and the dress; and the plaited hair and embroidery all conveyed with the utmost delicacy of finish. The other building—the Temple-palace of Seti (or Osirei) I.—was uncovered in 1857; it was finished by his son Rameses the Great, and is very rich and large; the bas-reliefs are the most beautiful in Egypt, indeed there is nothing equal to them in Egyptian art except the paintings in the tomb of this same King Seti at Thebes.

In earlier periods art was far more *naturalistic*; but what we may call Egyptian art *proper* was in the reign of Seti the most perfect of all; it is beautiful, living, and highly picturesque, although completely subject to the arbitrary rules imposed by the priests on the artists, in accordance with the elaborate theocratic system of government that extended through all the minutiæ of life. Here at Abydos stood, it is supposed, the City of This, the birthplace of Menes, and the capital of Upper Egypt long before the rise of Thebes, and at least 1300 years before the time of Rameses the Great, who lived about as long before Christ.*

I think the ride to Abydos was the prettiest and pleasantest we enjoyed in Egypt; we had good little donkeys, who took us there in about three hours and a half, through green fields of flourishing sugar-cane, bean, and dhourra crops, with here and there a grove of shady trees, and buffaloes in large herds feeding on the plain. The sun was hot enough without being fierce, and there was only too much of a cool breeze, delightful in the fields, but very disagreeable when we reached the ruined city, which lies under many fathoms of loose sand. The path was gay with passengers, all dark brown, and in the village we found troops of pleasant-looking women and naked shining-skinned children, who seemed more obliging than usual, offering us dates and water as we passed by. Then there were camels, old and young, feeding round a pretty little natural pond shaded by palm-trees.

We were very much detained by contrary winds the whole way down from Thebes to Cairo; day after day the same head-wind blew, with only the cessation of three or four hours now and then, and frequently with so much violence that it was impossible to proceed, when, after enduring a variety of unpleasant collisions with the small waves, we hauled to and lay bumping on the bank. The process of drifting down is not an agreeable one; the boat generally gets near the middle of the stream, and spins slowly round and round as it goes on, and in any wind it drifts with a kind of heavy lumbering motion, which makes many people qualmish. The sailors row a good deal, but in head-winds it is labour thrown away. We sometimes found pleasant walks on shore, especially in the lovely gardens of Siout and Minyeh, but the wind was often too high even for walking. We had intended to stop in coming down, to see the Red and White Convents, and many other things, but our many discomforts made us anxious to get on. One morning very early, however, we started to see the Cave of Diana, the Speos Artemidos, by no means to be missed by any traveller; it lies in the midst of

* Wilkinson's Chronology.

a wild desert ravine of broken rocks, and is excavated from the
mountain side, leaving in front a portico of eight square pillars:
there is an inner chamber containing a large niche, probably for the
statue of the goddess Pasht, " the beautiful lady of the cavern," to
whom the excavation was dedicated by Thothmes III. and Seti (or
Osirei) I. Lions and cats, the animals sacred to Pasht, have been
buried in numbers of grottoes hollowed out in these rocks, and some
of the larger tombs in the ravine contain a few hieroglyphics.

From this the deeply interesting tombs of Beni-Hassan are soon
reached; they occupy a long time in examining, for they are, next
to the Pyramids, the oldest records in Egypt, some of them being
of the time of Osirtasen I. and II., with the name of Suphis, the
builder of the Great Pyramid, introduced in one of the inscriptions.
Yet no colours anywhere in Egypt are fresher, and no paintings
more vigorously and admirably executed. They contain vivid representations of every trade, occupation, amusement, and mode of
life known to the Egyptians, besides a hundred other subjects far
too numerous to describe or even to mention. The porticoes of two
or three of the southern tombs are ornamented with polygonal
columns, the representation of the stalks of plants bound together,
with a lotus-bud for the capital; and one is considered to be the
original from which the Doric Temple at Corinth was copied; in
others the column is the same without any capital or fillet beneath
the abacus. It is wise and pleasant to linger among these tombs,
and to examine them narrowly; they should be studied in ascending the Nile, for the sooner the eye is accustomed to *good* hieroglyphics and the *best* Egyptian art, the better: after becoming even
only a little familiar with them, one's enjoyment of the finest and
oldest temples is doubled and trebled to what it is if the eye has
not learnt to distinguish easily between the ancient reality and
the modern imitation. One should never lose an hour of favourable
wind in ascending the Nile, nor stop for anything (even the all-
important daily milk!) should there be a chance of a good breeze;
but the few, very few miles gained by a whole day's tracking are
worth nothing in comparison to the knowledge thus gained in preparation for the Nubian and other temples. Thebes, indeed, on
both sides of the river, should be left till the last of all, unspoiled
by even a glance in ascending; and after it has been seen, the
slowest downward drifting without landing is scarcely enough
for arranging clearly in one's mind all the knowledge one has
gained there.

The last excursion we made before arriving at Gheezeh was to
visit the site of Memphis, the first city of which even a legend still

exists in Egypt: it is believed to have been built by Menes, the first king, whose date is given between 3640 and 2700 before Christ, and some hundreds of years prior to the building of the Pyramids. It continued to be the capital of Lower Egypt throughout the glory of Thebes and long after its fall; in fact until the rise of Alexandria robbed it of its commerce. It was still a city in the time of the Mohammedan conquest, 600 years after Christ; but, unlike Thebes, not a trace remains of its magnificent temples, and only a few green mounds and some broken statues guide the antiquary to its long-forgotten site.

A short ride from the village of Bedreshayn brings the traveller to that called Mitrahenny, where, prone on its face, lies the statue of Rameses the Great, forty-three feet high, and finely carved in a hard limestone, which was probably polished: the beautiful features (which can fortunately still be seen, from the ground sloping away from under the face) are in perfect preservation, and recall to the mind their brother portraits at Abou Simbil. There is also a broken statue farther on, about eight feet smaller, of another Rameses, and many fragments and broken bits of sculpture lie scattered about, besides smaller pieces arranged with some care by the villagers in a little mud-enclosure. We could not loiter under the fine trees that shade the village, nor even by the ugly ruin of the Sakkära Pyramid, for we were hastening on to the Serapeum, the happy discovery, made by Mariette in 1851, of the enormous tomb of all the Apis-bulls. This remarkable excavation is one long winding passage, sixteen feet wide and fourteen feet high, with large recesses on a level of some four or five feet lower at each side; in these recesses we counted thirty sarcophagi: only a very few were empty. It is almost incomprehensible how these sarcophagi, each thirteen feet by eight, and eleven feet high, could have been drawn along the passage; they are all of fine granite, some reddish from Assouän, some of a dark green nearly black, which stone is said, I know not on what authority, to come from the mountains of the Dead Sea. One sarcophagus is of basalt, with hieroglyphics remarkably small and delicately cut, and the granite is in some of them polished: they are I believe the finest sarcophagi ever discovered, and certainly wonderful masses. No Apis-bones have been discovered in them; all that have been opened were found filled with stones, as a mark of contempt. Apis was called "the living image of Osiris," and his name is probably an adaptation of a Coptic word meaning "conceal,"* as Osiris was concealed under his form; his body was black, Plutarch says, but he had

* Osburn.

a white triangle or star upon his forehead, the spot where the spirit was supposed to enter into him: on his back there was the mark of a vulture, a beetle under his tongue, and his tail was double,—all which was, of course, managed by the priests. In fact this Apis-worship shows what a monstrous system of priestly imposture the religion had become. How hard it must have been for the spiritually-minded, in these later times, to get at the ground-work of deep truth that underlaid many of the myths with which the priests had overlaid and so changed it, as far as the ignorant and vulgar went, into a degrading and gross idolatry.

But these are things to sigh over, and to think upon with an earnest, grave attention. What people find "so amusing" in the "bulls and cats" I never could understand; one would think that even the most frivolous would be sobered and the most trifling impressed into something like reverence after a few days at Thebes; yet even in the silent solemnity of the Valley of the Dead Kings-one's mind is jarred and worried with the strangest and most disagreeable contrasts. One may be lost to all the realities around, and then interrupted, as we were one day, by a voice calling to the unhappy dragoman, " I say—you there—awsk that feller oose tomb this is!" Being answered " Belzoni's tomb," the owner of the voice says he believes "that was the name of the king who built Abou Simbil;" and then he goes back to his dahabieh and his dinner, and perhaps confidingly remarks to his neighbour, after his champagne, " I say—wawt a bawr these tombs are! Egypt's quite a sell for a man like me!" in which latter sentiment we agree with him.

CHAPTER VI.

A MODERN EXODUS " IN HASTE."

"Nay, certainly, I have heard the Ptolemies' pyramises are very goodly things : without contradiction I have heard that."—SHAKESPEARE.

As we knew we should not have much time at our disposal for sight-seeing when once we had reached Cairo, we determined to visit the Pyramids from Gheezeh, this being a quieter and shorter ride than from the city. The heat was becoming greater every day, and those who wish to examine them in any degree of comfort, or see the view in bright tints, should leave their dahabieh before sunrise, taking breakfast with them. We did not start till 9 A.M., and only reached the Pyramids towards midday, when all the beauty of colouring had faded into the hot white glare, which is as painful as it is ugly. The path was for some way fresh with pleasant verdure, and crowded with Arabs, laden camels, and donkeys ; then at last we emerged on the dry loose sands, and had neither thoughts nor eyes for anything but the Pyramids. Their appearance, however, is very disappointing as one approaches them : I was not at all prepared to find how much so ; the deception caused by every line sloping away from the eye is inconceivably great, and not even a column raised beside them would correct the natural error, since the pyramidal form would still give the idea of something fore-shortened. I had to keep repeating to myself that the tower of Strasburg Cathedral might stand beneath the apex, and I found even then I did not quite believe my own reasoning about it.

We were soon in the usual mob of fellaheen anxious to be chosen as assistants for the ascent, on account of whom we had previously determined to forego a visit to the Pyramids unless we could join a party with gentlemen ; for they are an unruly and turbulent set, and only a very short time before a most unpleasant attack had been made by them upon a couple of gentlemen, when some blood was shed. The fellaheen had probably been roughly treated, but I believe that a little quiet firmness, with the declaration that you are English, and the determination not to be put into a passion by their noisy and extortionate demands, will soon secure the comparative comfort of the traveller. One must however make up one's mind to purchase the interesting result of examining the Pyramids by a thoroughly disagreeable process in every way. I am most glad to have *done* it, but nothing would induce me to repeat the operation, and I would earnestly dissuade any and every lady who is not entirely sure of her own nerves and self-control, and who is not very strong, from attempting it. The injury done to themselves in visiting the Pyramids by gentlemen who go to Egypt on account of delicate lungs or imperfect circulation is probably greater than the benefit they derive from the delightful climate, particularly if they indulge in the absurd schoolboy emulation of "trying to get up first."

The only right way to get through the ordeal is to be quietly passive in the hands of the three Arabs apportioned to each visitor. When once you have commenced the real business they are good-natured and careful fellows, proud of their knowledge of half a dozen sentences in half a dozen languages, and anxious to please you ; they know best how to tie up your garments so that they shall not impede your progress, and how to lift you with least exertion or disagreeableness to yourself, and the sole piece of advice I give to my countrywomen is, to *let* them lift you. Many of the stones are four feet in height, but the Arabs lift you at one jump with more ease than a stool or any other contrivance will afford you ; sometimes, too, they appear to mistake you for a doll or a swaddled baby, and you find yourself seized by the ankles as well as by the arms ! Even thus passively impelled upwards, the ascent is an enormous tax upon both blood and breath.

The now broken summit affords a platform of thirty-two feet square, with stones upon which and beside which you can rest comfortably; the view is fine, and interesting as being characteristic of Egypt, and should, I think, be viewed at the commencement of the traveller's stay in the country, thus taking in at one glance what you learn by slow degrees afterwards. Cairo, with its uncountable minarets, the most varied in form and the most picturesque in the world, rising upon the steep slope of the Mokuttum hills up to the citadel and the mosque of Muhammed 'Ali, is a remarkable view in itself; still more so the clearly-marked boundaries of the wide sandy desert, so melancholy and bare-looking, from the verdant, smiling plain studded with palm-trees which adjoins it; while the pyramids of Abouseer, Sakkāra and Dashoor, to the south, give a sort of still life to the scene. In the early morning or evening, doubtless, the view becomes as beautiful as it is striking, when even the featureless, desolate sand of the desert gains for a few moments the hues of a wild, stern beauty peculiarly its own.

An American gentleman arrived on the summit while we were there, and breathlessly informed us that the English Ministry was entirely changed, that England had declared war against nearly all Europe, and that the Old World was shortly going to pieces. Those who never stir beyond the reach of newspapers or letters can hardly imagine the avidity with which one seizes on all the news one can get after three months of exile from the civilised world, and it was curious to realise the vivid interest we felt in a thing of to-day,— whether one man or another was living " his little hour " in the new history of a tiny island 2000 miles away,—while so completely absorbed in personal interest in the events and actors of bygone ages. I *felt* the incongruity, but on the burning fiery furnace of that platform I could not *think*; my mind, too, was nervously fixed upon the horrors of the descent that awaited me. I found it by no means so difficult, but infinitely more disagreeable than the ascent. It was a very happy moment to me when I reached the bottom and found my sister standing, with the full complement of her limbs, in peace and comfort beside me: we had not felt legs or arms our own in either the up or down ordeal.

We rested some minutes in the shade before we entered the Pyramid. I think not less than eighteen Arabs went in with us; and it is impossible to describe the stifling feeling in the narrow passages, filled with noise, lights, heat, and smoke. I did not perceive in myself any sensation of horror or fear, so frequently felt by even the strongest-nerved travellers, but I confess that, according to the proverb of the " burnt child," the dread of fire came strongly upon me. We were above a score of persons, obliged to crouch quite on all-fours for many yards together, the flames of our candles flaring about in the draught which we made in passing, and my sister and I wore Arab-cotton dresses, on which one spark alighting —and many flew about—would have put us in a blaze, while any rush in those stifling passages must have been fatal to some one. The steep angle in which they dip, and their smooth surface, oblige one to have recourse to the barefooted Arabs for support, and their close company is considerably more disagreeable here than in the open air outside. But the passage is soon done; and after visiting a small empty chamber, nearly square, called the Queen's,—which is only interesting because it stands directly under the apex of the Pyramid,—you pass through a gallery twenty-eight feet high, the walls meeting at the top by progressive steps, and enter the King's chamber, an oblong room nineteen feet high. There are small holes or tubes in the walls of this chamber to admit ventilation, and over it are four large spaces, one above the other (which Sir G. Wilkinson naïvely calls *entresols*, in spite of their eternal darkness), intended to relieve the weight of the mass above them. In the two uppermost of these chambers the two stones were found on which the workmen had painted the names of the kings for whose mausoleum the Pyramid was built—Shofo (or Suphis, commonly called Cheops) and Nou (or Nef) Shofo, two brothers who reigned together, the one for fifty years, and the other for fifty-six years; their cartouches have been found in the rock-cut tombs close by, as well as the gold ring of King Suphis.

The chamber is formed of blocks of granite, which sparkle in the torchlight, cut smooth,* so exquisitely joined that the seams are almost imperceptible; at one end is the broken sarcophagus of the king, it is supposed, made of red granite, and still emitting a bell-sound when struck. It was a fine idea of those old Egyptians, as Herodotus tells us, that of admitting the waters of the life-giving Nile to enclose in its watery arms the dead body of the king, who in life "called the Nile his own:" thus insulating it from all earthly contact; but antiquaries have ruthlessly declared the tale to be less than a fable—a total impossibility. The overpowering feeling of immensity while thus descending lower and lower into the interior of the Pyramid is certainly very intense, and never to be forgotten; it is doubtless much increased by the quickening of the pulse, in the hurried rush down passages and up again, and by the difficulty of respiration. I felt something of the same kind afterwards in the cave of Adullam (near Hebron), the perilous path leading to which naturally hastens one's circulation a little; but there the habitual confidence of man in Nature and her glorious works has a soothing, strengthening influence, while inside the Pyramid one finds a vague feeling of fear steal involuntarily over one as one calculates the giant mass of human-raised Titan blocks around and above. I am sure the man who invented the horrible tale of the prison the walls of which gradually closed in day by day on the unfortunate prisoner confined within them had once stood in that King's chamber; and I remember comparing myself mentally to the little almond I had seen so gently and quietly cracked by the wonderfully-regulated

* The rest of the Pyramid is built of limestone.

power of the giant "Nasmyth's hammer," which but a moment before had pierced holes through a massive bar of iron as easily as a needle passes through fine cambric. The monstrous mass above me, however, remained unmoved, and the fate of the small almond was not mine.

The next half-hour was pleasantly spent resting under the shadow of one of the enormous blocks of which the lower tiers of the Pyramids are composed. Of course the finish given by the triangular stones, which made the surfaces of the sides smooth, must have added much to their appearance, but they are more picturesque as they are, with their rugged steps.

We saw the Sphinx in her very worst light, the glare of 2 P.M.: then all colouring is spoilt, the poetry of Nature silent, and the surrounding scene as ugly as it can be. And yet it impressed me as much as anything I have seen; like the Pyramids, it is impossible to form any idea of its size, from the fine proportion kept in all its parts, until the Arabs climb like ants over the neck and head. The features *have been* beautiful, but they are now so much destroyed that the mind must be full of those perfect faces seen in Abou Simbil, &c., to fill up the gaps for oneself: like them, it is more than wonderful how such exquisite harmony could be preserved in the 172 feet long of the figure and the 28 feet of the face cut out from the natural rock. In spite of fractures and discolourments it still retains its "mild and bland" expression: unimaginably grand it must have been when the bearded chin overhung the temple and the altar between its paws, and the group of lions crouched in front. It is believed to have been executed by Thothmes III., who was fond of architectural caprices, but we must all be thankful to him for a "caprice" so grand and enduring and noble as this. It is a marvellous mystery, keeping its own secret behind those wide-open eyes and within that serenely-smiling mouth, and one wanders round it vainly searching for the key to what one feels instinctively is full of a meaning now, and perhaps for ever, hidden beneath the eternal veil of sand.

That evening we went on to Cairo, and arrived at Shepheard's Hotel on the 25th of March, and for the next ten days we were employed in a ceaseless labour of shopping—wearisome enough anywhere, but at Cairo really dreadful. One hunted the whole day for some indispensable trifle, seldom having the slightest idea where to go to, and at the end of the day finding the thing in the first shop one had been in. We were soon in despair at the invariable answer to all inquiries for articles, that they had none; but a Cairo lady, who was so kind as to help us very much in our difficulties, assured us that meant only laziness, and at last we learnt to answer "We will help you to look for it," and by dint of opening drawers and searching for ourselves we sometimes found what we wanted. But one never could guess where to look for anything: for instance, we found books and trunks at the tailor's, boots and shoes at a watchmaker's, a French dressmaker behind a butcher's stall, and some strong, useful dresses at a warehouse for glass beads. Many things we never found at all, and we had to get on as best we could till they were sent out to us from England after some months of discomfort. Everything European was of course enormously dear, and our wardrobes, even the very queer medley they were, cost us certainly three times their real value. We were of necessity constantly in the bazaars, which, though very amusing to see, are tedious and provoking to the last degree when one wants to get any real business done, and excessively fatiguing. The sirocco and heat became very oppressive; the noise and bustle of the city after being so long quiet on the river was very trying to nerves that were already a good deal shaken. The hotel was full of passers-by, and the few friends we had came and went without being able to help us; the unjust demands of our *quondam* dragoman grew daily more annoying, and we soon perceived that the proceedings of the Arab court regarding the loss of the dahabieh might be far worse than the misery caused by any Circumlocution Office ever set up in a civilised country, where truth, honour, and honesty are at least words understood by all: they do not seem to exist in the modern Arabic used in Cairo.

Of the city, which we were longing to examine, we saw little or nothing; only once or twice, by way of rest after our weary work, we went up to the splendid mosque of Muhammed 'Ali, to enjoy the magnificent view. The famous view of Damascus is far more really beautiful, but there is a singularity and a grandeur about Cairo, the mingling of the works of man in the thousand domes and minarets with the desolate face of Nature, the verdant cultivation beside the barren waste of sand, that is unspeakably impressive. One day we paid a hasty visit to the four finest mosques of the city, those of Sultan Hassan, Touloun, El Azhar, and Hassaneyn; they are well worth seeing, grand, simple, and impressive, with bits here and there of admirable richness and beauty. We found most of the persons who admitted us civil as showmen and tolerably intelligent, and we were careful to show the decent attention due to their customs; so, not being provided with overalls, we walked through the mosques in stockings,—a not very comfortable proceeding. But one must have very little of the spirit of Christianity in one, and still less worldly good-breeding, if one refuses such conformity to their notions of reverence.

The minarets of the mosques of El-Azhar, "the splendid," Barkook, Nasr Muhammed, and Hassan, are beautiful; the domes, too, are sometimes elaborately and elegantly worked. But the buildings which charmed us most were the tombs of the Mamlook kings outside the town, full of variety and of singular elegance: they stand in the loose sand, and should be visited early or late to avoid the heat of the sun, but they will well repay a visit at any time, and artists would find among them subjects for many months of drawing.

One Sunday morning we got up an hour or two before sunrise, having arranged with a Copt dragoman to 'take us to the Coptic service, which was celebrated in a small old church while their large one was being repaired: it commences always at the first dawn of day. We found an oblong room with latticed windows, cleanly whitewashed and hung round with pictures of saints, some of which were not bad, and a part of it latticed off at one end for the women. On the north side there was a recess the whole length of the church, like an aisle, but nearly dark: one half of this was the chancel, enclosed within a screen; in front of the other half stood the Patriarch's chair and the reading-desks. As each Copt came in he crossed the church, and, going into the back of the recess, washed his hands in a little running fountain in one corner; then, returning into the church, squatted on the floor among the rest of the congregation. At first the service consisted of short readings of the Gospels, each portion read first in Coptic, then in Arabic, by little boys ten or twelve years of age, dressed in a kind of surplice over crimson silk, with caps, embroidered in gold, on their heads; these were the deacons. There were also several priests, who wore crowns with gilt crosses on their heads, and robes of various coloured stuffs. There was chanting besides, and bells chimed in now and then, sounding like cymbals. After about an hour of this the Patriarch,—the successor of the Apostle St. Mark, and the spiritual head of the Egyptian Church,—entered from behind the chancel, clothed in a magnificent mantle of green and gold tissue, with an enormous hood of the same, which almost hid his face; he held a beautiful patriarchal staff in his hand, with a silver crosier on the top, surmounted by the figure of a knight slaying a dragon,—that universal legend, found in nearly every country where any "ancient story" existed, typifying, each according to the local colouring in which it was found, the triumph of pure-hearted moral courage over brute force and wickedness. In his other hand the Patriarch carried a small gold cross, jewelled, and wrapped in a handkerchief of gold tissue, which each person who passed him stopped to kiss.

The readings continued for some time with many short prayers and sentences, the people responding with uplifted and waving hands, often repeating " Kyrie eleeson, Kyrie eleeson." After this the Patriarch preached a short but very energetic sermon, stopping continually, both in the reading and the sermon, whenever he saw anything amiss in the congregation ; calling out very loud orders to them, " Oh, ye donkeys, don't make such a noise ! " " Give more room to each other ! " " Oh, ye pigs, attend and listen ! " the people also frequently expressing their approbation of what he said in his sermon with a loud murmur of applause and the words " taïb, taïb." Then he retired into the chancel, and seemed, with the priests, to make processions round the altar, and to consecrate the holy Elements ; after which small cakes, circular, and stamped with the name of Christ, a cross, and some words were handed about, and bought by many (for five paras each) to take home. These are not consecrated, but, having been prepared for the Eucharistic bread, are considered semi-sacred, perhaps lucky. After a pause some members of the congregation went to the door of the chancel, where the Patriarch gave them the bread and the wine together in a spoon from a glass he held in one hand, at the same time laying the edge of his hand across the eyebrows of each while he gave his blessing. The people made numbers of responses in this part of the service, not one having any book, and they recited together the Creed, the Sanctus, and the Lord's Prayer, the service seeming, as well as we could make out, to be arranged very much the same as our own. The whole service was exceedingly *chaleureuse*, not merely a duo or quartette of priests, with the congregation as audience, according to the fashion of some of our churches at home, but all the people joining in very frequently, and with apparent devotion. At the end of it the kiss of peace was passed round, each one to his neighbour, the Patriarch kissing the priests and blessing them. The women did not enter any part of the church but that screened behind their lattice ; two of the priests carried the Sacrament to them ; and they joined in the responses very frequently.

The service is read in Arabic as well as Coptic, because very few of the people readily understand the latter now ; but the liturgy and all their religious books are written in Coptic, and they are instructed at school to pray, both in church and in private, in that language. The Copt is enjoined to pray seven times in the course of each day, and Mr. Lane says he believes there are very few who do not practise the rule; and the educated Copts repeat in their prayers the whole book of Psalms every day; they also keep long and rigid fasts. We heard afterwards that the Patriarch is much beloved by the people*; he is still a young man, and has a fine countenance, with a very black, thick beard, and bushy eyebrows, which he knit ominously when he scolded them. We were also told by those who knew him well that the present Patriarch is an earnest, energetic man, bent on reform, which he is endeavouring to carry out, as well as, by means of judicious and enlightened education, to elevate the minds of his flock. He entered frankly and earnestly into an elaborate argument, or rather explanation, of the difference between the Coptic and Anglican faiths with a friend of ours some time after, and seemed as much interested in the details given him as he was evidently pleased at the impression made by the Coptic service on an Englishman. We thought it one of the most interesting services we had ever attended.

The Coptic creed is very similar to that of the Eutychians (who were condemned as heretics by the Council of Chalcedon in A.D. 451), with some admixture of the tenets held by the Jacobites and Monophysites; their rites and ceremonies have been preserved with but little alteration for the last fourteen hundred years. The Copts are undoubtedly descendants of the ancient Egyptians, says Mr. Lane, but they are very far from being a pure race, having intermarried, long before the conquest of Egypt by the Arabs, with their Christian brethren of Abyssinia (who were Jacobites), Nubians, and Greeks. The name of Copt is thought to be derived from the ancient Greek name of Egypt, Ægyptos, or else from the City of Coptos in Upper Egypt, to which numbers of Christian Egyptians retired in the time of the Roman persecutions; the word is pronounced Gkubt or Gkibt, in the singular Gkubtee or Gkibtee.

After a fortnight's stay in Cairo, during which the examinations of our English servants and of the sailors were constantly repeated, each repetition bringing out some new variety of absurd falsehood in the history of the boat-burning, we learnt one morning from the English Acting-Vice-Consul that the story next to be adopted was that our maid had set the boat on fire, and that on this plea the dragoman Achmet Adgwa, owner of the boat, intended to sue us for 900*l.* damages.

On first arriving in Cairo we had been strongly advised to institute

* He died a few months after.

proceedings against Achmet for the recovery of our losses, which we estimated at considerably above 300*l.*, since our contract with him included our safe conduct and indemnity from accident during the three months of our voyage. Many said we owed at least the form of instituting such a claim to future Nile-travellers, the safety of whose persons as well as property is at the mercy of their dragomans and crews, who should, therefore, be made fully aware that they are held responsible for injury suffered by one or the other, unless caused by the traveller's own fault. But even the knowledge that we need not enforce the payment in the end did not reconcile us to the appearance of harshness against a fellow-sufferer; and we felt more disposed to exert ourselves to effect some compensation for his losses, with which experience had taught us so well how to sympathise.

But now the case was changed; from what we heard Achmet seemed to be restrained within no limits in the false and injurious stories he was spreading everywhere about us; we knew him, from his own account, to be possessed of property, in land and cows, unusually large for one of his class, and we heard now that he had expended much of this (as well as money begged and borrowed for the "maintaining of his cause") in bribing the members of the court from whom he hoped for a decision in his favour.

Under these circumstances the Consul was so kind as to step somewhat out of the course which he would have felt to be right in his official capacity, as he said, in consideration of our being ladies alone in a foreign land and among such a people, and he advised us to leave Cairo as quickly and as quietly as we could! He assured us that the final decision of the cause would not be at all affected in this country by considerations of truth or justice, and would probably be protracted to the very utmost limit that ingenuity could devise, or during which bribes could be supplied, detaining us thus prisoners during many a long month of summer heat in Cairo, to the great risk of our health, which had already suffered much from the shock and subsequent anxiety.

Unfortunately for us just at this time there was really no consul either at Cairo or Alexandria; our excellent friend Mr. Green had gone, and his successor had not yet arrived, and there was the same transition state of affairs in the consulate at Cairo; and thus, while everybody was acting for some one else, nobody liked to take any responsibility on himself, or to come forward in an affair not very simple, and not very distinctly his own.

We therefore lost no time in paying to our dragoman all that we owed him for the hire of his boat, and his wages up to the last day of our stay in Cairo, as if he had still been in our service there, which of course he could have no claim to ask; the sailors we paid up to the same day also, as we learnt that in the prison their supply of food depended on their own funds; and then, after passing the night in packing, we left Cairo by the early morning train for Alexandria, feeling even then how little pleasant it was for Britons to flee! especially when they had truth and right to stand on; but remembering also that " prudence is the better part of valour," especially when the Britons happen to be ladies.

But rest was not to come yet; we had a very fatiguing journey of thirteen hours (something was amiss in crossing the river, which detained us far beyond our time), and we hoped to remain a few days in Alexandria to obtain the rest which had become so needful for us.   However, a friend who was so kind as to act as our deputy in announcing our arrival to the Acting-Vice-Consul early the next morning, chiefly as a matter of precaution, brought us back a most emphatic message of advice to quit Egypt *immediately.* He was aware that an order for our detention had arrived in Alexandria, but it had not yet reached his office; and though the preferring such a claim on us, to use his own expression, was " simply infamous," there was too little hope of justice in an Arab court not to make it most important that we should not be exposed to the exercise of its power. His advice, therefore, was that we should go immediately on board any vessel in the harbour whose steam was up, without waiting to ascertain its destination; and he added significantly, " I trust the ladies will be gone before I am in my office." So warned, we lost not a moment in driving down to the harbour, leaving even the conveyance of our baggage to the kindness of a friend, who brought it after us to the Austrian steamer, which, fortunately for us, was just starting for Smyrna; nor would it be easy to express the immense relief we felt, after so much anxiety and turmoil, when the screw beneath our feet began to revolve, and Egypt—with all her inexhaustible and high interests, her indescribable beauties, her manifold charms, and, to us, her many troubles—was left on the far horizon.

CHAPTER VII.

WHERE HOMER LIVED AND SAPPHO SANG.

THE *Arciduchessa Carolina*, though a fine little boat and very clean and comfortable, did not prove a berth of roses to us; a terrible storm on the second day blew us back a considerable distance towards Egypt, as if our evil destiny wanted to force us into an awkward position, and instead of a three days' passage we had *the* benefit of five. On the evening of the third day, however, we were able to enjoy the exceeding beauty of the islands after passing between Scarpanto and the southern end of the Island of Rhodes. On the following morning our eyes opened on a grand mountain mass of violet hue—an *awful* colour, deep as the ripest autumn plum, mysteriously dark. The huge rock rose solemnly from the sapphire sea, which folded it round in waves of indescribable blue, while heavy masses of savage clouds now swooped down the mountain side, now rose and tore themselves asunder on the summit, leaving bare to view, ever and anon, the calm, pure snow lying in loving mantles half-way down the rock, answering to the glistening white masses and wreaths of surf thrown up again and again in ever-changing beauty at its feet. I saw this island twice afterwards; but never again did its sacred rocks impress me with such solemn beauty as then in that wild April storm-sky when I came up with my mind full of the grand old idols of Egypt, and remembered that *there* the Disciple whom Jesus loved—he who taught us that God is Love, and who showed to us that love whereby, when made perfect in our own hearts, we dwell in Him and He in us,—that *there* he dwelt in tribulation, but in patience, when the Spirit of the Lord came upon him, and he saw, with spiritual eyes, the " great city, the new Jerusalem," and wrote that heaven-born prophecy which " blessed is he that readeth ; "—for

this was Patmos. A large cave, in which the Beloved Apostle
is supposed to have lived, is still shown; a solitary and spacious
grotto above 700 feet above the sea—it is very probably a true
outline tradition. Nikaria, Samos, and Khio (Scio) were passed
successively, while the mainland presented an ever-changing view of
cliffs and bays, richly coloured, and in some parts wooded. They
were beautiful enough for any eye, but doubly beautiful to those
accustomed to the monotonous yellows and the arid white rocks
and sands of Egypt, however beautiful the colours in which sunset
and distance sometimes array them. Lovely the Bay of Smyrna
looked on the fifth morning when we landed at the quarantine very
early in the day, and willing were we to be pleased with the clear
water and the shining pebbles on the beach, the green vines and
meadow-land around us; but the quarantine itself filled us with
dismay. The dirty Hajj pilgrims who had crowded the deck of the
Arciduchessa Carolina" poured into the courtyard of the wing appropriated to us, which looked forlorn enough with the iron-barred
windows and doors, and the bare stone walls and floors of our
prison; the three English gentlemen who had come in the same
steamer were shown into one little room together; and to us, with
our maid, was assigned an upper room with a staircase to ourselves,
not so bad in itself, but that every room and the whole place was
pervaded by the most horrible smells one could imagine. We
passed the whole day sitting on the dirty floor, with nothing to do
or look at, or, what was worse, to eat, till sunset, when a boat-load
of beds and food, &c., arrived from the hotel; and we were then
allowed to have our luggage, which had been kept from us all day,
doubtless in order to see whether the plague would burst out of
the locks and straps in a visible shape.

We fortunately enjoyed a pretty view of the bay from the window
of a front room, and once we walked in a paddock of long grass
under the guardianship of a soldier, but it seemed bitterly cold
and damp to us after Egypt, and we counted the hours of our very
long five days most wearily. We were always expecting a visit of
inspection from the Turkish medical officer, but no one came; and
when we had fulfilled the law, the five days concluding at the very
same hour as that of our arrival, we were allowed to embark in a
little boat, which carried us across the lovely bay to the City of
Smyrna on the 15th of April. After this we never had any reason
to complain of the cold, for the spring changed at once into
delicious summer heat and sunshine.

We spent a pleasant fortnight enjoying the beauties of Smyrna.
The town is picturesquely situated at the end of the thirty-six

miles of winding gulf, the sea washing the very walls of the houses, whose bright red roofs, mingled with pretty trees and gardens, rise up a very steep hill, finishing in a forest of the finest cypress-trees in the world, not excepting those at Constantinople: it is really worth going to Smyrna only to see these trees. From the summit, which is crowned by an ancient castle and is the site of the martyrdom of Polycarp, a noble view is obtained; the town, with its bright colours and numerous churches, sweeping round at one's feet, and extending partly along a creek at the right, while sloping up from the water's edge, are rich meadows and fig-groves, dotted here and there with the summer residences of the wealthier inhabitants of Smyrna, and with a few villages. On the north, across the creek, the lovely mountains rise, backed by Mount Sipylus, of ancient fame; on the south the bay curves round westwards under the gloomy grandeur of fine purple and brown craggy mountains, on which, at this time, the snow was lying in light shrouds. All around the eye discovers remains of aqueducts and other ruins, through which the new railway steers its unwavering, narrow line. I should think that there are not a great many cities in the world that can boast a much prettier panorama than Smyrna.

As to the town itself, it does not possess many fine buildings; some of the bazaars are handsome and solidly built, and there are a few pretty churches. The streets are wide for an oriental town, and many of them are lined with European-looking private houses, which remind one of a French town; they are interspersed with trees and little gardens, and pretty *cafés* beside running streams. The bazaars are very amusing; there is nothing like a Levantine town for the jumble of languages one hears, and at Smyrna no one seems to think of troubling himself to select all the words of a *whole* sentence in any one language. Your true Smyrniote, being accustomed to think in all the eight or nine he knows, mixes them up at once into an *olla podrida* of language without the fatigue of separating them, for he is sure that to whomever he speaks one or other word will be intelligible. You ask the price of a thing—the coin will be in one language, and the number in another; you ask what o'clock it is, and the hour will be told in one tongue and the minutes in another, and so on. In a sentence of twelve words there are certain to be four or five languages mixed up, forming a jumble which is truly astonishing, and not a little perplexing at first.

We found the town well supplied with European goods, chiefly German, most delightful to us in filling up our many wants of the things not purchasable in Cairo; and the change was very agreeable from the cold, listless impassiveness of the oriental shopkeeper, who does you the favour of bestowing his goods upon you to his own entire ruin, as he assures you, though at double their value, and the brisk anxiety of the civil Levantine trader pressing his goods on your notice. Almost every shop is wreathed with strings of sponges of every variety of size, quality, and price: some nice little sponges are sold for a few halfpence, but a really good, fine sponge, fetches almost as large a price in Smyrna as in England. The Broussa silk and embroidery bazaar, which is handsomely built of stone, is exceeding gay and pretty; but the gayest of all the bazaars is that for made-up garments,—the stalls are filled with many-coloured cloths and waist scarves, embroidered turban stuffs, striped and flowered silk robes of the most brilliant colours, and gold-embroidered jackets, varied with antique arms, little glass cases of delicate porcelain and amber beads, Persian carpets and shawls, and table-covers of needlework; the sellers almost attack the unwary traveller, rushing at him with the articles generally bought by strangers, and shrieking to him on all sides, " Howadji! Señor! Ingleez! Franja! Monsieur! Signor!" &c., &c. Strings of camels pace along the streets—large, untidy-looking beasts, with long thick hair hanging down from their necks, very unlike the trim, closely-shaved, and more lively-looking camel of Egypt. Numbers of mules, and most gigantic donkeys, meet you at every turn. But the day for seeing Smyrna is Sunday, when all the inhabitants of the houses, high and low, sit outside their doors in groups, on chairs placed in the carriageless streets. You walk through the Armenian quarter after midday, and you have thus an opportunity of seeing whole families, of three or four generations, dressed in French fashions, but with the large, soft, lustrous eye of the East, and the languishing, graceful gait of the South; in the Greek quarter, blue eyes and more regular features make a pleasant variety, while each and all have coquettish flowers, freshly plucked, twined with an Eastern *abandon* in the dark tresses of both maid and matron. The Jewesses, alas! do not exhibit themselves in the same manner to the admiring passers-by; they are said, by those admitted to their houses, to be very remarkably beautiful.

We made one pleasant day's excursion to Bournabat, a village of the citizens' summer residences; each house has its own nice garden, but every one is enclosed in a high stone wall, making all the streets seem blind, and preventing any kind of view of the lovely mountain scenery to the inhabitants within them. But we learned that this had been, till within the last four or five years, a matter of necessity, not choice; since without these high walls no Frank was safe from insult from the Turks, even in their own gardens. The only exception to the rule was in a new iron-railed wall, just completed, round the garden of a Mr. Whittal, an English merchant of half a century's standing in Smyrna, and who is much respected and beloved by all classes. His house is the handsomest of the numerous good houses about Smyrna, and the garden is very large and charming; it has cost a large sum of money, and is still a costly luxury, from the enormous expense of keeping it watered: in dry seasons the water has to be carried out from Smyrna for weeks and weeks together, and of course the thirsty soil requires a vast quantity to keep gardens of such extent in order. Seeing us at the gate, the hospitable owner was so kind as to invite us in, strangers though we were, and to show us the house and grounds, and a small but handsome church which he has just built at his sole expense for the English community of Bournabat. In the course of the following summer, Mr. Whittal entertained Prince Alfred at a fête in his pleasant grounds.

We wandered about the village for some hours, peeping into a pretty mosque, and a beautifully clean bath, watered by the River Meles, on the banks of which the "divine Homer" sat and sang for all the generations of the world after him; and after resting in a *café*, and being refreshed with coffee and hot bread, which we took from the baker's oven—like all the shops here, open to passers-by— we rattled back in the rickety *char-à-banc* which had brought us from Smyrna: such a pleasant hour's drive, the lovely meadows between the fine wild mountains clothed in the richest and brightest spring greens, beds of wild-flowers on all sides, and the hedges filled with hawthorn, dog-roses, and acacia, all in full blossom, and the Judas-tree, with its tall spikes of bright lilac flowers on the leafless branches.

The next day a friend kindly called to invite us to accompany his family to the Armenian Church in the afternoon, as it was Maundy-Thursday, on which day, at vespers, the Patriarch washes the feet of twelve Bishops, to commemorate our Lord's act at the Last Supper. The church is spacious and lofty, half Italian, half Saracenic, built partly out of the ruins of ancient churches, and having itself twice fallen down, each time immediately after its completion, to the great delight of the enemies of the Armenians. It has no architectural beauty in the interior, but it is pretty and gay, like the temples on the top of a confectioner's cake, all pink and white paint and gold, with numbers of pretty silver lamps hung from every arch. The galleries were filled with women in bonnets and hats instead of the old-fashioned and more graceful black silk scarf; the floor of the church was closely covered with tarbooshed Armenians squatting,—

and as a great favour a bench was brought in, and placed for us near the altar. The service commenced with half an hour's singing, performed by twenty or thirty little boys and lads, dressed in flowered white muslin tied with riband, and each holding a lighted candle as tall as himself; *such* singing!—screamed at the top of their lungs with so much exertion that they all got red in the face in five minutes: each one on a different note and in a different key, following his own fashion and fancy as to tune, only getting in the words to something of the same time and swing, and keeping the nose steadily shut. Then came in the Archbishop, clothed in black, with a great black hood (which, however, he soon threw off, and then appeared in splendid robes of green and gold brocade), accompanied by twelve Priests or Bishops, each dressed in a different-coloured velvet robe embroidered with gold, and a large circular crown of the same colour as his dress, hooped with gold and surmounted with gold crosses.

After some more singing the Patriarch changed his robes before the altar to still finer ones of white satin covered with heavy gold embroidery; he put on a fine gold mitre, and advanced towards the people, holding a beautiful jewelled crosier in one hand and a gold cross in the other; he then preached a short but seemingly very earnest sermon in the harsh, nasal Armenian language. After this a huge silver basin was brought, which the Archbishop blessed separately with the soap and towels; he then seated himself in a squatting fashion on the floor beside it, while one by one the twelve Bishops sat for a few moments in a chair opposite to him, and placed one foot in the basin, over which the Archbishop poured some drops of water from a silver flagon; they then bowed and retired, kissing the Gospels and the Cross in his hand as they went. The service was then concluded. We had been involuntary witnesses of the preparatory process to the ceremony; for, while standing about, before it was time to enter the Church, we had seen the twelve Bishops previously washing the twelve legs, which were to be afterwards exhibited, in a very ordinary wooden pail in a small back room! They had incautiously left the door open, and we had reason to think the preparatory and more thorough ablution not at all unnecessary, and that it was a pity it had not extended to the other twelve.

On good Friday afternoon there was a grand procession from the Patriarch's Palace to the same church, the Bishops, dressed as on the day before, bearing pictures to excite the adoration of the people. We also went to several Greek churches, where crowds of people were streaming in and out to kiss some favourite picture in each;

in the Church of San Giorgio the popular favourite was St. George, but as no one could reach the saint comfortably, they kissed the dragon with as much complacency and doubtless with as much benefit. There was a very good performance of Rossini's 'Stabat Mater' at the French Church, but the crowd was so great that we could not even get inside the door. The prettiest and most interesting sight to me of all the gorgeous ceremonies was the Greek "Announcing the Resurrection" on Easter-morning; places were kindly obtained for us at the windows of the Greek Patriarch's palace, to which we went at a little after midnight. The crowd was then assembling in the court between the palace, the church, and the belfry (which was separated from the church,—a tall dazzling white building, like a tower of filagree sugar), and service was going on in the church. The crowd at last was packed as densely as it possibly could be, every individual bearing a long lighted candle, and nearly every one a pistol of some kind or other. Expectation and impatience got higher and higher, and the noise louder and louder, until about 2 A.M. the Patriarch and clergy came from the church in procession, carrying a huge silver cross wreathed in artificial flowers, and mounted a low platform; after some singing there was a pause, and then, in distinct, solemn tones he announced *" Christ is risen !"* In an instant all the bells burst out in loud peals, the people shouted like mad things, and every one waved his candle and fired off his pistol again and again: the waving candles had a beautiful and quite indescribable effect—it seemed like the wind passing over a field of fiery ears of corn, burning the brighter as they bowed their heads to the breeze. Then the people separated, and the strange sight was over, and the acacia-trees were left in silence and darkness: they had lent their own fantastic, fairy kind of beauty to the ceremony, for their white blossoms, illuminated by the thousands of candles underneath them, against the dark sky of night above their heads, looked like a white cloud bending down gently in fragrant blessing over the people. Despite our fatigue we had little sleep that night; for the whole population was in the streets, firing pistols, squibs, and crackers, without one moment's cessation, throughout that night and the next day.

Another but a sadder sight passed our windows on Easter Sunday-morning—the funeral of a young girl, the only child of a widowed Greek doctor, who is rich and much respected in the city; the funeral was therefore conducted in the grandest style. The procession commenced with a score of little boys, dressed in scarlet, carrying crosses and candles; then thirty priests, all robed in the richest brocades and the peculiar black cap of the Greek Church, one of them singing a sweet and solemn chant; then came the Arch-bishop, robed in brocade and mitred, carrying a gold crosier, a boy bearing his train; and after him the coffin—uncovered—painted white and supported by bands of white satin riband; within it lay the young girl,—embalmed, they said, and the face painted just enough to conceal the terrible colour of Death,—the body dressed in white satin, with a wreath of orange-blossoms on her head, and strewn over with white roses, buds and leaves. About a hundred gentlemen followed, wearing white hat-bands, foremost among them the poor father, bowed down with grief. The girl was very lovely, and she seemed sleeping to the measured sounds of the sweet chant sung by the boys who preceded her, and by the rich-voiced priest.

The whole scene was touching; but there is a horrible ending to it: at the grave the corpse is taken out of the coffin and stripped of all its fine clothes and ornaments, for which a regular scuffle then ensues among the gentlemen, and happy is he who can secure the white shoes, or the wreath, or any other morsel of the finery! The corpse remains in the grave for one year, when it is taken up, and the bones are put into a small bag, which is buried inside the church, the tombstone remaining as before.

All the shops in Smyrna were shut for the next few days, the people making holiday with every imaginable noise, and eating quantities of little pastry baskets filled with gay-coloured eggs; while at every door a lamb was tethered, all through' Easter Sunday, decked out with flowers or ribands, as on this day every-body gives everybody a lamb, and as few can afford one for each family of his acquaintance, the lambs just accepted are passed on in fresh presentation until they have changed owners through a score of hands; even so the custom is a great tax upon the purses of the inhabitants.

As we found that there was no steamer going to the coast of Syria for another ten days, we determined to pay a flying visit to the Island of Mitylene, where the English Consul had offered us the use of his vacant house for the summer months. We started at midday in a dirty French steamer bound for Constantinople, enjoying the lovely views of the gulf ending with the dark bold promontory of Kara Bonroun, which contrasted well with the yellow and red cliffs on the mainland. The wind freshened enough to make the passage very unpleasant, but we reached the island in less than eight hours. The day, however, had ended in rain, and the night was as dark as pitch. The steamer stops outside the harbour, nearly two miles from the shore: if a boat has been pre-engaged to come out for you, well and good; if not the chances are that you must go on to Constantinople, as, after dark, a Mitylene boatman would never think of an excursion on speculation. We had, however, fortunately an introduction to one of the few Mitylene gentlemen, M. Pinto, a fellow-passenger on the voyage, and he kindly landed us in his boat. The air on the island felt warm and balmy, perfumed with the fresh spring flowers, and we almost enjoyed groping our way up to the English Consulate, where we were received by the French Consul, who had kindly prepared supper for us. The house is spacious and comfortable; we found a good library, and all we could desire: our only perplexity being, that as neither of us knew a syllable of Greek, we had to send the servants to the French Consulate to get our common domestic wants interpreted.

The English Consulate commands a good view of this lovely island. The bright-coloured town curves round the little bay from which the mountains slope upwards, clothed in the rich hues of orange-groves, pomegranates, figs, and mulberries; grey rocks cropping out sternly at the tops among the dark shades of purple heather. An old castle on the left, and two quaint lighthouses on the right, add something to the beauty of Nature, while the eye travels on across the calm blue sea, caught here and there by a graceful lateen sail, till it reaches the coast beyond. Truly there can hardly be a more beautiful coast-view than that of these time-honoured mountains of Mysia, blue and hazy with light wreaths of white mist and snow. Rising straight up from the gulf of Adramytium at her feet, stands the noble and graceful peak of Mount Ida, clouds resting lightly on the summit, and shadowing the eternal snow on her crest: a fit resting-place for Jupiter and his attendant-gods, for the noble mountain—now de-poetised into the " mountain of goats "—was once covered with pine forests, in a lovely glade of which " Beautiful Paris, evil-hearted Paris" adjudged the apple to Aphrodite, " new-bathed in Paphian wells." I never looked at the grand old mountain without fancying I heard the sorrowful chant of " Mournful Œnone, beautiful-browed Œnone" repeating—

> " O mother Ida, many-fountained Ida,
> Dear mother Ida! hearken ere I die!"—

while one had but to walk through the streets of Mitylene or the villages near the town, to see girls beautiful enough for all the heroines of ancient song—even " the Greek woman" herself—with figures like statues of Phidias, and draperies that a sculptor would go wild to reproduce. Broken fragments of fine marble figures are frequently found beneath the soil on this classic ground: we saw two fine heads which had just been dug up, in one of which the gems placed in the eye-sockets to represent the dark iris of the eyes had fallen out, leaving round empty holes, shadowing the eye with a softer expression than the original gems could have done. A little patience and money would probably be well expended in collecting some of these remains. The natural marbles of various colours found in the island are also said to be valuable.

We saw a new hospital being built with the stones taken from the ruins of the Temple of Apollo, which was discovered in digging the foundations: it is a pity that some of the friezes could not have been secured for the Mitylene Museum—a praiseworthy institution, which ought to be supported by strangers, the native community being far too small to accomplish much. They have, however, acquired a wonderfully fine collection of scientific instruments for their college, into the uses of which the Lesbian youth of the present day, we were told, enter most heartily and readily. The institution appeared to us, in our hasty glance, to be unusually good.

Many excellent things are produced in the island, beginning with the delicious little beccafigues, of which a hundred may be shot in one tree in a few minutes of the first hour of a spring morning; then the figs, which are small but luscious, though not as far-famed as their Smyrniote neighbours; abundance of olives, the chief commerce of the island, and some tolerable wine; besides the innumerable *confitures*, on the manufacture of which the Mitylene matron prides herself, and of which every visitor invariably partakes, the mother or daughter of the house bringing various kinds on a silver tray before the inevitable coffee. An amusing story is told of the consequences of the rhapsodies written by Lamartine on the *confitures* he tasted on visiting the hospitable house of M. and Mdme. Pinto. A few weeks after the publication of the ' Voyage en Orient' letter after letter arrived by each succeeding mail, containing "*orders*" from Parisian confectioners for "Pinto's confiture," with special directions for its being exactly the same as that M. Lamartine had described; and for some months these letters continued angrily reproaching the astonished and indignant M. Pinto for not attending to their " commissions!" There are also abundant truffles in the island, and, it is said, " unequalled oysters."

Another product of Mitylene is the needlework of the women, which is really ancient, and very beautiful. It is rarely to be met with now, all the best in the island having been bought up; so that we thought ourselves fortunate in obtaining a few specimens of the pretty manufacture, which no modern Lesbian can imitate. At present the islanders do "*broderie Anglaise*," and despise the tasteful colours and elaborate patterns of their ancestors. If poor Sappho—"violet-crowned, pure, sweetly-smiling Sappho"—had only stuck to her needle instead of meddling with the Muses and Aphrodite, "the fatal fire" in her heart might have remained for ever unkindled by the rejuvenated old Phaon, and the rocks of Leucadia would not have been immortalised by a myth which I insist on believing, despite a whole library of commentators. By-the-by her marble coffin, which it is said she had prepared for herself before the fatal leap was determined on, is shown in one of the mosques here.

As we wanted to see something of the far-famed beauty of the Mitylene women, we gladly accepted an invitation to a Greek fête, given in honour of St. George, at a small village on the other side of the harbour. It did not seem to our ideas a very lively fête; the large gardens were filled with groups of men, women, and children sitting in family parties, eating dinners which they had carried with them, and listening to very barbarous music: there was no dancing or games, and we were disappointed at seeing no costumes except among the men, who still look picturesque. The women were altogether dressed in gowns *à la Européenne*, of the brightest possible colours, in thin sarsenets and muslins, and their pretty heads adorned with natural flowers. It is said that within a hundred years ago the women wore only a very short petticoat and an embroidered handkerchief over the bosom—the smallest modicum of a costume possible! They wear a great many jewels—strings upon strings of pearls most commonly, very often with diamond-clasps and earrings—and are certainly beautiful women, with very fine, lustrous dark eyes, and graceful movements; but their sweet mouths are sadly spoiled by the effects of the rouge which they all wear from their earliest childhood, the mercury in which so affects the health that there is scarcely a girl in the island above the age of sixteen with any teeth left in her head.

We took a very pleasant ride one day to the Porto d'Olivieri, the second large harbour in the island, in itself large enough to contain the whole English navy, even if half our ships were Great Easterns —Port Callone is still larger. We ascended the mountain behind the town on our good mules, enjoying as we went the most lovely and ever-changing views of the island itself, the sea, and the opposite coast; the road is a good one, well paved, and not broken into holes, sometimes steep enough for broad shallow steps. The whole way over mountain and dell offered a continual variety of rich colours, forests of pine and white cypress, olive-groves alternating with the fresh green of the newly-leaved fig-tree, in pretty contrast with crowds of luxuriant juniper, dwarf-oak, hollies, oleanders, myrtle, and many shrubs we did not know; while our mules stepped through the thickets of gum-cistus, both white and pink, growing in huge tufts everywhere; and every morsel of flat ground, or " smooth-swarded bower " was carpeted with the most brilliant beds of flowers,—" the crocus-brake like fire," and all the mountain slopes seemed striped like gay-coloured silks, with ribands of the brightest yellow, lilac, pink, and blue. Sometimes the rocks overhung the path in perpendicular bluffs, but in general the character of the island scenery is rather lovely than stern or grand.

We descended in about two hours into the olive-groves on the sea-shore, and alighted at some ancient baths, now used for a *café*. The shore, perfumed with flowering shrubs, is interesting from the multitudes of shells, sponges, and beautiful Medusæ of all colours and sizes; and the view of the tranquil water of the harbour—like a lake from which there is apparently no outlet, surrounded by the beautiful mountains—is very lovely indeed. The ancient towns of Hiera and Pyrrha stood at the lower end of the harbour. Passing thunder showers threw a thousand colours and changing lights over the scene, so that we forgave the wetting we got in riding back for the sake of seeing the beautiful mist-wreaths carried in haste over the opposite shore,—and the sun soon dried our garments. A short détour in returning brought us by the leper colony, encamped among the caves of a wilder and less cultivated valley: there are a great many of these poor creatures in Mitylene; they marry among themselves, and we saw two or three very pretty young girls in the group who begged from us; sooner or later, however, it is said that the taint invariably shows itself, and the inevitable disease slowly but surely eats into the whole body, till limb after limb drops off. It is not thought to be so very painful a complaint as its horrible appearance would seem to indicate.

We returned into the town by the sheds where the slave-market used to be held, and made our way into a small church filled with some splendid wood-carving; it is of a different style to the Venetian *chefs-d'œuvres* of Brustolon, but quite equal to them in execution. A transparent screen stretched across the church, composed of arabesques and wreaths of natural flowers; pulpit-stalls and reading-desks were all alike of the same exquisite workmanship. We heard there was a great deal more in two or three other churches, and that it was all the work of native artists of the olden days; it would be priceless to many a collector in England of such antique beauties, and I hope the pretty island may some day be robbed of it. Wood-carving is still a favourite employment here by the peasantry during the winter months: the peasants in the Island of Scarpanto also excel in this work. We may hope that Mitylene will yet regain her place in the commercial world: an island so easy of access, and possessing such harbours and so fruitful a soil, with an active, intelligent, and industrious population such as they are, ought indeed to be prosperous and important; but her vicissitudes have been many, though her name has been great, and at present she is under a thick cloud, called Turkish dominion. The birth-place of poets, musicians, philosophers, and historians—a stout member of the Grecian confederacy—she passed under the Romans, and long afterwards to the Venetians, under whose sway, probably, her fine castle was built; in 1465 she gallantly resisted the siege of the Ottoman Sultan Muhammad II., aided by a band of the Knights of St. John, until the city was betrayed to the Turks by the treachery of the Governor, who paid for his baseness by immediate execu-tion: not a Knight remained alive after its capture. A good half of her inhabitants were destroyed in the Greek War of Independence, and in the horrible massacres of that period, which were nowhere characterised by greater brutality; but now, after a long interval of peace, one hopes to see the beautiful island repopulated and pro-sperous, as some day—Inshallah—she will be.

The *Enphrate* steamer, in which we took our passage from Smyrna to Beyrout, is one of the finest and most comfortable of all the Mediterranean steamers, not excepting even those belonging to the P. and O. Company. We had the ship nearly to ourselves, except for the addition of the Hajji to Jerusalem—the inevitable nuisance in every Levantine voyage during the spring and summer. The pilgrims, who are continually going to or returning from every port in the Levant, live upon the deck, which is generally divided like a sheep-pen down the middle; they are expected to keep to their own side and within the railing, but, even if they do so, the sights, sounds, and odours proceeding from their locality are un-pleasant to the last degree. They lie all day huddled up on their mattresses, presenting every variety of Eastern costume and lan-guage,—grandfathers, parents, and children all pell-mell together. They bring their own provisions, and also plenty of small com-panions, on whose unfailing activity neither open railings nor ship-regulations have the slightest effect.

The day after leaving pretty Smyrna found us threading the islands we had passed by before—this time, however, going closer in shore, so as to catch a glimpse of Boudroum and Cnidus, and the glorious Cape Krio, which rose majestically, snow-covered, from the blue waters that foamed over its rugged feet. The evening brought

H

us to Rhodes, whose busy little harbour looked very pretty, with its
minarets and ships lighted up with lines of coloured lamps to celebrate the last night of Ramazān.   We were rowed on the following
morning in the gig of H. M. S. *Tartarus*, to the inner quay, where we
landed and found ourselves amongst crowds of gaily-dressed Turks
hurrying in great state to pay each other visits on the close of
Ramazān; from the beys, on richly-caparisoned horses, down to the
smallest child, all were in bright clean clothes, with natural flowers
in bouquets stuck into nearly every one's turban or fez.   It was
really gay and pretty; but nothing can save the streets of poor old
Rhodes from looking desolate and deserted when one compares it in
one's mind with its days of chivalry and splendour, the like of which
has passed away for ever from the world.   Passing by the barracks
of the Turkish soldiers, the ancient doors of which have been removed to Versailles, we found ourselves in the " Knights' Street,"—
once so grand, now so silent and sad.   There are but few remains
of the fine " Auberges," which belonged to the eight Languages of
the Order: only some richly-ornamented doorways and finely-carved
marble scutcheons in the walls, the armorial bearings on which
are still very perfect; but they are much hidden by miserable
balconies of old boards and broken lattices, which have accomplished the metamorphose of the palace of a monastic knight into
the hareem of a Turk.   The once noble church is now a heap of
unintelligible ruin, to which state it was reduced by a singular
accident: some rock-hewn caves had been used by the knights as a
storehouse of gunpowder in' the days of Rhodian glory, but they
had long been forgotten, when, in November 1856, a flash of lightning during a severe thunderstorm ignited the gunpowder and blew
the church, the palace of the Grand-Master, and a hundred other
interesting remains, into utter ruin.   We were told by an English
officer who witnessed the catastrophe that he saw the church *lifted
bodily* into the air, from whence it fell with a shock that was felt
for many miles round; every glass window in the town was broken,
and large stones wrenched from the walls beyond the outskirts of
the city.   One might almost say that by this powder Rhodes was
twice lost: 330 years before, the fortress was " heroically lost," and
obliged to capitulate to the Turks for want of the ammunition they
had buried and forgotten; and now the last memorials, even the
skeletons mouldering in the tombs of the gallant heroes of her siege,
were utterly destroyed by the very means which would have saved
them in their day of need ! *

* The town of Rhodes was yet further destroyed by a severe earthquake
in 1865.

The towers and minarets of the fortress-city mingle prettily in the views round the harbours of Rhodes, backed by the green hills and gardens which surround the town. People still amuse themselves disputing over which harbour the famous Colossus stretched his brazen legs, but the fact is that he was placed on the point of the rocky promontory *between* the two, called now the "Arab's Tower," but, in the time of the Knights, St. Michael's. It is still a massive square tower, and was topped by the bust and head of a man, covered with brazen plates, with an arm stretched out towards each of the harbours, and holding a lamp in either hand. He must have been a monster of ugliness, but he figures nowhere so amusingly as in the chronicle of the old British pilgrim Sæwulf, in 1182, who recounts how St. Paul addressed his 'Epistle to the Colossians' to the men of Rhodes, because they dwelt beneath the legs of the famous Colossus!

As the steamer allowed us but two hours of daylight, we could at this time see but little of Rhodes; but on returning in the following year we had the benefit of receiving much information from M. Salzmann—the best authority on the remains of the island; and I therefore defer my description of it till that time.

Nothing can exceed the beauty of the coast scenery of Asia Minor from Cape Krio onwards: the mountains are rugged, stern, and grand, the savage wildness at times changing into varieties of luxuriant, many-shaded woodlands, and green meadow-nooks—the snowy peaks in the spring and early summer rising behind the dark purple and red-browns of the nearer cliffs; and then the sapphire water—it is said by experienced sailors that the water near this coast is of a deeper and brighter blue than any other in the world, and one can well believe it. The beauty which extends along the whole coast attains its highest loveliness in the Gulf of Makri and the famous Seven Capes: the outlines of the cliffs and mountains are here both grand and graceful, and the blue distances on the other side of the Gulf lend much to the scene. Kastelorizo, Khelidonia, and Anamour are each very fine, and all abound in historical interest to the scholar. This little nine days' voyage in a fine steamer, coasting closely along under such beautiful scenery, is more than pleasant: we had lovely, clear weather, and fortunately always a calm sea. The fifth day was spent at Mersina, where, however, we did not land; and the sixth in the beautiful bay of Iskenderoon, where the Amanus mountains come down into the water, clothed in rich woods, and the beach is fringed with thickets of oleanders. The bay is enclosed by lofty mountains, the Taurus range, to the north, rising in the pale blue distance, covered with

H 2

snow, which seldom melts, even at the end of the summer. All these mountains are full of souvenirs of the misled but gallant Crusaders. Among their precipitous ravines, and in the hot valleys and plains between their heights, not hundreds, but thousands, lay down to die ere ever they saw the Promised Land of their enthusiasm; * and of those who survived many more passed along this great mountain-road, called the " Iron Gates of Syria," only to be slain before Antioch, Damascus, &c. Excessively hot is the Bay of Iskenderoon, and deadly the fever of the malarious plain on which the little town stands; but our walk on the sandy shore among the oleanders was delightfully pleasant.

Sunday we spent at Latakia, landing early in the tiny harbour behind a fine old tower, built on the rocks which rise insulated in the water; the shore was covered with something white, which I took for tombs,—when, as we came nearer, I saw them move, and discovered that they were living women, wrapped in the white *eezar*, or sheet, with which we were afterwards to become so familiar throughout Syria. Their faces were covered entirely with the *mandeel*, a dark-coloured cotton handkerchief of gaudy pattern, which is made at Manchester, and which we also now saw for the first time. The pretty town is surrounded with fine gardens, where we soon got quantities of roses and carnations. The streets are so frequently covered in with stone arches, even where there is no bazaar, that they are very shady and pleasant, and give a handsomer appearance to the small town than a fuller acquaintance warrants: the long vistas of arches are most picturesque, and great numbers of broken granite columns are still standing at the sides of the streets.

There are also some ruins worth seeing: one is a row of four columns with fine Corinthian capitals, still supporting a richly-carved architrave and frieze; another is a Triumphal Arch, or square of four arches, with fine friezes and capitals. Their beauty was much enhanced in our eyes from their being covered with luxuriant trailing weeds, springing from between the old stones, instead of the severe aridness of the unstained Egyptian ruins, to which we had been so long accustomed. The capitals and friezes are of very rich Corinthian, and well cut; and the stone, which appears to be a soft one, is of a fine golden-brown colour now.

It is difficult among the narrow winding lanes of modern Latakia to carry its topography well in one's head, at least in the visit of a day; but it would be interesting to map down the various remains

---

* The Crusaders frequently called even Northern Syria "the holy land of Jerusalem."

still *in situ* of ancient Latakia, or rather of Laodicea-ad-Mare ; there is still enough to show that a double row of granite columns once made an approach the whole way from the quay on the harbour up to the Corinthian Temple, whose remains are now quite at the back of the town, and at the distance of 1500 yards from the harbour. Numbers of these columns still remain, but the greater part have been broken off and rolled down to the sea, to be built into the foundations and walls of the castle in the harbour—the memorial left there by the Venetians, and where many of them, with their rough broken-off ends, are still to be seen.

From a large mosque on the hill behind the town a very pretty view is obtained : Mount Casius on the right, and the Lebanon on the left,—the graceful bays, where sponges luxuriate, sweeping into every imaginable curve on either side. From the gardens, on the south of the little harbour, the view is also very pretty. In short this Latakia is a gay little town, subsisting upon its merchandise of tobacco and sponges, and remarkably delicate silver-work ; the bazaars are uncommonly good for so small a place. The famous tobacco is brought in from all the north of Syria to be shipped from the port, and is, when the duty on reaching home is added, very nearly as dear as in London. The sponges are gathered off the coast, chiefly from the rocks near a little bay to the north, which is occupied exclusively by the divers and seamen. The cliffs above are filled with the rock-hewn tombs of the ancient Laodicea-maritima ; they are very simple, and, of course, all of them quite empty.

Tripoli, where we spent the next day, is a handsome town, and beautifully situated on a narrow strip of plain, at the foot of the Lebanon-range, which rises with abrupt loftiness directly behind the town—its strata most strangely and grotesquely marked, as if a boiling mass had been thrown out and suddenly cooled in its still seething commotion. Between the beach and the mountains are miles and miles of delicious fruit-gardens—oranges, apricots, and figs, hedged with pomegranates, tangled over with clematis, and watered by thousands of tiny streamlets from the Kadisha river. Five old castles remain ; the largest of which, on the seaside, built by Raymond de Toulouse, was still occupied and fitted with cannon in 1840, when the English knocked huge holes in its ancient walls ; the Saracenic doorway and the interior vaultings are good, and worth seeing. Another castle is situated in the pleasant valley of the Kadisha, a picturesque ruin, and a third crowns the mountain spur above the town, from whence there is a splendid view of the town and gardens, and of the river foaming through the rocks and woods, with the mosque and convent of the Derweeshes in a fine ravine.

We amused ourselves drinking coffee and eating ice in a *café* beside the river, listening to Arab story-tellers declaiming romances to large groups of well-dressed Tripolitans, seated in rows on stone divans along the streets, smoking nargilehs, and eating the excellent oranges, which are plentiful here. The little town is a flourishing one, with good bazaars; its best production is, however, but little known; these are carpets made by the peasant girls in some of the neighbouring villages. The process is very slow, as for each carpet the girls, or the family, gather, prepare, spin, and dye the wool themselves, which is then woven in patterns of their own design, and very tasteful they are, and the colours rich and brilliant. They are very strong and thick, as well as pretty, especially the finer sorts, and cost from 100 to 500 piastres,* according to their size.

The eighth morning found us outside Beyrout, where the swell—which is ceaseless in that bay—made every one so sick that we were thankful to get out of the ship, and to settle into the pleasant hôtel on the southern headland below the town, at Râs Beyrout. This hôtel is simply, almost scantily, furnished,—the open corridor is the only general sitting-room, but the semi-naked simplicity suits the climate, and we found it at all times a delightful residence, the heat of Beyrout being here tempered by the sea-breezes which blow all round it. Besides it was the cleanest hôtel we had been in since Paris; and it is an unspeakable comfort occasionally to get into a place where you can sleep in peace without battling with scores of fleas, or worse, and where there are plentiful signs of brooms and brushes.

* From about 1*l.* to 4*l.*

CHAPTER VIII.

THE "BEAUTIFUL GATE" OF SYRIA.

THE world must be very rich in beauty if there exist half-a-dozen places on its surface much more beautiful than Beyrout; but I for one cannot believe that there are: its loveliness is of many kinds, and though different pictures may combine to represent its beauties, no one will contain them all. Tripoli, Saïda, Hhaïffa, Smyrna, Mitylene rightly lay claim to many charms, but they do not surpass Beyrout. The amphitheatre of mountains, clothed in every hue, which change with every passing hour; the snowy summits towering up behind them; the rugged headlands of rocks, over which the sea dashes in ceaseless wreaths of foam; the city rising from the water's edge, and climbing up the slopes of hills, adorned with gardens, minarets, domes, mosques, castles, and palaces; the scattered palm-trees, and the bright colours dotting every street and quay, make a *tout ensemble* which fascinates the eye in the first moment, grows upon you under every changing light and sky, and rests in the mind an everlasting memory of loveliness.

To the north one blue headland stretches out beyond another, till the Theoprosopon (which forms one side of the Bay of Tripoli) arrests the view; from this the mountains reach back with majestic beauty to the far east, the various heights covered with every variety of green, from meadow grass to pine forest; tiny white streams dash down the sides, while crags, grey, white, purple, and yellow, break out from between them, and nearly every crag is crowned with the towers or walls of a monastery. In magnificent loveliness Sunnîn rises up behind them, the saddle-shaped summit covered with a thick mantle of snow, and the barren creamy-red sides stratified into terraces; then Kunîsyeh, more peaked and but little less lofty, snow-covered also; and then the mountain ranges gather round southward, still more richly clothed in wood,—and sloping down towards Saïda and Sour in blue distance, meet the clear blue sea at their feet. Râs Beyrout, to the right, throws out bold rocks to greet the waves, over which a coast road in front of rich gardens speckled with houses leads into the town. Lifted above all are the fine barracks, standing proudly on a hill in the midst, while a hundred palaces of the European residents and merchants of Beyrout attract the eye, each house surrounded with verandah-terraces of fantastic Saracenic arches, in various coloured marbles. In the foreground the once strong Castle of Beyrout is to be seen among the houses, and, on rocks jutting out into the little harbour, two other castles, now picturesque ruins, pretend to protect the crowds of oddly-shaped feluccas, stout merchantmen, and scores of little boats painted all manner of bright colours, that are jammed together in struggling confusion at the custom-house quays. Some way out of the town lies the white Lazaretto, among mulberry and fruit-gardens; while the golden-sanded shore curves round from beneath the old seven-arched bridge over the river, and sweeps away past myrtle-edged villages into the smiling little Bay of Jouneh.

In the early morning sun how clear and bright and beautiful it is! Later on how busy the gay boats, and how graceful the white sails flecking all the bay! At midday how refreshing and delicious the green woods and gardens! In the afternoon how tender and indescribable become the tints, and how enchanting the perfumes that spread through the air! And in the evening how unearthly the hues that steal over mountain, sea, and sky, dyeing the sea into a full larkspur blue, and the mountains into a soft grape-like purple, which seems, although so dark, to be semi-transparent, with deep crimson shining *through* the purple in some mysterious union; while the more distant summits become transfigured in a tender rose-colour, pure and lovely as a real, living, fresh-blossomed rose, and the white snow softens into a kind of pale glow, and seems ready to float away and dissolve in the rose-coloured and golden floods above. What scene on earth can be more exquisitely lovely than this? For many a month I watched all this day by day, with a thousand other changes; and, looking back through all I have seen before and since, nothing surpasses it in loveliness but the Great Desert and the Dead Sea (and they have much less variety, though not less glory of colouring), and one view of Broussa. Then at night, when the lights twinkled through the town, and the moon came out and seemed to turn the marble arcades and the minarets into molten silver, and illuminated the snow on the mountain-tops,—when the stars swam in liquid light over all, and the cool refreshing night-air came gliding by, laden with sweets— silent messages of whispered fragrance—and faint music stole up from the town, and the sea murmured below in soft plashings on the rocks;—then one sat and listened and looked, and longed to have it always night, until the glory of the dawn made one feel that joy is better than sadness, however sweet, and one's heart sang, "The earth is the Lord's, and the glory thereof!"

Behind all this, unseen from the sea or the town, is the delightful pine-forest made famous by the rhapsodies of Lamartine; it is a charming place, for though the trees are nearly all quite young, yet they throw a cool and refreshing shade upon the hot sand beneath them, and nothing can be pleasanter than an early morning or late evening gallop along the wide open glades, occasionally stopping at one of the quaint *cafés* for a glass of snow-lemonade, or pacing slowly under the sombre, fragrant trees on foot. The sand from the beach had blown over this part of the plain, rendering it quite a desert, until these trees were planted, to prevent its drifting; and it is to be hoped that the forest will be very much extended, to form shelter for the town and gardens on the rest of the plain from the south winds.

The hot season was now beginning, and it was time for us to secure a summer residence. Beyrout, however enchanting, did not suit us, as we did not choose to remain long either in a town or in an hotel, and except in the charming palace-houses of the residents, or in the Râs Beyrout Hôtel, it is too hot a climate to be healthy for European strangers in the summer; we were longing too for mountain air and a quiet home, so we lost no time in making inquiries and preparations for attaining both. First of all we engaged a dragoman, Habeeb Soma, the best of those at Beyrout, and whom we afterwards found, during the year he remained in our service, more honest than most of his class, invariably obliging, and particularly well-informed concerning the country; he was a mountaineer from near Bukfeyia, and used so guttural an Arabic that we found our very limited Egyptian vocabulary of little or no use to us; but as he spoke excellent Italian and tolerable French, we had no need of anything else, and he afterwards made great progress in English under the tuition of our maid. Guided by him we mounted some ugly but good Syrian nags, and proceeded to some of the neighbouring mountain villages.

We were informed that the abode most likely to be convenient to us would be apartments in one of the numerous convents which are strewed over the Lebanon mountains; we therefore first bent our steps to the Convent of Mar Ronkas, where we knew a European

family of ladies had spent the previous summer. At first we
followed a pleasant road among gardens and fields hedged with
prickly pears, and two large plantations of cactus (on which some
one was trying to cultivate cochineal), the scarlet blossoms of which
looked splendid. After fording the stream and pushing through
thickets of lovely oleanders, we began to ascend the mountain, and
The path became as bad as the scenery was beautiful; the horses
scrambled over rocks like cats, with occasional bolts, jumps, and
struggles that really astonished one; for this was one of the very
vilest paths I ever saw, and we were quite *new* to such undertakings.
The beauty of the scenery happily consoled us, and we reached the
convent at last. It stands on a little horn of the mountain, very low
down, but high enough to overlook the rich and lovely plain. We
pushed the gate open and found ourselves in a little court-yard full
of fowls, from whence we made fruitless efforts for about half an
hour to waken any of the monks : they were taking their siesta. At
last one of them appeared, and learning our wishes, set off for the
superior, who soon came panting up the steep, with his black gown
turned up in front, and the under-skirt carefully folded out of harm's
way during his digging and pruning. He made himself tidy and
then joined us, sitting in a pleasant window-seat while we sipped
lemonade, only one at a time, though, as they possessed but one
glass. The rooms he offered were tiny white washed cells, about
ten feet square each, with a hole for the window, and one little shelf,
and a saloon commanding but little view, and which was then filled
with silk-worms; we did not fancy the *gite*, especially as we foresaw that the good monks would inspect us from morning till
night as if we were beasts in the Zoological Gardens, and that it
would be impossible to have the cloisters to ourselves. The monks
seemed good simple-hearted creatures, employed in cultivating their
silk-worms and little herb-garden, and in prayer; we heard they
were very kind to the few peasants who lived near them, helping
them in the mulberry grounds, &c. They were very anxious to
have us as their guests, but our bodies being already immensely
impressed with the astonishing concourse of fleas in their little court,
we departed, determined to look a little farther.

Another day, therefore, we climbed the mountain to the village
of Beit Miry, of whose charms we had heard even in Egypt; the
road lay in the same direction, but instead of continuing to the left
to Mar Ronkas, we went straight up the mountain, through brushwood and thick beds of bright flowers and shady trees; then came
a pine-wood and a long delicious hill covered all over with a low
forest of myrtle just bursting into blossom and perfuming the air,

as we trod through it, most enchantingly. Next we wound up through mulberry-terraces to another pine-wood, from whence paths branched off to the two horns of the mountain, one leading to the fine convent of Deir-el-Kulah, the other to the village of Beit Miry*; here, under the pine-trees, is a spring trickling down the rocks, and giving birth to lovely branches of maiden-hair, and other ferns, sprouting from every little crack in the rock over which the water passed. Not knowing the path, which, indeed, had little to mark it, save all the biggest and roughest of stones turned out of the terrace walls, we rode in a steeplechase fashion through the mulberry gardens, till we arrived at the house of the Emir or Prince, which had been twice occupied by English families. Four very small rooms, built of unplastered stones, surrounded a little court, with the village chapel and priest's house; they were little stone huts and no more; they asked a high price for the rooms, and we felt exceedingly dismayed at the prospect of spending the summer in those dirty little holes. The Emir was very civil, and his wife, the Princess, came out to stare at us; she had been lying in one of the rooms on a couch covered with rich white silk, but was herself dressed in common cotton; she was old and very ugly, and wore the disgusting open costume of the Maronite women. This Emir was not one of the highest rank, but we were told by several people that he was very much loved and respected, and very kind in sharing his small wealth with his poorer neighbours. The meaning of the name of the village is " the house (Beit) of Emirs (Miry) or Princes."

Seeing a better looking house in the middle of the village, we rode on and asked if we could have it : it had a pleasant arcade-terrace, but was too small for us, and was not to be let till later, as it was then filled with silkworms, who would not *cocoon* for another month. The owner, a Druze woman, came out and invited us in to see the darkened rooms filled with the trays (made of mud mixed with straw) in which the silkworms were feeding, placed on a light wooden framework. The worms were still young, not being quite an inch long, and they were awake and feeding; we were requested not to speak loud or to disturb them, and we beat a hasty retreat, as the silkworm nurseries have a very disagreeable smell, and are horribly lively with fleas. The mistress wore the black serge veil, supported by the long silver horn* peculiar to the Druzes, and her face was of course hidden. They draw the veil across it so as to leave only one eye uncovered, and generally hold it in their teeth, a style that is more convenient than pretty; but indeed nothing can be more ugly than the horn itself; it might add

* Pronounced Bayt Mĕĕry.   † Called the *tantour.*

some dignity to the figure if it were worn standing upright, like a steeple, from the head, but it is fixed on the top of the forehead at an acute angle, looking like the sign-post pole over a barber's shop-door, and is worse than grotesque. Once put on, at marriage, it is never removed from the head, even at night.

All this time we had seen at the opposite extremity of the village a very large palatial-looking house, which we concluded belonged to some sheikh or emir of high rank, but on inquiry we found it had but just been completed, and was the property of three brothers, native merchants. We thought we would at least try if we could see it, and rode on to the door, where we found a large collection of horses, while seven Russian officers, who had ridden up the mountain, were smoking and chatting in one of the rooms. The house was large and very handsomely built; it contained six lofty rooms (one of which was thirty-six feet long), and a delightful arcade in the centre; the front windows had double arches with stone mullions, with deep recesses in the thick walls; there was a second terrace at one end, and a nice little garden attached to it. The view from the house was superb, overlooking the road up which we had ridden, with the whole of the exquisitely rich little plain of Beyrout spread out at one's feet, the river winding along in the midst like a silver ribbon, the town glittering in the sunshine, the beautiful Baruk mountains opposite, and a wide expanse of blue sea. Immediately behind the house rose a nearly perpendicular grey crag, two minutes' scramble up which led to the brow of the mountain, and opened out the magnificent wooded valley, or rather ravine, of El-Metn, on the opposite side of which rose snowy Sunnîn in all his majestic grandeur.

We were not long in making up our minds about this delightful spot, and the price, 21*l.*, was soon settled over lemonade and coffee; another half hour was spent in paying compliments before we descended the abominable path back to Beyrout: people said after-wards that we had given too much, but we were afraid of losing the house by hesitation. The canteen furniture belonging to the drago-man, which we had engaged for our future tour to the south, was sufficient to furnish the house enough for one's simple wants in that climate, with the addition of one table, some carpets, and the divans which already occupied the sitting-room. We took it for three months from the 23rd May.

Meantime we employed ourselves in exploring Beyrout and the neighbourhood. There is little to see in the town. We visited some Greek, Armenian, and Maronite churches, not particularly worthy of notice, and entered one pretty mosque with delicately

painted' arabesques covering the walls and roof of the interior:
service was going on, the congregation chanting and praying in
unison—the music of the chant was wild and harmonious. The
bazaars of Beyrout are not by any means handsome, but they
contain a very fair variety, and plenty of goods : one quadrangular
court surrounded with arches, where silk cord and tassels are
manufactured, is exceedingly picturesque, and parts of the cotton
and silk bazaar would supply endless subjects for sketches. Beyrout
is famous for its gold and silver-work, in which the jewellers display
a great deal of taste and tolerable execution; but they do not produce the best things at the first asking. There are also some very
good German shops for housekeeping articles, situated near the
Marina, where it was always a pleasure to go on account of the
lovely view from the quay of the mountains and castles.

One day, in order to save a long ride by a short cut across the
bay, we hired a small boat, and taking advantage of a fair breeze,
set sail for the Nahr-el-Kelb—Dog River; St. George's Bay, however,
is not a pleasant one for boating, and the heavy swell had a very
unpleasant effect upon our party, though it broke up finely over the
rocks at the entrance of the river and over the foot of the fine promontory; the surf ran high, tossing up over the volume of fresh
water which poured down to meet it, and we sped gallantly in on
the crest of a wave, not however without getting a very sufficient
wetting. This *embouchure* is really very pretty; the convents
perched on the summits of the hills give much life to the scene, and
the indecipherable tablets carved on the cliff-face by ancient
Assyrian and Egyptian conquerors (supposed to be those of Sen-
nacherib and Rameses II.) add historical interest to it: the fine
bold rocks and the winding ravine, with the full, clear river, and the
little Khan with its group of bright-coloured figures, and probably
a mule, or a horse and rider fording the stream instead of going
round by the steep, single-arched bridge in the middle of the
picture,—unite into a very pretty scene. The glen increases in
sternness and grandeur as it winds back, a few olives and mulberries
finding scanty standing-room on the edge of the river, while just
beyond the bridge are the romantic-looking arches of an old aqueduct
now filled up with tangled masses of luxuriant ferns, sweet-haw-
thorns, the splendid leaves of the Arab sweet-potato, and trailing
creepers hardly distinguishable from some long pendant stalactites,
gemmed with bright drops from the water trickling through. The
stream was bordered with flowers, among which flourished a
numerous family of enormous green frogs, who were croakingly
admonishing each other that some one would soon come to catch

them for his dinner. We declined making our luncheon on them, and preferred coffee and lemonade; after which we returned to our boat, and, tossing up on the top of a wave of river water, slid down the sloping surf on to the sea, and went slowly back to lovely Beyrout, which everybody should linger one whole evening in the bay to see.

We would not put ourselves again at the mercy of the swell in that bay, so we took horse the next day and proceeded to the same place by land in the morning. The road passes by the fine old bridge over the Nahr* Beyrout and the place where St. George of Cappadocia killed the " mighty worm" and rescued the Syrian princess: an indubitable fact, since it is witnessed by the stain of the blood which still remains on the spot where the holy warrior washed his hands, after finishing the dragon with a knife. Then we wound through some lanes, and came out on the sands, taking a brisk canter along the edge of the waves till we reached the promontory of the Nahr-el-Kelb: the pleasant sands were strewed with the remains of vessels driven ashore during the past winter, two of which were English. Several ships are lost every year in this bay. After crossing the beautiful river we rode a good hour farther along meadows and gardens to the village of Zouk Mehayl, where one of the chief manufacturers of pretty silk and gold stuffs had been requested to make us welcome. He took us to his house and spread piles of mattresses for us in the guest-room, his mother and pretty sister bringing snow-sherbet and coffee, and nargilehs for some of our party. We reposed for some time, for it was very hot, before we went up the village to see the *fabriques*: nearly every house, or even hut, in the place has its loom, sometimes many were at work together. The cloth is a woof of bright-coloured silks on a warp of thick white cotton threads, gold or silver thread being laid in with the colours of the pattern: it is shaped in pieces for cushions, slippers, bags, and caps, which are very pretty and durable, but somewhat costly, and they asked more for them here than in Beyrout. Some were also weaving silk scarfs and shawls—a poor imitation of the Damascus manufacture. Zouk is a thriving town, and very prettily situated on the side of the mountain sloping down into the lovely little Bay of Jouneh. We came home at a great pace in the cool evening air, thinking how charming a winter residence this bay would make for an invalid. It is a pity that this coast is not more sought by those who are obliged to seek a warmer climate than our own; there are many places on the coast which combine the advantages of the most delicious climate and magnificent scenery,

* River.

under a clear sky, bright sunshine, and sweet, but not relaxing air. Beyrout is said to be somewhat damp in the winter, but then the winter seldom lasts six weeks, and is not severe enough to render a fire necessary, though a brazier of hot coals in the evening may sometimes, but not often, be agreeable; and with a little notice and some pre-arrangements, houses might be found at Latakia, Beyrout, and its neighbourhood, Saïda and Hhaïffa, all most charming places. Living is certainly less, with a tolerably honest dragoman, than at Naples, Nice, or Malta; they are easy of access by frequent steamers, and the necessary comforts required for invalids can be had at Beyrout or from Alexandria, while, with a good dragoman, you have as little trouble in housekeeping as in an hotel. Of course these native-built country houses do not look very grand, but our experience can testify that a very little trouble taken, with the help of a dozen nails and a few yards of coloured flannel or cotton, will make the room not only comfortable but pretty also. The coast of Syria is at least worth thinking of by invalids for whom the ascent of the Nile is too expensive an affair: Cairo is very damp in the early part of the winter, and feverish, and few people like Alexandria; Corfu is said to be dull; and many persons are tired of the regular Italian watering-places, and are unwilling to encounter the enormous expense of a winter there. Of course, with the exception of one or two families at Beyrout, there could be no society, as the consuls are the only European residents at each place; but to some persons this would be a minor objection.

There are innumerable charming expeditions to be made from Beyrout; and while waiting for our house to be ready, we determined to initiate ourselves into the mysteries of tent-life in an excursion to Deir-el-Kamar,* the capital of the Druze country, which generally takes two long days' riding; but as we were *new* at mountain riding, we thought it better to devote four to it. The starting-day of any excursion in Syria is one that calls for extraordinary patience and good temper; even with these it is immensely wearying and provoking. We were ourselves dressed at 5 A.M., and our mules arrived soon after, but they were not finally loaded and despatched till near 11 A.M., and we followed at mid-day; we had eight mules, and a donkey to carry their master, and we took a cook, canteen, and three tents. This was our kit throughout Syria:—a large tent for ourselves, with double carpets, beds, dinner-table, and two folding arm-chairs, with another tent for our maid, and the kitchen tent; our personal luggage, which was packed in two tin

* Alas! thirteen months after, the scene of horrible and sanguinary atrocities.

travelling-baths in stout wicker coverings (a luxury with which I recommend every lady-traveller in this climate to provide herself), and a couple of portmanteaus. This luggage was carried on two mules, one of them surmounted by a little wooden cage, in which the Maltese dog, our inseparable companion and faithful little night-guard, was carried; he used to distinguish us at an almost incredible distance, and his bark of recognition, his voice of welcome in answer to our footsteps, was always the glad sound which announced that the tents were nigh and the dinner ready, at the end of a long, weary day's ride. Every one, even Mooslims, petted the pretty little thing wherever we went. His ancestors, of the noble Lion family of Malta, had some time ago settled at Smyrna, where this small scion of the house was given to me. He has long white hair, large black eyes, and a knowing little black nose.

Our road lay through the pine-forest; thence it turned off through many winding lanes, hedged with prickly pear, pomegranates, and hawthorn still in blossom, towards the mountains; in the gardens a few palm-trees are growing, but they look very stunted, sickly, and small, after those of Egypt. Leaving the olive-groves about Hadith, the road crosses a narrow sandy plain, and then begins to wind up the mountain. The beauty of the scenery compensates for all the *désagrémens* of the path. But before we ascend farther let me try and describe what is called a road in Syria, without understanding which no one can by any means fancy what travelling there is really like; how much it adds to the fatigue; how much it must necessarily occupy the attention, and, still more, how much time is consumed in its difficulties. The *best* of all the mountain-roads are staircases of paved stones, made chiefly by the Emir Beshir: these are all very well in going up, but in coming down most horses give you a kind of jolting bang on each step, which makes one feel sea-sick in a long descent. I had a dear old horse afterwards who used to come down quite gently on the step, but it is at the best a disagreeable jogging process. Very frequently these steps are broken or missing, and then one gets down as one can. More usually the path is the dry bed of a torrent, full of stones and big boulders, brought down and left by the rushing stream, loose and awkward to tread amongst; worse than these are long places like an old stone quarry, or as if the side wall, originally built of large blocks, had fallen down. Over these sharp edges, deep holes, and uncertain footing the horse feels his way as cautiously as if they were burning hot, and in descending it is somewhat dangerous. Nothing, however, is so bad as the dreadful smooth rocks at an acute angle, with perhaps a horrid cleft at the bottom, down which the unfortunate

animals slidder in a way that is apt to excite a very unpleasant
sensation in the region of the heart and throat—in excuse for which
it must be remembered that all these paths, except the staircases,
are made by Mother Nature: they are of any conceivable slope, and
of course the worst bits of path are always at the most perilous
spot,—a winding turn at the edge of a ravine, or overhanging a
yawning chasm. Then no one likes to feel the horse under him
gathering up his fore-feet for a jump or a drop, which, overdone by
an inch, will precipitate you, if not him also, to the bottom of the
mountain. True, the horses are extraordinarily sure-footed and
cautious, though they seldom seem to have a good point about them,
and they climb like cats; but accidents do occur sometimes, and a
lady's seat has a strong feeling of one-sidedness about it when both her
feet are hanging over a precipice, and only one shoulder seems really
over *terra firma*. The Arab saddles save some fatigue in this continual ascent and descent, and where it is very steep indeed, and
your horse feels as if he *must* topple back or fall on his nose, they
give better support and steadiness than the English saddle. Most
gentlemen bring their own saddles, but I believe those who do not
get on quite as well as those who do. We had English side-saddles
sent out to us, and our bridles were of anything—bits of rope or
leather, often adorned with fine tassels and amulets, fringe and
shells, &c., &c., over the head and neck of favourite animals, and
excessively pretty the harness often is when they are fresh and
good. Well, we have wandered far from our present road, but this
description is really necessary, and having been thus given once, it
applies to nearly *all* the paths throughout Syria.

The road to Deir-el-Kamar, however bad, is charmingly beautiful.
After resting a little at a fine fountain called 'Ain Bsâba, we wound
round a richly-wooded gorge on a path about two feet wide, and
through a pretty village called 'Ain Anoob, full of sweet geraniums,
where we looked up to the great English silk-reeling factory of
Shumlan, belonging to Mr. Scott, and down over all the road we had
come from Beyrout. Then turning up a breezy hillside, we found
our tents pitched in an olive grove outside the village of Anâb,
commanding splendid views of the plain of Beyrout spread out like
a map, the miles of olive and pine-woods and gardens contrasting
with the white town and the red sands, the blue sea, and the ever-
beautiful mountains. All the valleys on this road are richly wooded
and luxuriant with flowers; every stream teams with oleanders; the
pines perfume the air; and every height, if not covered with a
village, is topped by a convent.

Our day had been a short one, but we were very tired, and went

I

to bed at once, after dining by lantern-light under an olive-tree. The next morning, somewhat appalled by the difficulties, not to say dangers of the road, I remarked to the dragoman that I hoped to-day's would be better: "Mademoiselle," he solemnly answered, "la route devient toujours pire;" and with this consolation in my mind we started. Our way led over a hill that was literally rose-colour with wild flax; the old terrace walls were studded with cyclamen, and every here and there the wild hollyhocks shot up in spikes of fine lilac flowers, over a truly atrocious path. This soon opened on the Wady-el-Kâdy (the Valley of the Judge), a magnificent valley running N.E. and S.W., with a fine dashing river at the bottom; but before we had sufficiently enjoyed it we were descending the most fearful winding track through a pine-forest, throughout which, much as I have climbed and descended since, it is still a marvel to me how any one of us stuck on our horses*; however we reached the bottom in safety, and crossed a picturesque old bridge over the foaming river, and began to ascend the other side, amidst ilex and thorn, juniper, myrtle, and cypress, tangled over with wild vines; but we lost the track, and finally had to clamber up an almost impassable place, where one of our horses fell and threw his rider, but happily without hurting him. The summit gained at last, we looked over the sea on the right, with the bright red-sided mountain terraced with figs and olives, and noble cliffs of cold grey limestone; and on the left, down the fine valley of Deir-el-Kamar, Druze villages on every hilltop, the town itself standing out white and shining on a mountain spur, and at the head of the valley the famous castle-palace of the Emir Beshir, Bteddeen. We were soon in the town, which struck us as handsome and lively; the houses built of smoothly-hewn stone, frequently with arched and mullioned windows, each with its little balcony of flowers, among which we noticed several white lilies; we passed through some tolerable bazaars and a fine convent, from whence the town takes its name, there having been anciently a figure of the Virgin standing on the moon, carved on a stone outside the convent wall†; it had a small dome surmounted by a cross, and seemed well built. There were also one or two minarets and a gaily-painted Serai, or Turkish Governor's house for business‡; but we did not stay to see much,

---

* The *Times* correspondent gave (September 21, 1860) a detailed account of all this road, in which we were amused to recognise each particularly "bad step" that had horrified us when, like him, we took this path on our first Syrian excursion. † *Deir*, convent: *kamar*, moon.

‡ Afterwards the scene of the most atrocious part of the horrible massacres here.

as we wanted to reach Bteddeen early. The descent, however, from the town was so terrific (we took the wrong road, where no horses go, I believe), that we did not get to the bottom, and up the long, steep, zig-zag staircase leading to the palace till 2 P.M.

Bteddeen has been often described, but yet another description still may perhaps be pardoned : it is a pleasure to me to linger over the memory of its many beauties, all the more as probably ours were nearly the last European eyes that beheld them. We entered by a gateway under a succession of dark arches leading into a spacious square, the right-hand side of which was built on arches, forming the stables of the Emir's stud (usually of 500 horses it is said), over which was a terrace looking out on the glorious valley ; this square had been the tilting or parade-ground in the Emir's time. We crossed it into another square of the same size, in the midst of which stood a fountain in a bower of acacias in blossom, and at the opposite end the beautiful palace front itself, with an arcade to which a wooden staircase, fantastically formed and gaily painted and gilt, was attached. The walls were panelled entirely over with medallions of various-coloured marbles, and the doorways and windows adorned in the same way, the whole frontage being thus, with the floorings and balustrade of the terrace, a mass of marble mosaic in the most exquisite arabesques—in fact the patterns and execution of the Bteddeen mosaic are superior to, and more varied and delicate than, the best things of the kind in Venice, not excepting even the flooring of St. Mark's. In the centre of the terrace, against the wall, a beautiful little fountain still played, but some of the bits of mosaic had dropped out here and there, and were replaced by delicate sprays of light and tender maidenhair fern, bending down to the crystal stream, which seemed to brighten up under the smiles of the green fronds—a mark of ruin, certainly, but sacrilegious would have been the restorer's hand that should pluck out those graceful wreaths that hung there, hiding the decay of past splendour in their own sweet freshness. Off this terrace were several rooms, the ceilings, doors, and shutters of which were most elaborately painted in bright patterns, the gilding sadly dimmed, but enough remaining to show what charming little bowers, fit for fairy princesses, they had once been. From this we passed into the inner apartments, and went through the bath-rooms : they were considerably finer than any other thing of the kind we saw in the East, excepting one or two of the principal houses in Damascus : they were entirely of mosaic in marble, everywhere, except under each fountain, where porcelain tiles of a very fine make were used. There were plants—oranges, lemons, roses, &c.—growing in every room except the hottest, and fountains trickling or playing everywhere; and the large siesta-hall was divided down the middle by slender, clustered columns supporting a hundred vaultings. Many of these rooms opened into gardens of lemons and oranges that once were doubtless very charming, but they showed the want of care and the rude hand of the Turkish soldier more than the palace itself.

The commandant of the ugly soldiers quartered there had gone to Damascus, but after we had reposed some time on the terrace a lieutenant, dressed in a complete suit of primrose silk, brought us a pressing invitation from his chief's wife to enter the hareem, sending her eldest son, a boy of about ten years old, and an old black slave to conduct us there. We were shown first into a hall, full of marble columns, with a square gallery at each end, ornamented with marble and gilding, through which we entered the hareem court, where a large fountain was playing in the hot sun. In this court a number of immensely fat women and slaves, each dressed in a single loose garment of coloured muslin, were romping violently, throwing water at each other, and jumping in and out of the fountain, upon seeing which the boy who had come with us tore off all his clothes save a small pair of drawers, and jumped in with them. Not any of the women were pretty; they took very little notice of us, and only left off their romps now and then to come and stare at us for a minute. We were taken into a small richly divaned room, where the favourite wife of the commandant was nursing a fat baby, of which she was very proud, as it was a son. She was young and pretty, but her features were more like those of a boy than of a young woman, and her dress, of yellow Manchester cotton, was very ugly; her hair was cropped in a straight line on the forehead, as Mooslims generally wear it, and hung down behind in one long plait; afterwards she put on a blue velvet jacket embroidered with gold, and a dirty tarboosh. Two Christian women who were paying a visit like ourselves, and who were both very pretty, looked beautifully neat and clean beside the Mooslims. The wife asked innumerable questions, all of which we answered to the best of our Arabic powers, when we understood them, and then she showed us the other rooms, of which the ceilings were equally well painted; they all had plenty of mattresses spread on the floor, but the wife's room had an iron bedstead with mosquito curtains round it. We saw little to admire; they wore no jewels, and the only pretty thing was a hand-mirror, in a finely-worked filagree silver frame, which we wanted to buy, but she would not fiart with it.

We were glad to have been invited into the hareem, if only to see the view from the windows, so romantically beautiful in the long narrow ravine up which the castle windows look, due west, with the sea at the end; hill after hill bordering the valley on each side, the nearest one crowned with another small palace built for the Emir's mother, and the pretty white town farther on at the other side; both sides richly clothed with mulberry terraces and fruit-gardens, while from the stream at the bottom the steep zigzags up to the palace are so well seen that a knight of yore might have mounted the whole way without once losing sight of his ladye's eyes shining on him from her latticed bower, the rest of the fortress proudly and sternly guarding the narrow pass below the lofty cliffs. It is indeed a place for dreams of chivalry and fair ladies; but from such dreams nothing can awaken one more completely than the sight of the rows of Turkish soldiers, round, fat, and short, in tight blue trowsers, little close jackets, and small red fezs over their ugly heads,—nor can anything be less romantic than the stout, coarse females of the hareem. These soldiers blew a fine flourish of trumpets, and stared at us immensely when we left the fortress: they were probably the same garrison who butchered the unfortunate Christians in the following summer (June 19, 1860), and were ill-looking enough for anything; too horrible it is to think of the beautiful place, with the gnawed and mangled remains of human bodies scattered through its courts, and the snowy marble of those delicately-ornamented floors " pallid with horror, while the red darkened with blood." * The Turkish soldiers had done much to spoil its beauty, but the plundering Christian peasants are doing much more, and if we regretted then that we could not transport the whole place bodily to England, one is more than ever sorry now that ruin and desolation and a horrible memory has laid its heavy hand upon the once lovely and smiling spot.

The children of the town regularly mobbed us after dinner, bringing bouquets of flowers as we lay upon the sward outside our tents enjoying the beautiful view, the twinkling light, the large shining stars, and the multitudes of fire-flies that danced round us. Now and then a faint sound of singing rose from the valley, or a bird trilled a little evening strain; but the boys would chatter, for the American mission-schools have done much work here, and not a few could speak both French and English, which they were too glad to exercise upon the strangers. One of them had impudence enough to beg we would *lend* him fifty piasters, which he assured us he would certainly repay if ever we came back to Syria!

* Ruskin.

Every house in the little town had its flower-garden of roses, lilies, geraniums, &c.; among them we noticed a splendid double sweet-scented moss-rose of a fine deep lemon colour, which would make glad the heart of an English gardener. The inhabitants were nearly all Christians—chiefly Maronites, with a few Greeks under the Mutsellim; but the valley is full of Druze villages, as it is close to their chief stronghold Mukhtărah, and their Kūlwehs are seen everywhere, generally perched on some lofty or nearly inaccessible crag. The Kūlweh is their place of worship; there they meet every Thursday evening, and feast after service upon raisins, figs, &c. The meetings are conducted with such entire secrecy that little is known about them, and any one hardy enough to venture too near has invariably been put to death; but from what is known they seem to be more political than devotional assemblies; only the Akhals (or initiated) are admitted, and the affairs of the community discussed. A wonderful system of rapid and thorough communication is kept up, and the most perfect organisation and discipline reigns among them,—this is one of the things in which they are so far superior to their Maronite neighbours. They buy and sell much in the town, and are far neater and cleaner in appearance than the Christians. The bazaars were lively, and the people crowded round us with antiques, coins, &c., to sell, and sweet snow-water, which they pressed upon us, and for which they seemed unwilling to be paid. We got a fine antique bronze lamp, and a bronze ornament of two rudely-sculptured but very lively bulls, for a few piasters; they closely resemble some of the Phœnician bronzes in the fine collection at Turin.

The sun was too hot for us to linger, so we started off at 9 A.M. over the hill-top; there the fresh sea-breeze met us, as we looked down on the winding Da'mour, the ancient Tamyras, and retraced our steps through the Wady-el-Kâdy, till we reached our tents placed beside the fountain of 'Ain Bsaba among thickets of honey-suckle and wild geraniums; as the sun sank over the sea I went up and bathed in the bright spring, which is shaded over by noble trees. Late in the evening a terrible khamseen set in, and we had a wild night, the tents every now and then coming down over our heads as we lay panting and suffocating on our beds; they had been badly pitched on soft ground, where the pins would not hold, and two of them had been unwittingly placed on an ant-march, so that we, the unfortunate occupiers, were swarmed over, the whole night through, by countless multitudes of the black beasties. The khamseen brought up thousands of sand-flies, who operated vigour-ously upon our faces, for we had no mosquito-curtains then, and we became so ill with the unwholesome wind, that we got up at three o'clock to dress in hopes of getting off by daylight; but, *pour comble de malheur*, I was incautiously washing upon the grass, when a big black scorpion, astounded at the apparition, walked up to one of my feet and stung me, and I fell into such pain for some hours that dressing or moving was out of the question. We sent off to Beyrout for ammonia, but by the time it came I was better. The khamseen began to abate, and we reached the hôtel at midday, very ready for breakfast, and thankful it was no worse, for the black scorpions are the least venomous of the race. The yellow ones sting terribly, and cause fearful agony and swelling, but the wound is seldom fatal.

We found a large party of our Nile companions arrived at the hôtel in readiness for the French home-steamer; it was pleasant to meet with even such slight acquaintances in this distant land; but the change effected in them all since we had met in Egypt was more or less appalling. The nose of each one had been skinned once or twice or thrice; several were in the most brilliant process of excoriation, and every face below the forehead was painted in turkey-cockian hues! It was perfectly awful to look round the table at the indescribable varieties of RED that graced the board.

Two days after this we rode up to Beit Miry and took possession of our house, which we found indescribably charming and comfortable; the balconies were filled with carnations, and terraces bordered with hollyhocks and belle-de-nuit, and everything looked smiling; while just as we set foot on the threshold a volley of cannon sounded from the town-barracks and from every ship in the bay; resounding back in peals of thunder from the mountains all around us. We were a little astonished, and the villagers believed it was to welcome the English ladies; but in reality it was a royal salute on the landing of the Grand Duke Constantine of Russia.

CHAPTER IX.

OUR MOUNTAIN HOME.

THE village of Beit Miry runs along the top of a mountain ridge, something more than 2000 feet above the sea, which curves round in the form of a semicircle; the peasants' houses slope down on either side of the ridge, the Druzes mostly occupying the west, and the Christians the east end. Our house was planted on the end of the western horn, while the Christian Emir's house and the Maronite chapel faced us at the end of the eastern horn, just above a beautiful little pine-forest; the whole of the circle between being filled up with curving mulberry terraces and a few of the best houses. Beyrout is so charming till the end of June, that the *season* of Beit Miry had not then commenced, but by July eight or nine European families had taken refuge from the heat of the town and arranged themselves somehow in three peasant houses—miserable lodgings they were. There was only one other good house in the place, and that was not half as pretty, but from standing at the western extremity of the village it commanded the view in the northern valley as well as the southern view of Beyrout, and in this respect was certainly one of the finest spots in the whole of the Lebanon, indeed indescribably beautiful. Beyond this another smaller semicircle curved out from the ridge towards the south; this was covered with a forest of pines, planes, and some magnificent oaks, while, like a fortress crowning the summit, the large Convent of Deir-el-Khŭllah proudly surveyed the glorious country, itself a landmark for many miles.

Immediately above our house, on the top of the crag, stood a collection of Druze houses; about half an hour's steep descent below us was the palace of the Maronite Bishop, called Madrăss. When the Europeans had come up we used to think what a curious variety of creeds had met in that one small village—Druzes, Maronites,

Roman Catholics "united" and ununited, Greeks, Lutherans, English Protestants, and a few Mooslims. Perhaps the constant communication of the villagers with Beyrout, and the annual stay of so many Europeans among them, has done a good deal to improve the inhabitants of Beit Miry, but we certainly found them an honest (honesty, *bien entendu, à l'Arabe*), simple-minded, and industrious set. The Druzes are more industrious, the men much cleaner, and immensely finer-looking than the Christians, but the Druze women, on the contrary, look filthy and frightful beside the mountain Maronite women, many of whom in Beit Miry were really very pretty, and were always gaily, and generally cleanly dressed. A bright-coloured cotton gown, with usually a thick red woollen shawl wound round the hips, white muslin appearing at the neck (though the gown is always left wide open to the waist in front), a white apron sometimes, and invariably a white muslin veil, often very prettily embroidered in colours,—such is the costume of the Maronite woman, to which must be added string after string of gold and silver coins wound round the throat, falling over and below the bosom, according to the wealth of the owner, and among them, perhaps, two or three little triangular silver boxes containing charms, scraps of the Koran written on parchment. Her headdress is a red tarboosh edged with coins, a piece of bright-coloured crape or gauze tied round it, and then *the* Christian head-ornament, viz. from 100 to 200 strings of black silk cord, about two feet long, into which are woven at intervals little flat bits of gold, oval shaped, each string ending in a solid tassel or knob of gold or silver. I have seen as many as 3000 bits of gold on one headdress, but usually they carry from 1000 to 2000. These strings, which are all joined into one mass at the top, and are called the "*saffah*," are fastened to the back of the tarboosh, the long silk tassel of which hangs over them; an ornament of filagree gold, called the *koors*, is generally worn at the top of the tassel also; while from the front of the head, on one side only, a very pretty festoon ornament, of eight or ten chains of gold or strings of pearls, is added, each one strung with larger bits of gold than those on the *saffah*; a brooch of diamonds, or a bouquet of natural flowers, is stuck in on the other side. This head-dress is extremely pretty and graceful.

In this land of constant petty warfare and blood-feuds it is no wonder that the wealth of every family should be reduced to a portable form; nor is it any wonder either that husband should heap ornaments on his wife's person year after year to the utmost of his power, since at his death she retains no other possession, all the remainder of his property being divided among his children. It is thought unseemly for a man to propose marriage until he has funds sufficient to bestow on his bride a massive gold necklace of a peculiar pattern—*de rigueur* throughout Syria—and which costs at least 24*l.* In times of distress one of the coins, or if these are gone a piece of the necklace, is cut off and sold, but to be replaced as soon as possible.

The Druze women wear a long dark blue cotton chemise like the Egyptian women, and a square of the same stuff, which is drawn over the head and face, and over the tantour, if one is worn. The Christian women are generally very fair, though with dark eyes; the Druze women are dark, skinny, and ugly, and grow old much earlier than their Christian neighbours, because they do more hard work, and are more exposed to the weather, with fewer clothes to cover them.

Our housekeeping was soon arranged; we had eggs, milk, and fowls from the village, and meat, vegetables, and groceries from the town for the first month; after this we had abundance of meat and fruit, &c., from the village. Three or four Druzes went down every morning early to Beyrout with their mules, and, their commissions duly performed, returned in the afternoon. We seldom had occasion to find fault with them, but we had a great grievance in having every little package or parcel turned over and searched by the *douane* at the gate of Beyrout, even if our dragoman or cook accompanied them. Like Frank in the story, who would look, then touch, then smell, and finally succumbed under the temptation of tasting, large portions of our sugar, coffee, and fruit were mulcted by the soldiers, and very provoking it was to have one's peaches and figs arrive looking like *moulds* for their curious and presumptuous fingers. We applied to Mr. Moore, the Consul, to have a ticket of exemption given to us as consumers, not dealers, but nothing was ever done about it, and the food was too simple and good to admit of our hoping it might disagree with the pilferers.

It is not easy to say how happy we were in our mountain home; we were perfectly indifferent to society, as we had plenty of books (thanks to our friends), and many other occupations, besides reading, and sewing to replace the burnt wardrobe. In truth we found very close attention to study remarkably difficult with so beautiful a prospect ever enchanting and fascinating our eyes. Many hours that I intended to spend in reading found me looking and looking at the view, with my book in my hand; and yet we never could decide, all the months we stayed there, whether the landscape was most beautiful by morning or by evening. In every light and under every circumstance I longed to sketch its many beauties, but we had not been able to replace our paint-boxes since the fire, and it was not till ten days before we left it, probably for ever, that paper, pencils, or colours arrived from England. Our days passed in monotonous enjoyment, every little variety seeming only a fresh pleasure. We were up with the first streak of dawn, about four o'clock, and if Paradise is to be found in this world, it must be in the feel of the air early in the morning on those mountains. How the birds sang—how the fresh air came up, stirring all round one with fragrant perfumes—how the night clouds floated softly away —how the sunlight strode with majestic steps down the mountain side and over the plain—how the sea deepened and brightened from red to blue—how the sun caught the white line of foam on the rocky shore, and tipped house after house and village after village with gold! Truly this was what Hood calls

> " that breath in the air,
> A perfume and freshness strange and rare,
> A warmth in the light and a bliss everywhere,
> All sweets below, and all sunshine above."

Then we sat in the balconies among the flowers, or under our shady arcade, watching the villagers making very brief toilettes as they rose from their beds on the housetops (the children, like dogs, seemed only to shake themselves for their toilettes, while the family washing was invariably deferred till after sunset, when one bowl of water would be brought up for a couple of women or half-a-dozen children), or we watched the goats going by to fresh pastures, or the cows, of which there were not many, and the sheep on their way to be fed in the mulberry-terraces on freshly-gathered leaves, or strings of mules departing to some distant place, or the crowds of women going down in the cool early shade to the fountain to fetch up the water for the day, before the sun came on the spring; while we sat eating basketfuls of figs gathered before the dew was dry on their yellow skins, or of fresh, cool, golden prickly-pears. About eight o'clock a row of little round clouds, like tufts of cotton wool, rose up in a white line along the horizon of the sea, and the heat soon after became too great to bear out-of-doors; but the little clouds rose and rose and spread, whitening broadly on the sky, and by 9.30 or .45, as punctual as a watch, up came the delicious breeze from their bosoms, and seemed to whisper, "Never mind the sun, I'm here, and I'll keep you cool." And so it did; every day unfailingly it came, and every day it died away between four and five, when the sun' was going down, and the mountains beginning to cast long shadows on the plain. Then we used to go out and climb a new height, or dive down into a new glen or ravine each day; every day we found a fresh path, or no path, to take, but some fresh object to interest or some fresh beauty to admire, so enticing that we never came home till after the sun had sunk behind the resplendent sea, and the purple night clouds had come up, and the villagers were rolling themselves up in thick blankets on the housetops. Then sometimes the moon would shine with such loveliness, shedding floods of silver over mountain, sea, and plain, that we could not but pace our terraces till quite late, too full of admiration for sleep,—even when sleeping nature seemed near one; for as glass panes were unknown articles in Beit Miry, our windows had only iron bars to keep out animals, and wooden shutters in case of a storm; these, however, we never shut, and the fresh air of heaven blew over us while asleep, without a chance, at this height, of bringing fever or any other ill, so delicious is the climate by day and by night, never too hot and never too cold.

Even our little village had its legend of love and death. There was a small house, consisting chiefly of a verandah, half hidden among the mulberries between us and the pine-forest, which was occupied some few years ago by a half European and half Arab family. The great beauty of the daughter had attracted many suitors for her hand, one of whom was most assiduous in his attentions; these were at first accepted, but after some time the affections of the fair one were bestowed on a more fortunate rival, and partly in order to escape the unwelcome assiduities of the first lover, the family came up to the mountains for the summer. The inconsolable deserted one could not, however, resist the temptation of following his beloved mistress, hoping at least to gladden his eyes with the sight of her. Tying his horse in the wood below, he stole through the trees near the house, and beheld her standing in the verandah with his hated rival: the bright moonlight shone down on both, and the expression of her face revealed to him how hopeless were his own prospects. In a transport of jealousy he drew a pistol from his belt and levelled it at his rival; but, alas! the mad passions of his soul had unhappily been beating in his hand, and the ball pierced the heart of the unfortunate girl, who fell, bathed in blood, into the arms of her more favoured, but not less unhappy, lover. Maddened with horror and despair at the sight, the miserable young man discharged another pistol at himself, and in another second lay dead at only a few yards distance from his murdered mistress!

We had rigged a flagstaff soon after our arrival, and there we hoisted a grand red jack above the house. Of course we had no kind of *right* to do so (as only consuls are granted the privilege in Turkey), but we had carried our flag in Egypt, and intended to pitch it before our tents in travelling, and we had an idea that it might be of use to us in the mountains. Time proved the idea a good one, and we had reason to thank the kind friend who had provided us with the means of carrying it out. It led to an amusing consequence, for we found afterwards that every individual peasant who came down from the mountains, and all strangers from other villages, invariably stopped and asked who the great person could be whose house was ornamented with such brilliant colours; and that our dragoman and Arab cook, who were both mountaineers, and, consequently, tremendous gossips, for their own aggrandisement as well as ours, enlarged greatly upon how these English princesses had come all the way alone, over the wide sea and through kingdom after kingdom, to let their greatness sojourn for a while in the highly-honoured village; the which history was received with innumerable "Mashāllahs," and usually produced an amazing number of compliments.

The first Sunday after we arrived there the dragoman announced that the Maronite priest of the village wished to pay us a visit, and after the morning service he and a companion priest, or curate, arrived. They were dressed in long black robes of serge, with a scarf of the same wound round the waist, and the elder wore the regular mountain-priest's head-dress, a large globe of black serge: he had a fine open intelligent face and a long white beard; the other looked commoner, and wore only a red tarboosh with a black scarf tied round it. They congratulated us on our safe arrival in their village after the innumerable perils of which they had heard travellers tell, and invoked all manner of blessings on us while we sojourned near them. The old priest was pleasantly communicative as far as his limited subjects of interest and few words of Italian would admit: he told us that every priest must be seven years in the college at Antourah before he is ordained, and that in the act of ordination the bishop places one hand upon the candidate's forehead in blessing, while holding the chalice over his head with the other. They are supported by the voluntary contributions of their flock, but if this is not sufficient the bishop provides them with a small allowance. Each priest has a little garden which he cultivates for himself: he is not permitted to labour elsewhere for gain; but we heard of many instances where the priest helped a sick or unfortunate parishioner in his labour, and they seemed to be generally much beloved and respected in all the villages:

everywhere we were told of their being diligent visitors of the sick. They marry generally the daughters of a sheikh or emir, some one a little above the common peasantry; marriage being one of the privileges which Rome was obliged to concede to the Maronite Church, and the peasantry are very particular in having married priests for the confessors of their wives and daughters. We had not many subjects of conversation, but an *Illustrated London News* and some portrait photographs seemed to interest them very much, and they asked a great many questions. The convent bell sounded midday during their visit, and both priests stopped, even in the midst of a sentence, and bowing the head, said a short prayer, which they told us they repeated at every third hour in the day.

Many of the richer Arabs in the village came begging to see the English ladies, and were much pleased to examine us and our clothes, and our books and pictures, &c., &c.: they really seemed so much delighted that we had not the heart to send them away, however much they bored us. The woodcuts in a copy of Lane's 'Modern Egyptians,' representing the costumes of their Arab brethren, were viewed with clasped hands, and many " Mash-āllahs! " but they said if we had such good pictures why did we come so far and take so much trouble to see them? After my paint-box arrived I used to get repeated messages entreating me to take their portraits for them. On very pretty woman, rich in gold ornaments, came up early in the morning and sat till the afternoon, imploring to have her picture done, until I was really forced to do something like it, with which she was quite enchanted, the colours being very bright, and the bad drawing quite immaterial to her. That woman became a perfect torment to us afterwards, for having happened to see a pair of stays lying on the table, she became so mad to have them, that day after day she returned to the house with new and pressing entreaties, offering me at last coin after coin from her head-dress if I would only let her have the much-coveted articles to make her figure as enchanting as a European lady's! We generally found them very quick and intelligent in taking in new ideas, several of the girls learning to play " solitaire " after once seeing our maid do it, and more than one succeeded in accomplishing the triumphant one remaining ball, much to their own delight and our surprise.

Perhaps our favourite walk of all was along the back of the village, and through the cool, delightful shade of the wood, up to the Convent of Deir-el-Kullah. There was a little chapel half way along the path, shaded by a group of lofty evergreen oaks, under whose sombre shade we rested many an early morning and sunset evening; after passing which the path wound up the hill, with the loveliest views of Beit Miry and the coast, through the wood and over the roughest of paths; for all this wood has grown over the ruins of an ancient town, the smoothly-hewn stones of which would appear to have belonged to well-built houses. Then came the great square of the convent, where some civil black-robed monks bade us welcome, and conducted us to the corridor. Here we loved to sit, for the view, framed in the mullioned double-arched window, is as beautiful as the heart of man could desire: the deep richly-wooded valleys at each side, the cheerful villages, the green uplands, the blue and purple ranges of distant hills, the wide expanse of sea, and Sunnin, rosy and snowy, rising up a giant wall, beyond all. Many an evening we lingered here, sketching or chatting with the monks, and wondering if any earthly view could be much more beautiful.

This convent is built over the ruins of a very large temple, of which some huge columns and stones are still standing. A great many Greek and Latin inscriptions have been fixed in the modern walls (most of them upside down), all mentioning the god of sports, or *Baal-Markos*, the god to whom the temple was probably dedicated. Baal is the title of honour as lord, applied to all the chief gods before the second designation, as *Baal-Zebub*, *Baal-Peor*, *Baal-Beritu*, &c. In Phœnicia the proper name of the great Baal (the Bel or Belus of the Assyrians and Babylonians) was Melkartu. He represented the Sun, the ruler and vivifier of nature, the giver of life.

Close above our house there was a threshing-floor—a little circular bit of smooth ground in the midst of a wild conglomeration of rocks; and often in the earliest sunbeams we used to wander up there to watch the bullocks dragging the board round and round over the ears of corn, on which sometimes the three pretty little children of the Emir would sit, helping to press down the rollers on the straw, the under-side of the board being covered with sharp stones fastened on securely. In some parts of Syria they use knives or short scythes, which chops the straw while they press out the corn; and on a windy morning they would all be busy flinging up handfuls of it into the air, that the wind might blow away the chaff ere the corn fell back upon the threshing-floor.

Beyond this a rough path led through a deep, romantic, wooded glen, where, bending low under prickly oaks, terebinth, and hedges of juniper and clematis, we used to come out upon a luxuriant vineyard, truly "a very fruitful hill," and sit on the edges of an ancient winepress of hewn stones, which had probably been there since the days when the Prophet Isaiah sang songs of the spiritual vineyard in the deaf ears of the Jews. There were three or four of the receptacles for the grapes built up of stones, and hollows for the juice to run out of them into a lower place, hewn out of the rock; all were now tangled over with unpruned vines, honeysuckle, and clematis, making a bower of shade for the workmen when gathering the rich juice, and the mountain torrent dashing past wherein to cleanse the vessels. There were several of these wine-presses on the hills close to us: the upper one had legends attached to it, and stories of *jinns* and spirits and murders besides; and close to it ran the aqueduct which brings water down from Sunnîn, and, descending into the valley, used to carry a stream into Berytus, it is said. It is a pity it is not still kept in order, for water in Beyrout is very bad and very dear, and the aqueduct works to this day at Beit Miry, where we used to see a stream of pure water trickling through the interstices of the displaced stones.

One Sunday afternoon we descended the hill till we reached Madrass, the Bishop's palace, to whom, on a hint from one of his attendant priests, we announced our intention of paying a visit. He sent word that he should be delighted, and we walked through his pleasant gardens and into the well-built, commodious house, part of which is a residence for priests. It was a plain but well-finished building, with a good open staircase, on the balustrades of which crowds of snow-white doves were perched. The Bishop received us at the door of his apartment,—a good room, with a pink and white bed at one side, handsome carpets, and a large writing-table piled over with innumerable papers and letters and a few books. He was a very fine, noble-looking man, with bright intelligent eyes, an intellectual countenance, and a venerable white beard; he seemed in the prime of life, and perfectly conversant with the affairs of the day in Europe. He asked many pertinent questions about England, but considered her evidently a half heathen land a very long way off, whose only importance lay in her influence on the great European powers; but he really knew more of the details of the war then going on between France and Austria than we did, and had later intelligence: in fact it was very remarkable, as we often had occasion to observe, how closely the Syrians watched the events passing in Europe, seemingly beyond their personal interest. Here, and farther up in the mountains, it was the same thing: they knew as much, and more, than we could tell them, and the Druzes seemed absolutely to have the news of each engagement in the campaign before the Europeans themselves had had notice of the affairs of the very countries they represented.

The Bishop was very busy, but he talked a great deal, and begged us to come back soon; he asked many questions about English ordinations, and how and whence we got bishops, &c., &c.; he seemed very much interested when we told him of our great cathedrals, and his eyes brightened as he said he wished he might go to England to see them. We promised to pay him another visit, and to show him some *Illustrated News* pictures; but the very day we had appointed to go there was, alas! the day of our forced departure from Beit Miry, and we never saw him again.

Notwithstanding all the beauties and delights of our quiet mountain home, we became impatient to make some excursions from it before the summer had become quite too hot for travelling among the higher mountains; especially we determined that we must scale that snowy Jebel Sunnín, whose rosy crest was ever before our eyes in every walk. So we sent down to Beyrout for horses and mules, packed up our tents, &c., and set forth very early on the morning of the 6th of June, leaving the little dog to keep house at home with one of the men-servants, as we knew it would be too cold on the mountains for him.

The guide-books and travellers' account of the district we visited are so insufficient that we were obliged to trust entirely to the guidance of our dragoman, to whom every path was familiar; and we were not disappointed in the route he selected. Of all the wanderings we made, from north to south of Syria, no other seven days showed us such a vast variety of ever-changing panoramas of glorious and magnificent scenery as these did. The cedars of Lebanon have a grave, majestic beauty about them which nothing else can equal,—the wild and wooded sides of the Litaany,—the soft, sad tenderness of the Lake of Tiberias—and the flowery forests of Mount Carmel, each have their own peculiar loveliness; but the Kesrouân combines every variety of scenery in its stern grandeur and gentle grace, its rich colouring and wild contrasts, to say nothing of the exhilarating mountain air, cool, refreshing, and so fragrant with perfumed sweetness, that Israel, in the perfection of his blessedness, might well be said to " smell like Lebanon."

The blue morning mist was still veiling the valley with its beautiful bright haze when we skirted the valley of El-Metn, passing through the pretty village of Brumâna (where the Emir has a nice-looking house actually built with a sloping roof and glass),

K

and turned up over a sea-blown mountain brow into a pine-forest, where the rocks looked as if they had been burned like those of Nubia, and the path was, as we always observed it was under pine-trees, abominable.   On the left hand the Convent of Mar-Ishayr, the highest of all the convents seen from the mouth of the Nahr-el-Kelb, stands perched on an insulated peak—a fine situation, but they have no water, and are obliged to carry every drop they use up the toilsome ascent.   Then winding round two sides of a deep valley, we reached the large village or town of Bukfeyia, where we alighted to see the French *filature,* or silk-reeling *fabriques :* nearly all the workers were boys, each with his bundle of cocoons hopping about in a pan of boiling water before him.   After brushing off the coarse outer silk, the ends of the fine silk from three cocoons were instantly attached to a spool on the edge of the table, whence it passed to the huge wheel that wound off the large skeins.   The silk is sorted into yellow and white—the productions of a different variety of worm—and looked exquisitely fine and glossy ; it is not, however, considered quite equal to the silk of Broussa.   The refuse silk is used for tassels or other coarse articles.   The boys were mostly ugly enough—one was precisely a Thibetan Mongol, with sloping eyes and eyebrows, high cheek-bones, and a melancholy mouth with thick lips.   Bukfeyia boasts a fine palace, where the late Emir Hyder resided, and where the Emir, who is governor of the whole Lebanon, ought to reside ; but it was then empty : the reigning prince, being very unpopular among the Bukfeyians, was living at Beyrout. Bukfeyia is full of pretty gardens, and commands an extensive view, overlooking several valleys and picturesque villages.   The wood about it is more than usually varied, the pine and oak being mingled with poplar, willow, plane, ilex, arbutus caroob, &c., &c.

At midday we reached the foot of the mountain cliff where the large rich Maronite Convent of Mar-esh-Shouwyair stands proudly on the promontory looking up through beautiful valleys to Jebel Sunnîn.   We mounted the path, hoping to make a comfortable rest ; but the Superior was absent.   Most of the monks had gone to a funeral, and the younger brothers seemed so dreadfully frightened at the idea of admiting three women into their salon or their chapel, that we compounded with them for permission to spread our carpets in the cloisters.   They managed to bring the alarming daughters of Eve some cushions (upon which we immediately fell asleep), and when we left them they exploded into long fits of uncontrollable laughter on seeing us jump up sideways on our saddles, and we heard them still laughing and laughing as we descended the winding path. Then came a long narrow, beautiful ravine, on the opposite side of which, among thick mulberry-terraces, we looked down upon the Greek Convent of Mar Hanna * Shouwyair, a very large building, where the first Arabic printing-press ever set up in the Lebanon was made. This good work and the fine cultivation of the mountains all round these convents speak much in favour of the monks; nor did we ever hear a single word said against any one of the numerous convents of the Lebanon—nothing but respect and gratitude; and perhaps, until the government of the country is in some degree improved and the peasantry protected, and civilisation and education are in some degree spread amongst them, these fraternities of single men are the best methods of accomplishing any kind of cultivation in the unhappily wasted land.

From first to last, throughout Syria and Palestine, the one great feeling ever present to one's mind as one's eyes journey on, mile by mile, is the deplorable *waste* of land. When one sees what the rude industry of the ignorant and poverty-stricken peasant can accomplish; that smiling crops, delicious pastures, luxuriant fruit-gardens, and rich woods result from the meagre, clumsy work done by the mountaineer, unassisted by modern implements or knowledge, one cannot but sigh to remember our half-exhausted homelands, and think how small the capital, how slight the head-work, and how short the time that would turn the plains and mountains of Syria again into " a land flowing with milk and honey," and repay the workman, not tenfold, but a hundredfold. At present a little corn, mulberries and olives, figs and vines, are repeated, generation after generation, in the same terraces; but the amount of work necessary to convert thousands of miles of mountain and valley into fertile ground would be but small, and there are few crops to be found anywhere that could not be cultivated successfully either on the uplands or lowlands; while the climate is incontestably remarkable for salubrity, and a life in the hill-country would be by no means too hot for even a Scotch Highlander. Cotton could be admirably produced in the plains; and if the enterprise was commenced on a sufficiently large and imposing scale, a little firmness, resolution, and judicious conduct would undoubtedly insure success. It is true that the Turks do not particularly like or encourage European settlers, but the Christian Arabs are delighted to welcome those who they know will improve their condition,—will be their guardians and protectors,—and beside whom they could in some degree range themselves against the rapacious and sometimes dishonest cruelties of the government, and of their own lawless sects and tribes.

A *most* atrocious zigzag ascent led over the crown of the ravine,

* St. John.

K 2

and we found ourselves suddenly on a small meadow, where our tents were pitched beneath a group of truly magnificent oaks, commanding a view on all sides that was really sublime; Kunîsyeh, Nukh-el-Jurd, and Sunnin stood with numberless other heights majestically round us,—the feet of the two former clad in thick woods, which we were told abounded in wild boars. This place is called El-Merooj.

We went to bed very much tired, to be awakened from dreams of fine scenery and sunshine by torrents of rain—a very unusual circumstance at this season. Long before morning our tent, which was not a double one, had begun to leak; our clothes had got soaked through in the night, and we had no alternative but to remain in bed, as the only dry place, and to take our breakfasts in waterproof cloaks under umbrellas. Alas! the rain continued with unabated violence, and towards the middle of the day we unanimously agreed that we were exceedingly uncomfortable. However, at last a bright thought occurred to Habeeb. At a little distance there was a half-finished stone hut, built to shelter mules, with a roughly-made oven in one corner; into this hut our three beds, which had been kept pretty dry, were carried, and we followed them, conveyed on the back of a mule. The hut was unplastered and windowless, but dry: it seemed uncommonly like a dungeon, and I was in mortal fear of snakes; but we lit a charcoal fire in the oven, and were sleeping comfortably enough, when we were awakened by low hoarse sounds, perfectly inexplicable, and very alarming. We were at some distance from the tents and men-servants, and were beginning to feel a little odd, when the strange noises waxed louder and louder, shriller and shriller, and at last burst forth into the unmistakable crows and cacklings of a lot of cocks and hens that had been placed by some peasants in the oven, and were becoming roasted by the heat of the fire!

The rain, which is very uncommon indeed in June, continued to fall all night, but in the morning the sky cleared, and we mounted about eleven, and pushed on up steep paths, among loose rocks and crags of blue limestone of the most fantastic shapes, round the head of a valley tributary to the Nahr-el-Kelb, coming suddenly upon thickets of glorious and lovely rhododendrons growing in wild luxuriance among the rocks, with a beauty that made one forget cold and rain, and everything disagreeable. Beds of purple lupines, too, were dotted all along the path as we turned up a short pass into the great valley of the Nahr-el-Kelb itself—a most peculiar and magnificent valley, the mountain sides of all manner of rich, bright colours, with trees and meadows of fine corn up to the very summits; while half way down commenced, on both sides, vertical walls of blue limestone, straight and smooth down to the very bottom: it looks as if the mountains had turned bottom upwards by mistake. This part of the valley can scarcely be crossed anywhere, so unbroken are these rocky walls. We passed along opposite the pretty, scattered village of Biskinta, half hidden in woods and fruit-gardens, and then, having climbed up a very steep conical hill, we stopped at a little hut, placed in a wild, mournful solitude in the midst of a barren waste, where some shepherds were eating their dinner. Here we took shelter from a shower, and had but just rejoined the road when the rain increased tenfold, and a thick blinding fog came up the valley, only breaking here and there enough to give us glimpses of perpendicular depths below, from so dizzy a height and so narrow a goat-track, that perhaps it was as well we could see so little of the perilous way. We were now passing over the southern shoulder of Sunnîn, right up among the snow, when Habeeb suddenly stopped, and jumping down, exclaimed that here at last was a piece of sandy ground upon which we could pitch our tents, the ground everywhere else being as soakingly wet and dripping as we were ourselves. He spread a mat for us, and we alighted, huddling under one umbrella until the pitching of the tent was, with much difficulty, accomplished, a large fire lit, and our beds made, in which we immediately took refuge, and where we dined. We needed the fire, for the wind, coming off the snow, was horribly cold: we were now at least 7000 feet above the sea.

The morning proved fine, and we rode on, enjoying the sunshine along the ridge of the noble valley, catching once a most exquisite view of Beyrout, with the curving shore and blue sea, until we came to the famous Jisr-el-Hajar (bridge of stone), a grand scene indeed. This Neba-el-Leben (fountain of milk) is the chief source of the Kelb, and here the river rushes in three tremendous cascades from the top of Sunnîn, forcing its way through the limestone walls, under white masses of foam, and falls into a boiling cauldron just above the ridge, whence it tumbles down headlong into the valley in roaring torrents. The rock forms a natural but oblique bridge over the torrent, 163 feet span and 80 feet in height. The view from the bottom of the chasm is truly sublime, the mountains forming fine contrasts of browns and bright reds with the snowy summits and the stern grey crags; while all about the bridge and the cascades the loveliest flowers, including pink convolvulus and blue forget-me-not, grow in wild confusion. In a cavern under the arch, in the very midst of the deafening roar, some shepherds had made a home; the wife was churning butter from goat's milk in a very primitive churn—nothing more than a goat's skin filled with milk, which was tied on the end of a long stick, itself mounted on a tripod of sticks stuck in the ground, between which the skin was swung backwards and forwards.

After this we continued along the side of the valley under the snowy head of Sunnîn, rolling clouds of mist occasionally wrapping him mysteriously from sight; and passing over some very perilous places by the Neba-el-Asel (fountain of honey), for we had lost our path, we began to ascend the very steep pass which separates the valley of the Nahr-el-Kelb from that of the Nahr Ibrahim. It was very difficult and severe for the mules, and Habeeb watched his canteen with great anxiety. One block they scrambled up was very nearly four feet high, and our horses made a great fuss about it, although we dismounted to ease them. We were, however, well rewarded on reaching the top, for the scene was superbly grand, the snow all round us and under us, and a kind of glacier above our head. Then came a zigzag descent, which it is pleasanter to remember than it was to perform: the muleteers requested us to dismount, and after riding for some way we did so, for the sensation was not a pleasant one, when looking down the fearful depth as one's horse struggled over the masses of rock at the edge of the very steep and narrow path.

The valley of the Nahr Ibrahim, the ancient river Adonis, is wilder and sterner than that of the Kelb. We had intended on reaching it to have gone direct to Afka, the source of the river, but the inhabitants seem to be as wild and stern as the valley itself, and our dragoman declared himself afraid to venture without further tidings of their politics at the moment. War had just broken out between the Metouaalees, who chiefly occupy these mountains, and the Christians, and some sanguinary murders had quite lately taken place. We were not at all willing to give up seeing this celebrated spot when we had really got within reach of it, and we felt pretty sure that as English ladies we had not much to fear; so we told him to settle it as he pleased, and do the best he could, only explaining to him that we intended to go to Afka, and go we would, somehow or other; but, to give him time to gather tidings, we agreed to defer the visit till the next morning. So we turned away westward, and rode on for an hour or so till we came to a good camping ground, at a place called the "round meadow," just opposite the village of Amhaz, on the other side of the magnificent and savagely-wild ravine. Immediately above our tents were steep mountains, partly green and cultivated, but with masses of white and yellow crags breaking out on the side, some shaped like grotesque statues; and on the opposite side of the valley uprose stern walls, one above the other, of purple-grey rocks, almost vertical, yet here and there terraced with narrow ledges lined with trees that seemed to have no footing, and a thousand strange shades of colour blending on the mountain tops, till lost in the distant snow. We walked on a little beyond our tents, and there, turning a corner, was the sun shining on a mountain slope, one vast mass of glorious rhododendrons, " spreading their soft breasts unheeding to the breeze," and seeming like a soft veil of tender, delicate purple gauze drawn over the whole slope, so radiantly lovely one could never forget it.

The cold forbade all sleep: perished and frozen through the night, we gladly welcomed the morning light and hot coffee. Meantime Habeeb had consulted several peasants about our going on to Afka, and they all declared that it would be very dangerous; however at last, by good fortune, we captured a peasant whom Habeeb had known before, and believed trustworthy, and who was himself a Metouaalee,—a fine hook-nosed, dark fellow, with a long beard and good teeth, armed with gun and dagger, like every peasant and shepherd in the district,—and he engaged to conduct us safely there and back again. So we rode on along an excellent path for about two hours, enjoying the magnificent valley and the ranges of mountains before us (looking north-east), reaching right up to the snowy Makhmel, the mountain of the Cedars until we began a steep descent into the hollow where the source of the Ibrahim lay; the wood increasing till it became quite like a park,—pines, lignum vitæ, oak, terebinth, and fine lofty walnuts. We were fully occupied with the delightful view, when, on suddenly turning the angle of a cliff, we found the narrow path closed by fifteen men, who started up apparently from out of the rock, and pointing their guns at us, demanded our business; a parley and explanation ensued, and we immediately became excellent friends, the secret of which sudden transition we did not know till the day after, when the dragoman acknowledged that he had informed them not only that we were English, but also near relations of Mr. Wood, our late consul at Damascus, who did so much for the Metouaalees and Druzes that his very name is a passport still among them. We were equally innocent of the relationship and of the falsehood, but we reaped its benefit.

The mountains now rose in a close semicircle to the height of two thousand feet from the bottom of the deep dell, their nearly perpendicular sides dotted over with tufts of prickly oak and other shrubs the bottom itself filled with houses among gardens of pomegranates and figs, shaded by noble walnut-trees; while rushing out from a cavern under the great cliff was the cascade and source we had come to see. There was not very much water in it at this time, but we did not regret it; the divided cascades were prettier than a larger single one, and the sheets of foam were quite wide enough to be very grand and beautiful. The wild luxuriance of foliage about the boiling waters much increases their beauty, and the dark cavern, with the monstrous black mouth through which they pour, is fringed with tremulous maidenhair and other delicate ferns. A peasant told us that sometimes in summer the stream sinks into so small a compass that persons have crept into the cavern itself, where there is even now a small ruined building at the very back of the cave, probably a shrine or sanctuary for the most secret rites of the Greek worship. At the most picturesque part of the lower cascade, on a little cliff, are the remains of the old Temple of Venus, one hundred feet by fifty; little of ornamental work is left beyond bits of cornice, but all the stones we saw were of grey granite, smoothly hewn. This temple was a very famous and highly honoured shrine, for here, beside this foamy fountain, the beautiful Adonis was said to have received his death-wound from the boar, and here Venus is still heard, by imaginative persons, lamenting the untimely fate of the young hunter,—a victim to the cruel jealousy of Mars, who, distracted at the caresses lavished on him by the fair goddess, took the form of the ferocious animal he felt himself to resemble under such pangs, and pierced the youth with his cruel tusks. The despairing Venus metamorphosed his white and beautiful corpse into a white rose—a flower ever sacred to herself— which was afterwards changed into a red one, in consequence of a drop of her own rosy blood, drawn by the prick of a thorn, falling on the flower. Thus she still kept him beside her in emblem; but her grief was so great that the gods in pity permitted him to return to earth for six months of the year; the time of his departure from her side was announced by the sanguinary hue imparted to the falling waters, which then

> " Run purple to the sea, suffused with blood of Thammuz." *

At this moment, thus advised by Nature herself, the annual and solemn fête was celebrated, chiefly by women, who sat on the thresholds of their houses tearing their hair and weeping loudly. The statue of Venus was exhibited covered with a veil, the head leaning on her left hand, and the whole figure expressing sadness and weeping; on the day of her invocation it is said that a fire,

* Milton.

bright as a star, invariably fell precipitously from the sky into the water; this they believed to be Venus herself, but probably it was only an immense tear mingling in the blood of her lover. It is curious that the Jews should have adopted this Phœnician idolatry so entirely as to have carried its observance into the very courts of the sanctuary of the Lord God, where the Spirit shows them to Ezekiel " weeping for Tammuz," with their faces turned "towards the north,"* offering to her cakes and incense, and pouring out drink-offerings before her. The women during this festival wore men's clothes, while the men wore women's clothes, as was generally the custom where two persons (as Osiris and Isis, Venus and Adonis, Hercules and Hebe, &c.) were celebrated together: stores of dresses were kept in the temples for that purpose,—an allusion to this is made in Deut. xxii. 5, and 2 Kings x. 22, and possibly in Rev. iii. 4, in speaking of Sardis, a city consecrated to the double worship of Hercules and Diana. The celebration lasted two days: the first was spent in lamentations and wailings, as we have said; on the second they danced, shouted, and sang for joy, as if Adonis had returned to life.

So runs the legend,—under which one finds the natural fact of which the story is but the poetic clothing. Adonis, or Adonai—a Hebrew title signifying lord—the friend and favourite of Apollo, was made the personification of the Sun, or Summer, by the Phœnicians; the boar and the bear were both used as emblems of Winter, whose rude onset signifies in the fable the departure of the summer sunshine, vanquished by the cold blasts of winter. So the fable of the daughter of Plenty, carried off to dwell beneath the earth for half the year,—so the Tyrians, Romans, and Cappadocians kept some of their gods in iron chains till the winter was gone; then the gods were supposed to be re-awakened, and rose up endowed with new strength and power. In the Syrian mountains the winter is short, but the contrast must be quite terrible between the blazing and scorching heat of the long summer and the severity of the winter, especially in a place like Afka, surrounded by the loftiest and most snowy summits of the whole range; they might well consider it an annual death of Nature, and nowhere would Spring be more sudden, beautiful, and gladdening than here, more completely the resuscitation of a dead body. It is related that at the end of the days of mourning a dead man's head was thrown into the River Adonis, which carried it down to the sea: this is in fact precisely the same legend as that of Osiris, who, after being murdered by

---

* Ezek. viii. 14; Jer. vii. 18, xliv. 17–28. It was, in fact, part of the Astarte or Venus worship.

Typhon, the Evil One, was cast into the sea, and his mangled remains found by Isis on the Phœnician coast*—to celebrate which mystery the priests of Alexandria used annually to throw a head amidst great pomp into the sea, which held in its mouth a letter declaring that Osiris had come to life again. Both allude to the desolation of the earth at one season, and the return of verdure and fecundity at another.

The word Afka is said to be derived from the Hebrew Apheka, meaning to hold or embrace, in allusion to the embraces of Venus and Adonis; but as it also means a basin, it is more likely to describe the mountains surrounding or embracing the small deep well of the sacred glen, which is shaped precisely like the interior of a tea-cup, only with one side lower than the rest.

It is said that a good deal of these old ceremonials still remain among the wild people of Afka, but how much or what we could not learn; they were much more intent upon questioning and examining us than upon imparting any information, and possibly they might have resented any very curious inquiries respecting their religion, the peculiarities of which are, I believe, very little known. They are said, like the Shyites, to acknowledge 'Ali as the only true successor of the Prophet; but they have probably many other more peculiar doctrines of their own, besides their scrupulousness in what they eat, drink, or touch, which is carried to the very highest pitch, for they would die rather than drink from the same vessel that a Christian or a dog has touched. It is in truth natural that a band of lawless and savage men, living in secluded and wild mountainous districts, should have adopted local ideas, especially such as were sufficiently exciting to fascinate their untutored minds; but that any traces of such rites and ceremonies should have survived the fifteen centuries since Constantine destroyed the temple at Afka, is at least curious.

Wild and savage as the Metouaalees are, they were civil enough to us,—the men assisting us to scramble up and down the rocks by the waterfall, holding our horses, &c.; the women, who had never before seen a Frank lady, gathered round us with eager curiosity to examine our clothes, which appeared to be quite incomprehensible to them. Our large shady hats were subjects of great admiration, and they laughed long and loudly over the size of our waists, which they insisted on spanning with their hands, until their embraces became so troublesome that we mounted our horses, and, with many

---

* At Djebail, ancient Byblos. For a charming account of this festival of the finding the body of Osiris, see Ebers' admirable story of 'An Egyptian Princess.'—Tauchnitz.

lookings back at the beautiful and romantic spot, re-ascended the hill into the upper part of the valley. Here the cool fresh air was most refreshing after the suffocating heat of the pent-up glen, as we retraced our steps of the morning and passed on still along the south side of the Nahr Ibrahim (or River Adonis) towards the sea. We were half way down the very worst of all possible descents, jumping, slipping, and struggling among huge rocks and impossible crannies, when two of our horses took to fighting, and before the attendants could reach them one horse had toppled down part of the precipice, and was lost to view. We had many more miles to go, and the adventure was somewhat dismaying. However, some stiff bushes had kindly broken his fall, and the horse was picked up; the saddle, which had been a good deal broken, was patched together somehow, the things tumbled out of the saddle-bags were re-collected, and we continued our tortuous way, not pausing again till we reached a very beautiful spot, where the tents were already pitched, called Wätr-el-Jauz—the "country of walnut-trees," but the walnuts have now disappeared. Here we sat under the shade of a grove of fine willows, enjoying fresh views of the beautiful mountains. No day's ride had given us a greater variety of magnificent scenery than this one, and very lovely it had been under the cloudless sky.

But the next day was almost more beautiful, for after crossing the hill on which we had encamped the sea was added to the still more extended and splendid view. Habeeb averred that Hermon was visible, but we could not distinguish its cone. And then came an apparently endless descent of deep and very narrow ravines of great beauty, one after another, filled with flowers and fragrant shrubs and pleasant villages, with weird and savage rocks and stern grey crags, and such an abominable path that more than once we had to dismount and scramble down on foot. At last we reached Ghazir, a beautifully situated, large, and thriving village, full of fruit-gardens, roses, and myrtles, and with a great number of convents and French *filatures*. We rested here for an hour in a hospitable merchant's house, and then continued our way, descending literally through fissures in the rocks, till we had reached the sands of the sea-shore, and gladly found ourselves in the lovely Bay of Jouneh. Nothing could be prettier than the scattering of this bright-looking town over the steep cliffs, crowned with white convents behind it; the curve of the bay was so graceful, and the little gardens so rich and pretty, and the sea breeze so fresh and pleasant after the hot ravines we had came from. There were several ships in the bay waiting for corn. We turned off from the sea to pass through the atrocious paths of pretty Zouk Mehayl, and by the fine college for Maronite priests, called Antourah, most romantically situated in the bosom of a lofty gorge, surrounded by gardens of arbutus, ilex, and pomegranate, which we should have liked to see, had we had time enough.

On leaving Zouk we found ourselves in an extensive pine-forest on the upper side of the Nahr-el-Kelb, through which we descended by a winding path. Nothing could exceed the rich beauty of this narrow valley, the river winding at the bottom, and both sides clothed with wood. At the foot of the descent is one of the chief sources of the river, welling forth from a cavern, round which the ferns hang in green wreaths and garlands, as if veiling the source from common eyes. We had to scramble on stepping-stones through a swampy thicket of St. John's wort, rhododendrons, myrtle, and oleander, in order to reach it; but it was worth the trouble. There are much finer caverns with stalactites at another source of the same river, somewhere higher up in the mountains, but these we never reached, not having heard of them till shortly before we left Beyrout: they can hardly be prettier than these. It was half-past seven when we had regained the summit of the hill-side, for very steep and difficult it was to our tired horses and our tired selves, and the light was gone. We had still a long ride over the mountain, guided by a shepherd, and then came a descent to the river side, which in the darkness was really most perilous; it was terrific enough by day, and the shepherd seemed so shocked at the ladies having to descend it in the night, that he offered to stay with us, and very useful he was in encouraging the unfortunate horses, who would fain have stood still instead of struggling down the rocks, which in the darkness we could not attempt on foot: and had not the moon helped us in some parts we must have remained on the mountain all night; so we were indeed thankful to reach the bottom without any accident, and to find ourselves close to the mouth of the Kelb, looking doubly lovely in the moonlight. We pushed through the oleanders and forded the stream (though the current was very strong for the weary horses to withstand), finding our tents pitched beyond the river at the edge of the waves, and very gladly went to bed, after being thirteen hours on horseback. Late we stayed the next morning resting, with the tent door drawn back, watching the little waves curling up close to us, and the fishing-boats lazily sailing over the blue waters.

However we had still a long way to get home, so we mounted at eleven, and rode along the shore as far as Antēlyias, where we turned aside into charming gardens, bowered and hedged with myrtle and clematis, both of which the horses greedily devoured, and then up steep mountains, thickly covered with myrtle all in blossom, perfuming the air delightfully : a lovely ride, but the path turned round and round, till we began to fancy ourselves bewitched, and fated "never to return." At last, at near 4 P.M., we reached Brumâna, and completed the circle we had been seven days in travelling ; and in another hour we were very happy to find ourselves once more in our pretty home, where the little dog nearly went into fits, sobbing with joy at seeing us again.

CHAPTER X.

OLD PHŒNICIANS AND MODERN DRUZES.

ONE day early in July we had occasion to go down to Beyrout to despatch some business, and when there we found ourselves suddenly included in a hastily-settled ride to Saïda, the ancient Sidon. The opportunity of accompanying some friends was too pleasant to be resisted, and the arrangements were so managed that we were not to be troubled with mules and canteen; a Saïda gentleman, Signor Pietri Santi, then in Beyrout, having offered us the use of rooms in his house. The heat in Beyrout was now very great indeed, and the mosquitos almost intolerable: we felt them all the worse as there are scarcely any at Beit Miry, the blood-thirsty creatures seldom taking the trouble of flying so high above the plains. We therefore settled to make our journey by night, and to rest by day. We had, too, a glorious full moon, that lighted us through the narrow lanes of the town and the pine-forest, with a cool flood of silver-coloured light that was infinitely delightful, hiding much of the monotony of what is sometimes considered a tiresome ride, although there is really constant change, the steep rocky shore, here and there dressed with olive-groves, alternating with smooth curving sands. It is very wild, and perhaps dreary, by day, and to add to this impression, in one place where we were treading the broken rocks by the sea, a hyena bounded past, so close as almost to touch my horse's nose: he had been lying on our track, and we had unkindly disturbed him. Farther on, where the Khan Khulda marks the site of the ancient city of Heldua, we came upon camels swinging along under enormous burdens that seemed like walking houses, almost concealing the beast beneath, while at top of each lay the driver fast asleep, tied on to his own goods. We were told that they will often go on and on in this way, almost without any rest or food, for a week at a time. After fording the Damour, where we recognised the richly-wooded valley of Deir-el-Kamar, we stopped at Neby Yunus, the Khan of the Prophet Jonah, and, dismounting, fell fast asleep on the sand over our coffee. The light was breaking as we awakened half an hour after, and found ourselves in a pretty sandy bay, at a picturesque khan, beside a fine grove of tamarisk-trees, a sapphire-coloured sky over head, and the moon—one large mass of glowing silver, most wonderfully dyed and crimsoned with the flush of morning,—standing on the very horizon of the sea, while behind us, above the grove, the glorious "Daughter of the Morning" shone with steady golden light, seeming to grow larger and larger, when—all in a moment, up shot a flood of crimson and orange, lighting up the rocks and the sands and the trees and the sky; and the moon, after lingering a few minutes as if to rival the red light of day, sank down behind the waves, and when we turned round a moment after the morning-star was gone too. It was one of the prettiest scenes possible, a perfect picture of beauty, and the show was not yet over; for now dark masses, which we had taken for stones and rocks on the sand, wakened, stretched, shook themselves, and arose, and in two minutes their horses and camels and mules were shaken up and mounted, and they, with their bright-coloured burdens, rode off, clearing the place, and changing it really like a magic-lantern slide, or a dissolving view in a theatre. Then the sunbeams streamed widely over the bay, and down came troops of chattering girls, in wide scarlet trousers and white veils, to fill their pitchers at the fountain—the super-excellent fountain, for this water is sacred, and *must* be particularly sweet, the spring having appeared on the very spot where the good-natured whale was so kind as to come to shore and vomit forth poor Jonah (*Yunus* in Arabic) after his long and uncomfortable voyage in its stomach. It would be difficult to prove which is the truth, but another report says that the whale turned aside from the Great Sea into the quiet bay of Iskenderoon, and laid Jonah among the oleanders that fringe its shore, in imitation of Moses in the bulrushes; and if the whale was only careering about between Joppa and Tarsus, one place is as likely as the other.

Another mile or so brought us to the brow of the last headland, and to our first view of Saïda, and a lovely view it was: there she sat at the edge of the deep blue water, pale brown and purple mountains embracing her in warm, giant arms, with battlemented walls and towers round her, all white and glistening in the early sunshine, like a swan sitting by the sea-shore. We turned down to the beach and continued our road on the soft, slushy sand along the edge of the wave, sometimes stopping to pick up some particularly pretty shell, oftener to watch the colours of

> " the last foam
> That trembled on the sand with rainbow hues " *

caught from the bright morning sun. The view grew prettier and prettier as we distinguished the high castle above the town, built by Louis IX. of France, and the other fortress, standing on rocks which run far out into the sea, and are connected with the shore by a low bridge of nine arches. We entered the town about 8 A.M., and wound through the narrow streets and gay bazaars, and still gayer, thriving-looking people in bright, clean dresses, to the house of Signor Santi, where we were soon established in a pleasant saloon furnished with divans and mats: one expects nothing more in an Arab reception-room, unless it be a tray of pipes and nargilehs. The heat and the mosquitos drove away all thoughts or hopes of sleep, and we could only lie still and pant till the cool breeze of the sunset hour enabled us to visit some hospitable French Arabs living in the French khan, a huge building as large as a London square, erected by the Emir Fakhr-ed-din for the use of the French merchants in the seventeenth century. A large tank and fountain occupy the centre of the court in a garden of banana, acacia, and lemon-trees, which made the evening breeze come into the apartments laden with perfumes. Each family has its own suite of rooms, communicating with the rest by a wide corridor extending round the court on both storeys to walk and lounge in; it seemed to us a most pleasant residence, with a promenade on the house-top where one could enjoy fresher breezes and a lovely view of the city. Saïda is one of the prettiest towns in Syria; the mosques and baths are particularly picturesque, and almost handsome; the two castles, and the fine rocks with the breakers constantly dashing over them, and the rich fruit-gardens all around the city, form a most charming *tout ensemble*. The view from the Château of St. Louis is equally pretty and more extensive, the headland of Sour (the ancient Tyre) bounding the scene. This castle is kept in good repair, and was originally a strong fortress; that on the rocks, although very much shattered, is worth seeing. Saïda is a place for endless sketching, both within and without the town, and would repay an artist for a stay of some duration.

Warned by the heat and closeness of the house on the first day, we established ourselves on the following morning inside a Wely or Saint's tomb on the sea-shore, a little to the north of the town,—a

* ' Thalaba.'

spot to be recommended to future travellers, as we found the heat much less intolerable there than elsewhere; we were close to a spring and to the sea, and among lovely fruit-gardens. The tomb, which occupies one half of the building, is walled off, and locked up; the rest is a small square whose arched roof is supported by sixteen columns and is raised on steps at each side : such are most of the welys in Syria, and they are often very agreeable resting-places. In the afternoon we rode through some miles of the gardens, the richest, we were told, in all Syria; for here were not merely lofty trees tangled over with thick bowers of vines laden with luscious grapes,—orange, lemon, fig, almond, and plum-trees, fragrant with perfume and bending with fruit,—but bananas also, rare in this country, with enormous clusters of the rich brown and orange fruit hanging down among the splendid leaves and beautiful purple blossoms above them. The prickly-pear hedges were full of fruit, and roses and honeysuckles grew everywhere. But the glory of Saïda are her apricot-groves : from her—her sole commerce now—is exported the greater part of the *mish-mish* con-sumed in Egypt, Damascus chiefly supplying Syria; and there must be nearly as much mish-mish eaten in Egypt as we consume of oranges or apples in the whole of Great Britain. The fruit of all kinds grown at Saïda is considered of a better quality than any other in Syria.

Sidon was one of the most ancient cities in the world, and is one of the very few of those (such as Damascus, Hamah, and Hebron) on which a modern city or town, bearing the same name, exists at the present day. It was the chief port and capital city of Phœnicia, and the mother of a hundred other cities whose very sites have been forgotten in the dark ages of history. Six of the sons of Canaan,* the grandson of Noah, founded the principal cities of Phœnicia (Sidon, Arka, Sinna, Aradus, Simyra, and Hamath); hence their descendants were called Canaanites, the Greeks after-wards giving them the name of Phœnicians. Their coast extended from Mount Carmel to Mount Casius, along which numerous ports and cities were placed: the inhabitants of these appear to have attained a high degree of civilisation and even of luxury. Dismayed, however, at the extraordinary success of the divinely-supported arms of Israel, as step by step they victoriously subdued nearly the whole of Palestine, the Phœnicians emigrated in large numbers— " fleeing from the face of the robber Joshua," as they expressed it— and planted kingdoms and colonies throughout the coast of the Mediterranean, founding cities in Africa, Spain, Italy, Greece and

* Gen. x. 15-19.

L

the isles of the Ægean Sea. They need not, however, have been so much afraid, for Asher, to whom the land containing Sidon fell, never took the city, or drove the Phœnicians out of the country;[*] and God, in His anger against Israel for this, permitted these and some other tribes to dwell in the land in order "to prove Israel," and "to teach them war."[†] Unhappily the Israelites not only profited by their teaching in this and in other accomplishments,[‡] but they also learned from them their abominable idolatries: from them came the worship of Baal, the Sun,—the ruins of whose Phœnician-built temples abound in Syria, and especially about Hermon, or Baal-hermon; the Sidonians, however, called it "Sirion," or the "Breastplate." From them came also the worship of Astarte (or Venus), the enticing goddess, after whom even the heart of the wise Solomon turned from the paths of virtue, and to whose honour he erected an altar or "high place," on the Mount of Corruption, over the brook Kedron; and it was from Sidon, also, that Ahab, king of Israel, took the wicked Princess Jezebel for his wife, the great promoter of Baal-worship.

Sidon was in the height of her glory about a thousand years before the coming of our Lord; her colonies, of which Carthage was the chief, had then spread the knowledge of letters[§], science, and art over all the then-known world, and her ships had sailed round the southern extremity of Africa, in passing from the Red Sea to the Mediterranean.[‖] Her daughter Tyre was still more flourishing and renowned than herself,—"perfect of beauty," "very glorious in the midst of the seas,"—but she was slain, destroyed, "brought utterly to ashes;" and Sidon, conquered first by Tyre, fell successively into the hands of the Assyrians, Chaldeans, and Persians. Later on it became Syrian, Greek, and Roman, and was much occupied by the Crusaders. "Pestilence and blood" has been indeed "sent into her streets," and "judgments executed in her."[¶] "Blush with shame, O Sidon! thou city sitting beside the waters, the strength of the sea; thou mayest indeed say, I have not travailed, I have nourished neither young men nor virgins; for now none remain unto me: it is as though I had never brought forth a child!"[**]

We left the city at 8 P.M., passing through groups of people sitting in clusters in the streets and on the beach, smoking and listening to gesticulating story-tellers, and had a delightful ride along the shore, in the sweet, fresh, warm night air, by the light of the

---

[*] Judges i. 31, 32.　　　　　[†] Ibid. ii. 20–23, iii. 1, 2.
[‡] 1 Kings v. 6.　　　　　　　[§] Herodotus, book v. 58.
[‖] Ibid. book iv. 42.　　　　　[¶] Ezek. xxvii. xxviii. 22, 23.
[**] See Isaiah xxiii. 4.

magnificent moon. Twice we stopped at the roadside khans to drink excellent coffee, and morning began to break as we entered the olive-groves and gardens about Beyrout; they were gay with flowers —among them the colocynth (coloquintida), a queer-looking creeping plant with a fruit like green pills, now (happily) so much disused in medicine, that it no longer pays to collect it. We refreshed ourselves with quantities of the cool, sweet prickly-pear from the baskets of pretty women who were gathering them in the early dew; and as the blue mist cleared away the mountains looked so lovely, that we felt well repaid for the fatigue of the nocturnal ride. We reached the hotel at 6 P.M., and found occupation for some hours in ridding ourselves of the fleas we had gathered up in the khans *en route*; and at midnight we mounted again, to ride up to our dear little home at Beit Miry.

One morning at Beit Miry the Druze muleteer who had accompanied us to Deir-el-Kamar came to request the honour of our presence at his marriage, which was to take place that day; and on our promising to go to it, he left a present of an oke of pine fruit-kernels, as the Druze custom is to leave a gift with every guest invited to the wedding. We were summoned by a messenger, who said, "the feast was ready," at 2.30 P.M.; and on reaching the Druze quarter, a volley of muskets saluted us from a group of gaily dressed men surrounding the bridegroom, attired in new clothes, and looking very sheepish and uncomfortable. On arriving at the house, which was at the farther end of the quarter, we found the little outer court full of old hags, horned and veiled, cooking in stew-pans over fires made on the ground; the *cuisine* did not look very *appétissante*. The house consisted of only one large room, the roof supported by two pillars in the centre, and quite full of women, to whom we were introduced by the bridegroom's father, a venerable and handsome man, with a long white beard; his dirty old wife made many salaams, and kissed our hands, as did nearly all the guests in the room. There were both Druzes and Christians in the room—the latter dressed in gay-coloured coarse muslins and pretty white muslin veils, hanging down behind their heads, some of which were finely embroidered, with quantities of gold ornaments and bracelets; the Druzes in dirty blue or brown serge gowns, and veils of the same stuff in black, which they held over their faces when any men appeared; nearly every woman had a small infant in her arms, and the floor was strewed with bigger infants—small and large squalling alike most of the time. The Druze women are usually less pretty than the Maronite women, and their costume makes them appear still plainer: but they are finely made and

L 2

have good manners, though, like all Oriental women, less so than their husbands, whose open, free, graceful, and polished bearing is remarked by all travellers. A place was immediately cleared for us and a carpet spread, on which we sat to take ever so many glasses of *eau sucrée*, which we disposed of to the children, much to the delight of both children and mothers; but the heat became so intolerable that another carpet was placed for us on a shady terrace: whence we soon saw the bridegroom arrive at his own house, escorted by his friends, who fired muskets all the way.

Our seat faced the whole of the beautiful ravine of El Metn, and we presently saw some bright spots emerging from the thick woods at the bottom of the valley, and winding up the steep zigzag ascent on our side; this was the bridal procession. First came three mules, carrying the bride's bed and a great box, painted scarlet, and adorned with flowers, containing her wardrobe; then her father, with a snowy turban, mounted on an ass, followed by a number of relations on foot; and lastly the bride herself, surrounded by women, but without her mother, whom etiquette keeps at home. As soon as she entered the district firing began; after this a volley was fired at every zigzag on the road, the unceasing noise and shouting seeming much to annoy the horse on which she was mounted. She was closely veiled, first with yellow silk, then green gauze, and over both a white cotton eezar; and one of her hands, wrapped in a yellow cotton handkerchief, was held the whole time on the top of her head, in token of submission and obedience to her new duties; sometimes the weary arm was supported by a neighbour, but one or other hand was never taken down. When she came near the house the firing and shouting redoubled, and a score of persons went to meet her, among them the bridegroom, who bowed to her; then a very stupid sham battle ensued, one man on each side running into a vacant space alternately, and firing his musket in the air; this lasted about ten minutes, before she was allowed to proceed; her father lifted her from her horse, and the door was shut upon her and the women for a short time.

When we were summoned inside we found a gaudy shawl hung against the wall of the room, with her back to which the bride was standing on a pile of cushions, like an effigy in a church; she was unveiled, and proved very pretty, fair as an English girl, with light brown hair, the only Eastern characteristic in her face being the highly arched eyebrows, which are artificially formed in childhood. She was dressed in a red silk vest over a white silk chemise, and a green silk pelisse over that, fastened with large silver buttons, and several silver chains, to each of which hung a triangular silver case containing a *hezab* or charm, and a very massive and costly gold necklace; a muslin handkerchief lay over her head, but no *tantour*, the chief Sheikh of the Druzes having just published a command, we were told, that they should be given up by all but the old women. Here the unhappy girl was to stand for three whole days, with her eyes closed and her hand over the top of her head in the presence of the guests; even in the night, should any visitor come in, she must resume her place! The friends sometimes whispered in her ear, but she is supposed to be incapable of speech or sight till the contract is signed and her husband appears. During these three days no man enters the room. She looked very hot and tired, and flushed still more deeply as she stepped down from the cushions to kiss the English ladies' hands, in honour of whom she was allowed to lift her eyelids for one moment, and showed us her pretty brown eyes. After this her nearest relation, a very jolly looking woman, stood before her, and, pushing back the crowd a little, flourished each present brought by the guests, one by one, over her head, screaming out the name of the donor and the substance and value of the gift; and before she deposited it in the bride's pocket, spinning round between each announcement in a wonderful jigging dance, and giving the mountain cry of joy or triumph till we were nearly deafened. This cry is a very peculiar whistling scream, beginning on a high note and then jumping to the octave above, something like the Tyrolese *jodl*, only simpler, and never at any distance musical ; we sadly learned to know the cry well afterwards.

Having endured this as long as we could, our hands aching with squeezes and kisses, we bade them good-bye and departed, sending our present of three dollars in the evening, as we were told that was considered much more aristocratic and dignified than giving it at the time. The bridegroom and all his friends were sitting in rows on the house-tops, eating an enormous dinner spread upon nice mats; the dinner continues all day long, giving them fortunately something to do in the long interval before the contract is drawn; for the Druzes have no religious ceremonial of marriage. The bridegroom, a fine tall young man, seemed very anxious and curious about his bride, whose face he had never seen, and to whom he had never spoken; he was much pleased with the praises we bestowed on her, which, as Europeans, we could do—an Arab could not have spoken to him of his wife.

We learned on this day something of the division of property among the Lebanon mountaineers.   On the death of a man all his possessions are divided among his children, with no distinction of the first-born, the sons each taking twice as much as the daughters, who are supposed to be provided for by their marriage.   Should the land-property be too small for division, it is sold, and the proceeds divided in the same proportions; if there is any choice in the lots, the youngest child chooses first, and so on, the eldest coming the last; and if there are any young children, the largest portion is reserved for them.

CHAPTER XI.

THE BATTLE.

DURING the first six or seven centuries after the Resurrection of our Lord a number of sects sprang up in the bosom of the Christian Church, nearly all of them finding birth in the North of Syria and in Egypt. To say nothing of the Sabellians and Arians of Africa, or the Nestorians and Eutychians of Constantinople, the semi-converted Jews of Syria split into Nazarenes, Ebionites, and other sects, while among the Arabs of the north and north-east, Jacobites, Monophysites, Mariamites and Collyridians, Gnostics and Docetes, spread themselves over the mountains of the Lebanon, and the countries of Aleppo, Diarbekr, and Mesopotamia. These mountains, and the rocks of the desert, were soon thickly peopled with hermits and recluses, singly, and in bands, living in different degrees of asceticism. Those of the mountain tribes who had been converted to Christianity were united under a Patriarch (*Batrík* in Arabic), as their spiritual head, and were governed by Emirs or Sheikhs of the different districts.

About fifty years after the birth of Muhammad, and before the Reformed Religion taught by him had made any progress beyond the immediate neighbourhood of Medina and Mecca, or the confines of Arabia, one of those Christians who had retired into a cave in north Syria, in order to pursue his studies and meditations uninterruptedly, made himself remarkable by the peculiar sanctity of his life and the unusual depth of wisdom that fell from his lips. This man was called Hanna (the Arabic of John) Maroun,—the cave where he dwelt was close to one of the chief sources of the Orontes, the 'Ain or spring mentioned in Numb. xxxiv. 11.

About this time the quarrels between Constantinople and Rome for the spiritual jurisdiction of the Christians in Syria, broke forth, and emissaries from each were spread through the country, for the purpose of influencing the people. Hanna Maroun was at once elected by the united voices of the mountaineers as their adviser and leader. He immediately declared himself for the Latins, acknowledged the Pope as his spiritual master, and put himself at the head of a large body of followers. Those who acknowledged Constantinople as the throne of their spiritual and political head separated from the followers of Maroun, and gave themselves the name of *Melekites* (from *melik*, the Arabic for sovereign), which they bear to this day,* but they are more usually called the people of Roum, as members of the Greek Church, whence they then received their Patriarch and their tenets; they are of course now, as then, equally with the Maronites, subjects of the Turkish empire, but they hold the same doctrines as those of the Church of Russia, and look to her Emperor as their chief protector.

The tenets of the Maronites are simply those of Rome—their colleges and schools being presided over by teachers and priests sent from that city. They submitted more entirely to the Pope in 1180, giving up at that time the Monophysitism, which had till then tinged their tenets, and obtaining in return the immense concession of retaining many of their own peculiar customs,—a very remarkable, and perhaps unparalleled, concession on the part of Rome. They have a very large number of monks, who of course take vows of celibacy and poverty; but the parish priests are almost always married. The people communicate in both kinds, and their service is conducted in Syriac,—a language till lately well understood by them, but now entirely disused, since only three villages are existing where Syriac is still spoken,—the Gospels, and other parts, are read also in Arabic. There are between 90 and 100 convents, containing about 1500 monks and 500 or 600 nuns: the number of the Maronite population is differently stated, but is most probably about 233,000 souls. There are large numbers of them at Aleppo, Tripoli, Beyrout, and Saïda, but they may be said chiefly to inhabit the Lebanon, the Kesrouän district of which is almost entirely occupied by them: the principal number of their convents are placed there; and about the Cedars, and in the Kesrouän they have their great priest's college of Antourah.

Hanna Maroun died in A.D. 701, and was buried at Hámah, his tomb becoming at once, and for a very long time after, a place of pilgrimage to both parties among the mountaineers; his remains were believed to perform miracles, and were visited by pilgrims from even Egypt and all parts of Turkey. A convent was soon

---

* They also separated in the same way from the Copts in Egypt, and took the same name of Melekites. See Lane's 'Modern Egyptians.'

founded beside the tomb, the monks excavating cells in the living rock for themselves, and building up loopholed walls overhanging the ravine below—as in the convents of Mar Antoun and Khanobin; to this convent the Pope sent a present of a fine library.

Among these monks the belligerent leaders of the Maronites for the future were found. At one time, intoxicated with some successes over the partisans of Constantinople, the Maronites marched down to Jerusalem, when the Mooslims, taking advantage of their absence, seized and pillaged the convent, massacring the unfortunate monks that had remained there; after this the Maronites and Melekites wisely made peace, having enemies enough to contend with, without fighting their fellow-Christians.

The Maronites hastened to join the bands of the Crusaders on their arrival in Syria, and did them much service in replenishing their ranks, as hundreds and thousands of gallant Franks were slain in the field or died in the camp. At Damietta, in 1249, vast numbers of the Maronites fell fighting under the banner of Louis IX.; a fresh band, however, joined him afterwards at Akka, and there still exist in Paris copies of a letter written by Louis IX. to both the Emir of the Lebanon and to their Patriarch, *assuring the Maronites of the protection of France for ever:* it is dated May 21, 1250. Henri II. was, in 1520, addressed by Sultan Suleyman II. by the title of " Protector of the Christians of Mount Lebanon;" and Louis XIV., and still later Louis XV., repeated this assurance in letters addressed by them to the Patriarch of the Maronites in the convent of Khanobîn.

Certain it is that the Maronites have a strong belief that as they are now under the protection of France, they will one day be openly ruled by her: time will show how near this idea is to the truth. There are facts which appear to justify it, for gradually, cautiously, and silently the French have obtained a footing throughout the Lebanon, and nearly throughout Syria. There is scarcely a single large village in the whole of the Lebanon without a mission of one, two, or three monks, and a school taught by Lazaristes, and these are all Frenchmen; they have also missions and schools scattered throughout Syria; especially in the country round Jaffa and Jerusalem; and the Lazaristes teach so well and work their missions so thoroughly, that they are not only a good example to us, but they are sure ultimately of success; for the Arabs appreciate education: that is to say they love money with all their hearts, and even the poorest mountain peasant is glad to have his sons taught to count, to add up piasters, and to read and write; accomplishments which they acquire with remarkable facility. In the towns they teach

French also, which they gladly enough learn, to aid them in commerce, and to enable them to become dragomans. Unfortunately their French education usually renders the town Arabs pretentious and impertinent; the best example of which are the people of Zah'leh, where this education has been in full force for very many years, and of whom Mr. Porter says, they " are notorious for their pride, insolence, and turbulence. Family broils are incessant, and scarce a month passes without bloodshed." *

The French have also found another method of gaining substantial influence in Syria. Whenever their Lazaristes tell them of an unusually intelligent Sheikh or person of influence, they send him letters of naturalisation, and make him an *honorary* French subject: of course this includes, or would be found to include, the peasantry of whom each sheikh is chief, whenever the occasion needed. We learned also, on good authority, that the French consuls along the coast have an ingenious way of recommending the crews of boats to *buy* a flag, bearing the Jerusalem Cross, which is blessed by the Superior of the French Convent of the Terre Sainte, the Guardian of the Holy Sepulchre; under which they sail in double security, spiritual as well as temporal. France then claims them as *her subjects*, though of course they are in reality only Turkish subjects, and though all consuls are forbidden to protect any but their own lawful countrymen; and when France requires them they will be found ready for her service. Our informant mentioned sixty-four well-manned boats which to his knowledge carried the flag.

Nothing can be more mischievous than the various " protections " accorded by the European governments to subjects of the Sultan, Mooslim as well as Christian. They serve but to render them insolent when they have nothing to fear, and cringing when they have; and the protection is very frequently extended to most worthless individuals, merely for the sake of exercising and maintaining the right. It was reliance on this " protection " that made the Zah'leh people so insolent to the Mooslims, insisting on their dismounting from their horses on entering the town, and even calling their own dogs " Muhammad ": of course the greatest insult that can be offered to persons who consider dogs unclean animals. They have since been severely punished, and they most certainly brought the penalty on themselves.

The Maronites are industrious and docile; they are intelligent and capable of immense improvement; they are brave, but they have not the *pluck* and fortitude of the Druzes, nor the support of an admirable organisation, combination, and obedience, which is

* 'Handbook for Syria and Palestine,' vol. ii.

the very backbone of the Druze people;* nor have they by any means the high sense of honour which the Druzes undoubtedly possess, though, of course, there are honourable exceptions among them. The Maronite, when a little educated, prides himself on being *rusé*, but his *ruse* is a coarse affair in comparison with that of the Bedouin or the Druze; he is simply dishonest, though he has just wit enough to try to persuade you that cheating is the only thing of which he is perfectly incapable: if he cannot succeed in this he tries to prove to you what he gains is in some manner only his real due, or he assures you *tout bonnement*, that he felt that to your excellent heart and charitable disposition his profit would be equally a pleasure and a gratification.

When the Greek and Latin Churches of Syria forgot their differences and united in arms against the Druzes, they were frequently victorious; but the great Druze Chief, the Emir Fakir-ed-dîn, was so accomplished a general that the Druzes shortly recovered themselves, and held up their heads as proudly as ever. This Emir proved the Druzes capable of becoming active, and thriving in commerce, and he probably would have made them a great people had he not taken the unhappy notion of visiting Europe, where he wasted and lost both his patrimony and patriotism.

The custom of blood-feuds, which exists throughout the mountains, is a terrific promoter of discord; notwithstanding which it is undoubted by all who know the Druzes well that they would live in peace and harmony with the Christians if the Turks would let them; but these latter are unceasingly exciting them against each other, and urging them on to war for their own purposes. Of course it is all done in an underhand way, but the truth will out; and no one can be any time in the country without perceiving it.

One day our Druze muleteer, at whose wedding we had been guests one month before, was driving his mule along the narrow path, when another mule, driven by a small Christian boy brushed up against him. The Druze was a hot-tempered and foolish young fellow, and he immediately thrashed the boy with no moderate arm. The next day the victim's father and another man hid in a large caroob-tree, waylaid the Druze as he was going down to Beyrout on our commissions, and fully avenged the boy. The Druze went home with a bleeding head, a good deal hurt; upon seeing

---

* It is as well to note here that the Druzes have been an independent religious and political nationality for upwards of 800 years. Their creed is derived from the Bible and the Koran, interwoven with allegories. The religious duties of the Akhals are somewhat rigid.

which the women—never slow to join in a fray—took up the quarrel on both sides. They emptied each other's pitchers at the fountain, and finally broke a lot of them against the rocks—miserable, trifling squabbles, but from such bagatelles many a grave and mournful tragedy has arisen. We heard that the village priest was trying to make peace between them, and we hoped that there would be no worse results from this than from a hundred other petty quarrels we had heard of between Christian and Druze.

The week before an English friend of ours * had arrived in Beit Miry, and taken a house at the same end of the village as our own, but over the brow of the mountain, and therefore commanding the northern view of the valley of El-Metn; in the centre, in fact, of the Druze quarter. The moon was now, on the evening of the 13th of August, at the full, and we went over to see how gloriously beautiful the valley, headed by snowy Sunnîn, looked in the moonlight from his verandah: this was three days after the muleteer's quarrel. While we were enjoying what was really a magnificent and lovely scene, the mist wreaths, as we thought, which were lying rather thickly in the valley, rose over the moon, and advanced with steady steps, drawing a hard black edge across her face: she was half covered before we perceived that it was an eclipse, † and most curiously beautiful was the effect of the half-obscured light on the mountains. The villagers came out of their houses to observe the phenomenon, and seemed much alarmed by it. "They say," said our dragoman, "that these things always bring misfortunes, and that blood will soon flow;" and as if in sad confirmation of his words, before the eclipse was over we actually heard firing on the mountains opposite, and saw smoke hanging about in various spots —the villages on the other side of the Metn had taken up the quarrel! The Druzes about us seemed very much excited, but as we went home we heard that the Bishop at Madrass had ordered the culprits to come to him on the following morning, and that he would surely induce them to make satisfactory amends to each other.

And early on Sunday morning the good father did talk very earnestly to both. He desired his Christian son to apologise to the Druze whom he had beaten so unmercifully, which he promised to do; but he stipulated that the muleteer, as the first offender, should come to his house to fetch the apology; this the Druze stoutly refused. About 10 A.M. we were attracted to the window by the sound of loud and angry voices, and looking out we saw several

* The Honourable Roden Noel.
† This eclipse, which was total, was not visible in England.

Druzes collected on the roof of a house in the village, a few paces on our left, all shouting and gesticulating at once, and evidently restrained with great difficulty by some of the elders; they were all pointing and calling down the mountain side, where we saw, about a hundred yards below us, a no less eager crowd of Christians collected on a projecting knoll of ground on the path to Madrass, where, with their quick, eager movements, they looked just like a swarm of bees. We easily discerned similar efforts being made among them by the elders of their party, at soothing and appeasing their excitement,—they seemed to have formed themselves into a ring, through which they were determined not to allow any of the more impetuous ones to break, or to rush up to attack the Druzes on the summit: when presently up came the little party from Madrass with tidings of the conditions imposed by the Christian upon the apology he had agreed to make. The words were hastily shouted out to those above, and in another moment there came the report of a musket—a Druze had fired! And now, with a rush on both sides, the restraining elders were unheeded as the impetuous crowd swept by them—the Christians ran up the terraces from below, hiding behind the mulberry-trees to fire *up*, the Druzes from above firing *down* in answer,—and though numbers failed of their aim, we saw several deliver the fatal message of death or torture. Meanwhile there was a battle going on in the middle of the village, the Druzes from one end meeting the Christians from the other end; but this we could not see. The ground was so steep and the terraces stood so high, one above another, that on the mountain side there could be no coming face to face. It was completely guerilla warfare—each one fighting for himself, without leaders or plan, picking out any enemy he could see, and taking aim from behind a mulberry-tree or a bit of rock; but later on a small party on each side met on the open road and the rocks about the fountain, and fought for some time vigorously in the little dell. We saw some fall, and then the rest escaped through the pine-forest close at hand. All this time, high above the noise of the firing, there arose continually a horrible sound—who that has once heard it can forget how it thrilled through head and heart!—the war-cry raised by the women on both sides, as, standing on the house-tops, they watched the progress of the fight, urging on the men, hanging over the edge with eager gesticulations, or throwing their arms wildly in the air, more like frenzied demons than women. Added to these cries there came sometimes from one or another a piercing wail over the wounded or fallen; while many others followed their husbands with pitchers of water on their shoulders, giving them drink ever and anon in the heat of the burning sun, standing beside them when they took aim, and every moment shrieking out the fierce shrill scream which excited every man to do his utmost in shedding blood. Three of these women were wounded.

The principal Druze houses were, as I have said, on the little craggy rock exactly above our house; their rifles, therefore (and nearly all of them had rifles), were not more than seven or eight yards from it. Of course their houses were one of the principal objects of attack; so every moment the bullets passed over our roof, grating along the walls with that peculiar sharp *whitzzz* which it is far more agreeable to hear at a distance than within half a yard of one's ears; sometimes they passed close across the windows, and the answering bullets from below as often hit the walls of the house as others fizzed up over our heads in the open corridor. The Emir and another man were wounded by stray shots in the little house next to ours, and in fact there was scarcely a yard of ground anywhere near us free from bullets. We had previously agreed with our English friends—there were two English gentlemen then in Beit Miry—that we would read our Sunday service together; but now we earnestly hoped they would not expose themselves to the flying bullets in order to keep the engagement. However, afraid that we might need their protection, they never thought of breaking it, and they happily arrived at our house in safety and unhurt. Our dragoman wanted us to immure ourselves in a room lighted only by a door opening on to the corridor; but the excitement and interest of the battle was far too great for us too resist watching it for a long time from this open corridor or from the windows at all sides of the house. We were assured, however, that this fighting might go on for many days, certainly till night, and as we could do no good by watching them, we read our Sunday-service as usual. I do not think that any of us will easily forget that hour of prayer, and with what unusual meaning the petition arose, "From battle and murder, and from sudden death—Good Lord deliver us!" or how we thought of the same prayers rising at the same moment in hundreds of quiet churches in England, while our little congregation of five persons were assembled here, with the bullets falling thick and fast around us, and the voice of the reader frequently drowned in the sharp click of the muskets, the strange ring of the rifle-balls, and the shrill screams of the women! Fear, indeed (except from stray shots), none of us had thought of, nor had we any cause for it; we knew well that our being English ensured our safety among the Druzes, and that their respect for us would not fail : a remarkable instance of which was afforded more than once during the battle, when one of us leaned out from a window, and a Druze close by stopped, even in the moment of taking aim, and, lowering his gun, made a salaam to the "Sitt;" and they called to our servants to know whether some buildings on our ground belonged to us or not,—of course we said they did, and no one entered them. There was a French family spending a few weeks in some miserable apartments under our house, whereby, happily for them, they were living *under our flag*, and that flag afforded them equal security and safety with ourselves. A number of Christian women, as well as our landlord and his family, rushed into our house when the battle began, the women bringing their gold ornaments, and took refuge in these lower rooms;—not one of them was touched.

About three o'clock the firing suddenly ceased, and the subsequent stillness seemed almost stunning after the tumult and noise. We learned that the Christians had exhausted their ammunition, and therefore fled: the Druzes remaining masters of the field. Then came the saddest part of the day: several wounded and one dead Druze were carried past our house, borne on men's shoulders, bleeding and groaning, and the lamenting of the women was soon heard as, recognising their own beloved ones among the sufferers, they flung their arms over their heads, and sang a wild cry, half Druze war-cry, and half like the Irish *keen*. Druze reinforcements from other villages now arrived, and we saw some of the deserted Christian houses being sacked, and the furniture burnt: they said this was done only by the strangers. We opened the hall-door, and went out on the steps to breathe more freely in the now still afternoon air, when a venerable-looking white-bearded Druze, one of their chiefs, immediately came up and assured us, with the most expressive signs and words, that amongst them not only our persons but all our property also, was perfectly safe; that wherever our flag was unfurled everything would be secure, adding that it was already well known in the mountains. And they afterwards told one of the English gentlemen that they had for three days endeavoured to put off the war on account of the "sitteh Ingleez" who were staying among them, till we should have gone. This we heard also in other parts of the country afterwards.

The stillness and silence of the village in the afternoon was indeed a contrast to the horrors of the day: the Europeans profited by it in sending messages to each other, consulting what they should do. The Druzes were, of course, much elated, and as strangers came to join them from other villages, we heard that this battle was to be only the precursor of many others, and that they fully hoped to exterminate the Christians throughout the mountains. The other Europeans determined to leave the place at once—one family indeed had already gone; for, in the very thickest of the fight, about midday, these good people had the folly to fly, passing right through the combatants, and of course putting themselves in a hundred times more danger from stray shots, than they would have incurred by remaining quietly in their house. Their terror and confusion being too great to allow of a moment's thought of delay, they fled on foot in the burning sun, hatless and bonnetless, carrying their children in their arms, all the way down to Beyrout, a four hours' walk. On arriving in the town their alarm, increasing at every step, had filled their minds with horrible pictures, and they spread the intelligence that all the Europeans had been massacred, and their houses sacked. So far from this being the case, we heard afterwards that every single thing from their own deserted house was carried down to them a day or two later, not one object missing, even the lady's thimble and their provisions prepared for the day included! Except, indeed, their grey mare, which they had left tied near the house, and which we saw, poor thing, killed soon after by some three or four stray shots.

I am afraid that the prejudices of some of my readers may be shocked at my confession that my sympathy involuntarily sided with the Druzes throughout the day. Of course, in this particular instance they were in the wrong and the aggressors; but apart from the *cause*, the bearing of the Druze, speaking generally, is so much more akin to an English mind than that of the Christians, that one cannot well help such a feeling. The latter were quick and active, but the Druze has a fearlessness and nobility about him—a proud, steady step, a lofty head and eagle eye, a bold athletic form, and a free, open, but perfectly respectful manner, that makes one feel always at ease and safe with him. During the battle it was curious to mark the difference of the ingenious hiding and dodging of the Christian, and the daring boldness of the Druze; it reminded me continually of a battle between a cat and a bloodhound—if such a noble beast would condescend to do battle with a mere cat. The Christians of the mountains are well made, and have a soft, sleepy kind of beauty, set off by gay-coloured dresses; but if ever you see a noble form both of figure and face, full of self-respect and native dignity, and a neatly put on, clean, quiet-coloured dress, be sure he is a Druze, or a Metouaalee. These latter have but poor dresses. The dresses of the Christians are more costly than that of the Druze, but the Druze is much the cleaner of the two. Numerically, the Maronites far exceed the Druzes, but the minority of the latter are more than compensated by their courage, coolness, and organisation.

Mr. Noel now left us to see how things were going on in his own house, which he had given up to the shelter of very many women and children, with their little bundles of valuables and gold ornaments; and on going back he found his dragoman had brought in several of the wounded,. whose sufferings they did their best to relieve. That long night was a sad one, passed among the women and children, two of whom were wounded; many of the women were wailing for the dead, and amongst these was the muleteer who had begun the quarrel, and whose young wife had been married but a month before. Mr. Noel came back to us at nightfall for linen rags and medicine—a Druze dodged him in the darkness with his rifle cocked, and was just stooping to take aim when he called out "Inglecz! Ingleez!" upon hearing which the Druze started up and made amends by accompanying him to our door with many signs of respect, repeating "Ingleez taïb, taïb keteer!" (good, very good!)

A thick fog came up with the night, and shrouded everything from view, but we sat in our corridor watching the moonlight shining in strange brightness down upon the white masses and folds of the fog below us, and listening rather anxiously for any distant firing fearing lest the Druzes should think of pursuing the Christians in their flight. We heard nothing, however, until about seven o'clock, when the deep silence was broken by a horrible kind of sound—the Druzes were parading the village in a band, singing a war-song of triumph—very wild and simple was the air, and the voices sounded rich and sweet; but the *meaning* was too well expressed, and every note thrilled through one with a strange, sad horror, swelling loudly, and dying away softly, as they came to and fro. Often I think I hear that song still.

The chant had scarcely ceased when we heard, to our great surprise, drums beating, and the tramping of horses coming up the road. The firing of the battle had been heard in Beyrout; those who had fled had given the alarm, with all kinds of exaggeration, and the Pasha had therefore sent up a body of thirty cavalry to keep the peace. And at the same time the various consuls had each one sent up horses and mules to bring down their respective countrymen, protected by their own janissaries. In a few hours all the European families in the village, excepting ourselves, had quietly packed up and mounted, and before the sun had risen next morning they had all comfortably arrived in their homes at Beyrout. The English Consul alone had sent no help.

M

We had brought several letters of introduction to the consul, but during our long stay in the town he had never called, and we had had no communication beyond a civil note; in this time of danger and need, however, we fully believed and expected that assistance would be sent, not only to us, but also to the English gentlemen then in Beit Miry: so we sat listening for the arrival of more mules, but nothing was heard, and it became a matter of serious consultation what we should do. The French gentleman, whose family occupied the rooms under us, very kindly sent up to say he could spare us three horses if we liked to go down with them; but we had not the slightest idea of thus leaving our baggage behind us, having no fears of any kind for ourselves personally in remaining, while to leave our property at the mercy of strangers from other villages was not to be thought of. We knew that the Druzes had sent to summon their comrades from other mountains, and it was believed on both sides that a long and sanguinary war was only then commencing; and we felt that if we remained we should have no freedom in the neighbourhood for walking, and, knowing nothing, alas! of surgery, which we deeply regretted, we could not be of any kind of use among them. A minor but unpleasantly important consideration likewise influenced us: the Christians had carried off their cocks and hens, their gardens were trampled down, and it seemed very doubtful that we should get anything to eat; supplies from Beyrout were easily ordered, but if fighting continued, it was unlikely that any muleteers would bring them to us. Then our men-servants, being all three Maronites, not one of them could go in safety even to the fountain to fetch water, though the cook, braver than the rest, volunteered to do so, on condition that we would let him carry the flag in his hand! So, all things considered, we came very reluctantly to the conclusion that we had better go somewhere else, and accordingly a note was despatched by one of the descending parties to beg that mules and horses might be sent up for us.

We were not, however, uncared for: H.M.S. *Tartarus* had arrived some days before at Beyrout, and our friend Captain Mansell becoming alarmed for our safety, on hearing the alarming accounts carried down to the town, had himself gone to the consulate to seek for assistance. The Consul and Vice-Consul, the Secretary, and every one else was out; the consulate was locked, and not a janissary was to be found. It was Sunday, and some hours were lost in searching for them, and then in getting horses and mules, after which he took upon himself the dispatching of janissaries with the animals up the mountain. And as there are always more kind hearts in the world than one counts on, we had been remembered by another: a lady had sent out at daybreak to know if we had come down with the other Europeans in the night, and not hearing anything of us, and fearing that our consul had not sent up assistance, she requested a gentleman belonging to her husband's office to ride up at once, and invite us to her house. This gentleman readily undertook a long ride in the burning heat for persons in whom he had not the slightest interest; but we were yet more touched by the kind thoughtfulness of the lady who had sent him, to whom we were entirely strangers, and not even countrywomen. Many a traveller struck down with fever in Beyrout, and not a few of the poor and suffering in the town, have had occasion to bless her name.

In the meantime the Turkish Bey in command of the troop just arrived, sent three of his soldiers to our house for protection, and though we were considerably more afraid of them than of the Druzes, it seemed wiser to accede to the wishes of our servants, and to let them mount guard in the corridor, where they smoked and ate cucumbers the whole night long, while we were packing up our things. We had calculated that the mules might reach us by 5 A.M., and we were accordingly ready to start at that hour, but many another wearily elapsed ere our packages were fastened on the mules, and it was nearly 2 P.M. before we set off. Our escort was a large one, made up of English janissaries and some French kawasses, who had been left behind the night before, I believe for our protection. However, we saw no one from whom to be protected, and not a creature did we even meet on the road save a few miserable Christians, who had fled, despoiled of everything. That evening, with the war-cries and wailings of the battle still echoing in my ears, I sat long in the corridor of the hotel, watching the calm moonlight shining on the little village, now so far off, and our own deserted but beloved mountain home, and—strange and striking contrast!—looking at the " crimson and emerald rain " falling in showers of bright flakes from the rockets and fireworks of a splendid fête given by Count Bentivoglio, the French Consul, in honour of the Emperor's birthday.

Early the next morning the two gentlemen we had left at Beit Miry arrived at the hotel, driven down by the pangs of hunger! And in the course of the day we learned, on the best authority, " that one of the English ladies had been murdered in the battle, and that the other had escaped, with the maid, into the depths of the valley, where both the fugitives would be shot or starved to death!"

The question now was, what were we to do with ourselves? Travelling down to Jerusalem in August was not to be contemplated by any sane person, while the temperature of Damascus was much higher than that of Beyrout; where we found the heat so intolerably oppressive that we determined at once to go up as high as we could into the mountains. It was not likely that there would be any disturbance in the northern district about the Cedars unless the war became quite general, when, of course, the Metouaalees would join in it, but before this could take place we should be able to descend to Tripoli, or to cross the Bekâa to Damascus. Some of our friends had settled to go to the Cedars for some time, and as H.M.S. *Tartarus* was going to Tripoli, the Captain kindly invited us all to go in her that far, an offer which we were very glad to accept.

In the meantime a hollow peace was, after a few days, patched up between Druze and Maronite,—" till the next cocoons are gathered," we heard said on both sides, and too true, alas! it turned out to be. A good many small circumstances came out: the Governor of Beyrout had strictly forbidden the Christians to purchase arms in the bazaars, but Druzes were allowed to purchase them freely, and they did so, boasting at the same time openly in the streets of how many they had killed, and how they hoped to exterminate the Christians if the war continued; but these spokesmen were, I believe, the young bloods and boasting boys. From all we learned at this time and afterwards it was quite evident that the chief Druzes did not desire war: they were invited, dragged into it,—they are not men to brook even a small injury, and they resented it accordingly; but they would be men of peace if they were let alone.

It was not only in Beyrout, where it is more difficult than in most other places to separate gossip and *canards* from truth and facts, that we learned how completely the Druzes were favoured by the Government. The unfortunate Christians were seized, imprisoned, fined, when they attempted to obtain arms for themselves, while, as I have said, the Druzes notoriously purchased largely; the Christian mountaineers wherever we went were provided only with common old muskets, while the Druze had rifles in great numbers, and many of their sheikhs had revolvers, a weapon unknown to the Christians, for even the Emir of Beit Miry, but three hours from so large a European town as Beyrout, was astonished out of all Arab gravity at a silver-mounted six-barelled revolver, with which I was one day practising at a mark on one of the trees near his house. He implored me with clasped hands to wait while he fetched a beautiful little boy, his son and heir, to see the sight, and then when I had re-fired it for his edification he solemnly applauded his little son's question, as to whether the weapon came from Sheitân? I am convinced that the Emir himself believed that Satan reloaded it for me *ad infinitum.*

It is an unquestionable fact that the Turks do, and have always encouraged the Druzes against the Christians: they hate both equally; but their object is plain: the Druzes are exceedingly war-like and dexterous in fighting, the Christians are weak in war but strong in numbers, and they therefore try to make use of the Druzes to exterminate the Christians; and when they have done the hard work for them they will come in with a strong hand and get the small body of Druzes into their power. I believe that at least some of the Druzes understand their game perfectly, and see through it; they are quite willing to be assisted into getting rid of their hereditary enemies, whom the Turks are always representing as the authors of all ill against them, and they think they will take care of themselves afterwards. It will not be a very easy thing to exterminate the Druzes.

The horrors of the following spring completely confirmed all these reports: the Druzes paraded the streets of Beyrout with the Mooslims, the one boasting of the dogs of Christians they had slain, their boon companions applauding the deeds. It was reported by a gentleman who has lived long in the country that he had himself seen Mooslims ornamenting with flowers the muskets and knives of those who had killed the greatest numbers. Wherever the most horrible of the massacres and butcheries were perpetrated the Turks had encouraged the deed. At Deir-el-Kamar the Mutselim stood by while the Druzes disarmed the Christians, and invited the unfortunate 530 prisoners into the Serai, of which they after-wards opened the gates when the Druzes came in to slaughter them! At Hasbeiya the Turkish colonel collected the Christians into the Serai and there disarmed them: he himself admitted the Druzes in to kill the 700 unarmed men, besides the unhappy women, while his soldiers stood by looking on at the *battue!* These are but two out of numberless other cases; at Damascus the Mushir did everything to invite the Druzes into the town—there were 5000 of them armed within the walls on the day before the massacre—and while they did the horrid work the Turkish soldiers and Kurds carried off the plunder, the Mushir sitting at home in the Serai with the doors closed against every one.

On the very best authority the fact has been made clear that, in 1860, the *Christians commenced* hostilities. The Druze sheiks endea-voured by every means in their power to preserve peace, in all pro-bability because they felt their own weakness against the over-whelming numbers of their enemies in the Lebanon. When Kurshid

Pasha, *compelled* by the consuls to interfere, desired the Christian Emirs to send home the fighting men then assembled, they answered that they were confident of beating the Druzes, and would beat the soldiers also if they interfered to prevent them, knowing very well that the soldiers would do no such thing. So confident were the Christians, that they were careless; while the Druzes, fearful of defeat unless joined by their brethren of the Haurân, exerted all their strength, and improved every advantage they could gain. The Christians were everywhere beaten, and the Druzes were so much elated at their almost unexpected victories, that they pursued the Christians and committed barbarous atrocities such as nothing can justify; although, remembering their hereditary hatreds, and that the Christians had sought to exterminate them, some excuse may be found for their retaliation and revenge. At Hhaïffa and many other places the Christians committed horrible brutalities, about which nothing has been said; indeed, while deploring the misdeeds of the wild Druze of the mountains it would be as well to remember the acts of many armies of drilled and disciplined soldiery belonging to the most Christian countries of Europe —civilised Europe—and, not to speak of the atrocities of Austrian, Prussian, Italian, worst of all of French soldiers, to look back at some of our own in the unspeakable horrors that have taken place in Ireland, Scotland, and fair England! Of course the Druze, in giving loose to his passion, is very guilty; but he is ignorant and unenlightened: are we, when our passions are excited, pious and progressive though we be, much better? or were the Irish in 1641 or in 1798 one whit less sanguinary or atrocious in their conduct than the Druze?

CHAPTER XII.

LEBANON POLITICS.

WE were a party of seventeen guests on board H.M.S. *Tartarus*, and the vessel was so crowded that we were glad to find ourselves in our quiet tents on the pleasant shore of Tripoli, after twelve hours at sea. We spent the next day, while the horses rested from their journey up from Beyrout, re-visiting the town and mountains. Our tents were pitched in a garden on the sea-shore, close to the Castle of Raymond of Toulouse, and we rode thence by the bank of the Kadîsha to the fine ravine behind the town, and through the picturesque streets, till it was time to go to bed, as we were to be up and dressed before 3 A.M.; and so we were, but we did not start till past four, when the sun had risen. We had a very lovely ride of six hours and a half, over a wide undulating plateau with fertile fields, fresh, pleasant woods and purling streams, till the ascent, by a steep and rugged path, to a little chapel perched on the side of a very narrow grand gorge, where we rested for an hour or two. Here some very pretty smiling girls insisted on our admiring the valley, of which they seemed fondly proud, and the lovely views of Tripoli, with her rocks and headlands stretching out into the blue sea; they would also make us look at the chapel and their own cottage, the windows of both of which were filled up with human skulls, looking most dismal—and they showed us the curved iron bar hung in a tree, on which a hammer struck the call which served for a church-bell. Then came a tremendous ascent,—disagreeable enough to mount, but nowhere dangerous—zig-zagging up between two high mountains of curiously contorted strata, clothed with the white cypress, with which we were now to become daily familiar—now and then a pine, or a walnut, or a pomegranate, and every here and there tiny gardens perched on narrow ledges, bearing potatoes or cotton, or a few vines. Then, turning suddenly away from a strange peak, came Jebel Arneto, which looked as if it had been chopped off sideways, and meeting the upper streamlet of the Kadisha again bubbling by, we crossed the water-shed, and followed the brow of the mountain to Eh'den, a very large village, nearly hidden in groves of huge walnut-trees. The people crowded round us with warm and troublesome welcomes, as we made our way through them in order to choose a delightful camping-ground under some splendid walnut-trees, perhaps some of the finest trees in the world. As there was a good bit of ground, all the tents were set up in the same place, our three grouped round one enormous tree, with a mountain torrent tumbling and rushing down between them. The other tents were at some little distance, and afterwards, when another traveller came up from Tripoli, he chose the same ground, retiring to the back; nothing could be more picturesque than the whole group, with our flag in the front hoisted in a mulberry-tree, and the six or eight horses and twelve mules picketed beneath with their gay-coloured trappings and attendants, while round the kitchen tents there would always be half a dozen gossiping villagers in the brightest coloured dresses imaginable. The people of Eh'den are remarkably handsome, both men and women, and the children lovely: the women wear a singular headdress under their veils, made of silver, in the shape of the crown of a bonnet—sometimes with a kind of crescent-shaped horn.

This camping-ground was in fact on a wide terrace or plateau, running the length of the valley along the side of the mountain, which rose almost perpendicularly, like a wall, immediately behind us, with barely slope enough for the white cedars to grow in a feathery veil nearly to the summit. On the opposite side of the valley the mountain was still more richly clothed with woods, gardens, and villages, while between the two the gorge—which is called Wady-el-Kadisha—sunk suddenly down in a deep ravine, very narrow and very romantic, winding away westwards to the sea, which we saw at the extreme right; while the horizon, from the great height at which we were placed, was apparently some way up the sky. To the left the valley was closed by an amphitheatre of perfectly barren mountains, sloping down in bare terraces; * this was part of the great Makh'mel. On one side, at about half a mile from our tents, a copious spring gushed from

---

* On one of these terraces there stands a single cedar-tree, not very large, but the only *true* cedar we saw in the Lebanon besides the famous group in "Solomon's garden." It is said that there is another group in the Anti-Lebanon range.

the rock, bosomed in a nook of thick woods, dividing itself at once into two streams, one of which flowed down the gorge to the sea, and the other, passing just above our camp, ran down by the Pass we had mounted into the River Kadîsha.

We had intended to have gone on to the Cedars on the following day, and we always *did* intend to go on "to-morrow;" but the spot was so very beautiful, and our tents so agreeably placed, and the air so fresh and cool and pleasant, that we had been there nearly a month before we really made up our minds to leave it. We were, in fact, much in need of rest and quiet such as we found here : the horrors of war and bloodshed had been witnessed, but, in the excitement of the moment, by no means fully felt; in Beyrout there was still the daily and hourly anxiety for news from the surrounding villages, and the constant listening to the sorrowful tales of the unhappy burnt-out villagers who came to see our servants, and to reclaim the small articles of their property we had taken charge of; then came the new journey,—and it was only among the stern and lofty mountains, and the cool green groves of Eh'den, that we began to recover our usual calm enjoyment of Nature. The peasants of Syria declare that it is unhealthy to sleep under walnut-trees, and the dragomans always advise one not to do so; but the air of Eh'den is a remedy against everything—though we all fancied there was some truth in the idea. We were now 4750 feet above the sea, and though the sun was excessively powerful by day, and the tents uninhabitable where they were unshaded, we had plenty of cool resting-places beneath the trees, scarcely any mosquitos, and such cold nights, that we needed all the shawls and cloaks we possessed to keep comfortably warm ; nevertheless we managed to be scrambling up the mountain by 5 o'clock most mornings, and thought ourselves well repaid each day by the sublime and glorious sight of the sunlight breaking over the mountain, darting down into the gorge, and striding with lightning steps over the valley, bringing out a thousand brilliant colours which belong only to the gorgeous hues of Aurora, veiled and mystified by the blue haze and swansdown mists of morning. I could have watched that sunrise every day for years and never tired of its grandeur. There was only one thing better, and this was the sunset : every day it was the same, and every day it seemed to take one's breath away with its magnificence, as something too lovely and too glorious to be really of this earth ; then the gorge would fill up with haze as blue as the sea, and the walnut-groves would turn into masses of shining aventurine gold, and the mountains, yellow and bare by day, would flush over with a tender, transparent crimson glow melting into the golden light,—so delicate, so lovely, and yet so sublimely grand, that no words can describe it, and no pencil imitate its hues.

Eh'den is said to be one of the oldest villages in Syria, and is thought by some people to be the "Eden in Thelassar" * mentioned in Isaiah xxxvii. 12; the name is Syriac, and this language was spoken there till lately. It is a fine flourishing village, containing an active and industrious population, hardy and brave. The parish priest told us the boys were very intelligent and quick at learning, but in the Lebanon no girls ever go to school or are taught anything, —even the nuns only learn reading enough to enable them to chant the office in church. M. Regace, the Lazariste priest here, has two or three assistants in his mission, a large school in Eh'den, and one in every village in the valley. The people of Eh'den are well to do in the world; they eat meat always twice a week, and there are really no poor, because those who are richer help the poorer, lending money at a good interest, which the peasant repays by the proceeds of his land; he forfeits his property after some time if he fails to pay, but we were told that this seldom or never happens. The noble walnut-trees are many of them five hundred years old—they are found named, their position described, and the quantity of their fruit recorded in parchments of upwards of three hundred years old, in the possession of the Emir and other persons;—some of the trees have passed through the hands of as many as fifty families; the ownership of many of them is divided among perhaps a dozen different families, who collect under the branches, as we saw them doing at the gathering time, and divide between them the fruit that falls. One of the oldest families of Syrian *noblesse*, the Dah'reer, once inhabited a village filling up the now barren head of the gorge, but in a Metouaalee war the village was burnt, the family fled to Tripoli, and the soil has lain untouched ever since. This Eh'den, so famous for its vines and luscious grapes, and its flowers, and its summer beauty, is utterly uninhabited in the winter: it is so cold and so long enveloped in snow, that all the people, headed by the sheikh, descend to another village near Tripoli, where they live till the smiles of spring call them back to their vineyards; only the poor monks remain behind, and sometimes a peasant journeys up through the snow once or twice in the winter to carry them some little luxury to add to their store of bread, lentils, and wine.

Eh'den produces excellent potatoes, which are carried down to Tripoli and sent to Beyrout, for the natives never taste them, not having an idea how to cook them; nor do they care to learn, as the

---

* Both Schwartz and Jonathan the Targumist consider Thelassar to mean El Ashur, the mountainous part of Assyria, or the country round Adiabene.

Arab eats all his vegetable food, except bread and lentils, raw; and they are disinclined to eat or to do anything but what their fathers ate or did before them.

It was a pleasure to us to make acquaintance with the Sheikh, or Emir—the "pretty boy" mentioned by Lord Lindsay, now a man in the prime of life. He was the second son, but as his talents and intelligence were superior to those of the eldest son, his father gave him a better education, and associated him with himself in the business part of his position, and brought him forward to the Turkish authorities, so as to insure his being his successor. He speaks Italian and French well, has easy, pleasant manners, and is both lively and intelligent, as well as quiet and agreeable in conversation; in person he is tall, well made, and very fair. His name is Yussoof Karrâm; he is (of course) a naturalised French subject, and the Turks have made him a Bey. He has never been much farther from home than Beyrout, nor does he seem inclined to go; he says his duty lies in his government, which extends to several villages, and he will not leave it for a day. But his ideas are anything but *bornées* by the mountains of his native land; he showed himself thoroughly acquainted with European politics, and knew the names and characteristics of some of our Cabinet ministers; he is, in short, much too well educated for his personal happiness, for, except M. Regace, he has no real companion save a chance traveller, and he feels it impossible to marry among the uneducated, illiterate women of his own villages. He came to see us as soon as we arrived, bringing baskets of grapes and fresh bread, according to the hospitable custom of the village—the only place, by-the-by, where we experienced anything of the kind, for though of course we afterwards made a present to the bearer, the Sheikh begged us to understand that they only performed their duty to the stranger, whom they consider themselves bound to maintain till his baggage arrives.

We returned his visit on the following day; he came down to the courtyard of his house to receive us, with some seven or eight persons, and conducted us upstairs into a large, though low-arched room, with stone mullioned windows—the walls and floor of stones of two colours in patterns—and furnished with handsome Tripoli carpets and divans. His servants presented *eau sucrée*, then arrack, candied sweatmeats, and lastly coffee; after which came nargilehs for those who liked them. Of course we spoke of the war—of the patching up of which he had not then heard any satisfactory intelligence; he said one must not think the war in any way depended upon a personal quarrel anywhere—that was only the opening note on which others would inevitably follow; and he repeated most emphatically that the war really depended much more upon what was going on in the principal countries of the civilised world than on anything local; that the real fact was that, had the news of the Peace of Villafranca not been thoroughly spread through the Lebanon, the war would have been taken up on all sides, and become fierce and general, and that it was only because some were not aware of the Peace that it broke out at all—*else* this one would only have begun and ended a muleteer's quarrel. The Emir said also that did England and France go to war with each other to-morrow, or were the attention of Europe thoroughly occupied with some other war, the whole Lebanon would burst into a flame instantly, and not only the mountains but the whole of Syria would be utterly unsafe for Christians and Europeans, as, if anything really serious had once commenced, all the Mooslims would un-doubtedly join in the fight at once, while the Turkish authorities would try to exterminate all the Christians and Europeans in the country. He dwelt much upon the fact of how much the Turkish Government secretly encourage the Druzes, hoping to use them as tools to get rid of the native Emirs for them, after which the Lebanon would be more easy of access; but the Sheikh said con-fidently their mountain fastnesses would protect the Christians even after their leaders had fallen. He told us that during the late war between France and Austria the Turks invited all the Druze and Metouaalee chiefs to a secret conference in Beyrout to which not a single Christian was invited; he regretted much the recall of Lord Stratford de Redcliffe, believing that no one else could prevent such things and penetrate the secret, underhand doings of the Turks ; and he lamented loudly and bitterly that the famous Hatti-Humayoun had ever been obtained, since it was worse to have it the dead letter it is now than never to have had it granted, and he added that its very fulness of compliance ought to have prevented the Christian Powers from being deceived into putting any faith in it, as nothing could possibly induce the Turkish Government really to fulfil any-thing of the kind; the Christians have only been worse off ever since. Now, when seeking justice, they are always answered, " You have got your Hatti-Humayoun; what more can you want?"—although it be but waste paper, serving but to render the Mooslims more jealous and irritated than ever. We afterwards heard, both at Damascus and Jerusalem, exactly the same complaint made, in almost the same words as those used by the Emir, of the impos-sibility of getting any justice in the Turkish tribunals since the Hatti-Humayoun; however, he was but giving in his own way the usual Arab description of the Turkish Government, that "The Sultan goes to hunt gazelles on a lame ass," meaning thereby to express not merely its insufficiency, but its intentional inefficiency.

The opinions of the Sheikh Yussoof at least deserve the attention due to a man who, although naturally a partisan, is a liberal-minded enlightened person, and who is, next to the Bishops, the *chief* man of influence, and the only leader of the Maronites. His conversation wound up that day with the prophecy, only too sadly fulfilled, that this would be the last summer of peace in the Lebanon for many a day.

Sheikh Yussoof told us many legends of the Druzes, currently believed among the Maronites—of how they worship the figure of a calf made in gold or silver, and how they have various logs of wood concealed in their *hhulwehs*, each one named after the God of the Jews, Christians, &c.; these they take out on certain occasions and beat, saying that if any of the gods were true and real, they would save or avenge their types from these drubbings. But when the sacred manuscripts of the Hasbeiya Druzes were scattered abroad, and an explanation of much of their abstruse and speculative creed was thus obtained, nothing of an idolatrous nature was found in them. Had they really worshipped idols, something must have appeared of it in these books; and since then a key to various mysterious signs, not understood by all even of the initiated, has fallen into the hands of Dr. Vandyke of Beyrout, but nothing of idol-worship appeared connected with them.

Sheikh Yussoof thinks that the Druzes do not believe in the present existence of God; they say that in the beginning He created the world and all things in it—earth, air, sea—and then descended from heaven upon it; but the great wind, one of these created things, though small in the beginning, had increased meanwhile to great power and strength, and, catching the Almighty as He was reascending, killed Him, so that since that time there has been no God, and creation has been left to its own devices.

Hákeem, the founder of the Druze creed, taught that on the destruction or death of God His soul became incarnate in some other body—afterwards in his (Hákeem's) own body; that God in the beginning created a certain number of souls, which number has always and will always exist, neither increasing nor diminishing, as, if one person dies, the soul passes into another about to be born, and thus the original number always continues somewhere on the earth, to be collected and restored together at the end of the world. At that time the Druzes alone will be happy and blessed; the Christians will be punished for their heresies and contempt of the Druzes, by having two cantars of lead hung round their necks; the Mooslims will have two rotls, and the Jews two ounces, to carry in this uncomfortable manner.   They always favour the Jews above all other people, I know not why.   Much of their love for the English, at least in the present day, is said to arise from the respect and influence acquired by Mr. Wood, the late consul at Damascus, among them; and then, seeing that the English are neither Maronites nor Mooslims, they imagine they must be in some sort Druzes.

More interesting were the stories the Sheikh told us of the renowned Emir Beshîr, whose ancestors became Maronites many generations ago.   He spoke much of his greatness, of his unfailing integrity and uprightness, of his being enlightened so much beyond his age and position, and of how much he managed to effect against all difficulties; but he spoke also of the cruelty and revengefulness which tarnished his greatness, and was so strong a passion in him as sometimes to overbalance his high sense of justice, entailing the most horrible results.

Nothing earthly can persuade the Arabs that the Sultan is not the supreme governor of the world, or make them believe that his armies can be defeated, or that, if they were, it would make any difference in his position as Sultan over all nations.   For instance, the common people in the Lebanon firmly believe that the Queen of England sends some one of her nobles every year to kneel before the Sultan, with clasped hands and many prostrations, to beg from him the favour of being allowed to continue governing her country for another year; and they speak of it as an immense grace and kindness of the Sultan that he receives an envoy instead of herself in person, waiving that duty on her part because she is a woman, and has children to attend to!   They also believe that the Sultan kindly exempted England from paying tribute to him during the time of the Crimean war, because we brought our soldiers to assist his own against his rebellious subjects—an honour for our armies for which the ambassador had besought the Sultan on bended knees.

We often heard described the immense excitement of the Mooslims all over the country at the time of the horrible massacre at Jeddah; how they exulted over the Christians, assuring them that the time was soon coming for extirpating Christians throughout the Turkish dominions; and then, when the news of the bombardment of Jeddah by the English had arrived, how crestfallen the Turks looked, and how the Druzes went about saying, " Wonderful is the power of the English! Great are the English! We too are English ! "

Some days after we reached Eh'den the Sheikh invited us to dinner, sending his nephew and five of his head servants to conduct us in state to his house, where he came down, as usual, to the court-yard to receive us. As soon as we were seated in the salon a silver basin and ewer were brought, with embroidered towels, and water was poured over our hands by an attendant kneeling on one knee. When this had been performed for each of us, another attendant brought a silver incense-burner, over the perfumed smoke of which each guest bent for a few seconds, while another servant threw drops of orange-flower water over one's head and hands. Then came trays of apricots and orange candy, arrack and coffee, and after about an hour we went to dinner, which was served in European fashion, though the dishes were entirely Arab. The table was set out with flowers and fruit, and the dinner, which was handed round without being placed on the table, consisted of twelve courses of meat, prefaced by a thick vegetable soup—stewed meats, boiled meats, and minced meats, vegetables stuffed with meat, and meat stuffed with vegetables, two or three different pilafs of rice dif-ferently flavoured, and then two sweet dishes—one of square pieces of solidified cream—which I am convinced is the same as the " cream tarts " so often celebrated in the ' Arabian Nights '); the other of the favourite Arab *bakhalâweh*, a very light but rich pastry made with honey and almonds. These were followed by quantities of fruit, fresh and dried, besides many varieties of excellent Lebanon wine. We had coffee in the salon; and a band of servants lighted us home with torches and lanterns.

In return we invited the Emir and the French Consul at Tripoli, M. Blanche, to dine with us the last day of our stay at Eh'den; there were some other travellers there at the time, and we made a party of seven persons. M. Regace sent us a basket full of flowers, with which our tent was gaily ornamented, and our Arab cook managed to give them the same number of courses as the Emir had given us; but our dinner ended with real English plum-pudding besides, and excellent peach cream-ice, made by one of the drago-mans, and champagne. It is wonderful what skilful cooks these Arabs are, and how great a variety of dishes they make out of so few materials; their kitchen range, too, being only a pan of charcoal in the open air.

M. Blanche, a lover of the beautiful Lebanon, with the geography and natural history of which he is thoroughly acquainted, advised us to visit the old convent of Mar Antoun; so one morning we started on horseback at an early hour, for it was to be a long excursion. Our route lay along the Tripoli road till we came to

Jebel Arneto, where we turned off to the left and commenced descending the side of the valley, all bright and gay with vineyards, fruit-gardens, and flowers, with the blue sea in the vista beyond, till the valley narrowed to a lofty gorge, up which we turned: it was close by a huge rock, through which an open arch was cut, bearing a large white cross,—here began the convent territory. Through this arch the view was magnificent, the mountains of the winding ravine crossing each other at every step, with steep and generally inaccessible sides, covered with woods of low prickly oak and thorn, with juniper and white cypress; studded with caverns, and crowned with crosses. Perched on the edge of one projecting crest stood the convent, *se cramponnant* against the rock, and seeming to overhang the chasm below. The monks ushered us to a divân under a vine-covered trellis, close to a tiny chapel cut in the rock, the only part of the convent open to the unhallowed feet of women, numbers of whom come here in pilgrimage to obtain the miraculous cures for which the spot is famous. The convent, which is the largest in the Lebanon, containing one hundred and thirty monks, has a grand façade of arches built up against the mountain sides; the large halls and corridors are chiefly excavated in the rock, and some exterior buildings seemed to be well and ornamentally constructed. The gentlemen of our party were suffered to see the whole convent, except the enormous natural cavern, wherein unhappy maniacs are confined. The wretched patients are chained to the rock, and left there in utter darkness; if they show signs of improvement, the chain is knotted to a board; when they can undo the knot for themselves, they are supposed to be fit to return into the world; but I should think few of those poor creatures can ever come sane out of that dreadful place. It is a fine cavern, with stalactites forming within. On our return to the Pilgrim's resting-place the monks sprinkled us with orange-flower water, and gave us a luncheon of delicious honey, grapes and figs, and two salads, one of parsley, the other of raw tomatoes. We regretted that we, ladies, might not see the printing-press, where many monks are busily employed each day; all we saw of their occupations were some three or four spinning goats' hair in one out-building, while in another it was woven by hand into coarse cloth or carpets. The good fathers gave us a friendly farewell ere we commenced our ascent of the far side of the gorge—an ascent fitter for goats than horses; but very beautiful was the view looking back on the convent, and on all the various colours and forms in the valley below. At the top we were rejoined by one of our party who had scrambled on foot up to one of the numerous caverns to visit an old hermit, much reverenced for his saintly character; he, and two others, had once been monks in Mar Antoun, but finding that place too comfortable for their soul's welfare, they had, many years ago, retired into the solitude of separate caverns, their food consisting only of raw herbs and rancid oil, brought at long intervals up to the caves. The old man said that his only occupation was prayer, and that he endeavoured to entertain no thought in his mind but of God. He bestowed his blessing twice on his visitor with much unction, besides being very unctuous himself, placing one hand on his visitor's chest and the other on his back, so as to insure the blessing penetrating him through and through. The only thing in the cavern besides himself and his goulleh of water was a copy of one of Liguori's books translated into Arabic.

We then proceeded along the valley through the beautiful village, full of fruit and flower-gardens, of Forsraab, opposite to Eh'den, each succeeding view being more lovely than the one before; and crossing round the head of the valley, by the picturesque mill and under the walnuts and willows which overhang the stream, we scrambled up the other side, and reached our tents just as the afternoon mist—a very frequent visitor—filled the valley. Every one who goes to Eh'den should take this excursion, which occupies about seven or eight hours. The thermometer in our tent marked 45° that morning at six o'clock, but the heat in the midday hours was very great.

One of our favourite walks was to a small but very ancient convent, Mar Serkis (St. Sergius)—quite at the head of the valley, by the source, nestled into a nook in a wild little gorge of its own. The kind-hearted old monks always appeared quietly contented and happy among themselves, the want of comforts seeming to be atoned for in their minds by the fine view from their windows. They were very full of a new church they were building above the convent, but the one underneath it, said to be upwards of 500 years old, was more interesting to us. It is almost entirely excavated in the rock; is entered by a rock-hewn winding staircase, and is very venerable-looking and impressive, with its two or three sombre lamps shining dimly in the darkness, and a few Arabic prayers, written in the Syriac character, for its sole ornament. The source was always a favourite haunt of ours—its ice-cold waters gushing in full volume from the rock, under a pomegranate and some fine walnut-trees —on the one side tumbling rapidly down into a delightful little dark dell shaded over with white poplars and weeping willows, where it was immediately hushed into complete silence, like a child silenced in the midst of its glee, not uttering a murmur till another

N

" fount's young waters " had crept from under a rock to meet it, when they both went whispering and babbling and laughing quietly together over the rough way, till they came to the old mill, whence their course was a rapid and bounding one all the way to the sea. On the other side it glided into the white-cypress wood, and along a half natural, half artificial channel on the mountain side through the village, and down the Pass, till it rushed out, the full-grown Kadîsha, under the walls of the Castle of Raymond of Toulouse at Tripoli.

CHAPTER XIII.

SOLOMON'S FRIENDS AND SOLOMON'S WORK.

AT last, after bidding adieu to the Emir, we left our pretty encampment and the merry village with its handsome, gaily-dressed people. It was midday when we started, and we had a ride of two and a half hours to reach the Cedars, along a bare, barren road, crossing the low pass between the valley of Mar Antoun and that of Khanobin. Hill after hill of rock without the faintest trace of verdure was passed, till we arrived at the brink of an immense chasm, and, looking over the edge, beheld the village of Bscherreh hanging on the rocky side of the ravine, embedded in wood and garden. Just above the village the magnificent gorge closes round sharply, holding in its curve most weird-looking and fantastic rocks, and the beautiful Falls of the Kadîsha, which tumble down in masses of white foam to the gardens at the bottom; on the other side of the ravine the village of Hasroun lies on a shelf of verdure and luxuriance. We turned away from this beautiful view back to the hard, yellow, barren mountains on which the sunshine was pouring in fierce and pitiless rays,—when, in five minutes more, a general shout came from the muleteers, and the saïs beside me called out "Shoof! shoof! ya sitt! el Arz, el Arz!"* there, in the centre of an immense plateau, in the very bosom of the giant mountain which closes round three sides of it, lay a single black patch, so black and dark, I scarcely believed that these could be the cedars of Lebanon! We rode on quickly, and forgot all fatigue and heat and everything else directly we had reached their delicious shade, half an hour after our first view. It is difficult to describe the first feeling there: your head must ache with the scorching heat, your eyes burn with the unshaded barrenness of the last few hours—you must feel the soothing coolness of the shade stealing through your heated veins, you

* "Look, look, oh lady! the Cedars, the Cedars!"

N 2

must inhale the powerful and refreshing fragrance of the cedars, and see the venerable forms around you before you can understand that beauty and delight which there sink into your very soul. It is like passing from the noisy din and world-weariness of some great city's mart into the silent aisles of a vast cathedral,—only that here the solitude is more complete, the columns and arches are of Nature's raising, and the hymns are sung by sweet birds twittering and trilling from tree to tree, while all

"The forest leaves seem stirred with prayer."

Afterwards in the fiery heat of the Bekâa, the scorched sands of the desert, and the arid mountains of Judea, how often one's mind harked back to the cool green shades of the cedars: one then began to understand the glowing description of the Beloved whose eyes are like pools of water, and whose "countenance is as Lebanon, excellent as the cedars." (Cant. v. 15.)

It was hard to choose the prettiest among so many pretty spots for our tents, but we finally fixed them close to the little chapel in the centre of the grove, from whence we had a view of the sea. The chapel is a square construction of roughly-hewn stones, four young cedar-trunks forming the support inside. The altar was hung with pink chintz and ornamented with a cheap French print of the Madonna della Seggiola. Every morning at six o'clock an old Maronite priest came over from Bscherreh, a walk of two hours' distance, and chanted a short service ; sometimes a goatherd or two would join him, sometimes our servants or muleteers, but whether alone or not the voice of prayer and praise rose there every morning at dawn of day, and always sounded appropriate and *due* on what seemed holy ground, and instead of breaking the silence, really seemed to make the solitude more apparent.

The cedars form one group or grove covering an undulating piece of ground not a mile in circumference ; they are not scattered about, but stand in a dense mass, after passing the boundary of which there is not a shrub to be seen for many miles. There are about four hundred young trees, in themselves a beautiful and noble little forest, thronging round the patriarchs or "Apostles," as they are called by the Maronites. Of these venerable trees there are yet twelve, besides another as old, which has been lying on the ground for the last five or six years past ; there is another very old one, which has evidently been burnt, and of which so little remains that one cannot be sure of its generation ; but these "Twelve Apostles" are unmistakable, although the peasants believe that no one can count them—that some magic puzzles those who try, and that the numbers ever elude their grasp. The largest of the old saints is forty-five feet in girth, the second forty-two, while some of the branches we measured roughly at fifty-eight paces in length; whether they can have lived three thousand years, as the tradition avers, I am not called on to decide, and as the principal trunk of the fallen tree has been destroyed, it is impossible to find any vegetable history written upon its rings; but one likes to fancy the legend true, and to call them, as the Arabs do, the "Friends of Solomon;" while involuntarily one speaks of them in the language of his father David, as "the cedars which the Lord hath planted." One great charm of the encampment here, especially after the society of the good people of Eh'den, is the utter silence and solitude: it is such an indescribable comfort to encamp out of the sound of village dogs and jackals, and to be able to leave one's tent door open without fear of an intruder. Perchance in the morning a pretty boy or a rosy-faced girl would lead a couple of hundred goats down one of the little dells, their bells tinkling softly as they passed, but no other sound of man ever broke the silence. Nature herself, however, was never silent: the cicale here were extraordinarily loud, and the trees were full of little birds of the brightest green and gold plumage, with a sweet, clear note, while thousands of tiny lizards glided about everywhere; and to lie upon the soft and the dry bed of cedar-spines under the cool green shade, listening to all the sweet sounds, letting one's thoughts wander back into the long ages of which these trees are standing witnesses, looking out the while over the hot, barren mountains and down the many-coloured gorge to the snow-white coast and the blue sea twinkling beyond, with the horizon apparently half way up the sky (the effect of our own lofty position)—all this is recompense enough for any extent of fatigue and trouble incurred in reaching the spot. The place has but one drawback: want of water, the nearest spring being three quarters of an hour off; and also that only the commonest provisions are procurable at Bscherreh.

We were now 6100 feet above the sea, and we had expected to be colder than we were at Eh'den in the nights, but the equinox approached, and we were told that it would be warm after that,—and so it proved; the thermometer was at 45° one morning, and at 67° at the same hour on the next day! We had come again to the time of the full moon, and this was indeed the place to be "read aright" by its holy beams. Night after night we used to wander through the moonlit glades, watching the light silvering the mountain which stretches its giant arms with everlasting, strong tenderness round the ancient trees, and listening to the owls hooting here and there in the thick boughs. One night we had a still more beautiful and striking scene: it was the eve of the 14th of September, the date on which the Emperor Constantine is supposed to have seen the cross of fire shining in the the sky, in consequence of which miraculous appearance both he and his whole army received the Gospel of true Light, and salvation through Christ was proclaimed throughout his dominions. The festival is kept by beacon-fires lit upon every mountain-top in Syria, beginning with the cedar-mountain, besides bonfires in every village, handing on the good tidings, as it were, from one to the other throughout the land. It is a fine idea, and on a calm night it is still finer in reality; the flames of each fire as they rose and fell in the night breeze shining against the deep *azure* sky were exceedingly pretty, and every here and there a long train of flame was laid up the side of the mountain, like a fiery snake, which, catching the wind now on this side, now on that, seemed really to have caught also the wriggling, gliding motion of a living serpent.

Mr. Layard mentions a curious fact that occurred when he was at Kouyunjik, of a sweet smell proceeding from some wood burning on a fire made by his workmen: they had taken one of the beams from the excavation, just where an inscription on the building denoted that the roof had been made of cedar wood, brought from the Lebanon 3000 years before. This is doubly curious, because the cedars of Lebanon are *not* the red cedar so fragrant in burning, but a *white*, which gives out no particular fragrance when burnt. In one's encampment there the fire is always made of the small branches broken down by the wind; and some of the chips and shavings cut off from one of the oldest "saints," which lies now upon the ground, were put into ours, but no perfume came from it, save that of the fresh resinous smell peculiar to any kind of pine-tree wood. Perhaps that proceeding from the cedar wood at Kouyunjik was only this resinous fragrance, which, though very sweet, is not that of the red Indian cedar, to which we are accustomed as a perfume.

We wanted to see the celebrated convent of Khanobîn, which, though not the largest in the Lebanon, is the residence of the Maronite Patriarch; so we set off one morning at eight o'clock and and proceeded by the same road as we had come, descending to Bscherreh—a large village of very tumble-down houses, planted as thickly as possible with mulberries and poplars, but peopled with very plain men and women—a striking contrast to the handsome merry Eh'denites, with whom they are always at war, perhaps from jealousy or mortified vanity. Outside the village, built into and under and over the most extraordinary assemblage of insane-looking rocks, is the curious old convent of Mar Serkis, and a few minutes farther on comes the white foamy cascade of the Khadîsha rushing down amidst ferns and flowers—indeed this whole valley is smiling with flowers of all kinds and colours. Then we ascended the other side, and passing through the beautiful village of Hasroun found ourselves opposite to Hadshît—so close, as the crow flies, that the inhabitants of one village can speak to their neighbours of the other across the valley, while the splendid chasm between descends, first in green terraces and then in perpendicular walls of blue limestone cliffs, to the depth of a thousand feet. Hasroun is the most luxuriant spot we saw in the Lebanon—every inch of soil is cultivated, and the place is buried in thickets and forests of thorns, walnuts, planes, poplars, figs, and prickly oaks, tangled over and wreathed together with immense festoons of vines, besides those in more decorously-pruned vineyards; white and yellow clematis and honeysuckle were in all the hedges, and real fields of wheat and English-looking grass on all the slopes. Riding on over breezy downs we passed a gigantic cavern in the rocks on the other side of the chasm, and a lofty waterfall, which must be very fine in spring, as it has but one perpendicular fall; and then we looked down, first on the small convent of Mar Elisha, and then on Khanobîn, to which, however, we did not descend, as it would have taken us five or six hours more. It did not appear to us equal, either in size or position, to the convent of Mar Antoun, nor is the valley, at least as seen from above, as varied in outline or as brilliant in colouring as the other. We returned to Hasroun, feeling very much like cinders out of a furnace, and put ourselves to cool under a walnut-grove, where the people brought us great baskets of figs and grapes, for which we duly paid some trifle. If you stop *in* a vineyard you may eat as much as you like gratis; any fruit, however, that is carried away you are expected to pay for: this is in accordance with the old Israelite rule in Deuteronomy xxiii. 24. We were so much tired that we caught at the offer made by a peasant to show us a short cut to the cedars; but let all weary travellers beware how they lend an ear to such flattering tales of guides, who either scramble over tracks where no horses can follow them, or not unfrequently find themselves at fault, and leave you in the lurch. So it was with our guide, who led us for three mortal hours over the most thoroughly atrocious paths conceivable, and then deserted us, leaving us in such scorching heat, that not only ourselves, but even our dragoman and saïs and the two muleteers who had accompanied us, were made ill by it.

Our last afternoon at the cedars afforded us the extraordinary sight of what is called, I believe, a false sun : the mist had jammed itself up into dense masses, like a rough sea of ice-pack, filling up and smoothing over the whole valley, and extending over the sea beyond ; behind this the sun in due time sank,—but, ten minutes after, another sun of a flaming blood-colour rose, and after shining with an awful kind of dark brilliancy for about a quarter of an hour, it also faded away and died behind the mist-clouds,—very marvellous it was altogether.

We took leave of the grand old trees by moonlight, after a week's stay, mounting on horseback before 4 A.M., and began to ascend great Makhmel, or the Cedar-mountain.* The path was of course steep, and in some places so narrow as to be rather giddy work for climbing, but in no place in the least dangerous, or very fatiguing, except from the violent wind and the rarefied air. Just as it began to dawn we met a troop of goats, the goatherds singing in chorus to the music of a well-played reed-pipe ; very sweet and pleasant it sounded, and a very uncommon incident it was in Syrian travel. Most beautiful were the changing views at every fresh step in the ascent, the early light telling out the colours in the clearest and loveliest purity, while from each valley and nook wreaths of delicate bright *blue* mist rose like mysterious veils, slowly withdrawing as the dawn advanced. Suddenly the sun lit up the summits of the peaks, bathing each with its own flood of golden splendour, and, resting there, widened in a sudden sheet of light over the valleys below, flying over Eh'den with giant strides as we had so often watched it from the valley itself. The sun had but touched the upper valleys when we reached the summit—or rather very near the summit ; our companions ascended the highest peak, but the coldness of the thin air at this height rendered me incapable of going any farther, and our resting-place commanded such an ample view, that we did not regret much losing the northern part over the wide plain of Homs and Hamah, bounded by faint blue mountains, which can only be seen from the real summit. We spread our large map and compass on the ground before us as we gazed at the living map beneath—more living than a landscape usually appears, from the swiftly-moving light of the rising sun,

* Makhmel is the name given to this, the loftiest mountain in the Lebanon, by the people of the district of Tripoli ; the mountaineers themselves call it always and only Jebel-el-Arz—the mountain of the cedars ; its highest peak is called, as are *all* the highest peaks throughout Syria, Jebel-el-Khodib—the *summit* mountain. The height of the Jebel-el-Khodib here, which is now believed to be the highest mountain in Syria, has been lately ascertained to be 10,400 feet above the Mediterranean ; this Khodib is at some distance still farther north of the peak our party ascended, which was then believed to be the highest.

gliding, as it were, with vivifying beams over the picture—now
here, now there—waking up each portion, till it seemed really
living, breathing, under the rapid, silent changes.

We were seated on a narrow ridge or backbone between the
peaks,—beneath us, on one side, the two rifts of the Kadisha sloped
down to the Mediterranean, their blue and grey cliffs contrasting
most vividly with the orange rocks and red soil in the same gorges:
they were divided from the turquoise-blue—such a blue!—sea by
snow-white cliffs, sweeping in many a graceful curve along the
coast. On the other side of our ridge the mountain sloped more
precipitously and smoothly down into a region of sand, beyond
which came a range of hills, picturesque and rugged of dark
browns and purples, dividing it from the perfectly flat Bekka,*
stretching out in green and brown to the foot of the opposite
mountain range—the Anti-Lebanon—which was now of course
lying in deep dark shadow against the magnificently glowing
morning sky. A dark spot immediately under these mountains
was Baalbek; and as we looked the sun passed a giant step across
the whole plain, and brightened up the green plantations of the
village, so that, with a telescope, the temple was soon discerned.
Directly to the south rose our beloved Sunnîn, from this side a
ridge of rosy crags, rugged and jagged; beyond that, far away, a
graceful mountain stood quite alone—the blue cone, precipitous on
one side, sloping down gently on the other, striped with lilac shades,
it needed nothing to tell us that this was Hermon,—Jebel-esh-Sheikh,
the chief of mountains. To its left faint blue mountains faded
away in the distance, and these we knew were in the Lejah; to its
right one bright blue ridge, ending suddenly in the sea, was
Carmel. Then the sunshine shot down beneath us and lit up the
dark shades of the cedars, and the hard, white, solid little clouds,
like icebergs on the sea, expanded and joined the lighter mist-
wreaths that had risen from the valleys, and the distances became
hazy and the glorious colouring more faint. The fact is that for
really extensive views in this country the first hour of sunrise and
the last of sunset are the only times of day when they can be
perfectly seen; at all other hours the heat has thickened the air and
faded that brilliant colouring which is here the greatest charm.
The view from Mount Hermon is considerably more extensive, as
there are no intercepting peaks near at hand; but that from the
Cedar Mountain is certainly more varied and beautiful: and even if

* From the Hebrew *Bikha*, meaning plain, as this is *the* plain of North
Syria. From the Arabic *Bekâa* the Spanish *Vega* is derived—signifying a
plain between mountains.

it is not, as one traveller calls it, " the loveliest yet grandest scene that the world possesses," it is indescribably and grandly lovely.

We had a long, tiresome descent of nearly two hours before we reached our tents, which had been pitched near a clear and very cold source called 'Ain Ata, where we were thankful to creep under some fine walnut-trees out of the burning, fervid sun.   We had a fine view to look at all day—Hermon's graceful head towering up in the distance, while close to us lay nestled in a mountain basin the pretty Lake Yemouni, and fiery red mountains speckled with prickly oak rose all around us.   This spot is subject to sudden squalls, coming over the heads of the mountains ; our tent was not properly secured at first, and was rudely overturned by one of them, and we left behind us a variety of stains on the rocks and ground from the upset inkbottles that must have puzzled the goats for many days after.   We were glad of a good sleep that night, but on the next we mounted at 1 A.M., and started for the great plain of Bekâa, the heat of which no one would willingly encounter by day in the summer.   The road lay up and down steep glens and vales, thickly wooded with low trees and shrubs,—pine, prickly oak, and white cypress—all· of them twisted and stunted into strange, grotesque shapes, which in the deep shades of the waning moon and the starlight assumed most mysterious appearances :—now an old friar begging with his arms stretched out and his head thrown back—now a lady with a long train and a dancing step—now " bears with ragged staffs " on each side of the path like constables —now sturdy dogs, and, more frequently, cocks with or without tails, and their heads perked up till I half expected to hear the horrid *crow* close to my ear ; and in the lowest glade a gigantic knight on a charger seemed to approach, his black armour shining in the moonlight and a white shield glistening on his arm ; but his noble horse suddenly dropped his head, the knight mysteriously vanished, and the shield turned into the white, smooth trunk of an old gnarled oak !   We stopped for five minutes at Deir-el-Ah'mar, which seemed to be a hamlet inhabited by dogs only—no other living thing was moving.   The dawn was commencing as we arrived at the dead flat of the great plain, and very pretty it was to watch the light darting on Hermon and the great mountains we had just left, colouring the summits into a 'pink, brilliant as a rose-leaf, above the purple violet and browns of the lower mountains and the green plain on which we now cast long shadows behind us.   The morning-star was still shining with serene beauty as we turned aside to the single column in the plain, about which little or nothing is known, as neither inscription nor sculpture remains upon it, although little injured. It is of the Corinthian order, standing on a pedestal of steps, but is not nearly so lofty as that of Diocletian at Alexandria, which is eighty feet high; this column is only sixty, but there is something grand in its loneliness and silent mystery. Our horses evidently thought it uncanny, for they every one shied at it, and could scarcely be persuaded to go round it. The sun was shining brightly on the famous Six Columns of Baalbek as we reached the village at 5 A.M.; we got into a garden on the north side of the temple, but the heat was overpowering, and we had all fallen asleep before either our tents or our breakfast had arrived.

As the heat was very great here—96° in the shade each day—we did not visit the temple till after dinner; when we thought ourselves fortunate in seeing it *first* in the evening. It is a fine scene in the morning sun, but no single and incomplete architectural object can be more lovely than the Six lonely Columns standing with such dignity and majesty in the midst of the desolation and ruin around them, bathed in the golden glory shed by the setting sun, with the Temple of Jupiter seen through them, a mosque beyond, and the chain of barren mountains crimsoned into beauty behind them.

Baalbek has been so frequently and ably illustrated, by pen and pencil, in the last few years, that only a very few words are necessary to record the impression made by its graceful majesty upon the traveller. It is to be hoped that many more generations will see these ruins as they are—so enormous and ponderous were the materials used, that the puny hand of modern man can do but little to injure them—earthquakes are the only destroyers to be feared.

> " Time hath not harmed the eternal monument ;
>   Time is not here, nor days, nor months, nor years—
>   For sure those mighty piles shall overlive
>   The feeble generations of mankind. . . . .
>   A mighty mass remains ; enough to tell us
>   How great our fathers were, how little we.
>   Men are not what they were: their crimes and follies
>   Have dwarfed them down from the old hero race
>   To such poor things as we ! " *

Ascending a lofty flight of steps at the extreme east, the worshipper entered a magnificent open portico with a square hall at each end; thence he passed through a hexagonal court, surrounded with columns, into the great quadrangle, four hundred and forty feet long, across which a double colonnade † led to another flight of

---

* ' Thalaba.'

† Destroyed to build a Christian church, which in the time of Constantine the Great occupied this court.

steps, which gave access to the platform on which stood the Temple of the Sun. This edifice was surrounded by fifty-four columns of seventy-five feet in height; the loftiest, it is said, in the world, and appearing still higher than they really are from their (almost) extreme slenderness—they are but six feet six inches in diameter.* No trace of the cella of this temple remains, and there are some doubts that it was ever built; only six of the fifty-four columns of the peristyle are now standing (although the bases of a great many are still to be seen *in situ*, the present outside wall being built up between them), but these six are the chief beauty of Baalbek—

> " Flinging their shadows from on high,
> Like dials which the wizard Time
> Had raised to count his ages by."

The exquisite carving of their capitals is of the purest Corinthian; the acanthus-leaves are cut with remarkable freedom and richness, by no means overloaded, and the abacus, is supported by delicate volutes of the most graceful designs. It is curious to observe the effect of the weather upon these columns—on the north side almost every leaf and many of the volutes are perfect, while on the other they are shapeless blocks.

The whole of this temple and the Great Courts rest upon giant walls supported by the platform of Cyclopean masonry, justly considered one of the wonders of the world; in the western end are the three stones—rocks one ought to call them—from which the temple was called *Trilithon* by the Greeks; two of them are sixty-four feet, and the third sixty-three feet long; all three are thirteen feet both in height and in thickness. The platform, of which every stone is gigantic, is supported by three passages running under its entire length and breadth, vaulted, and of exceedingly fine workmanship, the enormous stones nicely and neatly joined; they are wonderful places to walk through : handsomer and of finer finish than the vaults beneath the Temple of Solomon at Jerusalem. Of course the beauty of Baalbek is in the temples, but the platform was, to me at least, a still greater interest; one had the same crushing feeling of the long ages of its past history come over one's mind that one had felt in the temples of Egypt,—and all in vain : for the shadows of its antiquity elude one's grasp. It is a relief to seize upon tradition, and pretend to believe it modern enough for Solomon's workmanship; one fancies, however, that one recognises the

* The usual proportion of a Corinthian column is 8¼ diameters to the height ; whereas the height of the columns of the Temple of the Sun are nearly 12 diameters ; those of the Temple of Jupiter have 10 diameters.

Phœnician (Canaanite) stamp upon its massive simplicity, which, though some may call it barbarous, became sublime in the hands of the Egyptians and Phœnicians. Perhaps Baalbek is much older than Tadmor, and was one of the cities already standing in the country before Joshua marked out the boundaries of the Israelites: it cannot be the Baalath built by Solomon when he built " Tadmor in the wilderness," both of them stone cities, because Josephus distinctly explains that to have been near Gézer, in the tribe of Dan; while the fact of the rocks of which it is built being so much more enormous than anything at Tadmor may be partly accounted for by the quarries at Baalbek being so much nearer to the building than those of Tadmor. Looking up from the exterior of these huge stones, and seeing the Six Columns shoot up skywards with their slender, tapering shafts, they have been not inaptly compared to " Ariel mounted on a mammoth's back!"

Although the ground has filled up the interior of the Great Court to such a height—at least twenty feet—as to render it impossible to form a correct judgment, one can hardly imagine that these beautiful walls were sufficiently high inside for the very great size of the area. The court was entirely surrounded with recesses, having six, four, or two columns in front of each, formed of Egyptian red granite and porphyry, quantities of the débris of which lie all about. Each recess contained a number of niches for statues, probably standing above others now buried, in which the priests or worshippers sat: these are all richly sculptured, many with eagles, fruit, &c.; but the Egyptian asp spoken of by some travellers we thought very little identical with its supposed original. This temple was dedicated to all the gods, with Baal as supreme, and is supposed to have been built, or at least the greater part of it, in the time of the Emepror Antoninus Pius, A.D. 138–161. I often pondered where the columns that Sultan Suleyman took in 1550 from this temple to adorn Santa Sophia could have stood: I conclude they were among these small ones closing in the recesses of the Great Court, as they seemed to have been the only columns in Baalbek of coloured marble, or of like dimensions.

The Temple of Jupiter is about two hundred feet to the south of the Temple of Apollo, beyond the grand court, and is said to have been built at the same time. The ground on which it stands is much lower than that of its imperial neighbour, but it has its own platform; it is larger than the Parthenon, but, probably from the very lofty columns near it and the impossibility of getting a distant view of the whole, it appears considerably smaller, and you have no idea of its real size till you come to measurements. Dr. Robinson remarks that nowhere else does it seem so impossible to reconcile the gigantic size of the fallen stones of the same entablature or column with those still standing, as at Baalbek; so perfect are the proportions that neither the size, nor any other one characteristic strikes the eye, in the perfect balance of the whole. It has another peculiar charm in its completeness, for although ruined and hidden, Baalbek still remains *as a whole*; perhaps no temple (always excepting the Theseum at Athens, which is six hundred years older than Baalbek) remains so complete, nor is the execution of the details surpassed by any other work of the kind. The cella is surrounded with forty-two columns, a triple row at the east end forming the portico, within which is the famous doorway, whose sides are formed of single stones forty-two feet high; it is covered, overloaded, all round with border after border of the most exquisite sculpture, fruit, flowers, leaves, and wheat-ears, interspersed with little Cupids and panthers; but the most interesting of the ornaments is the large eagle sculptured on the soffit of this doorway, holding a *caduceus* in his talons, and the string of garlands, upheld on each side by genii, are twisted in his beak. The ceiling of the peristyle is equally rich, and as a great deal of it has fallen, it can be closely examined; it is divided into hexagonal compartments, each one filled by a bust or figure carved in such high relief as to seem leaning out of its frame; the contours of the figures are very graceful.

These temples had been built about 800 years when they were turned into a fortress; they have sustained several sieges and much rough usage since. The Saracens and Crusaders built up walls within and without, which now remain to the extreme discomfort of the traveller; there is, however, a fine Saracenic palace or castle, close to the Temple of Jupiter, whose unadorned architecture contrasts well with the rich sculpture of its Corinthian neighbours; the walls are strong and massive, and the octagonal hall in the centre, which is gracefully vaulted, is remarkably handsome.

At a short distance from the great temple, standing alone among ruins, huts, and gardens, there is a little gem of a temple: it is shaped like a star-fish, the seven columns surrounding it being placed in a circle, and the cella wall receding in a semicircle between each. It had once a domed roof, and is most richly ornamented within and without with sculpture, the delicately-carved capitals of the fluted columns reminding one of some of the best things of the kind at Venice. The whole temple is only thirty-eight feet in diameter, and, alas, much destroyed; I am convinced it was intended for a *kiosk* or *boudoir* for the gods when they left the Great Temple to take a little recreation.

Then there are the quarries, to which we rode one evening, where the famous stone, sixty-eight feet long, and weighing probably 1100 tons, still lies unremoved. The peasantry believe that the genii, working amicably with the men of old, carried these stones for them, but, being one day offended at something, this stone was dropped in the quarry, and no human strength has been found capable of lifting it since. It is said to be the largest stone hewn for building in the world—the obelisk in the quarry at Assouân is, however, twenty-seven feet longer, and nearly as wide. These quarries point to such gigantic works, that one does not wonder they have given rise to legends of supernatural agency—adding the craft of jinns and genii to the might of the " giants who lived in those days." At Baalbek one learns to think naturally of the Rephaim, the Emims, the Zanzummims, the Zouzims, and the Anakims, whose fathers, it is said, won from Heaven the reward of a more than mortal strength for having given up solitude and celibacy on the tops of the mountains, and returned to a life of usefulness among their kinsfolk in the plains—the best argument for the " athletic religion" so much in fashion at the present time that I have ever come across. The quarries, which extend over a great distance, are very striking from their sharply-cut cliffs or clefts, and their deep caverns (some of which appear to have been made use of both as tombs and dwelling-places), some supported by pillars, others only open-mouthed. The rock has been left in strange grotesque forms; and has unusually brilliant covering,—orange and white, blue and gray, and a bright coppery green. From one of these wild mystic-looking nooks a very large eagle soared out slowly and calmly; he disdained to take any notice of our presence, but setting himself with much dignity on an adjoining point, his mate glided silently out of a hole close to us, and disappeared behind him—they were scarcely four yards from our heads.

One of the questions of interest concerning Baalbek is its name, which is generally believed to be its original, or at least an ancient one, to which the Arabs, when they conquered Syria in A.D. 630, wisely returned; but if the *bek* is a Phœnician (and hence Hebrew) word, it has not yet been found in the language. Some persons think that it may have been derived from the Egyptian *baki*, meaning city, and that the Greeks applied it when Cœlo-Syria fell to the lot of the Græco-Egyptian kingdom, in which case it would be as modern as their name of Heliopolis, and means only the same thing. Dr. Robinson, however, suggests that it is from the later Arabic *bakka*, a throng or crowd, and that it describes the place where worshippers of Baal met in a crowd. Others have tried to derive it from the same word as the name of the plain beside it—Bekâa—(*Bikha*, Hebrew for *plain*) as if to denote "Baal of the plain;" but this is untenable, as the *k* is not the same letter when used in Baalbek as in Bikha.

A little wely near the town is shaded by a cypress-tree worth seeing; though not nearly as tall as the splendid cypresses of Smyrna, it is so round, so full, and so luxuriant as to make a specimen fit for a picture—it is said to have been as large and full more than a century ago.

We left Baalbek at 11 P.M., after four days' stay; our dragoman was ill, and we took a guide, who led us for some time, up and down, over apparently barren mountains, but by so good a path that we did not suspect we were going wrong. There was no moon, only the beautiful stars and one radiant planet near Orion, about the heavenly birth and parentage of which the saïs told me a long legend, of which, unfortunately, I took in only about half. At last we reached the brow of the mountain, and turned into a tremendous ravine with a torrent roaring at the bottom; the road became a succession of smooth, sloping slabs of rock, and presently the guide sat down, and coolly informed us that he knew nothing about the route, and could only say that we were on a goat-path, where horses never passed, but which ultimately went down to the bottom of the ravine. The whole side of the mountain was enveloped in pitch darkness, so that we could not see one step before us, and it seemed more than likely that we should reach the bottom by an expeditious but not precisely agreeable mode of descent, as the path was nowhere more than two feet wide. We were benumbed with cold and fatigue, and excessively sleepy ; however, there was nothing for it but to go on, trusting to the sure-footedness of our horses. We finally reached the end of the path in safety, but I need not say that the four hours we were on that mountain side were neither very short nor very agreeable. Morning dawned as we emerged into the pretty plain of Surghâya, and the ride through the smiling green pastures was refreshing, with the wild craggy summits of the Anti-Lebanon towering over head, and Hermon filling up the end of the picture. We got to Zebdány at 6 A.M., a bright pretty place, with the hedges covered with sweet white roses and clematis, and English-looking gates, neatly made and painted, to the gardens. This plain is very rich and luxuriant; Bludan, the summer residence of the Europeans of Damascus, standing perched up, halfway to heaven, on a green plateau near the summit of one of the mountains. We resumed our route early the next morning, passing over the rest of the plain of the Bárada with its pretty waterfall and light Roman bridge, and the fine pass of Abila, the modern Souk; the steep cliffs, which close in with beautiful windings, are covered with tablets and tombs, some of them ornamented with columns and carved doorways; one of the tablets gives the name of the Roman legate of Syria, by whose order this road was cut through the mountain. This was the scene of an immense triumph of the arms of Islam under Khaled, in A.D. 634, over much more than ten times their own number of Christians.

The road was most lively with passengers; one troop we passed was of about two score of Bashi-Bazouks, going out to hunt, with falcons on their wrists and long spears in their hands; then strings of camels and Bedoueens, sometimes fifty in a string, and mules without end. Unfortunately we took a wrong turn, and instead of following our mules to 'Ain Fijeh, we went along green lanes and woods and streams till a peasant told us we were but an hour or two from Damascus, and we had to go back some miles before we could cross the river. It was midday before we came to a lovely village, wherein we rested, for we were faint with fatigue and hunger, having tasted nothing that day; then we ascended the hills on the other side, and found ourselves in the desert, El Sah'ra, over which the sun was pouring his fiercest rays as we paced along the winding track, across one featureless hill after another, the wretch of a guide continually refusing to go any farther, and having to be collared and thumped into obedience and utility. Probably this desert is green enough in the early spring, for between the loose stones like that of a sea-beach, over which we trod most laboriously, numbers of pale lilac colchicums were springing up at every step. Wherever one saw the soil beneath the stones it seemed as hard as the stone itself; and one could not help thinking of the curse with which God threatened the Israelites: " The heaven that is over thy head shall be as brass, and the earth that is under thee shall be iron." We were not of course entitled to the protection of Mooslim angels, or we should have been very thankful to be able to say with Muhammad, " the people in Syria are happy indeed, for the kind angels of heaven spread their sheltering wings above their head,"— certainly no kind angels sheltered us.

At last, fried and broiled, we descended into a fig-orchard, and soon came to the river; all the rest of the way was under the deep delicious shades of planes, walnuts, and fruit-trees, beside the rushing, tumbling stream whose cool sound was music to our burnt-up ears, we thankfully found the tents placed beside that never-to-be-forgotten 'Ain Fijeh.

The Temple of Fijeh is thought to be one of those built for the original Phœnician Baal-worship of Syria, like that of Afka, to which

o

it bears some resemblance: it is built in front of the living rock, which was probably cut out to admit of it, and was very simple, containing only one hall, about 30 feet square, built of very large stones, between which the trees have long ago pushed themselves. The temple stands half on a platform or ledge of rock which has been left bridging over the cavern, whence, out of darkness, mystery, and silence, not a gentle bubbling spring, but a full-grown river leaps into life, rushing past the rocks with a great song of joy for a few yards, when it tumbles headlong over a rocky ledge in masses of snowy foam; the trees everywhere crowding down its banks, bending over its waters, dipping in and playing with the laughing waves which seem to leap up to meet them, and arching over the broad, full stream in long vistas of watery loveliness and lanes of greenery. This source is remarkable for its size: it is the clearest water possible, and singularly bright in colouring, in the morning a full deep emerald-green—in the evening a sapphire-blue: it was impossible to help thinking of the two gems, so exactly did it resemble their clear hues by turns. Beside the spring, only two or three yards at one side, there is another temple, still smaller than that above the cavern: its very massiveness and simplicity telling of its extreme antiquity. One square column still stands, and there is a cornice, a bold but simple cavetto like that we saw at Afka, and afterwards both at Deir-el-Asbayr and Rukhleh; the whole building is very rough, but a huge, massive grandeur hangs about the now almost formless stones, and the situation is as romantic and poetical as can be imagined. It must have been in a spot precisely resembling 'Ain Fijeh that Egeria taught the Roman king those secrets which made Purity a Religion, and Virtue its own best reward. It is a delicious place—the valley, scarcely 200 yards wide, cannot contain itself for joy at its own luxuriance, but flings up orchard after orchard, vineyard after vineyard, upon the mountain at each side; and the river goes laughing through the woods, pouring out its richness as it goes, and merrily bathing the tree-roots that revel in its cooling stream. We scrambled up part of the mountain to look down on the tangled crowd of trees: the contrast of the beauty below and the yellow barrenness above is most striking. The village is a miserable concern, but we were pleased at seeing two newly-plastered Mooslim graves, with a little bed of bright flowers formed on the top of each: they were the first we had seen blossoming over Mooslims—but afterwards in Asia Minor it became a common sight.

We found the villagers so troublesome that day and the next

morning, that we moved off to a delicious little meadow of real thick springy grass beside the bright rapid river—a favourite bathing-place with travellers, about half an hour on the Damascus road, and settled ourselves under a rock to sketch: a goatherd politely brought up a goat, and feasted us on warm frothy milk from an ancient silver bowl, engraved with Cufic inscriptions. This spot has not the romance or the antiquarian interest of the fountain, but it is extremely pretty, the valley widening enough to let one see the deep blue-green of the river, and the splendid cliffs changing from yellow sameness into blue-grey crags, jagged and broken into rifts of the most picturesque nature. We had had enough of the desert, El Sah'ra, the day before, so we chose to try the lower or river path recommended by the peasants—a river path indeed, for it was chiefly *in* the river, across the windings of which we waded *nine* times, the horses nearly up to their middles, and scarcely able to keep a footing in the rushing tide; and then pushed through the *thick* groves, dividing the trees and hedges as we went, to the imminent peril of hats and habits that were already well soaked in the stream. At last we came out on the barren mountains, where an eagle welcomed us with a Jupiter kind of nod before he deigned to move on; and hurrying over the hills, we reached Kubbet-es-Seiyār nearly an hour before sunset. There was a furious wind blowing, but we found shelter in the pretty wely, while we sat down to enjoy the famous scene from which it is said Muhammad piously turned away: *se non è vero è ben trovato.*

The vast plain of yellow sand is bounded on all sides by mountains—Hermon on the right (west) towering up close at hand dark and craggy; to the south the mountains of the Haurān, in all the tender hues of distance; to the east the pass up which the road to Palmyra winds, joining the craggy Anti-Lebanon upon which we stood; at our feet, and extending to the middle of the plain, is the mass—*thirty miles* in extent—of gardens and groves in all the riches of the fullest summer foliage, deep and bright green of every shade. In the midst of this, almost buried as it were under the leaves, is the city, oblong-shaped, but with one suburb (the Meidân) stretching out a long thin line to the south: it shines with a dazzling, delicate white, like a city built of pearls, shooting up its tapering minarets and graceful domes, as if in jealousy of the poplars around it. Truly it is no wonder that the Arabs who first bore the banner of Islam through the wearisome desert of Arabia burst into shouts and transports of joy when they beheld these towers and palaces rising among the verdant plains and the murmuring streams that make such sweet music in the air; one might have thought the pretty buildings, like the walls of Ilion, had risen to the tune. One cannot take in a scene like this in a moment, and we had but just begun to understand it, and to feel satisfied with feeding on its beauty, when the sun sank behind Hermon, throwing one last gift over the city of such a crimsoning hue as turned the pearl into an opal, and lit up the trees into almost metallic lustre, bathing the mountains in a flood of peach-blossom that really made the whole view one of quite unearthly beauty. It lasted but a few minutes: the glorious sight passed away, the plain dimmed in shadow, and we descended the hill as quickly as we could to reach the gate before it should be closed for the night. It was just dark when we entered the city, and our first introduction to its long, narrow, winding streets, perfectly and entirely dark, save where a *café* or some miserable lantern made the rest of the darkness seem still darker, was not of the pleasantest; and certainly the last appellation any one would give them now is the word "straight," unless it meant a passage too narrow or *strait* to turn in. A succession of horrible yells and howls announced, every now and then that some one had gone over a wretched dog as we went stumbling on over the dust-heaps in the way. At last we reached a very small door, where our dragoman was waiting for us, and we dismounted at the hotel, which seemed to our tired eyes like an enchanted palace, with its brilliant colours, latticed windows, and lamps hanging between oleander and citron-trees, loaded with blossom, and filling the cool night air with fragrance. We went to sleep in good, clean beds, to the music of the falling fountain, which splashed gently over the marble basin in the centre of our apartment; and lay with a satisfactory feeling even in our dreams that, at last, we were in Damascus.

CHAPTER XIV.

THE FAIR CITY,

"Damascus is the mole on the cheek of Beauty—the plumage of the Peacock of Paradise—the brilliant neck of the ring-dove—and the collar of beauty."— *Arabian Poet.*

IT is curious that of the four oldest cities in the world—Sidon, Hamah, Damascus, and Hebron—not one has lost its first original name: Hamah became Epiphania under the Greeks, but retained the name less than three hundred years; Damascus is called by the Arabs of the desert *Esh-Sham*, but is known to them also, as to all the world, by the name used for it by Abraham the patriarch; it is the only large and flourishing city of the four, having 150,000 inhabitants, and immense wealth within its walls; while Hamah, the Syrian Manchester, contains only 30,000. In architectural objects of all kinds Damascus is incalculably inferior to Cairo, but in natural beauty, how far superior! so that although there are quite enough fine and striking buildings to lend variety to the scene, the eye does not miss the work of man among the enchanting verdure, rushing streams, lofty shades, and beautiful mountains that surround the city. I cannot understand any one comparing the bazaars of either Cairo or Constantinople to those of Damascus: the former have no pretension to building of any kind, besides being much diluted with the garb and features of the West, while the latter are entirely Europeanized. Damascus alone is thoroughly Oriental, displaying in its streets such an endless, indescribable variety of all nations and classes east and south of the Mediterranean, that it is impossible to weary of its sights or of its interests, in the amusement and pleasure of the moment; while looking backwards in the stream of Time, few places to the east of Europe can equal it in historical interest.

The Pachalik of Damascus extends up the whole country to

Hamah along the Orontes, and east of the Jordan down to Petra. There is a large garrision always kept in the citadel, and the town is governed by a Pasha of the highest rank, who is always a Field-Marshal (Mushir) and—far more important—the Emir-el-Haj, or Prince of the holy Mekka caravan. It is a city of very large manufacture, and there is probably none other existing, unblessed with water-carriage, with such extensive trade. Its silks supply Egypt, and travel eastward till they meet those of Persia and Kashmîr; its cottons and woollens, goat's or camel's hair stuffs, are used throughout the East, and also in Egypt and Arabia; its gold and silver ornaments and its arms supply the Desert, Arabia, and Syria, while its fruit is eaten from Tiflis and Baghdad to the shores of Europe. It is not easy to enumerate a hundredth part of the treasures that are displayed in the bazaars of Damascus: they are mostly divided, as in all Oriental towns, into classes—the silks in one bazaar, the spices in another, and so on; but many booths combine variety enough to dispel monotony. Among the finest and most costly things sold are the golden-wove stuffs of Mekka, which are very beautiful, and are chiefly used for the thick stiff cloaks of sheikhs and emirs, dyed in bright colours, violet, maroon, &c., &c. The carpets, silks, and shawls of Persia abound everywhere; they are of every class, and sometimes of great beauty. From Persia also come finely-ornamented nargilehs and embroideries of all kinds, Kashmîr and Bokhara shawls, old porcelain of great delicacy (as well as from China); arms from Baghdad and Kashmîr, and gold and silver ornaments of all kinds, vases, cups, incense-burners, perfume-throwers, coffee-services, and other objects. The bazaar of made-up and second-hand clothes is particularly amusing, and as gay as the saddler's, which is full of housings and trappings of horses and mules, from the finest gold and silver embroidery on velvet, enriched with pearls, down to the common bright crimson leather saddles, and the many-coloured harness of plaited worsted cords and tassels, decked with rows of white cowrie-shells and charms. Then the preserves and confectionery, gum, spice, and drug bazaars—always graver and more perfumed than the others—and the gay, lively cotton and printed muslin bazaar, full of colours and combinations of which one thought even Manchester must be innocent, but which are manufactured for the special delight of the Arab and the Kurd. Then come the narrow lanes of the red boots or yellow slippers, which seem numerous enough to shoe the population of Syria for twenty years; and the carpentery bazaar of carved, inlaid, and painted chests, so barbarously made, but so delightfully pretty.

Remembering the extraordinary vicissitudes which the beautiful city has undergone, it is more a matter of wonder that *any* architectural objects should remain in its streets than that there are so few;* one of the most distant possessions of Rome, farmed out and ground down for its revenues—the battle-field of Arabs, Saracens, and Christians, overrun by Kurds and Tartars, burned, and destroyed by Timour—it is a marvel that even the once beautiful church, parts of which are probably older than our era, should be still standing. The city walls have been preserved for convenience, and they bear, in some places, every mark of extreme antiquity; it is indeed very interesting to observe the different ages, which are frequently very distinctly marked in one small piece of wall, and to see how completely the old form realises in one's mind the stories of Rahab and the spies, and the two escapes of St. Paul. The moat is still wide around them, and in some places full of water, shaded over by trees; in others it is a dry receptacle for every kind of rotting filth and abomination—in truth, a ride round the outside of Damascus is a severe trial at all times to the olfactory nerves. The gates are mostly Roman, built over, added to, and altered by the Saracens, through whose tumble-down towers and broken battlements the fine Roman arch and bevelled masonry may still be distinguished; they are all of them very picturesque. The castle looks well, and would appear to have been once a strong building, and the serai is handsome.

There is not much variety in the minarets of Damascus, except those of the Great Mosque, which are models of elegance and delicate beauty, very graceful and rich, though airy; seen together they make a striking picture. The baths and cafés enliven every street: both are nearly always painted in broad, horizontal stripes of scarlet, blue, and white, which, though not in the least elegant or *recherché*—in fact it is somewhat barbaric—yet is very effective and gay. Wherever you go inside the city you look, at short intervals, into a dark cool chamber, in which are men smoking, lounging, chatting, and lemonade-drinking; or into a court shaded by delicious trees, with a bubbling fountain or a large tank of running water; or into a larger, airier, lighted hall, gaily painted within and without, where men are resting after the pleasant fatigues of the bath, wrapped in white garments, sipping coffee, and smoking nargilehs; the noise that proceeds from both café and bath duly announcing their neighbourhood. Near the outskirts of the town they are still prettier, at least in the evening, when they are

* A slight sketch of the history of Damascus in Note 1 may be found interesting to the general reader.

brilliantly lighted up with lamps hung in the trees, and always full
of people. One, by the castle, is particularly pretty, with rude
wooden platforms hanging over the rushing river, which seem as if
supported by the wreaths of creepers that have flung themselves
everywhere, and shaded by innumerable bending trees. Another,
near the Bab Tuma, where the river is more foaming and its voice
louder,—very rickety and wretched, but all the more picturesque
for that,—hidden under weeping-willows and poplars, pomegranates
and planes, presented an endless variety of costumes by night and
by day in the various groups enjoying *kief*. Near the castle, too,
is another sight, a plane-tree of which the trunk measures forty feet
in circumference, and within which several hermits have lived,
acquiring a *green* old age in a solitude they would not find there
now (although the little door is yet unremoved in case of another
occupant), since it is in the centre of a busy suburb, and always
surrounded by crowds of laden mules, donkeys, and camels with
their noisy drivers.

Except for the cafés and baths, the streets of Damascus are duller
than those of any other Oriental town, and people say they look
poor because they expect so renowned a city to look grand; indeed
I have heard persons who have come back from a hurried visit to
Damascus declaring that " the whole town was built of mud—nothing
but mud walls everywhere!" they had only glanced at the exterior,
and did not perceive that there was solid masonry beneath the
mud. This is a strange, anomalous taste in our eyes, but the
invariable Eastern custom: as soon as the stone wall is completed
it is covered with a coating of mud, which hides the more lasting
material, and looks tattered and miserable as soon as it begins to
peel. The new houses are being built with handsome projecting
windows, opening on to the streets, and the gaily-painted and gilt
lattices are extremely pretty; but this is quite a modern and
unusual innovation; in general the long lanes wind about between
high or low walls, all quite blind, except for occasional insignificant
doorways, topped with one small bit of carving, and an apology for
a window stuck in here and there, seldom anything better than a
rough hole or a long slit closely covered over by a ragged wooden
lattice.

But stop at one of these miserable little doors (that is if you are
fortunate enough to have so good an introduction to the inmates as
we owed to the English missionary, Mr. Robson), and let us see
what is within-side. A little room, or half dark passage, leads into
a small open court with a fountain and a *leewān* (a recess always on
the north side of every court, furnished with a divan, the *salon* used

by the inhabitants of the sleeping rooms which surround the three other sides of the court): this is occupied by the servants of the household; and from this another passage admits you into a much larger court, always paved with coloured marbles, and with one or more fountains shaded by pomegranates, lemon, orange, and oleander-trees; wherever you look, all is marble, both white and coloured. This court has also its raised *leewān*, splendidly ornamented on the walls and ceiling, and its divan covered with rich brocades; here you are received, and presented with lemonade, sweetmeats, and coffee. In most rich houses one of the rooms round this court is also a reception-room, of which the walls are entirely covered with marble mosaic and gilding, a fountain at one end, a divan at the other; coloured matting and handsome Persian carpets on the floor, and near the ceiling a row of windows, latticed with pierced marble or carved wood in patterns of fairy intricacy and lightness; the ceilings are always of wood most delicately carved, painted, and gilt. A closed door in this court leads by a little passage into a third court much the same, only handsomer than the others, where the ladies reside, and beyond which they do not come in Mooslim houses. The houses are mostly two stories high, but some have only one, the flat roof forming as usual the promenade; in Damascus the roofs of the hareem are generally covered with lattice or torn mats and green creepers.

One Saturday Mr. and Mrs. Robson were kind enough to take us to see some of the best houses of Damascus, which now generally belong to Jews. On this day they sit dressed in their finest clothes and jewels to receive visitors; at the first house we visited a large family were assembled round a widowed mother. The eldest daughter, who had been married four years, and was not quite eighteen, was very tall and slender, with a complexion as white as snow; her black hair and large bright eyes and small mouth made a beautiful face, though the highly-arched eyebrows (a painted line drawn after the hair is pulled out) added to the silly, inane expression of their faces. This girl was very lively, and never ceased asking questions and chattering, showing us all her ornaments, which were chiefly diamonds and pearls, on her head, neck, and arms. All the ladies were dressed in Manchester-muslin skirts of bright colours, and short silk or velvet jackets embroidered in gold; sky-blue and bright green seemed the favourite mixture of colours. The neck and bosom of each was covered, not concealed, by embroidered muslin, the skin underneath being frequently painted. On the death of the father the house and all its contents becomes the property of the son; the mother remains there only on sufferance.

In this one the master was only a child of twelve years old, but he exacted much respect from the servants (who sat in the room all the time, below the divan, and joined loudly in the conversation), and he was very finely dressed, wearing several diamond and turquoise rings, and an enamelled watch hanging by a pearl chain. He served us with sweetmeats, making a salaam to each before presenting the spoon, which we returned on giving it back; and after he had passed on each one made another salaam to his mother, the mistress of the house. They took us over the whole building. It is extremely handsome, no portion left unornamented, and all done in the finest inlay of coloured marbles, as delicate as any Florentine table: this is the old and good style; in the new houses the mosaic is only imitated in paint, put on by a pierced form—mere stencilling, in short.

The little son then conducted us to his grandfather's, a still more spacious, and handsomer house, with four or five large courts and splendid apartments. Here also even the upper apartments were very beautifully decorated, which is not usually the case, their ornament being generally confined to a little painting. The women in this house were very ugly, but gaily dressed; and a troop of romping boys and pretty girls burst in: the girls wearing very handsome belts of gold bosses sewed on velvet and set with jewels —the handsomest of these come from Baghdad.

But the finest house we visited belonged to a Jew named Lisbona —a handsome, portly man, who was sitting on the divan without shoes or stockings, chanting Hebrew from a big book on his knee. He was very jolly and talkative, and called to his wife and mother to join us; they apologised much for not being able to offer us coffee, as, being the Sabbath, they could not light a fire; and then made a close examination of our dresses, &c. The old mother wore a widow's headdress, a black *kefiyeh* thrown over and concealing the indispensable gold coins, and a huge bunch of short black ostrich-feathers laid on each side of the head and face; a large black tassel hanging from the back of her head, below which an immense number of stout black silk cords and tassels reached nearly to the ground—making altogether a heavy and really ponderous affair, only useful as a sort of domestic portable hearse of the ugliest description—so unlike our pretty, modest, English widow's cap. They showed us numbers of pretty things—nargilehs, zarfs, sugar-stands, &c., &c.—all in the finest silver filagree, so much better made than anything we had seen in the bazaars, that we begged Lisbona to tell us the maker's name, intending to buy some; but nothing would induce the excellent Jew to answer anything of the kind

until he had inquired again and again from each of us, and entreated
Mr. Robson to assure him of the fact, "Have you got money enough
to pay for them? Are you *sure* you have money enough?" and
when that was settled, he turned coolly to me and said, "Then
why do you wear that common thing on your shoulders? You
have got a beautiful dress—why don't you wear a nice shawl too?"
My dress was of stout English cotton print; but I had put on a
pretty silk shawl which had been given to me in Beyrout, and
which, being of native manufacture, displeased his sense of propriety, and made him think I was too poor to have anything better.
Of course I did not mention that my dress cost about a sixth part of
its price, and was intended for use, not beauty; but we took the
hint, and never paid another visit dressed in Arab manufactures.
These good people took a lively interest in us and our adventures;
but the women pestered us with ceaseless questions as to what we
had done with our husbands—where we had left them—what could
have induced them to let us go so far without them; and I do not
think they were ever persuaded that we had none; though, finally,
the old woman ran after us, emphatically entreating us, "Oh,
maiden! oh, maiden! if you really have not got a husband, *do* let
me send for such-and-such a marriage-merchant from the bazaar!"

The prettiest thing in that house was a fair, sweet-faced boy in a
side room, with one hand rocking a cradle containing a fat, pretty
baby, and holding in the other a fine Hebrew psalter, from which
he was chanting aloud. The cradle was of polished walnut-wood,
inlaid with mother-of-pearl, and had "Peace and happiness," in
Arabic, on each side. Lisbona and all the other Jews, on hearing
that we were "Ingleez," immediately inquired after Sir Moses and
Lady Montefiore, and sent scores of salaams and compliments to
them to be delivered without fail.

Then we went to a much smaller house belonging to a Christian
merchant, M. Freije, a rich and excellent man, with a lovely wife,
handsomely dressed, and wearing a pretty *soufah*, the same head-
dress as that worn by the Maronite women of the Lebanon, but
still handsomer; she had about 3000 bits of gold fastened to it.
She was busy superintending her household affairs, mounted on the
pattens, ten inches high, worn by every Damascus lady; but finding
us curious in pretty things, she kindly went to her coffers and
brought out several splendid dresses and velvet jackets embroidered
in gold—the embroidery on one jacket alone had cost 12*l.*; she also
showed us quantities of antique silver vases, zarfs, &c., and exquisite egg-shell and Persian china. Their house was being newly
ornamented—not painted, but an inlay of jet-black marble upon

white; it had rather a sombre appearance, although beautifully done, and was very much mixed with mirror and gilding—the present taste at Damascus, but which does not, I think, harmonise well with marbles. Then we went to see some Mooslims in a beautiful house, known to many travellers from its having been the hotel for some few years; the rooms were splendidly decorated with marble mosaic and incrustation of gilding, and the very large court was made lovely, like another of the houses we had seen, with several small *jets d'eau*, besides the large fountain, and a variety of fruit-trees and beds of flowers festooned together with thick wreaths of *convolvulus major*; the divans and hangings in the different rooms were all of the rich Damascus brocaded silk, some of them embroidered with gold, and the doors of the rooms were handsomely inlaid with mother-of-pearl.

An immensity of screaming to the unveiled women to get out of the way ensued on our appearance at the door; however, Mr. Robson being disposed of and imprisoned in one of the rooms, we were admitted, and found the lady of the house and a beautiful daughter of fifteen, both enormously fat, attired only in gowns and loose trousers of thin pink muslin, through which their stout brown limbs did look remarkably odd; they were at breakfast, and would take no refusal but that we must sit down too; so we were placed on little stools round the low *koorse*, or table, on which the tray was placed, and took a few mouthfuls of the fruits, the pilafs looking too greasy to be pleasant for one's fingers.

We spent a good deal of time in the bazaars, wishing to buy many things as specimens of Damascus manufacture, and I never tired, mentally, of watching the endless variety of faces, figures, costumes, and objects in the long, long alleys; then, too, the purchase of each article took as much time as buying a house full of things at home would have taken. I often wished one's home friends could have had Prince Cheri's telescope to see us, in our English dresses, sitting duly doubled up beside the well-turbaned, richly-dressed merchant, on his little counter, in solemn conclave over the price of a silk dress or a pot of confiture, or refreshing ourselves after the fatigue of each purchase with a saucer of pink ice and a cup of delicious coffee.

Most of the dresses made and sold at Damascus are of cotton, with the pattern thrown up in silk; many of the patterns are Oriental, but some of the prettiest are European,—these are about 2*l.* 5*s.* the dress; those of unmixed silk reach to any price, and are all of them costly; some are beautiful things, especially those which, like the scarfs, have silver thread woven in one way and gold thread the other. They make some good woollen articles, besides an immense variety of coarse stuffs of camel's and goat's-hair.

Many of the bazaars are lofty stone buildings, handsomely vaulted; some, less modern and less commodious, are more picturesque, as the Greek Bazaar; but the most interesting of all are the Shoe Bazaar, the Goldsmiths', and the Carpenters' Bazaar, in all of which ancient columns, half obscured by the booths, and beautiful vistas of arches, meet the eye at every step. The finest building in the bazaars is the Khan As'ad,—a model of that graceful, simple energy of style which is the best characteristic of the pure Saracenic architecture. The interior is a square of three domes around a large and lofty central dome, supported on square piers; these domes are pierced with windows, and the whole building is of alternate rows of black and white marble—ornament enough in itself. The goods of the merchants are ranged on the marble floor round the sides of the square, and a large fountain occupies the centre Nothing can be a finer study for an artist than the endless variety of bright-coloured costumes and wares grouped on the ground, contrasted with the grave severity of the black and white bands, while the slanting lines of sunshine fall in dazzling rays athwart the dark shadows of the pillars and recesses under the nine domes. The Khan is entered by a splendid doorway, as fine a specimen as can be found of the rich fretwork and interlacings, slender columns and mosaics, for which Saracenic architecture has no rival. This Khan is modern, but there is nothing of pure Saracenic more beautiful in Damascus.

Of course the Great Mosque of the Khalif Wālcd—once the Christian cathedral of the city—is the most interesting and beautiful of all; it is extremely difficult to see, as no Christian foot is allowed to cross the threshold, and they are very jealous of Christians even looking in; it would therefore be quite incomprehensible without Mr. Porter's plan, connecting the court of cloisters with the colonnades hidden in the bazaars. A hasty glimpse in passing by the outer gates is all the view one can obtain of the inside; of the outside, likewise, only a few fragments are visible, but these are beautiful. The upper part of a large gateway can be seen from the roof of one of the bazaars, which is delicately executed and in better taste, because not overloaded, than any of the work on the Temple of Jupiter at Baalbek; from another roof the capitals of several columns can be seen: they are in the purest and loveliest style of Greco-Roman art. Peeping in through some gates one can see the noble cloistered quadrangle, surrounded by Corinthian columns, and an exquisite fountain in Saracenic style in the centre; the gates themselves are of brass of very good workmanship, still bearing the figure of the sacramental chalice, now placed amid Arabic inscriptions, the additions of later years! The head of St. John the Baptist is believed to be really still in existence in the crypt of this church. May the day come—and that soon—when, in both Santa Sophia at Constantinople and in this Church of St. John at Damascus the worship of Christ shall be re-established, to endure throughout all generations, when the mists and veils that now darken the hearts of both Jew and Gentile shall have been torn away! For two thousand years the inscription (in Greek) on this portal has announced that " Thy kingdom, O Christ, is an everlasting kingdom, and Thy dominion endureth throughout all generations!" The Arabs believe that the time is at hand when Christianity will be proclaimed throughout the land, and Christian governors rule there; and we, too, look forward to the time when the Lord shall have "made bare His holy arm in the eyes of all the nations; and all the ends of the earth shall see the salvation of our God." *

Standing on that roof with these thoughts in one's mind, there was nothing more beautiful in our eyes than to look down at the crowded bazaar beneath one's feet, and to see, gliding quickly through the crowd of self-satisfied Mooslims, dark, reserved Jews, wild Bedoueen, and savage Kurds—the white cap and simple blue gown of a Sister of Charity. Wherever one went one saw them, generally in couples, hastening along with a basket on the arm containing medicine or food, administered alike to Jew, Turk, Heretic, and Infidel; every one who spoke of them used but words of admiration and respect. One day we went to see their abode, and found ourselves admitted to an elderly, happy-looking, sweet-faced Mother, who told us that they had arrived—six of them—on that day five years in Damascus, without any house having been prepared for them. Slowly and surely, with brave and pure hearts, they had laboured on, and much have they effected in those few years: now they have a well-built but substantial building† for their convent, rough, but clean and neat, containing seventeen sisters, two of whom are Arabs, and a school of about 150 children, besides many day-scholars, including Mooslims and Jewesses, and one Metouaalee. We heard these children read well and intelligently in some religious book, and saw their excellent writing. They were very clean and tidy, and remarkably well-behaved and happy-looking. Their dormitory, with rows of simple mattresses laid on the floor, their kitchens and play-grounds, were all perfectly

* Isaiah lii. 10.　　　　　　　　† Now utterly destroyed.

arranged. Bread, olives, and thin soup was their food, all of which the children learned to prepare. The upper classes were well advanced in French, and embroidered beautifully—an accomplishment which would insure their future support. It is impossible to see a more pleasing and interesting institution; and, for the first time in Damascus, one felt some hope of anything being accomplished towards the Christianising of the people. Well may English people blush, overwhelmed with shame, when we see such self-sacrificing and successful work, and remember that *our* Church has done nothing, absolutely nothing, in Syria.* I have said that the French have established missions and schools throughout the country, but God knows there is work enough and room enough for both to labour,—and where are ours?—a few excellent, hard-working men, sent out by the Presbyterians of Scotland and Ireland, are all that Great Britain has ever contributed to the land that gave birth to St. Paul and the Apostles. If *they* had stopped at home, what would have become of us, and how would the Gentiles have found salvation? Has England no yearning of love for the land of her Saviour? no debt of gratitude to pay back to the country whence her redemption came, and which lies now shrouded in mists of thick darkness? Let us imitate the zeal of our neighbours, and take example by the sagacity and liberality with which their missions are conducted: it is such poor, pitiful work to send a man, single-handed, here, and another there, and bid *them* "convert the land," while experience has indeed taught how little (or rather nothing) the most devoted efforts can thus accomplish here. If anything is ever to be effected, it must be by an organised body, whose labours may be directed simultaneously to the wants of body as well as soul—feeding, clothing, as well as teaching and civilising the natives; thus, and thus alone, may we, with God's blessing, look for some results.

The English Consul, Mr. Brant, from whom, as old friends, we received the kindest possible attentions, lives in a beautiful house of the old Damascus style, in the Mooslim quarter; the same house has been occupied for many years as the English Consulate, and

* In Palestine a mission has been established at Jerusalem for the Jews; but throughout the rest of the land the English are believed to be destitute of religion, and no sign of their worship appears in the length or breadth of the country to contradict the assertion. Even in Beyrout, where Englishmen congregate for commerce, and where numerous English travellers are continually passing and repassing, and where a Consulate (with now a Consul-general) has long been established, there is no clergyman to call them together, and not the slightest thing marks the observance of the Lord's Day, or their remembrance of Him in the land once sanctified by His presence.

has been over and over described; perhaps its chief charm is in the large size of the court and the tank in the middle, besides the remarkable variety of the trees and shrubs planted there—several kinds of acacia, orange, lemon, oleander, Japan medlar, varieties of roses and myrtle (on the perfumed berries of which I made my luncheon), besides a great many other shrubs. The large reception-room is very handsomely inlaid and carved, the cost of which, even many years ago, the Consul said must have been 800*l.*—now that everything is so much dearer, and labour so much more expensive, it would cost twice that sum and be badly done. With all this fine Orientalism around one, it was curious to see English curtains and table-cloths, to hear English music on an English piano, and to eat a thoroughly English dinner two thousand miles away from home. These things have a value we cannot understand until we have been out of England for a good long time: and I confess I was rather surprised to find how much I too enjoyed them.

One special pleasure Mr. Brant was so kind as to obtain for us was the permission to visit the renowned Abd-el-Käder,* and we went to his house one day, accompanied by Mr. and Mrs. Brant. We were taken first into the hareem, where Mrs. Brant interpreted in Turkish, which the first lady of the hareem speaks. She was sitting alone in a grand reception-room on a cotton quilt, with a dress of thick wadded quilting, and loads of white muslin folded round her head—the only handsome thing she wore was a gold tissue scarf round her waist. She was old, stout, and very ugly—but it is said that her husband has a great respect and regard for her, and that, although he consoles himself for the decay of her charms by those of many others, he always treats her with much affection, telling her his plans and consulting her about what he does: perhaps her being an Algerian Bedoueen, like himself, is an unfading charm in his eyes. She was suffering much from rheumatism, and said Damascus was a dreadful place, it was so cold nearly all the year. The younger females remove into the country to some of his gardens in the summer, but this one remains in the city. Her son, a boy of twelve years old, came in and sat on his heels beside her; she seemed very fond and proud of him, appealing to him about his father, of whom he spoke simply as "Abd-el-Käder:" we were told that they drop the expression of relationship in the case of a very distinguished person. The room was an odd jumble—the Damascene form and fountain furnished with French hangings, and filled with French china and ornaments: so, indeed, is the whole palace, and nothing can be brighter, gayer, or in worse

* Which means, "Servant of the Powerful One."

taste. The Damascene patterns, so pretty and so suitable in their place, are spoiled by the mixture, and utterly absurd are the French daubs of European ideas misapplied upon the Oriental walls; for instance, the lower part of the walls of one room, which would have been naturally a beautiful inlay of marble mosaic harmonising with the marble floor, was here replaced by painted views of Buddhists' pagodas, peopled with French shepherdesses and marquises, placed in the same accurate perspective as appears on the famous willow-leaf plate of long memory. Abd-el-Kāder is greatly, and naturally, blamed by his Algerian followers for having so entirely discarded the Bedoueen in himself, and above all for wearing the dress of a Damascene merchant; it may be urged that it is very fine to see him contented and making the best of his exile, and that it is wiser to "do in Rome as Romans do," but it does seem strange that he should carry the signs and characteristics of his long French imprisonment about with him, and thrust it upon the Orientalism with which he is surrounded, and which is natural to him. However, we understood that France is not a very palatable subject of conversation in the house, and of course we did not allude to it in any way.

The old wife appeared to keep up no kind of ceremony or etiquette, though she is said to be a severe and rigid matron over the younger wives; her slaves were all negresses, dressed in a single garment of pink cotton, and each had a nose-ring with one turquoise passed through the wide flat nostril, looking like a forget-me-not dropped on a bank of black mud; they stood at the lower end of the room, below the divan, chatting among themselves and laughing at our conversation, while they finished the sweetmeats we had left uneaten. We went into other rooms to see some younger wives of the Chief, and those of his sons—one of whom was extremely pretty, like a tiny wax doll, with pink cheeks, coral lips, black hair, and eyes that were half closed over by magnificent eyelashes, sweeping the cheek. It is said that he buys a new wife every quarter, and that he once replied to an English gentleman at Broussa, who asked him why he had so many wives, that he did not know how he could better expend *French* money than on such frivolous luxuries!* They are chiefly Circassians, but all those whom we saw were the smallest, most delicately-made little creatures possible.

After taking leave of the hareem we joined the gentlemen of our party in a marble-floored hall, daubed round with French figures, and the comfortable Oriental divan exchanged for hard French

* He has an income of 4000*l.* a year allowed him by the French.

P

sofas, on one of which Abd-el-Kader was sitting in European fashion. He came forward to meet us, and we were greatly struck with his appearance: he has a tall, majestic figure, fair skin, grey hair—that once was black—a long white beard, a forehead and keen piercing eye which could nowhere be passed unnoticed. I never saw more intellect marked in the one, nor a more truly eagle expression in the other,—as one of our party afterwards described him: " His every look is that of a prince, born and accustomed to command, acting upon promptly-formed judgment—in one word, a *Leader*." Abd-el-Kader is a man of much learning; he has written four large and profound treatises on Controversy and Philosophy; and he himself gives the daily theological lecture in the Great College at Damascus. His court is crowded every day and all day with persons soliciting audience of him, so that it is difficult to find him for even a moment at leisure. It is said that his Algerian followers are daily, but secretly, increasing round him, and that the last acts of his history are by no means played out; indeed a noble incident of that life has occurred since the above was written. England and France will ever remember his conduct during the Syrian massacres in the spring of 1860; it was not love for France, but the humanity of his enlightened mind and the fervent respect which he felt in his heart for the defenceless Sisters of Charity, which made him sally forth to their rescue, at the head of his own wild followers; nor would he have been a whit less forward to aid and support the subjects of England if the firm high character and unflinching conduct of the British Consul had not been protection and defence enough in itself.

Abd-el-Kader is regarded as a sovereign and respected as a man of sanctity by all Mooslims; therefore, when visiting Jerusalem some time ago, he was assigned a small suite of rooms in the mosque of the Moghrebins, a very holy place. One day when the British Consul was paying a visit to the Pacha of Jerusalem Abd-el-Kader was announced: the Pacha went to the door to meet him, and bowed down to the ground before him; he stayed but a very few minutes, when the Pacha accompanied him to the threshold, and there again prostrating himself to the very floor, he kissed the hem of his garment, which Abd-el-Kader did not withdraw, but, lifting up his hand, he stood there and addressed the Pacha in some such words as these: " I call upon you, oh Pacha! to remember what a responsible and important position you occupy; never forget how great is your duty, and how immense an account will one day be required of you for all the power bestowed upon you; fail not in any particular of your manifold duties; remember to give alms to the poor, to do justice to the widow, and to succour the oppressed "— the Pacha standing the whole time humbly before him, with folded hands and downcast eyes, in the attitude of a slave. Considering the high rank of the Pacha of Jerusalem, this scene was a very curious one.

CHAPTER XV.

THE QUEEN OF THE DESERT.

" The hue of youth upon a brow of woe,
    Which men called old two thousand years ago!
    Match me such marvel, save in Eastern clime—
    A rose-red city,—half as old as Time ! "

BURGON.

PART L—THE JOURNEY.

THE world-famous ruins of Palmyra are naturally a common
subject of conversation at Damascus, and although we had never
entertained a serious thought of reaching them, believing it to be
quite out of our power, we made many inquiries respecting them
from the Consul and other people; and one day Mr. Robson, the
excellent missionary, and his wife, showed us a portfolio of drawings,
conveying so grand an idea of the magnificence and glorious beauty
of the ruins, that we were seized with the most intense desire to see
them for ourselves: however, the more we asked about the journey
the more entirely impossible it seemed for us to accomplish it; the
fatigue and expense combined made it out of the question.

Now there happened to be some other travellers staying in the
hôtel, who were also very anxious to go to Palmyra, and among
them, happily for us, the famous artist, M. Carl Haag, to whom we
recounted the beauty of the drawings we had seen, and he too went
to see them next day; he came back still more enthusiastic about
the original objects than we had been. "If I am a ruined man all
my life, or if I walk there in Bedoueen sandals, I *must* go to
Palmyra!" he kept repeating all that evening. So we all agreed to
see whether anything could be managed for us, and the following
day Mr. and Mrs. Robson took us to see the Sheikh of the Anazeh,
who makes all the arrangements whenever any one does go to
Palmyra.

It must be explained that the fatigue of this expedition arises from the fact that no one has been allowed for many years to remain at the ruins more than twenty-four hours; twenty is the usual time. Of course you must be almost superhumanly strong to make the long journey there and back, fifty hours of camel-riding, and not require those twenty hours for sleep or rest,—while, as the ruins are three miles in extent, no one could take more than a glance at the principal objects, even if ten hours were spent in traversing them; and as the fear of Bedoueen *ghuzoos*, and the want of water, necessitate riding that part of the journey nearest to Palmyra at a stretch of twenty-four hours without stop or stay, both going and returning, few persons like to undertake it. Then the fee given to the tribe for allowing travellers to go there with safe conduct is usually 30*l*. each. We came, however, at a fortunate moment; the Anazeh tribe were encamped close round the ruins, and there was nothing to fear when once we had reached them. The Sheikh was im- mensely impressed with M. Haag's eagerness, and with the con- viction that all the world would· soon know from his drawings what a glorious place Palmyra is; and the Anazehs really love and value the ruins. And so, to cut a long story short, after many days spent in consulting and debating, with various pros and cons, he engaged to let us stay five whole days; and, if all the party in the hotel joined together, at the price of 15*l*. a head, he engaged to choose good dromedaries for us (on which *all* one's comfort, and therefore strength, depend), for which we paid 2*l*. each extra. It was also a golden opportunity of seeing a real true Bedoueen tribe in the desert, and we were promised to go among them as the Sheikh's guests, and live upon camel's milk and flesh, &c.

So, to our own infinite astonishment, as well as pleasure, it was really all settled: two days were allowed us in which to make arrangements for our departure on Friday, the 7th October, after the mosque prayers. Our little dog was consigned to the care of the cook, with the baggage, in which all unnecessary ornaments were safely deposited, that no sparkle of gold might tempt the passing Arab; and we spent the morning stuffing our saddle-bags with a change or two of linen, drawing materials, and one book each. Stout cotton dresses were put on instead of riding-habits, the provisions were stowed in the dragoman's saddle-bags, and we started on foot for the Sheikh's house, outside one of the gates of the city—the Bab Tuma. The Sheikh was ready, in his scarlet cloak and mash'lah, and having hooded his falcon—an indispensable companion—he took us to the court, where, indeed, was a scene of Babelar con- fusion. Eleven dromedaries were on their knees, all roaring, and growling, and groaning, as if they were being killed, after the manner of dromedaries the moment they are requested to kneel, and the whole time they are kneeling; all the camel-drivers and armed escort rushing about screaming and shouting—flocks of poultry at one side shrieking, gabbling, and cackling—pet gazelles were hiding in a corner—and a number of beautiful Arab mares were standing transfixed with astonishment at the unwonted crowd and noise. Our minds were soon concentrated upon the art of mounting, which is an ordeal for a novice, and on the first success of which the Arab prophecies whether you will make a good rider or not, and be worthy of his beloved beast. A couple of men held down each dromedary by standing on its fore-knees, while the Sheikh himself lifted us ladies, each with a sort of flying jump, into the middle of the seat, hastily settling our shawls, &c.; and while directions were shouted on all sides, with such earnest vociferation that it was impossible to understand one syllable of them except to "hold fast!" up jumped the animal, raising his hind legs first, when you go nearly over his nose, then his forelegs, jerking you as unexpectedly backwards, against the hinder pommel of your saddle, and affording you a knock on your spine that you remember against all future occasions.

By four o'clock we had all streamed in procession out of the gate—a goodly cavalcade of eleven dromedaries, besides the Argeels, their owners, who always accompany the camel, sometimes on foot, sometimes mounted behind the riders. The dromedaries carried our party, including the servants, the Sheikh, and the escort of armed Bedoueens, Anazehs and others—thirteen men in all; while several Damascus acquaintances accompanied us for a mile or two, after the kindly Arab fashion of leave-taking. Such a noise as we made altogether, for the Bedoueens had a darabouka (a drum) to which they sang lustily, shouting their good-byes on all sides, the whole way through the delightful gardens and green lanes that encompass the city! In two hours and a half we reached the village of Doumah, which stands on the edge of the gardens: it was all alive with men and women gathering the grapes, and spreading them out so thickly on the ground to dry into raisins, that we took them for red carpets; while many were crowding round the fires, by the aid of which they were turning the sweet juice into *dibs*—a luscious sweet in which the Arabs delight, and which is so often mentioned in the Bible, rendered, in our translation, honey. From this we passed out upon the great plain, and presently met the Baghdad postman galloping in at the end of his nine days' journey.

The sun went down at a little before seven; then suddenly the Sheikh uttered a command, and down went all the camels. "This is our halting place for the night," said he. "What, here—on the road? Shall we not go a little on one side and look for some shelter?" "Oh, no," said the Sheikh, "this is the best, for here we can see who comes, and we have to look out for robbers!" It did look astonishingly bare and strange for a night's rest, but in a few moments the dragomans had arranged our carpets, thick-wadded coverlids, cloaks, &c.; the fire, made of the dry thorns which grew all around us, was quickly lighted, and the kettle was boiling; cold fowl and hot tea were presented; then the camels were arranged, lying down in an external circle, the falcon unhooded and placed upon his perch, the saddle-frames built up into a wall, and our saddle-bags placed under our heads—the resolution was carried, *nemine contradicente*, that the Desert was both cheerful and comfortable—and before eight o'clock nearly all the party were giving loud and vigorous tokens of a profound sleep. My sister and I, however, were too new to sleeping *à la belle étoile*, and on so very hard a couch as that rocky road, to find rest easily; and we amused ourselves watching one of the camels, who, every now and then, would get up and hobble about with his one leg tied up close under him, till, finding he could gain but little by such limping amusement, he would lie down again and snore. Twice the practised ear of Sheikh Miguel gave the alarm of thieves, and prevented their approach.

Amongst the Bedoueens stealing on a large scale, involving danger and risk—such as coming by night into an encampment and silently making away with the camels—is not considered disgraceful; but all stealing from one another's tents without danger is considered entirely mean and bad; so bad that the punishment is cutting off the hand. The greatest penalty for grave crimes is beheading with a sword; for all lesser offences, such as stealing a camel, &c., branding with a hot iron is the usual punishment. False accusations are always punished by the infliction of whatever penalty would have been awarded to the accused had he been proved guilty.

The Bedoueens can be plentifully cool in their naïve impudence. Our good Sheikh had a little black negro boy—a slave—with him, whom he was taking to the tribe, thinking the winter in Damascus too cold for him; he had lately been ill, and the kind-hearted Sheikh got up early in the night, and taking off a cloak lined with fur, that he had to sleep on, wrapped it round the child; in the morning it was found that one of the Bedoueens had quietly appropriated it for himself as soon as the Sheikh had gone to sleep again. Of course this Bedoueen was not an Anazeh; our escort was purposely composed of Bedoueens of several of the minor tribes and villagers inhabiting this Desert, as the best security for our protection.

A few words about our friend Sheikh Miguel * may not be uninteresting. His eldest brother, Muhammad, is the head sheikh of the Mizrâb, one branch of the Sab'a, a powerful division of the Anazehs; he is himself of equal rank with his brother, but Muhammad always remains with the tribe, while Sheikh Miguel does all their business with the Government, and escorts travellers, for which purpose he lives part of the year in Damascus. He is like *all true* Bedoueens, a small man, about five feet three inches in height, slightly made, but erect, very graceful in all his motions, and with a light, easy step. His face is really beautiful—of a perfect oval; a long aquiline nose, delicately-formed mouth, small regular teeth of dazzling whiteness, and large black eyes that could be soft and sweet as any woman's, or flash with a fierce, wild eagle glance that really made one start. He wore a short black beard, and long crisp ringlets under his kefiyeh, which was of the very finest and brightest Damascus silk, bound round his head with the pretty *akgâl*—a double wreath of camel's hair tied and tasselled with coloured silks. His dress was a *kumbaz*, or long tight gown of striped and flowered silk, with wide, open sleeves hanging down to the knee; then his sheikh's cloak or pelisse of bright scarlet cloth bound with black braid, and three bars of broad black braid across the chest,—this, with the scarlet leather boots, worn over stockingless feet, and reaching to the knee, is the distinguishing dress of the Sheikh. Over all came a mash'lah †—a shapeless but very comfortable cloak—sometimes of thin white cloth, edged with colour, sometimes of coarse, thick brown and white camel's-hair cloth, sometimes of the same material in black, violet, or brown, with a handsome pattern in gold thread woven in upon the shoulders—this latter kind comes from Mekka, and are costly, but very beautiful. A silk scarf wound many times round the waist, into which a couple of revolvers and a big knife were stuck, and a sword hung round the neck by a crimson cord, completed his costume. As to his manners, the " best-bred " English gentleman is not more polished than he, and the Bedoueen chief joins an easy chivalrous grace to his quiet dignified demeanour, which has a double charm. From the moment we left Damascus and became his "charge" till we re-entered the city his kindness and thoughtful attention never ceased—morning, noon, and night,

* Pronounced Midgewell.   † *Mash'lah* means *to strip off.*

travelling or stationary, whatever we might be doing, alone or surrounded with Arabs, he had an eye and an ear always ready for
every want of ours; whatever little difficulty might arise, the
Sheikh was sure to be at hand to help one out of it. His conversation—of course through an interpreter—was always full of interest,
and more might be learned from him, I imagine, than from any one
of the ancient histories of the great Arab tribes, of which so little is
known. He and his brothers had all been taught reading and
writing, but he told us, as people say of vaccination, " they only
took with me." His Bedoueens and the escort addressed him
occasionally with "O Sheikh!" but most often it was "O Miguel!"
and they' talked and joked with him with a freedom that was sometimes rather annoying to us, for they never hesitated to interrupt
any of our conversations with him whenever they had a remark to
make. At home in their tents they observe some etiquette; when
the sheikh enters every person rises, and stands till he bids them
be seated, and they do not permit him, when encamped, to do any
menial work; but out in the plain a sheikh would be greatly
despised who made any difference between himself and his people,
or did not attend to his own camel, and eat the same food as the
others. The office of sheikh is entirely hereditary; but a very bad
or insane heir is set aside, and either the next of blood, or some one
remarkably distinguished by his prowess, is elected in his place.

The Sheikh awoke us all at sunrise on the following morning; our
toilettes, which consisted chiefly of shaking ourselves, were soon performed, and our breakfast of fowl, bread, and tea was likewise
quickly despatched. We were all mounted and away by seven
o'clock, and soon came to some ruins of an extensive khan and a
tower, whence we turned up the low pass of the Anti-Lebanon
mountains, called the Boghaz—or passage—rather slippery and
steep for camels. Their movements, either in ascending or descending, are very unpleasant to the rider: they make each step like
a stumble, jerking up or down upon it, shaking you all through,
and helping you to arrive at the camel's own opinion when he was
asked which was best for him to go, up hill or down, and he
answered, "May the curse of Allah light on both; for the flat plain
is the only place fit for a beast like me!" We here met a great
number of donkeys with long planks of timber lashed to their sides;
and as they dragged these loads over the rocky ground the roaring
noise they made was perfectly astonishing, and much alarmed the
dromedaries, who are very timid creatures, and are therefore very
unpleasant to ride past unusual sights or sounds, or in towns at
night. We passed the ruins of a temple, four columns and a

sarcophagus, and of some wells excavated in the rock with much care.

Descending on the other side we were *in' the Desert*, here narrowed between mountains to a valley of, we were told, ten miles wide. I need not say that our eyes were not of the smallest use in judging of any distance in the Desert; the atmosphere is so clear and so heated that objects at many miles off may appear quite close to you, and it is an ever-recurring marvel why you go on hours and hours and never seem to approach any nearer to the objects you have been looking at all the time. Another deception, which is frequently puzzling, is the magnifying of distant objects by the heat, so that a few tamarisk bushes look like a grove of trees, a horse seems a tall camel, and a camel looks like a walking tower. The Sheikh had some business to transact at a large khan which had for some two hours seemed under our feet, called Kuteifeh, and we had therefore the advantage of an hour and a half's rest on our carpets in the inner court; he despatched his business and said his prayers in the mosque, while we ate our luncheon, which was a sumptuous one, for we had nice cool oranges and fine raisins bought in the khan. Senân Pacha built this khan about three centuries ago, a handsome, solid building, with rows of fine arches; some houses have gathered round it into a small village, and there are gardens with pleasant trees, under whose shade we passed in leaving the place. Our course lay now nearly due east, and we soon crossed the track to Aleppo and Homs, which here turns off to the north. Our camels became very troublesome this afternoon, stopping to browse on certain aromatic plants which appeared on the plain, and as you have no particular bridle, and camels are remarkably self-willed, and reluctant to take advice in a language they don't understand, you have to sit still and bear it; but it is a very odd sensation when their heads disappear entirely under their bodies and their long forelegs go walking on over their own heads! After which they suddenly pull up these same heads, and look round in your face with such a meek expression of injured innocence, you are obliged to say, "All right, good drom, only do go on." The drivers make them go on capitally, either by requesting them to do so in the politest Arabic, or by enforcing their wishes with the bakourah (a hooked stick), as they sit behind you; but when the driver is walking your puny efforts of persuasion are ludicrously unsuccessful: mine were remarkably so, for my heel did not quite reach the neck of the beast, a good kick upon which tells him he is to quicken his pace, and no infliction of my bakourah ever had the faintest effect upon his mind or legs; indeed at last it became rather a favourite joke among the Argeels to see the "Little Sitt" beating on her camel with impotent fury. I had the most charming dromedary, a dear beast, whose sweetness was described in her name, "Helweh" (which means *sweet*),—she had the easiest, most elastic step, and the most delightful trot in the world; but to counterbalance Helweh's charms, my driver was a horrid old man, who would not walk much, and therefore was always sitting behind me and continually going to sleep, and whenever he did so his dirty head would drop on my shoulder, and get very roughly shaken off. He was besides the most garrulous old gentleman, and considered his conversation worth hearing; so whenever I was speaking to any one of the party, or the interpreter was telling anything particularly interesting, this old man elevated his hoarse voice and began a speech to another of his brethren, always choosing the farthest off, that he might shout the louder. One day I was so angry that I knocked him over the head with my bakourah, and told him to "hold his tongue," having learned to make the request in Arabic on purpose. I was rather ashamed of myself, but the other Argeels went into fits of laughter for ever so long, and afterwards they used often to inquire why I did not try him again, with many witticisms about his old head that I did not understand.

My sister's first dromedary was a very spirited, frisky creature, upon seeing which the kind Sheikh dismounted and put her on his own, a gentle black animal, called Simri (black), of which she became very fond, and she had a good, well-behaved young driver, who used to teach her the names of the mountains and the plants, &c., and, when she had repeated her lesson correctly, would call to all the others to come and hear the results of his good teaching. Occasionally she shared her luncheon with him, generally dry bread with a few raisins, and sometimes provided herself with lumps of sugar for him, and once, thinking to give him a treat, she gave him a stick of chocolate, all of which he received with true Arab politeness, and said "Taïb, taïb, kattar-herak,"* but he secretly imparted to the interpreter afterwards that she had given him some horrible stuff made of black earth!—this was the chocolate. Whenever we gave them anything they always divided it among the whole set, and seemed grateful and pleased. This is one of the delights of the Bedoueen—the *true* Bedoueen—not only that you know you may trust them, and that they are invariably respectful and polite, but that they seemed pleased and really grateful for little kindnesses. The Syrian seldom looks pleased, and scarcely ever says "kattar-herak."

* "Good, good, thank you."

The falcon-bearer was a true Anazeh, and he always had a good-natured word and an inquiry as to how we felt whenever either of us came near him; he approved of us mightily because we took to the dromedaries like " ducks to the water," and enjoyed it all from beginning to end. I can well understand the various accounts given by travellers of dromedary-riding: the fact is that your liking it depends wholly upon two things—first, the natural pace of your animal—and they all differ in this, more almost than horses; and secondly, the way in which your saddle is settled. The shedâd, the substruction of your seat, is simply an inverted V of wood, very smoothly made, with a stout back-bone along the top, at each end of which is placed a pommel about a foot high; fastened to the pommels over the top of the backbone is an open square frame, stuffed with camel's or goat's-hair—this forms your seat; across this, hanging down on each side, you throw first your saddle-bag, then a carpet, a wadded quilt, two or three cloaks and shawls, and, in short, as many things as you can heap up—the more the better, since these coverings make your saddle by day and your bed by night. You sit in the middle of the seat with a leg on each side of the front pommel, varying your position according to your pleasure, and you must lean a little forward always, or your back would rub against the hinder pommel. The saddle-bags are two handsome pouches of dark brown camel's-hair, adorned with rows of tassels of all manner of bright colours, little tufts of ostrich-feathers sewn on here and there, to draw off the " Evil Eye " from the good things within, and twelve or more long cords hanging from them nearly to the ground, ending in gay-coloured tassels—these keep up a continual swaying when the camel walks, and when he trots they have a very funny appearance.

We had plenty to look at on this our first day in the Desert. The mountains on each side were perfectly barren, but they glowed with fine colours; the ground was riddled with the holes of jerboas and rats, whom we sometimes saw running off into safety, and towards evening several pretty gazelles were seen dancing about in the thorns, and among the *hashish-el-kali* which covered the ground: this is the plant from the ashes of which they make potash for soap—the Damascus and Jerusalem soap being composed only of this stuff mixed with olive oil; it is the only trade the Desert Arabs carry on with the city, and the smoke from their fires for burning it is seen curling up in a dozen different directions at once: it is a dry, thorny, ugly-looking plant. We passed also a very large salt-marsh, glistening and sparkling in the sun as if it was a lake; then came the village of Jerood, and after 10½ hours of riding, independently of our rest at Kuteifch, we came upon the pretty village of Atny, where there was a stream and a good many trees. We got over a low wall into a small enclosure, where our night encampment afforded unlimited amusement to the villagers until quite late; and we spent a pleasant evening, chatting with the Sheikh over our dinner. Some time after a party of ten well-armed men mounted on horseback arrived, whose appearance the Sheikh did not much like; and so, to ensure their not attacking us on the morrow, he engaged them as guards extraordinary from the dangers of the road to Karyetĕen. This was not a pleasant resting-place for light sleepers. The jackals prowled round our little enclosure with the most horrible howls and cries; once or twice they leaped over the wall, and I had to throw stones at them to make them go away, and three times there came quite close to us the horrid yelling laugh of a hyena, which I confess made me feel a little queer.

We had now, too, arrived under the desert-dew, which fell this night so heavily upon us that in the morning the thick shawls above our coverlids were wet through, and I wrung a great cupful of water out of a bit of my dress that had unwarily escaped covering in the night. But the curious thing about this desert-dew is that no one ever catches cold from it; the Bedoueens never have rheumatism or coughs from it, and the most delicate travellers encounter it without harm. One of our party had a very weak chest and throat, my sister was very liable to cold, and I to fever, yet we slept exposed to the heaviest dews for fifteen successive nights without taking any remarkable precautions, and we never found the slightest evil result from it.

We started soon after sunrise, our ten new friends accompanying us, making a gay scene in the Desert, as they scoured the plain, *ventre à terre*, with their white mash'lahs and gaudy kefiyehs streaming in the wind behind them, pursuing one another in mimic warfare, then suddenly wheeling round, pursuer becoming pursued, and sweeping about in quickly changing circles, uttering their war-cries, and poising their long bamboo lances, as if to throw them at their enemies, quivering from end to end. These lances are twelve feet long, and are ornamented with bunches of black ostrich feathers at the junction of the bamboo with the long steel point; at the other end is an iron spike, used for planting the lance in the ground when the bearer is dismounted. The horses carry much more trappings than the camels, and their gay-coloured tassels sweep the ground as they gallop along, casting up clouds of sand in the air. They continued this for about a couple of hours, and then, getting tired of the play, galloped on before us, promising to send back a messenger if they found any dangers on the road. The Sheikh had judged rightly, however, and it was fortunate he had engaged them as allies; for on our return we found they had left us to rob three laden mules, and the next day they took possession of the English mail to Baghdad, kept the letters for a time, and appropriated a large portion of Government treasure.

It was terribly hot this morning, and we all suffered a good deal from the burning glare on the barren ground. It was amusing to see how by various degrees, sooner or later, each of us began to leave off looking much about, and gradually retired into his or her kefiyeh, becoming, as the heat increased, more and more transformed into the semblance of mummies; indeed our appearance would have been rather amusing in Hyde Park. I had a silk shawl folded thickly above my dress over my shoulders, then the white mash'lah, underneath a very thick, grey tweed cloak with a large hood, and our huge felt hats were covered with some yards of muslin hanging down, kefiyeh fashion, all round, the front part of which could be folded over the face; and in the middle of the day I always bound a blue veil several times over my lips and nose, as the only means of preserving them from blistering. Once or twice we tried to read —easy enough with the dromedary's even step—but the glare was so dazzling on the white page that we always gave it up after a few minutes. We put up two hares, and on the Sheikh shooting one we dismounted in the narrow shade of a low wall of what was once a large khan, called El-Kharab—the ruin—and made some coffee while the hare was being roasted whole. Feasting merrily upon its bones, which we handled Arab-fashion, we rode on after nearly an hour's delay—an hour that seems very short when it is thus snatched in the middle of a long day's ride for rest; but we forgot all our fatigues in the enchantment of the scene around us. The whole Desert gradually changed into a pale, sweet blue, looking so like the sea one almost thought it must be water; then the mountains, with their ever-varying crags, became dressed in their evening hues of brightest lilac, purple, and violet, tipped with gold, and the deep blue of the sky paled, as streaks of pink and crimson stole over its length and breadth. M. Haag went into raptures, and the Argeels' hearts were evidently softened, for, as the sun sank, they permitted us the pleasure of a delightful trot in the cool evening air, though they had complained bitterly in the morning, when we wanted to refresh ourselves under the burning sun, that we should "certainly kill the camels," and that we "might as well be a set of postmen at the rate we wanted to go!" The quick trot of a good dromedary is a delightfully easy, pleasant pace, and a great relief after some hours of the monotonous long swing of the walking-pace.

The first sight of Karyeteen was very pretty: the western sunbeams showing the bright specks of the white houses, which appeared to be lying under the mountain side, though in reality a long way from them. In the distance the faint blue summits of the mountains over Tadmor, our much-longed-for goal, were eagerly pointed out by the Argeels; for, be it well understood, Palmyra is but the Latin translation for the " Tadmor-in-the-Wilderness "* built by King Solomon (Tadmor and Tamar being the Hebrew for a palm), and no one but the European traveller ever gives it such an appellation; the Romans, indeed, called it Adrianopolis, but Tadmor has ever been in all the Eastern world its sole name, and Tadmor, or Tedmor, it is still called by all the Arabs of the " wilderness " around it.

It was moonlight ere we reached the large village of Karyeteen, and as we skirted the outer walls we heard nothing but the loud cries of numerous jackals. We were a very long time threading its lanes before we arrived at the Sheikh's house and khan—court within court—each one quickly filled with crowds of his relations and dependants, who came out to see us dismount in the outer court, and then pressed round us, trying to touch our faces and finger our clothes, and asking innumerable questions before we reached the large chamber prepared for us. Here, we saw in a moment, the people would be in and out all night; for they were already packing themselves in, in tight rows, to see us eat and sleep; moreover I felt the lively inhabitants of the mats, carpets, and cushions rubbing up their forces for the onslaught, and we therefore quietly escaped to a small terrace on the housetop, where, lifted up above them all, we reposed in perfect silence and quiet after our fourteen hours' journey. Our ten guards of the morning had announced our approach, and the village Sheikh had prepared a banquet for Sheikh Miguel: from our little terrace we looked down to the guest-chamber, where we saw the numerous guests crowding in relays round the enormous *pilaf* of mutton and rice, a bowl of which was sent up to us, with plenty of compliments, from the village Sheikh, on which we made a very good supper.

This Sheikh was a very tall, stout man, large-limbed and large-mouthed; he was wealthy and prosperous; but he looked unhappy and depressed; and Sheikh Miguel soon told us the cause: he had an only son, the delight of his heart, for whom he bought a

* 1 Kings ix. 18.

little black slave as a playmate. The two boys, one day, playing together, got hold of the Sheikh's pistols, and the slave accidentally shot his master's child,—the father, in a transport of blind rage, killed the slave, and was still miserable with grief for his loss.

All Bedoueen sheikhs have their black slaves, for they are the only servants they can have; no Bedoueen of any tribe will hire himself or herself as servant to any one, and however obliging they may be in lending assistance on some special occasion, the idea of rendering it constantly, or as a duty, would be most indignantly rejected by them all. But these black slaves are always kindly treated, and generally become very much attached and faithful to their owners. We used to see Sheikh Miguel giving his little black boy his food with much care, morning and evening; and the interpreter told us that the boy was most affectionately attached to the Sheikh, and that if his master was to forget him and give him nothing to eat, he would neither ask for food nor complain till he starved. They are really valuable servants, and sometimes cost large sums of money: we heard of one in Damascus who was so highly esteemed by her dying mistress that she had left all her children in her entire charge.

The banquet continued long after we had fallen asleep,—so numerous were the guests to welcome the highly respected Anazeh-chief. These entertainments are terrible affairs sometimes to the host, for an Arab invitation includes " you and yours," and your guest, therefore, brings his brother, and his cousin, and his cousin's cousin; and when you have invited a party of ten guests you may have forty or fifty, or, in fact, any number, all arrivals expecting an equal welcome, and, what is more difficult to provide, an equal share in the food.

We were roused from our slumbers at sunrise, but as the escort were not ready to start till nine o'clock, we might have rested longer; they were baking bread, I believe, for their journey, while we stood in the crowd below, baking ourselves in the sun. M. Haag made sketches of the faces around us—some superhumanly ugly, but some remarkably pretty. There was a young son of a neighbouring Sheikh, so pretty and so girlish-looking that we could none of us agree as to whether he was a boy or a girl,—there not being any remarkable difference in the costume at that age; and when I asked him which he was, he blushed every shade of red, and ran away laughing like a mad thing.

This Karyeteen is a large village with a mixed population of Mooslims and Jacobite Christians; the Sheikh's premises enclosing a rather handsome mosque, which seemed ancient, and some well-built houses. There are most copious springs and fountains behind the town, which supply innumerable rivulets and streams in the cultivated ground round the houses; they also fill a circular reservoir, a little lakelet, outside the village, where the caravan camels are all watered, surrounded by wild weeds and flowers. From this luxury of water Karyeteen is believed to be the *Hazar-enan* (village or enclosure of fountains—*enan* answering to the Arabic *'ain*) of Numb. xxxiv. 9, 10, describing the north-east corner* of the "promised land;" and again by Ezekiel (xlvii. 17) in speaking of the territory promised at some future time to the Children of Israel. Here Abraham and Lot probably rested on their way from Haran to the Land of Canaan; and Jacob, too, when he came out of Padan-aram with his wives and his children and all his property, to return to Isaac his father; for the natural highway from Mesopotamia into Syria led by the fountains of Tadmor and Karyeteen.

This was to be our grand day of twenty-four hours' fatigue, and we were all rather put out at our departure being delayed till the sun was high and burning, though not high enough to prevent the view of the long range of blue hills to the south-east from looking lovely as we emerged from the town: such tender and delicate hues one can only see in the Desert. We were now in the Wady-el-Kebeer (the great valley), which we were told was from twenty to thirty miles wide: its termination was to be Tadmor, and we looked eagerly on to the faint blue distance throughout the day Very early in the day the Sheikh pointed to a ruined tower on the plain, and said, "We shall halt there." It seemed quite close to us, but hour after hour we toiled on over the scorched-up, burning, barren ground, where scarce even a thorn was now growing, and we never, never seemed to come any nearer. There was no use in applying to our good Sheikh, for the Bedoueen has no idea of time or distance; and he invariably answered "Two hours—two hours," to everything. Before we understood this it was rather trying to have braced oneself up to hold out the time specified, and

---

* According to Mr. Porter this much disputed "border" is very simply described: the Mediterranean forms its western extremity, thence the only real valley opening into the eastern country is that of El-Husn, which separates the great chain of the Lebanon mountains (here called Mount Hor, probably some local name applied to one of the northernmost peaks) from the Nusairiyeh hills, which end at Antioch; this valley leads directly to Hamah, whence the border came through Zedad and Ziphron to Hazar-enan, "the goings out of it;" these two places are identified by Mr. Porter, with every appearance of probability, as Südüd and Zifroun, villages on the direct track between Hamah and Karyeteen.

then find it might be two, twelve, or any number of hours. It is the same with the Druzes and Syrian fellaheen: "I was born the year so much rain fell;" or, "That happened three years before such a pasha came;" or something of that kind, are their invariable answers; and in Palestine a fellah will tell you, "Oh, my father was quite an old man: he lived in the time of David!"

At length, near sunset, we found ourselves actually close to the tower, and some of us dismounted to examine it, while the dragomans made us a little coffee farther on. This place, El-Khasr, is called the Robbers' Tower, because it is a great place of rendezvous for *ghuzoos*, or plundering parties, and many an unwary traveller has been seized upon here, and dragged within its crumbling walls. Some fine work is still to be seen on the doorways, windows, and ornamental medallions of the picturesque ruin. The stone of the fallen columns seemed composed entirely of fossils, and we picked out some beautiful little shells with our fingers and penknives. Farther on, and in a line with the Robbers' Tower, appeared another, at some distance, still more ruined: the remains of a circular reservoir and of an aqueduct are found between them; the reservoir continuing filled with water for some time after the rainy season, adds another attraction to the Ruined Tower for robbers; our Sheikh therefore kept a sharp look-out while we pledged each other in spiced coffee, and watched our own shadows flying out to endless lengths across the plain, as the sun sank below the horizon. One has no idea of the beauty and poetry of shadows till one goes into the Desert; there I never wearied of watching them, and delighting in the new language they spoke to me.

The moon rose soon after we mounted again, and the little hasty rest had been so refreshing that we more than ever enjoyed the night; the camels keep better together than in the day, and the Argeels indulged in a number of wild songs, for the special encouragement of their creatures. Some of the tunes were pretty, wild, and sad, though monotonous, and the words poetical: the chief burden was in the style of "Go on, oh Camel, my love, my beauty, go on quickly, and the prettiest girls of the village shall come out to meet you; go on, and when you kneel the maidens will feed you with fresh sugar-canes, and stroke you with their soft hands," &c. Then they improvised verses about the riders, which elicited great applause and some amusement; they were chiefly personal descriptions, which we did not, of course, understand, but sometimes we caught allusions to incidents that had happened in the day, or to things we had said in our very meagre Arabic. M. Haug, who dressed like a Bedoueen, and was always full of jokes, was a favourite with them, and the chief songs were about him, with good-natured fun about his continually dropping asleep. The songs were very pleasant when the singers walked, or when you were listening to your neighbour's Argeel, but one soon wearied of the loud voices shouting in your very ears at the full crack of their lungs, when they twisted themselves up by the dromedary's tail, and arrived behind your own *shedad* : moreover, we were sure to lose, in the row they made, exactly the most interesting part of whatever conversation was going on amongst ourselves. And then, whenever one saw two of one's friends engaged in a comfortable chat, that instant one's driver was sure to send his camel rushing up, rudely dividing them, for the better arrangement of their own chorus, and one's apologies for the interruption were all the more supremely ridiculous, because we each knew that none of us had the slightest shadow of control over our own beast.

The singing one day ceased, on their understanding that my sister had a head-ache; but on being told the same thing the next day the dragoman overheard them inquiring from the Sheikh if the Ingleez women " always had *battal*," that is, good for nothing " heads ! " One must converse, if possible, in night travelling, for else it soon becomes difficult to keep awake, and a tumble from a dromedary is not the pleasantest thing possible. We were not quite enough at ease to twist back and lie half behind the pommel as an adept can do, though of course not when your Argeel is mounted behind you; but if one could manage this it would afford a delightful rest, for the camel's long, swinging, perfectly even step is the most sleepifying thing in the world, and at night, when you have not even your own shadow to watch, or if you are going eastwards and cannot see it, it really is the hardest thing to keep awake after a long day's ride.

The dromedary's pace is something under five miles an hour. One is apt to imagine it slow, for the stride is so long that they seem tardy, accustomed as one is to the short, quick step of the horse; but see the quick pace at which the Argeels walk to keep up with them, or, better still, dismount and try, and then see if you don't change your opinion. If one of the party lags behind or dismounts for only a moment, see how tedious the waiting for him again seems; or if you yourself lag a little, how soon your companions disappear into moving specks, and how long you are in overtaking them. Some of the dromedaries, especially those selected for the post, go at a wonderfully quick rate, but their gallop is a very rough pace; they cannot endure much of it, and die when at all overworked. Their owners are indeed most attentive to and careful of them; the camel becomes very quickly attached to a kind master, and they are very fond of these their valuable possessions. We found our dromedaries soon became acquainted with us, and would come when called by name to receive chicken-bones from our hands; sometimes they roused themselves, and made little observations upon us at night, and at Tadmor I woke more than once feeling my camel gently sniffing at my feet. Their proper food is chiefly barley, but on a journey they ought to have balls made of rice and dhourra mixed up with spices. Our men took none of this food with them, expecting to find supplies of it at Tadmor; there was none, however, and except what the poor beasts got in the khans and a few plants by the way, they had nothing whatever to eat, till we returned to Damascus, but the green stalks of the dhourra, which they like, but from which they derive little or no nourishment. Meantime they feed, as the natives say, on their own humps—that is, the humps gradually diminish in size: as long as there is any hump visible the camel can keep on; as soon as it disappears he languishes and dies. Every camel is branded with the mark of his owner and of his tribe, and it sometimes happens an Arab may be travelling among a distant tribe and come upon his own long-lost camel, either stolen or strayed, when the indelible brand proving its original owner, enables him to reclaim it. The most curious thing we heard about the camels and their masters, our interpreter vouched for as a fact, and by no means an uncommon one, that, so acute is the *smell* as well as the eye of a Bedoueen, they will tell, blind-folded, of any track of camels, not only how long since trodden, but even to what tribe the passing camels belonged!

Among the Bedoueens of this Desert the red camels are the commonest and the most esteemed; those of the Nejd (the desert about Baghdad) are generally black. It is of the latter that their tents and ābāych, are made, while the dyed colours are woven into their carpets and hangings, to form the stripes of their ābbahs and mash'lahs. The camel's milk is excellent when fresh and warm, but not when cold; nor is it rich enough to make butter. The flesh of a young camel is as good as beef; it looks coarser, but has no strong taste, and is considered a great delicacy by the Bedoueens.

The night was whiled away in hearing about all these things, and many a Bedoueen tale besides, while the glorious moon rode her course and then waned, and the morning dawn came. It was very cold that night, and we dismounted twice to try and warm ourselves; but in the morning, oh, how broiling hot it was! The low pass which opened into Tadmor itself seemed quite close to us at daylight; but wearily, wearily we journeyed on under the scorching sun till one o'clock. A mirage lent its beautiful deception to amuse us, and for a few moments it was difficult not to believe that we had water to pass before reaching the mountains, which had now swept round to the north-east, across our valley; they deepened into the very darkest violet, while to the left they faded into pale amethyst. Presently the Saracenic Castle above Tadmor became visible, and we all got excited and feverishly eager as the tombs cut in the rocks became more and more easily distinguished; then, as we began to ascend the pass, a few more, built like low towers, stood on the summits of the hill, like grave, silent, patient sentinels, beckoning us on to enter the City of the Dead.

Not all dead, however, for suddenly there dashed up the path towards us some seven or eight men, armed to the teeth, brandishing their long lances, shrieking, and yelling, and shouting, to welcome our good Sheikh Miguel: we had been discerned by scouts on the hill-tops, and they had galloped out to meet us. Thus accompanied we soon reached the finest and best of all the tombs (called by the Arabs the " Bride's Tomb," simply to betoken its great beauty, not because it is supposed by them to have been occupied by any bride), and we dismounted in order to examine it, and to rest a little in its shade while the Sheikh heard all the news of Tadmor. It was very bad news indeed for him, and a grievous disappointment for us all: the famine was so great in the land in consequence of the drought that the Anazehs, knowing nothing of their beloved Sheikh's approach, had broken up their encampment and departed only three days before, going towards Baghdad in search of pasture for their camels. We discussed the possibility of pursuing and remaining a few days with them, but the direction of their track was all uncertain; pasture might or might not have been found in this hollow or in that; and three days' start in the pathless desert made the overtaking them too doubtful and hazardous to attempt. So there was good-bye to all our promised plans, and our hopes of living among the Bedoueens themselves, feasting on camel's meat and milk, and seeing all sorts of Bedoueen games and sports: the Sheikh's new tent, too, which he had promised for our special use, had been carried off to be "seasoned." Altogether the disappointment was very great; but to the Sheikh himself it was much heavier,—he was longing to see his young sons, and he intended to take them back with him for the winter, to give them some education in Damascus: now all was frustrated, or at least deferred to another year.

We bemoaned his disappointment and our own for some time, and then turned to examine the tomb. It is composed of a square tower, thirty feet on each side, and eighty feet in height, divided into four stories; the lowest story has three huge blocks of stone in the centre, lessening in size one above another, through which a flat-headed doorway is cut, with deep mouldings and much ornament; above this is an arched window, the sides of which are formed of human-headed bulls, much resembling the Assyrian type. Under this a recumbent figure, like a swathed mummy, lies on a projecting slab, and a tablet, bearing an inscription in Palmyrene, with a Greek translation, says that it is the tomb of the Elabelos family, with a date of the Seleucidæ era, corresponding to A.D. 102. The chamber on the ground-floor is on each side divided into four compartments, which narrow pyramidally as they ascend; a fluted Corinthian pilaster ornaments each division. These recesses have several stone shelves across them for the reception of bodies embalmed and wrapped in mummy-cloth, of which large quantities lie about; at the end of the chamber opposite to the door there are two rows of fine busts, nine in all, standing on shelves, and other busts on the walls. But the chief beauty inside is the exquisite ceiling, carved in medallions, like that of the peristyle of the Temple of Jupiter at Baalbek, containing busts, birds, and flowers delicately sculptured upon a bright blue ground; they are somewhat broken, but we thought we discerned the eagle with Ganymede in one of them; a handsome cornice surrounds the chamber. One of the eight compartments is occupied by a small staircase leading to the upper stories, which are lighted by narrow loopholes for windows; the ceiling of the second is of elaborate geometrical patterns; the third had only a pretty cornice, and the fourth was quite plain; the recesses round this upper chamber are vaulted; all the ceilings are of enormous stones laid quite across the chambers, and like the rest of the building within and without, most beautifully united; the stone, too, is of the purest white. The general proportions of this building are charming, and the details are carried out with such artistic skill that it is a perfect gem. Sad and mysterious it looks as it stands there alone, in the middle of the pass, against the deep blue sky.

We were soon remounted, impatient to go on: only a few steps farther to the very middle of the Wady, and then—what can be more beautiful, more glorious in all the world than the view that burst upon our eyes! There—like nothing in Nature but the first time one sees the wide ocean spread before one—lay the desert in its apparently boundless infinitude, glowing in radiant colours of unnumbered variety; while, like jewels laid upon her bosom, stood Tadmor, though in ruins, still empress of the plain, majestically grand! First, though farthest off, the Temple of the Sun rose up in giant massiveness; then as we advanced another step the splendid Colonnade, with the Triumphful Arch, its noble gateway opened out: one building succeeding another, each and all dazzlingly white, save where touched with shining gold or rosy pink. How absolutely interminable it seemed as column succeeded column in endless succession, up to the very mountain foot, meeting other colonnades which branched off at right angles and then faded down in ruins,—lone columns standing up here and there, and those of the Amphitheatre curving round in a broken semicircle, amidst the miles and miles of scattered stones, broken pillars, fallen pediments, and huge blocks, which covered the whole ground! A few dark masses told out from among the light columns; these were the platforms of smaller temples and halls, and one the palace of poor Zenobia! On the left, above all this, the Saracenic castle looked down very grandly from its lordly height upon the elder ruins below, while green gardens of fruit-trees and graceful palms clustered together at the extreme right of the great temple.

On we went, our armed escort, in triumph at our safe arrival, screaming and shouting, and the horsemen, who had come out to welcome us, careering about on their wonderful horses over rock and ruin with utter heedlessness of all obstacles, like persons possessed; and as soon as we began to cross the plain and to near the ruins, the townspeople came streaming out in a great mob, shrieking their noisy welcomes, and crowding round the Sheikh as if they would pull him off the camel with their impetuous embraces, kissing his hands and knees at ever half-step. We rode to the eastern side of the temple and debated whether to encamp there in the shade, or farther off among the gardens; but the crowds of people soon decided the point: we saw we never should have had one instant's peace near the town. So we went on, the camels starting aside every now and then from the dead carcase of some wretched camel left mouldering in the way, till, down a little descent, we reached a small terrace, secluded and quiet, from whence a very low, ancient stone door, still turning on its original stone hinges, admitted us into a delicious garden of olives, plums, and pomegranates. The camels were unloaded on the terrace, and we ladies retired into the thicket of the garden to enjoy the welcome luxury of a good bathe in the little river which runs through it.

In spite of our fatigue we wandered out after dinner among the ruins, under the irresistible temptation of a full moon. Our last full moon had been spent under the Cedars: we had seen Karnak and Baalbek by moonlight, and we were thankful to see Tadmor also, with the Desert around it dipped in molten silver. The light and graceful colonnade, and the heavy masses of the great temple, are above all things lovely in the solemn holy light of the moon, and we could have stayed there all night had we not known that we were risking a good deal. We had taken the interpreter with us as our guard and guide, and we believed all the people to be asleep at this hour within the gates of the town; but as we were standing in the ruins of Zenobia's palace suddenly voices were heard. " E Wullah !" and " Mash'allah !" exclaimed the guide, " if these are stranger Arabs we are undone! and here they come!" He quickly motioned us to keep behind him, and advanced to meet them as two Bedoueens came tumbling over the stones, laughing loudly. They stopped short when they saw we had an Anazeh with us, and on being told we were friends of Sheikh Miguel they made a rough salaam, and said, " Allah give you peace!" but we took the hint that there might be others about, and quickened our steps towards the encampment without any loss of time. The Sheikh had been obliged to go into the village to eat *pilaf* and receive welcomes without end, and was much displeased with us for having ventured so far at night without him. Probably the Bedoueens knew he was in the village, as they were townspeople themselves, and had kindly followed us to relieve us of any superfluous articles we might have in wear, but finding one of the Sheikh's people with us, they did not dare to do so.

The Sheikh's tent having been sent away, we were under the necessity of sleeping here, as well as on the journey, under the unveiled stars; but it was no subject of regret to my sister or myself: we had become accustomed to our hard couches upon the dry stony ground, with sketch-books and saddle-bags for pillows; here we had the graceful branches of a palm-tree waving above us, and we slept well, night after night, in the warm, soft, delicious air.

PART II.—THE RUINS.

THE Temple of the Sun is of course the first thing to be thought of at Tadmor. It is an immense pile of gigantic masonry, enclosing a square of 740 feet each way, one-fifth larger than the court of the Temple at Jerusalem, the structure to which it is best comparable; for, unlike the beautiful temples of Greece, which stood with all their charms of light and oft-repeated shafts disclosed to the first and most distant glance of every eye, those of Tadmor and Jerusalem were jealously enclosed in a double row of cloisters against a high massive wall, the temple itself standing isolated nearly in the centre of this cloistered court; the whole structure is, like that at Baalbek, raised up on a platform of large stones, surrounded by a broad moat, now nearly filled up, but still distinct. It would be very interesting to ascertain whether there are the same, or any substructions formed beneath this platform, as there are under those on which both Baalbek and Jerusalem stand: so similar is the *idea* of all the three platforms, that it is probable they exist, but from the filling up of the ground the entrances are very likely hidden. The surrounding wall was seventy feet high on all sides; the flat surface broken by a row of pilasters, supported on a slightly projecting base, and a few false doors and pediments unsymmetrically placed. The west side was pierced by a magnificent doorway and portico; the latter has disappeared, and been replaced by a strong Saracenic wall with a lofty door. Through breaches in the external wall many of the columns of the cloisters may be seen, while above all the lofty columns of the temple itself tower up with much beauty and elegance.

As great things stoop to mean uses, this wall now encloses the whole town of Tadmor: the miserable hovels thickly fill up every portion of the court, clustering in the corners round the columns up to their very capitals, hanging on to the carved ornaments like decayed birds' nests, and poisoning the once sacred enclosure with fœtid squalor and indescribable filth. It is almost impossible to get any general idea of the ruins even as they are, through this horrible swarm; and probably before many generations have passed these people will have succeeded in destroying every vestige of the interior of this once glorious edifice.

The Great Portal was thirty-two feet high and sixteen wide, standing between two smaller doorways; the sides and lintel were each of a single stone, and all are exquisitely ornamented with bands of carving, in wreaths of fruit and flowers, quite as graceful and artistic as those of Baalbek, but not as deeply cut. One of the great sides of the central door has half fallen from its place, and leans like a tired giant against the Saracenic wall: all are blackened with the smoke of the fires which the Arabs, who make a dwelling-place of this portal, are constantly burning there. Above each doorway are two huge projecting brackets, which look very mysterious—possibly they once supported statues. A hundred columns, perhaps more, of the double cloisters still stand; but it is excessively difficult to see the half of them, even though one clambers on to the tops of some of the Arab houses.

Opposite the portal stood the Temple itself; the cella was surrounded by a single row of lofty columns with bronze capitals, all of which have of course disappeared, as the natives even now constantly throw down the pillars and friezes in order to wrench out the clamping irons between them. Parts of the beautifully carved entablature remain; the festoons of flowers held up by winged figures or genii are still quite visible; and when gilded by the rays of the western sun, with the bronze capitals shining in the light, it must have been a noble and striking picture; even now it is one of the finest bits at Tadmor, when the sun sinks low enough to illumine the lofty columns only, and the western wall throws the miserable wretchedness at their feet into shade. Several fragments are left, both here and in two small temples at some distance, in which a row of short columns are mounted upon others of ordinary size, forming, in fact, a clerestory, like that in the Hypostyle Hall at Karnak, and as is shown by Mr. Fergusson, like the House of the Forest of Lebanon (1 Kings vii.) at Jerusalem, and the Hall of Xerxes at Persepolis.

The Sheikh took us into the mosque, which was once the temple sanctuary: a large hall, with a single row of Corinthian columns on each side; but one cannot be sure whether these stand in their original positions or not, they are so strange a patchwork of various remains; capitals, turned upside down, now acting as the bases of some of them. At the north end is a large arch with much sculpture, which has probably been added by the Arabs; and at each side are two small chambers with richly-carved ceilings, one of which has the signs of the zodiac, with figures of the deities still visible, despite the efforts of the Mooslims to destroy them. On the soffit of the arch is the eagle with expanded wings, resembling the famous eagle at Baalbek. A small staircase leads to the roof of this mosque, whence the view is as grand as it is extraordinary: such a strange mixture of crowded wretchedness in the living present, contrasting with the faded witnesses of the splendour of the past; the gloom of the broken friezes and prostrate columns, and the majesty of those that still soar up against the cloudless sky with their richly-carved capitals; and then the graceful rows of colonnades in the plain outside, leading the eye into the boundless Desert beyond, dying away on the horizon in its garb of many colours. It is curious that an earthquake has so shaken the external wall of the temple that two sides—the north and the south—lean very considerably inwards, without the stones being relatively displaced; it is now as if they had been so built intentionally to give them an Egyptian or pyramidal air.

At about 300 yards' distance from the north-west angle of the temple is the grand Triumphal Arch commencing the chief Colonnade: a very curious and remarkably beautiful structure. The central arch is flanked by a lower one on each side; but between them, on either side, are inserted *two oblique* arches, projecting southwards, but so as to be invisible in a front view: taken with the central arch alone they are gracefully pretty, but then the side arches cannot be seen at the same time. Flanking the gateway on the south are three columns on each side, very curious ones,—round and square columns united together, the square sides facing each other, and the same with the round,— with *double* capitals placed one *above* the other; these capitals are in bad taste, but all else about the triumphal arch is very fine. The sculpture on the inner (north) side is rich and uninjured: endless varieties of wreaths and scrolls, and bands of fruit and flowers, and fantastic ornaments gracefully mingled, cut with equal skill as those at Baalbek, and in better taste, because not so loaded; heads are carved on the great door-jambs, and beautiful bits of sculpture lie in half-buried heaps all around. From this arch four rows of columns, forming a triple colonnade, ran towards the mountains for very nearly a mile in length!—not quite straight, for it bends slightly to the north-east, enough to prevent a vista to the very end. The columns are fifty-seven feet high, formed of three drums, of which nearly all the lower ones are now covered up with loose sand, while between the second and third a narrow stone is inserted, from which a bracket projects, probably intended to support a bust, as they are too near the top for statues. Doubtless this must have had a fine effect when the busts stood there; but at present they have a very singular and awkward appearance: several of them still bear inscriptions in Palmyrene, and also in Greek, giving the names of the persons whose portraits they bore. The capitals are of richly-sculptured acanthus-leaves, rather stiffly arranged; and on the abacus is an ornament very common at Tadmor—a row of oval balls with roses sculptured between each. The columns are united by a plain architrave, supporting a very rich entablature of the pine-cone pattern extending the whole way; above that came a frieze of billet moulding, with a row of the egg-and-rose moulding finishing the whole; only very few stones of this frieze yet remain *in situ.* A double gateway, one beyond the other, on the west side, ornamented with a broad band of the pine-cone pattern bent round the arch, and a well-executed moulding of the egg-and-rose ornament, leads to a row of columns placed in a semicircle, which is supposed to have been the Amphitheatre.

Nine of the columns here are still upright, and many others broken off; they have all brackets on each side, looking, in their present meaningless position, like the handles on a paviour's pound. A rich frieze still unites some of the columns, and finely-sculptured pediments and other stones are heaped up in huge masses on the ground. There is another gateway similar to this farther on, and opposite to it a colonnade branched off to the east, or a small temple may have stood here, for there are one or two tall slender columns, and some others supporting a second story of little columns. Not far from the great Triumphal Arch, at the entrance, are four monolithic shafts, only one of which is standing upright now; they are of dark red granite, with capitals and bases of the ordinary stone. This granite is said to be Egyptian, and to have been brought here by Solomon at the foundation of Tadmor; the tradition may be false, but it is not a bit more extraordinary than half the facts appertaining to Tadmor and Baalbek.

Between these two gateways, a little to the west, are enormous heaps of masonry: one heap is said to have been a Hall of Justice; the other, to which a street of columns appears to have led, has time out of mind been declared to be the ruins of Zenobia's palace. It has all the appearance of a palace; and the tradition seems confirmed by the very remarkable quantity of broken ornaments with which the loose sand is filled. If a stone is displaced hundreds of fresh pieces of glass, sometimes prettily shaped and of every colour of the rainbow, are turned up, with beads of all shapes. Many metal ornaments also, evidently for female use, have been found here, and are now worn by the Bedoueen women.

Towards the end of the Colonnade are four large square masses of masonry some twelve or fourteen feet high; and here, probably, was the central intersection of the city among the royal and public buildings; it is believed that these square masses were the pedestals on which statues or groups of statues once stood, or the bases of a four-sided triumphal arch like that at Latakia and many other places. These pedestals are found still existing at Shuhba in the Haurân, a city of unknown date; also in the centre of the ruins of Jerash; in the middle of ancient Antioch; and, I believe, at Bozrah.

About a quarter of a mile to the east of this there stands a little gem of a temple, almost perfect in form, though the sculpture is sadly mutilated; it is called by tradition the Temple of the King's Mother. It is very small, simply a cella with pilasters against the outer wall, and a portico of six beautiful columns and two half-columns, which (if my memory does not fail me) were fluted. The whole building is mounted on a small platform; the stones are, as usual at Tadmor, very finely joined, and the capitals are richly and well carved, preserving their freshness and sharp cutting still. The view from it is perhaps the best of Tadmor as a whole—it is superb. The little temple faces that of the Sun; the eye then sweeps up the whole length of the Colonnade, with the distant gardens seen between the columns, then the dark masses of Zenobia's palace, and interminable columns beyond, up to the fine mountains dividing the Baghdad desert from the Wady Kebeer, by which we had come.

One afternoon that we walked out here is worth a few words of record. The day had been changeable and stormy, but the sunset came with its usual magnificent glow, and the stones of the little temple seemed literally overspread with burnished gold, contrasting with the crimson and pink splendour of the western sky. Suddenly, and while the sun was still bright and warm, the great silver globe of the refulgent moon sprang up from the distant horizon, throwing an instantaneous flood of blue-white light over the immense plain, *meeting* the sun-glow in which we still stood; and scarcely had we time to observe the peculiar harmony melting into one another, when, with the rapidity of change belonging to an eastern sky, in the Desert especially, a densely black storm-cloud burst suddenly forth from behind the mountain close beside us, and pouring down over our heads came the dark, heavy shower, *actually falling between* the calm and lovely moonlight and the rich glory of the setting sun! It was, perhaps, just one of those moments in Nature which one might live a hundred years without ever seeing a second time; but it was something, once seen, never to be forgotten.

There is no spot like this small temple for obtaining a general idea of the immense proportions and mass of the Temple of the Sun, with the huge platform on which it stands; but it struck me still more here than even at Thebes and Baalbek how little these magnificent temples were built for external beauty. Exquisite and splendid as they were, *the* coup d'œil was always *after entering the doorway*, since in every case, the temples were shut in by a wall, above which only the most lofty of the columns towered. With the Greeks it was exactly the contrary—the splendour of their temples was chiefly on the exterior; and we moderns strive more for external rather than internal effect. One would have thought that the Temple of the Sun above all would have been more open than any others; but perhaps the ancients knew best: like the surpassing splendour and the golden lining to the House of the Lord in Solomon's Temple, the rays of the sun were collected in the temples of Baal between the shadows of the surrounding walls, and thus concentrated the attention of the worshipper on the immediate shrine of the deity. At Baalbek it is doubtful whether the walls on the west and north sides were ever built, or intended to be built, much higher than the bases of the columns; but I could not help fancying, as I thought over the other examples, that it had been as lofty as the rest, or as it is now. With the idea of concentration, these walls would be less required at Baalbek than anywhere else, for there the view is hemmed in by the lofty mountains that bend round three sides of the temple; whereas at Tadmor, Karnak, or Thebes, one can imagine the sort of want—almost a necessity—for the mind to feel some arrest or refuge from the boundless infinitude all round, before it anchored on the shrine of the holy Symbol within.

Between the giant and the little fairy-like temple there is a spring of good water, and a deep hollow, which for half the year is a small lake; it has been well lined with masonry, and the stream murmurs over the pavement with a pleasant sound. An aqueduct also crosses the plain here, which once carried water from the mountain to the Great Temple. Nearer, indeed quite close to the Colonnade on this side, are the remains of the women's Baths; they are much ruined, and covered over with sand; but two or three openings are still kept free with narrow stone steps, where the townswomen come all day to fill their pitchers: the water is of a high temperature.

Beyond the extremity of the Colonnade, among heaps of ruins of all manner of beautiful things, there are several temples (possibly mausoleums or baths, but they seem more like the remains of temples): one has a pediment elaborately sculptured; a portico of another seems to have stretched across the end of the Colonnade, some portion of which is still standing. A sarcophagus inside a small temple near this, sculptured on the sides with garlands of fruit and flowers held up by satyrs, it worth looking at. It is perfectly impossible to describe the details of the immense amount of ruin closely heaped together in this part—friezes and capitals and nameless fragments richly and beautifully sculptured with vine and acanthus-leaves, fruits and flowers, wreaths and medallions in endless variety, among scrolls of geometrical network and fantastic ornaments—all cut in that richly-coloured stone, which is in itself a beautiful thing. As you hold it in your hand or step over it, it is *couleur de rose tendre*, blushing at itself; as the sun shines on the vertical mass it is dyed over with gold, rich, luscious, and gleaming; while, at a few miles' distance, it is of a dazzling white. The buildings of Tadmor would be beautiful and grand in anything and anywhere; but they owe much to their material. In the stern, grim granite of our cold North, and in this vast and lonely position, they would be solemn and mournful—a very spectacle of grief; but in this lovely stone endowed with such rich and tender hues, the otherwise human-made thing seems spiritualised into a solid fancy—a dreamlike fabric of some delicate thought, congealed by a magician's hand into tangible stone. Sydney Yendys* has a fine simile of the Colosseum resembling an old gladiator, slowly dying, crumbling away in mouldering grief—a true picture of the ruins of the West, where Time flings funereal garlands of autumn-fallen leaves over her dead. Palmyra seemed to me, from the first instant I saw it stretched out before me in all its investiture of bright colours, like a fair maiden, a flower-crowned bride lying down in a repose that was really death, though it appeared only a deep sleep, with her white robes and her fair flowers still around her—*they* living, though *she* was dead—floating down the stream of Time—" the queenliest dead that ever died so young!" Yes, and even though

" The Crown is withered, yet the Queendom lasts!"

There are countless more ruins of temples, and colonnades, and monumental columns extending on all sides; but I spare the reader further description the more readily since I myself never got so far as to see the half of them.

Tadmor has been a good deal run down by those who have not seen it: the difficulties of getting there are so great that it was best to find out the grapes to be fed on when there were sour. Then it was thought a good way of exalting Baalbek to declare that even the city of Adrianopolis was not to be compared to that of Heliopolis: whereas the fact is that Tadmor is not comparable with any single group of temples such as Baalbek: there is scarcely another city in the world standing, with its streets and public buildings still distinctly marked out, without a modern city overlying the ancient one; it is not only a few temples, but a whole city, once vast and complete: and thus Nineveh, Persepolis, and Thebes are, perhaps, its only prototypes. I was once asked whether Palmyra was "not a broken-down old thing in a style of slovenly decadence?" It is true its style is neither pure nor severe: nothing over which the lavish hand of hasty and Imperial Rome has passed is ever so: but

* Sydney Dobell: Yendys being the former name spelt backwards.

Tadmor is free from all the vulgarity of real decadence; it is so entirely irregular as to be sometimes fantastic; the designs are overflowing with richness and fancy, but it is never heavy: it is free, independent, *bizarre*, but never ungraceful; grand indeed, though hardly sublime, it is almost always bewitchingly beautiful.

The union of the square-and-round column in one—one of the characteristics of Syrian architecture—is commonly repeated; the chief ornaments employed are the egg-and-rose moulding and the pine-cone, as I believe it is called usually: here, in the Colonnade frieze, this ornament is like a succession of pine-apples; but it is very difficult to see it distinctly, as, though much has fallen within reach of examination, it is also much worn.   The pattern might be a representation of fish-scales, when it would be in connection with the worship of Derceto, the mother of Ninus—one of the names of the sun in Phœnicia, where a fish was an emblem commonly adopted for Baal.   Or perhaps it is a pattern formed of the cone, under which form the Syrians adored the sun, and also Jupiter; as the Paphians adored Venus, mysteriously representing her in a pyramidal or flame-shaped stone.   That the pine-cone was a religious emblem throughout India and Assyria is well known; it was sacred to Bacchus for the intoxicating quality of its resin, with which the old Romans medicated their wines: the fiercely-burning, fiery characteristic of its balsam or resin was, it is supposed, used as a type of the life-giving properties of the sun.   Of the Phœnicians one cannot help thinking in looking at Tadmor: that platform chants the same mysterious strain as the platform of Baalbek; and whether these " great stones, and costly stones, and hewed stones " date only from the mighty hands of King Solomon, or they stood there for ages before, when there were giants in the land, they must have had the same origin as those at Baalbek.   The Phœnicians, or Canaanites, as they are usually called in Scripture, planted cities in the Haurân and the Lejah: may they not also have had a city here, by the abundant desert-spring, of which Solomon took advantage when he built his store-cities, " Baalath and Tadmor, in the wilderness "? It was in fact the bulwark or outpost of the kingdom of Israel, which extended to the banks of the Euphrates (Gen. xv. 18; Exod. xxiii. 31; 1 Kings iv. 21, 24), and had been built for the protection of his caravans bringing merchandise from India and Assyria.

At the foot of the range of hills we had crossed in arriving at Tadmor, and at the distance of a good mile from the farthest end of the Grand Colonnade, there is a hollow in which a little chasm opens, ending with a cave which is said to go some way underground, but which we could not explore, as we had brought no candles from

Damascus. From this cave the Râs-el-'Ain (the head of the fountain) a stream comes bubbling quietly out, and thence the little river flows for about three miles before it is lost in the thirsty sand. Nothing can be more limpid than this stream as it runs away over the little stones; it has no other beauty save the clusters of brilliant sulphur which cover the rocks of the chasm, for the water of the spring is saturated with this mineral, and is of a very high temperature; but it had cooled, and the taste of sulphur decreased, in the two miles of its windings, before it reached the spot where we encamped. Gardens and fruit-trees cluster round its banks and shade the waters, and certainly the sulphur does not lessen the luxuriance of the vegetation. We used to fill a large leathern bag, called a *zemzi-meer*, every morning, and hang it in the branches of one of the trees: in a couple of hours the sulphur had precipitated itself, and the water was perfectly cold and sweet. But before we left Tadmor we thought that the daily bathing in the hot stream, and the having no other water to drink, had made us all feel weak and languid. There were other causes for this feeling, however; the year had been one of excessive drought and consequent famine: the desert pastures had all failed, and there was but little food of any kind for the camels, of whom vast numbers had died, and the town was thickly strewn and surrounded with rotting carcases; for where they dropped down the bodies were left. The Tadmorites have an idea that the smell is wholesome, and when they are sick they go and sit beside one of the putrid carcases to inhale the beneficial perfume! Inside the town every one possessing a camel keeps it, like the Irish pig, with the family in their tent or hovel, or it lives outside the door, in the lane. If the poor beast dies there it stays, all the same; and unhappily, because one year lately some dogs went mad, the people shot them *all*, so that now there are only vultures to do the scavenger's work, so fearfully necessary everywhere, but especially under the powerful Eastern sun. There were scores of carcases within the gates; and as we were walking along the narrow lanes, especially once when darkness overtook us, it was impossible to avoid stumbling over and crunching into the disgusting heaps, and stepping not only over, but through them! It was only among the ruins that we ever escaped the smell; and in spite of the opinion of the Tadmor people, and of some French philosophers, I am convinced that we all suffered seriously from the horrible stench: the whole place was poisonous. Several of our Argeels got fever, and lay groaning and shivering by day and by night; the Arab remedy for which disease—on the homœopathic principle of "like curing like"—was to place the unhappy patient,

R

without any covering but his ordinary clothes, to lie in the full blaze of the midday sun! I need scarcely say that we did not observe any beneficial results from this treatment.

The people of Tadmor are unmitigated barbarians; they are fellaheen of the lowest order, permitted by the Bedoueens to live within the town on condition of their acting as purveyors for the tribes. The caravans from Aleppo and Damascus to Baghdad all touch there, and leave the kefiyehs and mash'lahs, &c., which the Bedoueen requires; then they tend the groves and gardens along the stream, one half of the fruit of which the Bedoueens buy, while the other half they take. The townspeople are a rough, rude set, and have all the vices of the Bedoueen without any of his virtues. It was a perfect ordeal to go even for a few moments inside the gates: men, women, and children would instantly pour forth from their hovels and mob us, examining our clothes, pulling us about, trying to feel whether our arms and legs were made of flesh and blood, like those of the Arabs, or of some Western substance quite differently composed; while they roared, screamed, and shouted in our ears enough to deafen us. One day that we wanted to climb up one of the houses to see the view, the Sheikh of Tadmor himself accompanied us, and two of our Argeels, in hopes of keeping the peace; but it was entirely useless; the scrambling process was difficult enough of itself, and with the whole population swarming round us to see the show, not even the whip of the Sheikh, nor the sticks of the Argeels, had the slightest effect in clearing the way. Several times they took us by the shoulders and turned us round to see our faces; and more than once I received a heavy thump on my head—for the purpose, I believe, of ascertaining that I had a natural head under my large brown hat, which was in itself a source of high astonishment to the savages. So it is not to be wondered at that we only thrice endeavoured to see the inside of the town, nor that we turned deaf ears to the numerous enticing invitations from the Sheikh to dinner, as well as to the more serious offers made to my sister and myself. The morning after our arrival, in our first walk out to the ruins, a crowd of townspeople mobbed us in the Great Arch; and several men eagerly begged to know how much our relations would expect for us. In spite of the assurance that Frank women were never thus sold, they continued to bid for us: one man enthusiastically rose to the sum of 10,000 piastres; but, like the fox in the fable, when told decidedly that he could not buy me at any price, he turned away and said, " I would have offered another thousand if her eyes had been black!"

The Sheikh of Tadmor himself held out tempting promises. He

had already four wives, who occupied, he explained, one large room in his house, each one with her family inhabiting a corner; but he was tired of one of them, and would willingly get rid of her; and he impressed upon us, with a bewitching leer on his coarse, ill-favoured countenance, that he did so much wish for an Ingleez wife! He rose to the astonishing price of nine camels, and added a tenth when he heard I was a good rifle shot! He was a horrid savage, this Sheikh Faras, cruel and mean, a very different character from his brother, Sheikh 'Ali, who was set aside from the sheikh-ship on account of his being lame and deformed, but who was the friend and adviser, the judge and consoler of all the townspeople: he could read and write, and had a great deal of intelligence and quiet good sense. A dreadful story was whispered to us of something Sheikh Faras had done a year or two before, when the Anazehs were encamped round the town, but both the sheikhs were away in war. Faras stole about a score of camels from the tribe, and was manufacturing a tale of how he got them, prior to bringing them home, when Sheikh Miguel unexpectedly returned to Tadmor without affording him an excuse for going out through the camp to the place where he had concealed them. The war was suddenly concluded, and the Anazehs did not move; four months after the miserable animals were found by accident, tethered in a small deep hollow as the wretch had left them. The poor creatures had gnawed each other as they stood tied together, and the skeletons, picked by the vultures, yet remained standing leaning one against the other, whitening in the sun!

There never had been known such a year of distress as the present one in this Desert. To the south of Tadmor, at this season, it is generally green with herbs, affording pasture to the camels: now it was all parched and burnt up; and though towards the east some of the ground appeared green and smiling at a distance, the herb was not high enough to be browsed on by any animal. Scarcely any rain had fallen in the preceding winter; the torrent-beds remained dry, and the ground unsoftened: now even the wells and springs were dry also. Another such year, they said, would be absolute destruction to the tribes, and their hearts were very sad and heavy; for the time of the early rains had come, but none had as yet fallen. The Anazehs, as I have said, had gone eastwards, in hopes of finding pasture; but the camels were so weak and so few, from the frightful mortality among them, that great numbers of their women had been left in the town of Tadmor to get on as well as they could till the next spring. Those women and children who had gone with the tribe had most of them walked, leaving their "carriages" behind them. These carriages, or *howdahs*, are wooden frameworks, covered with scarlet cloth, and gaily ornamented with ostrich-feathers and shells, placed over the back of the camel for the women and children to be carried in; but this year the camels' humps were so reduced that the howdahs could not be fastened on, and the weak legs had to be spared all unnecessary burden. All this distress falls most heavily on the sheikh; for should one of the Bedoueens lose his camels—their only wealth—the sheikh must set the example of giving him one of his own, and those who have most contribute in order after him, until the poor man has again as much as he had lost. The sheikh is essentially the father of his people; and in years of distress, when he has many losses among his own camels, and has to share what he has with those who are in want, he is sometimes reduced really to poverty. In time of war the sheikh takes by right a large proportion of the spoil; at other times what a man gains by his own prowess he is entitled to keep, though he generally makes an offering of some part of it to the sheikh.

One evening, just at dark, as we were seated round our dinner, a heavy cloud broke into rain: we hastily concluded the soon-diluted soup, and retreated under our carpets; but the Sheikh ran joyfully up the bank, and stood there with a light heart, watching the clouds, and listening to the thunder as sweet music, praising Allah for His goodness, and calling out to assure us that we should have a thorough wet night! We were as glad as we possibly could be under the circumstances: all the more readily as we had fortunately that day purchased a nice thick Tadmor carpet, which, however, did not prevent the rain from soaking down in little lakes beneath us. But the next morning all was dry; it had rained but an hour or two, and the Sheikh was as sad as ever: "Mashallah! it is God's will," was all he said, with the submission and acquiescence, not fatalism only, of a really good Mooslim, "and He knows best!" The very next day we heard a dreadful story. Some Arabs came in from a journey they had been making, and told the Sheikh that not very far from Tadmor, only three or four days' journey, they had come upon an encampment of black Bedoueen tents. Surprised at hearing no barking of dogs, and still more at seeing no smoke from the cooking fires, they approached the tents: still the same silence, and not a moving thing to be seen. At last they dismounted, stuck their lances in the ground, and entered one of the tents, with the customary "Peace be to all here:" it was peace indeed; for, lying on the ground, were stretched the corpses of women and children in every tent of the encampment!

It was an encampment of the dead! Their husbands and fathers had left them to seek food and water; but they never returned, and were afterwards found at various distances strewn about, as they had dropped by the way, lying dead beside their dead camels!

We heard while at Tadmor (for he never told us any stories about himself), two anecdotes, among many others, of Sheikh Miguel, characteristic of the courage and daring for which he is so justly noted: the real cool courage, free from all Arab boast or bluster. Some hostile Arabs of another tribe came down one night last winter, and stole all the cattle of the Tadmor townspeople. Sheikh Miguel was staying there at the time *en passant*, just as he was now staying there for us; but of course the affair was no concern of his; nor do the Bedoueens like interfering with each other's quarrels. So he sat in his tent smoking, not thinking to be mixed up in it, when Sheikh Faras and some of the Tadmorites came and petitioned for his help. He could not resist the appeal of distress, for he is a generous and most kind-hearted man, and in a few moments he rose and mounted his mare. Then turning round quietly to the Sheikh of Tadmor and his companions—great blusterers and little doers—he said, " You can keep in the valley; I will go up yonder mountain and bring back the cattle." He galloped off, and before long caught sight of the plunder, collected together, and guarded by seven or eight men. Though perfectly alone, he rode straight up to them, demanded in a loud voice, " How dare you take cattle when I am here?" and fired off his revolver among them. In a moment the whole set of men ran off, and the Sheikh himself quietly drove back all the cattle to the town.

Another time he happened to be quite alone with several camels and a large flock of goats, when a *Ghuzoo* appeared in sight at a distance; away flew the Sheikh on his swift steed directly towards them, beckoning with his hand as if encouraging those behind him to follow, and singing his own war-songs very loud. They recognised him on hearing them, and the whole body turned about, took to their heels, and fled away.

We had not as much of Sheikh Miguel's society during our stay at Tadmor as we should have liked; for by sunrise we were all out in different directions—sight-seeing, curiosity-hunting, and sketching; and though we took refuge in our pretty shady garden during the midday heat, he was then always settling business in the town, or surrounded by visitors and friends who came down to our encampment. The Bedoueens have little curiosity, thinking few people worth as much consideration as themselves, but the townspeople were glad enough of the excuse to come down and stare at the Frank ladies, asking endless questions about everything, and, if they could get an opportunity, feeling our dresses, inquiring how much they were worth, &c., &c.; they also particularly enjoyed seeing us eat, just as we like to visit the Zoological Gardens at home at feeding-time. We fed, indeed, on much the same food as themselves—Arab bread (which is always good when fresh), and, morning and evening, a fowl stewed in a basin of dhourra, called *bourghoul*, with sometimes a few dates. But what amused them was seeing us all eat together; for with the Arabs the men and women always feed separately; and our knives and forks astonished them not a little. They brought down quantities of curiosities to sell us; unfortunately they have begun to learn their real value, and where they used to ask a piaster they now demand a mejidi, and as often price bits of natural stone or pebbles quite as high as the real antiques. Sometimes these trifles are of as much value to them as the best antiques; for instance, a black stone marked with a cross in any way is called a "luck stone," and insures to the fortunate owner the fidelity and warm affection of her husband or lover as long is she possesses it. Anything bright or pretty they string together in long necklaces, with coins, &c., and sometimes they, unconsciously, possess very beautiful and valuable things among the veriest rubbish. Several women had some beautifully engraved gems and cameos, with which, however, they would not part at any reasonable price; some have ancient gold coins, and many small square pieces of stone, or some composition, with figures impressed upon them, which are supposed to have been Palmyrene weights, and have been picked up in great numbers in the ruins where the private houses of the city stood; they have also numbers of coral and agate beads, and sometimes some good uncut jewels, picked up generally near Baghdad. We were always looking out among the women's necklaces for the small Assyrian cylinders, some of the best of which have been so discovered; and one day the Sheikh took us into the town to the house of one of the richest women to see a cylinder she had, and which he thought she might be induced to sell to us. We made our way into a large windowless room, full of smoke, in which the mistress was weaving one of the excellent carpets the Tadmor people make, of brightly-dyed camel's hair, thick and close, striped with pretty patterns. Of course we were soon in the midst of a crowd, with all the women trying as usual to kiss us—a hobby of theirs that cost us a great deal of trouble in dodging round each other and making ingenious escapes. At last she brought the necklace with the cylinder of pale pink carnelian, cut with several Assyrian devices, one of them a priest in the act of making offerings on an altar before the sun. Seeing how much we were interested in it, she asked *un prix fou*, and we went off to pay a promised visit to Sheikh 'Ali, the Moollah of the mosque, who gave us coffee in a clean nice room—the only clean one we saw in Tadmor—and begged us to dine some day with him, enumerating on his fingers the various dishes he would provide for our entertainment. He was an intelligent old man, and seemed respected, for he was able to keep the crowd from tormenting us; and after some days he induced the woman to give us the cylinder at a reasonable price. We had the good fortune to issue from the great gate of the town just as Sheikh Faras was coming in mounted on his finest mare, a grey of beautiful and splendid form. She was considered priceless, and he would not have sold her for any sum; but Sheikh Miguel said if any misfortune *obliged* him to part with her, he would probably value her at 1800*l.* sterling. Very beautiful she was; and it was as great a surprise as pleasure when, in a fit of intense and very unusual politeness, he invited one of the gentlemen of our party to mount her. There was no bridle of any kind, but he vaulted on her back, and the fleet creature was off like an arrow in a moment, galloping over the heaps of loose stones and ruins without a check or stumble, while the Sheikh stood in the most amusing anxiety watching for his return and saying, "Where is he gone? how far will he go?" as if he thought her rider would run away with the beautiful creature in the wide desert: I believe he would gladly have done so, so delightful was her pace and her extraordinary fleetness. When he came back, the Sheikh actually offered my sister and me a ride also—a high honour, which we declined very unwillingly; but we were much penetrated with the compliment, as, among themselves, it is the greatest indignity for a mare to be mounted by a woman.

The Sheikh's pretty little son, a child of about eight years old, was riding home another spirited but gentle mare, with beautiful legs and a fine small head, and some of his followers were careering about, brandishing their long lances, while we lingered at the gate of the great temple till the sun was sinking; but this grand *double gateway*—one of the now old Saracenic work, and the other the still older structure of Imperial Rome—always interested us so much that we were apt to linger beneath its shadow. It was such a curious feeling to stand here in the very narrow space between the two lofty walls, looking through the inner one to the temple-columns towering up within, lighted up with the dying sun, and to think back over the magnificent processions of worshippers that had so often gone up here to the Temple of Baal—venerable priests and eager devotees, and the kings who reigned here sovereigns of the desert; and, in the centre of all, Zenobia, the proud empress, coming from her palace all down that pillar-shaded colonnade, in her beauty and her jewels, entering at this very portal to bend her knee before Apollo's shrine. So thinking, while our eyes watched the stream of modern life continually passing through—modern and savage, yet probably but little differing in appearance from the ancient inhabitants of this desert. The mind travelled back, far beyond the proud Roman, to Scripture pictures of camels and sheep and goats, and the Arabs, in their simple dress, like the fierce, robber-looking son of Ishmael, plentifully armed, as though "his hand was against every man:"—while we, the children of the far West and of to-day, stood there in the shadow of the Roman and the Arab, among the desolation of *all* the Past, and the degradation of the Present, gathering up all in one shadowy Thought,—the only eternal thing in the whole scene.

And so, wondering over the long past, we will go and visit the tombs of Tadmor. Very interesting indeed they are. There are two sets of them: some, far away on the sides of the mountain, are, like the "Bride's Tomb" before mentioned, built in the form of towers; the others are almost entirely underground excavations, with a few towers scattered among them, now so much ruined as to be little worth examination: these underground tombs are supposed to be those of the people—the towers those of the nobles. They are all built in successive stories, usually four in number, sometimes more; the form invariably pyramidal, though in some cases with interrupting stories of perpendicular sides. Inside in each story, a narrow passage or chamber runs across from end to end, with three or four compartments or cells on each side, each cell containing stone shelves for the bodies, which seem to have been run in on grooves when required, as the shelves were wanting in many instances. A pyramidal-shaped opening leads into a cell at the end of each chamber, originally closed by a stone door; and in some of the larger tombs this opens into other chambers. The compartments are separated by pilasters, and in one instance by fluted columns with very peculiar acanthus-leaved capitals. Staircases, usually still perfect, lead from one story to another; and, strangely enough, in some instances, on the second story, where the end cell is wanting, there is a doorway, high above the ground like those in the Round Towers of Ireland; the stone hinges for the door and the hollow for the bolt yet remain.

The ceilings of most of the chambers are richly ornamented with graceful patterns geometrically arranged, and many of them are still very perfect. In one tomb the ceiling is divided into diamond-shaped compartments, those in the centre contain sculptures of winged genii, and the others hold busts in high relief. Very rich cornices surround each chamber, and are frequently employed on the outside of the tomb also. In one there is a handsome variety of the egg-and-rose ornament, with a battlemented moulding above and below; all are delicately but vigorously executed. Each cell has its own loophole for ventilation.

In the inside of one chamber, over the doorway, we saw the sculptured representation of a mummy placed on a sofa with carved legs; the foldings of the cloth with which the mummy was swathed very distinctly shown, and the body garlanded with an embroidered band or wreath of flowers. The exterior of another tomb is distinguished on the second story by a pediment, and on the third or fourth story is a tablet for an inscription, guarded or supported on either side by the head of an aged man with a long beard; beautiful heads, and finely executed. These old busts have grand, calm, restful, mighty faces, with closed eyes, which one fancied seemed yet silently conscious of the unnumbered ages that have passed over them, and have left there an expression of grief, but also of noble, perfect rest, mingled into glorious harmony "of more than human beauty." Above these, again, were two kneeling figures, much destroyed, whether of men or women we could not tell; on a still higher story two small heads, with wings folded back, perfect and well sculptured; and on the highest story of all a row of small pillars and a cornice.

Outside the second story of another tower there is an arched recess, with a fine band of vine-leaves and grapes moulded round it. Within the recess lies the figure of a mummy, reposing on a carved sofa; and above that another figure, in a half-reclining posture, with three other figures standing behind it, all in good relief—the heads had been knocked off every one. A Palmyrene inscription is here carved under the couch; these inscriptions, containing the names of the dead and a date, are usually placed outside the tombs, and are very frequently both in Palmyrene and in Greek. All that have been found are prior to the date of Aurelian's conquest, and many of them date about the commencement of our era. The tombs are mostly lined with white stucco, on which a good deal of colouring remains.

The score of tower tombs scattered among the underground tombs in the other cemetery, near the Râs-el-'Ain, are believed to be of older date than these; but they are so much ruined, and so much encumbered with sand, that they are scarcely comprehensible—many of them have been patched with more modern constructions. In one of them we discovered two headless statues, life-size, represented on one stone—husband and wife, doubtless, sitting together—the male leaning back in a carved arm-chair; the female in a more reclining position, as if on a sofa, her left hand on the shoulder of her husband, and holding in her right a pine-cone like those so common in the Nineveh marbles; both are attired in graceful many-folded drapery, with rich bands of embroidery and jewels down the front and round the shoulders and necks of the dresses; the drapery is gathered lower down into embroidered boots.

The arrangement of the excavated tombs is that of a passage or passages, with a tunnel vault overhead, usually four cells on each side, and three at the end of the passage. The whole of this hill may be honeycombed with these tombs, concealed in the long accumulation of sand; those that are known have been discovered by such accidents as that of a camel falling into a hole, which proved to be the hollow before the entrance, or gazelles taking refuge there from the hunter; many of the tower tombs are full of gazelles' bones and horns strewn on the ground. In all the tombs we saw heaps of human bones, but tossed together—thrown away after the mummy-cloth had been unrolled from the bodies; for the Bedoueens set great store by this gummy cloth, with the old spices still adhering to it, to use as plasters for their sick horses. We saw no bodies yet lying there, but the Sheikh told us he had seen many; and there is no question but that in numbers of the upper stories, now inaccessible from broken staircases, or in the tombs below the present surface of the ground, vast numbers of mummies must still lie untouched. The Sheikh mentioned having seen some in perfect condition with bronze lamps on their bosoms; and many gold ornaments have been found in them, some of which are now worn by the Bedoueen and Tadmor women; we remarked, indeed, how much more elegant and tasteful some of their ornaments were than the usual run of Arab women's things.

These tombs are all far away from the ruins and the town, and stand on the sides of a sand-blown valley. The dead calm, the lonely silence, and the utter desolation of the place are very striking; and to the most thoughtless, sitting there among the dead, and looking out over that grand and lovely view, a thousand painfully interesting thoughts and questions cannot but be suggested. The illimitable desert spread out beyond the mass of once luxurious palaces, crowded temples, and busy streets, with these tombs full of fleshless bones, that seemed scarcely farther removed from life than the now empty, ruined buildings, alike wrapped in the same mantle of deathly silence—the warrior, the ruler, the merchant, the prince, and the people—all now swept away, with only the shadow of the shadow of their earthly glory yet remaining! Where are their immortal souls now stored, waiting the great Day of Account? And what has He, the All-merciful, in store for those who knew not His revelation, nor His gracious Promise, nor even of His imposed Laws? What shall be the portion reserved for guiltless ignorance? The answer of unwavering trust, even in such unfathomable mystery, came in the wide-stretching desert all around us, boundless as His mercy; in the unmeasured sky above, trackless and incomprehensible as the mystery of Eternity; and in the all-glorious colouring in which that scene was clothed by the Hand of Love that showers mercy and blessing alike upon the evil and the good; and who will one day "bring the nations" into the city which will need no sun nor moon, for the "glory of God" will lighten it.

To make up for our terrible disappointment in not seeing the Anazehs, the Sheikh good-naturedly told us a variety of customs common among them, and one evening we got him to describe their favourite "sabre-dance." The men stand close together in a half circle, elbow touching elbow, jerking themselves quickly to and fro in concert with a sideway movement, while a woman, generally the wife of the Sheikh, stands alone in the middle, swinging a sabre rapidly round and round in her hand. From time to time one or another of the men darts forward, and pretends to seize the hem of her dress. If the woman is awkward, or the man not excessively agile, a hand or a finger is cut off, or a wound of some kind given, and these accidents frequently occur; but in spite of this they are very fond of the dance. It requires, of course, great nerve and skill on the part of the woman; the women of the tribe, however, are not wanting in these virtues. In time of war a curious custom prevails among them. The most beautiful woman of the tribe, or rather she who combines with beauty the most sense and courage, and has therefore most influence among them, is placed on a camel which is adorned with colours, scarlet cloth, shells, feathers, &c. The camel is then led out among the warriors, and placed in the very thickest of the fight, where the woman remains, inspiriting and encouraging them by her songs and her exhortations. At the conclusion of the battle, whoever has fought the best comes to her, and with his sabre cuts through all the legs of the unfortunate camel, when of course the woman is precipitated to the ground. If this valiant man is one of her own people she is his lawful prize and well-earned wife; but if the enemy are the conquerors she is taken away by them, and must afterwards be ransomed. A married woman is very rarely selected, never but when an unmarried girl cannot be found sufficiently courageous and spirited; but this is very seldom the case. While she is thus placed on the field of battle, the rest of the women guard the tents, assisting in the fight as much as possible with stones, which they are most expert in throwing. If their enemies are the conquerors they are quickly expelled, and their tents plundered and stripped of everything in a moment; but if their own people win the fight the women instantly rush out to the tents of the defeated and strip them; it is the women always who are employed as plunderers of the tents.

When the warrior returns from a distant fight it is the invariable custom that his own tent is the last he comes to, and in this tent the wife must remain: brothers, sisters, every one in the encampment goes out to meet him, but the wife must await the meeting with her husband till all the others have seen him. It is sometimes a hard rule to keep, for there is much love among them; but any deviation from it would be considered a great breach of propriety.

When a woman is newly married she is, a few days after, dressed out in her best attire, with all her richest ornaments, and taken round by her husband to visit every tent in the tribe, or at least in the encampment, in turn. She has to drink coffee with every one, in token of their friendliness and acceptance of her as a wife among them. Nor is the choice of a wife quite so simple an affair among them as we are apt to imagine. The Anazehs are exceedingly proud, and particular to an extreme degree about descent and pedigree. The rank of husband and wife must be equal; and if marriage with a stranger is in question, there is as much search and inquiry made about the age of the family and the pureness of her descent as in the case of any Spanish grandee; and if every step in the pedigree is not satisfactorily ascertained, the engagement is broken off. We saw one girl at Tadmor who was really extremely pretty, with soft sweet eyes and long black hair reaching to the ground. She was immensely admired by and spoken of among the Bedoueens who frequented the town; she was of a good station among her own people, and not a word had ever been whispered against her; but she belonged to a tribe which the proud Anazehs consider inferior to their own, and not a man among them would think of marrying her. The true-blooded Bedoueen, in fact, values no one but one of themselves; and to marry a woman *not a Bedoueen* is considered a grave dishonour, of which expulsion from the tribe is almost invariably the consequence. Moreover a Bedoueen man of a high tribe, such as the Anazehs and Shemmaars, &c., would think himself utterly degraded if he condescended to dishonour a woman of any other race, blood, or religion but his own; stranger women, prisoners in their hands, would be made to labour, and possibly be harshly treated, but they would be safe to the last from dishonour or insult. The real Bedoueens are not in the least affected by any display of dress, or ornaments, or riches, or rank in any out of their own tribes. We were told of a Pasha who had charge of some Government negotiations with one of the more northern tribes, who was exceedingly surprised that no one but those commissioned to deal with him had the curiosity to come out and look at him. He had taken great pains to attire himself grandly, and to have his standing and rank duly blazoned forth among them; but he had the mortification of finding they did not care one jot about it at all, or value it in the least.

The most flattering description a Bedoueen can give of a woman is that " she has hair like a mare's tail," and " a neck like a camel's." We wished to have heard more of their love-songs, but translation is very difficult in Arab songs, where much depends upon the play of words, and even of letters; and it is scarcely possible for any foreigners, however fluent in the language, to enter into the beauties of the verses. The Bedoueens are all extremely fond of poetry, and we used to like to listen to them, sitting round their fire every evening reciting and singing song after song, while one of the party ground coffee in a mortar, beating time, as all expert coffee-pounders do, with the pestle, in a tuneful cadence. Many a night we went to sleep to that pretty, quiet music. They have as many love-songs as war-songs, and often they recount the exploits and describe the beauties of a favourite mare, sometimes of a camel; but there is never anything coarse in their songs, as there almost always is in the songs of Egypt; nor even in the talk of the men among themselves, as they sit chatting together, is there ever a word which a woman need blush to hear.

Unfaithfulness on the part of a wife is immediately and invariably punished by death; her head is cut off, if not by her husband, by her father or brother; her crime is looked on as the dishonour of her whole house and family, and by them must be wiped out.

The Anazeh women have not good tempers, and the men do not consider them patient or gentle enough to be fit to milk the dear and precious camels; this office is therefore always performed by the men. But they are allowed to ride them, and are most expert and fearless in doing so. It is very pretty to see them mount, as they are accustomed to do without stopping the camel; they place one arm on his neck, which he bends down as he walks along, and then resting one foot for a second on his knee as he crooks it forward, they spring up standing on his neck, and so get into their places, the camel assisting them with a little jerk for the second jump; they are quite at ease when mounted, and think nothing of standing upright on his back while settling their children in the *howdahs* as he strides along. We could not hear that they had medicine of any kind for the camels when sick; and all they do in cases of sores is to burn the flesh round the sore with a hot iron—an operation we were twice obliged to witness, to our own sorrow.

The dress of the Anazeh women consists of a long robe or chemise of dark blue cotton, reaching from the throat to the feet, and confined by a belt of embroidered leather; over this a *kumbaz* or pelisse of some bright colour in silk or cotton, according to the wealth of the wearer; yellow leather boots if she is rich, and as handsome a necklace of varieties of things strung together as she can obtain; over this a mash'lah of white or striped camel's-hair cloth, which must, as well as her kumbaz and chemise, be long enough to hide her feet, and the sleeves of the blue chemise must also be long enough to trail on the ground behind her; she ties up the ends when busy. On her head she wears, if she is rich, triangular gold ornaments hung at each side of her face, with from ten to twenty short gold chains and coins depending from them, long earrings, and, in "full dress," a nose-ring, generally of turquoise. Her veil, called the *shembar*, which is placed across her face close under her eyes, and reaches to her knee, is of dark brown crape, and she wears a gay silk *kefiyeh* over it, bound with a rope of dyed camel's-hair prettily twisted up. Zenobia is a common name among them to this day; they call it *Zenobeeah*, which is said to be the original pronunciation. They have mostly black hair, but the lighter and redder it is the more it is admired, and they are always washing it with *henna* to give it a red tinge. They use kohhl on the eyes, and all the Bedoueen men use it also; it is considered a great preservative in the glaring sun, and I certainly found it very cool and pleasant on the lids, keeping them from blisters. If a Bedoueen woman appeared without kohhl on her eyes she would be thought as untidy and undressed as an Englishwoman without shoes, and they always have a little bottle containing it close at hand.* There is a great knack in applying kohhl; the eyelids are closed lightly upon the freshly-blackened pin, which is drawn quickly from between them, darkening the edges of both lids at the same

---

* *Keren-happuch*, the name of one of the beautiful daughters with whom Job was rewarded for his patience, is the Hebrew word for the little bottle containing the kohhl.

moment. The use of this substance has been always general in the East : Herod the Great, we are told, painted his eyes with kohhl, and also dyed his beard and hair with *henna ;* but it was considered very effeminate, and St. Cyprian indignantly denounces it as " the devil's grease."

They are very much afraid of the " evil eye," and the women wear certain round stones hung to their waistbands to preserve them from such a misfortune. They have generally a number of silver bracelets, which come from Baghdad, and the name of their husband is invariably tattooed upon the back of the left hand. A line upon the temples and the chin is all the face-tattooing in which they usually indulge; they express great surprise at our dislike to it, as their idea is that it imitates the blue veins showing through the skin, and is therefore a natural ornament.

There was an old hag of a woman at Tadmor who was much considered by the townspeople, on account of her having twice made the pilgrimage to Mekka; she was in consequence called Hajji Elleerieh—but we called her " Meg Merrilies." She was the greatest chatterbox woman could be, and had quantities of legends and stories to relate. She was a very successful curiosity-finder, and we used to take her out with us sometimes, hunting along the ground where the ancient houses had stood, in hopes of finding coins, bits of porcelain and glass, &c. One day, when she saw me busy cleaning a pretty little pebble I had found, she began with, " Oh, lady! I have found something much prettier than that; it must needs be a stone belonging to some *jinns,* for I never saw anything like it before." She would not for a long time tell us any more about the wonderful stone; she said she was afraid, and she knew we should not believe her if she told us all she had seen : however, after a whole day's coaxing and flattering, she told us that she had been out one day among the ruins of Zenobia's palace, not long before, about midday, when, the sun being very hot, she sat down by a low wall to rest. Presently she heard the hissing of serpents close to her, and turning her head to look over the wall, she saw, at a few yards off, two serpents fighting; their heads were curved far back, as their bodies glided and wriggled about, facing each other; and every now and then they would dart like lightning one at the other, each trying to seize his enemy's head. At last one gave the other a mortal bite, and he fell bleeding on the sand. Then she made a noise, and the victor glided frightened away, while she went to look at the dead snake, curious to see for what they had been fighting. And lo! out of his mouth came the apple of discord—this little white stone! and she opened her hand,

and showed us a large, round pearl; a costly one in any place, but doubly valuable in my eyes with this marvellous tale attached to it, and, above all, for having been picked up in Zenobia's palace. The Bedoueens did not know it was a jewel, nor had any of them ever seen a pearl before; and as it is too fine a pearl to have belonged to any traveller passing by, I am morally convinced, and always shall be, that this identical pearl was dropped off the necklace of the beautiful Zenobia herself, just before she left Palmyra for ever! I need not say that we bought the pearl. The Sheikh said that, although the old woman was a great rhodomontader, he did not think the story of the serpents untrue; it was not a story that she would have invented, and he had himself more than once seen serpents fighting in the manner she described for some such object as a bit of stone.

One of the gentlemen of our party was anxious to get up to the fine Saracenic castle which overlooks the town, and Meg Merrilies offered to show him the way; so one afternoon they set off together by a path that she assured him was quite feasible. She missed it, however, and after two or three hours' walk they arrived at the foot of an almost perpendicular cliff. She wanted to go back, but he insisted on proceeding, and, taking off his shoes, he managed, being an expert Alpine climber, to ascend the rock. She scrambled after him by another way, a long time after, holding on with her long hands, which were like eagle's claws. He entered by a loophole, for, though the castle is nearly perfect, the drawbridge and all legitimate entrance is destroyed. He described it as the gloomiest castle he had ever seen, with numerous vaulted chambers and extensive dungeons, occupying a very strong position. Meg Merrilies most unwillingly followed him, and kept on exhorting and conjuring him "not to be afraid of the jinns," of whom she was herself evidently in mortal terror, and when she came down she gave us a most lively account of all the trouble she had had in persuading him to go on, describing his misery and the dread of the awful jinns, and all she had done to soothe and comfort him! She would stop on the way down the mountain continually to gather the potash plant, and when she had got a good bundle in her veil, she addressed him with, "Oh, young man, in the flower of thy blooming youth! carry this load on thy back for me, for thou art young and strong, and I am old,—and then I will *perhaps* give thee part of the profits of my bundle!" He good-naturedly helped her, but her version of the story to us was that he was so completely worn out with fatigue and terror that she was obliged to carry the "welled"*

* "Young man."

(who is about six feet high) on her back for a long distance. To this castle, in seasons of drought, the people of Tadmor go in grand procession, dressed in their best clothes, and when there they sacrifice a lamb, and offer up prayers for rain.

Our promised five days had expired, but most reluctant were we to leave the enchanting spot. Every day new points of view were to be seen, other tombs to be examined, and fresh sketches to be taken; we therefore made a joint petition in due form to our good Sheikh for leave to stay longer; he was, as usual, full of kind desire to accede to our wishes. The tribe was indeed gone, but he had heard of nothing but peace round the place, and if we liked to stay we might do so as far as he was concerned; but the matter was more difficult with the Argeels: they earned more per day in Damascus than we gave them, and, the time of our contract having expired, they wanted to go back. We made them a handsome present, however, to be divided among them, as well as ten piasters a day for the food of each camel, and they agreed to stay a few days more.

Our English ideas of the desert—the expression we use for the *ne plus ultra* of all that is horrible—are so vague and so unlike the truth, that I despair of making any one understand by words alone the exceeding and glorious beauty of the scene around us. At home we think of the desert as of a white sea of gloomy though glaring barrenness,* a wearying monotony of ugliness; instead of which no scene in nature can be clothed in more brilliant, more varied, or more quickly changing colours. In the narrow space between the foreground and the horizon, when laid down on paper, no brush could ever be made to lay in the countless streaks of variegated colour filling up that space; in despair of catching them by any other means, I have scribbled down upon the margins of my drawings a score of descriptions of the view at that moment before me,—such as this, beginning with the foreground:—" Brown, dark red, violet, lilac, gold, rose, crimson, pale green, orange, indigo-blue, sky-blue;" these all blending into delicious, strange, incalculable harmonies, ever and ever changing. Each effect seemed the most beautiful, and one wished it to last for ever,—when, in another two minutes, all would be changed into something so much lovelier still, one never knew whether to admire or wonder the most. Many and many a time, anxious though I was to draw all I could,

---

* Many of the deserts of Africa are, I believe, like this. Where the sand is loose, and consequently wind-blown, of course nothing can grow; in the Great Desert the sand binds, and much of the varied colouring is owing to the appearance of the thorns, &c., growing upon it.

s

my pencil remained still in my hand while I was engrossed in watching the rapid and beautiful changes which no brush could copy and no tongue describe. Then the mountains that approach Tadmor on one side would shine out in shades of violet, purple, and a delicate misty lilac, of such brilliant hues that one felt startled at the sight; and, late in the day, the ruins used to look literally like things built of pearls set in burnished gold, as they stood against the background of wine-empurpled mountains, or, as sometimes, on one of the fine dark stormy evenings we had, against a sky of deep sapphire blue, unlightened by the sunshine which touched accidentally on their fair whiteness only. It seemed, indeed, to my fancy as if the ruins sometimes, in the very intensity of their glowing colours, found a silent voice, unheard by the ear, but understood by the mind that listened to their "eloquent teachings:" as if they were the clear upper notes, the sweet treble of the deep harmony evoked all around in the sublime colouring of Nature. Holy and noble indeed are these colours, which God has given to clothe and invest His creation: "of all God's gifts to the sight of man the holiest, the most divine, the most solemn;"* and they who see the fair things in the Desert in their most radiant brilliancy, as though they were fresher there from the Creator's hand than in any other place, may well fancy with me that one heard them saying—

> "Though heedless man might quite forget Thy praise,
> We praised Thee; and at rise and set of sun
> Did we assemble duly, and intone
> A choral hymn that all the lands might hear. . . .
> We, the Seven Daughters of the Light, to praise
> Thee, Light of Light! Thee, God of very God!"†

I often thought, too, of the legend, which may be truth, of how Solomon built a palace here for the daughter of Pionkh, King of Egypt, who sighed for her native deserts even among the fair palaces and gardens round about the hill of Zion, and how she dwelt here in the Desert, so like and yet so unlike her own grand, wild, and impressive wilderness of sand; the one grand in barrenness and desolation, the other sublime in beauty and fruitfulness. The sky, indeed, was the same over both: unclouded and serene, and with that most exquisitely lovely hue that ever earth has seen; and what must not that sky have been to the men of those early days, with simple minds but high thoughts, who, intimately persuaded that directly behind its slight though ever undrawn veil Jehovah and all His angels were assembled in awful majesty, "looked upon every cloud that passed as literally the chariot of an angel,

* Ruskin.   † Hon. Catherine Maynard.

and every ray of the morning and the evening as streaming from the throne of God!"* No wonder, in truth, that they worshipped that sun, from whose light and warmth all generation seemed to proceed, as God, or at least the chief token of God; more wonder if they had not done so; and no wonder either that, when they raised such buildings to His honour, and filled them with the shining gold and the ivory, and the gems and the incense, and all that could intoxicate and enchant the senses, the rough and rude-minded son of the Desert asked no question and wondered no more, but fell prostrate in awe-struck adoration before the shrine of Baal!

Here, too, most probably came the Magians of old, passionately yearning after light—a light more tangible and nearer to their hearts than the purely spiritual religion they had been taught to follow—with their pulses beating high, and their hearts big with expectation and hope, which the Divine spark was working out within them, as they followed the Star which their science had told them must have brought a message to them. Reverently they followed the high and holy and solemn messenger, not pausing in their sacred journey even at this famed and beauteous shrine; but, laden with the best that they had, the poor outward symbols of that which was better within, they followed steadily on till the beautiful angel of the Lord (as they in their simple creed believed that Star to be) stopped above the low hills of Judæa. Then with the un-questioning, childlike humility of the true philosopher, they, the great priests, the Wise Men of the East, knelt down with exceeding joy before the little Child, and recognised in Him the Divine Man, the Day-spring of a new and brighter day, which should give light, not to the children of Abraham only, but to all those who " sat in darkness and in the shadow of death," and would "guide their feet into the way of peace."

M. Haag's beautiful sketches proceeded with great rapidity: the people molested him very little, and I am certain some of those who did see him at work believed that his drawings were done by magic. It was a great thing to get out of the way of the rude curiosity of the townspeople; for though we always had a man of the town or one of the Argeels for our protection wherever we went, they bored us dreadfully when we were within reach. My companion was generally a fine young Bedoueen, so very black, but so erect and handsome, that we called him " Black Adonis." He used to lie on the sand close to me while I drew, twisting up and smoking cigarettes; but after a day or two he began to be interested in my performances, and got nearer and nearer: at last I was

* Ruskin.

s 2

amused to find him gazing intently over my shoulder, looking up when I did, and watching my pencil as it moved. I doubted whether he really understood the picture, and, to prove him, I made a long line which did not exist in nature, when a deep grunt just at my ear startled me into the sense of my error: I rubbed it out, and was rewarded with a " taïb, taïb;" and for the next three hours that young savage sat there, forgetting to smoke, looking on with the deepest attention, keeping up a running accompaniment of grunts, and rebuking me with an indignant " la, la " (no, no), when I put in a figure that I had seen sitting there the day before, but which was not there now. At last I gave him a bit of paper and a pencil, and said " ente amel soora " (*you* make a picture),—he burst into a long, low, grave chuckle, and said " Anazeh fingers too big;" but we were fast friends ever after : and I heard him relating my invitation to his fingers, with much gusto, that night round the evening fire.

One afternoon my sister and I went out together, with only the guide, a Tadmor man, to carry our sketch-books, and stationed ourselves at the Temple of the King's Mother. Beyond this neither man nor woman of the town would go alone after dusk; they said the place was full of jinns,—but the jinns were of flesh and blood: stray Bedoueens of small tribes might be, and were almost always, lurking about to plunder any thing or person they could find, and they were gentlemen not to be lightly adventured with. We had plenty of time, as we thought, before us, and we settled quickly to work, my sister choosing a fallen capital for her seat, which the guide was moving a little into position, when a serpent of deadly venom darted out from behind it, with head erect and hissing tongue: fortunately the guide had a huge stone in his hand at the moment, and the creature was crushed at once. The man said it was an evil omen; but he lay down beside us, and was soon fast asleep, and we sat drawing, and never looking round, till, all of a sudden, we saw two mounted Bedoueens not very far from us, and coming in the direction from Baghdad! It was rather a startling sight at this distance from protection, and we wakened the man, who immediately seemed in an awful fright, and hid himself in the inside of the temple. It was too late to hide, we knew, and moving would be more likely to attract their keen eyes than keeping still; but I am free to confess that for once my heart did beat uncommonly quickly (though we both assured each other there was on danger whatever), remembering very well that we were two miles from our people, and that the sun was fast sinking behind the mountain. But, to our immense relief, the men passed on without seeing us, and as they skirted the town, and turned down towards our camp, the guide pronounced them Anazehs.

So they proved to be, as we found when we got back to the camp, and bad news they brought, viz., that they had seen hostile Arabs on the way—at some distance, indeed, but possibly scenting us from afar. So the Sheikh issued his decree at once, that off we must go at sunrise the next morning. We ate our last dinner, much to the joy of the Tadmorites, who had sent down a formal message that morning to the camp, saying that they did hope we would soon "move on," for that we had eaten nearly every cock, old and young, in the town, and they could not supply us with any more! We were, indeed, aware we had eaten the *old* cocks, but were all unconscious of having ever tasted a young one. So we had to make the best of our departure, and to believe it was time to leave: we were all feeling ill and languid, from the heat, our overtaxed strength, the sulphur, and the carrion; and the camels were evidently getting weak from want of proper food. The precious sketches were packed up, we made our last notes by starlight, filled the saddle-bags, took a farewell bathe in the sulphur stream, and lay down for our last sleep in the air of the warm, sulphur-scented stream.

THE RETURN.

THOUGH brightly still shone down the moon's soft ray
Upon the hard rough pillows where we lay,
The wary Bedoueen watched her orb decline,
And waked the sleeping camp from dreams divine.
Then, one by one, each prostrate figure rose,
Around his head the gay kefiyeh throws,
And as the bright light reddened into morn,
And flushed with crimson hue the sand and thorn,
We bade adieu to that strange resting-place,
And tow'rds the West again we turned our face.

But first our way we slowly paced beside
The tepid stream, where maid and stripling tried
'Mid thirsty beasts the hideous skins to fill ;
Then by the mighty Temple Wall, where still
The lingering shades in cool grey masses hung,
And gazed aloft, where early sunbeams flung
Their light upon the carven columns tall
Which tower up above the huge, grand wall,—
Across the plain, by many a look delayed,
We passed beside the long, long Colonnade,—
All solemnly serene those pillars stand,
As some fair forms uprisen from the sand,
Which, ever gathering round their long-hid feet,
Pays thus with jealous care its homage meet.

There, lost in boundless blue infinitude,
The Desert lies with every colour hued,
While over all the last faint shades of night
Dispersed before the morn's triumphant light.
And there the Temple, all her grace displayed
By bright Hyperion's first and latest rays,
Gives back the mute response of golden praise
Which pitying Time upon her stones hath laid !

Then past the stone heaps, once the Palace fair
Of her whose feet in jewelled sandals bare
To worship proud within that glorious fane—
Imperial Princess of the Desert plain !

Oh ! slowly then we clomb the barrier hill,
Where stand a hundred tombs of ancient story,
With one long gaze regretful eyes to fill—
Fit place of farewell to Palmyra's glory !

Here stood the sad dethronèd Queen, and wrung
Despairing hands where golden fetters clung,—
Here stood to upbraid those mountains stern and great
She deemed sure guardians from the younger world,—
Here gazed upon the splendid home where late
The widowed Queen her own proud banners furled,—
Now—o'er Palmyra, Roman eagles wave,—
Her Temple courts profaned—her Queen, a slave !

But yet, I trow, the anguish of that gaze
Dwelt less upon the pride of brighter days
Than on the Tombs—now of their treasures reft—
Where thrice four hundred years of honour slept ;
And half in envy burned as she descried
The Tomb of that first Queen—th' Egyptian Bride
(For whose delight 'tis said King Solomon raised
This home, more lovely far than that she praised
On mighty Egypt's shore of still unrivalled fame) ;
And thought how calm she slept—untouched by shame,—
With those proud hearts that Death alone could thrall—
Closed eyes that wept not for their Daughter's fall !

'Tis said Zenobia made another home
By Tiber's banks, in stern, ungrateful Rome,
That on her brow, divinely calm, there reigned
The impress of serenest peace unfeigned :
Not such the mark that guilt or shame confers,—
Nor chains nor fetters could that soul degrade,—
Erect, she bore the vassal's sign—and made
The shame Aurelian's—and the triumph hers !
Yet oft I ween, when Evening's golden haze,
In clouds of sunlight wrapped her wondering gaze,
Rome's cruel walls no more the heart enthralled,
By memories fond to that loved home recalled ;
Beneath the shade of waving palms she dwelt,
Before Apollo's sacred shrine she knelt,
Her homage paid as fancy saw again
The crimson glory flood the Desert plain, ¡

The pearly columns shine with roseate hue
Against the violet hills and deepening blue,
And cried, " What though my voice no more I raise,
This ceaseless beauty offers up glad praise !"

And we too turned away—our last look bent
On those old Tombs,—while, like a bright dream spent,
The wild, free life upon the Desert plain,
The beauteous and sublime infinitude,
The gorgeous-coloured ocean, rainbow-hued,
Those rosy Temples with their golden stain,
All lovely things we shall not see again,
Sank down behind the barrier hill, which closed
From view the living Tomb where calm reposed,
In marble letters writ upon the sand,
The dim but yet proud story of the land :—
And, happier far than they who here adored
Mysterious gods, and their dark aid implored,
We lifted up our hearts in mute appeal
To that true Son of God whose righteous Heel
Hath trodden down the Serpent's sinful head,
O'er Death's dark shades His healing radiance shed,
And spread from north to south, from east to west,
The Faith which makes both Jew and Gentile blest !

Then passed we to a narrow vale, among
Dark violet mountains, where light mist-wreaths clung,
Gazelles and jerboas bounding through the thorn
Brush off the sparkling dew-drops of the morn,
And, dancing lightly on the path, the bird,
The camel-lover's * little note is heard.
So slowly paced the camels one by one,
So, one by one, each long slow step was done,
Each measured footfall's swinging cadence sung,
As higher sunbeams shortened shadows flung :
The wild fierce rays seemed scorching every brain
As all around they scorched the barren plain ;
And then on either hand th' unbroken walls
Of purple crags grew streaked with shades of red,
And darkening browns upon the lilacs spread,
As blazing up the midday sunshine falls.

And still the same slow step went calmly on,
And, one by one, th' unmarked hours were gone,
Till, blessèd sight ! blue waters coolly lave
The purple mountains' feet with rippling wave,
Delicious creeks and little bays appear,
And seem our hot and burning eyes to cheer,

---

* *Habeeb-el-gemmal*, the lover of the camel : a little black and white bird,
that is always dancing on the path, about a yard before the camel as he paces
along, especially in the morning.

And all th' horizon gleams with shining lakes—
When lo ! they quickly vanish like the flakes
Of snow that fall beneath an April sky,—
And all the Desert seems more hot, more dry.

At last the boundless, unflecked dome of blue
Deepens behind us into sapphire hue,
While radiant westering floods of brightest gold
In warm embrace sweet rosy clouds enfold ;
Dark hues of plum upon the mountains shed,
And on the Desert plain a ruddy sea is spread
O'er which the long blue shadows fleetly fly ;
Then darkening clouds were all around unfurled,
And sank the sun into another world,
Whence long, long after o'er the eastern sky
Sweet pictures of bright pink and gold he flung—
The evening echoes of the hymn he sung
At break of day,—like Farewells floating back
From lips unseen upon a winding track.

A moment on the soft warm sand we lay,
The fragrant coffee made, and longed to stay,
But as the deepening night around us came
A distant spark revealed a hostile flame.
And quickly quenched was ours, and we had gone
With slow soft footstep calmly striding on,
And aught but whispered tones the Sheikh forbade,
Lest we by tell-tale winds should be betrayed.

For now the night-breeze fluttered o'er the plain,—
Now fragrant with sweet-scented herbs it came—
Now whistling with a hard and rustling tone—
Now sighing with a low and tender moan,—
Anon a swift and savage gust would rise,
And with a solemn fury sweep the skies ;
Then hush—and softly clinging round the face
A sweet and balmy breeze with loving grace
Would breathe—most like a cloud of rosy hue,
Alone and matchless in a heaven of blue ;
Or, like the memory bright of one sweet day,
Shining throughout the weary life-long way.

So with the same long step we glided on,
And, one by one, th' unmarked hours had gone,—
No change came o'er the darkened way,
Save where the stars moved on in bright array,
Or flung themselves athwart the gleaming night,
And fell with glittering glances out of sight.
So ever " ohne Hast und ohne Rast,"
Till since the dawn full twenty hours had past,
And by the Robbers' Tower we glided fast,
Lest lurking Bedoueen the troop descry,—
When suddenly the red Moon leaped on high,
And, in black masses mingled on the ground,
The silvery beams our shadows all confound,—

Dismayed we thought discovery sure at hand,
And listened for the Arab's rough command;
But all around unbroken silence spread,
And nought disturbed us as we onward sped;
One enemy alone appeared unsought,
With whom we each with painful efforts fought,
While every hour he more victorious grew,—
Sweet Sleep! unwelcome then, though friend most true!
The pitying Sheikh the camels bade to kneel,
That we a hasty hour of rest might steal,
And in a shallow wady on the ground
All soon were wrapped in dreamless sleep profound.

While there we lay and wearily reposed,
Th' eternal eyes of every star was closed,
And night's cold grey had turned to ruddy morn
When we awaked to find the Desert thorn
Was bending o'er our heads its little arch:
Then hastily we rose—resumed our march,
And chased our own blue shadows flung before
The rising ray,—no living thing moved o'er
Th' unchanging yellow sand, till formless shade
And quivering air the midday hour betrayed;
When lo! a cloud of moving dust appears,
And to our little band it quickly nears,
　　Now circling round in front and flank,
　　Then swerving off as though they shrank
　　With pity from our little troop,
　　Then turning back with sudden swoop,
　　In narrowing circles wheeling round,
　　And hoofs scarce lighting on the ground,
　　With tightened bit and poisèd lance,
　　With savage shriek and fiery glance,
　　With angry words and hostile mien,
　　On, on, they came, Wild Bedoueen!
　　Our guns were fired—and quickly they
　　Reined up,—and then we guessed the play
Which welcomed us in Desert style to share
Their homely shelter from the scorching glare:
With kindly toil they led our beasts to drink
Delicious draughts within the lakelet's brink,—
This done, our steps to Karyeteen we pressed,
And in the spacious khan at last found rest.

We were not destined to find much repose at Karyeteen, as we were obliged to keep in the shelter of the guest-room from the heat of the sun, and no entreaties, coaxings, persuasions, objurgations, or anything else could keep the people out of the room. They made us very comfortable upon cushions and mattresses; but, seating themselves beside us, if we closed our weary eyes for one moment, a finger stole up to feel our cheeks, or stroke our hair, or pulled at our dresses to see how they were made. At last we gave up trying to sleep, and retired into another room for the still better refreshment of a good bath; our dragoman standing outside the door *en garde*, about forty or fifty women crowding round him and abusing him for keeping them out and preventing their climbing up to the windows to look at us. " I tell you the Sitts are bathing!" " E wullah! isn't that what we want to see ?" And at last they tried to break open the door. We then returned to the guest-chamber, where fresh and fresh relays of people came in to inspect us as we lay on our cushions; my sister patiently answered as many of their questions as she understood, while I amused myself with writing the foregoing lines, as a history of our return ride.

Towards sunset they brought us a banquet of meat and rice in various shapes, with vegetable-marrow and lentils, ending with a huge dish of fine dates stewed in butter, or rather oil, smoking hot; very good it was, but one could eat but a little of it. It was rather a picturesque scene, for the room was a large one, and the whole town seemed crowded in to inspect the Franks feeding. The dinner was placed on the ground, and lighted up by two brass candelabras, each of them five feet high and handsomely made, which threw bright lights upon the swarthy faces ranged around us, with the many-coloured kefiyehs of the men, and the gold ornaments of the women. Some of the men were very handsome; and they were highly delighted when M. Haag made a hasty sketch of one or two.

We mounted as soon as it was dark, a large caravan of camels and donkeys accompanying us out of the town, as they had asked permission to benefit by the Sheikh's escort. The donkeys seemed like so many mice running beside the camels, but the long strings of baggage camels, tied in dozens and scores, were very troublesome, for our dromedaries were continually getting entangled among them; and as there was no moon and the night was very dark, they fell very often. It was so cold by midnight that, coming after our many sleepless hours, we were all continually falling asleep, and at last the whole party got down to walk, so the Sheikh said we had better have tea, and we lit the fire, and then Sheikh, Argeels and all, went fast asleep, and we slept till near sunrise, to the Sheikh's great annoyance, for the night's halt had been quite unintentional, but a very great relief.

Our journey back was not so pleasant as the journey there, for the camels were so weak they would lag, and we had the sun nearly all day in our eyes, which is much harder to bear than when it is behind one; moreover we were ourselves pretty well tired out. But we had a lovely view all day of the snowy mountain range reaching up to Homs, a beautiful feature in a desert-view: the snow had fallen while we were at Tadmor, but, curiously enough, although it had been very thick on Hermon as we left Damascus, it seemed to have almost quite melted away as we returned. We were joined in the course of the morning by an armed Arab, mounted on horseback, who would answer no question as to where he was going, or to what tribe he belonged. The Sheikh looked grave, and after some time offered him a piece of the bread he was himself eating, but the Arab declined it; and there could not be a more unfriendly sign. After an hour or two the Arab was suddenly missed from us, and the Sheikh became anxious, still more so when at dusk he was descried at a distance waiting for us with two other Arabs; of course there might be two dozen concealed. So we were desired to close in a compact body and to ride on quickly, the Sheikh advancing in front, and we got a little excited, and some of us hoped to see a little " fun;" when, on reaching the men, the Arab's companions turned out to be two of our own escort, who had ridden on while we had delayed to let our camels feed on some tamarisk-bushes we had happened to find: the stranger wished us good-bye soon after. There is no doubt that he intended mischief, but if he belonged to a Ghŭzoo, he probably told them we were too strong a party to attack; and so ended our last chance of an adventure.

We rested that afternoon at Atny, and, starting again when the moon got up, mistook our way into Jerood, and got into an encampment of Bedoueen tents, setting all the dogs into a chorus of furious howls; a great annoyance, for they run at and bite your camel's legs, and make him wrathful. The camels stumbled and fell a great deal, but the night work was pleasanter than the very hot days; indeed I always enjoyed the night journeys, both in the Desert and in Syria (when I was not sleepy), almost as much as those of the bright-coloured day. The night was so clear and light, and the sky so *blue* instead of black, that one can still see something of the scenery, although the contrast of the silver moonlight and the densely black shadows are deceptive; and then one can think so quietly and uninterruptedly, with one's head cool, and one's eyes unscorched, while truly there was always food for thought around one, above all in the full, softly-glowing, God-created lamps of Night that shone in the sky. In the far East it is easier than under our gloomy skies to understand how naturally the men of old turned to them for worship; and how they yearned for the changeless purity and Eternal Order they saw there and nowhere else. Often I thought of the child with his pure heart so fresh from the Hands of God that he saw Him everywhere, and asked if the stars were not "gimlet-holes to let the glory through," and felt how fully his innocent eyes had seen, in spirit, the glory revealed in their beauty; as the miracles manifested through the simplicity of Christ's human life: the Divine Glory within it revealing the Light which was already shining in the darkness of the world that comprehended it not.

It is beautiful to look out at any moment of night upon the glowing stars, but you cannot read their meaning clearly unless, night after night, you have watched "the bright procession" move "down the gleaming arch:" till you have seen the whole "celestial army" sweep across an "endless reach of sky," and pass out of our poor human sight to rise in other skies. Not till you have learned the bright lesson of the "marshalled brotherhood of souls,"* moving calmly, silently on, held up in the Hand of God the Father of all, "binding" their "sweet influences"† into one harmony, as He permits the souls of some to ride in majesty through the world, and others to shine meekly and dimly, but in His sight not a whit less radiantly. If there was one thing more in my mind than another, by night and by day, in all my long rides through the Desert, it was the oft-repeated words, "Heaven and Earth are full of the Majesty of Thy Glory!"

These are some of the thoughts that occupy one almost unconsciously in the long silent hours of Eastern travelling; and difficult as it is to carry the mind of the reader along with one in descriptions, and hopeless as it is to paint in expressive words the scenes that met our eyes, it is yet more impossible to make them enter into trains of thought that arise from the accidents of the atmosphere and the silence and the beauty around one. I ought to apologise for trying to do so.

We found the Bourghaz pass perfectly stifling, and were thankful that the good Sheikh ordained a rest for the sake of the camels, under the shade of the thick lofty trees about Doumah, which had seemed hopelessly far off. My sister's camel, the dear Simri, had lagged latterly very much, and she dismounted, hoping thus to relieve the tired beast, but within a few yards of Doumah the poor thing knelt down on the road side, and lay there till she died two days after. We had a most refreshing meal of grapes and delicious fresh lebben (sour milk) under the trees before we remounted; my sister was given a very fine white dromedary, and we all set off racing each other at a brisk trot.

We had a grand entry into Damascus; about two hours' distance

* Buchanan Read. † Job xxxviii. 31.

from the town we met the beautiful and almost priceless mares of the Sheikh out exercising, and he immediately mounted his favourite, and galloped wildly and gaily all round the cavalcade. The dromedaries knew very well how near they were to home, and they went merrily along while the Argeels brushed them up, re-arranged their own kefiyehs, and then burst out into choruses of songs, screaming and shouting, and some of them standing up and dancing on the camels' backs amid peals of laughter, while the darabooka played unceasing rub-a-dubs of the noisiest description. Very merry and bright it was; the road was lively with people, to whom the astonishing fact of our long stay at Tadmor was again and again related, and a thousand welcomes were shouted to Sheikh Miguel as one after another recognised him. Most cool, refreshing, and delightful did the green trees overhanging the rough paths, the bright gardens, and thousand rushing streamlets appear to our desert-used eyes. I need not say how still more welcome the excellent hôtel beds felt to our wearied bodies as we sank to sleep to the music of the fountain in our room, after fifteen days' absence. But I may add that, for my own part, I would willingly undergo twice the fatigue again to re-visit that magnificently lovely Tadmor.

CHAPTER XVI.

STRONGHOLDS OF NATURE AND ART.

WE stood much in need of rest after our return from Tadmor, and we were not sorry to spend a few days in the hôtel, varying our time with pleasant rides in the suburbs of the city—the justly famous gardens of Damascus. We are told that one might take a new ride every day for four months among these charming groves, fields, and orchards, with pleasant-looking villages every here and there; the roads, too, are mostly excellent, and there are many fine views of the city to be seen from between the trees. A net-work of little canals and channels of water extends over all the cultivated plain, cooling the air and soothing the ear with the pleasant murmuring of the streamlets to which all the glorious verdure is owing; miles and miles of those tiny rivers are spread over the ground, every one coming originally from the Bärrada, the river whose course we had followed from 'Ain Fijeh. This river is the Abana of Scripture, which Naaman considered, with natural pride, as fine a river as any in Israel; the Hebrew name meant "the clear" river—the Arabic means "the cold." The other "river of Damascus," the Pharphar, was described in Hebrew as "the fugitive;" while its Arabic name of the Awaj signifies "the tortuous." The latter is not as long a river as the Bärrada, and contains scarcely a third as much water; it rises on Mount Hermon, and both rivers after passing Damascus are lost in marshes on the sandy desert beyond. The Bärrada was named Chrysorrhoas by the Greeks; it flows on the north side of the city, while the Awaj passes on the south.

There are many varieties of trees in the gardens of Damascus, but the most numerous are the apricots, the dried fruit of which forms so very large a part of its commerce. The apricots are either dried in the sun and then pressed flat in slight wooden boxes, or else they are stoned and mashed into a thick paste, which is dried in masses a yard or two long, and is exported in large rolls looking like brown leather,—this is called *kumrredeen*—the apricots dried whole are called *mishmish.* It is said to be a lovely sight to look over the plain of Damascus in the spring, when the innumerable apricots are in flower, the effect being exactly that of light snow resting on the trees; but many persons think it more striking when the fruit is just ripe: then the trees glow as if illuminated with thousands of tiny lamps hung among the branches, giving a most curious golden gleaming effect from the heights above.

The gardens are separated by primitive walls formed of cakes of mud, sun-dried, about three or four feet square and six inches thick; they are generally topped with dhourra straw or palm-branches, and have a most curious appearance. There is something of the same kind used in Greece, but in smaller cakes.

One of our pleasantest afternoon rides was to the village of Jobah, lying hidden among walnut-groves, at about an hour's distance from the city; this place has been time out of mind held sacred by both the Jew and the Mooslim, on account of a very ancient synagogue built over the cave, in which it is believed that Elijah hid himself from the persecutions of Jezebel. We were invited to descend into it, without shoes, through a narrow hole with nicks, instead of steps, cut in the rock to tread on; but we declined to enter, hearing that there was nothing to see within. In the centre of the synagogue there is a space railed off where Elijah is said to have anointed Hazael king,—here no one entered, but otherwise the floor was quite covered with people. A school was going on in one corner, numbers of women were tailoring and making shoes, and men reading aloud in groups.

Passing through the streets on our return to the hôtel, we met an infant's funeral: the father, preceded by a little boy dressed in his best, carried the child laid out on his arms, with an embroidered handkerchief thrown over it, but the small face left uncovered; it seemed smiling in its sleep. Two friends followed him, and they were all chanting a not inharmonious hymn, or more probably verses from the Korăn. The simplicity of the funeral, and the contrast of the little dead face and the bright colours of the dresses, were quite touching. The Arabs all dress in their finest cloths at a funeral, and the widows sit in their richest silks, with all the gay colours they can put together, for three days after the death of the husband: it is partly from the idea that he is gone to happiness, but more to do him honour and pay respect to the corpse.

The hôtel at Damascus is a good specimen of the modern style of ornament in houses, and is both clean and comfortable. A miserable little passage is as usual the entrance from the street ("called Straight") into a large court, with a lofty leewän on one side and a good room at each corner: in the centre a tank of water is shaded by pomegranate, lemon, and oleander-trees. Opposite the leewän is the best room, which my sister and I inhabited: it was forty feet high, with a floor of variegated marble, and a roof ornamented in the old delicate style of painting, which is now disappearing before a gaudy, coarser kind. A fountain played in the centre of the apartment, which had three alcoves on raised floors,—two of them, screened off by curtains, formed bed-rooms, and the other was fitted up for the general sitting-room; the walls were painted with a stencilled imitation of the beautiful old marble mosaic, and the upper windows near the ceiling were closed with carved lattices of intricate Saracenic patterns. It made a very pleasant room, but when we came back from Tadmor we felt half suffocated from sleeping under a roof with closed doors and windows after being accustomed to the open air! It seemed very absurd to have caught the Bodoueen dislike to a house, but we had dreadful headaches, and were glad when the nights were once more passed in our airy tents.

We mounted donkeys on our last evening in Damascus and strolled through the streets. They were generally very dim, sometimes pitch-dark except for the lantern carried by one of our attendants, to prevent our stepping on the horrid dogs lying asleep everywhere; but here and there one came on a brightly-illuminated *café* or a barber's shop, or that of a grocer or tobacconist, noisy with late bargainers and coffee-drinkers. The bazaars seemed endless in their darkness, a single oil-lamp now and then revealing a figure rolled up in a dark *abbah*, asleep on the boarding which served as the counter by day; the shop itself being closed in by a heavy wooden lid, which is lowered by night over the recess and locked. Sometimes a long vista of arches ended picturesquely in a brilliantly-lighted *café*, or a group of white-turbaned Turks sitting on the ground smoking nargilehs. But the prettiest sight was afforded by the various Mosques, most of them lighted with hundreds of hanging lamps and filled with rows and groups of men kneeling in prayer: in one, which was much less illuminated than the others, the polished marble floor shone darkly, like a lake of black water, reflecting back the few lamps like stars, and throwing out finely the figures of the Mooslims, dressed in bright colours and white turbans, standing in groups, or prostrated in prayer. As one passed quickly by it gave one the impression of a dream, the beautiful Mosque with its numbers of slender columns and horse-shoe arches in party-coloured marbles, and the dim light shining on the worshippers, chanting their prayers in a wild and sweet harmony.

We left Damascus on the afternoon of the 2nd November, by the Bab-el-Salahîyeh, our last view of the fair city having been from the same point as the first; then we descended into a lovely winding glen, full of thick foliage and the rushing, tumbling stream of the Bärrada, and emerged from it on to the Desert and the desolate Sah'ra mountains just as darkness fell upon us. The country was so hideous that we were rather rejoicing that the young moon gave scarcely light enough to show it in its dreary loneliness and silence, when—voices called to us to stop. The dragomans immediately fell back to ask what they wanted, and we soon guessed they were the robbers or Syrian banditti which, as we afterwards learned, infest this road. Fortunately we were, every one of us, dressed in the white mash'lah of the country, and we believe that they mistook us in the dim light for men; at all events they seemed to think we were too strong a party for them, and let us alone, and we made the best of our way on. Of course, as *contretemps* always come together, one of the horses was lame from a bad shoe, and we could only go at a walking pace; and the fun of the thing was that, though we all showed our pistols and revolvers, not one of us, even the dragomans, had remembered to reload them on leaving Damascus. We expected the robbers would pursue us in great numbers, but they kindly changed their minds if they had such intentions, and we heard no more of them. We continued the dreary road, however, with the pleasing expectation of finding they had possessed themselves of all our baggage and tents, which had been sent on before us; so that the little dog's bark and the mules' bells seldom sounded more melodiously in our ears than they did two hours later, when we came upon the tents near the village of Dimâs.

The ride of the following morning led through a charming green vale, full of sweet bright flowers, and lively with caravans of camels bringing corn from the Haurân. Two men among the camel-drivers recognised one of the horses, which had been purchased in Damascus, as having belonged to a brother of theirs, and fell to kissing and hugging the pretty creature most enthusiastically, to the apparent delight of the horse, and the immense surprise of its rider, until the origin of their affection was explained by the dragoman. We crossed a circular plain with a pretty lake at one side, and then reached the Druze village of Deir-el-Ashayr, where the villagers were so poor that they could not even give us milk or bread or fruit. But we had an interesting temple to examine, under whose shade we rested for some time, admiring the fine view of the Anti-Lebanon

T

mountains, with the whole valley of Zebdany lying at their feet, and Bludân perched on a mountain nook among dark green woods. The temple is small, standing on a platform of fine blocks of stone which measures 126 feet by 69, and about 20 feet in height, curiously finished with a simple but bold cavetto cornice, exactly the same as that at 'Ain Fijeh, only *inverted*. The platform reminds one in miniature of those at Baalbek and Tadmor, and in the extensive ruins strewed at one side of the temple a large court leading up to it is still traceable. There was an entrance under the platform into a vaulted passage, as we are told; above there are the remains of a hall with three small chambers at one end, and a portico in front. Only one column of this is standing, but two capitals lay on the ground carved with a simple circular horn or roll, something like the Ionic, but very rude. This temple is the more interesting as it is one of the semicircle of temples closing round the foot of Hermon, all built to face the sacred mountain,— and was most probably, therefore, one of the Baal Temples—like those of Baalbek and Tadmor; the style of the building is simple but good, strongly resembling that at 'Ain Fijeh, except in the Ionic kind of capital.

We rode on through a wild pass of rocky hills, covered with prickly oak and hawthorn, where we saw hundreds of goats with long black silky hair. They came at the herdsman's call, and gave us plenty of milk, which we drank from a fine old silver bowl engraved with Kufic characters. Early in the afternoon we reached Rukhleh, a Druze village, where our tents were pitched, but we rode on half an hour farther, or more, to examine some other temples of which the villagers told us; we found the remains of three temples, which seemed all of them to have been turned facing Hermon, but they were now only such heaps of jumbled stones that one could make out little or nothing of them. The faces of the cliffs in these little valleys are quite full of tombs, which ought to be much more narrowly examined than they have been as yet. We entered one large excavation fronted by two arches; it contained places for five bodies, and two huge stone sarcophagi with high peaked lids, broken, but unusually deep; three or four bodies might have lain in them. There seemed to have been a bracket carved in each angle of the cave, but we could find no further ornament or inscription. There were stone sarcophagi lying about in many places, and several hewn in the rock under one's feet, so that now the lids were gone, they were open pits into which one might unwarily step. We passed soon after this by the face of a rock, smoothed to about thirty feet high, with a rude pilaster at each side, and the remains of an altar before it. Close in front of the altar was a large deep hole, which the guide said was the opening of a passage hollowed underground for several yards' distance; one could not help thinking it might have been made to carry off the blood or water from the altar: it was a curious, mysterious-looking place altogether. Passing back to our tents, we saw a well-cut bit of frieze, and then the mouldings of an arch built into a terrace-wall—in fact the whole of the valley seemed strewn with architectural or sepulchral remains.

Then we went to the large temple, of which a great deal still remains *in situ;* it was placed with the angles to the cardinal points in order that the S.W. side should face the Baal-Temple raised on the highest point of Hermon. In the centre of this side is sculptured in high relief a face, five feet in diameter, supposed to be the representation of Baala (or Baltis, the feminine of Baal), who was called by both the Phœnicians and Hebrews "the queen of heaven." * The remarkable face on a temple at Kunawât in the Haurân is the only other example that has been found of this singular and interesting subject: this one is a good deal defaced, but there is a soft and solemn grandeur still expressed in the large eyes and mutilated features. Several mouldings surround the face, wide at the top and narrowing under the chin, showing that it was to be seen from below: the innermost moulding seemed to represent thick curls—the outer one was of the egg-and-dice pattern; there was something touching in the large sweet face, still looking out through centuries of long years at the setting sun, whose last rays were now passing a mellowing tint over the unchanging features.

The style of the temple is massive and simple: a lofty triple doorway stood on the N.W. side, a smaller one on the S.W. side, and the S.E. end terminated in an apse. The lintel of the great doorway has fallen, but it lies on the ground, showing the figure of a large eagle well sculptured on the under-side; the wings are expanded, and the claws hold a long wreath of palm-branches, and a laurel-crown sculptured on each side of the eagle; these ornaments closely resemble those around the eagle on the famous onyx of Augustus in the Imperial Cabinet at Vienna, but the bird itself is very different. Palm-branches and laurel-leaves were sculptured on other stones near by. A row of columns extended through the centre of the temple, with the same rude Ionic capitals we had seen

* Jer. vii. 18; xliv. 17; 1 Kings xi. 5, 33. Her great temple was at Sidon, but there were very many others raised to her in Syria: she was also called by the Hebrews Ashtaroth, by the Greeks Astarte, and by the Assyrians Mylitta.

T 2

at Deir-el-Ashayr; the rolls, which formed the volutes on two sides of the capital, passed horizontally along the other two sides, and were bound in the centre of each by a fillet, with leaves curling up from underneath them: on the other two sides, besides the volute at each end, were scrolls and other ornaments. Dr. Robinson thinks that Banias may be the site of " Baal-gad," in the Valley of Lebanon, under Mount Hermon (Josh. xii. 5): I should like to suggest that if Baal-gad be not a collective name for the *whole group* of Baal-Temples * that encircle the N.W. and S. sides of Hermon, which seems the most natural interpretation, it may be applied with more probability to the numerous remains—of four at the least —of temples at Rukhleh rather than to Banias. Banias, though certainly " under Mount Hermon," is completely south of the range of country usually called " Lebanon;" while Rukhleh, on the *northern* foot of Hermon, seems to be more indicative of a land extending from "Mount Hermon unto the entering in of Hamath," a place precisely to the N.E. of Hermon, and therefore " toward the sun-rising."

Winding glens, thickly wooded with prickly-oak, led from Rukhleh to Kefr Kook, the Lebanon mountains opening before us as we advanced towards the sea, and the double peak of Jebel Niha forming a pretty point in the view. As we came to Rasheiya the view extended far up northwards, and the snowy summits of our beloved Sunnin, Kunisiyeh, El-Jurd, and Makhmel came in with much beauty. Rasheiya is very picturesque; the houses overhang each other on the sides of a steep hill rising out of vine-terraces, and crowned by the Emir's Palace, a castle-like building looking very grand in contrast with the low stone village houses. We spread our cloaks under some shady rocks while we had our usual luncheon of fresh *leben*, and looked at the silver ornaments which are largely made here. Presently the Emir's brother came down to visit us, with numerous attendants, and invited us to rest in the palace, which we declined. He seemed very intelligent, and sat a long time examining with pleasure the few things we had to show— lunettes, travelling-fans, measuring-tapes, &c., and our large map of Syria, which always delighted the Arabs. He left us at the sound of the bugle in the castle, and we went on, an hour farther, to a large pool of brackish water in a little plain, where the mules, released unusually early in the day, enjoyed a thorough scamper and gallop. We had to send back to Rasheiya for water, which makes this otherwise pleasant spot an awkward camping-ground; there is

* The same word precisely—*gad*—is used here in the Hebrew, as in Gen. xxx. 11, where it signifies an indefinite number.

a large pond here, but it was then too brackish to use; we had chosen it in order to shorten our expedition to the summit of Hermon on the following day, which would, we knew, be very fatiguing.

We started at 8 A.M.—much too late—on the following morning, sending the mules by Rasheiya to Hasbeiya. The path commenced among pretty woods and tangled vineyards, until it became very steep, and had to be ascended in zigzag, the horses slipping continually, and the saddles occasionally coming off, not having been properly secured with braces across the chest. With *good* horses three hours is ample for reaching the end of the path; after this the ascent is really difficult and very bad, a long, steep slope of loose, small shingle, in which both man and horse sink up to the knees, slipping backwards at every step. All dismounted but myself; my gallant old horse, a Crimean charger, carried me, with the aid of two strong human arms, to the top of the second summit from the north, whence all the northern view is shut out; thence we found grassy dells and little hills along the lofty ridge to the highest and most southern summit. Here we stopped a couple of hours to enjoy the magnificent view, for seeing which we were highly favoured by the weather. The heat was tempered by a cool, gentle breeze instead of the terrible wind usual at this height, and the distance was perfectly clear and cloudless.

To the south-east the Haurān lay mapped before us, blue hills on the horizon faintly bounding the far, far distance, deepening in colour as they swept round to the south; Damascus lying, gem-like in its verdure, on the barren country towards the north. Then came the long white ridge of the rugged Anti-Lebanon; the heights of Makhmel and Sunnîn, &c., all rosy beneath the snow, headed the confusion of peaks, and slopes, and craggy heights of the Bârûk range, occupying the whole of the western country between Hermon and the blue sea; while we looked down into the very heart of the deep narrow ravine of the dashing Litaany, with its sharp, sudden bend towards the sea, half hidden in thick woods. Saïda and Sour lay underneath the cliffs, range after range of mountains filling up the space between the Litaany and the coast, till Carmel ran a deep blue promontory into the sea; then came the purple and green mountains of Galilee to the south, among which Tabor, and Hattîn, and Jermûk stood conspicuous, while, paling in blues behind them, lay the Judean hills, the mountains of Gilboa and Samaria. At our feet the lake Houleh ("the waters of Merom") seemed close to us, and beyond that, shining in clear blue serene loveliness, the beautiful lake of Tiberias sank deep down in the dark purple mountains, like a sweet smile on an aged, rugged face. From thence one could trace the winding hill-tops of the Ghor, the valley of the tortuous Jordan, till it was lost in the faint distance of the Dead Sea mountains. Just underneath us the craggy summits of the lower spurs of Hermon clustered over Banias : on one of these it is supposed Christ our Saviour was transfigured.

Hermon was to the Israelites the principal mountain in the land ; it stood like a sentinel commanding their northern border, and they did not much concern themselves about those beyond it ; it is, however, supposed to be about 300 feet lower than the Cedar Mountain. Its beautiful cone, snow-covered nearly throughout the year, is seen from many parts of Palestine ; we saw it distinctly from the Dead Sea. It is so much loftier than any of the more southern mountains that it naturally takes the name of Jabel-esh-Sheikh— the chief or prince of mountains ; this is its commonest Arabic name, but it has many others. Its ancient Hebrew names have much the same meaning, Hermon and Sion both signify the " upraised," the " lifted upon high," the chief thing: so Sion was the name given Jerusalem to express that which excelled all others ; and it is perhaps in the same sense that the word is applied in Ps. cxxxiii. 3, where it expresses the fact of the loftiest mountains catching the most dew from the clouds. The Phœnicians called it the " Breast-plate," in the language used by them at Sidon—*Sirion*; and in that used by the Amorites—*Shenir*; both words, in the two dialects, having the same meaning. It is natural, also, that Scripture should mention names peculiar to these tribes of Phœnicians, as Hermon appears to stand over Sidon, and the possessions of the Amorites extended to the skirts of the mountain itself.* It may be worth noticing also that in the days of Abraham the Amorites were settled in the mountain of 'Aim Jidi, on the coast of the Dead Sea,† from whence on clear days Hermon is well seen—almost the only view of it to be obtained from the south of Palestine. An old pilgrim tells us that every morning at sunrise a handful of dew floated down from the summit of Hermon, and deposited itself upon the Church of St. Mary, where it was immediately gathered up by Christian leeches, and was found a sovereign remedy for all diseases : it was of this dew, he naïvely adds, that David spoke prophetically in his Psalms.‡

A massive wall once encircled the highest peak of the mountain, and a temple stood here. The ground is covered with the large hewn stones of the outer wall ; a few of them were bevelled, and we saw some bold, simple sculpturing on some of the others, the style reminding us of Dier-el-Ashayr. That a temple dedicated to Baal

---

* Deut. iv. 48.   † Gen. xiv. 7.   ‡ Itinerary of St. Antony.

once existed here is to be gathered from the name of Baal-Hermon applied in Judg. iii. 3, and 1 Chron. v. 23, and St. Jerome testifies to the fact;* nor could one stand on that summit and look from east to west and from north to south without feeling that worshippers of the sun could not have left so grand a spot unconsecrated to their god. One seems, standing here, to enter into something of the feelings of the untutored child of Nature who daily witnessed the incomprehensible mystery of the sun's all-glorious course, and believed his quickening rays to be the source of all the life and well-being of the world around him. The stones of the old wall were mostly covered with a very minute lichen of a bright scarlet colour; while between every stone grew tufts of a velvety thorny plant, very dense and tough, covered with the tenderest little pale, fragile blossoms; a kind of *immortelle*, which fell or blew away at a touch or a breath; they grew on the Cedar Mountain also, and we afterwards found them near the Dead Sea.

We refreshed ourselves with a little snow or ice melted in some wine which we had fortunately carried up with us, and at two o'clock commenced our descent, which, after the first half hour, became really terrible. We thought it quite hard upon the horses to have taken them to the summit on either side, but from Hasbeiya it is really a cruelty. We were three long hours and a half descending that gully, jumping and scrambling from stone to stone, the horses following as best they could, often standing still, trembling, and casting imploring looks at us, as if for help. The walls of the ravine closed in boldly and sometimes quite perpendicularly on each side. Numbers of caverns and holes were observable, which are, they say, infested with bears and jackals; eagles' feathers, often bloody, lay about on the rocks, and numerous lovely fossil shells, which we could not stop to detach, lay half imbedded on their sides. Alas! the sun set when we reached the beginning of a path, and we were soon in darkness, though when the moon rose she lighted the rough path every here and there, and showed Hermon towering up very grandly over our heads. The descent was very steep, but most of it seemed richly wooded, and, we doubted not, commanded fine views by daylight. About half past eight we arrived at the village of 'Ain 'Ata, where the people seemed to commiserate us very much for being so late on the road. It was vexatious to find that our tents had passed through this village, and that had we been better informed of the distances we might have been saved all the long additional and disagreeable descent which we were compelled to make in the dark. How we ever got safely over the succeeding

* Porter.

road is a mystery to me; it seemed nothing but a succession of smooth beds of rock turned up at a steep angle, down which the poor horses slipped and sliddered hopelessly. Hill after hill had to be passed, until at last we reached the town of Hasbeiya, the rows of lights in the houses on the terraces looking very pretty up and down the sides of the mountains. We descended to the very bottom, and learned there, to our intense vexation, that the tents had gone on two hours farther, and there was nothing for it but to follow them through a very narrow ravine along the edge of a dry torrent bed. The path was frequently not eighteen inches wide, and darkly shaded with trees, and at last my poor tired horse slipped his hind legs over the edge, was too worn out to recover himself, and fell, turning over in the air, on to the rocks below! We were both of us soon picked up, and I remounted for the very long two hours which ensued—very thankful to have escaped without serious injury; but I was so much bruised that I could not stand unassisted for three days after. At last we reached a thick grove of fine old olive-trees, and after firing pistols and shouting repeatedly, to our great joy we were answered, and soon after reached our tents at exactly one o'clock in the morning, having been seventeen hours on horseback, and without any food but a bit of Arab bread.

Our tents were pitched in a delightful spot near the village of Kaukaba, not only under the shade of the olives, but on rich green-sward, an uncommon luxury in the East, with the waters of the Hasbâny close by, coming from a large spring, one of the most northern sources of the Jordan; the rocky vale between us and Hasbeiya was filled with tall white asphodels and fern, and every little crevice held its bunch of pink cyclamen. The fair of Souk-el-Khan was going on a mile farther down the valley, and we had plenty of gaily-dressed passers-by: this fair is said to have been held annually since the time of the Romans. After some days' rest we went into Hasbeiya to pay a visit to the Emir, whose palace stands, with much the air of a fortress, above the town on the steep mountain side. The castle walls are quaintly ornamented with square bay windows, supported on carved machicolations, and brightly painted—pink, red, blue, and green. We dismounted in a small court in front of the building, in which several servants and gaily-caparisoned horses were standing. We had omitted to send beforehand to announce our coming; but the Emir received us very graciously, and led us into the palace by a long flight of steps, and through several darkish passages and chambers, till we reached his reception-room, a small and ordinary apartment, with the daïs railed off, below which stood a crowd of attendants. This Emir is called

Sa'ad-ed-dîn, and is chief of the ancient family of Shehâb. They are now Mooslims; but having once, some generations ago, been Christians, they are much despised by the true believers. He looked about fifty years of age, small, and not handsome, with a crafty expression of face. He made us many pretty Arab speeches, for which he is rather famous, assuring us that he had never admired his palace until we praised it, and that our words had made it lovely, &c., &c., and then he offered to show it to us, stating that it had been built by the Crusaders about a hundred years before his family came into possession of it, and that they had occupied it eight hundred years. It has been a fine old building, but is now much decayed and dilapidated. He took us through a handsome inner court and up two stories of staircases to a lofty leewän arch, the entrance to the hareem—the most perfect specimen of Saracenic architecture possible—a fairy-like structure of rose-coloured limestone, inlaid with various polished marbles most delicately and tastefully carved; the deeply receding arches, with honeycombed semi-domes, were supported on slender spiral columns, with wreaths of flowers twisted round them: there were many richly-carved medallions, and in the centre a broken fountain; the whole thing was both rich and elegant. The hareem apartments seemed gaily painted, and a number of female slaves and handsomely-dressed little girls kept peeping out at us. The Emir's father, too old to govern now, but consulted on every occasion, sat in one of the courts wrapped up in fur. Sa'ad-ed-dîn himself was shabbily dressed; but his servants were all well clad, and seemed respectable Arabs, not slaves. He accompanied us down to the court, standing while we mounted our horses, and sent a janissary to guide us to the Druze Khulweh (place of worship), to which my sister rode with a friend, while I remained sketching in the town, not being as yet very active again.

They found it rather a long mount up to the Druze settlement, but the way commanded wild and beautiful views of the mountains. At last they reached some low houses and an arch, under which was a strong screw press, for extracting honey from the comb, the janissary said; above this was a well-built stone terrace in front of the chapel, called a Khulweh, which means " solitude." Some very old Druzes, with long beards as white as their turbans, came forward to meet them, and led them into a small enclosure, shaded by a large oak-tree, where eight others were sitting in conclave on a stone divan; they were most cordially welcomed, and carpets spread for them to rest on, while the old men reseated themselves in European fashion on the divan. One of them was said to be a hundred years old, and had a white beard reaching below his waist; he was bent, and rather deaf, but with all the fire of youth in his clear blue eye. They said he knew the English were always good friends with the Druzes, and, in reply to the request of their visitors, professed themselves happy to show the inside of their chapel to them; so the oldest Druze led the way into the chapel. In the outer passage they took off their shoes, and thence went into a room where two rows of pillars supported an arched roof; the floor was covered with thick carpets, a divan of cushions round it, and piles of small cushions in the corners; they apologized that it was very poor, and that they had no ornaments to show, no hanging lamps, like the Christians, or fine priests' dresses. They said they had no distinguishing dress for those in authority, and no ceremonies; they only prayed the prayers transmitted from generation to generation, and read from the sacred books; they had, they said, thirty Priests or Ukkals (the initiated), who lived in this chapel during the winter. They insisted on their visitors eating or drinking with them: it was " their rule," and they " must," a refusal would pain them so much; so they brought an osier tray heaped up with raisins, figs, and roasted maize, of which they partook; but the Druzes were much grieved that they could not stop to take a real dinner with them, and implored them to return on another day: they made the servants fill their pockets with all that remained of the dried fruits. Opposite the window of the room there was a very strong-looking door of polished metal or stone, which they saw by the outside must have led into a room which had no outer windows; this was probably the *real* chapel, into which they never admit a stranger, and the outer room perhaps had only been passed off upon their visitors to prevent their asking any more questions. This was the very Khulweh plundered by Ibrahim Pasha, when their sacred books were scattered about and many of them burned. Their visitors left them with many salaams and good wishes, and returned to Hasbeiya, where the Emir came out to salute them as they passed by. I had in the mean time been sketching on the road, to the immense surprise of the people, who crowded round me, explaining to each other what I was doing, and at last fell into a discussion which greatly edified me as to whether I was man or woman—" welled " or " bint;"—they became quite excited in their perplexity, and propounded the difficult question in a loud voice to every fresh arrival. When I stood up and they saw my long riding-habit, besides the hat, which they admired greatly, they were overcome with astonishment; but they agreed then that I must be a "bint," not a " welled," while the dragoman chaffed them for their stupidity.

From Kaukaba we determined to make a long *détour* to see the natural bridge over the Litaany, so we left our tents the next morning at 9.30, and ascended the other side of the valley, passing the mines, whence the workmen brought out huge cakes of pure bitumen to show us; there are about thirty pits containing bitumen of the finest quality lying in horizontal strata. At the top of the hill came lovely views, looking back, of the Lake of Galilee, and looking forward, of the ravine of the Litaany, into whose depths we saw more distinctly as we rode along the uplands, and over brow after brow of the mountains, until we reached Yah-mour, a miserable Metouaalee village. Thence the mules were sent on by a more practicable route, while we descended a break-neck path, cut out of the rock, and overhanging the river, to the natural bridge of El-Kouweh—a scene of splendid beauty, enthusiastically admired by Dr. Robinson—where the grand cliffs rise perpendicularly about 400 or 500 feet at each side in masses of grey limestone and bright red soil, with oak, oleander, ferns, crocuses, and cyclamen bursting out from every crevice. The bridge, which is formed by masses of rock which have tumbled down, is about forty feet high : some fine fig-trees grow under it, leaning over the madly-rushing, foaming water, which throws up its white spray among their branches. It is a glorious spot, and we lingered there long before we commenced the very steep and difficult ascent on the other side ; this surmounted, we found a good path up the pretty, wide green valley of Mushgharrah, along which I imagine many a band of Crusaders passed wearily. The wady opens up into the Bukaa, with a fine view of the Anti-Lebanon range, which was then crimsoned in the setting sun. Mushgharrah is situated at the foot of Jebel-Tom-Niha—the twin peaks—to the west of the valley of the Litaany ; the village is large, and thickly shaded with trees ; at the bottom of it, beside the dashing river, is a bright little cemetery under fine walnut-trees, and near it a picturesque waterfall, embosomed in foliage, rich ferns, and flowers ; travellers should encamp in this pretty meadow rather than mount into the village as we did. Opposite to the village, on the very summit of the mountain, are two thick groves of aged trees, doubtless one of the " groves and high places " of Baal-worship ; the peasants have many legends about their sacredness.

Our ride of eight hours on the next day was one of much beauty. An excellent road led through the whole valley, and we had pretty views in every direction ; by-and-by we crossed a ridge which divided the valley of the Litaany from the district of Esh Shŭkîf, when we found ourselves among the rich red soil and stone pines familiar to us at our beloved Beit Miry. We then followed a very tortuous path over the shoulder of Jebel Rihân, with beautiful views of the lakes Houleh and Tiberias, and of Hermon, looking excessively grand under a dark stormy sky, with thick black clouds gathering about his head, from whence peals of thunder saluted us at intervals. We passed a rock thickly incrusted with a brilliant sulphur-coloured salt, and quantities of fine fossil wood; while all the paths were shaded with myrtle bushes in full flower, from which the mountain takes its name of *rihan*, the Arabic for myrtle: the horses ate the flowers most greedily. Then came two hours of descent among a forest of prickly oak and arbutus, but in which all the really fine trees had been burned for charcoal: several were burning as we passed, the fire lighted round the roots and left to burn till the tree falls. The sound of a pipe attracted us, and we searched the bushes till we found a shy shepherd-boy playing really pretty airs on a rude pipe of two reeds, surrounded by his goats, who seemed enchanted with the melody; two of them were standing on their hind legs with their fore paws on his shoulders.

We found our tents pitched on the hill-side by the black-looking village of Jermuk. A rich valley lay beneath us, closed at the southern end by the noble Castle of Belfort, called Kŭlat-esh Shŭkîf, which we were very anxious to visit, as a spot famous in crusading annals, and because it is frequently mentioned in the old chronicles by the same name as our own. The thunderstorm we had been expecting broke upon us in the night, and we were nearly drenched by the morning, our tents not having an outer cover; we therefore determined to push on to the castle, contrary to the advice of the dragomans, as we thought it quite as unpleasant to sit in the rain inside as outside the tent.* So we wrapped ourselves up and started: whereupon the sun came out approvingly, and turned the clouds into a beautiful fresh day. We sent the tents by a different route, and followed ourselves a pretty path, over breezy downs, through two villages, Nŭbatîyeh and Arnoun, to the foot of the castle hill; thence we had an ascent of about an hour, partly on foot, to the summit.

This castle is well worth a visit. It is perched on the brow of an absolutely perpendicular cliff, rising 1500 feet from the bed of the Litaany, which dashes in white foam over the rocks at the bottom of the chasm. The other side of the ravine is not so lofty, but beyond it the country slopes up to the foot of Hermon, in every variety of colour, and the chasm of the river is thickly

* I may as well remark that the rain of this night and the day on Sunnîn in the month of June, was the only rain we had during all the months we were travelling with tents.

wooded. There is a deep moat round the other three sides of the castle, only a' very narrow ledge on the river side being left for entrance. Some of the towers are sixty or eighty feet high, with sloping masonry at the foot of each, resembling the Tower of Hippicus at Jerusalem. Much of the foundation of the castle is built with massive stones, bearing the Phœnician bevel; probably the Crusaders only added their own work to an already strong and ancient fortress, since, commanding, as it did, the principal road from Sidon to Damascus, and to Laish (Banias), it could never have been left unfortified; and the name still used being the same as the Hebrew, seems to indicate that it was a Hebrew fortress. Shŭkíf means to overhang, or to look out from, and is used to signify the same kind of overhanging or projecting rock in Numb. xxi. 20. The walls are very thick, and a great number of finely-vaulted chambers remain uninjured, as well as five or six staircases. In the centre is the now ruined chapel built by the Crusaders, with a groined roof, and a little ornament remaining on the doorways and walls. How many an ardent prayer may have arisen under its arches for the restoration of the Holy Sepulchre, and victory against the infidels, before the pious and valiant knight went forth to conquer, or—far more often—to die!

Various are the stories connected with this castle and its possession by the Crusaders and by the gallant Saladin. It must ever have been a place of great importance to either party. The view from it is very fine indeed, and the two sister fortresses of Banias and Hunîn are easily distinguished. We sat here a long time, sketching, and thinking over its old history, with visions of the pious Louis, and Philip Augustus, and our own brave Cœur-de-Lion, and listening to the utter silence of the lonely spot, when, from the ruined keep of the castle, a huge eagle, disturbed by the unwonted voices, uprose on

> " proud and ample pinion   .   .   .   .
> Sailing with supreme dominion
> Through the azure deep of air,"

and flew majestically over to the opposite heights.

A quarter of an hour farther, the river, which flows due south from the valley of the Bukaa, turns at a sharp angle to the west, and the chasm, scarcely three feet wide at the bottom, bends round, presenting a lovely and splendid picture. The sides are richly covered with wood of many kinds, and, as far as we could see down by leaning over the edge of the cliff, bright with flowers. This is one of the finest spots in all Syria, and it is indeed of very singular beauty.

We walked down to Arnoun, and then descended a very rough path, full of lovely views, to a delightful old bridge, at the very foot of the castle cliff, called Jisr Khurdeli, of high, pointed arches, half hidden in trees and oleanders. We had a steep ascent on the other side, ere we reached our tents, placed on the top of the ridge of hills between the Litaany and Hermon, near a village called Khurbeh. The great mountain was densely shrouded in clouds, and for the last hour or two had appeared awfully grand and black; but the sun set just as we reached the tents, and the whole scene was in a moment transformed as if by magic. The thick clouds changed to sheets of rose-colour and gold, and, breaking asunder, revealed the majestic mountain standing in the midst, robed in a mantle of deep, dark violet and indigo blue, from whence the snowy cone shone out like silver. The glorious colouring lasted about a quarter of an hour, and then paled and darkened away, till, from behind the immense mass, the moon rose like a globe of fire, her beams touching all the mountain-tops and the white villages in the valley below, where only the screaming jackals disturbed the exquisite beauty of the night.

The wide valley which we had to cross the next morning—the Merj Ayûn, or meadow land at the southern end of the Wady-el-Teim—was delightful ground for cantering on; indeed nearly all the roads in this part of the country are good, as they pass usually along wide valleys. These paths not being known to dragomans, we had brought an old guide, on muleback, all the way from Mushgharrah, who was clever at avoiding any "bad steps." In consideration of his venerable white beard I had addressed him with "O Sheikh!" which so delighted him that he stuck close to my side ever after, and insisted on talking to me. He was a fine, intelligent old man, and knew the country thoroughly. He told us quantities of stories about the mountains and the flowers and the people, and asked numbers of questions about the "Ingleez;" what did we do? how we did dress? what did we eat? &c., &c.; and concluded all by telling us he knew very well how to go to England,—viz. "you must go to the great water with many mule-loads of figs and bread and clothes, and get into a great ship, and the ship would wabble very much—here he nearly fell off his mule, with the excess of the wabbling—and then would go "aha-ha-ha-ha" . . . . a note prolonged for about two minutes, to signify the immense length of the journey. We volunteered a letter of recommendation for him to future travellers, and parted, the best of friends, for—oh rare exception!—the old man was actually contented with the money given him, and did not ask for more baksheesh!

We came after a couple of hours to the dyke of the Hasbany, whose windings we followed, looking down on the river, tumbling over black basaltic stones, and, by-and-by, reached a bridge with an unpronounceable name, which belonged to a tribe of half-breed Bedoueens in the neighbourhood—Jisr Gkhujar—where there were delicious nooks for bathing under thickets of nebbk and oriental plane, gay with oleanders. In half an hour thence we reached what is called the Source of the Jordan, a beautiful spot, where the water wells out with wonderful copiousness from under a grove of lofty valonidis oak-trees, in a wide circle of clear crystal water, one one of the largest fountains known.* Above this is a hill of rubbish, covered up with trees, and stones, and huts, which cover the ruin of Dan, the northern limit of the land of Israel,—"from Dan to Beersheba;" a good situation for an important town, the hill being just high enough to command the whole plain, with the " Waters of Merom," now Lake Houleh, beyond, and the mountains closing in a fine circle all round it. It was from this place that Abraham chased the Mesopotamian chiefs who had taken his brother prisoner, and pursued them as far as Damascus; from here that the Children of Dan expelled the careless colonists from Sidon, who had settled in the " place where there was no want of anything that is in the earth," and set up a city and an altar for themselves; and here that Jeroboam erected a golden calf to save the people the trouble of making pilgrimage to Jerusalem. The meaning of the Hebrew name Dan was " Judge," and thus the Arab of to-day does but translate the ancient word into his own language, calling it Tell-el-Khady, the hill of the judge. From under this hill another, or part of the same, fountain flows out, and the old pilgrims, Arculf in the sixth century, and Sæwulf in the tenth century, relate that these two fountains were called Jor and Dan—the union of the two waters making the river Jordan! This was always the frontier town of Palestine, and our next twelve or fourteen days were spent in Galilee.

The two hours after this lay through a charming forest of lofty oaks of several kinds, the vallonea, or " oaks of Bashan," plane, caroob, and the bright foliage of the nebbk, covered with its pretty little fruit, which we pulled and ate as we rode along; the trees were tangled over with vines and wild roses, making bowers from

* There is another source of the Jordan on the eastern side of Banias, called Lake Phiala, from its circular shape—mentioned by Josephus.

one to the other. Then we passed all through Banias, and fixed our tents in an olive-grove on the other side of the town, by the bank of the stream, commanding a beautiful view of the castle and country. This village is so infested with serpents and scorpions in the summer that every house has a sort of cage, made of branches and dried leaves, erected on poles above the roof, into which the inhabitants mount by a ladder to sleep,—very odd these airy bedrooms look. The people are disagreeable and troublesome to strangers, and we had several alarms of robbers during the three nights we stayed there, besides paying a large price for the permission to encamp under the olive-trees. But it was a delightful spot: the ruins of the old citadel were close by, and the path led through an ancient square tower of bevelled stones, over a picturesque bridge, under which a cataract of foaming water, the Za'areh, dashed down to the Jordan; the rocks over which it tumbled, and the old stones of the bridge, were thickly hung with long streamers of vines and blackberries, bending down to catch the light spray from the water, and with lovely fronds of hart's-tongue and giant maiden-hair fern; then the stream tumbled on under an arched avenue of large plane and willow-trees, which met and interlaced at the top, shading a pool that made a bathing-place *par excellence.* It is no wonder that travellers coming up from the arid, stony ugliness of Judæa should think Banias a perfect paradise of loveliness, and, as Josephus calls it, a " place of great pleasure, famous and delightful;" its freshness and luxuriant verdure are remarkable even to eyes lately come from the thick foliage and flowers of Damascus.

Quite on the other side of the town, at the foot of a cliff of bright red limestone, one of the lowest spurs of Hermon, are the remains of the old Greek shrine of Pan, from which the place derives its name—Pan being the Grecian representative of the Syrian god Baal. A deep cave and a very copious spring made the spot suitable for the commemoration of that sylvan god; and though not now a pretty place in itself, it must have been a fine one when the cavern was open and the sculptured niches perfect: still more so when the " beautiful temple of white marble " erected by Herod the Great, in honour of Cæsar-Augustus, was standing. Now the cavern is half filled up, and the water only oozes out at some distance: the niches are broken and hidden under the heaps of *débris* of stones, broken so small that the ruins of a temple are scarcely discernible, and the only "odour of sanctity" to be perceived at present is a handsome little Wely, dedicated to the Mooslim St. George, called El Khudr. This Tomb is prettily built with twisted and sculptured columns, and we found in it a carved stone, hollowed at the top, which seemed like the remains of an ancient altar. The view from it is fine. We scrambled down the hill, and followed the stream into its delicious and lofty thickets of ash, bay, laurustinus, myrtle, vine, clematis, nightshade, ever so many different roses, and a thousand other plants, shading the little cascades of water and hiding many remains of ancient buildings.

But the grand object at Banias is the noble Castle of Subeibeh, which stands on a cliff something more than 1000 feet above the town. It took us nearly two hours to reach the top, partly on foot, for the way is very steep. It has been an enormous castle: but its chief merit is in the splendid workmanship of the masonry. The stones are very large, and nearly all of the Phœnician bevel; the plan of some of the towers and sloping substructions closely resembles the Tower of Hippicus, while near the west end a Saracenic hall has been built, like that at Baalbek: the groined roof supported upon a central pillar. At the eastern end the castle expands into almost a second castle, mounted on much higher rocks. There are some remarkable cisterns hewn in the rock, one so vast that it must have been able to supply a large garrison for a year or two; this is finely vaulted over, and has two stone staircases descending to the bottom. Altogether this has been, I suppose, not only the finest fortress in Syria, but probably was one of the most ancient strongholds in the world: indeed it is said to be " the most perfect specimen extant of Phœnician military architecture." It commands a noble view from one side, but is not in itself well placed for modern warfare, as, instead of being an isolated eagle's eyrie, like Kulat-esh-Shukif, Subeibeh is commanded on three sides by mountains closely bending round it: for the ridge on which it stands is like one finger running out in the space between two other fingers, both of which are loftier than itself. Some peasants were cultivating tobacco in the light soil on the summit, and in the turned-up earth we found bits of ancient pottery and glass, some of fine colour and delicate texture, with the iridescence of time very beautifully marked upon them. The slopes of the rocky hill are now thickly wooded, and the whole place was spangled with flowers.

The prophetic blessing pronounced by the patriarch Jacob on his death-bed comes naturally to one's mind in Banias; for the little colony of Danites seem to have been planted here exactly in the spot where there could be " a serpent by the way, an adder in the path, that biteth the horse's heels, so that his rider shall fall backward." The children of Israel were always subject to the incursions

U

and raids of the Syrians of Damascus, the Assyrians, and others; and whether they entered the land of Israel by one side or the other of Hermon—whether they swept down the Bukaa and the Wady-et-Teim, or chose the shorter route through the upper part of Ituræa, the men of Dan were always lying in ambush, as it were, under the foot of the mountain, to intercept their progress, or to attack them from behind; and thus make them "fall backward." But Banias had a deeper interest for us than any mere historical one: this was the first place in which we came upon the Footsteps of our Lord,—for it is the Cæsarea-Philippi of the Gospels,—a name given to it when it became part of the territory under the jurisdiction of "Philip Tetrarch of Ituræa, of the region of Trachonitis." It was here that the Son of Man pronounced a special blessing on the ardent Peter's confession of His Divinity, and promised that His Church, built upon a rock, should be sustained through all ages: "six days after" He went "up into an high mountain apart, and was transfigured before them": most probably, from what can be gathered from the Gospels, it was to one of these lofty peaks that He went, wooded and lonely, immediately above the town, as no change of place is mentioned between His coming to Cæsarea-Philippi and His going up into a "high mountain." Hermon was, both in reality and in name, the loftiest of all the mountains of Syria—*the* "high mountain" *par éminence:* it had also always been considered a holy mountain, probably from the worship carried on in the temple upon, and those all around it; and perhaps St. Peter alludes to this, as well as to its after and holier consecration, when in his second Epistle (i. 18) he calls it the "holy mount."

It was to Banias that Agrippa II. withdrew with his sister Berenice when he found the Jews would not be ruled by him, nor submit to the Romans; the city was afterwards visited by both Vespasian and Titus when the Roman army was encamped on the plain of Esdraelon previous to the Fall of Jerusalem: and it was here, 1100 years after, that Baldwin IV., King of Jerusalem, disgraced the word of a Christian and a knight, by carrying off the numerous herds of the Arabs and Turkomans to whom he had vouchsafed his royal protection: a treachery amply avenged by Nour-ed-din. The coins of Cæsarea-Philippi are still extant.

On leaving Banias we retraced our steps to the Jisr Gkhujar, and thence crossed the valley to the opposite side, among herds of buffaloes and the fine horses of a Turkish Bey, put out at grass among the rich pastures, and guarded by the tents of the Bedoueen shepherds. A number of buffaloes followed us up the long and steep ascent to the Castle of Hŭnin, and made themselves very disagreeable companions on the narrow path. This fortress is small and poor after Shŭkif and Subeibeh, and much ruined: it is a jumble of Phœnician, Roman, and Saracenic masonry. A fine hall yet remains, which has been a mosque, and is now a cow-stall; the most curious thing about the castle is the large deep moat, which seems to have been hewn out of the solid rock. We passed on by a very pretty path with fine views, shaded by arbutus-trees full of red berries, and found our tents on a bleak barren spot beside a pool of very dirty water, the only water in the neighbourhood: close to a village called Meis-el-Jebel, of strict Metouaalees, the only village of that sect down here, I believe. A storm passed over our heads without breaking, presenting a beautiful scene of stratified clouds—five and six layers piled over each other on one spot with the thunder growling through them.

Early in the morning we rode on to Kedesh, the royal city of one of the Canaanite or Phœnician kings smitten by Joshua (xii. 22), a " fenced city," and a " city of refuge " of the tribe of Naphtali (xix. 37 ; xxi. 32) ; and a holy place, as its name signifies in Hebrew, the name which it still retains. We were very anxious to see the ruins here, and dismounted at a small square edifice built in a very massive but simple style, wholly unornamented, save one bold moulding. The entrance faced the south ; inside, the four angles are filled up with solid masonry, continued between each to the height of about three or four feet; the lower parts contained three cells for bodies on each side—these had evidently all been used as tombs; in some of them the lids of the sarcophagi were yet remaining, and all of them were full of bones; some of them may have been brought in by jackals, but among them were human bones. In all there were eleven sarcophagus beds, the place of the twelfth being occupied by the doorway. The conjecture of its having been a synagogue seems more than extraordinary, as no Jews could ever have met for prayer in such close proximity to dead bodies. The style of the building appeared to us Roman.

Somewhat further on were several sarcophagi—two of them double ones, with places for two bodies, cut in one stone and under one lid, which was peaked and sculptured all over with a pattern of pine-cones or scales. The sculpture on the sides is almost quite worn out and corroded by the weather, but in some lights one can indistinctly see an eagle sculptured at one end. On other sarcophagi, wreaths of leaves or pine-cone, bound together with fillets or ribbons, are really distinct; at the angles we all thought we distinguished rams' heads with horns curling round, or ends of ribbons united with the wreaths; there seemed also to have been rams' heads between the wreaths.

Beyond these, some parts of a temple still stand on a platform; a triple doorway, handsomely ornamented with egg moulding and wreaths of leaves, resembling those of Baalbek, is much worn; on the lintel of one of the side doors we espied an eagle displayed, but without crest, or streamers, or wreath, sharply carved and still very clear, a double rose and other flowers sculptured on each side of him; and in a small niche a graceful-looking little figure in a toga or flowing drapery. On the ground lay some capitals of rich acanthus leaves; and half buried in the soil, and overgrown with thorns, we found a stone, which we thought looked like the slightly curved side of an altar. We made our saïs and some others dig it out and turn it up, and found that it had indeed been an altar, ornamented with three cones on each side at the top, and having a depression in the centre; on one side was a representation of itself, and on the other, between two palm-branches, a Greek inscription, in which the word ΘΕΟΙΣ was alone distinct. It appeared to us that all the buildings here, and all their details, are indubitably Grecian or Roman; and we sought in vain to discover any of the grounds upon which Dr. Robinson founds his "conviction" that the sarcophagi were of Jewish tombs, or where he found the "splendour" of which he speaks so strongly.

Here lived Barak, a man of much consideration among the children of Israel, whom Deborah the prophetess desired to go with his 10,000 men to Mount Tabor, and thence to give battle, in the name of the Lord, to Sisera the Phœnician general, which he did, near the River Kishon. Everybody remembers how the defeated Sisera was treacherously assassinated by Jael, the wife of Heber, the Kenite, whose tent was pitched under "the terebinths of Zaanaim, which is by Kedesh.* Curiously enough, all about Kedesh there is still a remarkable number of lofty terebinth trees— fine, large, old trees, with their pointed leaves and pretty bunches of red berries, which turn green when they are ripe enough for eating, and from which the Arabs press an oil, good for burning, but which is very irritating if applied to wounds; from the stem a great deal of gum exudes, smelling strongly of turpentine. It is curious that, though the Arabic name for these trees is *Butm*, they call the young, tender, bright green foliage in spring " tarabinth," a name we often heard used for them at Beit Miry. The inhabitants of Kedesh-Naphtali were among the first Jews carried into captivity by the Assyrians.

* Wrongly translated the " plain of Zaanaim," Judges iv. 11.

Our road led us up and down deep and wild ravines in steep, zigzagging paths. We stopped for luncheon in the village of Alma, where in the cemetery we saw a long plait of woman's hair bound upon one of the tombs, perhaps all the mourner had to offer; flowers lay upon another, twined into a wreath; and upon a third, a covered tomb, was a pottery vase full of ashes, in which incense had been burnt. Splendid views of the Lebanon and beautiful Hermon made the road pleasant: and late in the day we reached Safed, a city set upon a very high, steep hill, up which our weary horses toiled. The hamlet at the bottom was full of gaily painted houses and little gardens, neat and tidy enough to do credit to an English gardener; but, indeed, all Safed is neat, being inhabited chiefly by Germans and Poles, thrifty, industrious, and thriving. The town was almost entirely destroyed by an earthquake in 1837; it remained in ruins for many years, and all the houses are newly built or building. We saw numbers of very handsome girls and boys in the village.

Safed is one of the "holy cities" of the Jews, and Israelites from all parts of the world come to reside here. It once possessed celebrated schools, at which many a learned Rabbin was educated, both before and after it had been one of the chief strongholds of the Latin kingdom of Jerusalem: now the streets are full of foreigners, and the variety of costumes and countenances is very grotesque. The views from it are magnificent, extending over what was the Kingdom of Bashan to the east, with the lovely Lake of Tiberias at one's feet, and the mountains of Hattîn and Tabor to the south: on the other side are the stern, wild-looking hills of Jermuk, very dark and bold. In truth the view from the crumbled Castle of Safed is one of the loveliest in Syria; for all the country round it is varied and mountainous, with rich woods and green valleys. The path by which we left it wound down a steep ravine with ever-changing views of the Lake, while from every crevice between the broken rocks bloomed an infinite number of giant pink cyclamens and purple auriculas. By-and-by we came into a green grassy valley, and were slowly crossing it, when suddenly a Bedoueen appeared in the distance, and soon after another and another. They reconnoitered us a little, and then rode straight down upon us. As this part of the country has a tolerably bad character, we all thought we were *in for it*, and closed up in a body; but they only parleyed with our guide, kissed him, and rode off. We, however, took the hint, and waited till our baggage came up, uniting our forces for our mutual protection. Turning round the next hill, we looked down upon their encampment of black tents, with large herds of cattle; and further on we found a delicious valley of nebbk trees, where scores of graceful camels with their young ones were feeding. A lovely scene it was, increasing in beauty as we reached the shores of the Lake, so dear to the heart of the Christian, constantly trodden by the feet of our blessed Lord, that one almost looks to find some visible trace remaining of His Presence.

CHAPTER XVII.

HIS OWN CITY AND HIS EARLY HOME.

" But all things feel
The power of Time and Change! thistles and grass
Usurp the desolate palace, as the weeds
Of Falsehood root in the aged pile of Truth."—*Thalaba.*

THERE are few places about which the reports of travellers seem to differ more completely than the Lake of Tiberias. Miss Martineau says she thought, at first sight, that she had never seen a sheet of water with so little beauty: Lord Lindsay calls it lovely: Dr. Robinson says its attractions lie in the associations, not the scenery: while Strauss pronounces it the most beautiful place in all the earth. Much of these diversities of opinion arise, doubtless, from the road by which it is reached; but very much more is owing to the season at which it is visited. Most persons go there late in the spring, hurrying over the end of their Syrian tour, after witnessing the Easter ceremonies at Jerusalem; doubtless then, and for probably six or seven months after, it is intolerably hot, feverish, unhealthy in the extreme to strangers, and very dreary; grey vapours, hot mists and fogs, thicken the air and obscure the delicate tints of the colouring. The fact is, that in spring and summer the barren mountains of Palestine have *no* colouring: they are veiled in a monotonous dust-coloured mist, neither interesting nor striking. At all times of the year the basin in which this Lake lies is very hot, for the country rises in a steady though gentle ascent, from the coast of the Mediterranean to the brow of the mountain which forms the western shore of the Lake; while from that brow the Lake is sunk down 653 feet below the level of the sea, the cliffs on the other side rising to about 1000 feet. The thermometer in summer frequently rises above 100° in the shade, and fevers are prevalent: the hot and cruel blasts of the sirocco commence in the spring, filling the air with the burning sand of the Desert, but ripening the melons (for which Tiberias is famous), tobacco, and grapes, a month or six weeks before those of Damascus or Saïda. Towards the end of ,the year the southern and eastern winds die away, and pleasant breezes from the north and north-west take their place, laden with the cool freshness they gather from the snowy summit of Lebanon; and it is said that snow has occasionally fallen on the Lake in the winter.

We arrived there on the 17th of November, and found, although the full sunshine was intolerable and the air altogether oppressive, yet it was not sufficient to make any of us feel ill; we were, on the contrary, very comfortable in the shade: there was sometimes a refreshing breeze, especially on the water, and the colouring of the scenery was really beautiful:· the mountains, arid and barren masses of rock on the eastern side, were clothed nearly all day in delicate lilacs and purples, sometimes rosy, sometimes golden; the water was always of a light greyish blue; the nebbk and walnuts that fringe the western shore were in their highest luxuriance, and the blossoms of oleanders were absolutely glorious.

The Lake is about twelve and a half miles long: the miserable town of Tiberias with its broken walls, the single dome of the Hot Baths, and the hamlet of Mejdel, all on the western side, are the only signs of humanity to be seen around its waters,—north, south, and east, the same silent, arid, almost desolate aspect meets the eye; the little sail of one rickety old boat, on rare occasions, is seen on its sacred waters; and the most really beautiful object in the panorama is the lofty cone of glorious Hermon, snow-crowned, and, for most part of the year, snow-covered, filling up the whole of the northern end of the Lake. Probably few places in Palestine present a more striking and complete contrast in its modern appearance to what it once was. In the time of our Lord seven or eight cities graced its banks, several of them magnificently adorned with stately palaces, spacious halls, theatres, forums, racecourses, and splendid temples; the wares of every known country, from the far shores of Spain, Greece, and Egypt, to those of Persia and the Indies, mingled in the market-places with those of Damascus, Tyre, and Jerusalem, while the white sails of numerous ships crowded its waters, carrying merchants or their merchandise, fishermen, or troops of Roman soldiers. Now, not one stone lies upon another of all the edifices that lined the shores; silence reigns on all around; and the dis-appearance of Sodom and Gomorrah is not more complete than that of the cities of the Lake.

It was in Tiberias that Herod Antipas held his court when

Tetrarch of Galilee, and it is said that there, seated on a throne of Parian marble inlaid with precious stones, he gave the fatal order to Salomé, the daughter of the miserable Herodias, for the execution of John the Baptist, while not one of the dissolute crowd gathered around the person of the infamous king put forth a hand to save the stern saint. Well might it be said of the inhabitants of the voluptuous cities then standing on the shores of the busy Lake, that they were "a strange intermixture of Hebrews without faith, Romans without honour, men without courage, and females without modesty." Among such as these, how must the gentle spirit of the pure and holy Jesus have been bruised, stricken, and afflicted! Yet here He, who came not to do His own will, was found more often than in any other place. Here, after He had "increased in wisdom and stature," He removed from the home of His childhood, and dwelt in Capernaum, thenceforth called "His own city," with the sufferers whose infirmities He had taken and whose sicknesses He had borne, the woman whose sins He had forgiven, and a few poor fishermen who had left all to follow Him as His companions and friends. Here He was especially the Son of Man, the Friend Who sticketh closer than a brother, encouraging the weak fears of one, healing the little daughter or faithful servant of another, restoring the lost, and taking little children in His arms, binding up the broken-hearted, bringing good tidings to the meek, and opening the prison to those that were bound—the Comforter of all that mourned, changing the spirit of heaviness into the garment of praise—the Consoler and Giver of Rest. Here, too, He was essentially the Divine Teacher, whose lessons sunk into the hearts of His hearers by their homely words and examples taken from all that' their eyes gazed on day by day; the Conqueror also of the spirits of darkness and evil, and of the stormy wind and sea; the Anointed of the Lord proclaiming the acceptable year, as well as the day of vengeance of our God. Here, "the people which sat in darkness saw great light,"—and thence, He departed and began that long journey which was only finished on the Cross of agony. Every spot seems living with Gospel associations—and here, more than in any other place, save Jerusalem, the natural features of the landscape bring to mind His discourses and daily teachings. This is the great charm of the Lake of Galilee.

We reached the shore at 'Ain Tabighah; and pitched our tents beside the bubbling, rushing stream, which gushes out from among thickets of nebbk and agnus-castus; the hum of the tent pitching soon died away, and we wandered out to the low rocks and loose stones upon the sandy beach, just at the edge of the water, and spent

the evening in watching the lovely scene before us.   The hills that
sloped down from Safed, backed by Jebel Jermuk, and Kurn
Hattîn, all green and verdant, swept round on our right at the back
of the little plain of Gennesaret, to the mountain behind the town of
Tübariyeh (Tiberias), now dark and purple in the shade, while the
dark brown town, and the white Baths, were distinctly to be seen
beyond the luxuriant foliage of the little plain; on the left, every
gully, ravine, and crag of the rugged mountains of Bashan were lit
up by the dying rays of the sun, while to the south both sides united
in the blue, clear distance of the Jordan hills at the foot of the Lake.
The flowers of the agnus-castus perfumed the air, the fish sported
visibly in and out of the waters, and not a sound was heard but
the bubbling of the fountain and the little tinkling bells of the
mules.

This 'Ain Tabighah is the only creek on the shores of the Lake
where, from the shelving, instead of rocky, nature of the beach, a
boat could be drawn up on the land; and it has, therefore, been
conjectured (with good reason) to be the scene of the second miraculous draught of fishes; it is also with much probability considered
as the home of Simon Peter, and Andrew, James and John.   It is
now agreed upon by most learned men that there were *two* Beth-
saïdas—one of which was exalted into the dignity of a city by
Philip, the tetrarch of Gaulanitis Ituræa and Trachonitis, and to
which the name of Julia, the daughter of Cæsar, was given by him
after he had enlarged and embellished it.   This town, of course,
stood on the *east* side of the Jordan, where only Philip had jurisdiction: no more than a few heaps of stones now mark the spot, but
much more is probably hidden under the mound that covers the
site.   Looking down from the hills above, we had been able to
discern the place with the river flowing past it into the Lake: there
is a deep ravine behind it, and some uplands of green grass, on
which, or on the grassy meadow between it and the river bank, it
must have been that the multitude was miraculously fed by our Lord;
and from thence that He "passed over the Lake to Capernaum"
(John vii. 15, 17).   The other Bethsaïda was called "of Galilee"
(John xii. 21), thus implying that there were two towns of the same
name, and that this must have been on the *western* side of Jordan;
it probably stood near the beach, since its name, "house of fish,"
seems to denote a village of fishermen.   It has been supposed to have
occupied a position near this little creek, though no remains of
buildings have fixed the spot.   It was to this place, when sad and
lonely at His absence, knowing, indeed, of His Resurrection, but no
longer dwelling familiarly with Him, as of old, that seven of His

disciples returned, with their hearts full of deep but awed affection, pondering over His sufferings and their own weakness, and recommenced their old occupations. Here therefore, close by that little creek, after a night of weary and fruitless toil, they saw Him standing on this shore, in the dim twilight of the dawn, and heard His sweet, gentle command to them, to cast in the net for the fish they sought: then the loving heart of St. John quickly recognised his Lord, and St. Peter, trembling with eagerness and affection, threw on the rough garb that lay beside him, and hastened through the shallow water to the spot whereon He stood, yet durst not ask Him, Is it Thou, O Lord? Here, too, the solemn question came to Peter, "Lovest thou Me?" to which the zealous disciple, his heart beating with the joy of having again found his Lord and Master, readily answered "Yea, Lord;" and a second time, thinking, perhaps, that the strength of his love was doubted, or that the Saviour desired, as the affectionate disciple would have done himself, another assurance of his devotion, he answered with the same readiness,—but when yet again, the third time, the question was repeated, Peter paused; had he been unmindful of its true meaning? did the love his Lord demanded imply another kind of love, than the half careless mind though ready heart had fathomed? Pangs of conscience perhaps struck him, memories of opportunities wasted, warnings forgotten, advice and precepts thrown away; a horrible remorse arose from the threefold question, when he remembered how three times he had denied his Lord in public, while again, in the stillness of the morning, the crowing of the cock sounded in his ears: and who can tell whether in that moment visions swept not across his mind of future sorrow, and pain, and suffering, and something told him of a love, so far exceeding all he *had* felt that it would enable him to bear agony and wrong in patience and gladness of soul;—and so, with a heart bursting with humility and self-abasement, and yet of profound love, he answered, "Thou only, O Lord, knowest! fain would I have this love, but Thou only canst give it, or keep it in me. I am Thine, do with me as seemeth good in Thy sight;" and Jesus gave him His divine command. He laid the Cross upon his shoulders, and put the Cup of which He had drank into his hand, and when He had done this He said unto him: "Follow Me unto the fountains of living waters, where God Himself shall wipe away all tears from thine eyes."

There was not the faintest ripple on the water as we rode along the shore the next morning, skirting the hillside, to the ruins of Tell-Hûm, the difficulties of exploring which are recounted as very terrific by most travellers, owing to the dense crop of thistles, about

the height of a man on horseback, which flourish over the ruins:
now, in the autumn, they were all dead, and gave us no inconvenience. The site, which is close to the beach, is covered thickly
with heaps of hewn stones, of a very dark limestone, almost black;
those *in situ* are only foundations with bases and plinths of columns,
while masses of ornamental lintels, doorposts, cornices, and friezes
lie on the ground confusedly piled up. There was one acanthus-
leaved capital, and many stones with the egg moulding and a profusion of other ornaments. Among the broken columns were several
bases composed of one square and two round columns combined,
one side of the square being rounded out into two half-circles, and
all cut in the same block,—the same combination as we had seen on
the Triumphal Arch, and other buildings at Palmyra: Dr. Robinson
and Mr. Porter say that they are indicative of a Jewish synagogue.
But our interest soon centered in a large stone, on which, stooping
down into a hole, we saw some curious figures, and immediately got
three men to upturn it for us, in order to obtain a more distinct view;
and of which, in spite of the burning midday sun, I took a careful
drawing. The stone was of a very white limestone, about three feet
and a half long and eighteen inches high; on one side was carved,
not in high relief, the representation of a temple on wheels, with
pilasters against the wall, the capitals of which were a rude kind of
double nick or tooth, something like the usual top to a Greek altar:
the door, a double one with panels, has one side sculptured so as to
appear ajar, or pushed a little open outwards; in the tympanum
was an ornament resembling rays, or possibly leaves. The roof was
arched over with regular depressions on the arching, to our minds
unmistakably representing curtains pressed down, or drawn in
with cords; two wheels, with six spokes in each, were carved
beneath the side. Beyond the temple three large *half*-acanthus
leaves were rather richly sculptured, with a border of leaves
curling up from under them. The stone was broken at each end.
It occurred to us each at once, Should Dr. Robinson be right in
supposing that a Jewish synagogue stood here, might not this be
a representation of the Ark? possibly part of a panel or a frieze
commemorative of the return of the Ark to the people of Israel when
it was sent back by the Philistines*? or of "the Ark of God set
upon a new cart," and brought up by David from Kirjath-jearim to
Jerusalem, with music and dancing, and the sound of the trumpet;†
the half-acanthus leaves may have been a comparatively modern
representation of the flowers, and wreaths, and green branches spread
in the way? In the Mishna we are told that the sanctuary of

* 1 Sam. vi.   † 2 Sam. vi.

Shiloh "was a structure of low stone walls, with the tent drawn over the top." * The Ark was undoubtedly only covered over at the top by hangings, *one* of which was hung entirely *inside* the woodwork, the others were thrown over it.† In the embellishment of the sides of the edifice the artist may have added imaginary pilasters, according to the buildings of the time in which he lived; but the *fact* of the open roof, with only the curtain of fine linen and embroidery between it and the sky. he was not likely to forget.

I cannot but hope that the account given here may arrest the attention of some scholars whose researches have been directed to the subjects connected with Hebrew archæology, and that some interesting result may be drawn from the consideration of this very remarkable stone.‡

It would seem, from the expressions used by Christ in upbraiding the cities in which His mighty works had been done, as if Capernaum (Capher, *a village*; näum, of *Nahum*, a proper name), had been a city superior ("exalted to heaven") to the others; but so immediate had been its downfall, and so complete was its abasement, that Josephus only mentions it as "a village called Capernaum." The splendour that evidently once existed here, from the unusual profusion of ornament, seems to indicate that Tell Hûm must be the site of a city more than ordinarily handsome. It is also worthy of mention that Josephus, being wounded in a skirmish fought where the Jordan falls into the Lake, "not far from the banks," was carried, naturally, to the nearest place for aid, and that place was Capernaum§; and if Capernaum stood upon an elevation, as has been thought probable from our Lord's custom of singling out those characteristics of places which most obviously struck the eye, Tell Hûm is the *only* site between the Jordan and Mejdel, where ruins have been found, that is placed on a hill: the city which once stood here, whichever it was, must have been much more conspicuous than any other, except Tiberias, on the western side of the Lake. There are no

* Mishna, ed. Surenhusius, vol. v. p. 59.

† See Munk, pp. 155, 156.

‡ The Jews first commenced the institution of synagogues in their towns after the Captivity, or about the time of Ezra. They were at first only rooms, and afterwards buildings, set apart as places of meeting for the purposes of joint prayer and religious instruction. Each synagogue was served by several ministers, under one chief or principal, one of whom recited the prayers and expounded certain chapters of the Pentateuch, or Prophets. At other times the synagogues served, then as now, as school rooms for the children, who were gratuitously taught to read by the scribes and doctors who frequented the synagogue, or by the ministers attached to it.—*Munk.*

§ Joseph. Life, 72.

other ruins between Tiberias and the Jordan to be at all compared, either in extent or richness, to those of Tell Hûm; but beyond it, two miles further north, there are heaps of hewn stones, enough for a town, called by the Arabs *Kerâzeh*, exactly answering to the description given by St. Jerome of the situation of Chorazin. Probably the positions of Capernaum and Bethsaïda will never be ascertained; but the remains at Kerâzeh deserve to hold a place as one of the three, all the more as there are really *no* remains of ancient buildings at 'Ain Tabighah, unless, indeed, the ground has closed over them.

We were unable to make any investigation to the north, beyond a general view, and, much to our regret, we found it impossible to ride to Kerâzeh or to cross the Jordan; Bedoueens were encamped at both, the two tribes were at war with each other, and we could not find a guide to take us to either in safety. Two men offered themselves for the purpose, announcing that they were Bashi-Bazouks, but we had no means of ascertaining that they were such, and it would have been highly unsafe to venture among the Bedoueens without protection. So we reluctantly turned round and rode back to 'Ain Tabighah, whence the tents had already gone on. as we thought a second night in such close neighbourhood to the Bedoueens might be too strong a temptation for them to resist, and we had been warned by several prowlers coming in the previous night about the tents, who received a somewhat warmer reception than they expected.

In about a quarter of an hour, passing along a rock-cut road, we had reached the little Plain of Gennesaret, a semicircular plain left by the suddenly receding hills, and covered with rich vegetation, the only flat meadow land on the borders of the Lake, except just where the Jordan falls into and runs out of it. On the north side of the plain a few stones lie scattered about, and a few more, it is said, lie under the trees and little mounds further on; if this be really the site of Capernaum, as some believe, never was there a city more entirely levelled and annihilated! The principal argument for this idea is that here, gushing from the base of the cliff which borders the plain to the north, is a fountain or spring containing numbers of very tiny semi-transparent fish gliding about among the pebbles: these have been suggested to be the same as the fish alluded to by Josephus, similar to some in a lake near Alexandria, which fountain, he says, the people of the country called Capernaum. The spring is shaded by two fine fig-trees, whence its name, "'Ain et teen" (*teen*, Arabic for fig); a number of camels were browsing on the nebbk bushes and drinking from the clear water, while the baby camels were gambolling about the plain. A little further on, some old walls are all that remain of a khan mentioned by many writers even 300 years ago, as Khan Mineyeh. This little plain, once the rich garden of whatever city stood here, is now covered only with deep thickets of oleanders loaded with blossoms, giant thistles of beautiful colours, nebbk and agnus-castus, whose pretty spikes of lavender flowers made the air fragrant; the shore was one mass of tiny shells, which the muleteers kept picking up, begging us to admire them; we brought away great numbers after strolling over the plain. Mejdel, the modern representative of the old Magdala, from whence Mary Magdalene is said to have derived her name, is only a collection of wretched hovels, which looked picturesque enough at the moment, from a large caravan which was resting there, laden with apples and pears, *en route* from Damascus to Nazareth. We found our tents pitched by the cemetery on the site of ancient Tiberias, a little to the south of the modern town, and close to the edge of the water; this position was very quiet, cool and pleasant, free from all the annoyances and uncleanness for which the town is so famous.

We engaged the one fishing boat of Tiberias to take us on the following morning to the ravine directly opposite the town, Wady Fik, the site of ancient Gamala; but finding that some Bedoueens were encamped between the shore and the Tombs, we turned southwards, and in two hours reached the pleasant grassy banks where the Lake passes quietly into the Ghor, or valley of the Jordan: we landed on the eastern bank of the river, and walked across the meadows between one or two of its windings among nebbk trees and flowers and dhourra fields. The banks were bordered with thick cane-brakes, with their long lank leaves floating like streamers on the wind and the waters, and we heard the wild boars moving about in the depths of the brake; a camel was suckling two pretty little camels under a tree, and kids were sporting in the stubble. Then we got down to the river's edge and began picking up lovely shells, when presently I saw a little snake, about two feet long, come swimming slowly towards me; its body was lying in curves just under water, and its pretty head stood erect some three inches out of it, perking about from side to side in the most knowing fashion, but very gracefully: it stopped and regarded me with wonder, and I threw a little stone at it to see what it would do; the creature swam rapidly to shore at my very feet, stopped a moment, turning round for another look at me, then rushed among the pebbles and darted away into a hiding-place.

We sat down under the shade of the rocks, and one of our boatmen walked knee-deep into the Lake with a little net; in a few minutes he had a dozen fish, each about the size of a mackerel; the other man collected two or three sticks and built up a little pile over a morsel of charcoal, on which he placed the fish; the sticks were lit with his cigarette, and in five minutes he brought them to us nicely broiled: most excellent they were. One could not help remembering the "fire of coals" (charcoal), and "the fish laid thereon," and the blessed invitation of the Risen Lord to His apostles, "Come and dine," while we could look round at the very mountains and Lake that had met His own human eyes, and feel that we were indeed seeing the same objects, breathing the same air, and treading the same shell-covered shore that our blessed Saviour Himself had done. We went very slowly back to Tiberias late in the afternoon, enjoying the sweet, gentle air and the lovely view—the sunshine purpling the barren eastern mountains, and illuminating the old fortress above Gamala, Safed Castle standing up aloft on the left, while the golden clouds mantled in long ribbons across the head of noble Hermon, and tinged all the snow with beautiful rose-colour. If any one wants to *feel* the beauty of the Lake of Gennesaret, let him spend a November or December evening on its bosom, watching the varying scene, till all has faded into darkness; till he has done that, he has not understood that Lake; here above all places one realizes in the scenery, over which the familiar associations of Scripture have cast their halo, that

> " The colouring may be of this earth,
> The lustre comes of heavenly birth."

This Lake is literally teeming with fish: we had four kinds at dinner, caught by a man standing on the shore in front of our tents; but as no one catches them in any other way, of course very few, comparatively, are taken. Josephus says the water in it is very remarkable for its coldness and "subtle flavour;" we thought it, however, particularly flat and mawkish. The bread made by the Polish Jews in the town is delicious. Tubariyeh, as it is called, is most melancholy-looking, from the utter ruin caused by the earthquake of 1837, when several hundred houses were thrown down, the walls crumbled into heaps, the towers broken into gaps, and the place more than half destroyed. This is one of the four *holy cities* of the Jews, in one of which they expect the Messiah will come upon earth; the chief part of the population is composed of Jews from Poland, Bohemia, Russia, and Spain. When the Jews ceased to fight for Palestine as their country, many learned rabbins retired to

Tiberias, where a celebrated academy was founded; and here, about the year A.D. 180, the holy Rabbi Judah, who traced his descent from one of the skeletons restored to life by Ezekiel, made the famous collection of Jewish laws and traditions known by the name of the *Mishna*. The Jews in Palestine were united into a sort of religious society, under a *Nasi* or patriarch, who resided at Tiberias. The town was originally built by Herod Antipas, who bestowed lands and privileges on the Jews to induce them to settle there, in spite of the repugnance they felt for a town, the foundations of which had been laid among many ancient tombs. The hot baths close by are said to resemble those of Aix-la-Chapelle, and not far from them, to the south, is the site of Tarichæa, the unhappy town taken by Titus, aided by a small fleet, when the whole Lake was discoloured with blood, and 6500 corpses left upon its shores, while 30,000 still more unfortunate Jews were taken captive and sold in the market-place of Corinth.

The governor of the town came down to our tents on Sunday morning, to answer our inquiries for a guide to Um Keis, the ancient Gadara in Gilead, on the eastern side of Jordan; he brought a man whom he warranted a safe guide, as he declared him to be one of the Beni-Sahkr Arabs who inhabit the mountains about Um Keis—a great and noble tribe whom we were anxious to see; but the man turned out to be one of the pretended Bashi-Bazouks at 'Ain Tabighah, and we therefore thought that he was likely to make a very indifferent guard or guide. The next morning the governor, meeting one of the dragomans in the town, whispered to him that the man was altogether a rogue, but that he knew of no other more honest to go with us, so we were obliged to give up that expedition also, and a very great disappointment it was. In consequence of this delay it was late before we started for the caves of Wady-el-Hamân, of the fortified caverns of which Josephus gives such an interesting account (B. J. i. 16): Herod the Great only succeeded in dislodging the banditti who inhabited them, by letting his troops down in chests by ropes, from the brow of the perpendicular cliffs above; he subdued them, but not one yielded to his entreaties that they would save themselves by surrender; one father slew his wife and seven sons, before he threw himself down the precipice, rather than yield to the hated Roman.* It was a steep and hot ride up the romantic glen of the little river, the horses barely finding room for their feet along the mountain side, after which we had a great *pull*

---

* These caves had been the scene of another bloody massacre of Jews, who had taken refuge in them in B.C. 160, by the troops of Demetrius, King of Syria.

on foot up to the caverns. They are natural caves artificially deepened, with internal passages and staircases communicating with each other hewn out behind and in front of the rock: story after story, one above another, here and there a strong wall or a tower, a passage or a bastion, prettily built of yellow and black stones in alternate layers; there were cisterns also in each, but all were now full of the bones of bears and jackals, and crammed with bats, smelling powerfully and sickeningly. We reached the bottom with some difficulty, and continued our way as best we could through the thickets in the ravine, where monstrous boulders were lying, and whence the cliffs on either side rose, often quite perpendicularly, to the height of six or seven hundred feet. Then we turned up suddenly to the left, to visit the remains of Beth Arbel (Hosea x. 14), the Arbela of Josephus. The ruins extend for a considerable distance in heaps of broken stones, with here and there a roughly-built arch which looked Roman; but in the midst of them there is an important ruin, which has been suggested to be that of a Jewish synagogue. The columns of two portals, one within another, still stand erect, remarkable for being dissimilar in the pairing, a round and a square column supporting the same arch; an acanthus-leaved capital lay on the ground, and a slab on which two small columns with their bases were sculptured in high relief, one of a close spiral pattern, the other enriched with vertical flutings filled with roses or quatre-foils. Probably many more pieces of sculpture are buried under the débris. It was a noble site for a city, overlooking the ravine below, and the blue Lake to the right, as well as the sites of more than one of the cities that surrounded the Lake; Safed sitting aloft in her shining whiteness seeming quite close on the summit of her peaked mountain—" a city that cannot be hid :" and Hermon filling up the distance.

We were now in the plain or plateau where it has been conjectured the Sermon on the Mount was delivered beneath the two horns of the curious-looking mountain called Kurn Hattin: it seems a very long way from the Lake and from Capernaum, near which such numbers of people were more likely to have been collected than on this rather out-of-the-way upland. But here, certainly, the dreadful battle of Hattin was fought by the Crusaders against Salah-ed-din in 1187, when Guy de Lusignan, the King of Jerusalem, and the Grand-master of the Templars were both taken prisoners. Here also, only a few years ago, Agheel Agha, the Sheikh of the Hawâra Arabs, fell upon the Governor of Tubariyeh, and killed him and ninety of his followers. We plodded on through fields of stubble and tall thistles, teazles and wild caraways, with the round ungraceful hump of Tabor as our goal. But, alas! our long détour had taken more time than we had counted on, and the sun set ere we had crossed the desolate, lonely hills and reached the Khan of Tughjar, a place famous for robbers, but beautifully situated in a park-like country of noble oaks. Our guide would not face the Bedoueens whom we found encamped at the foot of the mountain, and we had no idea how to reach our tents on the summit; it was very unsafe to go up to their camp without a guide or *introduction*, but we could not help ourselves; we had not shawls or cloaks enough in which we could lie down till daylight, and we were besides dreadfully hungry, so we rode boldly in among the open tents and glaring fires, and were soon in a crowd of men, women, and children: we told them we had a letter to Agheel Agha, their chief, and wanted a guide up the mountain. They gave us water, and three men accompanied us beyond the savage-looking camp, but it was impossible, in the thick darkness, to ride; the guides felt with their hands in advance, and then called to us to come on, but they were often at fault, and then we had to retrace our steps amid the dense thickets of trees. After three whole hours of groping, clambering, and scrambling of a very unpleasant nature, we gained the summit, and arrived at our tents at 10 P.M. When we saw the side of the mountain by daylight afterwards, it seemed a miracle how we had ever got up it in the dark; even the regular path is bad enough.

Tabor* is an isolated hill, clothed on two sides with a thick covering of oaks, some of which are said to be peculiar to this mountain; they grow only too closely, but there are many noble trees amongst them, besides quantities of terebinth and nut-trees, with lentisk and other shrubs, while the rich, soft grass is covered with gum-cistus, gigantic cyclamens†, and white crocuses. The other sides of Tabor are entirely bare; it is said to stand 1400 feet above the plain, and 1860 above the sea. It was probably the boldness and peculiarity of its outline, and the impression of strength and mightiness that the mountain gives, rising abruptly from the very flat plain, that caused the Prophet Jeremiah to say the King of Babylon shall come up " like Tabor among the mountains " (xlvi. 18) to destroy Egypt. Except for its delicious verdure

* Archbishop Mislin says that the word Tabor expresses something of the purity or light attainable at an elevation, figuratively speaking, a sort of "excelsior."

† We found great numbers of the leaves of the cyclamen measuring eight and nine inches in length; they were like thick, soft, green velvet, most beautifully marked and mottled.

and lofty trees it has no great beauty, and its outline is remarkably ungraceful. It seems to have beeen always a gathering place for the northern tribes of Israel, standing as it did on the line that divided Zebulon from Naphtali, whence they descended, sword in hand, into the rich plains below; and it probably soon became one of the "high places" of idolatry (Hosea v. 1). A strong fortress, it is believed, has ever existed on its summit, and extensive remains, possibly of the fortifications erected by Josephus, are still to be seen. All this entirely precludes the idea of this mountain having been chosen for the scene of the Transfiguration, which was evidently on a place apart from the world. The view from the summit—our first into the south of Palestine—is fine; the plain of Esdraelon lies immediately below, with "Little Hermon" (Jebel Duhhy) and the graceful mountains of Gilboa beyond; Carmel and the "great sea" on the right; the Jordan with the hills of Gilead and Bashan, and a corner of the Lake, on the left; to the north, Hermon, Safed, and Hattin, with some of the mountains behind Tyre, shut out the Lebanon. One feels one has left the romantically beautiful country north of Hermon, but the country one now sees is very verdant, and not less interesting.

A Russian hermit used to live on the top of Mount Tabor: he was the son of the Archimandrite of a monastery in the Crimea, and took holy orders at a very early age, the intention being that he should succeed his father at the head of the brethren; but soon after he had settled down in this quiet life, a vision, as he thought, appeared to him, in which he saw a mountain of most peculiar form, and heard a voice saying, "Arise, my son, and behold thy home upon earth." The dream was repeated seven nights running, and at last the dreamer did arise; he knew not where to go to find the mountain, and no one gave him any information about it; however, he set out, and went first to Mount Athos; there was no mountain there like that in the vision. Then he went to Mount Sinai, and then to Mount Ararat in Armenia; but none answered to the picture in his dream. He travelled far into the East, then into the West; eleven years of journeying, and at last he stood before Mount Tabor. "This is it," he said, "I have found it, this is the strange shape I saw in my dream; I have sought and found nothing like this!" so he ascended the mountain and never left it again. Many years he lived there, studying and praying, and doing all kinds of good works; attending to the sick, and labouring among the peasants and shepherds around him. They soon loved him with grateful affection, and sought him in every sorrow and difficulty, and he never wearied of

administering to them. One winter's day a panther approached
the cave in which he lived : he threw him a piece of bread, and the
panther crouched down at his feet; he soon became quite tame, and
thenceforth, wherever the hermit went, the beautiful creature was
seen at his side, following him like a dog. Mr. Rogers, the English
Consul at Hhaïffa, who told me this story, frequently saw them together on the mountain; he had learned the history of his dream
and of his wanderings from the hermit himself. He lived to be very
old, but had died about two years previous to our visit to Mount
Tabor.

We should have been glad to stay here for some days, but we
had not time enough to spare, and were obliged to go on at once :
our mules, therefore, were sent on the following day direct to
Nazareth, while we descended the north-east side of the mountain
and rode away over wild valleys and among pleasant woods to the
camp of Agheel Agha-el-Hâsy. We were curious to see something
of Bedoueen life when actually in camp, and as the Consul at
Hhaïffa had been kind enough to give us a letter of introduction to
him, we took advantage of having some friends with us at the
time, with whom it was both pleasanter and safer to go than by
ourselves. The Hawâra were not, indeed, a tribe that we at all cared
to visit, but we were not sure of another opportunity of seeing the
inside of a camp, and we therefore determined to go. The Hawâra
Arabs are not, in fact, a real tribe: they were formed only a few
years ago by Ibrahîm Pacha, who appointed Agheel as their
Sheikh, and gave him the rank and title of an Agha: he is of good
family, but a Syrian, and originally an Osmâli or Bashi-Bazouk, the
generic name given to any of the Arabs of this country who
attached themselves to the Government and fought for pay. The
tribe is composed of fellaheen or peasants, chiefly Egyptians, or of
any one discontented with his former position who chooses thus to
enrol himself in a new confederation : many are scamps and ne'er-
do-wells from Barbary and Tunis, united under a bloodthirsty
chief, with the title of Hawâra, or "destruction."

We sent on one of the dragomans with our letter and to
announce our coming, and some Bedoueens came to meet us: wild
and ill-looking men, who seemed to us quite *vulgar* when we
thought of our dear Anazehs. They led us into the camp, and we
dismounted among a number of tiny baby horses tethered in a ring.
At the door of a low tent, somewhat larger than the others, stood a
tall, heavy, stout man, with his back to us, dressed in a long blue
cloth coat or *kuftan*, the sign of a Turkish agha: he wore also a
kefiyeh and the red boots of a Sheikh. He was busy giving

directions to his black Nubian slaves about preparing his tent for our use, and scarcely condescended to turn round and look at us; at last he nodded carelessly enough, a half salaam, to a gentleman of our party, but he took no notice of us, and went on talking in a monotonous, oily, lifeless kind of voice, while he fingered his beads. The slaves hung a variety of gaudy Tunisian shawls round the inside of the tent, and placed carpets and couches of cushions for each of us on the ground, some of which were pretty and embroidered. Agheel waited till we were seated, and then he squatted on a bit of stone outside the tent: we begged him to enter, but he said it was "not the custom, and his people would think he gave himself strange airs if he entered a tent when his guests were inside; in fact, he only sat down anywhere in sight because we were Europeans; had we been Arabs it would have been impossible." We had scarcely any conversation, for he did not seem disposed for any; he spoke sometimes to the dragomans, but he asked no questions and had evidently no curiosity whatever about us, and the only remark he made was, when we took off our hats, he laughed a long unctuous chuckle, saying, " Europeans always uncover, Arabs never do." We mentioned Sheikh Miguel of the Anazehs, and Mr. Rogers of Hhaïffa, but though he listened, he made no answer, and there is scarcely any expression on his sleek, fat face, with his small, sunken eyes, low forehead, and thick lips, smooth but repulsive; if it has any expression it is one of mingled sensuality and cunning.

The tent which he had given up to our use, of course his own, was about six or seven feet high, of dark-brown camel's or goat's hair, " black as the tents of Kedar," closed on three sides, but open in front, and supported by three poles; the earth was left uncovered between our couches, and a skin of fresh water was brought in and placed in one corner for our use. A sheep was killed according to custom for guests, and in about two hours the dinner arrived, a metal basin having been handed round just before by a black slave, and water poured on our hands; then came a huge wooden bowl containing a heaped-up mountain of stewed rice, covering over and hiding lumps of boiled mutton, with the bones broken small : but it seemed to us as if the meat had been taken off: at least we never could find any, though we gnawed the bones for some time perseveringly, throwing them to the dogs when they were done with. There is much knack in taking up the rice: the fingers should be lightly closed so as to grasp a little ball of it, as otherwise the hot grease only runs down the hand and the food is spilt; the rice was very good, but we burned our fingers so horribly in getting at it, that we soon gave it up, and left off nearly as hungry as when we began : the Agha and the slaves, with a rudeness very unlike the fine manners of true Bedoueens, stood round us laughing at our awkwardness in this new experience. They gave a small piece of bread to each of us, and then the bowl was lifted up and carried to our servants, after which it was given to the slaves, one of whom brought us a calabash of water, and tried with much energy to rub the grease from my fingers with a morsel of dirty soap.

A few minutes after, the Agha got up from the fire outside the tent beside which he was sitting, and asked if we wanted anything, and then went away to his own dinner and to sleep; sending us, alas! as a compliment, two large mash'lahs and a cloak from his own person. They were very splendid, for my sister's was lined with wolf-skin fur, while mine was of sky-blue silk embroidered with gold; and of course we were very grateful when a slave laid one upon each of us; but the consequences were fatal. There we lay, " martyrs all o'er," as the hymn says, a prey to thousands of fleas, every now and then pacing up and down in the open air before the tents with our maid, trying to cool our unhappy skins; and we looked the next morning as if we had had erysipelas, and we thought that morning never would. come : but of course it was very interesting, in a natural history sort of way, to have ascertained that fleas belonging to Bedoueen tribes are, like those children of nature, far more agile and sanguinary than their civilised and domesticated cousins. We had a little lamp of olive-oil in an earthen cup brought to us at dinner-time, and two bits of candle, for which we built small towers of stones by way of candlesticks, much to the amusement of the Nubians, but the stars gave plenty of light. However, we were very glad when they paled, and we could send word to the Agha that we wished to go on to Nazareth; there was nothing to stay for, as we had discovered they would not show us any of the amusements we had hoped to see; the Hawâra considering it unbecoming in men to dance. We begged to see his mares, to which the Agha consented, not very willingly, and four were brought up and walked past us as quickly as possible. He said he had no more of his own, but he showed us a horse completely covered with saddle-cloths and trappings of gay-coloured tassels, &c., which the gentlemen requested to have removed. He hesitated long, but at last gave the order, and for half a second they were lifted up; the horse was a fine creature, and he probably feared if we saw his good points, that we might cast the " evil eye " of envy upon him. Thinking to please him, we asked to go to the hareem, but he did not seem much gratified: however, we were taken to a tent close to his own, in which we found his two wives, who kissed our hands. The first wife was handsome enough to have been really beautiful, if she had not been tatooed all over her chin, cheeks, and lips; her features were well cut, and her eyes large and soft; she was showily dressed all in silk, but very dirty, and had a very fine Bedoueen necklace of coral and gold coins, among which were many Napoleons and Austrian eagles, eight or ten bracelets, very fine onyx rings on every finger, and gold ends to the long plaits of her hair. She looked very sad, however, and seemed filled with sorrowful envy of the younger second wife, who, though dressed in cotton and with few ornaments, was very happy and merry nursing a ten-days-old son, tightly swaddled up, but with its little eyelids carefully painted with Kohhl. We left them very soon, and returned to take leave of the Agha, to whom we paid the usual compliments, which he only received with a stolid smile, and we parted with little regret on either side, the Nubians only appearing interested in our departure on account of the baksheesh. The fact is, that encamped, as he always is, in one or other of these valleys, just in the route of travellers, he is continually being visited by Europeans, who are moreover sent to him frequently by the Consuls; those, however, who see Agheel Agha, and the Hawári tribe only, have little idea of the fine manners and high breeding of a *real* Bedoueen.

We were guided over the hills by a guard of honour of several Arabs with their long lances, and came in sight of Nazareth in an hour and a half. This first view was rather striking: the hills closing round the city " like a rose enclosed in its leaves," as old Quaresimus says, in an almost circular basin, very fertile and full of olives at the bottom, but the hills are flat-topped and barely covered with a scrubby thorn, so that the town and hills are all glaringly white together; there is but little beauty in the view, but all is gentle, harmonious, pleasing: just the kind of scene one would wish to see round the earthly resting-place, for thirty years, of our Blessed Lord. The views from the hill-tops are on every side extensive (the city stands 1237 feet above the sea), and beautiful in their variety: the hills of Tabor and Tiberias in front of the heights of Jordan and Bashan: Hermon standing up proudly to the north-east, and to the north-west the rich plain of El Buttauf, and thickly wooded hills sweeping round to meet the forests of Carmel with its sea-washed bluff: then the plain of Esdraelon and the mountains of Gilboa and Nablous, blue and graceful in the distance. The town is a pretty one, containing a few goodly houses, and some mosques, round each of which fine cypresses cluster; olive-groves and walls of prickly pear surround it.

Our tents were pitched close to the fountain, the mouth of which is a long hole sunk in the ground, and paved in with stones : this, as it is the only spring in or near the town, must be (happily without question) that from which the Blessed Mother of our Lord, and He Himself, in the life of loving obedience that He led when "subject to His parents," daily drew water, like the hundreds of women, girls, and boys who now throng around the fountain at all hours of the day, and even of the night. The women of Nazareth are certainly handsome; they have fresh, bright complexions and merry faces, but they have been a good deal overlauded by travellers in my opinion, for, like that of the rest of the women of Palestine, it is a coarse, bold, unlovable style of beauty. They wear a curious head-dress of large silver coins overlapping each other, and sewed on to a cushion which is put round the face like a bonnet: the colours of their dresses and wide trowsers are unusually gay, and they add a gaudy cotton scarf hanging down from the back of the head. The Greek Christians are the best-looking, but even they, like most Syrian women, are very untidy and rather dirty, and extremely unlike one's idea of the Blessed Virgin; indeed, three or four Jewesses in Jerusalem, some of the women at Nablous, and the' sweet-faced, soft-eyed, gentle-looking women of Suediyeh, near Antioch, are the only women I saw in Syria who made me think of *her* face.

We went, of course, to the Latin Convent to see the Grotto of the Annunciation, so often described: the church was full of people attending the funeral of the Superior, who lay, with the head uncovered, on a bier in the centre of the church, and I could not help thinking that the happy look of peace on the wasted and care-worn features was a better explanation of the "scripture fulfilled" in this place than all the sights of the Virgin's kitchen and the angelically-upheld column, &c. &c., shown to the faithful pilgrim.

The Protestant Bishop in Jerusalem has established a Mission here, which appears to be well worked: the clergyman, Mr. Zeller, has a school of sixty boys, including Mooslims, and both Greek and Latin Christians, who read the Scriptures in English as well as Arabic. Mrs. Zeller teaches a few girls, the number of whom are constantly increasing, and who are, indeed, as many as she could manage unassisted; they had also established evening classes for. young men, which seemed to be successful so far, and from which they hoped much. There is a small church in which the service is performed in Arabic.

We rode the next morning along a pleasant path to Sepphoris, a town built by Herod Antipas as the capital of Galilee, but destroyed by the Romans to punish a revolt of the citizens in 339; it was called by them Diocæsaræa. A square tower or fortress on the top of the hill is interesting from the lower part being built of stones with the Jewish bevel on them, a good deal less "rough" and prominent than the Phœnician or Roman. Further on there are very picturesque remains of an old Gothic church, the cathedral of the town when Sepphoris was the seat of a Bishop. Then we rode on through charming olive and caroub groves, and drove across the pretty plain of El Buttauf; the wild caraway plants reaching above our heads and the thistles to the horses' shoulders; underneath the shrubs several sarcophagi, handsomely carved with wreaths, like those at Kedesh, lay almost hidden, and also some wells. On the other side of the little plain, rising a few feet up the hill-side, are the ruins of a lately deserted village, believed to be the real Cana of Galilee: its name has been time out of mind, as it still is, in Arabic, Kana-el-Jelil, and all the early pilgrims in Palestine so accounted it by the unquestioned tradition of the natives, until the journey of Quaresimus in 1639, when the monks at Nazareth chose to find another at a village called Kenna, a few miles to the south-east, more easy of access from their own convent. There is no water in the village itself, but at some little distance in the plain there is a deep well, a shadow of a reason for the previous collection of so large a quantity of water for the marriage-feast.

This Kana-el-Jelil is one of those sites of the truth of which the traveller longs to be assured; the winding valley with the pleasant flowery meadows at the bottom, the wooded hill-sides, the unbroken stillness and yet cheerful loneliness of the spot all seem most thoroughly appropriate to the place where, doubtless, the feet of our Blessed Lord frequently wandered, watching the lily of the field and the fowls of the air, the ripening of the grape and the growing of the corn, conscious of the glory of His Father in each and all, and conscious of that hidden glory in Himself which He waited to manifest because His " hour " was " not yet come." And dear to the heart of every Christian must be the place where He sanctified all human relationship by His loving Presence, and consecrated to Himself those human joys and natural instincts, through which, by not destroying, but ennobling man's nature, the human heart ascends to immortality and infinity.

We returned to Nazareth by Kefr Kenna, so as to be quite sure of having been at least along the road travelled by the Saviour.

CHAPTER XVIII.

THE ROYAL CITIES OF ISRAEL.

In about an hour after leaving Nazareth, we found ourselves safe at the bottom of the rocky ravine by the so-called Mount of Precipitation (the most unlikely of all the monkish traditional sites we had yet seen), and entered the rich, fine Plain of Esdraelon: it was a pity to have to ride over it when covered only with stubble and dead thistles, but at any time and under all aspects it is a place of so much historical interest that one is apt to forget the present in the past. We took the path down the eastern side, passing close to the mountains of Little Hermon (Jebel-el-Duhhy) and Gilboa* on the left; both of these run out in promontories on the plain, and both are of graceful outline, but Gilboa is by far the more so. On the northern end of El Duhhy, lying on a little grassy slope half-way up the hill, there is a small quiet hamlet, with white houses shining among the trees; this is Nain; still bearing the name it bore when our Blessed Lord made the widow's heart to sing for joy. Lower down, and more to the east, then wrapped in a dark shadow, is Endor, where the prosperity-spoiled Saul heard his doom, and the sombre voice of the spirit announced to him, "to-morrow shalt thou and thy sons be with me;" and so on the morrow, and only at a few miles' distance, was the prophecy fulfilled: for "the men of Israel fled from before the Philistines and fell down slain on Mount Gilboa," and David, forgetting all the injuries done to him by the ungrateful Saul, sang in the sorrow of his affectionate heart, "The beauty of Israel is slain upon thy high places! how are the mighty fallen!" The dry and barren sides of the unsmiling mountain recall vividly to the mind the curse which came upon it, that there should be neither rain nor dew, nor green crops upon the soil where the father and son had fallen. On the southern side of El Duhhy is yet

* Gilboa means the gushing-out fountain.

another site of interest: a little village prettily nestled in a green nook of trees at the foot of the hill, Solem, the ancient Shunem: and one could readily fancy, while riding oneself among the wide flat fields, how the Shunammite's child was sun-stricken, and the reapers carried him home, and then the mother urging on the tardy steps of her ass, all across that wide plain, to the home of the good Prophet, on that side of Carmel—there, on our right,—and her joy in his restoration to life.

A low, round, isolated hill, called El Fouleh " the bean," stands in the midst of the way, bearing the ruins of a strong castle called the Château de Faba by the Crusaders, where Richard of England, surprised by the Saracens at daybreak, leaped from his bed and slew four men in his tent, taking captive seven more. A little further is the point of Gilboa, where the miserable mud hovels of Zureen huddle together over the royal city of three kings of Israel, first planted here by the wicked king Ahab. Though the whole place is filthy, and the people crowd round you as if you were part of a wild beast-show, and though there is neither tree nor shrub nor any plant on the hill save a few hedges of prickly pear, it is one of the most interesting of sites mentioned in the Old Testament to stand on. Not the faintest trace remains above ground of the palace of Ahab, whence Jezebel was thrown from a window, trodden under foot, and gnawed by the dogs of the foul city: but one looks down into the green " valley of Jezreel," * between Gilboa and Little Hermon, where the smiling vines of Naboth grew which Ahab coveted to his cost; the very same valley where sixteen years later Jehu, the avenger appointed by the Lord, came up with his company and met the son of Ahab in the very vineyard and shot him there, while the King of Judah, who was on a visit to his brother-in-law of Israel, tried to escape yonder across the plain, but was overtaken and slain at Megiddo (now Lejjun). Seemingly just under one's feet among the green grass, at the bottom of the hill on which one is standing, a spring of clear water attracts the eye, now called 'Ain Jaloud, but in the Bible the well of Haroud, where the Lord delivered the Bedoueens of Midian and Amalek into the hands of Gideon and the three hundred who had lapped the water of the spring. Further on in the valley, nearer to the Jordan, is a curious-looking low hill, covered with the ruins of Bethshean (or Scythopolis, as it was called after the captivity), whence the grateful men of Jabesh-Gilead fetched the mangled corpses of Saul and his sons, and buried them under their own village tree. Burckhardt says that this once great city was three miles in circumference; many

* Jezreel means God sows.

columns (easily distinguished from Jezreel) and a very perfect theatre still remain; this city was the seat of an archbishop in the time of the Crusaders. A little to the south, near the Jordan, so that the mountain of Gilboa hides it from Jezreel, it is supposed, lay the Salim or Ænon, where John baptized the multitudes who flocked to him; and across the Jordan, recognised by its band of rich foliage bordering the sacred stream, one can just see the ruins, or rather site, of Pella, the place of refuge of the Christians during the siege and destruction of Jerusalem. This is all seen in looking east; while, to the north, the mountains of Galilee stand as a great wall across the country, only breaking down before they reach Carmel, which is green and smiling at every season of the year, stretching back southwards along the whole side of the Plain of Esdraelon, even to the wooded hills of Samaria, with the Kishon running near its verdant foot the whole way. This was the great battle-field of the wars between Judah and Israel—the plain of Megiddo where Barak triumphed over the Philistines—where Josiah was killed by the King of Egypt, for whom the mourning and lamentation was so great, that the " lamentation of Hadad-Rimmon " (a town on this plain) became a proverbial phrase for the expression of any extraordinary sorrow: as Zechariah uses it to describe the mourning of the repentant Jews, in the day of their restoration, for the crucifixion of their Messiah; the name of the plain is also taken by St. John in the Apocalypse, as a type of the great gathering-place for " the battle of the great day." [*] The name Esdraelon is but the Greek form of the Hebrew word Jezreel. We were to see this plain again in the spring, standing on Mount Carmel, with our thoughts full of Elijah the prophet and his good works; now we were thinking chiefly of all this kingly strife and of the tents of Issachar resting in the pleasant land.

The palm trees of 'Ain Jenîn—the En-gannin of Scripture and Ginea of Josephus—were a pleasant sight at the southernmost point of the great plain after our long ride: very bright and refreshing to the eyes were the green gardens of the town, watered by the abundant springs from whence it has evermore been called " the fountain of gardens," and plentiful indeed seemed the supply of cabbages, cucumbers, sweet lemons, melons, &c. &c., that we saw in the streets as we passed along to our tents. This place used to be considered very unsafe, and travellers generally found some of their property appropriated by the villagers, but a new Mutsellim has brought the people into better order, and it is now as safe as any other town in Palestine. This was to be our last night in Galilee,

[*] Zech. xii. 11; Rev. xvi. 16.

and in the land of Issachar, on the morrow we were to enter the kingdom of Samaria and the tribe of Ephraim.

There could scarcely be a prettier combination of mountain and meadow, wood and rock, with the bright sand of the beach and the blue sea in the distance, than the scenery throughout this next day's ride, changing at every quarter of an hour; the sun was very hot, and the eight hours were fatiguing enough, but on the whole it was a delightful ride, full of variety and beauty. The road was generally excellent, frequently passing under the shade of thick olive-groves, gay with women and children gathering the fruit shaken down by the men from the fine old trees; others were picking up the broken sticks or storing the olives in sacks: while the hills and plains were alike gay with the large white stars of the sweet-scented crocus, and real English daisies, not, indeed, very " wee " or very " modest," but fine luxuriant things, golden-eyed and " crimson-tipped." The whole day was a continual change of hill and dale and valley: we crossed one little round plain, or basin, rightly called Merj-el-Ghuruk, the Drowning Meadow, as it is under water throughout the winter, but which was now full of stubble; near to this is the Dothan where poor Joseph was sold to the Ishmaelites, (whose caravans still take this road from Egypt to Damascus,) and where the servant of Elisha was allowed to *see* plainly that if God be for us none can be against us. Beyond this is a fine old fortress called Sanour, which is supposed to be the ancient Bethulia, the scene of the acts of Judith while the army of Holofernes was lying encamped in this little valley extending to the fountain near Dothan: then the venerable woods of Jeba, till, coming down into a bare, rocky valley, we found ourselves at the foot of the least pretty side of the City of Samaria, still called in Arabic by its Roman name of Sebaste; a steep hill, surrounded by such ancient terraces, that they look now like natural formations of the rock. There are many ruins scattered about on the hill, chiefly of decapitated and sunken columns, but neither the broken colonnades nor the Church of St. John are very picturesque or interesting: the church, a semi-ruin of the Crusaders' time, and now a mosque, is poor, ugly, and of a debased style of architecture; a scrap of moulding here and there, and a few small lancet windows, are all that there is to see, except some marble tablets, with oddly sculptured crosses on them, the tombs of some Knights of St. John of Jerusalem, and the entrance to the cave or tomb in which St. John the Baptist is said to have been buried. The finest view of Samaria is from the hill on the south-west side, from whence one readily sees how splendid a site it was for a city, and how grand it must have looked when encompassed by colonnades and triumphal arches, and crowned by one noble temple, such as Herod the Great built in honour of Augustus on the summit of the hill, with the thick olive-groves richly grouped about its feet. Samaria must have stood there like a crown or a wreath round the top of the mountain, the " crown of pride to the drunkards of Ephraim," now " trodden under foot :" a " glorious beauty on the head of the fat valley," now withered as " a fading flower and as the hasty fruit before the summer."* Ephraim seems to have been most famous for its rich vineyards ; but, in sad consequence, so habitually drunk were its sons, that their chief city, Sichem, had acquired from the Jews of later times the contemptuous *sobriquet* of Sichar †, from the word *sichar*, to drink to inebriation. Omri, King of Israel, left his royal abode on the beautiful hill of Thirzah, a few miles off, for this place, which he bought from Shemer, and made it his palace and the seat of government, which it seems to have been for many years after, although Jezreel was also occupied by some of the kings. Two hundred years after its erection Samaria was taken by Shalmaneser, the King of Assyria, who removed the inhabitants and placed colonies of his own people in the half-ruined houses. In the time of the Maccabees it was again destroyed, and after having been slightly rebuilt by Gabinius, the Roman Governor of Syria, Herod the Great embellished it with fine buildings, and called it Sebaste (Augusta) after Augustus Cæsar. It is called by the Arabs Sebaste or Sebastîyeh.

Noble and grand as Samaria must have been, the site of Nablous is more picturesque and beautiful. The town is fixed on a low eminence filling up the centre of the narrow valley, almost hidden by, but with its domes and minarets rising out of, the rich olive gardens and deep foliage of all kinds; the one is proudly " set upon a hill," the other lies nestling in the shade. There are not many cities older than Nablous, for the " place of Sichem " was known in the days when Abraham pitched his tent in the forest of terebinth, called Moreh, or Moriah, as it is written in the Samaritan scripture ; but the city was probably founded by Shechem, son of Hamor, the Prince of the Hivites in the time of Jacob, and it was here that the bones of Joseph were buried after they had been brought up from Egypt. The possession of the "land of Israel" was declared by Joshua when, after crossing the Jordan and taking Jericho and Ai, he advanced straight to this valley, and having ascended Mount Ebal, built an altar, on which he offered sacrifices, and read out to the people all the words of the Law of Moses. Abi-melech the unworthy judge, and Rehoboam the wicked king, were both proclaimed

* Isaiah xxviii. 1–4.   † John iv. 5.

here, and Shechem was for some time the capital of the kingdom of the Ten Tribes; it had originally fallen to the lot of Ephraim, but was afterwards chosen as a Levitical city. When the Assyrians came to Syria under Tiglath Pileser, all the wealthy or influential inhabitants of Samaria were carried off, and made emigrants by force, to the countries watered by the Euphrates, while their places were filled by various peoples brought from other parts of the vast Assyrian empire. Again, in the invasion of Shalmaneser, the same thing took place, and more strangers were brought into the land: probably it was chiefly the men who were carried off, while the Assyrians who took their places married the Samaritan women who had remained in the country. These people, who went under the generic name of the Cuthæans, each served idols after the custom of the several countries they had come from, until, having suffered much from wild beasts and disease, they began to think that they must be offending the "God of the land;" so they petitioned for the return of one of the priests who had been carried from hence into exile, and under his instructions they "feared the Lord," keeping up, however, their own idolatry at the same time. The restored priest of Samaria, who established himself at Bethel, probably taught them to worship Jehovah under a visible image, that of the golden calf set up by Jeroboam: until the good king Josiah, by breaking all their images, forced them, ostensibly at least, to worship Jehovah: they are believed at this time to have received the Pentateuch from the hands of the King of Judah. It was in consequence of this strange anomaly, the mixture of idolatry and true religion, that the Samaritans or Cuthæans were refused a share in the building of the Temple under Zerubbabel, and although closely intermixed with a few of the old Jewish families of Samaria, they were ever cordially hated by the Jews. In the time of Darius, Manasseh, the brother of Jaddoua, the High Priest of Jerusalem, who had married the daughter of the Persian Satrap of Samaria, Sanbalat, got permission from the Persian King to set up a rival Temple on Mount Gerizim, of which he was himself to be High Priest; a few years after it was established, the people of Shechem (a mixture of old Assyrian colonists, a few older Ephraimites, and those Jews who did not choose to conform themselves to the stricter laws and vigorous reforms of Ezra and Nehemiah) declared it their opinion that Moses had clearly indicated their mountain, Gerizim, as the place whereon the sanctuary was to be established; they rejected all Jewish traditions, as well as the Books of the Prophets, accepting the five Books of the Pentateuch as the only really sacred Scripture. Seventy-six years later the Samaritans applied to Alexander the Great to accord them the same favours as he had accorded to the Jews, but as they could not reply with a direct affirmative to his question whether they were Jews or not, he said he would tell them his wishes at another time, and meanwhile, accepting their addition of 8000 men to his army, to whom he afterwards assigned lands in the Thebaïd. On his return from Egypt he found the governor he had left in Samaria had been foully murdered, and he expelled the Samaritans entirely from the city; they settled at Shechem, at the foot of Gerizim, and when Antiochus Epiphanes forbade the celebration of the Jewish religion under pain of death, they declared themselves descendants of the Baal-worshippers of Sidon, and dedicated their temple to Jupiter Olympius. This temple was completely destroyed by John Hyrcanus, the Jewish prince, in B.C. 129, but the Samaritans, with their hatred to the Jews redoubled, continued to perform their own rites on the ruined site of their 200-years old temple. Vespasian rebuilt the city, and called it Neapolis (whence its present name of Nablous), but it is believed that the temple on Gerizim was never rebuilt. The message of salvation through Christ was first taught here by the Saviour Himself in His memorable conversation with the woman at the well, and afterwards by the Apostles, and Christianity appears to have flourished here early, bishops and martyrs bearing witness to the true faith. One church was enclosed in a strong fortress built by the Emperor Justinian, and there were probably others. The Samaritans had colonies in Gaza, Damascus, Cairo, and even in some parts of Europe, but the little community of 133 souls at Nablous are all that now exist in the world. They believe Mount Gerizim to be the Moriah on which Abraham was ordered to sacrifice his son Isaac, because of its original name, but the distance from Beersheba would appear to be far beyond the foot journey in three days, of men laden with wood.

The first person we saw, on reaching Nablous, was Jacob Shellaby, a Samaritan who went to England some years ago, and having interested very many clergy and laymen in the present state of the Samaritan sect, returned to his home with a rich harvest of subscriptions to aid in their education and general improvement. He speaks English well, but he can neither read nor write in any language, even Samaritan, although he professes to be able to do so; as he is the showman-general of the place however, and we then knew no other, we set out under his guidance to see the schools, &c. He took us first to his own house to show us a large stone inscribed with Samaritan characters, which he says he found fixed in a wall in a dark lane where a Samaritan synagogue once stood. He told us the inscription was of the Ten Commandments, but on his

Y

producing a copy of a translation made by Mr. Rogers, the English Consul at Hhaïffa, we found it was a short summary of the first chapter of Genesis, in which the name of God is given as "the Ancient;" but it is written *Shema*, which Rabbi Schwartz says, quoting from the Talmud, was the word used by the Samaritans to express GOD, from the name of the idol worshipped by those who came from Hâmath (see 2 Kings xvii. 30), an idol made in the form of a goat.   The idol of those who came from Cutha was in the form of a cock, and called *Nergal*, which meant a bird, and Schwartz says that they had a bird carved in wood always fastened on the upper end of the rolls of the Law.   Dr. Levisohn, however, a Jew, who since his conversion to Christianity has devoted himself to the study of the Samaritan Pentateuch while living in Jerusalem, and who maintains that the Samaritans are but Hebrews of the tribe of Ephraim, declares that this is all Jewish fable, that they have no carved birds on the Law, and that the word Shema here used is *Ha-Shema*, "the Name," a reverential manner of alluding to a name too holy to be expressed more definitely.   The Samaritan language is the same as the Hebrew, but written in a different character: the Samaritan character was formed on the model of the more ancient Phœnician, while what is now called Hebrew, or square writing, was modified from the Samaritan, little by little, under the influence of the Chaldean writing, with which the Jews had become familiar in their exile; the more ancient Samaritan finally disappeared among them, and was replaced by the Chaldean character, which is retained to this day, and to which the Palmyrene was closely assimilated.*   It is interesting to observe an incidental proof that this change had been fully established before the Christian era, in our Lord's reference to the *Yod*, as the smallest of letters (Matt. v. 18), which it is in the later writing, but was not in the Samaritan.   When the Asmonean or Maccabean princes restored the Jews to be a free and independent nation, and established a coinage of their own, they inscribed it with the more ancient character, from a natural wish to return to the purer times of Israel's glory; five final letters have been added in the later writing: while the earlier is evidently an alphabet more suited for carving upon wood or stone.

We obtained from Shellaby a copy of this inscription, but we learned afterwards in Jerusalem that though genuine, it is impossible to be sure that the stone is very ancient, as up to fifty or one hundred years ago it was the Samaritan custom to place such

---

* The square Hebrew commonly in use was probably not in use before the time of Christ.

inscriptions on the lintels of their doors, and to use them as ornaments on their walls; this one, therefore, may have belonged to
some Samaritan house, taken down to make way for the mosque
which now stands on the site of the old synagogue.

We then went to the school, which is held in the outer room of
the synagogue. Shellaby said that he paid the schoolmaster
entirely from his own funds, and that there were usually about
twenty scholars; at this time there were only ten or twelve,
but nearly half the number were girls, quite a novelty in a
Samaritan school. One pretty little creature, who wore quantities
of rings and gold ornaments, and was about seven years old, read to
us with much clearness and fluency from the Samaritan Pentateuch,
blushing immensely at this exhibition of her accomplishment. She
is the first Samaritan girl who has learned to read, and he said she
had been in school only eight months. She, as well as all the other
pupils, had the most extraordinary ears: large round constructions of flesh falling forward like elephant's flappers; they were
intelligent-looking children.

The synagogue is a small low room, with two recesses, in one of
which the Law is kept behind an old curtain, embroidered with a
pattern something like censers. It is rolled round two tubes of
metal, and each end of the vellum is cased in metal: it was wrapped
in a crimson velvet embroidered cover: the handwriting on the roll
is remarkably fine and firm; the parchment on which it is written
is old and torn, and has been remounted on another vellum, now in
its turn alike old, dirty, and ragged. The Law is read out from a
copy in a book, in order that the ancient roll may not be handled.
Shellaby affirmed in the most positive and solemn manner that this
was really *the* ancient copy—the Roll of the Pentateuch, written, as
they declare, by the hand of Abishua, the son of Phinehas, the
grandson of Aaron—that is, about three thousand years old—
though most of the Samaritans believe that it was written in the time
of Moses. Amram, the High Priest of the Samaritans, however,
assured us later on that *the* old copy has *never* been shown to *any
one* but a member of their own congregation, and as we found afterwards that there was little dependance to be placed on Shellaby's
word this is probably the truth. Numbers of dirty, torn books
were lying on a shelf at the end of the room, seeming still
less cared for than the dirty room itself. A few tin lamps and a
broken stool, besides one desk, were the only furniture or ornaments.
The men and women sit separate. They assemble in synagogue
every Saturday, and the Roll is read through once in the course of each
year. The priesthood is hereditary, descending from father to son.

Y 2

Almost at the summit of Mount Gerizim, at the foot of the crowning knoll, there is a level piece of ground, to which the Samaritans ascend four times a year—at the Passover, Day of Atonement, Feasts of Tabernacles and of Dedication,—and where they pitch their tents; a small pit in the ground is lined with stones, a fire lighted within it, and the paschal lambs, suspended from sticks laid across it, are roasted, or rather baked, in the hole: there is another small pit, where they are cleaned, and a trough into which the calcined bones are afterwards thrown; when all is ended the oven is unbuilt, and the stones dispersed, lest infidel hands should touch them. The Passover is eaten standing, with a staff in the left hand, while, with the right, each person seizes from the animal whatever portion of meat he can reach; they afterwards wipe the grease from the hand with handkerchiefs, which are then thrown into the fire, and the remaining bones are burnt. They have no objection to Mooslim or Christian being present at the sacrifice, but they must not taste the lamb: and they have been sometimes obliged to pay a penalty of five thousand piasters to a Turkish governor, rather than allow him to eat the smallest morsel of it.

A little above this place there is a natural ledge of rock cropping out, divided at rather equal distances by chance cracks; these, they say, are the twelve stones brought by Joshua from the Jordan. They also declare that a sloping mass of bare, smooth rock near this is the spot where Abraham commenced the offering of Isaac, and they show the natural cavern evidently existing underneath as the pit into which the blood was intended to run off. This sloping rock they believe to have been also the scene of Jacob's vision of the heavenly ladder. Some old ruins on the summit of the mountain (which is 2650 feet high) have been thought to be the remains of the Samaritan Temple, but Dr. Robinson considers them to be some of the stones of the fortress built by Justinian; the church which then stood there is now represented by a small Mooslim wely. Probably the Temple of the Samaritans enclosed the sloping rock, and that they had chosen it in imitation of the Sacred Rock in the Temple of Jerusalem: they entertain the most profound reverence for it, never approaching it without taking off their shoes: and it is said that they always turn to it, as the Mooslims do to the Kiblah, in prayer; there are some very old-looking remains of walls near it.

The view from the summit extends over an expanse of sea, with Jaffa among its green gardens and light-coloured sands; it prepares one for the Judæa one is to enter at a very few hours' distance: so barren and dreary are the mountains all round, one is glad to have one last view of pale, blue Hermon.

The eastern end of the narrow valley, in the centre of which Nablous stands, opens out into a small circular plain called the Wady-el-Mokhna : just before the plain commences there is a semi-circular recess exactly corresponding, on each side of the valley—and hence it *seems* self-evident that this was the spot (as no other appears as suitable), where Joshua assembled the children of Israel, and, ranging six tribes in the one recess on Mount Ebal, and six in the other on Mount Gerizim, with the elders and officers, the judges and the Levites assembled round the Ark in the centre, read out "the blessings and the cursings" and all that was "written in the book of the law." How often, in after times, did these two mountains that then echoed back the solemn words of warning and of promise, resound to the tumultuous shouts of the idolatrous multitudes who brought "strange gods" from their heathen homes to be worshipped in the once holy valley!

Just at the commencement of the little plain, the *eye*, as it were, of the valley, are the melancholy remains of "Jacob's Well;" somewhat further on a little wely marks the site of Joseph's Tomb ; and on the slope of the hill, to the east, "before the city" of Shechem, is the village of Saleem, the ancient Shalim; there Jacob pitched his tent and built an altar to the Lord God of Israel, "the parcel of ground" which he bought and gave to his son Joseph, and in which Joshua laid the bones which he had brought up from Egypt.

But nearly all one's interest settles in "Jacob's Well," of which now, alas! one can see only the site, as even the hole, still visible, is but the choked up entrance to the vaulted chamber above the well, part of a church which was standing in the time of Bishop Arculf, A.D. 700. It seems strange that a spot, reverenced alike by Christians and Jews, Mooslims and Samaritans, and a site in which all traditions have ever and ever agreed without shadow of doubt or question, should have been allowed to fall into such a miserable state of ruin and decay. We inquired in Jerusalem whether we might be permitted to restore it into use and order, but we found that only two or three weeks before the Greeks had bought it, intending to build a Russian convent around it. The well is said to have been excavated entirely in the solid rock, with the sides hewn smoothly and regularly in a perfect circle : the last measurement known of it gave nine feet in diameter and seventy-five in depth : but it was then probably much filled up at the bottom. There are few sites more interesting to a Gentile than this, few where the scene around has been so little changed in the long intervals of ages ; we looked now on the fields that were then "white already to harvest:" yonder is the path by which the "disciples had gone away into the city to buy meat:" women carrying pitchers on their heads were passing to and fro: and towering grandly above us was the head of "this mountain" of Gerizim, to which the Samaritan woman pointed as she spoke of the Temple wherein "our fathers worshipped." One fancies one hears the grand message of universal salvation in the spiritual religion of the true and pure heart, echoing silently, as it were, still in this quiet spot: one enters into the mingled astonishment and joy of the woman, who perhaps had felt something stirring in her heart, a groping after something better and holier than the jumble of idolatrous fetishes around her, who, accustomed only to the harsh bigotry of the narrow-minded Jews, heard now for the first time that religion was confined neither to one place nor to one name: that God was not "like unto gold or silver or stone, graven by art or man's device," but a Spirit "in whom we live and move and have our being;" that Messiah was come neither to judge nor to condemn, nor to destroy, but to save men, to gather them into one fold under one Shepherd, Whose yoke was easy and Whose burden was light, Who was ready to lay down His life for His sheep, and to be "indeed the Saviour of the world."

The Crusaders had a church in Nablous, which is now of course a mosque, but the nearly perfect doorway is well worth seeing: it is in the Gothic style, then prevailing in France, with a good dash of Saracenic about it; it is very richly and well carved. We found the people of Nablous, unlike their former selves of even only ten years ago, remarkably civil and obliging: the present governor punishes any instance of incivility in the severest manner, and it is now an agreeable resting-place for travellers: we stayed two days, and walked much about the town, admiring the handsome and well-dressed women and children. Seeing we were strangers, some men invited us into a large court filled with some hundreds of water-skins, for the making of which Nablous is famous; the roots of the red-oak, which grows very plentifully in the valley, being used for the tanning: they are then sewn up at the extremities, filled with water, and laid out to season them. I never saw anything look more horrid than this immense family of black sheep, all lying on their backs, with their heads cut off and their legs in the air! The chief trade of Nablous is in soap: there are four large manufactories, and heaps of ashes and refuse nearly as large as those of Jerusalem.

We traversed the whole town on leaving it, and met so cold a wind as we rounded the stern cliff of Gerizim, that my lips were cut and chafed. This whole day's ride was very dreary; the little valleys between the hills would have been cheerful enough in summer, but they were now filled with stubble or with yokes of patient oxen turning up the soil with a primitive plough, or rather a couple of ploughs employed on each field closely following each other. Scarcely three trees were seen in the whole day, and the hills were barren, rocky and ugly to the last degree; one narrow winding glen, Wady-el-Haramiyeh—the Robber's Valley—was all the beauty we had: there the rocks were relieved by olives, the ground sprinkled with starry crocuses, and the terraces covered with tangles of red hawthorn berries and a beautiful yellow bell-shaped clematis, with a drooping head and pretty leaf. We stopped beside the fountain of Yebroud, and had enough to do to warm ourselves in the very cold night, which we were glad to shorten in our impatient anxiety for the memorable day which was to give us our first view of Jerusalem. Yebroud seemed as if it must be a pretty place in summer, and soon after leaving it we came to a fine *barranca*, where the perpendicular walls of four small valleys met in a little plain full of trees: but after this all was utterly stony and hideous, however interesting from the numerous sites mentioned in the Scriptures still to be traced on the country. After three hours' riding, we came to a conical steep hill, called Tuleil-el-Foul—the ancient Gibeah—so long the home of Saul and the seat of his government. We insisted on mounting it, as we felt sure it would command a fine view of the neighbourhood of Jerusalem, nor were we mistaken; for after we had seen all the views about the City many times over, we always returned in thought to this one, as, with two exceptions, the most beautiful of all, for from no other place is the simile, used by the Psalmist, of God's love encompassing His people " as the hills stand round about Jerusalem " so well illustrated as from here. We looked over Scopus, to where the domes and minarets of the holy City seemed rising directly from thick olive-groves, enclosed and surrounded in the embraces of the wild hills and blue mountain ridges on all sides: Jericho and Bethany were alike hidden, but the Mount of Olives stood up proudly with the little Church of the Ascension on the summit: while under the stern range of the Moab mountains lay the Dead Sea, in a sweeping curve of the most lovely turquoise blue, calm and peaceful, scarcely sad, but lying among the dreary, barren mountains like the smile óf peace on the rugged face of a dead man. I never afterwards saw the Dead Sea without remembering the peculiar feeling of solemn but tender beauty that it gave me from Tuleil-el-Foul.

Passing the desolate hill where stood Nob, " the city of priests," destroyed by Saul, we came to the brow of Scopus, where hundreds of small stones, mounted in threes and fours upon each other, told of the farewells or first views of generations of pilgrims to the Holy City. The view is here confined to the City and its own olive-groves, with a few of its domes and minarets rising above the walls, which are more quaint than grand, for they have a very fanciful Saracenic parapet above them, the olive-trees looking so infinitely sad as they grow out of the white stony ground; the half-ruined tower in each garden, the dreary heaps of grey ashes by which one passes, and the utter silence, so unlike the outskirts of a great city, all combine to press down with a very solemn, very sad weight upon the heart, yet strangely harmonising with the instinctive feeling of its beauty, with the prettiness of its graceful minarets, and the happy peaceful feeling of being, at last, in the haven where one would be. The quaint expression of old Fuller came naturally into my mind, describing the arrival of the way-worn Crusaders at the longed-for goal: " All had much ado to manage so great a gladness! "

We went into the City for our letters, and then, passing along the northern wall, descended into the valley of the Kedron and climbed the Mount of Olives, on the summit of which our tents were pitched. The first sight of Jerusalem from here would be solemn at any time, but we were greeted with a scene of such glorious magnificence as probably few persons see twice in a lifetime, and which it is hopeless to render into words: floods of flame and fire had spread over the Mediterranean Sea, above which heavy clouds of a deep plum colour were closing down, crimsoning the brown plains below: the City domes seemed stained with absolutely bloody tips, above which a strange, orange glow was hanging in the air: the bare flat hills on each side paled off in indigo and pale blues: while behind us were the mountains of Moab*, wrapped, covered in a mantle of silky, shining gauze of the most exquisite shade of peach blossom, like the petals of a rhododendron, which seemed absolutely unearthly; this gradually deepened into violet, and the glory of it faded away: the stars came out, and the new moon rose, and everything relapsed into silence and darkness, broken only by the howling of the jackals and a light here and there in the City, while the wind blew with a bitter whistle through the tents; but never, while life lasts, shall I forget our first view of Jerusalem by the sunset light of the 30th November, 1859.

We stayed here for some days: the nights were bitterly cold, for Olivet is nearly 3000 feet above the sea, but the days were lovely,

* " Une ligne droite, tracée par une main tremblante," as Chateaubriand well describes them.

and the quiet enjoyment of the sacred view, which we could now study at leisure and in all the changing lights, was worth almost any discomfort. We found reason afterwards to rejoice that we had been thus able to get the general topography of the City, and the relative position of the hills within, and of those without its walls, thus thoroughly into our minds; for the narrow tortuous streets, and the constant up and down of apparently steep hills (which are on so small a scale that one cannot at first rightly distinguish one from the other), is so very confusing to the mind, that one needs to be really conversant with the general lie of the ground, before one can understand or reckon up the connection of the details. But yet without this, there is an inexpressible pleasure in the feeling of a rest on the holy mountain, while encamped under the shade of the olives, gazing on the City, which from this point is really beautiful; only one thing was still more impressive to us wanderers, and that was the descent on the following Sunday morning, by the steep winding path on the hill-side, across the narrow Kedron, through the gate of St. Stephen, till "our feet stood within the gates of Jerusalem!" along the Via Dolorosa up to the little Hebrew-and-English church, where the familiar prayers of our beloved service fell with holy sweetness, "sweeter than honey and the honeycomb," on the long unaccustomed ear, and we sang those words, to the well-known notes, that recalled many a happy Sunday in Christian England, in company with fellow-Christians met together on Mount Zion, literally from all the quarters of the globe—"the holy Church throughout all the world doth acknowledge thee!"

CHAPTER XIX.

THE SEPULCHRE OF ABRAHAM AND THE SEA OF LOT.

As the Syrian winter does not commence till January, and December is the best of all months for travelling in those regions where the heat is intolerably oppressive during the summer, we thought ourselves fortunate in having secured it for a visit to the Dead Sea, as we were not inclined to make the hurried excursion which the heat renders imperative upon most travellers. We therefore only remained a few days on the Mount of Olives, and started afresh on the 5th of December for Urtass, skirting the Holy City, passing over the plain of Rephaim, and by the rich woods of Beit Jala, along the rocky hills of Bethlehem to the Pools of Solomon. Between Beit Jala and Bethlehem a little Mooslim wely marks the spot where the beloved Rachael died (a site on the authenticity of which there is happily no doubt), whence Jacob went sorrowfully on, and pitched his tent beside the little tower built for the flocks of the neighbouring herdsmen to take refuge in: close to the spot where, many hundred years after, our Tower of Refuge[*]— a "strong tower of defence"—was born in the mean and miserable stable of an inn, taking for His earthly mother one yet more weak, tender, and pure than the dutiful and affectionate Rachael.

Our tents were pitched in the gardens of Urtass, and on the morrow we borrowed a labourer from the owner of the rich valley to be our guide among the mountains: the man was instructed by

[*] Genesis xxxv. 21. Migdol Edar means the "tower of the flock :" not only every vineyard had its tower of defence, but there were small towers or fortresses built for the shepherds and their flocks to sleep in on cold nights, and into which the flocks could be gathered on a sudden alarm from the raids of the Bedoueens. The Targumist Jonathan, says : "And Israel pitched his tent at the Tower Edar, the place where the King Messiah will manifest Himself at the end of time, as saith the prophet Micah ;" in that remarkable verse —iv. 8.

Mr. Meshullam, in case we were attacked by Bedoueens, to say that we were friends of his. Our dragoman was not particularly willing for the expedition, as these Bedoueens of the Ta'âmreh tribe are remarkably unruly and belligerent, but as Mr. Meshullam, who is thoroughly acquainted with the whole country, had not seemed to think it unsafe for us, we determined on proceeding, and continued our route over as dreary a succession of barren stony mountains as one could see anywhere; there was not even the common little thorny plant among the pebbles, although in the valleys, and under the stones which encumber every slope, the ground is mostly as rich as any soil in Syria. We passed round the foot of the Frank Mountain, an odd shaped hill like a cone with the top cut off, familiar in almost every view about Jerusalem. Its Arab name is Jebel-el-Fureidis, the Mountain of Paradise; but in its present barren condition it certainly does not merit such a name, whatever it may once have done when crowned by the palace of Herod and beautified with his gardens; it was probably then a delightful spot, the fine houses and palaces built beneath the hill encircling it with splendour; its having been fortified by the Crusaders is the cause of its present name. These barren and dreary hills and dales are the commencement of the wilderness of Judæa where most of the history of David and Saul was enacted, and we were now on our way to the Cave of Khurieytîn, which is believed to be the cave of Adullam: it must be undoubtedly near it, if it is not the cave itself, and it is a fine specimen of the enormous caverns with which these limestone hills are riddled in every direction.

We were in the middle of one of these silent desolate valleys, when a Bedoueen, dressed in a couple of unshorn sheepskins, suddenly started up and stopped us, informing us that the paths here had not been made for travellers, but for Arabs (their usual formulary when they intend mischief), and then another and another head appeared, peering over the brow of the hill. As we were entirely at their mercy, the only plan was to make friends by the mammon of unrighteousness, and we therefore engaged Sheepskin as a guide: once in our service, we knew he would be faithful to us. Soon after we came to a deep, narrow ravine, on the perpendicular cliffs of which not even a thorn was to be seen: here we dismounted, and proceeded along a little ledge, about two feet wide, left on the side of the cliff; and a very dizzy path it was, overhanging the precipice. Across it lay a single block about six feet high, over which we had to be pulled up on one side and let down on the other, after wriggling over the top, between which and the overhanging rock there was a space of only a couple of feet: it was not exactly pleasant, but Sheepskin's foot and |hand were firm, and grasping tightly his horny fist, without venturing to glance below, the last jump, an oblique one, over the chasm, and in at the mouth of the cave, was successfully performed. A low passage leads into a rather fine hall, arched at the top, about 120 feet long by 40 wide, with many recesses, from whence winding passages lead for an untraceable distance under the hill, one of which has, I believe, been followed to an opening near the top of the hill. The hall is large enough to contain a great many men, but not 400, I should think, unless they were packed as closely as the bats which hung like thick curtains, one overlapping the other, on the sides of the rock: we were careful not to disturb them, as the Bedoueens said they were very vicious. It is scarcely worth encountering the peril of the way to see the cave, except for the association of David and his mighty men with it: Adullam is said to mean " to quit the true road," and certainly if this is Adullam there is no true road at all to it.

When we had made our way back to the horses, another Bedoueen joined us, demanding baksheesh as well as those who had helped in getting us to the cave and had held the horses; this we refused, and rode off a few paces, when the disappointed Arab wrenched a bag from off our maid's saddle, and ran down the ravine with it! The other Bedoueens pursued him, the dragoman succeeded in knocking him down, and the others gave him a drubbing; while to impress them with a sense of our power, I fired three shots over their heads, and told Sheepskin when he came back that I could fire six shots all at once at bad men. He looked grave and astounded —as well he might, for I soon remembered I had told him *sixty* instead of *six* in my bad Arabic, and doubtless he thought my little revolver a gift from Sheitân himself.

He was dismissed in content, and we proceeded on our way to the ruins of the ancient Tekoa, a hill on which a Christian town, founded by St. Saba, existed for six hundred years, but which has been deserted since 1138: the only ruin of interest is that of the church, in which lies a noble font of rose-coloured limestone* sculptured with Christian symbols: it also has a *seat* round the inside. From this hill there are lovely views of the Dead Sea, which shone as blue as the Mediterranean in the mid-day sun. Tekoa is interesting as the birthplace of the prophet Amos, who was, in the time of Jeroboam II., keeping his father's sheep, and feeding on wild figs in these hills when the Spirit of the Lord came upon him.

The country becomes prettier between Tekoa and Hebron, as the valleys are full of terebinth—then crimson-tipped with the autumn

* There is much rose-coloured limestone in the hills about Tekoa.

tint—lentisk, and oak, and the hill-sides were clothed with vineyards which were now, however, very nearly leafless: only great bare stems straggling about on the ground. The country seemed very silent, for there are no villages, but we stopped among a flock of sheep and milked some of them into our tin mugs, by way of luncheon, as we found no water till late in the day, when, reaching a small village, a woman drew some and then coolly demanded my sister's gold bracelets in payment! They were uncouth people, for the children spat at us as we passed! the only real rudeness we ever experienced in Syria. The villagers were busy with a number of little new-born lambs, which they were laying out on soft mats in the sun. At last we turned into the valley of Eshcol, rich in fine vineyards: and Hebron opened out at once, rising up one side of the valley, enclosed in olive-gardens. It is a very large town, handsomely built and rather picturesque, as every house has one or two little domes, and the windows are furnished with brightly painted shutters. The mosque is in the centre of the town, which forms a good picture, although the hills around are each one uglier than its neighbour: they are but shapeless brown undulations of no external interest till one remembers that there, on the brow of one of them, Abraham stood to watch the burning cities of Sodom and Gomorrah.

Between 2000 and 3000 years before Christ, Palestine and the neighbouring countries were inhabited by eight different races of men of giant stature: one of these races, the children of Anak, had inhabited, we know not how long, the hills and valleys about Hebron, when a tribe of strangers, probably from the shores of the Persian Gulf, arrived in the country, over which they soon spread themselves; they did not, however, destroy the children of Anak, who continued to dwell in the land for at least a thousand years after; these strangers were called, from the country of their adoption, the Canaanites, and afterwards the Phœnicians. Some time after a little band of travellers one day passed by, going down into Egypt because there was a famine in the land of Canaan; they returned in two years, but they were now very rich in gold and silver and cattle, and so numerous that they had to divide themselves into two parties; he who chose for his portion the borders of the river Jordan, where it afterwards became a lake, was called Lot; and he who pitched his tents under the fine oaks in the valleys about Hebron was called Abraham. And here, nearly a hundred years after this, Abraham was laid by his sons in one of the caves* on the hill-side which he had bought from the children of Heth, a

* Machpelah means the *double* cave.

family of the Canaanites * settled there. By this time the children of Anak had built the city which they called after their forefather Arba—Kirjath-arba—" which is Hebron ;" and the valleys had been named after Abraham's friend, Mamre, who belonged to the Amorites, another family of the Canaanites.* Damascus was at this time a city also, but which was the oldest of the two we shall probably never know.

Hebron seems to have been in the centre of the land assigned to the tribe of Judah on the partition of the country, and after Joshua had slain its Canaanitish king ; and thence Caleb, to whom the valley was specially given, drove out the original inhabitants, the children of Anak. Hebron was afterwards apportioned as a city of the Levites, but in 400 years it became again a royal city, as David was there " anointed king over the house of Judah " and Israel, and there he reigned seven years and a half until he had taken the stronghold of Zion and made it " the habitation of the Lord." Long after, the sacred caves containing the bones of Abraham and Sarah, Isaac and Rebekah, Jacob and Leah, were enclosed within massive walls ; and it is believed that these sepulchres still remain intact and unrifled of the dust which has lain there for more than three thousand years, for although the Idumeans and the Mooslims have alike at different times had possession of the city, the bones of the Patriarchs are sacred alike to all. The Crusaders in 1167 built a church over the tombs, calling it the cathedral of the " bishop of St. Abraham : " but it was soon after turned into a mosque by the Mooslims, to which they gave the name of the " Mosque of the Friend of God "—*Mesjed 'l Khalil 'l Allah.* Neither Christian nor Jew have ever been admitted into the enclosure since the day when the Mooslims took possession of the city, nor, indeed, are Mooslims even of very high rank allowed a sight of the real sepulchres : all they ever see are a set of marble tombs, built on a higher story, as it were, in the building, each one over that which it represents below.

The structure enclosing the caves is a very remarkable one ; it is of an oblong form with a wall of massive stones, hewn smooth and beveled identically the same as those in the substructions of the Temple at Jerusalem ; and there is no reason to doubt the tradition that these walls were built by David when he reigned in Hebron. There are fifteen pilasters against the two long walls, and nine against the short walls : at each end there is a lofty staircase and a

---

* Heth and Amori were both sons of Canaan, grandson of Noah. Both families were settled in the mountains about Hebron and 'Ain Jidi : they were therefore brothers of the founders of the cities of Sidon and Hamath.

Saracenic door. Jews are allowed to ascend only to the third step of the flight, and the guards are very chary of letting one even look in at the doors. The stones of the walls are some of them twenty feet long, but they are mostly squares, or nearly so, of from three to four feet: against these in the outer angles Jewish men and women are usually to be seen kneeling in prayer, rocking themselves and weeping. These massive walls have been heightened a few feet all round with a very poor Saracenic wall, plastered over, and castellated; at each end is a minaret, while in the centre, the dark tiled *sloping* roof and arched window of the Christian Church rise up, looking more incongruous and unusual than one can say after seeing all the flat-roofed towns and villages of Syria and Palestine.

At the bottom of the valley is the Pool of David, not hollowed in the rock, but built round with stones of the ancient Jewish bevel (since plastered over by the Arabs) with two staircases down to the water: it is 130 feet square: it contains only rainwater and is very dirty: there is another smaller tank some way further, built in the like manner, and, doubtless, it was over one of these that David caused the murderers of Ishbosheth to be hanged.

Sheikh Hamzeh, the Wakeel of the Bedoueens on the west side of the Dead Sea, lives at Hebron for the purpose of making arrangements for travellers desirous of going into the Desert, and we spent one whole day in bargaining with him. The price was fixed, after a great deal of bother, for 600 piasters, including baksheesh. Sheikh Hamzeh and Abou Dahouk, the son of Sheikh Salâm, the famous chief of the Jeh'aheen Arabs, were to accompany us themselves with ten Bedoueens. We were to have five full days, and to go where we liked, and camp wherever we chose. So we started at mid-day, Sheikh Hamzeh, a most courteous, white-bearded old man, leading the cavalcade, and never failing to make a salaam and say " Marhaba! " whenever he came near us, though it might be twenty times in an hour. Abou Dahouk was most anxious to enter into conversation, and was as polite and well-mannered, in his simple way, as any English gentleman. Abou Dahouk was the name of his grandfather, father, brothers, and cousins. It means the father of David, and so strict is the custom of calling a son after his father's father, that every Arab is called among his friends "father of so-and-so," even before he is married, in boyhood or babyhood: since, if ever he has a son, that must be the child's name. Our dragoman, Habeeb, was always addressed among his intimate friends as " Abou Faras :" his father's name had been Faras, and therefore if he ever married his son would bear the same. " I have gotten a man from the Lord," seems among the Arabs to invest the mother with peculiar dignity (Gen. iv. 1), and a wife does not bear the name of her husband, but that of her son. We used to be amused to hear the English Consul's wife always addressed by the natives as "Om (mother of) Iskender" her eldest boy's name being Alexander, and they would inquire from her after the child as "Abou Jacobi," his father's name being James.

The road from Hebron soon changed from dreary hills to absolute desert, with nothing particular to look at save the openings of a few caves here and there, the scenes, doubtless, of many of the adventures and escapes of David during his wanderings in the "wilderness of Judæa." One cave was fronted with columns, and we regretted not being able to examine it: the Arabs call it "the mother of bells," and seemed to regard it with interest and respect, so it may contain some remains of interest. The word here translated *wilderness* or *desert* should not be misunderstood to mean a sterile place: the root of the original Hebrew word *midbar* means to conduct, to lead, and describes an open country fit for the pasturage of flocks: they were frequently fit for cultivation, but were left open for the occupation most congenial to the early Israelite. Soon after we came to Tell Ziph, the site of the city whose inhabitants tried to betray David into the hands of Saul; and in half an hour more to Carmel, where there are ruins of some interest: an old tower of the same masonry as the Tower of Hippicus, and the remains of several churches and other ruins of some extent. It was in this place that Amaury I., King of Jerusalem, occupied, in A.D. 1172, so saith the Chronicle, the identical dwelling-house of Nabal, the churl whose beautiful Abigail became afterwards the wife of David!

We went on over still drearier hills, till, turning suddenly up a low rise of coarse, gravelly sand, we found ourselves close to the tents of the Jeh'aleen Bedoueens, a small number of whom were encamped in a shallow wady below; there were about forty long, low, black and brown tents placed in two rows: a few horses picketed at a little distance, some dogs, and one baby-camel: the camp camels were all in another wady. The Bedoueens were soon swarming around us, and were immensely excited at our little dog, whom they firmly believed to be some kind of lamb; these good people are such troublesome beggars, and so handy in assisting one to give them what they want, that our servants dared not even take their tobacco bags out of their pockets, and with all their care one of the silver spoons was missing before morning; while a boy kindly picked up a torn bit of newspaper from outside our tent and offered it to us for six piasters! we made the little dog growl at him in return, and he ran away in the greatest terror.

Abou Dahouk left his horse here and continued all the way with us on foot, walking beside our horses and assisting them in difficulties: about every ten minutes he looked up in one's face and inquired " Ya sitt, taïb?" a sort of Bedoueen cabman's " All right, mum ?" For some six hours we went on and on, over the same uninteresting downs of bare sand, without seeing a bush, scarcely even a tuft of thorn, and with no variety in the shapeless hills to break the monotony : one never seemed to know where one hill ended, or the next commenced, except by following the rings or long lines of white rocks cropping out, in unnaturally regular bands, round or up the slopes. This was the desolate scene of the wanderings of St. John the Baptist, and well the dreary view harmonised in the mind with one's idea of the stern Saint—a scene far more dreary, forbidding and harsh, than the finest picture of Spagnoletti or Salvator Rosa; they painted the ascetic under the gloomy terrors of darkness ; more picturesque though less terrible to endure than the fierce rays of the scorching sun upon the shadeless, glaring mountains of sand. At last we turned into a very narrow little ravine, the bed of a winter torrent, where a few seyâl trees had procured it the name of Wady Seyâl. The path was rough enough, but nothing to what followed when we had entered the Wady-en-Nemrîyeh, the valley of the Leopardess, which was too magnificent to be dreary ; the monotonous slopes were left behind, and there were now only lofty walls of 1000 feet high, meeting at the bottom in the wildest confusion. Every mule had to be unloaded at the very beginning of the ravine, the first ledge being too narrow for a loaded mule to hold a footing: and there were many places where they could not scramble up or down with any weight to carry beyond their own. We had been slowly getting down the zig-zag for more than an hour when the path was reported good enough for us to mount ; but at the very first step the horse our maid was riding slipped over a smooth slope of rock and threw her on her face, which was severely cut. She lay so long insensible, that we had time to realise in its full horror the sensation of helpless solitude in a desert in time of need : we had no water : however, the only thing we could do turned out to be the best cure of all, and that was to wash [the wounds with pure wine, after which they heal with wonderful rapidity. Fortunately we had not much further to go, for the tents were pitched on a small level spot in the very heart of the ravine, close to the only spring to be found for many miles. I do not think there is in all Syria a finer spot: the cliffs went down about 300 or 400 feet beneath us as perpendicularly as a plumb line: they towered above us about 1000 feet more: while seen through the narrow

z

opening at the eastern end, the Dead Sea lay in calm loveliness, with the opposite range of the mountains of Moab, varying, with the light of evening, from every shade of the brightest rose-colour to the deepest violet. In the very middle of the blue lake the end of the Lisân or *tongue**, shone out in the most staring white. The silence of this valley, or rather chasm, was almost oppressive; yet it did not quite want life, for the trickling of the little stream fell loud and clear on the ear, and every now and then a little gazelle would come and stand daintily on the very edge of the cliff overhanging the tents, and look down with wonder on the unusual scene below.

· We left it at nine o'clock the next morning, and rode for a couple of miles, due south, along the foot of the mountains that border the lake, but at a long distance from the shore; then we turned suddenly up a zig-zag cut out of the cliff, which is here about 500 feet high, with 300 or more above it a little further back. How the horses ever got up that zig-zag I don't know, but they seemed to cast reproachful glances at us at every fresh pull. We found a level plateau at the top, sunk down, however, so as to afford no view on either side: here and there among the sand and white stones there were lumps of stone as black as coal, increasing in number at every step: they rang with a metallic sound at the touch of the horses' hoofs. Soon the whole ground sounded like the crackling of volcanic scoria; yet amongst the very blackest of the stones lay thousands of tiny, delicate, white snail shells such as we had seen in the Tadmor Desert, and in other desert places since; and our Arabs picked up great lumps of gypsum, which they offered to us as valuables. We met a couple of goatherds, whose shining bodies were nearly black, and almost naked: they were overwhelmed with astonishment, not merely at the unusual sight of travellers, but at their being ladies! Sheikh Hamzeh engaged one of them as guide, and he led us to a little spring at the foot of the mountain, now called Sebbeh, once crowned with the famous Jewish fortress of Masada. He told the goatherd to show us the way up, but for some time the only answer he got was that woman's foot could never mount that rock. It certainly looked rather appalling.

The rock on which Masada stands is a perpendicular of 1500 feet high, facing the Dead Sea: it projects from the line of cliffs, and would be entirely separated from them by the deep chasm which runs behind it, but for a narrow connecting neck of smooth sloping rock; up this neck we were to climb. Sheikh Hamzeh and the Bedoueens took off their sandals and abbahs, and we pinned up our riding habits closely around us (they were, nevertheless, in rags when we

* Joshua xv. 2.

descended), and then we slowly crept up the slope. Above this there was about fifty feet of naked rock *wall* to be got up somehow: once there was but a ledge of some three inches wide to stand on whilst Abou Dahouk scrambled up the smooth face seven or eight feet higher, and then, leaning over, pulled us up by main force: one false step and we should have gone to the bottom of the chasm. We found a paved path at the edge, probably the road leading to the "White Promontory," on which Flavius Silva raised the bank for his battering rams, and were soon on the wide plateau above. Safely landed there, it may be interesting to relate, in a few words, something of the magnificent tragedy* which has made the name of Masada famous for all history.

Simon Maccabæus, the last of the seven hero-brothers of Judah, built this fortress about the year 140 B.C.; but it is probable that it had always been a fortified retreat during the wars of the country. Little is known of its history till Herod the Great took possession of it, enclosed the flat top in a strong wall, rather less than a mile in length; on this he erected thirty-eight towers, and added a lofty and magnificently-furnished palace for himself: the rest of the ground was left for growing corn, as the soil was rich, and a great number of tanks or reservoirs of water were hewn in the rock, so that the garrison holding it could live independent of supplies from the outer world. To this inaccessible fortress he intended to retire in case of revolt among his subjects, or any other great danger. There were but two ways of ascending to it: one by the narrow neck we have described, which was defended by a tower, and the other by a zig-zag path up the cliff facing the lake, called the *Serpent*, the danger of which Josephus describes as "sufficient to quell the courage of everybody by the terror it infuses into the mind ... for that he who would walk along it must go first on one leg and then on the other, and there is nothing but destruction in case your feet slip." Herod laid up stores of all manner of arms in it, and vast quantities of food. A few months after, he made good his retreat from Jerusalem when that city was attacked by the Parthians, and having placed his mother and his beautiful betrothed, Mariamne, in the stronghold, he went himself to Rome, while Antigonus besieged Masada in vain for three months. A hundred years later, the imperial army having got possession of the fortress, a band of the Zealots, maddened by the outrages of the infamous Florus at Jerusalem, managed to get into the citadel—probably by ascending the Serpent in the night—and massacred the whole garrison. Within the next five years Jerusalem had fallen, after indescribable sufferings; and of all their fortresses,

* Josephus, 'War,' vii., viii.

z 2

Masada alone remained in the possession of the Jews. To this, Flavius Silva, the Roman envoy and Procurator of the miserable country, determined to lay siege, and led his army there early in the spring. In the meantime the cisterns had been filled by the winter's rain; and such is the dryness and purity of the air, that the remains of the corn, wine, oil, and dates, stored up by Herod, were found to be perfectly fresh and good, while the supply of arms was sufficient for ten thousand men. The Romans surrounded the whole rock, and, blockade being useless, they at last succeeded in building a bank of earth and stones just above the *neck*, on which to place their battering rams and other engines. The garrison made an ingenious machine of wood and earth to resist the ram; but the Romans set fire to it, and then the soldiers within knew that resistance was hopeless. Their commandant was Eleazar, the grandson of Judah the Galilean, one of the first of those who had encouraged the Jews to resist the cruelties and impious demands of the Romans: neither flight nor submission entered into the mind of his noble descendant; he knew that on the following day the Romans would make a general assault on walls that would crumble beneath their irresistible power, and he determined to unite the whole company in one grand sacrifice. Assembling his garrison at nightfall around him, he made, with all the eloquence of a dreadful enthusiasm, one of the grandest appeals on record; he described to them the horrors that awaited them should they fall into slavery and dishonour, and dilated upon the blessed assurance of the immortality and rewards promised to the soul that should escape unstained from its earthly bonds; and having worked them up to a state bordering on frenzy, he conjured them to meet an awful but triumphant death with unfailing courage. The little band of heroes were not unworthy of their noble leader: death was easier to every true Jew than impiety or dishonour; the liberty of the soul was sweeter than the freedom of the body. Without one instant's hesitation each man embraced his wife and his children, and in the next moment stabbed them to the heart; then, choosing by lot ten men to complete the dreadful sacrifice, they lay down beside the corpses of those dear victims already gone, and, one by one, each offered his throat to the knives of the chosen ten, who, after piling up all their wealth in one heap, set fire to it and to the palace. One was again chosen to consummate the bloody deed—to put an end to his companions and lastly to himself: and when the morning dawned of Easter-day A.D. 73, the sun rose on nothing but smoking ruins and bleeding corpses! The Roman mounted the breach with a shout of triumph but only an awful silence met them, broken at last by the appearance of two women and five children, who had concealed themselves in one of the cisterns, and now came forth to relate the speech of the heroic Eleazar, and to point to the ghastly heap of immortalised patriots! Thus closed, with an awful grandeur, the last scene of the long tragedy of the Jewish War of Independence.

Masada must have been abandoned soon after, for even tradition is silent as to the bloody spot. Nearly eighteen centuries passed away before Mr. Eli Smith and Dr. Robinson, coming in view of the mountain, conceived that it might be the long-lost Masada; and in 1842 two travellers, Messrs. Walcott and Tipping, having succeeded in climbing to the top, discovered the remains of the fortress and palace. It has since been ascended by three or four other travellers who agree in thinking that the ridge or *neck* on the western side, " fit only for a rope-dancer's foot," as says De Saulcy, is covered with the remains of the mound built up by the Roman general. On reaching the summit, the gateway formed of a single pointed arch is the first thing seen; it is neither handsome nor particularly well built: the stones have several marks rudely scratched upon them of crosses and circles, one of which, the circle with the cross beneath it, is said to be the sign of the planet Venus: this is the best piece of building on the whole plateau. There are four sets of ruins, but they are all of the roughest character, and either Josephus's account of Herod's palace must be enormously exaggerated, or the remains of it have totally disappeared. Had the Crusaders ever fortified so remarkable a mountain some tradition or record of it would have been handed down, or some token of their building would remain apparent: but certainly none is existing there now. The work is very rude and coarse: the stones are not large, and the interstices are filled in with little loose bits without being mortared or even mudded over: inside the largest building, which has a semicircular apse to one of the rooms, the walls are plastered over with a hard cement, into which common bits of stone or fragments of pots of any shape are stuck in rude stripes or diamonds, with a rough attempt at arrangement of colour, but nothing could be coarser or rougher in appearance: there is also a pavement of the same kind of coarse pebble-mosaic. The cisterns, which have been evidently very large, are now filled up, from the ground and stones having fallen in; and the only sign of life was an eagle, who, disturbed at our approach, soared up into the sky, dropping a feather at our feet: this we carried down as a trophy.

It is worth a great deal, even such an ascent as it is, to stand on the blood-stained soil of Masada; but it is really worth double the toil to see the view from the summit of that rock: one of the things to remember through life. Somebody says there is no "beauty" in it: I can only suppose he saw it in the spring or summer, when Syrian views are colourless; but to me every other view I have ever seen fades in my memory when I think of the wild, stern, peculiar magnificence of that scene. The great Desert is indeed far more impressive from its apparent infinitude, and nothing, in my opinion, can come up to the strange beauty of Palmyra, standing in the midst of its many-coloured ocean: nor, perhaps, to the lovely luxuriance and wealth of Nature displayed at Broussa: the view from the Second Cataract of the Nile has something of the same character, untouched by aught that is human, while the vast extent of the scene there makes up for the variety in this:—yet here, with every trace of man, past or present, seemingly swept away, with the vaporous colouring and quivering mists rising from the hot and accursed sea, and with the great variety in its outlines of land and water, this view is beyond all others for the splendour of its savage and yet beautiful wildness. To the south, Jebel Usdoum, the Mountain of Salt, believed to be the site of Sodom, seemed closed beneath us: a compact low mountain, standing out in the water, in front of range behind range of other mountains, stretching away to the south and curving round the end of the lake: there the pale grey shore was backed by a range of low, dazzlingly white hills, shining and sparkling in the sunshine, for these are the famous salt-hills: the mountains of the east side of the sea come down to meet them in ranges of varied form, while behind all rose up the noble blue line of the mountains of Edom, among which is Petra. The whole length of the sea, from end to end, lay before us, with the Lisân, or large tongue of white land, only a few feet above the water, stretching out from the south-eastern side: Kerak, the scene of so many events in ancient and modern history, was visible on the mountain over it; while from three several fissures in the rocks, curls of vapour rose up in the still air from the hot mineral springs of Calirrhoe, and from others of which we did not know the names. Utterly barren and treeless was the whole view, save the beautiful thickets of foliage that marked 'Ain Jidi to the north, and that lay in two of the wadys opposite: but the most striking peculiarity in the view was the leaden colour of the lake itself: it seemed formed of some liquid thicker than water, with trails of scummy matter meandering over it. It was mid-day—and yet the colouring was superb: the dark hues of Jebel Usdoum and the snow-white glitter of the salt-hills contrasting with the vaporous purples and lilacs of the eastern shore; the dull yellow-white of the Lisân and of the coast beneath us was very remarkable; while all around us the rich brown rock of Sebbeh, the burnt appearance of the crags and the lumps of black stone filling up the deep rents and chasms, made an extraordinary scene, but a perfectly *dead* one: one longed for even a ruin in the distance to give some sign of man. The Arabs who accompanied us, and who had never been up there before, appeared much impressed with the grandeur of the view, but, with the instinct of nature, were still more interested in the accursed sea itself, repeating vehemently again and again, "Moieh battâl, battâl!" (good for nothing, bad water).

We retired with cautious steps down the side of the rock by which we had mounted: I cannot say it was by any means a pleasant operation: and thankfully availed ourselves of the clear, cold water bubbling from the spring at the bottom of the *neck*—for there *is* a spring, although its existence has been strongly denied; and probably an unfailing one, as we found plenty of water in December, and the goatherd said they had not as yet had any rain. The horses were sent on to descend the zig-zag we had walked up, at about a mile and a half distance, and we descended by another "serpent" to the bottom of the chasm—may my feet never pass down such another! The Bedoueens said the goats had made the path, and certainly it was only fit for them; we were heartily glad when we reached the bottom, though we had a long way to walk before we met the horses, and plenty of time to observe the stupendous cliff of Masada, much bolder and loftier and with a finer crowning crag than any other on the Dead Sea. The northern face has several caverns in it, which must have been occupied by hermits who had little temptation to "look back:" for no one would willingly retrace any of the steps that led to them.

Perhaps the shore, along which we had now to ride for a good four hours, is one of the most remarkable features of the Dead Sea; it is about a mile in width from the foot of the mountain to the water's edge, and more than double at the mouth of the Wady Seyâl, the delta of which is cut through in strangely regular terraces by the action of the winter's torrents; the ground is a chalky mud, sometimes so soft and slimy that it will not bear the weight of a foot. It is strewn with lumps of white gypsum, brown pumice, black bitumen, salt, and sulphur (but the bitumen was in pieces not quite "as large as a horse," as old Mandeville describes the lumps that "the water casteth out every day"). Nowhere was the ground level for the space of twenty yards: it was altogether a succession of fissures and mounds, intermingled with quicksands, like a field that has been long under water, and cracked in the drying of the hot sun: such, I believe, it is, for this plain is usually flooded in the spring. Down in the deepest part of the wady we found several trees: some were " sont " (mimosa) trees, with tiny leaves and long straight thorns; the others, our old friends the nebbk, here called sidr. The mimosa, called *sont* or *sunt* in Egypt, is believed to be the " shittim wood " of Scripture; it is here called " seyäl," nearly the same word as the Hebrew *esal*, mentioned in Gen. xxi. 33, 1 Sam. xxii. 6, and xxxi. 13: it is probably a tree of this kind, therefore, to which each of those passages alludes. There is a wady on the east side of the Dead Sea, called Wady-*el-Esal*, and on the west as we have seen, called *es Seyäl*: the one on the eastern side is said to be also full of these trees. When we came to the large depression on the shore called Birket-el-Khulil, we found the ground covered with a crust of salt; and the smell, for the next two hours, of sulphuretted hydrogen was very strong indeed, and immensely more nauseous than that of the springs of Tadmor: it is said to be emitted from the ground, not the water. The shore was thickly strewed with trees: bare, black skeletons, encrusted over with a mantle of salt; they are brought down by the Jordan and the winter torrents in the ravines between the mountains.

The splendour of the sunset colouring had scarcely faded when the full moon—a globe of pure fire—started up from behind the eastern mountains, and spread a broad flood of silver and gold over the sea and land: even the Bedoueens seemed subdued into silence by the superb loveliness of the scene, and left off singing, to repeat again and again, in low tones, " Quiyis, quiyis keeter!" and the sweet cool breeze tried to console us for the excessive fatigue which had now overtaken us. About seven o'clock the welcome sound of rushing waters met our ears, and we were soon struggling up the steep ascent, too steep to ride in the dark, to the " fountain of the kid," 'Ain Jidi, where our tents were pitched, just beyond the thick bosquets of deliciously shady trees that cluster round the spring. We were thankful indeed to see them, all the more when we heard that the servants had had rather a skirmish in getting there, the Rashaidya Bedoueens of the place having refused to admit the Jeh'aleen Bedoueens, as escort, into their territory; nor would they, even to the last, allow the camp to be placed very near the water. We went to bed, rejoicing in the prospect of a quiet Sunday's rest on the morrow in this beautiful spot.

Nothing could be more delicious than the climate here: although, probably, oppressively and most unhealthily hot in summer and spring, it was now quite perfect, warm, fresh, and balmy. We could gladly have stayed for many days, enjoying the superb colouring and the pleasant trees, but that no food being procurable nearer than Hebron, for either man or beast, we could have only one day to linger; and the Arabs were unwilling to grant even that much use of the spring. Soon after breakfast we heard loud and angry words: the Rashaidya Bedoueens refused to let our men take any water from their fountain, and, after some blows, out came the long knives (yataghans), and a serious storm seemed impending. They demanded the payment of tribute for entering their territory, and we did not choose to pay a single piaster beyond the sum agreed upon with the Jeh'aleen Arabs for our safe conduct throughout the journey, as we thought the quarrel might be a *ruse*, got up by the Arabs together for the extortion of money, and that our yielding would be a bad precedent for future travellers. But for peace' sake we made them a present of a kid, and took some of them as guards in a walk along the sea-shore, after which they might be supposed to deserve a baksheesh. Sheik Hamzeh and Abou Dahouk came too, and took as much care of us as if we were wax dolls, besides helping to collect plants and bitumen, &c., and teaching us with much care the Arabic names of each.

'Ain Jidi is the Hazezon-Tamar—" the pruning of the palm "—which was occupied by the Amorites, when Chedorlaomer, the King of Elam (Susiana), came up to chastise his rebellious tributaries, the Kings of Sodom and Gomorrah and Zoar, &c., and smote them. The Kenites dwelt here on whom Balaam looked as he said, " Strong is thy dwelling-place, and thou puttest thy nest in a rock." And here the Moabites and Amorites gathered together before they went up to Jerusalem, in the time of Jehoshaphat, from whence not one of them ever returned. Solomon sings of its delightful vineyards: Josephus and Pliny tell of its palm-groves and balsam. Hasselquist found vines there in the last century, and the zakkhoum still bearing its healing oil; but both vine and palm-tree have now entirely disappeared. The tangled woods round the stream are of acacia, nebbk, mimosa, jujube, tamarisk, and almond-trees; while the ground is strewed with wild mignonnette, growing plentifully among the strange fantastic grass and huge boulders that cover the little plateau. Besides these there is the henna, with its small bright green leaf (translated in the Bible as camphire, copher and cypress), to a branch of which Solomon likens his beloved among " the vineyards of En-gedi;" and large thickets of the Sodom apples*, mentioned by Josephus as " the ashes," or " remainders of divine fire reproduced in those fruits," the *Asclepias gigantea* of botanists,

* Deut. xxxii. 32.

called by the Arabs *osher*. This plant grows about twelve feet high, and has large oval leaves, growing in pairs, very thick and fleshy, of a pale bluish green : they discharge quantities of acrid milk when broken, which the Bedoueens are most careful not to touch : it has a horrid smell.   The fruit, which also hangs in pairs, is a large blue-green globe, about ten inches long : it is evidently filled with air, and very light; when torn or burst open the thin rind is seen to contain a small pod filled with seeds, imbedded in delicate white silky threads, which the Arabs use as matches for their guns.   Perhaps the fruit looks more tempting in the spring, but in the autumn the plant is as ugly and poisonous-looking as one can imagine.   The small plant (*Solanum Melongena*), which is also called Sodom apple, grows plentifully here.   It is remarkably pretty, the large, rough, hairy leaves and the thorny stem bearing both the purple flower and the golden fruit at the same time : the fruit, which is like a very small lemon, contains only brown gum and a few seeds.   The water of the fountain is of 81° Fahr. temperature, but when cool it is excellent drinking.   The source is five hundred feet above the lake.

'Ain Jidi is exactly opposite the ravine of Wady Mojib, on the eastern coast, the River Arnon of Scripture.   The view from the fountain is beautiful, but by no means so fine as that from Sebbeh : Jebel Usdoum stands out well, but from hence it hides the salt hills at the southern end of the sea : the three promontories we had rounded between Sebbeh and 'Ain Jidi rose grandly, one behind another, with the ruined fortress crowning the last and loftiest. This was the view, with the still, sullen-looking lake below, which met the eyes of the Essenes, those earnest strivers after purity and holiness, who inhabited these caves in the time of our Lord.   Here, too, long after, came many a Christian hermit to spend the evening of his days, in silent communion with his God, apart from the noisy world : and in the short, sweet twilight I almost fancied I heard them—the

> " anchorites beneath En-gedi's palms
>   Pacing the Dead Sea beach,
> And singing slow their old Armenian psalms,
>   In half-articulate speech ; "

but, alas ! no sound of Christian prayer or praise rises now from the shores of that beautiful but desolate lake.

All sorts of stories have been related of the horrible aspect of the accursed Sea, of the lurid glare that illuminated its banks with supernatural light, of the strange sounds and terrible forms that were seen around its shores ; and until lately it was really believed that no bird could fly over its waters, and that every creature, man or beast, that inhaled its malaria either perished or went raving mad, as if its very atmosphere was impregnated with the visible wrath of God. The story of the malaria ought to have been proved false by the remembrance of how many hermits and recluses lived beside its waters, especially congregating at the very spot where the odours are stronger than at any other: many of them may, indeed, have been mad, but not from the effects of the climate, although doubtless it is one of the very hottest and most oppressive to be found in the world throughout the summer. The smell of the bitumen and sulphur, the slimy ground, the sparkling salt hills, and, more especially, the singular thick, viscous appearance on the surface of the water, are all extraordinary and strange enough; but there is nothing, really nothing, about the lake, as we saw it, bearing evidence of the miraculous vengeance of an angry Deity, however frightful and awful an appearance it may occasionally wear when the hot mists and vapours are lifted from the surface of the water, in the middle of summer, by the sirocco of the Desert, and hang in dense rolling masses over the lake alone. Such was the description given to us by the Bedoucens; but this is not of very frequent occurrence, and is confined to the hottest part of the season only.

This lake has had a great many names; in the first books of the Bible it is usually called "the salt sea," and "the sea of the plain," while Joel, Zechariah, and Ezekiel call it "the eastern sea:" the Greeks and Romans spoke of it as the "Lake Asphaltitis:" Eusebius and Saint Jerome write of it by its common modern name of the "Dead Sea," applied because its waters hold no living thing within them. The Arabs have but one name for it—Bah'r Lout— or the Sea of Lot; and for the asphalt or bitumen cast up upon the shores they have retained the old Hebrew name of *humor* in their word *hamr.* After the earthquake of 1837 such an enormous lump of bitumen was detached from the bottom of the lake, and floated on to the shore, that the Jeh'aleen and Ta'amreh Arabs sold 18,750 lbs. weight of it in Bethlehem and Jerusalem, where it was carved into plates, vases, &c. &c. Deeply interesting are the scientific speculations as to the formation of the lake, sunk as it is at 1371 feet below the level of the Mediterranean; and many savants find it difficult to conceive that even the rapid evaporation, caused by the extreme heat of the depressed valley, can be sufficient to carry off the immense bulk of water poured into its bosom by the Jordan.* It has even been imagined that some subterranean communication or

* Six millions of tuns per diem, it is said.

channel empties it into the Red Sea; *I* have, however, no business to meddle with these difficult questions. It was enough for us to think back upon the affluent fountains of the river we had seen pouring out from springs shaded over by luxuriant trees and flowers: to remember the green meadows through which it wound its way into the silvery Lake of Tiberias, teeming with countless multitudes of fish, and the pleasant cane-brakes at the southern end of the lake, whence it flowed, as from its cradle, between lands of richest verdure and wealth of wood; while now the *riante* brightness of the sacred stream was suddenly quenched as it laid itself down in the deep silence and stern solemnity of its tomb in the Dead Sea:

> " Besando su sepultura,
> El Jordán viene á morir."

Beyond this tomb there is yet one more thought on which to meditate in reverential silence: the mysterious prophecies of Ezekiel and Zechariah, of the "living waters" that shall one day "go out from Jerusalem, half of them toward the eastern sea," down through the "desert" plain and "into the sea, and the waters shall be healed; the fishers shall stand at En-gedi, and shall spread forth their nets, and the fish shall be according to their kinds as the fish of the great sea, exceeding many."[*]

We left 'Ain Jidi, very regretfully, early in the morning, and turned many a loving glance at her fresh bright trees as we toiled up the wady behind the spring: such an ascent as it was! worse than that of Wady-en-Nemriyeh, without the wild grand beauty which there compensated for its difficulty. Within a few hundred yards of 'Ain Jidi, the mules had to be unloaded, and all the heavy part of the luggage carried up on the backs of the staggering muleteers, whose strength seemed to us marvellous, in men who never taste meat; the Bedoueens are wonderfully firm of foot, and surprisingly active and agile, but they have not this kind of strength in their muscles, and do not carry burdens as this class of men do. We were just one hour mounting the zig-zag ascent, and when we reached the top we found the Sheikh and the muleteers dancing about in the liveliest manner, congratulating each other upon having surmounted these difficulties without accident. We had then a monotonous ride of six hours among the utterly barren rounded peaks of the wilderness: they can be compared to nothing as well as the waves of the sea in a violent storm suddenly turned to stone; not a weed is to be seen, nor any change of colour save bands of

---

[*] Zech. xiv. 8; Ezek. xlvii. 8, 10.

white rock cropping out in ribbons along the mountain sides, and here and there a few black stones. We followed a N.W. course all day, and at five P.M. came to a miserable village, called Beni-naim, at so short a distance from Hebron that probably no travellers had ever encamped there before; so the people tormented us so much with their pertinacious curiosity; they informed us that this was the burying-place of Lot, and they showed us his gigantic tomb, into which, however, we were of course not admitted. An hour and a half's ride through narrow wadys, green with prickly oak and thorns, brought us to Hebron in the morning.

While the tents were being pitched we yielded to Sheikh Hamzeh's earnest entreaties to take coffee at his house, and alighted there: he soon brought in his three wives and a pretty sister to make many salaams and "mar'habas," and then showed us his beautiful boys with much pride. The children at Hebron are very remarkable for their beauty, superior even to those of Bethlehem; and, like them, they are dressed very gaily and handsomely. The Sheikh gave us excellent coffee and sugar-plums; and then dinner was brought in on a metal tray and placed before us with plenty of hot bread: the first dish, called *mafrukka*, i.e., half-baked bread shredded into hot butter, with abundance of sugar, was excellent; then came poached eggs swimming in oil, and cakes of quince jelly: the tray was passed out, when we had done, to the servants, and then to the Bedoueens. We gave dinner to the Sheikh and Abou Dahouk in the evening, seated on the ground by our tent: they had behaved so well and been so untiringly attentive to us that we were anxious to testify our satisfaction in a pleasanter and more uncommon way than only the inevitable baksheesh. They were very much pleased at our invitation, and conducted themselves with the utmost good breeding and grave politeness, only showing a little puzzlement as to how to carry the spoons to their mouths, and at the unaccustomed heat of the soup, as they never take any hot liquid or food except coffee, which they sip: we had Mooslim-killed meat on purpose for them: but they took more kindly to the mishmish and rice: the rest of the escort were feasted on a sheep, at the same time, in the cooking-tent. We parted with many "katter hērraks" (thank you), and Abou Dahouk expressed his firm resolution that soon, very soon, he would go to England: he would begin at once to wear grand clothes and to speak English: he seemed to think that putting on a Frank dress would make the speaking English much more easy. We were much amused to hear, six months after, from some gentlemen who went down to Sebbeh, that the Arabs of his tribe, the Jeh'aleen, were singing a long song, describing in flowery language the two

"*Sitteh Ingleezeeyeh*" who had sojourned among them (the poet did not record at what period of the world's history); princesses they must have been, for they had given food and drink and a feast to the poor Jeh'aleen, and refreshed them with coffee: not common coffee only—but actually coffee *with sugar!*

Hebron stands 3000 feet above the sea, and after the delightful climate of the Dead Sea we were so dreadfully cold, that we were very glad to leave it, and to bend our steps along the Jerusalem road, trodden probably by the feet of nearly every person we read of in Scripture from the days of Abraham to the Christian era. In half an hour we had reached the noble oak (*Quercus pseudo-coccifera*), which the Hebron people believe to be the tree under which Abraham received the angels: it is a very fine lofty and beautiful tree, one of the finest trees in Syria: the trunk is 23 feet in girth; but it is needless to remark that it is not of such great antiquity, being yet in the prime of its life; nor, as this is the prickly oak (the *sindian* or *ballut* of the Arabs), could it be the terebinth (*butm* in Arabic) under which Abraham pitched his tent. The branches were full of fruit: they bend down more weepingly than those of the smaller and younger trees of the species; it is beautifully placed among the vineyards of the rich valley of Eshcol.

About half an hour further we turned off the road to visit some ruins that are said to be those of the singularly beautiful basilica built by command of Constantine "over the terebinth of Abraham," in order to put an end to its worship by the common people and to destroy the idolatrous altars set up around it. The remains consist of the three lowest courses of two sides of a building 290 feet long; many of the stones are more than 16 feet long by 4 feet wide, and by their size and workmanship appeared to us to be of a higher antiquity than the time of Constantine; near the top of the hill there are several ruins and some broken columns which seemed more like work of that age. Here we had an extensive though not pretty view, catching sight of the Mediterranean and the Dead Sea, on either hand, at the same moment. All the hills along the road have once been terraced and planted, and then the country may have been pretty: now the hill-sides have returned into almost their natural condition, and are varied only with a scanty sprinkling of prickly oak, arbutus, and juniper, with here and there the winter-crimsoned leaves of the *butm* or terebinth; and despite the verdant nooks where the plough is occasionally used, the whole road seemed very bare, bleak and dreary. It became still barer and still drearier as we neared Bethlehem, a handsomely built white town lifted up on the very end and ridge of a rocky spur, which runs out into the valley due east; there are gardens round Bethlehem and the glorious olive-groves of Beit Jala are not far off, but the whole scene is one of intensely dreary, rocky barrenness. And yet, so much is everything in Judæa changed, that Bethlehem was formerly distinguished by the name of " Ephratah "—fruitful; doubtless every hill was once clothed with forest and every valley full of foliage or smiling fields; indeed, there are some living even now who have heard their fathers tell of the fine trees that shaded the road the whole way from Bethlehem to Hebron, where now nothing better than a shrub appears; and one chief source of labour among the fellaheen is digging up the huge roots of the trees from the old broken terraces and ledges of the rocky hills to sell for fuel in Jerusalem: we were told that almost all of these roots were of oak.

Bethlehem * is one of the brightest villages in Palestine: it is in truth a town of considerable extent, of substantially and smoothly built stone houses; and the people, who are all Christians, are a race apart, marrying chiefly among themselves, and taking much pride in their origin; they are the descendants of the Crusaders and the beautiful women of Bethlehem, *then* degraded and despised, but now proud and haughty. They are excessively quarrelsome and unruly, but also very industrious, and a handsome, bold-looking, blue-eyed people: the children especially are, many of them, remarkable for their beauty, which is set off by the scarlet or crimson mash'lahs they all wear, neat and clean of their kind. The women wear a quantity of silver ornaments, and headdresses, shaped like bonnets, of silver coins sewed on, overlapping each other: their dress is invariably a thick gown of dark blue woollen drugget, striped with crimson, and a coarse white linen veil, with coloured fringe, drawn over the head, but not covering the face.

The church at Bethlehem is said to be one of the oldest in the world, and there is no reason to doubt the assertion: much is believed to remain of that erected by the Empress Helena, though much was added by the Crusaders; it is a large building, consisting of a nave with four aisles, separated by rows of columns, monoliths of red limestone, veined with white and polished: the Corinthian capitals, which are peculiar and handsome, appearing quite poor through their veil of whitewash; the columns have been painted over with figures of saints, and the upper part of the walls and the roof were once covered with a fine mosaic of high antiquity,

* Beit-lahm, as it is called in Arabic, means the " house of flesh." Bethlehem, in Hebrew, means the " house of bread."

of which but a very little yet remains.* The Greeks occupy the centre chapel in the choir, adorned with quantities of gilding and a very rich screen; the Armenians are on the south side, and the Latins have a large chapel to themselves at a few yards' distance, dedicated to St. Catherine. From the Armenian Chapel, a small semi-circular staircase descends to a pair of fine silver doors, which open into the Grotto—an irregular, oblong cave, with a recess not three feet high, scooped out at one end, where sixteen silver lamps are always burning over the inscription on the ground, in silver letters, " *Hic de Virgine Mariâ Jesus Christus natus est:*" over the recess is an altar used in turn by the three communions. Upwards of forty lamps of gold and silver hang from the roof of the cave; they are always lighted, and are all gifts from the pious of other lands, mostly from France and Russia; a marble trough in one corner represents the Manger, and pictures are placed above the altars; the cave is lined with marble, so that, if it is the real place, little of Nature remains visible in it.

We passed through the Latin Church to descend into the grottos still lower down, dedicated to martyrs and saints, and to the tomb containing the so-called bones of the Innocents: then came the cave where there is every reason to believe St. Jerome spent great part of his life, and where he wrote most of his books; it is now neatly whitewashed and lined with a stone vaulting, which robs it of all reality; indeed, the sacred sights enclosed in the church at Bethlehem pleased me as little as those at Nazareth, and I was most glad to leave them and to sit outside our tents among the fig-gardens, listening to the shepherd boys, leading home their sheep and goats, and singing as they went. It was so dreadfully cold, that we were glad to close in the tent at night with a good charcoal fire.

We sent our dragoman into Jerusalem, early the next morning, to engage a Bedoueen guard for our journey to Jericho, and we pursued our way for three hours, over very ugly, bare, and barren hills, towards Mar Saba: we looked down upon two camps of the Ta'amreh Arabs in wadys below us, but they did not molest or notice us: and once we had a lovely glimpse of the Dead Sea. Then we descended suddenly upon the Convent of St. Saba, perched on a lofty cliff, running out between two deep wadys, one of which is the Kedron: two high towers first meet the eye, but on approaching nearer, one is bewildered with the pile of massive walls, domes, battlements, staircases, and five splendid buttresses supporting the

---

* The fragments still on the wall have been admirably reproduced in a 4to. volume, "Sur les Eglises de la Terre Sainte, par le Comte Melchior de Vogüé. Paris, 1860."

building on the edge of the precipice from the giddy depths below; a small garden of orange and pomegranate trees is enclosed within the walls, and the monks were busy at sunset in feeding flocks of little black and yellow birds, which were twittering about the place. They keep a vigilant watch from the towers, and no Bedoueen is ever knowingly admitted within the walls on any pretence: but they have more than once succeeded in robbing the convent. The original cave was selected by the holy Saba in A.D. 483, and his sanctity and wisdom drew several thousand disciples round him there: he was not often allowed to rest in solitude or retirement, being frequently compelled to take an active part in the troubled scenes of the Holy City, and having been made Archimandrite of the anchorites in Palestine, he went even to Constantinople to implore justice and favour from Justinian for them and for the clergy of Syria. The Emperor came out to meet him, prostrated himself at the feet of the holy man, and granted all his petitions. Many men of note have since that time lived within these walls, and the library is said to contain MSS. of great value. The monks observe a very severe rule, but they are hospitable and kind; willing to admit guests of their own sex, or to do any service in their power for those to whom their rule does not permit entrance.* We only needed water, but they sent us hot bread and some wine, and they are willing to supply any travellers encamped outside with food if they desire it.

On the following day we found a good, but often very steep road, leading over wearisome, sand-strewn, desert hills; the alternations of ground seldom extending more than two or three hundred yards each, were more tiresome, undulating as regularly as the waves of the sea. The whole range of mountains in this "wilderness of Judæa" has been aptly described as a multitude of gigantic limekilns, yellow and white towards the south, about 'Ain Jidi, red and pink towards the north; the variety of colour alone saved them from being painfully monotonous. Soon after leaving Mar Saba we had a sudden glimpse of Jerusalem, between two steep and lofty cliffs: the view was striking, the city standing so completely alone and lifted up on her own mountain, like a queen, but so *triste* and desolate, in strange harmony with the utter barrenness around, that it seemed, as Chateaubriand well expresses it, "the City of Desolation, in a desolate solitude." Dr.

---

* A vulgar trick was lately played upon the monks by some travelling lady. who entered the monastery in men's clothes, concealing her hands in her pockets while going over the whole building; but whilst taking coffee her sex was discovered, and she was immediately expelled by the justly offended monks.

Barclay supposes somewhere near this to have been the spot where
" Abraham lifted up his eyes, and saw the place afar off " (Gen.
xxii. 4), and that thence he went up the valley of the Kedron to the
foot of Moriah : from this place Mount Moriah, and that only, can
be seen ; and the valley is strewn at the bottom with large building
stones of high antiquity, called by the Arabs " Khirbet Ibrahim :"
it does not seem the road he would have taken from Beersheba, but
the idea is worth considering.

Somewhat further on we came to the tomb of Sa'a-ed-deen, the
herdsman of Moses ; and soon after to the Tomb of Moses himself,
according to the Mooslims ; a large pile of building, but partly
ruined ; it is visited every year by thousands of Mooslim pilgrims.
From near this tomb a splendid view of the valley of the Jordan,
the plain of Jericho, the Dead Sea, and the Moab mountains, opens
suddenly before one : very rich and lovely was the bright green of
the plain, from the thick groves of nebbk, which is at this season in
very full leaf, and the ribbon of foliage on the banks of the Jordan
winding down the centre of the valley. We descended upon the
plain by a good path, and were more than an hour on the sand
before we reached the trees, among which our tents were pitched,
beside the fountain healed by Elisha, now called 'Ain-es-Sultan : it
is a lovely spot : the clear, pure, warm stream of this source, and of
another a little further on, called 'Ain Douk,* gushing out over the
plain, carry delicious verdure wherever their waters pass. The
nebbk† here forms lofty trees, the lower growth tangling into
perfectly impenetrable thickets, for the slender and somewhat
pendent branches are thickly set with long, sharp thorns : in
spring, when the leaves have fallen, the tree looks like a heap of
thorns thrown together for burning ; now they were charming, the
gay little rosy yellow fruit hanging among the small leaves, which
are shaped like hawthorn-leaves, and of a very bright green. Then
there was plenty of agnuscastus, still in flower, and quantities of
the smaller " Sodom," or " mad-apple," as the Bedoueens call it,

* The "fountain of watching," or, "of the watch tower." The ruins of a
castle are still to be seen on the rock above the spring : this was the castle
to which Ptolemy, the Governor of the district, invited his father-in-law,
Simon Maccabæus, and had him assassinated during the feast ; and when John
Hyrcanus besieged it to avenge the murder of his father, Ptolemy brought
John's widowed mother and brothers on to the battlements, and scourged them
cruelly whenever he made an assault : the dreadful sight compelled John to
withdraw his troops, although urged by his mother to persevere ; Ptolemy
managed to escape, but not before he had had the heroic woman and her sons
put to death. (Josephus, W. I. ii. 3.)

† Called, by the Arabs of this neighbourhood, the dôm : its botanical name
is, I believe, *Rhamnus nabeca.*

with its purple flowers and golden fruit, tempting enough almost to provoke to taste: they declare that if the goats browse on it, they go mad for five days. The sun left us under the shadow of the Quarantania mountain only too soon, but for an hour or more after we were in shade, the mountain-tops and lake and the bright trees on the plain were all lit up in glorious colours, and made an enchanting scene. How fortunate are those who come to Jericho in December! Instead of the "suffocating air, like the blast of a furnace," such as most travellers experience there, we revelled in the moderate warmth and the refreshing shade of the thick foliage, we enjoyed the gentle bubbling of the fountain and the sweet singing of the birds, and even tried to forgive the abominable jackals who howled all night most cruelly, for the caves in the mountain of Quarantania are favourite abodes of these beasts.

There is no plain more often mentioned in Scripture than this one of Jericho, yet upon none have the historic evidences been more completely swept away: it is so well watered by the streams of the Wadys-el-Kelt and Es Sidr, and those of the fountains of Es Sultan, Douk, and some others, that there is no lack of verdure; but such is the neglect and utter waste both of land and water, that scarcely a tenth part of the plain is cultivated: the climate is quite tropical, and the soil is so rich that a very short time, two or three years of care, would restore the whole valley to the "divine region" it once was. It is now overrun by very unruly Bedoueens. On the western side the fine mountain of Quarantania rises abruptly from the plain, marked with the openings of scores of caves and grottoes once inhabited by hermits. Between the foot of the mountain and 'Ain-es-Sultan, are many ruins and some large mounds: this is all that remains of what is believed to have been the ancient City of Jericho taken by Joshua, the fortifications of which he forbade the Israelites to raise again: the city, however, was either not wholly destroyed or else soon rebuilt, for it is mentioned by its name of the " city of palm-trees " in Judges i. 16—afterwards as having been taken by the Moabites (iii. 13)—and as the place where the messengers of David tarried till their shaven beards had grown again. Hiel of Bethel did, in the time of Ahab, rebuild the fortifications, and the curse pronounced by Joshua was fulfilled in the fact of his losing one son at the commencement, and the other on the completion of the walls. A school of prophets settled here, and much of the history of Elijah and Elisha took place at and near the city. By a pass between Quarantania and Wady Kelt a path leads in six hours to Beitîn, the ancient Bethel; it was by this road that the Israelites

" went up to Ai," and " made it a heap for ever, even a desolation unto this day."   Little more is known of ancient Jericho, but one would like to excavate these large mounds and seek for further remains.

Right across the centre of the plain runs a stream called the Kelt : upon the banks of this, a mile and a half east of 'Ain-es-Sultan, stood the fine city of Jericho, built by Herod ; it was adorned with a splendid palace, an amphitheatre, and a hippodrome : to this *new* Jericho our Lord came when He visited Zaccheus the publican ; here he healed the blind man, and told the multitudes that followed him that the Son of man was come to seek and to save them that were lost ; here, too, John the Baptist preached to them repentance and good works, baptizing them in the Jordan, as the type of the new birth and purification of the heart : his own coarser food and coarser garments contrasting with the voluptuous luxury, delicate living, and " soft raiment" of the " king's houses " and the palace of the infamous Herod—great only in wickedness.   Herod, indeed, was, among the " generation of vipers" against whom St. John warned them, and before whom he " spoke the truth, boldly rebuking vice ;" near this, too, on one of those mountains on the east side of Jordan, was the fortress of Macherus, where this bold and mighty man was put in prison, and where he " patiently suffered for the truth's sake."   In this City of Jericho, Herod had his brother-in-law Aristobulus " playfully drowned" in bathing* ; and here he himself died in great torments a few years after.   Vespasian destroyed the city and Adrian rebuilt it ; the Crusaders burned it to the ground.   Now the most miserable of all wretched villages stands upon the site, bearing the name of Er Riha, a word that means *smell* ; the squalid hovels of the filthy, savage-looking people are hedged round with the dry branches of the nebbk, forming a most impenetrable barrier ; once it was surrounded by a forest of lofty palm-trees, and by large gardens of the balsam, which was so precious that a handful of its gum was a present fit for a crowned head.   Judæa derived great part of her revenues from the balsam grown in the gardens of Jericho and 'Ain Jidi, and Pompey carried a tree of it to Rome as a trophy for his triumph.   Not a palm-tree remains in the land, and the only apology for the balsam is the zakkhoum, which grows abundantly ; it is a thorny tree or shrub, with tiny leaves growing on very thick twigs : the oil pressed from its fruit, which resembles an olive, is much sought after by the Arabs for healing wounds, even though this tree is said by the Koran to grow in hell, and its fruit to form the food and drink of the damned.

Somewhere rather nearer to the Jordan must have been the City

* Josephus, 'Antiq.' xv. iii. 3.

of Gilgal, the first encampment of the Israelites in the Land of
Promise, where the Tabernacle remained till it was placed at Shiloh:
here Saul was made king over Israel, and here also he learned that
the kingdom would be taken away from him because he had not
believed that God desired obedience more than sacrifice from his
people. It was strange they should bring the unholy spoil of the
Amalekites to the very neighbourhood where Israel had received so
great a lesson on the sin of covetousness*, and had been so signally
taught that their conquest of the heathen nations who had inhabited the land of Canaan was to be a religious enterprise, done
only in purity of heart, not for self-aggrandisement, but for the
glory of God alone.

We rode early the next morning to the village of Er Riha. Our
Bedoueen escort were soon stopped to pay the tribute due to the
Arabs of the village for conducting strangers through their territory: twenty piasters for each of us, and a sheep added to the
bargain. We were glad to leave the noisy crew, and ride on along
the bank of the Kelt, which some have supposed to be the "brook
Cherith," where Elijah was commanded to go, although the Bible
distinctly says, "which is before Jordan," and " before" means to
the east of Jordan.† One would rather look for Cherith among
the little known valleys, which we see with longing eyes on the
opposite side of the Jordan, among the barren mountains of Moab:
now inhabited by such wild Bedoueens that their exploration is
nearly impossible. It is interesting to remember, in thinking of
them, that the word translated as "ravens" in our Bible, who
brought food to Elijah, also means Arabs.

Deceived by the clearness of the atmosphere and the level plain,
the Dead Sea appeared so near to us that we expected to reach it
in half an hour: it was, however, a ride of two hours and a half,
before we had arrived at the shore, passing over low undulations,
covered with sharp cones, little queerly-shaped peaks, and much
sandy mud. The shadeless plain was very hot under the mid-day
sun, and the horses occasionally sank so deep in the mud that our
progress was slow; but the view was interesting: we soon recog-

* The Valley of Achor is believed to be the same as the Wady Kelt.

† Of the three words used in Hebrew to denote the East, one means literally
the *sun-rising*, while the two others signify *in front*, or *in face of*, and some
difficulties have arisen from the translation of the latter in our Bible, as in
Num. xxi. 11; but it is easy to remember that the spectator is always supposed to face the sun rising, and therefore the "right hand" denotes the
South—the "left hand" the North—while " behind " is the West. The word
Saracen, signifying " men of the East," was derived from the Arabic *Sharak*,
corresponding to the root of the first of these three words, *sarak*, the sun-rising.

nised the headland of 'Ain Jidi, and the well-known cliff of Sebbeh, with Jebel Usdoum behind it, apparently forming the end of the sea; on the left the wreath of warm vapour showed the ravine of Callirrhoe; and one point of the mountain range, which appeared to be higher than the rest, we chose to fancy must be Pisgah. While we looked at the view our dragoman built us a grand little tent with driftwood and shawls, under which we spread our carpet, and made our preparations for bathing in the lake: the water was as cool and refreshing as its clearness had looked inviting, and very pleasant it was to float upon the strangely buoyant water. The taste is quite indescribable: the first sensation is of the saltness of brine, very naturally, for, whereas there is four per cent. of salt in the ocean, there is twenty-six per cent. in the water of the Dead Sea; the next is of a sickening, greasy, bitter flavour which is most disgusting: of the many descriptions of it, M. de Saulcy's is much the best—"a mixture of salt, colocynth, and oil." The strangest part is the sensation on the skin afterwards: without any touch of a towel one was instantly dry all over—literally "dry as a bone"—drier than anything one could think of, and yet greasy withal: not exactly sticky, but oily: the most disagreeable feeling inside one's clothes and gloves. The salt dried on one's hair and clothes visibly, just as it lies on all the driftwood on the shore, but a touch brushed it away. We picked up a small fish quite dead, and a number of very tiny black shells, similar to some we had found in the Lake of Galilee, with indubitably *living* fish in them; I have it noted in my journal that they were still alive thirty hours after: but the Bedoueens said these had been only lately washed in from the Jordan, and that they could not live long in the Dead Sea water. Chateaubriand relates that he heard a murmur in the water, which his guides told him arose from millions of little fish rushing into the lake: I conclude he means that they were singing their little death songs. Certainly all the shells that we picked up on the shore at 'Ain Jidi contained only dead fish: but probably some current washing round from the mouth of the Jordan along the curves of the northern end, enables the fish to live in that particular spot; those we picked up were stationary, adhering to the stones. About twenty feet from the shore there is an islet of mud, which is said to be covered with ruins of great antiquity, but we saw none from where we stood. We gathered great bunches of tiny pink flowers, something like heath, very dry and very pretty; they made the shore quite gay, and we put bowers of them on our horses' heads in the hot ride of two hours more to the bank of the Jordan, where we were glad to undress again, under the shade of a friendly tree, and wash off the uncomfortable feeling of the " bad water;" the Jordan did not look as inviting as the Dead Sea. It is muddy and of a dark leaden colour, and we found the water very cold, but it was refreshing and pleasant.

We had skirted the band of foliage from the shore of the lake delighting in the varied tints of orange, red, and greens of every hue, against the background of dark blue mountains behind it: now, descending into the depth of the *ghór*, or deep valley which the rushing Jordan has worn for itself, we entered into the charming shade of the tall fine trees—poplars, willows, tamarisks, planes, terebinths—and a thick jungle of agnuscastus and everlastings, both in blossom, the fine tall canes waving their beautiful flowery heads and flaunting leaves in the breeze, "the reeds shaken by the wind."* The river turns in a sudden bend at this spot, the bathing place of the Greeks, and the eddy is strong and dangerous; but, a few yards further on, the path between the trees on the opposite side shows that it is one of the fords of the Jordan. Perhaps no one at home can quite enter into the feeling with which one bathes in the sacred Jordan: when one has "come up to Jerusalem" all through the Holy Land, following each hallowed footstep, and remembering each sacred story, noting sadly the ruin and desolation that are spread over every historic site—apt illustrations of how the Light has shined and yet the people still sit in darkness—and then one comes here where the river has been passing on with the same steady, ceaseless rush, ever renewing the same lovely thickets, since the day when the Ark of God passed over, and since the Son of God fulfilled all righteousness. One can hardly help fancying oneself no longer only a silent spectator of the distant scene, as, plunging into the river one seems to enter into the past, and to be united something more than spiritually, to the sacred histories of the stream: truly we have each our "Abana and Pharpar" at home in which we may indeed wash and be clean, without or within; but a new feeling rises in the heart, and a new prayer murmurs on the lips, as we feel the water of that hallowed river pass over us. "Among all the travellers who visit the Jordan, is there one, however far removed from superstition, who is willing to turn away without having bowed his head in these sacred waters?" †

The plain of the Jordan, now called El Ghôr, would appear to

---

* These reeds are the *Arundo donax*, the "pride of Jordan," in which the young lions lay when they mourned—because the floods came and hid the reeds, and they were chased away. (Zech. xi. 3.)

† Miss Martineau's ' Eastern Life, Present and Past.'

have been always the most important plain in Israel, as its name in Scripture is *Ha-arabah**, *the* plain par excellence: and the river is the only really large one in the land of Canaan. Its three sources we had seen already, at Hasbeiya, at Tell-el-Khady, and at Banias; but the ancient inhabitants reckoned only the last as its veritable source; the Hebrew name is Yarden, the descender, and the old Arabic writers preserved this in the word 'Ordoun for the upper part of the stream: below the Lake of Galilee it is called Sheriat-el-Kebeer, the great watering-place. The valley is enclosed between ridges, rising with steep precipitous sides, between 1000 and 2000 feet (the eastern side is the loftiest), the breadth of the valley here is about nine or ten miles; but it becomes very much narrower farther north. The river is itself sunk below the level of the valley between *two* sets of banks; those confining the water are low, the upper ones are much higher, and at a considerable distance from the stream: the continuous rush of its volume of water has worn this track for itself; lower down, all along the Jericho plain, there are *three* sets of terrace banks; the middle one is covered with shrubs, canes, and low herbs. The average breadth of the river is about 150 feet. The one remarkable characteristic of the Jordan is its being tortuous beyond all other rivers in the world, I believe, so that in its 60 miles' course (as the crow flies) between the two lakes, it winds to the length of 200 miles; it is still stranger that its fall is 660 feet, without a single descent of any very sudden depth, but all one continued downward slope; it is probably from this peculiarity that it bore the name of "the descender." Its valley, from being so much depressed below the level of the Mediterranean, is of an intensely hot climate: "a gigantic furnace," as poor Van de Welde calls it, in the vivid account he gives of his own sufferings there: he was in the Ghôr in the month of May, when, of course, the inevitable sirocco was constantly upon them, and he says that the heat was considerably worse to bear than anything he had ever felt even in South Africa.

We turned regretfully away from the "sweet and sacred river," at about an hour before sunset, and adapted our speed to the short time we had in which to find our way to the tents before dark: it was a lovely evening, and even our dragoman forgot his usual fears "*de se casser le cou*," and galloped on merrily. We put up a hare and a gazelle and plenty of *khuttar*—the sand-grouse—some of which were shot; and then the two Bedoueen Sheikhs went off, darting about, pursuing each other with war-cries, making their long spears quiver in the hand from end to

* Joshua xviii. 18; Josephus, 'Wars,' iv. vii. 2.

end, and turning them cleverly over their heads as they wheeled smartly round, each by turns pursuing and pursued. The next evening, for we spent a quiet Sunday beside the fountain, they offered to exhibit one of their dances, and we were summoned to sit at the tent door as soon as it was quite dark. Here we found a wild-looking group ready for us, standing by the light of a huge fire of dry nebbk branches piled up high, the sparks of which went flying about, lighting up the pretty trees above us, and illuminating the eager faces of the swarthy Bedoueens who stood in a row before us, with the muleteers and our servants squatting on the ground in a ring around them. One of the Bedoueens stood opposite the others, and whichever way he swung his body or threw himself, they did the same, while he improvised a long song, with a verse for each of us, bringing in our names as the Sitteh, Habeeb, Suleimân, Nakhleh, Marshet, and so forth, the others repeating the final words of each line, or answering by a rhyme: the verses were about our journey and their good wishes for us, &c. All through they beat time loudly, throwing one fist into the palm of the other hand, bringing out between each verse a strange hoarse sound, like a camel's grunt, " Adjjä, Adjjä," to each beat, and swinging or rocking the body vigorously from side to side : sometimes they suddenly dropped on one knee, and seemed to feign to strike the one opposite, but they never touched each other.

We left 'Ain-es-Sultan early the next morning, and turned westward up the pass of the Wady-el-Kelt, the " going up of Adummin," that is, " the red pass," which was on the western border of Judah ; the word is the plural of the same Hebrew root as Adam, Edom, &c., all meaning *red*. St. Jerome says that the name refers to the blood so often shed by robbers on this road ; but in the Septuagint it is given as the " pass of the red ones." It is a steep and rugged ascent, with sharp angles turning on the edge of the cliff, with the 400 or 500 feet of chasm below : but the road is everywhere protected by rough walls : it bears traces of the old Roman work at intervals all the way to Jerusalem. From the summit we looked back once more over the plain, now beautiful in the morning light: the orange and green foliage by the winding river, like a green serpent on the sand; the blue sea and the stern and lofty cliffs, with the cleft of Wady Hesban, through which, probably, the Israelites arrived at the Promised Land; the eastern and western mountains gradually closing in at the far north, with the castle, Kulah-er-Rùbud, standing up prominently on one of the cliffs farthest north; the castles of Jericho and El Hajla on the plain, and the ruined arches, aqueducts, and nameless buildings at the foot of Quarantania, with all the delicious spread of verdure far away across the plain; make a fine and striking picture.

Everybody knows how gloomy and wild is the road from Jericho to Jerusalem: chasms and ravines succeeding one another with dreary monotony, now bordering the road with precipices, now sunk between walls of naked rock that, collecting the sun's rays and seeming to exclude the air, produce an atmosphere of scorching, suffocating heat, and a dazzling glare that makes this day's ride one of the most trying in Syria: even at this season we found it, to a certain degree, distressing. It retains as ever its bad name, and no part of it can be traversed in safety without a Bedoueen escort; the ruins of two large khans are on the roadside, and probably one of them marks the site of "the inn" alluded to in the beautiful parable of the Good Samaritan. An ancient fountain further on, usually called "the fountain of the Twelve Apostles," is believed to be the En-shemesh of Joshua xv. 7. One can well fancy the weary followers of our blessed Lord, and He Himself, resting at the end of the day beside this fountain, in the shade of the rocky height behind it; and then, because "The Son of man had not where to lay his head," lying down beside the trickling water, and sleeping by the roadside as one sees people doing twenty times a day in Syria. Surmounting the steep path above this spring, Bethany and Abou Dis, supposed by some to be the "village over against Bethany," come in sight at once, and formed a sad, but pretty picture in the evening light. Very mournful are the bare heights about here, but fig-gardens and fruit-orchards are now beginning to fill up the valleys; and the bottom of the curving slope, on which Bethany nestles with a look of meek, quiet confidence, is filled with luxuriant plantations.

There are few places which hold such a tender, homelike association with the life of our Lord as this little village, where, as in His "own city," among the poor fishermen on the banks of the Lake of Galilee, He had a resting-place with Lazarus and the loving Mary, who, here, in the house of one Simon, anointed His sacred feet with precious ointment. Bethany and Bethphage are reasonably supposed to have been different parts of the same village, or rather that Bethany was the name not only of a village, but of a district: Beth-hina, in Hebrew, meant the "house of date-palm:" a species of palm, mentioned in the Talmud, as having a remarkably hard wood, "hard as iron." Beth-phage means "house of figs," and is spoken of three times in the Talmud as close to Bethany: that they were close together, we learn from Mark xi. 1, and that palm-trees grew there and on the Mount of Olives we know from

John xii. 13, and Nehem. viii. 15, as Bethany stands on the north-eastern slope or end of the Mount of Olives: not a palm remains in existence now, but the figs grow luxuriantly. The houses are rudely built, chiefly of old materials, sometimes with the ancient Jewish bevel, loosely put together: a ruin on the top of the hill appears to be the remains of a tower of which the once massive walls have quite fallen down.

A tomb, excavated in the rock, is shown as that of Lazarus; of course such sites can seldom be ascertained with perfect certainty: but there seems no good reason for doubting this tradition, one more likely than most others to have been preserved; the objection that it is now within instead of outside the village seems over critical, as, in the lapse of eighteen centuries, it is far more probable than unlikely, that the houses should have gathered round the scene of so remarkable a miracle. The tomb stands now at the north-western corner of the village, and where (should Bethabara have been at "Jacob's ford," as Origen says) it would be passed by one coming by the path *over* the Mount of Olives to Bethany: this is the road that, coming down from the north, our Lord would have chosen without diverging to enter into the city where they "sought again to take Him," and where Mary, "going unto the grave to weep there," would meet Him when He "was not yet come into the town." The entrance is by a low doorway cut in the rock, and a passage with several steps descending into a vault, with another vault immediately below it reached by a few more steps: some masonry inside may have been added since: the tomb is alike sacred to Christian and Mooslim. The village is now called El Azarîyeh from *El Asar*, the Arabic form of Lazarus.

We stayed a couple of days at Bethany, studying the three paths to Jerusalem, round and over the Mount of Olives, delighting in the quietness of the spot, and in the views of and from the village. There is nothing more striking or more beautiful in its mournfulness than the view of the Holy City, which, by the sudden turns of the lower road from Bethany round the projecting spurs of the southern shoulder of Olivet, bursts twice upon the eyes of the pilgrim; and most thrilling are the remembrances of all that met the eyes of the blessed Saviour as He passed along that same old road in His last and most memorable entry into Jerusalem; but descriptions of the actual scenery would be useless after the vivid picture drawn by the graphic pen of Dr. Stanley.

It wanted three days of Christmas, 1859, when we took up our abode in Jerusalem.

CHAPTER XX.

ANCIENT JERUSALEM.

" The perfection of beauty—
    The joy of the whole earth ! "

" ¡ Ciudad de las tristezas ! "

JERUSALEM, with its mixture of Past and Present, is not by any means to be realised to the mind's eye by a rapid description, nor can it be understood at a glance: weeks, and even months, are absolutely required to take in the details which make up the whole; and these must be weighed and balanced, examined and considered, unless the traveller desires only to follow some one particular crotchet, or submits passively to the dictates of some one particular theory. If he chooses to think for himself, or to compare the thousand-and-one opinions of those who have gone before him, he will soon find himself launched into a maze—a labyrinth—a confusion worse confounded —from which he will at last turn away in despair, almost with a feeling that as they cannot all be right they must all be wrong. The most trustworthy method for a scholar is to come here with only the Bible and Josephus in his hand, and to study the ground with these guides only; but even then the results would probably be far from satisfactory until a generation or two has passed away, during which the building of one or another house, the clearing of this or that locality, may give from time to time glimpses of the foundations which lie concealed under the thirty or forty feet thickness of débris heaped over them—the seal on the long closed book of the Past— the sod growing over the grave; in this way only can a knowledge of the true facts of what has been ever be attained. So much, bit by bit, has been discovered in the last few years, and each discovery has made its predecessor so much more comprehensible than it was before, that one may reasonably hope that many further truths will cóme to light : if only the eyes that see them and the mind that connects them are unbiassed and unbound to some one prejudice.

It would be very presumptuous, and quite as useless, for me to attempt a detailed description of Jerusalem; but as most of those who are anxious to glean a more distinct image of that one holiest spot on all the earth, have derived some faint idea of the locality from the various accounts of travellers or from panoramas, models, drawings, and photographs, we may as well try to add some touches to the picture, and to bring out here and there a strong light or a dark shadow. I need hardly say that this small work has no pretensions whatever to any kind of learning: its only aim is to give an outline of what appears to be the plainest and most nearly indisputable evidence towards the elucidation of the great whole: to assist those who are at home in the realising of what they cannot see, and perhaps to guide the traveller, who can give but a few days to his examination, in the unravelling of the tangled knot. There will be scarcely one word on this controverted subject that some one would not dispute, if they thought it worth the trouble; but as I do not pretend to have discovered any one single fact, nor to cling to any one particular theory, I shall be the first to rejoice at any absolute mistake being corrected by abler heads and hands than mine.

Jerusalem was one of those cities founded by the sons of Canaan, the grandson of Noah[*], of which we have already spoken in mentioning Hamath and Saïda; it seems to have been always regarded as a sacred place, as would appear from Josephus having reminded the Jews, during the siege[†], that when the Egyptians came up and took possession of "Queen Sarah," Abraham ["]spread 'out his hands towards this holy place" to obtain God's assistance, and so the King of Egypt, "adoring the place, fled away." It was probably the Salem where Melchi-zedek worshipped the true God, himself both king and priest, having been called to the true faith, although surrounded by idolatrous Canaanites, and therefore "without father or mother" in his faith[‡]. Perhaps the remarkable circumstance of this single instance of an altar raised to Jehovah, caused the rock to be looked on as holy: and it does seem as if some special reason must

[*] Gen. x. 16. 1 Chron. xi. 4.

[†] Joseph. W. v. ix. 4.

[‡] Munk considers that this Melchi-zedek was a Canaanitish priest of the god "Elioun, father of Heaven and Earth," according to the description given by Philo of Byblos and Sanchoniathon of the mythological gods and goddesses of Syria: the words used in the Hebrew by Melchi-zedek are not those expressing the name of Jehovah, whilst Abraham in his reply takes care to precede the same "El Elioun" with the name of Jehovah, as though he wished to declare *his* GOD to be the one true and only Most High God. Josephus evidently also believed him to be a Canaanitish priest. War, vii. xi. 1.

have existed for Abraham's having been desired to take Isaac a journey of three days' distance in order to sacrifice him on that very hill. Abraham gave it a name indicative of that perfect unquestioning faith in Almighty God, of which he had given so signal a proof on the rock, *Jehovah jireh*, the Lord will provide: the period at which this name became transmitted into that of Jerusalem, and the exact meaning of the latter, are both disputed points. It is generally believed to be a combination of the last syllable of the new name given to the rock by Abraham, prefixed to that borne by the city in his time, Jireh Salem; thus signifying that the Lord will provide peace, and prophetic of the daily Sacrifices to be there offered for a thousand years, by the people He had chosen, and of the Lamb, Whose death on that spot should make our peace for ever with God. It was also called Jebus, from the name of its founder, and Zion to denote its pre-eminence and excellence. It is spoken of both by Isaiah (xlviii. 2, lii. 1) and Nehemiah (xi. 1, 18) as "the holy city," Kodesh, the name which it has retained in Arabic, El Kodds: which appears in Herodotus under the Greek form of "Kadytis."

It is only in reaching Jerusalem from the East, that the length and breadth of the Holy City is seen at one glance: from the South, only the part outside the Zion gate, and the walls and towers on the Western side are visible at the first view, crowning the brow of the hill; the view from the Jaffa road, which has first met the eyes of pilgrims for more than a thousand years, and is therefore in some sort hallowed, is the least striking of all; little or nothing is there seen but the Western wall and the old square Tower of Hippicus at the Jaffa Gate, and these rise from the uneven plain apparently undivided from it by any valley or ravine. From the North road, the whole of that side is well seen at once, relieved by the olive-groves before; yet little more than the wall itself can be seen, with the top of the Greek Convent, and a few domes, among which those of the Mosque of Omar and of the Holy Sepulchre are conspicuous above the others.

Every traveller, from whatever side he arrives, should ascend the Mount of Olives before he loses himself in the confusion of narrow streets and crooked houses within the gates, and should, for some hours, study attentively the general features of the view before him, the different elevations within and without the town, the chief buildings, and all the details he can distinguish. Let him sit there from the moment when the first silvery shining ray darts over the mountain wall of the eastern Desert, tipping here a grey dome and there a gilt crescent, till the sun has waxed high and strong, and pours down in the naked, white, shadowless light of noon: let him stay there till the dark red hills and the grey rocks melt into a maze of deep violet, and the white stones turn rosy, and the old walls change into piles of yellow gold, and the sun goes down behind the far away hills, putting out its fires in the " great sea," yet lingering to throw back grand loveliness of rose and lilac upon the Moab mountains, whence he will come again in the morning. Then the quiet city gradually sinks, as it were, into the deep shades of the ravines on each side, and the Turkish soldier's shout for the Sultan comes up upon the last ray of sunshine ; a twinkling light appears in every building, till all is hushed and dark and silent, save the horrible dogs quarrelling in the valley of the Kedron below. It is surprising how necessary it is to watch this view for a whole day, as the varying light brings out one point after another : one such continual comparative observation does more for the right understanding of the whole, than a hundred disjointed, quickly-caught views of passage.

We will sketch in slightly what we see: the bare hill to the south of the city, with one miserable wind-worn tree on its brow, is the Hill of Evil Counsel (where Caiaphas and the elders are said, upon no authority, however, to have taken counsel together, Matt. xxvi. 3) : it is rocky and irregular, sloping off to the west and dying down in the plain of Rephaim ; on the north, long ridges of low barren hills or plains, stony and bare, though dotted with olives here and there, stretch one behind another : they seem to rise gently from the city, until the monotony is broken by the low peak of Neby Samwel, marked by a tower, the ruin of an old convent church, since converted into a mosque.

Between these two sides of the picture the Holy City stands, apparently on a square, rocky hill, enclosed in crenelated walls, with here and there a bastion or a zig-zag : very quaint and very sad those old walls look, and yet something proudly, too, they stand. Beyond them, a long, dull, flat ridge rises slightly towards the west, and two deep narrow ravines sweep round the holy mountain : the one is the Valley of Jehoshaphat, or of the Kedron, commencing from some distance to the north of the city, and running along the eastern side of it to the south : the other is the valley of Hinnom, coming round from the western side and uniting with the Kedron at the south-east corner, embracing at that point, between them, the spur of Mount Moriah, which is called Ophel. Furthest from us, on the western wall, is the Tower of Hippicus. Near it, to the right, are the Latin Convent and the two domes of the Church of the Holy Sepulchre ; to the left, on Mount Zion, the extensive Armenian Convent, the domes of some new Synagogues, the English Church,

and the tomb of David are seen (the last outside the wall). These
are almost the only buildings on which the eye can rest among the
confused mass of little brown and white domes and grey walls: nor
are any of these seen at first, for the Mosque of Omar, in the famous
Harâm, the second most beautiful building in all the world, rivets
the spectator's whole attention. The wall enclosing the mosque
occupies more than half of the eastern side of the city: in the centre
of this space stands the mosque, an octagonal building, pierced with
seven windows on each side, narrowing above into a small circle
also pierced with windows, and surmounted by a most graceful
dome, bearing aloft the gilt crescent of Islam: the whole building is
cased entirely in encaustic tiles, chiefly blue, green, purple, and
yellow, formed into intricate and delicate arabesques, and so mingled
that it is impossible to say whether the building is green or blue;
the cornice is replaced by an Arábic inscription in large and prettily
interlaced letters. The mosque stands on a marble platform, which
is reached by broad flights of steps, and round the edge of which
are several groups of slender arches and small houses, while little
circular *mihrabs*, or praying-places, shaded by a light canopy of
fretted stone, are dotted over its surface. Round this platform are
grassy slopes, with noble cypresses and a few other trees, the bright
and dark green of which contrast beautifully with the white and
coloured marbles of the buildings.

At the southern end of the enclosure is the Mosque of El'Aksa,
ornamented with a dome and covered by a sloping roof. The
Mosque of the Moghâribeh, the College of the Dervishes, and the
Serai, the residence of the Pasha, stand on the west and north sides;
while the whole extent of the eastern side of the city is only broken
by St. Stephen's Gate, and the long-closed "Golden Gate," with its
two round arches and small domes.

This is the view over which Jesus wept, when He beheld its
beauty, and thought upon its ruin and desolation: and strange
and thrilling indeed is the feeling it gives to one now: the gloomy
ravines lose much of their effect seen from above: the surrounding
hills are one and all the very dreariest, barrenest, and ugliest one
can find anywhere, and yet—the whole is beautiful: and even the
fastidious and trifling are impressed by it.

There are two other views of Jerusalem which specially deserve
mention, all the more as they are seldom seen by travellers: the one
is from the easternmost point of Scopus, whence the plateau of the
Harâm is well overlooked, and the upper part of the city, Mount
Zion especially, appears as a good background to it, while the olive-
gardens seem richer than usual from being taken in perspective,

and contrast well with the bare hill of Olivet rising on the left, the ever-beautiful Moab mountains behind all. The other is, in my opinion, the *prettiest* of all the views of Jerusalem: it is from the eastern end of the Hill of Evil Counsel, and should be seen when the city is overspread with the bright rays of the western sun, when the Mount of Olives appears more lofty than in the earlier light, and the elevated position of the city is well displayed by the deep shadow of the ravines of Kedron and Hinnom.

It is believed that the present enclosure of the Harâm is about the same size as that of the Temple of Solomon; the marble platform on which the Mosque stands, as the Temple stood, was rendered necessary by the inequalities of the summit of Mount Moriah, and because it was not naturally large enough to contain all the Temple . buildings; in fact it acted in something of the same way as the platforms beneath Tadmor, Rukhleh, Baalbek, &c., but that here it was only required for giving the Temple a level standing-place on the summit of its own stronghold; in the others it was required also for elevating the Temple to view. But this platform was not intended to *cover* the sacred rock, a rock sanctified to the Israelites by two of the most holy and sacred events in their history: one, the binding of Isaac for sacrifice; the other, the appearance of Jehovah to David in the threshing-floor of Araunah the Jebusite*; and it was therefore left to be seen naked and natural in the Holy of Holies, the place of solemn sacrifice and communion with Jehovah. The platform was consequently sunk about twenty feet lower than the summit of the rock: and as on the south side the mount slopes down suddenly, while on the north side it is scarcely of a lower level than the summit, the platform was supported on the south side upon rows of arches, closed in by the exterior wall, which is consequently very deep without and shallow within. As there is no doubt that these substructions supporting the platform must have been made previous to the building of the Temple, they are intensely interesting as being indubitably of the time of Solomon, made "immovable for all future times." (See the interesting account of these foundations in Josephus, xv. 11, 3.)

These substructions were entered from the exterior by a door in the south wall, which is now closed up, but into one of the halls under the platform the Mooslim pilgrim is allowed to enter, because a stone niche, lying here on its back, is an object of devotion among them as the so-called "cradle of the Lord Issa" (Jesus); the vault of this hall within is supported by a single column, short, but

* That these two places were the same is an immemorial tradition, confirmed by 2 Chron. iii. 1.

2 в

enormously massive, which used to be a monolith, with a curious capital of leaves ranged in a stiff row all round it: they are more like feathers than leaves, and have a very Egyptian look about them: the capital is carved in the lowest relief possible, as if intended to be further adorned by colour.* The double passage leading from this hall to the platform, by an inclined plane, occupies but a very small portion of these arched vaults: they appear to have been built in chambers, divided by very thick walls of enormous bevelled stones rather roughly chiselled; into these no one is allowed to enter, but from a loophole in the wall of the hall before mentioned, one can have a good glimpse into their gloomy but grand recesses. It is outside this part of the Harâm that the wall of Solomon's time appears in such beauty:† It reaches from about the last sixty feet of the east wall to some short distance on the southern side: there are sixteen courses of stone still uncovered, but, on the southern side, they are soon hidden beneath the accumulated soil, or else have ceased; while on the east the rest of the wall has evidently been rebuilt, as small stones and fragments of columns are jumbled in with many of the very large stones of the original wall: the broken columns are of porphyry and verde-antique, and doubtless ornamented the Temple itself or the cloisters. The masonry of the angle is most beautiful: the finely-closed joints, the finish of the bevelling, and the smooth faces are so wonderful in these enormous stones that the words of the Psalmist naturally occur at once to the mind of the traveller, "That our daughters may grow up as the polished corners of the Temple;" besides the solemn thought of that Saviour, who has become "the chief corner stone."

Go from this angle down into the Valley of Siloam, where the valley of the Tyropæan falls into it, and climb up the opposite cliff face, the eastern end of the Hill of Evil Counsel: look thence at this magnificent Temple wall, a marvel of masonry, great even now: fancy what it must have been, when it was complete in the same grandeur all along to the western side; fancy, beyond this, the Bridge (the remains of which were so happily discovered a few years ago), crossing the (then) deep valley of the Tyropæan to the cliff of Mount Zion—still steep and lofty—connecting the Temple with the Xystus (the house of archives; is it any wonder that the Queen of Sheba was overwhelmed with admiration when she saw this "ascent" by which Solomon went up from his palace to the Temple? but still more when she looked on the other side of the

---

* The drawing of this capital in Mr. Fergusson's Handbook is very inaccurately done.

† See Dr. Robinson's 'Bib. Researches,' vol. i. 288.

Temple and saw, extended right across the valley of the Kedron, another but much loftier Bridge, uniting the Temple to the Mount of Olives! This Bridge we are told was constructed upon two rows of arches, of which the upper row was much smaller and closer than the lower; and over it, in grand procession, the High Priest went with the red heifer to sacrifice her on the summit of Mount Olivet; the point of its junction with the Wall of the Temple is distinctly traceable if compared with that of the Bridge on the other side, and some day it is to be hoped the foundations may be discovered on the slope of the hillside, or at the bottom of the valley.

At the north-western corner of the *enceinte* of the Harâm the rock rises to a considerable height above the level of the platform: it has been cut down vertically: below it the rock-surface is perfectly level, and has been thought by some persons to be the threshing-floor of Araunah, partly, I believe, from tradition, and partly because Josephus, quoting Hecateus of Abdera, seems to describe the altar as being *near*, not *in*, the Temple itself, although contained within the same surrounding wall. The Serai, or Pasha's palace, stands on the summit of this corner rock, considered to be the site of the fortress of Antonia, "the Tower of the Corner," which was originally built, it is believed, by Judas Maccabæus, and reconstructed with great splendour by Herod. From the roof of the Pasha's house a beautiful view of the Harâm is obtained, of course in better detail than that from the Mount of Olives: the light colonnades and the *mihrabs* are much better seen, and prove to be mostly exquisite specimens of Saracenic work; one, opposite the eastern door of the Mosque, is called the "Judgment seat of David:" the delicately-painted roof is supported on seventeen slender marble columns, no two capitals of which are alike, and all are richly sculptured; straight simple leaves round one, like an Egyptian capital, basket-work on another, trellises of vine-leaves on others, and so on; they have probably all been taken from some much more ancient building. The next in beauty stands on the top of the steps opposite the Mosque of El Aksa: it is called "the Pulpit," and is most richly carved in various coloured marbles.

The magnificent Mosque in the centre of the platform is believed to have been commenced by the Khalif Omar, and very much enlarged, beautified and enriched, in fact, quite rebuilt by the Khalif Abd-el-melek in A.D. 686. It was seven years in building: the Mooslims believe it to stand over the rock on which Jacob was sleeping when he saw the vision of the heavenly ladder: but it is still more sacred to them, as to us, from having been the sacred rock beneath the altar in Solomon's Temple, whereon the daily sacrifice was offered. During the time of the Latin kingdom in Jerusalem this Mosque became a Christian Cathedral, where the service was daily sung and an altar erected on the summit of the rock: the building was called by the Crusaders the "Temple of the Lord."

The fanciful and intricate patterns of the porcelain walls of the Mosque, the graceful letters of the inscription round it, and the tracery of the windows, are still more beautiful on a closer inspection: nothing can be more perfect of their kind, or more peculiarly charming than the harmony of the colours; the windows are filled with stained glass of the very richest and most brilliant tints, that even the palmiest days of the mediæval ages could produce in Europe, and the effect of the dim religious light upon the interior of the dome, which was once entirely gilt, on the adornment of the walls and columns, and on the bare, naked, rough rock below, is singularly beautiful. Two rows of columns encircle the centre, forming a double corridor, and support the clerestory and the dome: these columns have evidently belonged to some other building: their capitals are mostly of acanthus leaves. The Rock itself is enclosed in a metal screen of lattice-work about six feet high, and to it, we are told by the Bordeaux Pilgrim in A.D. 333, the Jews came every year, anointed the stone with oil, wailing and rending their garments, thus proving its authenticity in their minds: it had been for many years polluted by an equestrian statue of the Emperor Adrian elevated on the very rock itself. The Bordeaux Pilgrim specially mentions that this Rock adored by the Jews was *pierced*: below it is the "noble cave" spoken of in the Mishna, into which the blood, &c., from the altar drained, and descended thence by a conduit into the valley of Siloam, the gardens in which were enriched by this drainage: and this appears to be corroborated by the special name of the valley being Kedron, which comes from *kedar*, meaning dark, gloomy, sad, filthy. The gardeners, it is said, paid as much money as a trespass-offering for a share of it to fertilise their gardens, which were called the "king's gardens." (Nehem. iii. 15; Jer. lii. 7.) Dr. Barclay, Signor Pierotti, and others have themselves passed up from the mouth of this passage in the Pool of Siloam to the "noble cave," and the latter gentleman has also ascended by a branch subterranean conduit, hollowed in the same way from the valley of Siloam to a spot under the so-called Hospital of Omar, some way to the west of the precincts of the Harâm, and not far from the bridge of St. Gilles.

The Mosque of El Aksa stands at the southern extremity of the Harâm, over the substructions built by Solomon: it was a Christian basilica of seven aisles, and is so much more church-like in the interior than even the Holy Sepulchre, that it is striking to the European eye. Most of the columns are of marble, chiefly of dark green serpentine: two of them standing about the centre of the nave are very thick square monoliths, and some are supposed to be Jewish, on account of the lowest fillet of the capital and the upper fillet of the base being carved on the plinth; these two are both ornamented with very peculiar leaves, not in the least conventional, but well-carved examples of the commonest weeds in Palestine; the arches are supported by beams of wood laid across from capital to capital, which gives a most singular appearance to the structure. Several recesses, chambers, and additions at the southern end of the Mosque form other mosques, and there are many *Kiblehs*, or prayer-niches and pulpits, that have been given by pious khalifs. In the Mosque is a well, descending into the vaults of Solomon, some of which were probably used as reservoirs of water. The Mosque of Omar is lovely and beautiful; that of El Aksa is grand but *triste.*

Near the northern end of the Harâm, in the eastern wall, is the Golden Gateway, now much sunk below the level of the soil and overgrown with picturesque wreaths of caper and other plants: the architecture is more rich than chaste, and only the general effect is good. Outside, two small arches are ornamented with wreaths of leaves and various mouldings bent round the arch: within, there is a large hall, with two rows of lofty columns down the centre and a rich cornice round the wall. Some of the bevelled stones used here are as gigantic as those of the time of Solomon: one of those in this hall is the second largest in the Harâm; the largest of all is in the eastern wall.

Leaving the Harâm, there is a deep ditch or fosse immediately beyond the northern wall, believed to have been excavated to make the walls of the Temple or the Fortress of Antonia still loftier from the outside: it seems also as if it had been intended to have been filled with water, as the sides, roughly built of small square stones, some of them bevelled, and filled up in the interstices with loose pebbles, have been caked over with mud or cement. It is now half full of rubbish, and looks most melancholy; several small arches or open passages round it may have been for conducting water to or from other reservoirs; these may have been " porches " in which " impotent folk " sat to ask alms of those who came down to draw water. There is no sufficient reason, I believe, for the tradition which supposes this to have been the Pool of Bethesda, but the construction reminds one of the description given in Scripture.

This fosse is close to St. Stephen's Gate, at which the Via Dolorosa commences; after a short distance along this line, there are portions of very ancient walls, and the remains of the only fluted columns existing in Jerusalem; just beyond them, beside the Serai, a mean and modern-looking Roman arch crosses the road, called the Arch of the Ecce Homo, as the monks say that it was from the window above the arch that Pilate exclaimed to the multitude "Behold the man!" A convent for the *Filles de Sion* was being built on the north side of the street when we were in Jerusalem, and in digging the foundations, the architect, Signor Pierotti, came, to his great surprise, upon a pavement of good-sized flags, and afterwards upon a covered passage of very large stones, of the time of Herod, similar to those in the Wailing-place of the Jews and at the South-East corner of the Harâm, bevelled and finely joined; this passage has square openings carefully finished in the top, and is about fifteen feet high and eighteen feet wide.* The "pavement called Gabbatha" must have been somewhere close to this, as the Governor's or Pilate's house was close to Antonia (Dr. Barclay believes it to have been an apartment belonging to or adjoining the tower of Antonia): and the passage may possibly be the "certain, dark subterranean passage" mentioned by Josephus (War, i. iii. 3) as the scene of a dismal tragedy.

The Via Dolorosa then passes by a very pretty old Saracenic house, built of alternate grey and red stones arranged in patterns: this is believed by the poor pilgrims to have been the house of Dives, the rich man in the parable, and the dogs who lie under the archway below the house to be the descendants of those who licked the sores of Lazarus: doubtless, both house and dogs have an equal right to their ancient pedigree.

The Via Dolorosa then turns up the hill, and arrives at the back of the Church of the Holy Sepulchre: passing round to the front or south side, we find a small square, entered by a door at each side,

---

* In continuing this excavation last December (1860), Signor Pierotti came upon a quantity of water shut up in a rock-cut conduit: for several days about 250 gallons were drawn out per diem without lowering the level of the water; it was at first very brackish, but it soon became quite drinkable; after this a heavy fall of snow caused the superincumbent earth to fall in, and the works were discontinued. The most interesting feature of the discovery was the intense excitement it caused among the Jews: a tradition of ancient standing exists among them that when three springs are discovered in Jerusalem or in its immediate neighbourhood, the Messiah will come, and on hearing the news they flocked to the spot in excited crowds of both sexes; many wept for joy, others knelt down and prayed, all tasted the water reverentially and carried home bottles of it as relics. It was not, however, really a spring, but only an accumulation of water which had been collecting there, perhaps for hundreds of years, and is now, I believe, dried up.

of only three feet high, through which a Jew could pass only at the
peril of his life, as the crowd of pilgrims, bead sellers, &c., would at
least do their best to tear him to pieces. Parts of the Greek convent
surround three sides of the square, which was evidently a court or
cloister in front of the Church: the bases of several columns are
still *in situ*, and one column has a rich basket-work capital, of which
there are several examples in Jerusalem. A double portal once
gave entrance to the Church, but one of the doors is now walled
up: they are both deeply receding, each as six small columns of
porphyry alternating with verde-antique, the capitals very richly
carved with leaves and flowers and feathers bent sideways, as if blown
round the capital. The arches are surrounded with bands of the
most delicate and finely-carved sculpture, besides a row of the book
moulding (resembling a row of books set edgeways), and lintels most
richly carved, one with a fanciful arabesque, the other with a representation of our Lord's Triumphal Entry into Jerusalem. Over the
door are two windows similarly ornamented, and a smaller one
further to the right; the whole façade is horribly spoilt and mis-
used. Above it the dome over the centre appears, and on the left
the tower, now broken down nearly to the height of the Church
walls, but still picturesque. The large dome over the Rotunda, the
subject of so much discussion, is behind this. A row of sixty small
capitals surround the smaller dome, sculptured with remarkable
delicacy; they *may* have been taken from Herod's Temple, as the
tradition says, but, at least, they are evidently a vast deal older than
anything else in the building.

Inside, the whole church, although covering what those who
worship there believe to be the most sacred spot on all the earth, is
in the most painful state of dilapidation and dirt. The Rotunda, or
Round Church, built over the Holy Sepulchre itself, never was
handsome or solid, and is now crumbling to decay. It is surrounded
with a double gallery, apparently supported by pilasters, which are,
however, only painted, and that very rudely, on the wall: everything about it is coarsely done, in imitation "compo style," now
falling to pieces, to say nothing of the dome above, which, as everybody knows, is much torn away, leaving free entrance to the air,
light, and rain.* The Sepulchre stands in the centre, enclosed in a
high structure or chapel of polished yellow marble, with pilasters
and twisted columns, topped with confectionery looking plaster
angels, and bunches of artificial flowers, besides numbers of pretty
silver lamps hung in festoons in the front. The Tomb of our Lord,

---

* The cupola was repaired, at last, under a protocol signed by the Governor
of Palestine, and the Consuls-General of France and Russia.

in the interior, is covered with slabs of marble, and therefore quite hidden from view and touch : silver lamps are ever burning here ; a priest keeps watch beside it by night and day, and the sweet-smelling flowers of the mimosa are daily strewed upon the marble, and bestowed afterwards on some few of the pilgrims.

At the western extremity of the Rotunda are two ancient tombs hewn out of the living rock : these are very interesting here, being perfectly natural and unadorned, and as there is no reason for sup-posing them counterfeits they testify incontestably to the fact of there having been sepulchres in the rock of this place. The Church of St. Helena, furthest to the East, from its remaining, like these tombs in its original simplicity, is more impressive and striking than the rest of the building : it is a crypt of simple, massive architecture, round arches supported on very short, thick columns, with the curious basket-work capital of which we have spoken before. It is impossible not to believe that the form of these came originally from the " nets of checker-work " made " for the chapiters that were upon the top of the pillars," in the Temple built by Solomon (1 Kings vii. 17). Descending several steps more, we reach the Chapel of the " True Cross :" a vault in which the Cross is said to have lain hidden and forgotten for 300 years ; it is rudely excavated, and is believed by some people to have been an old cistern.

The Chapel of Calvary is at the southern side of the church, near the entrance door, but above a very steep staircase : the rent in the rock is shown, like every other relic here, enclosed in metal cages or hidden beneath slabs of marble. The chapel is dressed up with all manner of tinsel ornaments, artificial flowers, pictures, &c., but there is one beautiful altar, sent from Italy, with fine groups of figures round it in relief : it is of bronze gilt.

The Greeks have the centre of the church, and show " the centre of the world," in the middle of it, as well as the tomb of Adam (Melchizedek lies close by) ; their church is a mass of gilding and carving and marble ; the Latins have a plain, ugly chapel on the north side of the Rotunda ; they have also an organ (on which they play most extraordinary things by way of sacred music), and some good singers in their choir. The services of each Communion are celebrated at different hours on the same spot, viz. the space between the Holy Sepulchre and the Greek Church ; an altar is here erected and dressed, and seats are arranged for each service. There are also large aisles and passages and chapels innumerable, besides a host of "stations" for the pilgrims, each containing some "relic" of our blessed Lord or the Virgin, in which none but the most credulous of all can believe. These shrines are dilapidated and dirty, and form a strange jumble of architecture; there are five periods very distinctly discernible in the construction of the building—1st, that of Constantine, A.D. 330; 2nd, after the destruction of the Basilica by the Persians in 614, when it was rebuilt by Modestus, the prior of the Greek convent; 3rd, when having been destroyed by the Khalif Hakem in 1010, another church was built by his mother, Miriam, assisted by the offerings of all Christendom; 4th, when it was completely remodelled by the Latin kings of Jerusalem, after A.D. 1099, and so remained till, 5thly, half the building was burned down in A.D. 1810, and was soon after patched up into its present condition by a Greek architect.

Directly to the south of the Church of the Holy Sepulchre, there is a large green field, one-half of which has lately been bought by the Russians, the other half was given by the Sultan four years ago to the Emperor of the French. On the northern side of this field two aisles of an ancient church are still standing, beside which the soil has accumulated to the depth of some forty feet or even more: these are the remains of the Church of St. Mary ad Latinos, and the Hospital for female pilgrims, dedicated to St. Mary Magdalene: both were built in A.D. 1048. A little further on is the gateway which once gave entrance to the fine buildings of the Knights Hospitallers of St. John, constructed at the same time as the churches, but much enlarged and beautified during the Latin kingdom in the Holy City. The gateway is a fine object from the street, with its broken wreaths of flowers and queer figures illustrating the signs of the zodiac, but the interior has till lately been used as a tannery, and the whole place is so filthy that explorations are more than difficult; we managed, however, two or three visits, and penetrated to a very picturesque square, still quite perfect, and closely resembling that at Rhodes; it consists of two stories of Saracenic arches, four at each side, forming a double corridor, looking like a khan. There are numbers of fine vaulted chambers and halls further on, without much ornament, and buried in soil and rubbish: but interesting as the dwelling-places of that noble band whose best blood dyed the soil of the Holy Land.

But something else far more interesting than even these historic ruins has lately been discovered in this field: the Russians were excavating part of their newly-acquired territory, or rather digging through the accumulated rubbish to see at what depth the real soil lay, when at about thirty feet deep the spade struck on stone, and a few turns more laid bare some depth of wall, built in precisely the same style as the Wailing-place of the Jews, and other Herodian masonry: this piece of wall is in the form of a right angle; only a very few stones were uncovered, but these appeared to be about six or seven feet long and three or four feet high, all bevelled; but it was not easy to get at them for examination. Their grand interest is that they lie exactly *in the line supposed to be that of the Second Wall*; these stones lie further north, but parallel to the Sook-el-Kebeer (the Bazaar) of the present city, about half a dozen feet to the west of it, in the middle of which, some time ago, Signor Pierotti came to stones of the same style of work in an excavation he had occasion to make for the Pasha.* At the time these stones were apparently unconnected with anything, but taken now with the stones in the field they lead directly to the arch, a little further to the south, built of large stones more rudely fashioned, but so much covered up as to be more than half concealed, which was long ago pointed out as the Gate Gennath from whence the second wall started. Another link in the chain of evidence seems to be, that in digging the foundations of the house of the late Dr. McGowan, about fifty yards to the west of the buried gate, various stones, bearing the mark of high antiquity, were found at a great depth, which appeared to have formed the lower part of a wall; while one has only to climb up some roof or eminence in this neighbourhood, to see that a line drawn from Hippicus to the remains of the Bridge at the south-west angle of the Harâm† *exactly crosses over this deeply sunken Gate.* The Gate is placed at right angles to the line of the Wall, according to the usual custom, it seems, of placing the gates of such walls in the return of a projection or recess: as may be seen now in the walled up " Gate of Herod," the "Gate of the Mogharibeh," and others: as well as in the gates of a later age, like those of Damascus. Gennath meant the Gate of the Gardens, for which a natural situation would have been on the slope of the Tyropæon: they are not likely to have been very extensive in so small a city, placed on such rocky ground.

The identity of the Gate of Gennath is one of great interest, because on it depends, in a great measure, the probable truth or falsehood of the site of the Holy Sepulchre. Supposing the line of

---

* Signor Pierotti holds the office of architect to Sooraya, Pasha of Jerusalem.

† The words used by Josephus are as follows: "Now that wall" (the first) "began on the north at the tower called Hippicus, and extended as far as the Xystus, a place so called, and then joining, to the council-house, ended at the west cloister of the Temple. . . . The second wall took its beginning from that gate which they called Gennath, which belonged to the first wall: it only encompassed the northern quarter of the city, and reached as far as the tower Antonia:"—(Whiston's Josephus, 1860 v. iv.) Another translation is given that the wall was " carried in a circle " to Antonia: the result will be nearly the same.

the second wall to be identified with that of these ancient stones in the Russian territory, I think any unprejudiced observer must acknowledge the distance between that line and the site of the Church to be more than "fifty yards," named in the Talmud as the prescribed distance from the walls of the City for the interment of criminals: a Talmudic yard being equal to two feet, the distance would be consequently only 100 feet. It is true that our Lord was not buried in the place where criminals were usually interred, but in the tomb hewn for the "rich man of Arimathea;" the bodies of criminals would probably have been removed further from the city than those of men less unclean and impure: and the objection that none could have been buried so close to the walls must fall to the ground. The place chosen for the crucifixion of our Lord was certainly not the usual place of the execution of criminals, since it is not likely that in that spot a "rich man" would have made a "garden;" even though it were but a graveyard, he would have chosen some place he could visit without risk of becoming unclean. The usual place, the Talmud says, was to the south of the city; but this would have been too far to reach, hurried as they evidently were to get all concluded. The priests, as Dr. Barclay observes, were afraid of the voice of the people, and would not have hazarded sending Him right across the city, as the path from the Judgment Hall to the Dung Gate would have led: it was not only "nigh to the city," but the priests, it is said, looked on, reviling Him while He hung upon the Cross; and one need only mount on the roof of the Serai, or on the Church of the Holy Sepulchre itself, to see how well they could have seen all that took place on its site from the wall of the Temple, without leaving its precincts, and thus defiling themselves on the eve of the Passover, by approaching an execution or entering an unclean place.

Along this second wall were the towers of Phasaelus and Mariamne, "hard by" to the Tower of Hippicus, "on the north side" of "the old wall;" the palace of the king (Herod) "adjoined thereto," and was so near to the Temple that "the fire which began at the tower of Antonia went on to the palaces, and consumed the upper part of the three palaces themselves." The identity of the Tower of Hippicus with the citadel at the Jaffa Gate has been little questioned: it is a remarkable building, and the peculiar circumstance of its being formed out of the living rock to a considerable height, faced with stones, is a feature by which Josephus has happily caused it to be recognised without doubt. A short time ago some stones fell out from the inside of an upper chamber in the tower, and with them a few arrows fell also: and on peeping through the hole thus made, a great store of arrows were seen laid up in a recess, prepared for feathering, and closed up there perhaps by mistake! The wood was in most cases uninjured, and some of them were given away; but on finding the Christians very eager about them, the Mooslim guard walled the remainder up again. From this Tower of Hippicus, the third wall, built by Agrippa in the time of Claudius Cæsar, A.D. 41–54, commenced: it went north-wards to the Tower of Psephinus, an octagonal tower elevated at the north-west corner of the city, and very lofty, affording a view of wide extent. Accordingly, at the north-west corner of the hill, in its natural position, situated on the highest point of the city, there is a ruin of a tower, plainly octangular, but of which only one side is now standing entire, answering to the dimensions given by Josephus, and incontestably containing many stones of an ancient bevel and very large size, coinciding, in fact, with Herodian work. Josephus says that "the third wall . . . reached as far as the north quarter of the city and the Tower of Psephinus, and then was so far extended till it came over against the monument of Helena . . . Queen of Adiabene . . . it then extended farther to a great length, and passed by the royal caverns, and bent again at the tower of the corner at the monument, which is called the Monument of the Fuller, and joined to the old wall at the Valley of the Kedron." (War, v. iv. 2.) It is a curious coincidence that close to this ruin of Psephinus, under the roots of a remarkably fine terebinth tree, which every traveller will remember, some workmen discovered, two or three years ago, a large Tomb, apparently Jewish, with ornaments of circles and triangles, &c.: and a tradition is attached to the spot among the natives that "a king of the country" lies buried there; why should it not be the tomb of one of those Davidian kings who were not buried on Mount Zion, but in "a garden," such as this slope probably was then, as it is now? A deep fosse, cut in the living rock, flanks the whole of this northern wall, until it arrives at the "royal caverns" not long ago discovered by Dr. Barclay: these are huge caverns running under a very large portion of Bezetha, and about (as well as I remember) 1000 feet in depth—that is, speaking roughly, half as far as the Via Dolorosa: they are lofty and wide, with several branch passages, and are evidently the quarries whence came all the stone used in the building of the Temple, and whence no sound of "hammer nor axe nor any tool of iron could be heard in the house while it was building." The quarrying marks of the workmen are still to be ob-served, and the sizes of the blocks such as are seen in the wall of the Harâm are easily traced here: one almost fancies one can match the blocks to the spots from whence they are cut. An ancient excava-tion, very lately discovered, at the north-east angle of the present wall of the city, may possibly be the "Fuller's Monument," as it seems to fall in with the place described by Josephus: there is also an ancient double cistern, close to the wall, between the Damascus Gate and this angle, about which there is an Arab tradition that it was "the tomb of a dyer." If these points have been rightly assigned, the third wall would appear to have been almost identically on the same line that the modern wall occupies at present. Dr. Robinson has carried it out about half a mile to the north, but it seems most difficult, after seeing the supposed remains, to give credence to his theory; the bit of "the wall" is only about three or four yards long, formed entirely of small insignificant stones, unlike any really ancient work, and without a single other piece to carry on the line to the Valley of the Kedron: while the foundation of the "tower" has much the appearance of an old cistern. The wall was dragged out here to meet the so-called Tombs of the Kings; but at the time when Dr. Robinson wrote, the "royal caverns" had not been discovered, and there is now happily no need to choose for them a position for which little evidence can be adduced: besides the impossibility of conceiving that such a "wonderful" wall as this is described by Josephus to have been, could have so wholly and entirely vanished without leaving a trace even of its "solid towers" and "beautiful stones." Had the wall stood out here, Titus would have looked into the town from the brow of Scopus, where his army was then placed, and would certainly have had no need for the reconnoitring ride which was so nearly fatal to him; while, on the contrary, the artificial filling up of the valley for the approach of his battering-rams, is easily discernible to a practised eye within this distant wall; and if, on the taking of the third wall, as soon as the camp of Titus was removed within it, he came face to face with the "faction in the Tower of Antonia," how could the wall have been out here? (Joseph. War, v. vii.)

The conflicting opinions concerning the original sites can never be really settled till the actual foundations or remains of the different buildings in question are seen, by dint of extensive ex-cavations. Every step made underground is, or ought to be, so much gained towards the elucidation of the truth, since that truth can never be attained by reasoning alone, especially when the reasoning is framed to suit preconceived notions: while least convincing of all it is to talk of this line or that being impossible, because, had the walls so run, the city would have been such an odd shape, &c. &c.; and arguments founded upon the consequent

smallness of the city are the last to impress one after a glance at
the localities themselves. Our minds have been so filled from
childhood with the vastness of the subject, and our memories are
burdened with such a variety of far-reaching histories and details,
that, looking at them through a mental perspective, we fancy that
so vast a history must have had as vast a theatre. We have every
proof that Josephus's numbers as to persons are almost always
exaggerated, to harmonize with his descriptions of buildings
when constructed by persons whom he wished to flatter; that
he exaggerated immensely in his numbers relating to the inhabitants of Jerusalem was but an error naturally due to his
wish to magnify the greatness of the conquest, as well as the
sufferings of his countrymen. As the first wall of Jerusalem
included the whole of Mount Zion and Ophel, there must have
been nearly as much ground contained within its compass as there
is now in the modern city, in which there is so large a proportion
of waste land: and when the second wall enclosed the " northern
quarter," there must have been quite as much. The natural
dimensions of the city are declared by the summit of the hills
which time cannot change for any historian, and the history must
be fitted to the facts, not the facts to the history: but instead of
this, endeavours of every kind are now made, in order to accom-
modate preconceived notions, to stretch the city on the rack of
theories, and torture it into whatever size or shape may suit the
fancy of the reasoner.

Unfortunately no one now investigates the subject with a
thoroughly unprejudiced mind: not merely must the " true
Protestant " avoid every place venerated by the Roman Catholic,
but even the ancient sites of Jewish history must be dragged into
the abysses of party feeling and garnished with party names.
That much has been overlaid by a very grievous and blind superstition is, indeed, too true: but is it any reason for sweeping away
the whole fabric that the pinnacles are ill-built or may be formed
of unworthy materials? I would not have an inch of ground
taken upon tradition only, for it is better and best to have a reason
for everything, and there should be no limit to honest and earnest
inquiry; but it is more than melancholy, it is pitiful, to see reason
and study laid aside because Protestantism has fixed on one thing,
and it would be " Romish," and therefore " superstitious," to believe
anything else. In Jerusalem people are mourned over nearly as
lost sheep, or as brands in the burning, if they choose to think and
study, to read and examine for themselves: if they will not throw
themselves down with unquestioning faith before the Protestant

idol, they are supposed to gulp down at once the whole draught of superstition, no *via media* is possible, or rather none is permitted; and if any one, great or small, hesitates to declare that the site of the Holy Sepulchre could only have been within the second wall, he is at once believed to be lying under the deepest folds of such darkness as encompasses the Spanish or the Russian pilgrim.

I believe myself that Dr. Robinson, as not only a learned, but an honest and honourable man, would be the first to disapprove of the Protestant banner set up in his valuable book, and the last to think that the pure faith of the Church, in England or in America, would be endangered, if even the time-honoured spot, hallowed at least by the prayers and tears of fifteen hundred years of pilgrims, should in time prove to be the true, real, and unquestionable site of the Holy Sepulchre of our Lord.

Returning into the city the traveller may walk along a very distinct, deep depression running the whole way across Jerusalem, from outside the Damascus Gate to the Gate of the Mogháribeh, and through that into the valley of Siloam: as elsewhere this is very much filled up with the accumulated soil, but it is still a broad and deep valley, into which the wet of even a single rainy day drains so much that it quickly becomes an almost impassable morass in some parts; the southern half of this valley contains a number of very interesting objects, besides its being itself the ancient Tyropæon mentioned by Josephus. From the extreme end the remains of the ancient Bridge and the Wailing-place of the Jews are seen; the latter, believed to be a portion of the ancient Temple Wall, is a sad and melancholy place, which no one, I think, can visit on a Friday without feeling that the sorrow of the Jews is real and unaffected; their lamentations are probably not only for their desolated Temple, but they pray here, as Catholics do at a particularly holy spot, bringing their private troubles or trials to "lay them before the Lord" with tears and sobs: many pass the entire morning, reading and reciting psalms and prayers, beneath the sacred stones, and, whatever may be the cause of their emotion, the effect is real enough.

Close to this is the lane leading to the very beautiful "Bab-el-Silsileh," the Gate of the Chain, into the Harâm: a lovely little fountain stands close to it, and in the fine old Hall of Justice at one side a handsomely carved sarcophagus may be seen, which was brought from the "Tomb of the Kings." Then comes another beautiful Arab fountain close to some ancient Baths, from which the Mooslims say there is a subterranean conduit connected with that under the "noble cave;" the Baths are now deserted and broken; a few steps further on is the old Cotton Bazaar, also deserted, and another pretty gate into the Harâm, said by an ancient tradition to be the "Beautiful Gate of the Temple." Fine old Saracenic arches enrich this long street at every step: at a third pretty fountain, spoilt by whitewash, a lane turns up to the so-called "Hospital of St. Helena," probably a confusion between the Empress and Sultana, the wife of the Sultan Selim, who erected it to serve as a khan for all pilgrims. The exterior of this building is beautiful of its kind, rich and yet simple, of the same style as the Mosque of Sultan Hassan at Cairo: within are numberless halls and chambers and terraces, with vaulted ceilings and marble columns, and here and there a pretty bit of carving; from the roof a fine view of the Harâm is obtained. Soup and bread are still given away from the original funds, though they have been much diminished by the Government: still very many are fed every day: we tasted the soup when cooking in an enormous caldron, and thought it, as well as the bread, very good.

A branch of the valley of the Tyropæon is observable through the Jews' quarter to the end of the Bazaar, where it is for a few steps steep enough, but it soon stops, and all is level ground for a considerable distance within the Jaffa Gate: while the measurements taken at different times on reaching the actual rock beneath the Armenian Convent, the English Church, the Latin Patriarchate, the Casa Nuova, and some others, were all so nearly the same as to show that there is no great depth of soil accumulated here. It was probably this connecting neck which caused the northern hill to be called by many writers Zion, as well as the southern hill: William of Tyre says that "the City is built on two mountains divided by a moderately deep valley; the western mountain is called Zion, and the eastern, Moriah. On the mountain of Zion is the Church of the Holy Sepulchre, standing on its eastern declivity."

Passing out of the Jaffa Gate one turns to admire the fine massive construction of the ancient Tower of Hippicus, the long slopes of masonry in the fosse below, and the large bevelled stones of the walls, with odd holes left in many of them, nicely though roughly squared, probably made by the instruments used for quarrying or carrying the stones. They look like the holes for supporting the scaffolding, which are left in the walls of even the best finished buildings in Spain, to the great astonishment of the traveller. The Damascus Gate, called Bâb-el-Amud, or column, because it has two small columns at the inner side, is interesting from the two very ancient chambers adjoining it; these, as well as an external piece in the gateway, all have massive,

bevelled stones, some of which are identical with those at the
south-east angle of the Harâm, and some with the masonry of the
Herodian period; indeed this spot is remarkably interesting as
showing the style of four several periods—the wide bevel of the
most ancient Solomonic or Phœnician—the narrow bevel of the
time of Herod—the unbevelled stone of the Romans,—and the arch
above of the Arab. The castellations and battlements of this gate
are so quaint as to be quite ludicrous.* The Gate of St. Stephen
is not particularly handsome; it is called by the Mooslims " Bab-es-
Sitt Mariam," the Gate of the Lady Mary, as that leading to the
Tomb of the Blessed Virgin. This gate is ornamented with
medallions of two funny-looking lions, whose origin is accounted
for by this fable: Sultan Suleimân the Magnificent, while contemplating the sacking of the city, had a dream, in which he saw two
lions on the point of springing at him, with the intention of
tearing him to pieces, whereat the good Sultan was so much
alarmed that he cried out for help, and on being awakened
related his dream. One of his attendants wisely explained to him
that this was a heavenly message intended to prevent his destroying a city rendered sacred by the presence of so many of the
Prophets and of the Lord Issa; whereupon Suleimân renounced
his project, and instead of ruining the Holy City, surrounded it
with a new wall (the present one), and had these lions sculptured
upon one of the gates in commemoration of his dream. So runs
the Arab legend: while exact likenesses of the lions may be seen
on several coins of the Seljukian Sultans.

The Zion Gate is the most ornamented of all, of course entirely
in the Saracenic style: it has several of the pretty medallions
formed of those delicate and elegant intricacies which are one of
the great characteristics of this style, and all of which M. Salzmann
ingeniously finds have been taken from various sections of the
Arab's favourite fruit, the water-melon. The double triangle,
which is seen everywhere, has, however, a more ancient origin than
anything purely Saracenic: it is believed throughout the East to
have been the signet seal of Solomon, and is therefore dear to the
Jews: it is also commonly called the Shield of David. It was a
cabalistic sign, as well as the usual symbol of recognition in the
secret language of the Pythagoreans, and is said to have been the

* While writing the above, news has reached me of the discovery of an
ancient gate of Herodian work, encased in the Saracenic work of Sultan
Suleimân's wall, close to the Damascus Gate which is said to envelop it in all
its parts. The details of this and some other interesting discoveries made by
Signor Pierotti will be given to the public before long.

2 c

sign among the ancient Indians expressing the trinity of fire, water, and air, or spirit.

Outside this gate is the reputed, and probably the real, Tomb of David, into the chamber of which not even the Pasha is allowed to penetrate. The old Sheikh of the mosque politely allowed us to see the imitation room above the real tomb, and then showed us the so-called Cenaculum, a very pretty old Latin church, with fine vaultings and pointed arch windows, with the billet moulding common in all the buildings of the time of the Latin kings of Jerusalem; the columns with handsome and fanciful capitals, one of pelicans, another of vine-leaves, another of fruit, but all sadly disfigured with whitewash. The tradition respecting this site, that it was that of the upper chamber of the Last Supper, is as old as the fourth century.

One of the most interesting of all the ancient places about Jerusalem is the great sepulchre called the " Tomb of the Kings," about half a mile, or rather more, to the north of the Damascus Gate: a large square has been excavated from the rock, forming a court (now sadly filled up) in front of the entrance, the sculpture of which, although not apparently of a very early date, was till lately an object of much interest and beauty, when an American knocked the greater part of it down, in order to take a few bits to his own country. (What a pity it is that there is no law for inflicting similar injuries on the persons of such depredators!) The maiden-hair fern and some shrubs have done their best to re-ornament the excavation, but the two columns supporting the rich frieze, and nearly all its ancient beauty, are gone. The tomb was closed by a most curiously-fitted stone door, which could only be opened by means of a lever removing it along a grooved passage, and was secured in its place by another slab, also sliding in a groove, placed at right angles to the door: the whole arrangement was carefully concealed by a huge flag-stone. Besides the ante-chamber there are five other chambers branching off, containing fifty or sixty receptacles for bodies. Some marble sarcophagi have been found within these tombs, all of them richly carved with wreaths of flowers, and therefore probably not very ancient: one of these may be seen in Paris, another I have mentioned before, and broken portions of others lie about. Dr. Robinson identifies this tomb with that of Queen Helena of Adiabene on account of the description by Pausanias of the miraculous opening of the door on the same day and hour annually: but the authenticity of the story is doubted by many scholars, and might apply with equal force to any other tomb in the place to which some concealed bolt had been attached.

There are many reasons both for and against the identification, and it is much to be hoped that learned men will not rest satisfied with any one idea merely because Dr. Robinson has uttered it. The mind of the honest inquirer in Jerusalem is half wearied and half provoked at the continual answer now given to everything, viz. that as the champion of Protestantism has settled such and such a question, there is no further need for discussion, especially if the reason given for such a decision happens to be unsatisfactory to his mind.

Many other very handsome tombs, of apparently more ancient date, lie dotted over this low valley, the first beginning of the slope of the Valley of Jehoshaphat; they are all without the faintest trace of inscription of any kind, and it is much to be feared that nothing certain will ever be known about them. One is a large grotto cut out of the living rock in a very pretty corner of the vale, its roof, till lately, supported by two massive square columns, with a side gallery, and a pulpit, or stand for the singers—for the excavation was once a Jewish synagogue. The Emperor Adrian permitted the Jews to return once a year, on the 9th day of the month Ab, to the Mount of Olives, to gaze on and to weep over the beloved and Holy City, and also allowed them to have a synagogue to the north of Jerusalem; and the Jews still come here to pray once a year in the month Sivan on the day of Pentecost: that is, they did so till a year ago, but since that the Austrian Consul has, with unpardonable Vandalism, chosen that particular spot as the quarry for the new hospice, as if the whole valley was not equally fit for the purpose, and has nearly destroyed the old synagogue; it is now almost filled up with the chippings of the stones, but is still picturesque with almond-trees and caper bending down over the opening.

The so-called "Tombs of the Judges" are further north; they have, here and there, a good deal of ornament, but it does not appear to be of a very ancient date: possibly they are the tombs of Asmonean kings and princes, and it is to be hoped that they will some day be much more uncovered; even as they are, they are very interesting. Scores of tombs are to be found throughout this valley excavated in its rocky sides; after which it opens up a little branch at the northern end of the Mount of Olives, all filled with olive-groves and patches of corn, the prettiest bit of country in the immediate neighbourhood of Jerusalem: the valley soon narrows into the deep ravine separating Bezetha and Mount Moriah from the Mount of Olives; at the foot of the latter is the so-called Tomb of the Sitt Mariam. This chapel is deeply sunk below the present level of the ground: but whether it is really a grotto excavated in the

rock, or that the ground has accumulated round it, and the long
steep steps descending to the chapel have been since added, is
doubtful. It is rather an impressive place in its darkness and
roughness, contrasting with the exquisite gold and silver lamps and
other ornaments which have been presented to the shrine. The
altar is divided by a low wooden screen down the middle: half is
Greek, the other half Armenian; the noise must be perfectly stunning when both are chanting with their usual energy doubled, in the
hope of drowning each other's voices. The Latins have three small
altars in the church, and the Mooslims a niche for prayer close to
the altar, in memory of the " Sitt Mariam, the mother of our Lord
Issa."

Very *triste* and mournful is this valley of the Kedron, especially
after mid-day, when all is in shade: steep paths wind like ribbons
over the sloping sides, and a few olives grow here and there
between them, under which violets and scarlet ranunculuses
blossom in the pleasant spring time, followed by quantities of
asphodels; two small bridges cross the bed of the torrent, in which
there is never any water, save a little stream after some days of
rain in the winter, nor does the water ever flow for more than a
day, or a day and a half: the word translated " brook " in the
Bible, properly means such a torrent-bed as this, so common in the
dry soil of Palestine. There is no site from whence the sadness of
Jerusalem is more impressive than from this spot: the sudden slope
on one side is crowned by the bare smooth wall of the Temple, even
at this distance plainly patched and time-worn, with the walled-up
gateway seeming strangely silent and lifeless: on the other side,
the white road and widely sprinkled olives and figs on the mountain slope are seldom enlivened with passers-by, though there is
something cheerful and encouraging in the group of smiling houses
and the little domed mosque that mark the (reputed) site of the
Ascension; while below, the eye rests lovingly on the little
enclosure of venerable olive-trees within the garden of Gethsemane.*
Those who cannot venture upon the pleasure of believing in the
truth of any reputed spot in Palestine, for fear it might be a
mistaken one, object that this group of trees is too near the
highway to have been the place of our Lord's retirement; but at
that time the whole hill-side was probably covered with wood, in
which but a few steps would be necessary to find solitude and some
sort of concealment, especially if, as is almost unquestionably the
case, a wall enclosed what is particularly described as a garden: and

* Gethsemane means the "Garden of the oil-press."

the expression used, that "He went forth . . . over the brook Kedron, where was a garden," seems to point to this bridge as the one nearest the city, and to some place directly at the other side of it. How many years this tradition has lasted I do not know; but one thing is evident—that there are no other olive-trees nearly so old in the whole neighbourhood of Jerusalem: and if some trees have been known to live for 1000 years, surely these carefully cherished and tended trees may well have borne the burden of eighteen hundred years. But at least, it would be strange indeed if their drooping forms and "color di mestizia" did not touch the heart with a deeper feeling here than in any other place where, if not the very spot where the blood of our Redeemer was shed for us, His holy Footsteps must have often and often passed on their mission of Love and Mercy. The monks have sadly disfigured the place with gaudy pictures, and utilised the ground into plots of impertinently gay flowers and fat cabbages; but one forgets these incongruities in the silence and sadness that reigns around, while sitting under the shadows of the venerable trees; and once while we went there holy strains filled the air, for the old Archbishop (sent on a special mission from Rome) was chanting a Litany of the Passion of our Lord, kneeling on the moist soil, with his silvery hair uncovered, in the midst of a band of French pilgrims, beneath a dark and cloudy sky, that seemed in unison with the sorrowful-looking trees, and with the sweet and solemn harmony.

About the centre of the short valley of the Kedron are the singular monuments to which the names of Absalom *, Jehoshaphat, and Zacharias have been given: they are most picturesque and fine excavations, all three being cut out of the living rock; and the mystery that hangs over their origin and date endows them with double interest. The strange mixture of Doric architecture and some other style less easy to name, with an air of Egypt through both, is thought to point to an Herodian age; in which case the "Tomb of the Kings" may be thought, from the strong resemblance between them, to be connected with that royal line of Idumeans. The "Tombs of the Prophets," as they are called, are also interesting from their unusual arrangement: they are excavated in the side of Mount Olivet, in long parallel lanes of concentric semicircles, with various other branches and small cells, a circular hall giving entrance to the whole; the opening is choked up with trees and shrubs, but it is

---

* The real tomb of Absalom was in "the king's dale," which, according to the Talmud, is the same place as "the valley of Shaveh," "the vale of Siddim," and "Succoth;" and is in the Ghor or valley of Jordan. (2 Sam. xviii. 18; Gen. xiv. 17, 3.)

worth visiting from its great extent and curiously theatrical form; the entrance is just opposite to the south-eastern angle of the Temple.

Descending the valley and following the bed of the Kedron, between the hill of Ophel and the strange, uncanny-looking village of Siloam, with its half-built, half-excavated houses, the little dell is arrived at where the Valley of Hinnom sweeps round from the west, and passing the south side of the double hill, falls into the Valley of Jehoshaphat. This is the spot where the ancient horrors were enacted by the idolatrous Israelites of offering their children to the gigantic brasen idol of Moloch, on whose burning hands these unhappy human sacrifices were laid: the "king," as his name signified, of idols, or rather of abominations, and the chief deity of the Amorites. On the eastern slope above Siloam, tradition says that Solomon's strange wives and women lived, and there he built altars for them each to worship the idols of their own country; the vile place, we are told, was "on the right hand," that is, the south, "of the Mount of Corruption"* or the Mount of Olives, the hill to the east of Jerusalem. A whole neighbourhood of horror and corruption this part must have been, for at the mouth of this Gehennam, or Valley of Hinnom, was "the potter's field, bought to bury strangers in," and called in the Aramean dialect of the day, "Hākl-dâm," the field of blood. The whole cliff face above it is pierced at every few feet with a multitude of rock-cut tombs: about 800 have been counted immediately about this spot: in one very peculiar-shaped tomb, to which the name of St. Onofrius has been given, there are seventy recesses for bodies; the under part was used as a cemetery for those who died of the plague some few years ago, and each inner place is still filled with bones and skulls and bits of clothing; the workmanship of the excavation is good of its kind and very simple, a well-cut cornice outside and some small pillars with rude capitals. Above this is a large ruin, half excavation, half building, originally a cistern, but since that a church dedicated to St. Bridget: from it there is a beautiful view, but a sad and funereal one. Wherever the eye can reach, far and near, above and below, one sees tombs—tombs—tombs everywhere; all the southern side and the bottom of Hinnom is lined with tombs†; on both sides of the Valley of Jehoshaphat, from its very first rise on the north, even from the foot of Scopus, into the dark ravine of the Kedron, the tombs lie as thick as the ears of wheat in the corn-field; under the very wall of the sacred Harâm they cluster in long rows; while on the plain to the

* 1 Kings xi. 7, 8; 2 Kings xxiii. 13.   † Jer. xix.

north, and on the plain to the west, they cover the ground with their white and melancholy faces. At the foot of the Mount of Olives the white stones form a complete pavement to the hill-side; many a poor Jew has laboured all his life, early and late, to gain enough to bring him to the beloved and Holy City, merely to lay his bones, a few days after, in the holy ground; for they believe that those who are laid in the sacred soil lie at rest in their graves, while all who are buried in strange countries must work their way underground to that Holy Land whence alone they can rise! Nor is this idea of the valley confined to the old Jews: the Mooslims also, and even the early Christians, had a strong belief that the awful Judgment of the Last Day will take place in this dark ravine: strange indeed it is how widely spread was this tradition. Solemn and mournful it is to see how these acres of graves mingle in every view of the city, and to think of how, like silent " watchmen set upon thy walls, O Jerusalem," the whole city is encompassed, enwreathed, as it were, with " an exceeding great army " of the dead; a City of the Dead it seems, for the dead are more numerous than the living. And looking at those gloomy valleys one cannot help thinking of the " great multitude which no man could number, of all nations, and kindreds, and people, and tongues," the Jew and the Mooslim, the Greek and the Armenian, the Syrian and the Egyptian, and the little band of the children of the West, all lying waiting, waiting for the opening of the Great Book, and the awakening of the heathen, —"multitudes, multitudes in the valley of decision," or judgment, where the corn shall be threshed from the chaff*,—waiting, for the day of the Lord, and for the glories of the New Jerusalem.

" If I forget thee, O Jerusalem, let my right hand forget her cunning. If I do not remember thee, let my tongue cleave to the roof of my mouth; yea, if I prefer not Jerusalem above my chief joy !"

* Joel iii. 14.

CHAPTER XXI.

FROM CHRISTMAS TO EASTER IN JERUSALEM.

WE had thus reached Jerusalem only two days before Christmas, when, through the kind introduction of a Roman Catholic friend, we received an invitation from the Latin Patriarch to attend the Christmas services at Bethlehem, which, delighted to be enabled to spend that; night on the real and long-hallowed spot, we gladly accepted, and accordingly mounted our horses on the afternoon of the 24th. We found the whole road from the Jaffa gate gay with crowds of pilgrims, on foot and on horseback, on donkey and mule-back, men, women and children, including Franks and dragomans of all countries hastening to the same goal. The wind was piercingly cold on the plain of Rephaim, and as we turned over the brow of the Mar Elyas hill, the rain came up in light, chilly showers: not enough, however, to damp the spirits of the Bethle-hemites, who were waiting in two parties, one of about fifty men, and the other of about one hundred, standing beside their horses, to receive the French Consul and conduct him into the town; he comes here this day in state, as representative of the Imperial Protector of the Holy Places and Christians of Syria. Very picturesque indeed they looked, with their gaily-tasselled horse trappings, the scarlet dresses, and white or yellow *kefiyehs*, which nearly all the Bethlehem people wear.

We alighted at the Convent, which appeared to be in the wildest and noisiest state of confusion with its hosts of guests, and were shown into a small dormitory, where we waited till the good brothers summoned us to supper—cabbage-soup, cold fish, and raisins. The service, which was held in the Latin Church of St. Catherine, commenced directly after, but we did not go into the church till nearly ten o'clock. It was crowded to excess with tightly-packed rows of peasant women in their white *eezars*, and men in bright-coloured *mash'lahs*: the gay *kefiyehs* were removed, and only white cotton caps remained. We were conducted to seats which had been provided for us near the altar, immediately behind the state chair of the French Consul: we were surprised at the reverence paid to him throughout the service; they were continually bringing him the cross or relics to kiss, censing him specially, and bowing to him repeatedly, whenever any of them crossed the chancel. The service was very grand and splendid: the Patriarch was re-attired six or seven times in exceedingly rich robes, his mitre sparkling with the very large jewels with which it was inlaid, all which accorded well with his superb face and figure, majestic, haughty, and proud, yet with a sweet smile, and a very intellectual countenance. He sang his part of the service beautifully and reverently; indeed the singing would have been altogether charming, had the music been less incongruous: but it wandered from opera to opera, and from overture to overture, until, just at the moment of the elevation of the Host, every solemn thought and feeling took flight as the organ struck up " Strida la vampa," and Patriarch and Priest seemed to melt away into the figures of Azucena and Manfredo, with the gipsy band around them! But we thought we had never seen a Romish service so reverently performed : in no one of the assistants, even among the small choir boys, was there an irreverent look or gesture, so unlike many of the Church ceremonies on the Continent; the secret of this we learned the next day, on visiting the Latin seminary, where they are all under the watchful eye and training of the Patriarch, and a most devout and serious-looking set of young men and boys they were. The Bethlehem peasants joined in the responses and hymns with energy and apparent earnestness; they are a rough, passionate set, and disturbances among themselves are very frequent, and often break out during these services: especially when strangers join them, and, consciously or unconsciously, give them offence, when a serious *émeute* sometimes ensues.

About 2 o'clock A.M. the wax Bambino, which had till then adorned the altar, was laid with great ceremony in the arms of the Patriarch: the procession moved slowly through the church to the chanting of hymns, and descended the narrow steps to the Grotto of the Nativity, where no one was admitted besides the clergy and the French Consul, but ourselves and two of our friends, and as it was, the Grotto was more than crammed. The Bambino was laid on the silver star, which is supposed to mark the holy spot, and was afterwards removed to the marble " manger:" the Gospel narrative was read aloud, a few prayers offered, and some hymns sung, and this part of the service was simple, intelligible, and really impressive ;

the rough cave and small space contrasting with the exquisite gold and silver lamps and crosses, the rich embroideries, the apparently devout faces of the assistants, and the sweet harmony of the chanting. The service was finished in the upper church about 3.30 A.M. We went back to the dark dormitory, and waited more than an hour in silence, thinking over the service which had certainly been, on the whole, fine, and in some ways, striking; but how completely the whole scene vanished—like a cloud of its own incense—from my mind in the hours that followed!

While our companions were attending another mass, we mounted our horses and rode slowly out of Bethlehem; the night was so bright and clear that the sky was more blue than black, and after the exciting, sleepless night, and the noise and bustle in the Convent, the calm silence and fresh air was most soothing and delightful. Then, away from all human interventions and interruptions, one felt really alone with God and the great Past; all the intermediate centuries seemed to fade away into a further distance than the mere time in the face of unchanged and unchangeable Nature, and the chords of all that is dearest to a Christian's heart seemed to ring as if touched by a living finger; the "bright procession" of the stars shone brilliantly in the clear heaven, over these wild and lonely mountains—the very same where, eighteen hundred years ago, on this very winter night, "shepherds were abiding in the field, keeping watch over their flocks by night,"—like that boy whom I hear singing to his sheep in the valley below, and doubtless watching with deep attention those same stars, among whom a new and sacred meteor had appeared to guide the sages of the East to this very spot. There, on that silent hill-side, they stood when "the glory of the Lord shone round about them," and the "multitude of the heavenly host sang, Glory to God in the highest": and the poor shepherds were no longer afraid, for they knew that these were indeed "tidings of great joy," and their hearts told them that now God was beginning to "comfort Zion," and to make her wilderness and her desert like a garden: that joy, and gladness, and thanksgiving, and the voice of melody would sound there, for that the "Redeemer was come to Zion," and the everlasting light was shining through the darkness around them.

Already, as we skirted along the hill-side, the light of morning was breaking in blue, misty haze, when, with all the suddenness of an Eastern sunrise, in a moment up shot the bright rays from behind the dark wall of the Moab mountains, straight and stern barrier though it seemed to be, and spread in one lightning glance over the whole country; the night was gone, the beautiful stars had vanished back into heaven, and the sunlight in vast tides of brightness had come in—

> " In its sumptuous splendour and solemn repose,
> The supreme revelation of light :"

it lit up the hill-tops, and brightened the terraces and the little meadows, while all the distant mountains of the Dead Sea deepened into hues of blood-red and deep purple. Then I looked back to Bethlehem, white and radiant like a pearl of great price, as the bright beams shone on the convent walls where many hearts were then bowed in prayer: the vines and the corn around it soon lightened up in yellow sheen, and I thought of Ruth, the gentle, brave-hearted girl, and half fancied I saw her following after the broken-spirited Naomi, as she turned back to the home of her child-hood: I seemed to see her threading the oak woods of Moab, de-scending those steep and rocky mountains yonder, crossing the rushing river and the wide, hot plain of Jericho, cheering and supporting her mother-in-law across the barren, desert hills and vales of Judea with firm but tender words: herself strong in the unselfish, earnest purpose of her heart, until the instinct of her guileless purity had led her to her kinsman Boaz, and she went singing through the golden corn with her heart full of the glad promise within her. I thought of David, the beloved of God, chant-ing on those breezy hills his own sweet hymns and psalms, which not only Judah and Israel, but all Christendom, as long as the world shall last, will sing with him in hallelujahs of glad praise; and of her, another meek and guileless Virgin yet more pure and more lovely than even Ruth of old, who arose and went rejoicing in God her Saviour into the hill-country of Judea, and bare a Babe in the little Bethlehem-the-fertile, the city of Ruth and David, by whom she and all the whole world shall be blessed.

And so we went up by Solomon's aqueduct and the rich groves of Beit Jâla, while the light broadened on the mountain tops all round : and when we mounted the steep, rocky path to the Convent of Elijah, Zion, the blessed and the beautiful, burst upon our eyes, lifted up on the " glorious holy mountain between the seas." The western wall lay all in dark shadow, but the south wall glowed like bright metal in the golden light, which touched the domes and minarets; there the fair thing stood, bathed in splendour: all the rocky country, and the desert hills, and the dark mountains of the Dead Sea, all in deep shadow, and only these two cities of Jerusalem and Bethlehem, with the little plain of Rephaim at our feet, shining in the newborn light of day. And it seemed to me as if the very trees around me sang, Behold "the tender mercy of our GOD, whereby the day-spring from on high hath visited us, to give knowledge of salvation unto His people for the remission of their sins—to give light to them that sit in darkness and in the shadow of death, and to guide our feet into the way of peace"—"for thy light is come, and the glory of the Lord is risen upon thee."

That scene—a type, as it were, of all the Christian's hope, assured to him by the blessed event of this day—was one moment in a thousand never to be forgotten: the light of it was still shining round one's heart, when, three hours after, we joined, with all the little community in Jerusalem, in the service of that glad Christmas morning in the Hebrew and English Church on Mount Zion.

A few days later, we spent a pleasant afternoon with the Latin Patriarch, Monsignore Valerga,* at his palace at Beit Jâla, to which he had kindly invited us. Here he watches over a seminary, chiefly of Arabs, preparing for the priesthood. His career has been more than usually interesting from the adventures he met with as an intrepid missionary among the wild Kurds, by whom he was twice taken prisoner in the Desert, receiving some severe lance wounds, and a bullet in the neck which could never be extracted. He reads Hebrew as well as Arabic, and speaks some of the dialects of the latter; and he showed us a genealogical tree he was compiling from some old Arabic histories, alleged to have been written before the time of Muhammad, giving many of the names mentioned in early Scripture history, from which he was trying to trace out the origin of the great Bedoueen tribes. Some of these names are, according to his view, identical with those of the descendants of Esau —as, for instance, the two greatest of all the tribes, the Shammah (Gen. xxxvi. 17) and the Anazeh (verses 20 and 29)—*zeh* or *zie* signifying *tribe* throughout Western Asia. He appeared to be a well-read man on other subjects, though perhaps most conversant at present with the questions regarding the policy of Rome, embodying in himself all the magnificence of the thrice-holy Throne he so triumphantly upholds in Jerusalem. He was so kind as to take us over the seminary, which appears to be well organised: a very simple building, but airy and comfortable; and we heard that the education which the students receive is both substantial and extensive. We were present at the evening prayers in the chapel, which were reverently and well sung by the students, and we were much pleased with the intelligent brightness of their countenances.

* He died in 1872. I have quoted his theory without wishing to commit my readers to its truth, as it is more than doubtful whether any authentic Arabic histories of an earlier date than Mohammed are extant, or even ever existed.

The chapel, which is pretty within, is ugly enough without; it occupies the centre of the group of buildings which are surrounded with gardens, wherein cherries were being cultivated for the first time in Palestine. The land was not obtained without a very fierce struggle, in which the Patriarch acted with the firmness and adroitness of a practised diplomatist, and finally obtained all he wanted. During our stay in Jerusalem he allowed us to pay him many visits, and we always found him kind and friendly; to us he never showed any of the stiffness and pretension of which he is accused; his conversation was invariably that of a man enlightened and without bigotry, and he was far more ready to promote and encourage discussion on the authenticity of the "holy places" than many of the Protestants who have set up a Pope for themselves, and would impose his infallibility on every one else.

The Patriarch has established large and flourishing schools, of which we heard an excellent report: and also a sisterhood, *les Sœurs de Saint Joseph,* for attending the sick and poor at their own houses; they have a large field for work, and seemed to be doing well.

On the last day of the year we went, by the Patriarch's invitation, to see the ceremony of investing a French gentleman with the Order of the Knighthood of the Holy Sepulchre: but the ceremony was wholly unimposing, and its uses and duties are now merely nominal. A short address was made to the candidate in Latin, and the Creed repeated, during which the Sword and Spurs of Godefroi de Bouillon were fastened upon the newly-made knight.* We went into the Sacristy, the first day we saw the Holy Sepulchre, to examine these relics; and I thought the old Franciscan monk who showed them would have embraced us both, he fell into such an ecstasy of joy and respect, when he heard that we were ourselves descendants of that great and noble warrior king, the flower of all chivalry: he who refused to wear the crown he had justly earned in the city where his Saviour had worn a Crown of Thorns. Alas! after having, as in duty bound, devoutly kissed the relics belonging to our illustrious ancestor, the Patriarch assured us that there was no authority for believing them to be the real sword and spurs of

* The investiture of this Order of Knighthood is now but a compliment, or a gift, I believe, in return for a certain sum of money: the new Chevalier informed us that he had undergone no fasting or preparation of any kind, and undertook no special duties even in behalf of the Holy Sepulchre. Yet one must hope that, like the words which the sentinels of the Crusaders' armies in the Holy Land had to cry aloud every quarter of an hour through the night, even the Knights of the nineteenth century would at least in the depths of their hearts "Remember the Holy Sepulchre!" which, even in olden days, was hardly in a state more disgraceful to Christendom than it is at present.

the Conqueror of Jerusalem, as they are of a much more modern construction, and that Chateaubriand had been the first to discover their claim; indeed it must be acknowledged that they are strangely small, and the sword must have been a most insufficient weapon for a warrior who could cleave a camel in two at one blow.

There are many noble memories, and sad ones too, connected with the brief reigns of the Latin kings in Jerusalem; but one of the most touching has always appeared to me that the seven Christian kings, the successors of the noble Godfrey, used to be crowned at the altar in this little chapel: and then, solemnly and humbly ascending the steep steps of the rock on the other side, laid their earthly crowns on the altar of Calvary!

Up to the year 1808, the tombs of Godefroi de Bouillon and his brother Baldwin I. were to be seen at the entrance of the small chapel to the east of the great south door: they were modest structures, with penthouse roofs raised on four little columns of white marble, with the touching inscriptions known to all the world; while opposite the southern entrance were the tombs of their seven successors; but the spiteful Greeks took advantage of the terrible fire which in that year destroyed nearly all this part of the church to clear away every vestige of the tombs. It is said, however, that long before this, in the invasion of the ferocious Mongols in 1244, the bones of the heroes of the Western world had been already torn from their resting-place and scattered to the winds by the barbarians of the East.

We spent the 13th of January pleasantly enough in accompanying the English Consul and Mrs. Finn to pay the annual complimentary visits to the Greek, Syrian, and Armenian convents, as this was their New-Year's day. A narrow lane near the English Consulate divides the largest of the Greek convents from their Patriarchal Palace, the convent extending until it has enclosed the western end of the Church of the Holy Sepulchre, of which the Greeks have the largest share. We were received at first by one of the Bishops, and then by the Archbishop (the representative of the Patriarch, who lives at Constantinople) in a large corridor: a few good pictures of saints at one end, and a gigantic clock, was all the furniture it contained: this had been fitted up for the Grand Duke Constantine in the foregoing summer. From this we were conducted into the grand saloon, a well-furnished, handsome room, with green divans, on which we ranged ourselves in a row, a preliminary struggle having taken place as to which of the gentlemen should take the lowest seat: the contest ended in the old Archbishop clasping Mr. Finn round the waist with his fat arms, and depositing him in the seat of honour. Numerous compliments passed in Greek and Arabic, partly with the aid of an interpreter; while *shibouques*, curaçao, and sweetmeats were presented with the coffee by two deacons. All the ecclesiastics were dressed in full black cloth gowns edged with fur, and the black, saucepan-shaped, tight caps peculiar to the Greek Church. This old Archbishop is known generally by the name of the "Fire Bishop," as it is he who annually produces that astounding miracle for the edification of the mob assembled in the Holy Sepulchre. Two pretty little gazelles were playing about the room, and a little toy ship was tossing on some blue waves in the middle of the table; these occupied us during a not very entertaining visit, and, as we took leave, a jocose deacon performed a wonderful whistling of birds, ending with the yells of a hyena, "done to life," for the amusement of the visitors: it sounded rather odd in an archiepiscopal palace.

This convent is enormously rich; the chapel belonging to it contains some very old, and a few really good, pictures, with massive gold glories studded with jewels: two of them were found some years ago buried under the ruins of an old convent on the plain of Jericho at Beth-hogla, where they had long lain forgotten. In these Greek pictures only the face and hands of the subjects are seen; the rest of the figures are always covered with plates of gold or silver of rich beaten work. There is also a valuable library, containing some 2000 volumes, and 500 manuscripts, about 100 of which are Greek, written on vellum. We saw a noble copy of the Gospels in Greek, with golden initial letters and enriched with very tasteful and well-preserved illuminations: this was pronounced by Mr. Coxe* of the Bodleian Library, to be of the ninth century. But the most beautiful of all is a large copy of the Book of Job in Greek, the Scripture written in large characters with very long notes in smaller writing; with hundreds of curious portraits of poor Job enduring his various misfortunes, seated on a circular dunghill, his body "powdered," as the heralds say, with carefully painted sores, and brilliant sky-blue hair and beard contrasting with his otherwise melancholy appearance! he did indeed look as little like "the Morning-Star of Song" as possible! The illuminations are much spoiled, but they are most highly finished, illustrating the various wonders of Nature mentioned by Job and his friends; and which are doubtless explained in the Commentary. The book concludes with illustrations of the last chapter of Proverbs, displaying the "virtuous woman" at her various employments.

We then crossed the nice convent-garden, gay in summer with

* The old fathers were continually quoting "Howadji Coxe of England!"

peacocks and canaries, and after a short walk reached the convent, where Mar Gregorius*, the Patriarch of the Syrians, resides. He received us in the outer court, and seemed proud to show us the new buildings of his convent, a hospice for Syrian pilgrims ; the rooms are small and very plain, but neatly finished ; a not very common characteristic in this country. The good Patriarch is really an interesting person : he has but lately returned from India, where he went to collect money for the building of his hospice. A few years ago the Kurds committed such terrible depredations upon the scattered Christians and Nestorians of Diarbeka and the country around it, that pilgrims ceased entirely to come thence to Jerusalem, and the Syrian convent, which depends, like all the other convents, mostly on their alms and fees, was nearly ruined. In this emergency, the Patriarch thought of applying to the Christians of the primitive church on the coast of Malabar—the Christians of St. Thomas as they call themselves—and to them he actually went in person, relying on his own prestige as a Bishop coming from Jerusalem. The English Consul gave him letters to the authorities in the States under British protection, and the event proved that the hopes of the courageous old man were well founded. The Rajah of Travancore, a Christian Prince, received him with royal honours, turning out the soldiers and firing salutes of cannon ; and he afterwards assisted the Bishop to collect a very large sum of money in his territory. He showed us with great pride a roll of paper containing a sort of panoramic representation of his travels, and the procession in which he went to the church at Travancore, done by a native artist. There was the long boat, the head of the Patriarch appearing at the cabin window, with a deacon holding cross and crosier at each end, and the eight rowers, all done in fiery reds and yellows; followed by the same head appearing in a palanquin, in the midst of a long train of blacks carrying drums and some other wonderful musical instruments, and a great many brilliant umbrellas, one of which, made of straw, had greatly delighted the good Bishop. As a border, round the paper, were very Chinese representations of the houses and trees he had passed on the road, and of the ladies in each house lighting lamps to illuminate his passage : while groups of cannons, shaped like drums, were being everywhere fired by matches a deal bigger than themselves or the soldiers who held them. The good old man seemed immensely impressed with the wonderful riches of the country, and especially with the gaslights in the streets. He has a very interesting face, very fair, with soft, bright

* His baptismal name was Nour-ed-din—" the light of religion "—but it is customary to take another name on becoming a bishop.

eyes and a fine white beard; he wore a violet-coloured cloth gown over a red satin underdress, and a wonderful globe-shaped headdress covered with black crape, with a smaller black knob fixed in the top like a door handle. We afterwards learned that his extreme pale- ness was owing to the attentions of a would-be successor, who flavoured the Patriarch's soup one day with corrosive sublimate, from the effects of which he was, with the greatest difficulty, restored by the physician of the English Mission.

As a mark of great favour he then showed us a tiny copy, about two and a half inches square, of the Four Gospels, written very beautifully in Syriac; it was on parchment, each page bordered in lines of blue and gold; the first page illuminated simply but prettily, and the commencement of each paragraph written in red. He said it was known to be more than a thousand years old; so we begged one of the priests to read us the last chapter of the Gospel of St. Mark, which he did, translating it into Arabic, as we wished to see whether it contained the final seven verses in our version, said by Tischendorf to be modern interpolations: the Syriac was identical with our own. But Dr. Rosen, the learned Prussian Consul, told us that this Gospel, though certainly 1060 years old, was originally translated from the Greek, since written Syriac, as it is now, is not as old as the Christian era: his opinion was that without doubt these final verses were interpolations. The book was enclosed in a beautiful case of silver-gilt, embossed with figures, and closed with curious clasps.

The Patriarch then took us into the church, which they believe to be the very same as the house in which "Mary the mother of John whose surname was Mark" abode. The font in which she and Mark were baptized stands at one side of the church, plated over with silver, and just outside is the door in the wall, now built up, where St. Peter is said to have come knocking, to the alarm of Rhoda; the doorway is evidently of the time of the Crusaders. More interesting antiquities were a Byzantine picture of the blessed Virgin over the altar, said to have been painted by St. Luke himself; it is a very sweet and well-painted face, one of the very dark Madonnas frequently seen in the East; and some fine old copies of the Gospels and prayers in Syriac, with interlinings and headings in red.

In the street we soon after met a very brilliant procession of the Russian Bishop, Kyrillos, returning from the ceremony of laying the first stone of a new convent, church, and hospice, on a very large scale, outside the walls to the north of the city. The Russians have lately purchased much land in and about Jerusalem; indeed the Greek Church is obtaining vast acquisitions and influence in

2 D

the place, neither secretly nor silently. After the coarse, unintellectual, white-bearded faces of almost all the Oriental clergy, it was delightful to meet the figure which now presented itself, with a face sweet and pleasing enough anywhere, but which was rendered much more so by a singular and graceful costume. Young and very fair, with blue eyes, his intelligent and refined features beamed under a tall straight cap, round which a black scarf or veil was smoothly folded, the ends hanging down behind over a quantity of very long and glossy golden hair, flowing straight down over his shoulders: while the breast of a full, graceful robe of light purple satin was adorned with four or five jewelled stars and orders, the episcopal golden cross hanging from a gold chain over all. He carried a golden-headed staff, the finely-worked crosier being borne before him: and altogether, surrounded by a troop of grave, intellectual-looking ecclesiastics, and a host of Russian pilgrims, with his gentle manners and animated countenance, the Bishop made a picture more like dreams of olden times than anything one is likely to meet now-a-days—at least in any other city than Jerusalem. He is a man of much influence in the Russian world, being a great favourite in the Imperial family.

We went on next to the grand convent of the Armenians, which occupies, with its many buildings and gardens, a very large portion of the south-west corner of Jerusalem. A numerous retinue of priests, &c., were grouped round the Patriarch as he stood in the hall of reception; we had heard of the Armenian as the richest of all the communities in Syria, but we were not prepared for the noble gallery through which we passed into his *salon*; the gallery must be about 250 feet long, and is very lofty; it is well finished with marble pavements and coloured walls. The Patriarch seemed quite to enjoy the fun of receiving so many visitors at once; he is a jolly kind of old man, but with a coarse, heavy face, very unlike our Syrian friend, Mar Gregorius; we were told he is not a man of any learning, and is only interested in counting the riches of the convent, every *para* of which passes through his hands. A great variety of sweet-meats, and little cakes, besides the usual pipes and coffee, were handed round, and the room was perfumed with burning ambergris; and there was altogether more ceremony than with the other patriarchs. Mr. Finn told us that on a visit he had lately paid him during an illness, the Patriarch had received him in bed, attired in the same black robes and mitre-shaped cap of blue velvet that he now appeared in, tucked up under three or four thick and heavy cover-tures, though it was in the middle of summer: the old man, nevertheless, insisted on performing the usual ceremonies, struggling up on his knees and feet, under all the bedclothes, to make the proper number of bows and salaams!

The Babel of tongues which had amused us in the other visits was still greater here, for the Austrian Consul, a Venetian, and his wife, the Contessa Pizzamano, a Florentine, having joined us, added German and Italian to the Armenian, Turkish, Greek, Arabic, French, and English, in which the conversation had been previously carried on! One envies the Consular dragomans the ease with which they slip from one language to another, almost in the middle of a sentence, until they really seem to be speaking all the eight languages at once.

Of course the Patriarchs truckle to the Pasha of Jerusalem, upon whose free admission of the pilgrims nearly all their riches depend; on this subject we heard a characteristic story of the excellent Sooraya, the Pasha now governing Jerusalem. One day, in passing through the Bazaar, a fanatic Armenian pilgrim struck the Pasha and endeavoured to stab him: a European gentleman who was walking beside him, threw himself between them and warded off the blow: upon hearing of this the Armenian Patriarch came down into the street, and knelt down at the Pasha's feet, with servile gestures, entreating him to come into the convent. The Pasha turned away in disgust and refused, though he had really been on his road to him, and that evening he wrote a letter to the Patriarch expressing his strong opinion of the unbecomingness of a dignitary of the Church kneeling down at the feet of the secular authority. On the following evening he went to visit the Greek Patriarch; but he for some private reason, or rather intrigue of his own, did not particularly wish to see the Pasha; on entering the saloon, the attendants came to beg he would excuse the Patriarch as he was already in bed. The Pasha walked up to the unlighted candles on the table and put his finger on the wick—then turning to the attendants he said, "Tell the Patriarch that Sooraya Pasha desires to see him at the Serai at midnight,"—and he abruptly left the convent. Then he said to the gentleman who was with him, "I was disgusted at the Armenian Patriarch for kneeling to me yesterday evening, because I hate cringing and servility—but I hate a lie still more: those candles were still hot and soft, and were blown out as I came up the stairs: so the Patriarch will have to walk to my house in the night for his pains."

No one knows better than Sooraya Pasha what good manners are, or understands better the good breeding which marks a *gentleman*, whether his face is black or white, or his creed that of East or West. He is not fond of our countrymen, because unfortunately many of the specimens he has seen he has found rude, rough, and bearish; that is to say, paying no attention to those ordinary rules of good breeding which are at least due to his rank : but he thoroughly enjoys a conversation upon subjects of universal interest with an enlightened or well-educated European.   He speaks French well and with a good accent, but he considers it *" une langue d'amitié,"* and will only speak Turkish to his general visitors, when he receives them as Pasha of Jerusalem ; the language of his Government is the state language for state visits.   He is not fond of the European Consuls in his city : very naturally, for their chief and almost only intercourse with him is their application for the redress of wrongs committed against individuals under their protection ; and in Jerusalem they are inevitably, one and all, more or less mixed up with the small quarrels and questions of the place : each, of course, anxious to persuade the Pasha to see everything that takes place through the spectacles of the particular Government which he represents.   The Pasha is very earnestly anxious about the good of his own rule, and is very resolute to hear for himself, and, if possible, to see with his own eyes, all that happens ; he frequently perambulates the city at night in the dress of a Turkish merchant, with a single attendant, in the style of Haroun-al-Raschîd ; and sometimes makes discoveries which are very astonishing to those not in the secret.   He is himself a fine-looking handsome man, slow in manner and reserved in conversation like most of the Turks : but he is not to be surprised into a *gaucherie,* and is one of those men who always know what to do, and when to do it.

One little illustration of this I heard from an eyewitness : an English traveller (whose name I do not know) came to call on the Pasha. Either from ignorance or from that bull-headed, stupid passion that our countrymen indulge in of showing themselves superior to all the formalities and common courtesies of society, he appeared dressed in a rough shooting coat and high riding boots : the Pasha had risen to receive him, but the moment he saw this costume, he turned with dignity to the gentleman beside him and said, " Je dois me retirer," and instantly left the room.   He was indeed extremely annoyed at the disrespect, almost tantamount to insult, so rudely shown to him and to the Government he represents : but the only remark he made was, " Je croyais que c'était un monsieur qui désira me voir : mais je comprends maintenant que c'est un homme qui n'a jamais vu la bonne société."   If travellers do not choose to encumber themselves with dress clothes, they ought at least to be contented not to thrust themselves upon those whose station demands that respect and courtesy which all men of good breeding ought to be, and always are, willing to pay. It is, moreover, very incomprehensible why Englishmen should think it becoming to be offensively and systemati- cally rude to the Turks, while they really do manage to be decently respectful to the authorities of other countries, such as Austria, Greece, Naples, Spain, &c., whose Governments they despise, perhaps, equally with that of the Sultan.

After this digression we must return to the Armenians, whose very splendid church we visited next; it contains a shrine over the spot where St. James was beheaded, and the own particu- lar chair of that Apostle—a chair that was probably made by a French carpenter about three hundred years ago. The shrine is enclosed with doors of tortoise-shell, inlaid with mother-of-pearl, of very beautiful workmanship; the columns and walls are loaded with gilding and pictures, and the roof is hung with a profusion and confusion of ostrich eggs and silver lamps hung upon silver chains in festoons, which has a *bizarre* but very elegant effect. The mosaic pavement in the chancel was the best we had seen in the East : it is quite equal to that of St. Mark's at Venice, and is in better preser- vation. The most curious thing in the church is a large curtain occasionally drawn across the chancel, of very ancient and exqui- sitely fine embroidery; it is covered with portraits of saints, &c., and the whole genealogy and life of the Virgin illustrated in groups of figures. In the convent garden are some splendid pine-trees of an uncommon kind, branching and shady; a great delight to eyes accustomed to the treelessness of Judæa : a fine cypress is growing up in the very centre of each pine, tree struggling with tree for the mastery.

The Armenians were the first to introduce printing into Jerusalem, and they have now quite a fine printing-establishment in this convent; at the moment of our visit they were printing a "Guide- Book to the Holy City." They gave us as a specimen a paper prepared for the pilgrims, containing a few prayers, a receipt for a gift of money, and the picture of an angel holding the decapitated head of St. James, their patron saint, on a dish; there was a pretty ara- besque border round it of roses, the type of which we were surprised to see was engraved on mother-of-pearl and ivory.

The Armenian Patriarch had a fine engraving of our Queen and another of the Prince Consort in his *salon,* and more than one of the high dignitaries we saw that day inquired about Prince Alfred who had then lately visited the Holy City. It was, indeed, very plea- sant to hear how favourable an impression our Sailor-Prince had made wherever he went in Syria: how he charmed everyone with the sound information and bright intelligence which he inherits from

both his royal parents: how his unaffected boyishness won all
hearts, ready as it always was in an instant to change into the
demeanour of a Prince when the occasion required it: and of his
consideration for and attention to all around him in the midst of
his own merriment.   His visit called forth much kindness from the
European Consuls and some others in Jerusalem, who vied with
each other in.sending furniture and European comforts to the
English Consulate to prevent the difficulties and inconveniences that
must inevitably occur in such an unlooked-for event: even an old Turk
sent up a precious morsel of embroidery of gold and precious stones,
an heirloom in his family and a gift from Sultan Selim.   The Pasha
of Jerusalem sent horses to meet the Prince and his suite at Jaffa,
and for the Prince's own use he sent a horse which had been a gift
from a Turk of very high degree, and was considered priceless.   The
unhappy animal was covered with housings, loaded with gold of
nobody-knows-how-many-pounds' weight, and had, according to
the Turkish fashion, been fed up to its furthest limits—in
fact blown out with fat.   The day was intensely hot, with a
sirocco blowing: no one seemed to know that the Turks never
gallop their horses for more than a few. minutes at a time, and the
journey was in itself twelve long hours; all the horses, and indeed
the riders also, suffered very much, but on the following day the
Pasha's precious animal expired! a loss for which the gold-mounted
revolver, afterwards presented to him by the young Prince, must
have been considered by the Pasha as a poor consolation.   The
presents given by him, indeed, gave satisfaction to none of the
natives in Syria: they were really handsome as coming from the
young Sailor-Prince, travelling as such; but the people could not
be made to understand the difference between a Prince travelling in
state and *incog.* as it were.   Nor could they ever realise the fact of
his being *on service*; and therefore as the son of the great Queen of
England, and received as he was in Jerusalem with all the honours
due to Royalty, the presents appeared poor, and afforded an unfortunate contrast to the lavish profusion with which the Russian Grand-
Duke had thrown about his diamonds only a short time previously.

   A day or two after this we heard that there was to be a very
grand wedding of a Russian lady in the chapel of the Greek
Convent, and as the bridegroom was an Ionian gentleman, and therefore under the protection of the British Consul, whose presence
was necessary at the marriage, they were so kind as to send us an
invitation to the chapel, on hearing that we wished to see the
ceremony.   Unfortunately on the day appointed there was a
continual down-pour of rain, which in Jerusalem is not a very

convenient accompaniment to " going out." There are two sedan
chairs in the city, but both of them are private property; every lady
resident there has her own donkey, but there are none to hire, so that
if you choose to go out you must walk, and there are few things
much less agreeable than a nocturnal promenade by the light of a
lantern, picking one's steps along the filthy streets of an Eastern
town, disturbing the dogs and cats, with a shower-bath pouring
down over one's head. The inner chapel was only about twelve
feet square, and being filled with the bridal party we had to
uncloak and ungolosh in the muddy outer court before we could
mix with the gay dresses within: but as everybody was in the
same plight it did not much matter. The Metropolitan Bishop of
Petra officiated, assisted by various bishops and clergy, himself
handsomely robed as well as the bishops: the rest wore only the
every-day black gown, and observed no order. All of them
continued chatting among themselves, and laughing, scarcely in an
undertone, during the whole service: nobody seemed to know
exactly the right order of the service, and they kept correcting and
expostulating with and advising each other all the time: the
difficulty, we were told afterwards, was to decide which piece
should be in Russian and which in Greek; and they all laughed at
every mistake. After several prayers and some reading to which
no one seemed to attend, and at which no one knelt, the hands of
the bride and bridegroom were joined by the Bishop, who then
blessed two wreaths of coarse artificial flowers (answering to our
rings) touching the Gospels with each flower; then presenting one
to the bridegroom, he crossed him with it on the forehead,
shoulders, and chest, doing the same with the wreath of the bride,
and then again changing the wreaths and crossing his hands and
theirs: last of all he laid each wreath on his own head, where
it looked supremely ridiculous, the gay flowers on the snowy locks
with the satin ribbons streaming down. Then came a great many
prayers and blessings, no one kneeling: after which the Bishop of
Petra put himself out of the way in a little pew, and the other
bishops and priests, joining hand in hand with the bride and
bridegroom, walked or rather scuttled in a ring round and round
the altar, chanting a psalm, two gentlemen walking behind bride
and bridegroom, holding the wreaths above their heads; a ceremony that was remarkably undignified, for they all laughed the
whole time. Then the Patriarch took a common glass tumbler in
his hand, and administered the Holy Communion in a spoon to the
newly-married pair and to the Russian Consul, mumbling something out of a book, while all the priests laughed and chattered on,

and finally exploded in fits of laughter because the Bishop of Petra had tumbled down with the glass in his hand and broken it. The whole service was so entirely irreverent, and the attempts at chanting so ludicrous that we were quite glad when they all disappeared, the lights extinguished, and all hands had hurried away to the banquet : nor did we care to see another Russian wedding—though I would fain hope that the irreverence of this one was exceptional. The Greek ceremonies at Jerusalem are by far the least reverent or edifying of any, but the services of the Russian Church impressed us more than anything of the kind that we witnessed in the East.

The next ceremony at which we *assisted* was a very different scene : it is the custom among the Protestants living in Jerusalem to keep the anniversary of the arrival of Dr. Alexander, the first Anglican Bishop in Jerusalem, as a festival by attending morning service together in the Hebrew and English Church : they meet in the evening in the girls' schoolroom, the walls of which were prettily ornamented with palm branches and wreaths of passion-flower, with words formed of olive-leaves. The Bishop and Mrs. Gobat, kindly invited us to join them, and we gladly availed ourselves of the invitation. We found the assembly were chiefly of Europeans, with the addition of converts from the Spanish and German Jews : in a smaller room upstairs the Christian Arab congregation were feasted together, the men on one side, the women on the other ; the Bishop made them a short address in Arabic, to which they seemed most earnestly attentive : they were, of course, all in their native costumes. The medley of tongues in the room below was curious : one of the clergy addressed the meeting in Spanish, another in German, the Bishop having read a chapter in the Bible in English, while the singing of psalms and hallelujahs was in Hebrew,—the wild melody of the old chant was one of the sweetest I have ever heard ;—and German hymns were added at the end. For once the petty jealousies and narrow-minded bigotry of the small *cliques* that poison the Holy City and seem to set its very stones at enmity and evil-speaking one with another, appeared to have died away, and peace and Christian feeling reigned over all. There were other strangers besides ourselves, and some travellers from the New World of America, as well as the still newer of Australia : and one could almost believe the legend of the Greeks, in looking round, that Jerusalem is the " centre of the world."

There are schools provided by the three Mission Societies, for which funds are collected in England, all under the general super-vision of Bishop Gobat : a large but uncommonly ugly building, a perfect eyesore in the view, has been erected for the boys outside the city walls on the south-western brow of Mount Zion : it contains several airy rooms, capable of holding a great many more children than they have in the school at present : a garden is attached to it, leading into the quiet little English burying-ground (already beginning to be sown with one or more infants from every family of the European Protestants living there), in which some curious remains of ancient baths have been found. The girls have a school near the Hebrew and English church; and there is a very small infant school under the care of a young Russian, who was educated in the Bishop's school, which seemed to be getting on very well.

The Prussians have a very successful establishment of Deaconesses, which appeared to be doing good work, Pastor Fliedner having himself gone to Jerusalem at the special request of the late King of Prussia to commence the institution ; his niece is one of the sisters : they have a large building, under the care of five sisters, a beautifully clean, well-arranged house, including a girls' school, a dispensary, and a hospital where men and women of all or any creed are taken in, and seemed to be most kindly and well nursed. The sweet, cheerful faces of the sisters must in themselves do good to their patients : and their pretty blue dresses and neat caps are much to be preferred to the black costume of the Latin Sœurs de la Charité. Another institution, belonging to the Anglo-Prussian mission, is the House of Industry, where a number of boys and Jewish converts learn carpentering and shoemaking, and earn a good sum by the variety of pretty things they make of olive wood.

Besides these there is a school for Jewesses, which interested us very much : it was founded a few years ago by a Miss Cooper, who went to live at Jerusalem in order to devote herself to the improvement of poor Jewesses, her cherished purpose from her earliest years. Her income was *very* small, but by means of extraordinary self-denial and frugality, she contrived to house and feed one or two poor girls, spending the whole of every day, not devoted to them, in visiting the Jewesses in their miserable homes, helping them with her own hands, working for them, and teaching them to work for themselves : and though for several years she met with but little encouragement or assistance from others, the persevering earnest labours of this single-minded woman, working alone, in poverty and weak health, effected a real change in the idle, dirty, ignorant state in which she found the Jewesses of Jerusalem sunk. After some years had passed away, she received some small grants from the London societies, and was able greatly to enlarge the number of her boarders, several of whom she had the happiness to see comfortably and honestly settled. She had just succeeded in providing a good house for her little family of orphans when her worn-out frame sunk under a slight fever: she died a few days before we reached Jerusalem. Just before her death she had placed the school under the care of the Jews' Society, endowing it with all her little fortune; and delightful it was to see the bright happy faces of the orphan girls, and the large room filled with the strangely-dressed Jewesses, who came daily to work there for several hours. Some of them thus earned enough to keep their families from the state of beggary not unusual among the Jews of Jerusalem.

These institutions are all for the very poor: but Jerusalem stands most grievously in need of a thoroughly *good* school for children and youth of a higher class than these; every year the number of Europeans resident in the Holy City increases largely: a great many European shops are now open, and families are beginning to settle there; very few of these can afford to send their children away to Europe for education, or are inclined to do so, yet they earnestly crave the benefit of such teaching. Jewish converts, with the love of learning so remarkable among the Hebrews, are always most anxiously desirous to secure the practical and wholesome education unattainable among themselves: while a very large number of both Jews and Mooslims would thankfully entrust their children to a Christian school, rather than lose their only chance of improvement. The Greeks and Armenians have already commenced institutions of the kind, while the Latin Patriarch has, as we have seen, opened an establishment at Beit Jâla, where the thoroughly good education given has induced several members of other communions to join it, not, as they say, "to learn the religion," but for the sake of the grammar, geography, languages and arithmetic taught there. For girls, if their parents do not send them to the schools of the Latin Sisters, they must go without any tolerable education of any kind. The absolute necessity of distinguishing between class and class is more felt in the East than we can well imagine at home, and consequently the necessity of schools for a superior class is far more imperative there than in England.

An English college was opened in 1854, with a very few resident pupils and several day scholars; the education was of a more advanced nature, and was chiefly for young men intending to become missionaries; lectures were given on the fundamental principles and history of the Church of England, and a course of critical lectures on the Greek text of the New Testament were delivered by the Principal, which excited much interest among the residents in the city: in fact, the college answered well, and might have been the means of accomplishing much, but the excellent Principal was obliged to return to England, and funds enough could not be collected for obtaining another. It is difficult to overrate the importance of both a school and a college at Jerusalem, or the benefits that would arise from such an institution; like the Theological Seminary at Beit Jâla, it would form a nursery for those well-trained labourers in Christ's vineyard, the supply of whom from England has been so sadly small; it would serve also for those who, having been educated for the ministry in European schools, desire to perfect themselves in the languages of the countries to which their lives will be devoted: besides the advantage of studying Eastern manners and habits, and becoming themselves acclimatised before they begin to work in hot countries. In a city where Hebrew Greek, Turkish, Arabic, Amharic, Syriac, Hindoo, Russian, German, French, Spanish, Italian and English are daily spoken, there ought to be uncommon advantages of education for missionaries to the heathen nations around, besides the wild field of work among Jews, Mooslims, Druzes, Metouaalees, &c., in Syria itself. In fact it is impossible to say into how wide-spreading and valuable an institution such an establishment might grow: in the meantime, it is lamentable to see the children left untaught and untended from the want of a tolerably educated schoolmaster. How many young men there are in England who, having had the advantage of a grammar-school education, might devote themselves to this good work: there are plenty of families capable of and willing to pay a reasonable sum for good schooling, and if any one, with knowledge enough in himself to impart well and thoroughly such an education as our middle-class schools in England afford, holding the sound religious principles of the English Church, and with temper and self-respect enough to keep out of the miserable *cliques* and parties that disgrace the Holy City, would only go there and begin, he would succeed in supporting himself comfortably, and would, with God's blessing, confer a lasting and incalculable benefit on the Christian community of Jerusalem.

The "Maison des Filles de Zion" was instituted four years ago by M. Ratisbonne, a converted Jew of Paris, for the purposes of spreading conversion and education among his brethren: the difficulties, however, proved so much greater than was expected, from the intense aversion of the Jews to any approach to image worship, that the unoccupied sisters, finding nothing to do in their chosen line, opened a school for the daughters of the higher classes in Jerusalem, which, for lack of any other, is attended even by some of the children of Protestants. A small house was found for them, in which they made a nice little chapel, enriched with pretty gifts of pictures, &c., but lately money has been collected in France for building them a convent in the Via Dolorosa, close to the Serai, the residence of the Pasha; the building that the monks call the House of Pilate. The so-called Arch of the Ecce Homo here stretches across the road, and it was in digging the foundations of the new convent that a pavement of very large flag-stones was found, as well as the smaller side-arches which stamped it at once and indubitably as a Roman triumphal arch of a not very early date. The Latin monks at once seized on the pavement as the veritable *Gabbatha :* and what was their joy, when, a few days after, a hewn stone was discovered, about two feet long and one foot thick, bearing an inscription in some unknown and curious characters. At first the story went that they were Samaritan letters,—they were quite as like Chinese; but before long the true story was hit upon. A sister, who had the good of the Mission much at heart, and who suffered constantly from fever and ague, had for some time past had dreams: and, one night, the whole Passion of our Lord revealing itself to her, she beheld Pilate's wife sending him the message that he should "have nothing to do with that just man," written on a piece of stone which she at once recognised as the identical stone so lately discovered! the words in which this advice was conveyed being "Judex iniquitus," and signed "Claudia Procla!" Here was the whole truth miraculously revealed, and great was the rejoicing at this fresh proof, as they naïvely said, of how good "le bon Dieu" was to His people in Jerusalem in thus constantly assisting them to unravel every mystery. It was indeed, to say the least of it, a valuable illustration of the manners of that age, that a lady, desirous of sending such a message in all haste to her husband, should be obliged to have recourse to such a ponderous billet-doux : but *there* was the benefit of the miraculous assurance of what would otherwise have appeared strange. Not feeling perfectly satisfied with this sapient explanation, we obtained, through the kindness of the French Consul, a tracing of the inscription and sent it to Dr. Rosen, who saw immediately that it was Cufic of a late date, and translated it thus,—"The son of Obeid Allah, the son of Shem, the son of Muhammed," the last word being incomplete from the breaking off of the stone : it was probably an inscription stuck into a wall to announce the name and generation of the occupant of some tomb close at hand. And so ended the pious *trouvaille* of the Filles de Zion!

The English Consul, Mr. Finn, whose heart and soul are entirely devoted to the good of Jerusalem, and who is esteemed and respected by all who really know him, has established a library and a museum in connection with the Jerusalem Literary Society; both languish sadly for want of funds, and the antiquities of the latter are wholly undisplayed and concealed, from the want of a place in which to keep them; yet among them are many objects of great interest and value. Mr. Finn is naturally and justly anxious that Syria should not be entirely stripped of her own antiquities for the enrichment of cabinets in other countries, where one or two isolated objects convey little of the intelligence they bear when collected with many more of their kind. At least a specimen of every coin and curiosity should be left where they form links in the chain of the history of the past; but money is required to secure them, and hundreds of opportunities are annually lost for the want of a few piasters. Among the objects already collected are several very fine and perfect Osteophagi found in the Mount of Olives; one with a pent-house top and much ornament, mostly like wheels, on the sides; another with a double top, the under one flat, the upper one rounded: some curious ancient lamps in pottery and in bronze: two very beautiful, delicately-fine glass vases found at Tyre; and a splendid bronze helmet found on the other side of Jordan among the Mountains of Moab; the form is said to be Greek, and from the style of the figures, which stand in fine relief around it, it is judged to be of the time of Demetrius, B.C. 160. There are also some slabs from Nineveh, some fine specimens of ancient mosaic of different periods, and a few Hebrew and other coins.

In fact there is no place in the world where the interest and memorials of religion and of history harmonize to such an extent as in Jerusalem; and no place, surely, can be so delightful a residence as this, where it is impossible to walk a yard within or outside the city walls without coming to some fresh subject of interest; or where one can never raise one's eyes without beholding some place or view entwined in the deepest fibres of the Christian's heart. Without natural beauty, with many discomforts, and with a bad climate in winter, we yet found in a very short time that the city had taken such firm hold upon our affections that it was impossible to leave it; the longer we stayed, the more we loved it, and we lingered on from week to week till four whole months had passed away; till Christmas and Lent and Easter were over; till we could say with the " beloved " in the song, " lo, the winter is past, the rain is over and gone—the flowers appear on the earth, and the time of the singing of birds is come; " then we rose up, and sorrowfully went on our way.

1 believe it is impossible for any one to understand this who has not stayed there for some little time: the hurried traveller, rushing

through with only a week, or, as it very often happens, only three days at his disposal, has so much more to see than he can possibly manage, even physically, that he has little time for any real comprehension, and still less for any right feeling of such scenes.   Travellers mostly go there in the end of the spring, when Jerusalem is very hot, dusty, and continually oppressed with sirocco; they are disappointed with the want of natural beauty, and are at once tired out and unnerved with the many discomforts of the place, and with the vexatious feeling of trying to realise their old associations through the thick veil of ruin and superstition which has overlaid them. They are confused with the modern life and secular scenes, carried on under the shadow of those ancient names which they have been accustomed to consider all their lives as set apart for sacred things and thoughts; and a vague feeling of irritation arises unconsciously in the mind of each, wondering at his own coldness and undevotional feelings in that spot where he had expected, of all others, to feel impressed and hallowed: till at last, knowing that 'he has honestly tried to feel aright, he consoles himself with thinking the fault must be in the place, not in himself, and he goes away declaring it is " a dreadful place,"—" not fit to live in "—&c. &c. &c.

We had at first some comfortable apartments near the new Austrian Hospice, but which were situated at the very bottom of the Tyropæon Valley: and as I had taken the " Jerusalem fever," as it is called, immediately upon arriving, we became very anxious to get other lodgings.   After some time the English Consul kindly obtained for us the use of a charming house, at the moment untenanted, standing on very high ground near the Damascus Gate : the change was of great use to me, and the improvement in our position was most enjoyable; our windows commanding the whole of the Mount of Olives and Bezetha, the Mosques of Omar and El Aksa, and the Moab Mountains ever dyed in radiant colours in the background.

The climate itself would not be much in fault at Jerusalem during the winter if the houses were better arranged, but every house in the city, however small, is built over its own cistern; many have three or four, and even more, the whole supply of water for the consumption of each family in a year being contained in them. These cisterns are stone chambers, generally vaulted, into which the rains that fall on the flat terraces drain.   Then the walls and roof of every house are built of porous stone; they are very thick, and the rooms very low, and altogether they are as gloomy as they are damp and unhealthy : while the eternal expanse of white plaster everywhere, varied only with stains from the damp, is most depressing.   Moreover they are all so ill built, especially in the roofing, that, except the house of Dr. McGowan, which is built *à l'Anglaise*, the gallery at the Armenian convent was literally the only room we ever heard of in the city into which the rain did not enter. Of course ague is the inevitable consequence of sleeping in this damp atmosphere, and scarcely a creature escapes it in the winter: even infants of a week or two old take the disease, and many fall victims to it. Dr. Barclay told us he had never known Jerusalem in the winter without from two to three thousand cases in it under medical treatment. The most successful system of cure appeared to me to be that of taking plenty of food and quantities of wine; the long-kept drinking water is, I am sure, very provocative of the disease. I feel convinced also that much of the quarrels and hatreds between set and set of every communion arise from the unconquerable depression and lassitude caused by this miserable complaint, and which unfortunately is scarcely shaken off under the balmy skies of the early spring, before the sirocco begins to blow. This dreadful wind continues usually, in fits of three days at a time, from about the middle or end of April till July, and adds to the languor and lassitude which overcome both man and beast, an irritation of the nerves which extends to both mind and body; it appeared to me to be as severe and intolerable at Jerusalem as in Egypt. The south wind is only hot and drying: it is the east wind, blowing over the desert, which is so malignant, and which fills the air with a thick, fine dust that veils the view, darkens the sky, and penetrates everywhere. One day, February 8th, the air was so completely thickened as to assume almost the brown appearance of a London fog, and from our house we could not see even as far as the Mount of Olives. Some of the dust was collected, and on examination in the microscope, it proved to be the same kind of thing as had fallen three years before, when specimens were sent by Dr. Roth to the great Liebig; viz. a dust composed of very minute shells, unbroken, and not of these latitudes, but from the islands of the Indian Ocean, blown here in one of the great circular storms, about which we are daily gaining more information. It was curious that the dust, when placed in water, did not sink in the shape of sediment to the bottom of the vessel, as sand or long-dead shells would have done: but being still alive and full of air they remained floating on the water. We heard afterwards that this wind had reached to Malta, and carried some of the same shell-dust to that island.

We had seen two heavy showers of sleet in the early part of February, and once the snow had lain on the ground for about an hour; but very little had fallen in the time of the "early rain" (which is always in the month of November), and the people were much distressed for water. There were but nine days in January in which any had fallen, and there was much suffering in consequence; many of the poor Jews, who had no cisterns of their own, had to pay three piasters * for a skin holding about two quarts, since, when the cisterns are empty, all the water has to be fetched from below Siloam: on this account the " Dung Gate," which is always kept closed, was opened to give greater facility to the troops of donkeys who brought up the skins. Public prayers were offered repeatedly by Jews, Mooslims, and Christians for rain; the Jews also ordained a fast: but scarcely as much rain fell in February and March combined as had fallen in January—and by the end of March the " latter rain " is over. We had one storm of thunder and lightning and a great deal of south-west winds, called by the Arabs " the father of rain," but in this case he was not paternal, and had brought but little with him.

It is easy to understand the immense importance of rain to the inhabitants, and the wisdom of having provided the number of vast cisterns believed to exist beneath the Harâm : from whence all these are fed is still a mystery. The magnificent aqueduct from Solomon's Pools, which is supposed to have supplied the temples and poured a continual stream into the " noble cave " for its cleansing, has been allowed to get choked; yet there is water in many of the cisterns now; there is, therefore, some reason to suppose that another subterraneous passage will be found some day carrying water from a concealed fountain without the walls. Water may be heard at any time rushing by underneath the ground just outside the Damascus gate. The finest of all the reservoirs of the city is an enormous place, excavated wholly in the solid rock which rises only a few feet directly behind the eastern end of the Hóly Sepulchre : it is worth seeing, and is considered to be as old as the time of Helena; but, although her name has been attached to it, it does not probably owe its excavation to her : the water stored there was so low when we visited it that we descended upwards of twenty steps of the fine massive staircase before we reached it; and it was said that so many had never been uncovered before. It is close to the Convent of the Copts, in which there are several interesting fragments of early Byzantine architecture.

The fountain of the Virgin and that of Siloam both lie in the valley of the Kedron at the foot of Ophel; they are connected by an underground conduit, and, as we have said, with the " noble cave" beneath the Sacred Rock; the first is reached by a double flight of stairs within a cave, and is very picturesque from the figures of the

* A piaster is about equal to two-pence.

women always washing there : the pool of Siloam is an oblong basin, with some old shafts of columns stuck in the modern walls : it is pretty, but from being open to the sun does not give the same idea of refreshing coolness as its sister fountain. Below these is the Well of Nehemiah or En-rogel, called by the Arabs the Well of Job; it is arched over with large hewn stones of great antiquity, about which the weeds and flowers nestle luxuriantly. After two days of heavy rains that had taken place in February, this pool, which is 125 feet deep, became quite full, and numbers of people went down out of the city to bathe in it; they were disporting themselves very happily when suddenly the water fell, and down they all tumbled with it to the bottom! and there had to wait till ropes could be fetched to pull them out; probably some subterranean passage had been choked and was then suddenly relieved.

The streets of Jerusalem are less filled with beggars and repulsive objects than those of most Spanish and Italian towns; nearly all the horrors, in fact, are collected together at one gate, that of Zion, which one avoids as much as possible. These poor creatures are the lepers, for whom rows of huts are built just within the Wall of the City, in which they hide their wretchedness, except when begging in little groups of hideousness outside the Zion and the Jaffa Gates. We learned from a physician, who had paid a good deal of attention to the disease, that the suffering is not at all equal to what one would suppose it to be from its dreadful appearance; sensation becomes deadened as the malady proceeds, and the flesh to be eaten away has long before ceased to feel; at one time he had been sanguine as to the possibility of arresting the disease, but one system that he had tried after another having ultimately failed, he now, he said, believed it to be entirely incurable and unmitigable, but not contagious in the ordinary sense of the word: although probably one sleeping or living constantly with a leper, and breathing his breath, might become affected by it. The children of lepers he had frequently seen apparently sound and pure, but he was convinced that the soundness never continued long after they had reached the age of puberty. The Arabs all dread it as most strongly infectious, and any person in whom the disease shows itself is instantly chased from all communication or intercourse with his people; and sometimes leprosy declares itself in some family till then wholly untainted by it. He related some touching stories of mothers who had brought him their handsome fine-looking children, whose features were just beginning to show the taint, and of their agonised entreaties to him to cure them, and how he had, in consequence, consulted with medical men in every country on the subject—but all in vain.

2 E

There is also another set of these unhappy creatures near the Gate of St. Stephen, but they will probably be removed whenever the Emperor of the French really commences the restoration of the Church of St. Anne, of which the Sultan has lately made him a present. The church, which was built during the twelfth century, is in very bad order, and is indeed little more than a shell: the façade is good, with some nice work about the arches, which are ornamented with the pretty billet and book mouldings: inside it is poor and modern and much defaced, having been occupied latterly by an Arab school; the proportions, however, are very pleasing; and there is a fine apse at the east end. Beneath are the grottoes, entirely closed from both light and air, in which St. Joseph and St. Anne are said to have lived, and where the Virgin was born: the rock is much chipped, and the fragments are sold or given away in large quantities, as the possession of a morsel is believed to ensure good health to any young mother.

Of good architectural work, of about the twelfth and thirteenth centuries, there is indeed no lack in Jerusalem; the Holy Sepulchre exhibits a vast number of very beautiful details, beside those of St. Anne, the Hospital of the Knights, the Church of the Flagellation, and many others. Perhaps there is nothing more striking than the score of small but exquisitely worked capitals on the columns which surround the Arab-built Church of the Ascension on the summit of the Mount of Olives: the Empress Helena is said to have erected a handsome church here, but nothing remains of it, unless it be these fragments, which some have thought must have been copied or perhaps borrowed from a building of a yet more ancient date. Adjoining this church is a mosque with a picturesque minaret, from whence there is a glorious panorama over the Dead Sea, the intervening mountains and the Holy City. I must again repeat that, to be *enjoyed*, it should be seen in the autumn, not the spring.

An interesting visit may be made to the Convent of the Holy Cross, about three quarters of an hour's walk due west from the Jaffa Gate: the view as you suddenly descend upon the convent is pretty. The church is supposed by competent judges to be the oldest in Palestine, having been built before the Church of the Holy Sepulchre was completed by the Empress Helena. It was founded by the Georgians—the earliest Christians of the Greek or Anatolic rite in Palestine,—and the walls are covered with frescoes of their saints, each holding a scroll, containing probably his own name and history, written in old ecclesiastical Georgian. These frescoes are mostly as brilliant as they were fifteen centuries ago, and though many of the figures are too grotesque and rude to suit our modern eyes, they are all full of life, vigour, and expression. The most ludicrous are those of the earliest date, where all the saints have long thin spiderlike legs: St. Jerome has his lion, and St. Anthony a beard that reaches below his knees. On the other side the figures are interesting as examples of the ecclesiastical vestments worn at that period; the procession ends with the figure of a Georgian queen who gave the stone for the building, a model of which she holds in her hand. The church is seventy feet long, with nave and aisles divided by four square pillars, with strange battlemented capitals, frescoed all over; it has a small dome over the centre. The whole of the church is floored with a very fine mosaic, chiefly white, which is the most ancient: but in the middle there is an Arabesque pattern in black and red, of cocks and flowers in medallions, very spiritedly done: it has been cruelly mended with blue tiles in modern days. One part near the door is strangely stained, it is said, with the blood of the monks slain by Chosroes the Persian: the church was spared, however, when all others were destroyed, because he used it as barracks for his troops.

The convent has undergone many vicissitudes: it has just been restored by the Russians, and is both handsome and commodious: the young students, who were forty-six in number at the time of our visit, are said to receive a really good education, such as will fit them for profitable employment afterwards; it includes modern Greek, French and Italian, with arithmetic, geography, and drawing. The dormitories, class-rooms, &c., are all large, airy, and well, almost handsomely, built; there are apartments provided for the Greek Patriarch, but he always resides in Constantinople. The belfry is exceedingly pretty of its kind, which is the filigree confectioner's style of work common in Russian buildings. Some fine olive-groves and gardens are rapidly growing up round the convent.

A quarter of an hour's walk further on is the Church of the Visitation, where the faithful may be edified by a grand picture of the Virgin Mary attired in a cloth riding habit, with a hat and feathers, ascending the stairs of Elizabeth's house, Joseph giving her his arm with an air of great politeness, and Elizabeth receiving her with outstretched hand in splendid robes of the eighteenth-century cut!

One day, towards the end of March, we made an excursion with our kind friend M. de Barrère, the French Consul, to 'Ain Karim, supposed by the monks to be the "desert" frequented by John the Baptist: the village is situated in a little branch of a deep long glen, running from south-west to north-west, called Wady Beit

2 E 2

Hanina, and the views about it are very fine. The mountains are, as usual, very bare, rocky and dreary looking: but the bottom of the valley is filled with vineyards and fig-gardens, and olive-groves rise up the hill-sides, where a few little villages lie dotted about. This fertility probably gave rise to its name—*kerem* being the Hebrew for a vineyard or orchard. The path was very bad, but the ride was pretty, and the view on arriving at the brow of the mountain, looking down upon the little nook in which 'Ain Karim nestles, is very fine. There is a large Franciscan convent here, built from money collected in Spain, and inhabited by Spaniards only, where visitors generally stop: but we went on to a large house belonging to the First Dragoman of the French Consulate, who received his master with a salute of five or six muskets, and had the French ensign flying over the house, the windows of which command a view of the glen right up to Neby Samwel. Near this is a Grotto where the Virgin visited St. Elizabeth in her "country residence," over which the Crusaders built a church, now in ruins: in the village there is another Grotto, where St. John the Baptist is said to have been born, and over which a really fine church has been erected; it has a beautiful mosaic pavement, and quantities of pictures and marble sculptures: lamps are arranged over the holy spot as at Bethlehem, and an inscription in silver declares " Hic Præcursor Domini natus est."

The village was full of flowers, and seemed both gay and flourishing—a pleasant place to stay in: we did not leave it till late in the afternoon, and then, as we mounted the hill-side, and turned round to take a last look at the valley, we found the opposite mountains darkened over with shadow, and behind them, far away between two heights, lay the Mediterranean, glowing in the most wondrous way beneath the sinking sun, literally,

> " a leaf of gold
> Of Nature's Book, by Nature's God unrolled ;"——

it was soon hidden from us, but altogether it was a grand and beautiful scene, in spite of the barren, wild, featureless mountains all around us.

Another very pleasant ride we took was to Neby Samwel as it is called, the only mountain approaching to a peak, and the highest near Jerusalem: it lies at the north-west end of the same long glen, Wady Beit Hanina, but the valley here is neither as rich nor as smiling as at the end near 'Ain Karim ; it would be utterly dreary from its extreme stonyness, were it not carpeted, in the spring, with brilliant and lovely wild flowers, growing more thickly than the grass: even in the depths of winter large white and pink cyclamen and white crocuses are seen in every nook.

The village is small, but from being entirely built of ancient materials, large hewn stones, many of them bevelled, it looks better than it really is: many of the houses are partly excavated in the steep rock, at the summit of which stands the mosque, once a Latin church built by the Crusaders, but now much ruined. The minaret can still be ascended, and the view from it is very fine: not, however, equal to that from Tuleil-el-Foul. Jerusalem is just seen and Bethlehem may be guessed at; the Frank mountain, and all the various confused crossing ranges of mountains between Hebron and Jaffa, Jericho and Jerusalem: while to the north "Gibeah of Saul," "Ramah of Benjamin," Rimmon, Beeroth, and Gibeon are close at hand, stretching round to the west, where the plain of Philistia begins, on which Ramleh, Lydda, and Jaffa are distinctly seen.

Neby Samwel is supposed by Dr. Robinson to be the Mizpeh where the people elected and Samuel crowned Saul king over Israel. Two thousand years later, when the unfortunate but noble king of England, Cœur de Lion, had been forced by his companions into a treaty with Saladin, instead of conquering him by force of arms, he was led to this, "the Mountain of Delight," as the old Chronicler calls it, to see the Holy City; but the king, in the bitterness of his disappointment, covered his face with his shield and burst into a flood of manly tears: and although permitted by the gallant Saladin to enter those sacred walls as a guest, he turned away and refused to tread the holy ground to save which from the feet of the infidel he had in vain shed his own and his faithful soldiers' blood.

Long after, old Sir John Maundeville thus writes of this spot: "Two miles from Jerusalem is Mount Joy—a very fair and delicious place. There Samuel lies in a fair tomb, and it is called Mount Joy, because it gives joy to the hearts of pilgrims, for from that place men first see Jerusalem."

The arrival of the pilgrims, intending to assist at the Easter ceremonies in the Church of the Holy Sepulchre, began very early in the year to make a difference in the appearance of the city: those from Russia and her dependencies arrive at all seasons, but they become very numerous about the latter end of January, and in this year (1860) on account of Lent commencing in February, they were earlier even than usual: almost before one thought the Christmas holidays were over, the streets began to fill with the sleek, cunning features of the Armenians, the fair stolid faces and thick dresses of the Russians, the lank locks and high fur caps of the Circassians, the coarse, heavy, greasy garb of the Bulgarians, and the shivering, dark-faced Copts, while every variety of speech, from soft to hard, guttural to liquid, struck upon the ear in the various languages they spoke.* The Russian and French steamers are loaded with these hajji, who find shelter in the Holy City at the numerous Greek and other convents. Doubtless there are some who undertake this pilgrimage, partly at least, in hopes of gain, and as a pretext for soliciting alms, but vast numbers come purely from religious motives: who would not do the same, if they could implicitly believe, as these poor creatures do, that their eternal salvation is absolutely secured by the washing in the sacred river, the obtaining of the Holy Fire, and as a reward for the perils and dangers bravely incurred, the hardships and sufferings cheerfully borne of their long and very painful pilgrimage? Whatever may be said of the deplorable superstition under which they labour, their faith in the providence of God, and the intense earnestness of their piety, is as remarkable as it is exemplary: we were told of a thousand instances in which these poor creatures have sold all their little possessions to purchase the means of transport to the sacred goal; for their own support on the journey they provide little or nothing, trusting to the alms of the charitable; and one might almost envy them the perfect simplicity of faith and trust, with which they expect the Hand of God to be used almost visibly in *their* service, while they are doing so much in *His*—as they think. "The Lord will provide" is their simple answer to every anxiety; the same conviction has moulded many a lovely character in every clime and creed, and the same trustful faith has been answered by a blessing on many a noble institution.

What little money they can scrape together before starting is kept with the utmost care for the payment of the enormous fees extorted from them in the convents and for the indulgences to be purchased at the various shrines, all which they are assured are indispensable for the completion of their salvation: they frequently bring ornaments in gold and silver, or pieces of fine embroidery, with them to sell or barter in Jerusalem to obtain the requisite sums. When all is concluded, the title of hajj, the odour of sanctity exhaled from them, and above all the comfortable assurance of their

---

* These people are generally profoundly ignorant peasants, knowing nothing but what the Priest tells them: we heard that the Greek clergy in Syria always told them that the English are a people subject and tributary to Russia, like most of the provinces they come from—and that Russia allows us to send a few people to live in the East, but that very soon she will not permit us to do so any more!

being marked as pious pilgrims by the angels of death, are sufficient reward for all they have undergone.

In consequence of the variety of communions into which the Greek Church pilgrims are split, there are only two occasions on which we can see them all united together, not only in one spot, but actuated with one idea, and combining in one action : these are the Washing in the sacred Jordan, and the Descent of the Holy Fire in the Sepulchre. We determined to see both. Formerly all the pilgrims endeavoured to go down to the Jordan on the same day, the Monday in their Passion Week, and much inconvenience arose from the multitudes assembled there : but of late years the Pasha and the Superior of the Greek convents have combined to organise them into separate bodies of from 500 to 800 persons, each body marshalled in a great caravan ; these set out at the beginning of each week in Lent. We took the opportunity of the mid-Lent caravan, joining a large party formed at the French Consulate, with all our arrangements for the little trip made in common. As too close vicinity to the pilgrims is not agreeable, our tents were pitched at 'Ain-es-Sultân, and a very pretty encampment they made, with the flags of three or four nations flying above them. To avoid the annoyance of the caravan on the road, we had preceded them by a day, and we intended to do the same in returning : we had therefore a day in the plain of Jericho at our disposal, which we employed in visiting the various ruins to be seen there.

The first was the Greek convent of St. Jeronymas—the Kusr Hajla of the Arab—the Beth-hogla of Scripture : the ruin is mounted on a low hill, and shows that the convent must have been extensive and handsome. Its interest at present is in the variety of frescoes, still remaining in fresh and brilliant colours, on the walls of the chapel and some of the chambers : they are open to both rain and sun, yet there they remain, bright as ever ; four or five hundred years ago the monks who worshipped there passed away, and have been long forgotten : not a trace of their individual history remains : but alone in the wide and silent expanse these lifeless images endure, while the ghost of such a " grave Jeronomyte," as spoke to Monckton Milnes, in the Escurial, whispers

——" *these* were the *living* men,
And *we* the coloured shadows on the wall !"

The names of the pictured saints are still visible, and the representation of the symbols peculiar to each, and of their priestly dresses, is very Greek, and interesting to the archæologist.

We then made a *détour* to revisit the head of the Dead Sea, and both here and at 'Ain-es-Sultân were exceedingly struck with the change produced by the difference of the season from that at which we had formerly seen them. Instead of the glorious colouring and vivid green foliage in which we so much delighted, and the descriptions of which must, I fear, have wearied my readers, we found now only dust-coloured mountains, a thickened atmosphere, and a completely obscured distance; Hermon was invisible, and the southern end of the Dead Sea had faded into only a faint bank which fitly closed in the unlovely mountains around the heavy, leaden-coloured lake. On the plain the change was yet more apparent: the splendid orange tints which had then varied the band of green on the river banks had disappeared: and, what was much worse, only the green of the early crops smiled upon the ground; the lovely foliage, so peculiarly vivid of the nebbk, was altogether gone, and the trees looked nothing better than tangled masses of straggling thorns: the bright flowers and fruit of the smaller Sodom apple were few and far between, and the large leaves hung withered on the bushes: not a blossom of the agnuscastus was to be seen; nevertheless in their place, wherever the plain was cultivated, the crops were full of blue bells, ranunculuses, speedwell, violets, and campanulas, in bright and lovely luxuriance.

We gathered a great many of the Jericho roses* as we rode along; very ugly and unfloral they look: but they are curious things from their opening out in water, many hundred years after, in precisely the same dry freshness as on the day they were gathered: they are interesting too from the fact of their having been added to the blazon of so many of our oldest families, both in England and France, when the head of the house returned from pilgrimage or from a Crusading campaign.

We found the sun so oppressively hot that we were glad to take refuge in the ruins of another convent, close to the Jordan, dedicated to St. John the Baptist by the Latins: some massive buildings still remain, and we ensconced ourselves in a large vaulted hall, which we found cool and pleasant. This convent was built over that very remarkable cavern which, for about six hundred years, always contained seven virgins; when one of them was about to die, her next door neighbour excavated another cell beside her own, and no sooner had the sick one expired than her body was immured in her own cell, and on the same day another virgin, in the tenderest years of infancy, arrived to take possession of the newly-made cell. The seven virgins watched over the linen which had wrapped the dead Saviour in the tomb, and their ghosts

* Anastatica hierochuntina.

are supposed to haunt the convent ruins still. As we left it before nightfall, we did not, unfortunately, see any of them.

We rode back to our camp at sunset, passing on our way through the cavern of pilgrims arrived at Er Riha, where the motley company had just settled into their tents, some hundreds of which are pitched, for those who can afford to pay for a place in them, on the banks of the Kelt close beside the village: there were also about fifty green tents for the band of 200 Turkish soldiers who are sent down by each caravan. The arrival of the French Consul, with his kawasses, made some commotion among them: the officers all came forward to greet him, and the confusion was so great between the noise of the pilgrims, the soldiers, and the villagers, that we were very thankful our own encampment was pitched at so great a distance from them.

Our night was a short one, for we were on horseback before four o'clock the next morning and had to go some way across the plain in the darkness: our servants and the kawasses carried lanterns, lest any of the party should get entangled in the straggling branches of the nebbks with their terrible thorns: a necessary precaution, as our cavalcade consisted of about seventeen persons, and the path was often narrow. We were some way beyond Er Riha before the growing light showed us a long black line, winding like a snake over the plain: most curious it looked, and still more so when we were able to distinguish that this was the caravan. We were soon in the midst of them, but many had reached the river bank before we got there—and what a scene it was! For two or three hundred yards before the actual bank, the ground was thickly covered with men, women, and children, each standing beside his horse, mule, or donkey, in various stages of undressing; till leaving his heap of clothes on the grass, he rushed into the water. We made our way to a little rise among the trees which had been kept clear for us, whence we could look down at ease upon the struggling crowd: the Greek Bishop had just given his benediction to the people and to the water, and the mass had rushed in pell-mell, husbands and wives each with their party of sons and daughters, helping each other, for the head must be bathed three times in the name of the Holy Trinity before the body is immersed: every one crossing himself many times, and most of them repeating prayers aloud as they undressed, and a few praying while in the water. The gowns or shirts they each wore were carefully preserved to serve them as shrouds in their coffins, but almost every one had handkerchiefs or sheets, &c., to dip in the sacred stream and take home to their relatives and friends for the same purpose; most of them carried away branches of tamarisk, or poplar, or the long canes as memorials, making the caravan look quite green as it passed back. There was more bustle than solemnity about the whole affair: they had come, and gone, in little more than an hour's time, and the appearance was that of a people who had something to do and to get it done, rather than of being engaged in a religious rite. In the previous year the good Russian Bishop, Kyrillos, came down himself with the principal band, erected an altar under the trees and commenced mass at ten o'clock the evening before, and not an individual was allowed to enter the water before he had confessed and received absolution from the Bishop. This must have had an excellent effect on the pilgrims, and one can hardly fancy anything more impressive than the psalms and prayers rising among the trees beneath the open sky, and the rushing sound of the holy water chiming in with the beautiful chants of the Russian choir. The Bishop was much annoyed when he heard that no mass had been said for them, and he declared they should never go down again without himself or some one deputed by him, to give them a really religious service and to keep order, as he had done, dividing the men and women into separate bands. Two or three poor creatures who had come the whole distance on foot, died on the way back to Jerusalem, of sunstroke or fatigue, after the sudden cold bath; and one sick man who had been warned not to risk the chill, said he only wished for baptism, and death as soon as possible after it: his wish was fulfilled, for he died upon the river bank.

The caravan proceeded back to Jerusalem without stopping for an hour's rest, and we therefore remained through the heat of the day at 'Ain-es-Sultân, to let them pass: after this we found our ride home pleasant, and the coming in sight of the city under the rays of the full moon was very beautiful and striking. It was midnight when we entered the Damascus Gate.

A curious ceremony is still observed at the Holy Sepulchre, though few persons are now aware of its origin, which is however attested by an Arabic inscription near the entrance door. On the first Saturday in Lent, the Latin Patriarch, attired in very grand robes, and accompanied by the French Consul in uniform, walks in procession to the door of the church, which is closed just before he appears: his attendants knock: it is opened from within, and the procession enters, chanting the Te Deum in chorus, as a hymn of praise that the Christians have prevailed over the Mooslims, and have entered the holy place in triumph! The custom is said to date from the time of the Crusaders, and the right of entry to all pilgrims is thus celebrated still, in their behalf, by the Patriarch: he then visits every "station" in the church, chanting a Litany and a hymn appropriate to each; this is done frequently throughout the year, but on this day it is especially grand.

On the following Saturday, the Greeks and Armenians make the same procession (their Lent commencing seven days later than ours), but without the same hint of the closed door. It is curious to follow the gorgeous and grand procession of each communion, resplendent in gold and jewels and all manner of colours, passing to each shrine with all the *éclat* of a fresh scene on the theatre: the rush of the pilgrims belonging to each, crowding round them, and then the sudden ebb, as they hurry on to the next "station," and the half-hour of silence and solitude till another scene comes on the stage. We thought the Latins the best drilled, and the most civilised and reverential; the Greeks are very splendid, but noisy and irreverent; and the Armenians, though perhaps the most solemn of them all, make such a terrible screeching and yelling as quite to mar the effect. Their jewels are exceedingly fine.

On their first Sunday in Lent (our second) the Greeks and Armenians perambulate the Holy Sepulchre between lines of soldiers, precisely as they do on the Easter Eve, with the grand exception of the heaven-sent Fire: we had places provided for us in the Latin gallery as the processions took place at a much earlier hour than our own service. The Greeks, carrying about a dozen or more silken banners painted with representations of the life of our Saviour, proceeded three times round the Rotunda, each Bishop holding in his hand a jewelled cross and a small picture, which the pilgrims scuffled up to kiss, as well as the hands of most of the Bishops themselves: there were evidently favourites among them as the people crowded much more to some than to others. Nothing can be more splendid than the robes of the Greek Bishops: the gold and silver tissues for which Russia is so justly distinguished, and the silks of richest hues, embroidered in gold and loaded with jewels, cut in the forms one sees in ancient frescoes, each bearing its own symbolic meaning, form altogether a very grand picture. A great many of the Greeks are fine tall men (of various countries), with interesting and intelligent faces: the Russians are usually less so: their faces are fair, but their features are coarse, although the long, flowing, light hair combed back over the shoulders has always a peculiar and graceful effect. The Archbishop of Tabor, the chief officiator of the day, was a figure not easily to be overlooked as he walked along; very tall, and with a fine thoughtful face, his dark beard flowing down over the jewelled crosses on his breast, wearing a circular crown, enriched with emeralds and surmounted by a cross in rubies, while his superb robes, stiff with gold, swept behind him as he passed slowly by, with a huge pastoral staff in his hand.

The Armenian Bishops and Priests came round a quarter of an hour after, more slowly, and more solemnly, arrayed chiefly in green and gold, and red and gold, with their mitres and the astonishing black silk hoods which tower up from the forehead into a point—so singular, and yet not ungraceful in its way.

The service that pleased us almost more than any other in Jerusalem, and seemed to us the most solemn and impressive, was that of the Russians, conducted by Kyrillos (the Russian Bishop mentioned before) in a small church close to his own convent. The Liturgy generally used is that of St. John Chrysostom, but during Lent it is changed for that of St. Basil, of which the Bishop had kindly sent us a French translation on the previous evening. The whole service was performed in a reverent and untheatrical manner that was very delightful to witness. The Russian Bishop, shocked, as he well might be, at the horribly inharmonious screaming of the Greeks, has imported a choir from Russia: and in no country or church have I ever heard sweeter or more devotional singing than that of the seven men's voices, unaccompanied by any instrument, repeating a hundred times the "Kyrie eleison," and the "ameen" of the litany and prayers, between the beautiful anthems. The service is very fatiguing, for there are no seats in the church, nor do they ever sit on the floor: but the whole congregation stand throughout the two hours or more, only occasionally kneeling down, but making frequent genuflexions down to the very ground. The vestments were most magnificent, but it was pleasant to forget them, in the apparent earnestness and devotion all around; as, indeed, it was pleasant also to forget the fearful garlic of the Russians and Greeks in the clouds of sweet incense, which were, nevertheless, rather suffocating.

Some days after we inspected the ecclesiastical wardrobes of the Bishop, which he was so good as to have displayed for us during a visit we paid him at his convent: there were fifteen or sixteen sets of robes; in England we should scarcely know what to do with such stuff, since, besides its splendour, it is too thick and heavy for any one but a man to wear.

My readers would be dreadfully weary if I were to detail to them all the various ceremonies of the Holy Week, celebrated in the Church of the Holy Sepulchre: a few of the principal ones will suffice. Perhaps the *prettiest* of all was that of Palm Sunday, when a grand high mass is said before the Holy Sepulchre itself, after which the Patriarch pronounced a solemn benediction on scores of green palm-branches, which he then presented to the clergy and assistants, the French Consul, and others, one by one. We were surprised at his sending his secretary to us to say that he wished to give them to us also, as a mark of his regard, and we were glad to receive them not only for this, but as appropriate *souvenirs* of this day spent in Jerusalem. The palm-branches used on this occasion are all grown in a garden at Gaza, where one family of Christian Arabs have had for many generations the hereditary right to supply them.

The services on Good Friday were really impressive; we were at the door of the Holy Sepulchre before 6 A.M. and found it closed, as the service had commenced some time earlier; but the French Consul had left two kawasses to conduct us into the chapel of Calvary, where chairs had been provided for us beside his own. The chapel was almost entirely dark, and densely crowded; the vestments used by the priests were all of black velvet embroidered in silver. The Patriarch had given up his place to Monseigneur Spaccapietra, an old Archbishop, who had lately arrived on a special mission of inquiry from the Pope: a fine-hearted and enlightened old man. The service, which was most solemnly and reverentially conducted, consisted of the Gospel narrative of the Passion of our Lord, and the words of the Saviour, of the people and of Pilate, recited by different voices. The old Archbishop chanted the Scripture with much earnestness and simplicity—but he was in Jerusalem for the first time in his life, he was worn out with a severe attack of the fever and with fasting, he was standing on the very spot where, the tradition of his church told him, the Redeemer had suffered, and when he came to the portion describing the consummation of that awful Sacrifice, the gentle-hearted old man was so completely overcome, that he laid his head on the altar and sobbed aloud; and a thousand times more impressive than all the splendour of the services on the previous days was it to see the aged, silver-haired Archbishop realising the sacred and sorrowful story with such an intensity of earnestness as made the solemn words themselves come doubly home to the heart.

In the evening the church was so densely crowded that it required all the efforts of the six kawasses of the French Consul to get us to our places and to preserve us from utter suffocation: the people of Bethlehem come over in great numbers to attend the Franciscan service, which is given entirely for them; the Patriarch and all the superior clergy disapprove greatly of the sacred farce

into which it has degenerated.   Unfortunately the Franciscans and
the Patriarch are often at issue concerning the services, and it was
on this account that the Pope had sent Monseigneur Spaccapietra
to decide between them; both, however, agreed in denying the
power of the Pope over either of them on the subjects in dispute.
The service is performed by the Franciscan monks, and consists in
the taking of a figure of the Saviour down from the Cross, and removing each nail and the crown of thorns, with many kisses. After
this six or seven short sermons were preached in various parts of
the church, each in a different language, by monks appointed to
the task, who are at least supposed to have studied the language
they preach in; when we had heard the French sermon we did not
regret that the crowd prevented our getting near enough to hear
the others.   The last was preached in Spanish, before the Sepulchre,
which was dimly illuminated only with the torches and candles
carried in the procession, the whole of the Rotunda remaining in
darkness: it had a very fine effect.   This service was not over till
near midnight.

On the Saturday, Easter Eve, some curious ceremonies are
observed.   After the customary benediction of the baptismal water
for the year and the lighting of a new lamp, the priests assembled before the entrance of the Sepulchre; twelve or thirteen
chapters of the Gospels were read recounting the events of the
week, and when that part of the narrative was reached describing
the placing of our Lord in the Tomb, the Patriarch, dressed in a
plain white robe with a priest on each side of him in a white
surplice, laid themselves flat on the ground on their faces, before
the door of the Sepulchre.   Psalms and hymns were chanted for
about half an hour before they rose, and throughout the mass that
followed the two priests knelt on one knee at each side of the door
of the tomb, exactly as the angels are always represented in old
pictures of the Entombment.

The services of these days were dreadfully long, and the poor
little children of the French school fell asleep with their heads on
each other's shoulders, like rows of little scarlet ninepins, but else,
every person joining in them had the appearance of thoroughly
reverential devotion.   The good Patriarch is rigidly strict in his own
fasts, and by the afternoon of this Saturday he was so weak
that his voice was nearly inaudible and his face flushed with fever.

On the following Friday evening we went again to the Holy
Sepulchre to see the Good Friday ceremonies of the Greeks and
Armenians;   the Greeks of course take the precedence, but the
Armenians join themselves on at the latter end without much

confusion. As the French Consul did not wish to parade himself and his kawasses in the church this night, we were placed under the care of Signor Pierotti, who is so great a favourite with the Turkish authorities and with many of the Greeks, that everything was thus made easy for us. The church *belongs* to ten Turks, one or more of whom must be present on all the greater days of ceremony : there is also a guard of a few soldiers appointed by the Pasha, who are always to be seen sitting in a recess at the entrance; it is by their permission that any one enters. The officers and the Bimbashi (the chief of the battalion) were most polite and pressing in their attentions to us the moment they saw we were friends of Signor Pierotti's, and insisted on our taking their chairs to stand upon when the crowd became too dense for us to stem or to see through.

The ceremony began in the square before the door of the church, with a very long procession, from the convent, of the Greek Bishops and clergy joined by a number of Copts, chanting all the while they perambulated the little square lighted by the lanterns and torches they carried in their hands; then the Copts entered the little chapel which belongs to them on the north side of the square, in the south wall of the church, and the Greeks entering at the great door went into their own large chapel in the centre, under the second dome, which was most brilliantly illuminated with a circle of lamps round the lowest edge of the dome and a double cross across it, which showed well against the dark height above it. After a long service here the procession ascended to Calvary (which the Greeks share with the Latins). Both chapels were at once crowded to that degree of denseness that neither hand nor foot could move save those of the celebrants, and as every one held a lighted candle in his hand, the heat was suffocating, as indeed it had been almost to fainting, on the Good Friday night of the Latins. All the clergy wore splendid copes of black velvet richly embroidered with silver. After some prayers the Russian Bishop, Kyrillos, mounted one step of the altar, and, facing the people, addressed them in what appeared to us an unimpassioned almost monotonous manner, but it must have been effective, for, one after another, most of the Greeks around us were moved to tears. After this they descended to the 'Stone of unction," where an old and much respected Bishop again addressed the people— this time with much energy and warmth—to which they listened with earnest attention.

We then mounted into the gallery of the Latins which the French Consul had kindly engaged for us, and waited there till the procession came round: it was really very grand indeed: the Rotunda was brilliantly illuminated, and several rows of silver lamps and flowers were hung round the sepulchre itself in festoons; the Bishops appeared innumerable: among them the venerable Bishop of Petra and the Archbishop of Tabor with his long dark beard were striking objects. All were most splendidly attired in robes and copes of every hue covered with gold and silver embroidery, and all bore crosses or pictures of saints in their folded hands, which the pilgrims pressed forward to kiss: some of the Bishops had kawasses on each side of them, and as they went they chanted the Te Deum and some psalms with an earnest heartiness that seemed as if the procession was not all for show— there was no irreverence this day—each one looked grave and serious. Several ancient banners, said to be some of those used in the armies of the Crusaders, were carried round at the head of the procession; they represented scenes of the Passion, some of which were very well done in painting and embroidery; after them came a really interesting relic of olden times, the alleged history of which is believed to be correct: this was the banner of the Emperor Heraclius, which was borne before him when he entered Jerusalem bringing back the "true Cross;" this relic is considered too precious to be seen by any one except on this day, for all the rest of the year it is most carefully locked up; it was now borne by four Bishops, whose pious hands each held a corner, and had been placed on the altar of Calvary during the service; we could see that it was a most singular piece of embroidered work, representing the Saviour in his Tomb, with an inscription surrounding it as a border. The procession went round the Rotunda three times, and then a very short service was performed within the Sepulchre itself; it finished about 1 A.M. We walked round the church before going home to see the curious sight of the Greek pilgrims covering every available morsel of ground to secure places for the "Holy Fire" on the morrow; they had been in the church the whole of this day for the purpose, and now one and all, men and women, boys and girls, lay in heaps, like mere bundles of clothing, fast asleep, with here and there a foot or a leg sticking out from the heap. Great numbers of the Latin pilgrims also consider it a meritorious act to spend one night in the church: some few employ it in prayer and devotional exercises, but the greater part retire to the Latin gallery, where quantities of cushions are provided, and sleep away as comfortably as possible. The church is never left unguarded; a few Priests or monks of both communions are invariably there by night and by day.

The morrow—Saturday—was of course *the* day for the Greeks; and at a very early hour travellers are obliged to take their places in the church before the crowd becomes too dense or too uproarious for Franks to penetrate. But the full glory of that strange, wild scene of tumult, called the "Greek Holy Fire," has passed away; the ceremony is conducted with as much splendour and superstition as ever: but in the previous year, 1859, Sooraya Pasha, having witnessed the whole affair with his own eyes, was so much shocked and disgusted with the make-believe miracle, and with the disgraceful scenes which took place under the excitement of religious frenzy, that on this occasion be concerted plans with the French Consul, and lined the whole church with his soldiers, separating the pilgrims into such small bodies, and keeping such strict order among them, that neither enthusiasm nor confusion could break out into anything very frantic.

The Superior of the Greek convent had had the extreme politeness to place the whole of the upper gallery round the dome of the Holy Sepulchre at the service of the French Consul: the key was sent to him the day before, and a guard of soldiers waited to conduct us through the crowd in the large convent up to the rickety, dilapidated, half-ruined place it was, so that we were not obliged to go there more than an hour before the service commenced; chairs were already placed for us, and lemonade and coffee followed; the gallery was the most delightful place to see from, as we could thus walk round the whole building and see the crowd on every side. Very amusing indeed it was to watch the pilgrims being packed more and more densely into their places, after having struggled and fought to secure the nearest spot possible to the hole in the marble wall of the Sepulchre whence the Fire was to issue; the soldiers allowed them to struggle to a certain point, beyond that, when mischief seemed brewing, the combatants were separated and stopped. Every few minutes some man or group of men amongst them seemed trying to excite himself and his neighbours up to howl and yell and dance: sometimes they made short runs, in the wild manner described by former travellers, sometimes one man running with two others, or even three, standing on his shoulders: but their frenzy and excitement seemed *put on*, as if acted, and soon came to an end, the warmth of their religious feelings was damped or blighted by the presence of the Mooslims, and the flames of its fire in a manner quenched.

Not the least amusing part to me was the crowd of spectators in the lower gallery: such a motley company as they were: the venerable Roman Archbishop Monseigneur Spaccapietra and his

2 F

Maronite secretary, beside a number of noisy irreverent Americans, and two or three grave Presbyterians. Then came the French caravan, a score of gentlemen organised into a travelling party under the special protection of their Government, and therefore of course occupying the best places in the Latin gallery: next to them a young Austrian baron, keeping somewhat hidden behind a column lest some fanatic in the multitude might recognise him as one of the Jews who are forbidden to enter the building: he was safe enough where he was, but if a Jew were seen in the crowd he would most probably be torn in pieces. Close to him were the fair, quiet faces of the Comte de Paris and Duc du Chartres; and beyond them a number of young English gentlemen, one of whom, before long, got into a squabble with an unfortunate monk who had remonstrated against the overbearing insolence with which the Englishman, according to the custom of John Bull, had endeavoured to take the best place from one of the French caravan, and who so far forgot himself and the place he was in as to strike the Franciscan. The French Consul had much ado to soothe, scold, and appease the wounded feelings of the poor monk into forgiveness and forgetfulness of the insult, while we blushed for shame at the unseemly conduct of a countryman: but alas! such occurrences are but too common among those who would be the first to revenge any disturbance or irreverence shown by a foreigner in our churches at home, but who have the stupid folly of thinking they assert the dignity of their own religion by deliberately insulting those with whom they do not agree. Whatever they may believe or disbelieve themselves, it is simply disgusting to see an Englishman walking about the Church of the Holy Sepulchre with his hat on, or to hear loud voices profaning the sanctity of the place; and one grieves to think, however wanting they may be in sentiments of piety or religion, that they should not have learned either good taste or good feeling enough to keep away from places sanctified to others, unless they can refrain from such conduct as is not only unchristian and ungentlemanly, but indecent.*

* I once saw an American, when the Chapel of Calvary was full of devout pilgrims, deliberately lay Murray's Handbook open upon the altar, and, standing on the upper step, place both elbows beside his book, and in that position proceed to read aloud Mr. Porter's remarks upon the time-honoured spot! I saw the colour flush deep into the cheek of a Franciscan monk beside me, and a Greek turn away with a bitter scowl, and I could not help wishing to ask that man, however little reverence or devotion he might have in himself, if he had ever heard of that charity which "doth not behave itself unseemly," or of that "knowledge" which is "puffed up," while "charity edifieth," or if he thought he was practising the golden rule of doing to others as we should wish them to do to us.　　　　　　　[Having

The crowd had now become quite dense, and were so well packed that there could be no more striving to get near the wall of the Sepulchre, or to displace the three happy men—wild, insane-looking creatures they were—who had had their hands clenched in the sacred hole for several hours: cries were continually being raised, and the same words constantly repeated with a sort of scream; of course we supposed these to be, as they have frequently been reported by travellers, expostulations with, and reproaches to the Almighty for delaying to send down the Fire, but previous experience of Latin misrepresentation of all Greek doings made us inquire from a Greek gentleman on whom we could depend the meaning of each cry as it arose; it turned out that the exclamations were " This is the house of God—this is the tomb of the Saviour—this is the day on which He rose from the dead—let us raise up our hearts unto new life;" and then they all beat their breasts; then another cry came still more frequently, " Life was dead—was buried in the grave—now is new life come to us from the tomb—let us live unto God—life and light are come to us;" again and again repeated. Sometimes the words were in Russian, sometimes in Greek, but the sense was the same. They were repeated louder and louder, quicker and quicker, and the excitement became greater, those on

---

Having said thus much, I feel in duty bound to relate an anecdote of an Englishman: he was standing in the midst of a crowd of Greek pilgrims, all kneeling at some sacred service *with his hat on ;* many of them were giving visible signs of discontent and anger at the insult, and to be the object of wrath to such a crowd might not improbably lead to some very disagreeable consequences: a friend of ours went quietly up to him and remarked that the pilgrims were beginning to notice it; the Englishman abruptly advised him to mind his own affairs, upon which our friend coolly lifted the hat from his head, and said gently, " You have forgotten, sir, that you are in a church ;" in an instant the natural answer of a " true Briton " was prepared in a doubled fist; but better thoughts came in another moment, the direction of the uplifted arm was changed, with the candour of a gentleman, he held out his hand to our friend, and said, " You are right—thank you for reminding me of it."

I am convinced that there is nothing like a sojourn in the East for enabling one to value and thoroughly appreciate the sterling qualities and noble character of our countrymen: their integrity, truth, and *solidity* shine out in brilliant and glorious contrast to all other human surroundings; but why, oh, why, should so many of them consider these virtues incompatible with good manners, moderation, and consideration for others? Why should one always have to blush for the rough, rude, coarse bluntness for which they are notorious in every place where they pass; and why should their dignity and independence be uniformly supported by manual violence and bluster? We laugh at the French for their vainglory, and at the Yankee for his bragging and boasting; but dear John Bull is often worse than either of them, for he behaves exactly in the same manner " according to his kind ;" and if he wishes to prove he *is* better, he ought to *do* better.

the outside of the crowd almost beyond the Rotunda, struggling, jostling, and fighting with each other, when the procession appeared and slowly edged its way round the building, the soldiers, by main force, keeping room for it to pass.   Arrived at the door of the Sepulchre the Bishop of Tabor took off all his rich vestments, and clad only in a white surplice, entered in alone and closed the door behind him.   Now the multitude did indeed sway backwards and forwards in one intense frenzy of excitement, but, in three minutes, a deafening shout arose, and the sacred Torch was thrust through the hole! in less than four minutes the tapers of the whole crowd were lighted from end to end of the Rotunda, and in another moment had run round the more distant parts and into the small Greek gallery with surprising swiftness, for not only were whole bundles of tapers lighted at one touch, distributed from one to another, but others were let down by cords from above, and were drawn up with many crossings and much rejoicing.   The whole thing lasts literally but a few minutes, for not only are the tapers short and thin, but most of them are blown out directly after they have been lighted, to be carried home as precious relics, and burned beside the death pillow of the owner: hundreds of handkerchiefs and sheets are held in the flame to have a hole or two burned in them, after which they serve as shrouds, ensuring a welcome from the angels for the souls of their fortunate possessors.   Of course, as is well known, none of the educated Greeks believe in this absurd "miracle," which the "Fire Bishop" does not hesitate to acknowledge proceeds from the application of a lucifer-match; but these miserably ignorant pilgrims still devoutly believe in it, and the delusion is encouraged for the sake of the fees, by which the convents are supported.   It is curious indeed to see the complete change that suddenly comes over the lately expectant multitude: the expression of every anxious, haggard, and eager face has given place to the look of triumph and rejoicing, the intense happiness of success: now their long, weary, and often painful pilgrimage is over, and every object is accomplished: all the sacred places have been seen and kissed with reverent eyes and lips: the sins of a life have been washed away in the cleansing waters of the Jordan: the grave-clothes bathed in the sacred stream are secured, and now is added the holy taper lighted by the miraculous Flame which arises from the Tomb of their Saviour, which is to cheer them through the death struggle, and light them along the Valley of the Shadow of Death into Abraham's bosom.   Easter is entirely forgotten; for the "Fire" is the real object, so directly obtained from Heaven that the commemoration of the Resurrection is quite secondary.   This afternoon many hundreds have left the city, and begun their home-ward journey, unmindful of the Sunday that is to follow. Deluded, superstitious, and ignorant indeed they are; but perhaps the eyes of the Almighty Father may discern underneath all this, buried and hidden from the sight of men, some faithful and loving hearts more worthy of His blessing than many an enlightened, self-esteeming, and well-informed Pharisee, who looks upon them only with contempt. These poor pilgrims in truth we may regard with that love and "mercy which rejoiceth against judgment," though one would not willingly express one's opinion of those who keep up what they know too well to be a falsehood for their own "filthy lucre's sake:" indeed one might say, as Sooraya Pasha said after contemplating the frantic scene that so much shocked the gravé Mooslim—"Vous croyez que c'est une maison du bon Dieu, et que cette cérémonie est une chose religieuse—je vous dis que le bon Dieu ne peut pas être ici, et que, tout bonnement, ce n'est qu'une profanation horrible! "

On this same day, April 30th, 1859, as the Pasha sat looking on at the tumultuous scene, and stroking his beard with astonishment, a fanatic Russian pilgrim thrust his flaming torch into the Mooslim's face, growling out, "Dog of a Turk!" Signor Pierotti, who was standing beside him, instantly knocked the Russian on the head, and the kawasses rushed up to seize hold of him; but the Pasha interfered to prevent them, and only said to his friend, "Monsieur, il faut avoir patience avec les fous! "—a piece of advice which the traveller will do well to keep in his mind in modern Jerusalem.

CHAPTER XXII.

THE JEWS OF JERUSALEM.

" Glory, honour, and peace, to every man that worketh good; to the Jew first, and also to the Gentile."

" The cedars wave on Lebanon,
   But Judah's statelier maids are gone !"

THE population of the Jews in Jerusalem is variously estimated, and probably differs much from one season to another: the numbers usually given are from six to ten thousand, and these are divided into two classes—the Sephardim and the Ashkenazim; the first are descendants of those Jews who were driven out of Spain by Ferdinand and Isabella in 1497; they amount to two-thirds of the whole, and, although they have been in Jerusalem ever since, but very few of them speak Arabic: bad Spanish is their language; the Ashkenazim, are those who come from Germany and Poland. Some few of the Sephardim are able to support themselves, but many of them and all the Ashkenazim are maintained by alms; each family obtains but little, and the poverty and suffering among them is very great, yet scarcely any of them ever attempt to earn a piaster for themselves; they are paupers, with the slavish disposition and bad habits of that class in every country, deepened and degraded by the inactivity and indolence common to the Oriental. Nevertheless, when incited to work, when interested and encouraged, they are found to be as intelligent and industrious as those whom adversity, example, and necessity have taught to be independent in all other countries. They arrive yearly in large numbers, and would naturally increase very fast, but the dirt, even among those who are better off, and the state of degradation in which they all live, carry off a much larger number than the annual incomers. There is a great improvement in the feeling of the Arab-Christians towards them in the last few years, and even among the Greeks and

Latins; but it is extremely difficult to persuade them that these modern Jews whom they see coming daily from Europe, speaking only European languages, are of the same nation as the children of Israel: and, in fact, very few of the Arabs are ever brought to believe it.

They are one and all most grossly and deplorably ignorant: they bring no money with them, or, if they do, it is soon gone, and they all live upon what the Rabbins give away, implicitly obeying them in the smallest trifles, and submitting to the strictest surveillance, for fear their miserable pittance should be stopped. Large sums of money are sent yearly from the richer Jews of other countries for the support of their brethren here; the Rabbins, however, waste and appropriate the lion's share of these, and at the best the funds are quite inadequate to the support of so large a number. The Spanish Jews have a poorhouse, containing four or five rooms, and two closets; in one room of which eleven persons were living when we were in Jerusalem; they had each paid forty piasters on entrance, which entitles them to remain there for life; they had no means of livelihood, and were not allowed by the Rabbins to accept relief from any hand but their own: so they lived miserably on the scanty alms doled out to them.

A Prussian gentleman, himself a Jew, who was on a visit to the Holy City, told us much of the utter degradation and shocking dirt in which he found his brethren living; of their want of principle, their avarice and covetousness, their perfect shamelessness when convicted of falsehood or perjury, their cringing servility even to one who has boxed their ears in public on some such conviction; and he declared that the chief Rabbins were among the very worst. This is probably true, for the Rabbins seem only anxious to keep the people from improvement, and throw every difficulty in the way of their doing any work except under their own direction; nor is there work enough in Jerusalem to support the fourth part of them, unless they are put to agricultural employments.

Their ignorance and consequent superstition are really appalling, and are an immense hindrance to helping them in any way: anything given to them is immediately sold to enable them to observe, not the law, but some custom connected with a superstition, so low and gross, that even the Rabbins can hardly be supposed to countenance them, or at least to inculcate them; for instance, after a child is born, even though the parents lack bed and bedding or a morsel of mouldy bread, a lamp must be kept burning for forty days beside the infant to prevent the approach of evil spirits; and this is invariably done, whatever starvation and suffering may be the consequence of it. They believe most strictly in purgatory, and declare that the body remains sensitive and conscious of what befalls it, and in torment after death, until the prayers of the children shall have released the soul from suffering; the prayers of more distant relatives may avail, but it is a source of deep sorrow if a man or woman in dying leave no children to pray for their souls. The transmigration of souls is also believed among many of them: we heard of a Jewess from Adrianople who applied to the Rabbins to rid her of the soul of a man who, she firmly believed, had possessed her; she said she had drunk some water in which this man's soul had found refuge, and he having thus gained an entrance into her body, she could not get rid of him; he had told her that on account of his sins neither heaven nor hell would receive him, and that he would not leave her body, because, if he did, he would have to enter that of a dog, where he would be continually disturbed by its barking!

One of the women working in Miss Cooper's school was divorced by her husband just before his death, as a mark of affection and kindness on his part; he had had no children, and she would consequently have been obliged to marry his next brother, who was still a child; he, therefore, set her free that she might avoid years of waiting, and might marry again by her own choice. Before dying he desired that his corpse might be dragged from one door of the synagogue to the other by the feet, in expiation of his sins. On the day of his burial it was raining heavily, and a covering was laid over the bier, in order, as they said, to keep his clothes from being wetted, that he might present a decent appearance fit to come into the presence of God.

Ludicrous and degrading as these superstitions are, surely they ought to rouse something better than disgust in the mind of the enlightened Christian; if the heathen have claims on our benevolence, our kindness, our teaching and example, how much more have these poor outcasts, now indeed erring and miserable, but once the Chosen People of God our Father. If, in the end of time, the veil is to be lifted from their eyes, and their hearts opened to acknowledge Christ Jesus as their Saviour, our part, at least, meanwhile, should be to raise their moral position, enlighten their ignorance, and make them meet to receive His Holy Word.

Of course the observances commanded in the Mosaic Law must be respected, and, therefore, all gifts should be prepared accordingly. A Jewess cannot rightly wear a flannel petticoat if it is sewed with cotton thread instead of woollen, and a strict Jew will always refuse a blanket, lest thread or cotton should be mingled in the yarn. Much of their poverty arises from the early marriages customary among them: the German Jewesses marry at twelve years old; the Spanish Jewesses are forbidden to do so in Jerusalem before thirteen, but they evade the law by marrying outside the walls. They have large families and little food of either body or mind to give them.

An excellent hospital was established near the Zion Gate by Sir Moses Montefiore, and we heard much of its good management; an equally good school, however, which had been instituted by him for young Jewesses about the same time, had come to an end before our visit to Jerusalem, owing, I believe, to jealousies and squabbles among the Rabbins.

Their synagogues have had many vicissitudes: one was erected in 1267, in which Ashkenazim and Sephardim worshipped together, but the Mooslims turned it into a mill: it was restored to the Jews a hundred years after, but the Mooslims burned it in 1721, when forty rolls of the Law were lost in the flames. At the requests of the Russian and Austrian Consuls, Muhammad 'Ali gave them the site again in 1836, and a synagogue now stands upon it. There are, indeed, four standing altogether, neither handsome nor particularly interesting; in only one were there seats provided for the congregation, who are expected, in the others, to squat on the pavement. Papers, containing the name of God and some extracts from the Talmud, are pasted upon the walls: a recommendation to alms-giving, for the good of the donor's soul, is placed over the poor-box: and the Ten Commandments hang above the chest in which the Law was kept. These were all in Hebrew: the sermons, I believe, are given in Spanish or German. There are two new synagogues building; both of them very handsome, good work and tasteful design.

The most interesting building to us in the Jews' quarter was, on account of its great antiquity, the synagogue of the Karaite Jews; from the accumulation of the soil it is now quite underground: it is very plain, but contains some fine old manuscripts, most beautifully written and well worth seeing: one was a copy of the Pentateuch, more than 500 years old, with notes, and the number of words and letters in each page written in lines forming fanciful patterns, a different border for each page: the object of this strict enumeration is to prevent alterations or additions—even to " a jot or tittle "—creeping in: there were also a few bits of good illumination in it. The desk on which the Law is placed was covered with a very fine piece of most curious ancient embroidery, quite peculiar of its kind. The Karaite Jews are an interesting people; they reject the Talmud and all tradition, declaring the Mosaic Law, as given in the Pentateuch, sufficient in its own integrity, and they endeavour to live up to it with an earnest and sincere devotion. They are, in fact, the

Puritans among the Israelites, and are by some supposed to have
been the "just men" and "devout men" mentioned in the Gospels:
by others they are believed to be descendants of the Sadducees.
There used to be a large body of men at Cairo, but they are now
much dispersed, and though there are very many in Turkey, only
six reside at Jerusalem.

We were very anxious to see the Passover kept in Jerusalem, and
were glad to receive an invitation to the house of one of the most
respectable Jews for that evening: the night of our Good Friday.
We went there between eight and nine o'clock, and found the whole
family, including four generations, assembled in the principal room,
which was well lighted with lamps and several wax-candles; these
they were obliged to ask the Mooslim kawasses who came with us to
replenish, when they burned out later in the evening, as the Jews
cannot kindle a light, or do any kind of work during the feast.   We
were placed upon the divan at one side of the room, the women
of the family, with the servants and children, remaining together
at the bottom of the room; only one of the women, the venerable
mother and mistress of the house, was seated with the men and boys;
these were all together in one corner, with a small table before them
covered with silk and velvet cloths, richly embroidered with gold,
some of which were heirlooms of great antiquity.

A little boy, the youngest member of the family, then asked,
" What mean ye by this service ? " (in accordance with Exod. xii. 26);
upon which all the males stood up, rocking themselves, without
ceasing a moment, and recited very rapidly, in Hebrew, the story of
the deliverance of Israel from Egypt.   Then a boy repeated a very
long legendary tale in Spanish, with a rapidity that was perfectly
astonishing.   All had books before them, and continued rocking
their bodies to and fro, while only one was speaking: this is in
illustration of the text, " All my bones shall praise Thee."   After a
long time the men sat down, when a long white and black cloth was
placed upon their knees, and the old mother brought in a metal
ewer and basin, and poured water upon the hands of each, which
were wiped in the cloth, while they continued reading out aloud.
Then the master laid a white cloth over one shoulder, and removing
the coverings from the table, he took one of the large cakes of
Passover bread, till then concealed, and, breaking it in half, tied it
into the end of the cloth and slung it over the shoulder of the
youngest boy, who kept it for ten minutes, and then passed it on to
the next, and so on : all continuing to recite from the books without
stopping; after this the mother brought another basin, and the
master took up a glass vessel containing a mixture of bitter herbs

and vinegar, and some other ingredients, and, separating ten portions from it with his fingers, threw them into the basin—these represented the ten plagues of Egypt. There were plates of lettuce and other herbs, and the bones of the roasted lamb, in dishes on the table, besides the unleavened bread and four cups of wine; three of these at certain parts of the ceremony were passed round, and partaken of by each individual, including the women and baby. One cup of wine remained untouched, which was said to be for the Prophet Elijah; and we were told that in most families, towards the end of the supper, the door of the room is opened and all stand up, while the Prophet is believed to enter and partake of the wine: among rich Jews this cup is frequently of gold, with jewels. Some other dishes were laid on another table containing nuts and dried fruits, of which they afterwards partook: except in this the females entered into no part of the ceremony. All were dressed in their best and gayest clothes, with jewels and flowers in their hair. Before the conclusion they expressed to each other the usual wish, that at the coming of the next Passover they might all be in Jerusalem, while the customary prayer was offered, that by that time the Messiah might have come to redeem Israel.

Passover cake is made of the finest wheaten flour and water, rolled into a very thin paste, and quickly baked. Many Jews go out in the previous year to watch the growth of the corn until it is reaped and threshed, and stored away in a clean place: it is ground with much care, as, if water should fall on it, fermentation might ensue, and it would then be unclean; or if a mouse or rat should come near it, it would be equally impure; very often a patch of corn is sown separately for the Passover bread, and is then carefully watched. The ovens in which to bake it are hired by the synagogue authorities some days before, and are thoroughly cleaned out, plastered within anew, and large flagstones laid down, on which to bake the bread: these are afterwards taken up again, and locked up in some place belonging to the synagogue till the next year. Many of the Jews have a totally distinct set of vessels for use during this week, to prevent the slightest taint of leaven on the food: some even keep a room locked up the whole year, and only open it for this week; and on our expressing surprise, we were told of a Jewish family in Germany who kept a small house set apart for this purpose. All these minute observances make the Passover bread very expensive and difficult for the poor to obtain for a whole week's sustenance; the synagogue gives away a rottl to each person, and the richer Jews also give it away to their poorer brethren; but, at the best, they are always very poor and starving after Passover, having spent every piaster they can beg or borrow to observe the feast with due honour.

It is extremely difficult to persuade a Jew to come to the house of a Christian for work or presents, and nothing will induce them to enter it on any pretext : they have such a passionate horror of the cross, that they are in constant dread, even amounting to terror, of seeing it by accident : they firmly believe that we look upon the figure of a cross as a fetish, and that every Christian is *compelled* to have one in his room as well as to carry one upon his person ; nor are they ever convinced to the contrary ; if they cannot see it on you, they still believe that you carry it concealed somewhere. The reason of this is their rooted conviction that it was the form of the idolatry practised by the Canaanites, and against which the Jews were particulary warned ; the converted Jews like to wear a cross, but it is with a feeling of self-imposed humiliation, and is done as a proof of the depth and intensity of their conversion. They say that the Egyptians were all Christians! and worshipped the cross, and that it was for this reason that the infant Moses refused to go to an Egyptian nurse, as his eyes always met the cross upon them ; and so the princess had to send for a Hebrew woman at last, on whose breast he could lie in peace. Mrs. Finn once, during the dangerous illness of one of her children, after many prayers and entreaties, at last persuaded a young Jewess to come to her as wet-nurse, and rejoicing in her unusual success, she took her up to the child's bedroom : no sooner had she opened the door a few inches than the Jewess uttered a loud shriek, and rushed out of the house, never ceasing to run till she had reached her own, where she sobbed violently : she had caught sight of the corner of the iron bedstead, and, without waiting to see more, believed it to be a large iron cross hung up for her special annoyance, the mere glance at which would bring more fatal consequences to herself and all belonging to her than the worst *mal occhio* ever seen ; there was no use in explaining it to her—she would never enter that house again. Perhaps this horror and hatred of the cross explains why St. Paul, in writing to the Hebrews, writes entirely of sacrifice, but never once mentions the cross ; and it accounts in some degree at the present day for the unsuccessful efforts of nearly all Roman Catholics in the conversion of the Jews.

Yet, however rejected and abhorred by the Jews, let us never forget that it was through them that Cross came to us by which all the world may receive salvation ; they were the good olive-tree on whose " root and fatness " the wild olive and the Gentile were grafted* ;

* Rom. xi.

upon the Law given to them our Christianity was raised up, and the Jew was our schoolmaster to bring us to Christ; from their fall came the riches of the world, and through their unbelief we have obtained mercy, that through our mercy they may obtain the same. What shall we say to those who gain everything and give back nothing? Ought it not rather to be that from every " uttermost part of the earth" something of our abundance should be gladly spared for the sons of those from among whom came the humble but glorious Twelve who carried and spread the seed, the rich harvest of whose labours we reap? If we have received of the Jew spiritual things, is it a great thing if he shall reap our carnal things? Theirs was the land, and theirs it will be again, by the same sure promise whose fulfilment is certain; theirs was the Zion which "the Lord shall comfort," and theirs were the " waste places," and the " wilderness," and the " desert," which " He will make like Eden, and like the garden of the Lord;" the land which their fathers possessed they shall possess, although " desolation and destruction, and the famine and the sword " have come upon them; while our part is to remember that " this cup of His fury " will be transferred " to the hand of them that afflict " His people, and the blessing of Him who charged us to " help one another" will be given to the Gentile who tries, in all humility and faith, to enable his poor Jew brother to possess his own : to show him the light of truth by the hand of real charity: and to help him to raise up and exalt himself from the low and degraded condition of the Jews now living in the Promised Land of Israel.

Another reason also exists for endeavouring to raise the Jew to independence: when, by God's grace, they have hearkened to the teaching of the missionary, when his eyes are opened, his heart softened, and his ears unveiled, what is to become of the Jew? The doors of his home are closed against him, his kindred have become his bitterest enemies, and the misery, which he feels he might bear for himself, becomes impossible to face when he looks on the wife and children around him, who will be left destitute and starving from the moment of his listening to the voice of faith in his heart. In Europe this struggle is sometimes a terrible one, but there the honest man can always earn a crust; in Jerusalem who can describe its sufferings to those from whom the lowest and meanest source of maintenance, that of alms, is taken away? At present, if a Jew is converted, he struggles on miserably for a short time, until he and his family are forced with deep reluctance into exile, and they pass away to Europe or some country where they can support themselves by their own labour, instead of remaining in the land of their fathers, where they would be not only examples to others, but also firm ground from which to work for the conversion of their brethren.

Knowing this well, the Societies who have planted the missions here supply something for the support of the newly-converted Jew at first: this, however, cannot long be continued, and is at best shifting the evil to another hand; honest labour is the mainspring of that independence which makes a man, and which the Jew, long bowed down under the heavy consequences of the curse, almost requires to enable him to listen to the truth asserting itself in his heart, instead of continuing to lean only on the effete traditions of the fathers of his race. Mere alms-giving in this case has another evil also: it enables enemies and opponents to say, however unjustly, as the Latin Patriarch said to us one day: "We cannot make converts as you do, we have not the funds; your mission is endowed with the power of money: with the Jew and with the Turk words can do little." It was useless to contradict the assertion, though entirely untrue, but the utmost care is needed to give no colour to such an accusation.

And, therefore, those who look on the Jews as their elder brethren, as the chosen of the Lord, whom in the time of gathering He will not forget, have united in more than one place to teach them how to work, and to supply them with the means of labour, so as to enable them, as Jews, to earn their daily bread by the honest industry of their own hands. I have already mentioned, far more cursorily than it deserved, Miss Cooper's work-school for Jewesses*; I have now to tell of another plan.

Eight years ago, that is in June 1852, a piece of ground to the north-west of Jerusalem was hired by some Christian residents in the city; olives, mulberries, and vines were planted as far as the small funds then in hand allowed, and Jews were for many weeks each summer employed in the care of it. For four years this continued, the Jewish labourers varying from twenty to two hundred in number, not indeed according to the applications made, which were very numerous, but according to the amount of work which the varying funds enabled the managers to give. By 1857, the sale of the stones taken off the ground, and contributions remitted from England and India, cleared off the purchase of the land; a deed of trust was executed, and trustees both in Jerusalem and England were nominated; and though constant applications for work were

---

* There is also a society called the "Sarah Society," formed of ladies for visiting the Jews at their own miserable homes, taking them food, clothing, and medicine: they work, as Miss Cooper did, unobtrusively and quietly, saying little, but effecting much.

necessarily refused, and such numbers were turned away for whom it was impossible to find wages, that the good effected could not be very extensive, yet the experiment had at least drawn out the most satisfactory proofs, against the common cry, that Jews are willing to work even at an occupation to which they are wholly unused, and that they are capable of and willing to learn agricultural labour. Some few were also taught building, as the plantation had to be walled round, a cistern built, and a small house erected for the superintendent. From the year 1857, up to the present moment, Jewish labourers have been employed on this land, which may be called the nursery of Jewish field-labourers; but owing to the smallness of the funds at command, the number has been trifling, sometimes only two or three, sometimes seven or eight at a time. The grand thing would be to get any sum, even a small one, secured to them annually: as, at present, never being able to foresee when ten pounds or one shilling may be remitted for them, or how long the proprietors may have to go on without receiving anything, it is impossible to incur the requisite expenses at the proper times; a particularly unfortunate disadvantage in a country where everything must be paid for, or contracted for *at a year's advance*, and in an agricultural undertaking, where everything depends upon seizing the right week for the putting in of seeds and plants.

In the meantime, a converted Jew of Spanish family, Mr. Meshullam, had settled in the vale of Urtass, near Solomon's Pools, then a desolate valley about fifty or sixty yards wide, between rocky, cold-looking hills of limestone, but which was once unquestionably the place where Solomon in his days of glory had made vineyards and orchards. Thousands of years they had lain in stone-covered neglect and desolation, till the hand of culture was once more laid upon them. The grateful land returned almost at once into fertility and productiveness; a "garden" instead of a "wilderness," an "Eden" instead of a "desert place."

After a few years it became known that the Greeks had cast longing eyes on the little glen now smiling in fresh richness, and were bargaining to buy the whole valley from the Arab Sheikhs to whom it belonged. Had they succeeded, not only would all the nine years of labour then spent by Mr. Meshullam upon the valley have been thrown away just as its value was rapidly increasing and the enterprise was beginning to pay well, and his large family have been thus cast adrift upon the world, but the plan· ever dear to his heart and to many others for enabling his brethren to support themselves by agriculture, would have had to be recommenced in some other and perhaps less favourable place. Such a golden opportunity could not be lost, at least, if any amount of exertion could save it : nor was it. After endless labour in reasoning with and persuading the people of the neighbouring hills against the intrigues of the Greeks who have a convent close by, the Sheikhs were brought to promise to sell the chief portion of the valley for 150*l.* It was all done as quietly and silently as possible on account of the vigilance of the Greek rivals, but, on the 12th of May, 1856, a message was brought to Mr. Finn, the British Consul, to say that the consent of the Sheikhs was gained, and that they would come into Jerusalem on the following day to conclude the purchase.

This message was very joyfully received, for it is a rare and diffi- cult thing to get an Arab to sell a square inch of ground : but where was now the money to effect it ? It was necessary to lay it down in good coin before the eyes, and into the very hands of the Arabs ; but not one piaster had Mrs. Finn been able as yet to secure for the execution of her darling project. She had long been ardently desirous of establishing a Hebrew farm settlement, and she felt that here was the one golden opportunity. What was to be done ? at the slightest appearance of hesitation or indecision, the Shiekhs would have been off in a moment, and the land would have been in the possession of the Greeks in less than twenty-four hours, and the opportunity lost, perhaps for many years, of acquiring a suitable bit of ground for the long-cherished plan. Yet to accomplish it now seemed well-nigh impossible.

That evening a number of travellers were met together at the British Consulate, when one of them accidentally mentioned having passed through Urtass in riding to Jerusalem, and asked some questions about the place. The history of Mr. Meshullum's efforts came out. The wished-for purchase was mentioned as well as the difficulty from the want of funds, but little was said of Mrs. Finn's anxiety and almost despair for the requisite money. However, before leaving the house, one of the travellers—may the blessing of a good deed rest upon him !—offered 50*l.* as a loan during a six-weeks' excursion to Damascus towards effecting the purchase. This was something : but the horizon was yet clouded and dark. Early in the morning the Sheikhs arrived in Jerusalem to execute the sale, and the drawing out of the papers commenced. This is not, however, the really important part of the sale, for even if the deeds are signed, the Arab will often bring back the money in his hands, and the sale is null : the sale really consists in his verbal declaration before witnesses that " I, the son of ——, the son of ——, sell this land to ——, the son of ——, the son of ——," and so on ; this engagement is never broken, especially if there be witnesses of repute to guarantee the transaction. While the papers were being written out, a matter of some hours' toil, Mrs. Finn sent for the Rev. Mr. Nicholayson, the first of all the missionaries in Jerusalem, and the most venerated by all classes and all religions, a cautious and sagacious man : he came, and willingly put his hand to the work. They then sent for Mr. Bergheim, the banker, himself a converted Jew, and explained their object; he ran home, and soon returned with 50*l.* in a bag, which he advanced, joyfully and gladly as a loan, to buy a bit of the land of his fathers, for his despised brethren. Mr. Graham (the Lay Secretary of the Mission) gathered the other 50*l.* in small sums, chiefly as loans also, and the purchase-money then stood complete. Two or three of the English residents, who loved and laboured for the Jews, assembled at the Consulate, and the actual sale began.

This Arab sale, which is called " the sale by the broken group," is a curious affair: should the price be only a distinct number of piasters, the money might be returned at any change of mind in the original owner, or at least disputed afterwards. The custom is therefore to buy for a definite and *also for an unknown sum* ; a quantity of bazaar trinkets, small coins, and trifles are collected in a handkerchief, which is rolled up, thrown into the air, and the scattered contents scrambled for by all present.

An exciting scene it was : the group of picturesque Arab Sheikhs, headed by a wild Bedoueen, a notorious robber but a powerful chief, whose presence was a guarantee for the truth and fidelity of all the others: and the little band of Europeans, some of whom had long planned, worked for, and earnestly desired this happy moment: some who loved the Jews, and some who had themselves been Jews; all assembled in the little room at the Consulate, with the precious money counted out in little heaps on the table between them. Mrs. Finn brought out some of her own European ornaments, on which the Arabs look with profound respect as things of untold value, and tied them up with the rest of the things in the handkerchief: " the broken group" was thrown on the floor, and one and all scrambled pell-mell for the contents; the heap having been so skilfully thrown that Mrs. Finn could pounce at once upon her own things. A happy day it was : and it is pleasant to add that within the time specified by each kind lender, the money was re-collected in large and small gifts, and the loans repaid.

The crops of the valley thus satisfactorily purchased, paid well during the first five months, notwithstanding the expenses attendant in commencing on the new part of the ground: this was cleared and walled, old terraces were repaired and fresh ones made, besides

2 G

all the sowing and planting that the funds would allow: the re-claiming was commenced in June, and by October the land was rich with crops; preparations were then commenced for a poultry yard and dairy, when a miserable accident, in February 1857, brought it all to a temporary stand-still. The water from the Pools of Solomon, which happened to be unusually full, was let out from an opening secretly made in the lowest Pool by an enemy, and rushing in torrents through the valley, carried away crops and trees, and, cutting deep channels right down in the soil, washed away great quantities of the earth itself: leaving the discouraged proprietors to the mortification of seeing their own turnips and potatoes, picked up by the Bedoueen at the mouth of the valley by the Dead Sea, exposed for sale in the Jerusalem market! Some hundred pounds' worth of damage was thus effected, for which no redress has ever been obtained, and from which the little gardens were but slowly recovered; gradually, however, they were restored to order: tanks were repaired and a small aqueduct built: a two-roomed house was erected out of stone quarried on the spot, and an old ruined tower filled with bee-hives: the gardens have ever since been thriving well, and producing a very profitable return for the money spent upon them during the last four years.

The prices of labour and of building materials have risen so much since the work was begun, that the cost of bringing the valley into thorough order has greatly increased in proportion: Russians, Greeks, Latins, and others are employing, at high prices, all the available hands of the Jerusalem district, while hitherto numbers of applications from Jews for work have been obliged to be refused, because they could not be paid for their labour. The object for which the valley was purchased will never be attained until cottages can be provided for the Jewish labourers to live in: they cannot of course walk out from Jerusalem, a distance of about seven miles, to their daily work; but, if residing on the spot, the long-cherished hope might be realised not only of giving them daily employment, but of settling *Christian Hebrews as independent farmers and land-owners in Palestine.* The Jews would ever be, and are, most gladly and joyfully welcomed as labourers both in Urtass and in the Plantation we mentioned before: but the little colony in the cottages would be confined to Christian Hebrews, for whom, in time, and by God's blessing, a schoolroom and a church might be erected.

One bright morning, early in April, we rode over the pleasant plain of Rephaim, down the hill to Rachel's Sepulchre, and then crossing the wild rocky hills behind Bethlehem, turned suddenly to the south-west, and found ourselves in the midst of verdure and luxuriant cultivation, that brightly contrasted with the country we had just passed over: this was the valley of Urtass. We crossed a pretty cascade, which was conducting the water from Solomon's Pools into the gardens and fields, and in a few minutes were seated in the shade of Mr. Meshullam's house, eating excellent bread and butter for the first time since leaving England; and looking out on the very fine vegetables and fruit trees loaded with white blossoms. As the afternoon drew on, the rich scent of the hawthorn came up the breeze, the finches sung little trills to each other in the trees, the sweet notes of the cuckoo echoed from hill to hill softly but clearly, and we fancied ourselves carried back to the time when the Land was flowing with milk and honey, instead of her now widowed, barren, desolated state. Then we wandered down among the shrubs and trees, treading over carpets of the lovely Syrian campanula, pink flax, blue and scarlet pimpernel, to inspect the marvels that energy and a little agricultural knowledge has obtained from the soil of the Holy Land, in the valley which has lain fallow since the gardens of Solomon, the King of Israel, withered and died. They are marvels indeed: the beans, planted in February, had eight, nine, and ten stems to each root, each stem from two to two and a half feet high and loaded with pods: from the peas we picked a great basketful in five minutes, which proved at dinner to be of the very best kind: above them stood a mulberry-tree, planted but seven years ago, whose branches extended thirty-five feet from tip to tip, and whose stem measured, at two feet from the ground, one yard and a quarter in circumference: the branches were then covered with fruit, which it was expected would be ripe in ten days. A little further, there was a peach-tree which had been planted just fourteen months before, a tiny seedling: it was now seven feet high and covered with blossoms. The mustard plants which had been in the ground barely three months and a half, were in bushes about six feet high, with woody stems, two and a half inches in diameter, with nineteen branches proceeding from the first foot of the stem, every branch a mass of seeds. The pigs were feeding on turnips nine and eleven inches round, and we gathered flowers of the cabbages, looking like bunches of cowslips tied on a stick, each head from ten to fourteen inches in height. A still greater proof of the wonderful fertility of the valley is that the vines, planted in this same year on the newly cleared hillside, were bearing little bunches of grapes already! the terraces on which they were growing having been to all appearance only rock up to Christmas, less than four months ago.

The Jews have a legend that the cauliflowers in the valley of the

2 G 2

Kedron, formerly grew so tall, that the gardeners had to get up ladders to reach their heads! and I began to think we had got into some such region of agricultural enchantment; the statements I have made might seem like extravagancies of the like kind, but I have been careful to state nothing that I did not see with my own eyes, and measure with my own hands; and those who have witnessed the effects of heat and water, combined upon a virgin soil, will bear witness to the possibility of the assertions made. Mr. Meshullam is doing his best to import foreign seeds and plants, and to set the example of scientific agricultural work as far as he can.

Many interesting Scriptural memories are connected with this place: it is believed to be the "rock Etam" where Samson dwelt: perhaps a place containing many ravenous birds, as the word Etam is supposed to come from the Hebrew for an eagle. It is also unquestionably the place where Solomon made him "a garden and orchards, and planted in them of all kinds of fruits," and "pools of water to water therewith the wood that bringeth forth trees;" and to this "very pleasant" place Josephus tells us Solomon "drove in the morning, sitting high in his chariot;" for the kings of all other countries hearing of his wisdom and virtue had sent him "chariots and horses, and as many mules for his carriages as they could find proper to please the king's eyes, by their strength and beauty. And he made himself a chariot of the wood of Lebanon, lined with gold, and with a canopy of purple silk supported by pillars of silver: and in this chariot he used to go out every morning, clothed in a white garment, and drive to his garden; for he had laid causeways of black stone along all the roads that led to Jerusalem, upon which he could drive his chariot with ease and swiftness: while he was surrounded with a band of young men in the most delightful flower of their age, eminent for their largeness, and far taller than other men: they had very long hair hanging down, and were clothed in garments of Tyrian purple, and they had dust of gold sprinkled every day on their hair, so that their heads sparkled with the reflection of the sunbeams upon the gold."* And riding along that pleasant path one could well fancy the goodly sight of the glorious king and his train, besides indulging very earnestly in the wish that the smooth causeway of black stone was still in existence.

Some ancient remains are, however, still existing, though long since concealed and overlaid by the soil brought down by the mountain torrents in winter, for the valley is very subject to such inundations; two days of rain in the beginning of February in this

* Josephus, Ant. viii. 7.   Eccles. ii. 4, 5.

year had brought down such quantities of water, and filled up the lower end of the valley with so strong a current, that a powerful man could not swim across it. Of course these torrents tear much away, but they also bring much down, and in some places the accumulations of soil are very remarkable. There is a low projecting cliff about half-way down the valley on the north side : this promontory has from time immemorial borne the name of the "Promontory of the Baths ;" just at this part the valley is occupied by a very large building arched all over and finely built, upon which the soil now lies to about the depth of twenty inches; this long-buried ruin has been always called by the Bedoueen and fellaheen of the districts the Baths of Solomon ; ancient coins, bits of glass and mosaic have been frequently found there, and the other day a large piece of finely carved cornice and a capital were dug up of remarkably pure and fine Corinthian.* A small aqueduct, still visible, led to this ruin from the copious spring close by : and, in short, it is incontestable that some "baths," and those of some consequence, existed here. It has therefore been suggested with much reason that this was the "Emmaus" of Luke xxiv. 13 ; Emmaus being the Greek form of the Hebrew word Hamath, and the Arabic Hammâm, which are indiscriminately applied to naturally or artificially heated baths. The remains of no other baths of any kind have been found near Jerusalem, and the distance of "threescore furlongs" agrees perfectly with the sacred narrative ; it is more likely than that the two Apostles walked back from 'Amwas after it was "toward evening" and the day was "far spent," that is, *halfway from Juffa*, distance of twenty miles, and yet arrived in Jerusalem while "the eleven" were still "gathered together :" having walked in the one day forty miles. One may well fancy the walk by day of the Apostles over these pleasant breezy hills, passing by the place where their Lord was born, talking together of all that had happened, and then the return in the cool evening with a far greater "burning" in their hearts than before, for joy that their "faith was not in vain," and that Christ was risen indeed. The view that met their eyes was in some way different, for, as we have said before, there is reason to believe that all these hills were once covered with woods; in Urtass in particular wherever the hillsides are cleared for planting, the old roots of the oak-trees are found thickly neighbouring each other, and are of such size, that one, not un-

---

* Since this was written a marble-lined bathing-place has been uncovered,; with a cemented one adjoining it, another large and deep tank, two or three brass bathing implements, many small gilt and coloured mosaics, some Cufic and Hebrew coins, and some marble fragments of columns.

usually large, that we saw lying on the ground, was sufficient for four camels' loads!

We had already paid three visits to Solomon's Pools, but having now explored the wonders of the gardens of Solomon we proposed to examine his Pools with more attention than we had as yet been able to do: Signor Pierotti, who has made accurate plans of them, kindly accompanying us to explain the subterranean buildings. Having dismounted at the old khan, we walked for between two and three hundred yards, in a line exactly due west from the N.W. angle of the wall, when we came to a very small hole, the only entrance to the sealed fountain. Down this hole we dropped ourselves, with some difficulty, to about the depth of twelve feet, and, being safely landed on a hillock of mud at the bottom, found that we were standing in a large vaulted chamber of solid massive masonry, in length about twice its own width, and opening at one side into another vaulted chamber smaller than the first, along the centre of which a tiled conduit led the water from a source in the rock at the further end; the tiles of this conduit are peculiar—neither Roman nor Arab—they are therefore believed to be Jewish, as well as the very ancient solid arches of the chambers. There are three, if not four, sources for the water which, united, flows along a vaulted passage, between four and five feet high, opening out of the east side of the first chamber. Signor Pierotti kindly walked through the water (which was then about a foot deep) for some distance with a candle that we might see how finely built the passage is: he has walked along the whole length to the wall of the khan when there was not much water in it, and found that after some few yards its course turns slightly, but on the whole it maintains a due easterly direction till it reaches the khan, whence it turns suddenly south to the first Pool, and the passage becomes very low: at intervals along its length there are small chambers on either side. Altogether it is a fine work, and it would be difficult to doubt that one sees here the original work of the mighty Solomon.

After following the line of the subterranean conduit above ground, we next descended the steps into the chamber at the north-west corner of the First Pool, which receives the surplus water from the commencement of the great aqueduct: the steps led into a little passage, running east and west, a low arch from which led into a large chamber, at the end of which we saw another large vaulted chamber: both were finely built and filled with water three or four inches deep. The aqueduct runs along at the north side of the Pools, the surplus only passing into the upper or First Pool.

Below the Third Pool, a strong wall has been built across the valley as a guard in case of the escape or overflow of the water from the Pools : here we found the remains of a grand stone staircase, and close beside it we went down a passage on an incline to a high vaulted chamber, through which the water from the Third Pool runs ; and at the north end of this is the great filtering chamber, through which the water passed before it could enter the aqueduct. The scientific knowledge displayed in the formation of this aqueduct is said to be very great; especially in the mode of propelling the water up the steep ascents, by means of repeated air chambers admitting the force of the air before each rise.

Passing by Urtass on our way home from the dreary hills about Solomon's Pools, one is again struck with its fruitful appearance : the luxuriant richness of one or two small gardens * in other spots, render assurance doubly sure that the " pound " is only " laid by in a napkin" and hidden in the earth. In general, nothing throughout Palestine strikes the eye of the pilgrim half as much as the indescribable stoniness and desolation of the country he is passing through; and nothing, by a natural analogy of contrast, rises so constantly to his mind as the expression of the " milk and honey" of the Promised Land: the striking contrast has to be reconciled by the memory of the long and awful history of the " Chosen People," whose ingratitude and wickedness caused the present melancholy condition of their loved Judæa : for fifteen centuries they possessed this glorious Land; they passed from it without leaving a single memorial upon the soil they had so long occupied, and in no other country have they achieved a conquest or established an empire. Yet ever imperishable, in the history of man, will the name of the Hebrew nation remain : a nation without a territory, a people without union ; instead of dumb and lifeless monuments like those of Egypt, Greece, and Rome, they are themselves the living ruins of their nation, scattered to the north, south, east, or west: united only by an invisible chain, a law, a principle. They own no country, for their mission was not of this world, but of that above : to know God and to teach Him to others. Their being commenced with the Patriarch who was called from a far country to proclaim, among the idolatrous peoples of the earth, the existence of the Creator : it finished at the coming of the Messiah ; and no sooner had the seeds of this faith

---

* Such as that belonging to a Greek Priest, near Mar Elyas, called " Benjamin's Garden," the cultivation and fruitfulness of which in a very few years is wonderful. Dr. Hooker says he would engage to supply the whole population of Syria with food from the produce of ten well-cultivated miles of the valley of the Jordan !

been carried over the pagan world, than the corporate existence of the Hebrews terminated; they are are now but a religious society scattered even into the uttermost corners of the globe, waiting the fulfilment of those glorious Promises which shall restore strength to Zion; waiting till the Lord shall comfort His people, and redeem Jerusalem: till her city shall be no more termed Forsaken or Desolate, but, breaking forth into joy and loud songs of praise, she shall be called " Hephzibah "—for " the Lord shall delight in her."

CHAPTER XXIII.

THE CAVE OF ELIJAH, AND THE PULPIT OF CHRYSOSTOM.

THE last days of our long stay at Jerusalem were come only too soon; we revisited our favourite spots, said good-byes to all the kind and valued friends we had made in the Holy City, and on Monday morning the 16th of April, at a very early hour, sallied forth for the last time from the Damascus Gate, with eyes ever turning back full of deep affection to the mountain hallowed by every sacred association in the heart; it had been a happy home and a resting-place to us in the midst of our wanderings, and we were very sad indeed at leaving it. We had chosen the upper road of the two leading to Jaffa, as the most interesting as well as the prettiest, and we soon found ourselves passing over pleasant valleys and breezy hills flourishing with corn and olives, and now in the spring-tide gay and gaudy with flowers. How lovely they were! and how pleasant the bright morning air and the extensive views over Judea! we passed to the right of Neby Samwel, beyond which was the hill on which once stood the royal city of Gibeon, whereof "all the men were mighty." A rich little plain lies below it, now green with corn, over which Joshua drove back the five kings of the Amorites with the king of Jerusalem at their head, chasing them along "the way that goeth up to Bethhoron;" up in the village is a fountain or "pool," probably that beside which Joab and Abner sat while their soldiers fought and slew each other, twelve on each side, "followed by a very sore battle that day." One other recollection clings to Gibeon, better and holier than all these strugglings and fightings, in the prayer of Solomon for "a wise and understanding heart," granted to him here, where he had come to sacrifice "a thousand burnt offerings": "for that was the great high place" after the destruction of Nob, and before the Tabernacle was removed to Jerusalem.

The two Bethhorons, to one of which was the going up and to

the other the "going down" of the army of Joshua (x. 10, 11), still retain their ancient name in the Arabic, Beit Oor el fŏk—the upper, and Beit Oor el taht—the lower. There is a splendid view from the upper one, which we enjoyed from under a thick grove of olives, while examining the massive remains of portions of the ancient city wall, formed of very large stones, which are still *in situ*. The villagers brought us a large bowl of delicious olives, which we quickly demolished, and a number of eggs roasted in hot ashes. The country after leaving Bethhoron is singularly devoid of villages; but it was smiling enough in the fresh spring greens, and the view over the plain of Jaffa, or rather of Sharon : on which Ludd, the Lod of the Old Testament and the Lydda of the New Testament, is situated. It was late in the afternoon ere we reached it, but we dismounted to see the Church of St. George, a rather picturesque ruin of the time of the Crusaders : the eastern apse, part of the choir, a group of many clustered columns with marble acanthus-leaved capitals and one lofty pointed arch remain to make a pretty picture. The town is very prettily situated among its rich gardens and cornfields, palms mingling with the olive-trees; the people were all busy making matting from the palm-leaves, which they weave very dexterously and well : it is the great place in Syria for this manufacture. Ramleh, which we reached after dark, is a large and pretty town, still more richly placed among cornfields and fruit-gardens : the roads are hedged with prickly pear, and sycamores, figs, caroubs, and the ever-dear palm come in to diversify the olive groves. We encamped on the plain, which seemed very wild and bare in the night, as the wind came soughing across its dry and grey thorn bushes. In the morning we went to see the vaults on the north side of the town, which are remarkable for their size and good masonry : they are long tunnels well arched over, sunk below the level of the ground, with staircases descending into them : they are considered to be of the tenth or eleventh century. A little further on stands the beautiful minaret, or tower, built in 710 A.H., *i.e.* 1310 A.D., by the order of the Sultan, as an inscription over the door testifies. This place is believed to have been a spacious khan, which goes by the name of the Church of the Forty Martyrs; much of the cloisters or open corridors still remain round the quadrangle, and below the surface of the ground are the large cisterns or granaries, like subterranean galleries, built of good close brickwork covered with cement. There was also a mosque, but it is now gone : a stone lying on the ground reports that "Sultan Bibars . . . Prince of the Faithful, came out from Cairo . . . and came to Jaffa, and conquered it, by the will of God, in three hours,—then he ordered that this cupola should be built above the blessed candlestick and this door in the mosque," in the year 1267.

Ramleh has always been a place of some consequence, since it was founded by the Khalif Suleimān in the eighth century: it was the head-quarters of our own Cœur de Lion for a long time, and it was in this place that St. George was first declared the patron saint of England—a very sorry kind of saint, I fear, he was. Thence all the way to Jaffa the country is altogether pleasant meadow-lands and wheat-fields, with groves of trees, till the excellent road brings one to the delicious orange gardens which extend for some miles from the town. The oranges were then in their finest ripeness, and every branch was covered with flowers, which spread their enchanting fragrance over the whole country, and delighted us even in the pitable plight we were in, for an Oriental shower had soaked us, *jusqu'aux os*, and our dripping drapery and drenched appearance would have been very ludicrous if it had not been so very uncomfortable. Rooms had been prepared for us in the Latin convent at the request of our kind friend the French Consul at Jerusalem, and the good monks brought us a plentiful repast; but almost before we had emptied the water out of our boots, the storm had increased so much that the Russian steamer in the roadstead sent up to say she must go away or go to pieces; and we had to make a hasty descent into a small boat, and a perilous little voyage over the Jaffa rocks, before we were tossed and pitched and then thrown into the steamer, amid the tremendous surf and waves caused by the storm. That evening is not a pleasant one to remember.

Early next morning we landed at Hhaïffa, one of the prettiest places on the coast of Syria, and were soon comfortably installed in the English Consulate by the kindness of its owner Mr. Rogers. Hhaïffa is situated on the north side of the promontory of Mount Carmel, commanding the coast up to the headland of Tyre, and the plain watered by the Kishon on which Akka is situated; then come range after range of the Galilean hills, and Hermon rising his grand head loftily and majestically behind all; it was now completely covered with snow on summit and sides. A good road leads up to the large convent which is finely placed on the very brow of the mountain; it was built from the alms collected by one monk who begged for fourteen years through Europe, and in the end obtained half a million of francs for the purpose. It is a most comfortable abiding-place for strangers, and we were charmed with the good monk who showed us over the convent; the church is built over the cave inhabited by Elijah, which the monks say has ever since been occupied by some holy men of one creed or another; the church is ornamented with imaginary columns and marbles done in coarse gaudy painting.

At the foot of the mountain near the sea-shore is a very large cave, partly natural and partly artificial, where it is said Elijah taught his disciples; and a little further on there is a more curious spot: a cave with a smooth bank of rock immediately below it, down which the Druzes roll themselves, on one day in the year, in accordance with some strange superstition; on that one day they flock here from the surrounding mountains in great numbers.

We rose early the next morning in order to ride to the site of one of the most interesting episodes in Bible history—Elijah's sacrifice; it is a long ride, but one is richly repaid by the delicious fertility all round one, and the pretty views on all sides. There is nothing grand here: but for quiet, tranquil beauty, "the excellency of Carmel" is very charming, and among the many changes in the sacred sites, it is pleasant to find this mountain still worthy of its name: a full orchard, a fruitful field, is the meaning of the word. Having crossed the town we were soon upon the mountain, winding up its steep sides, among thick, low woods of prickly oak, laurustinus, and other shrubs, with quantities of honeysuckle, and the ground variegated with all the hues of the rainbow from the innumerable varieties of wild flowers which grew everywhere. We still looked back over the plain and the blue sea, until reaching the brow of the mountain we lost it on this side, to find it again on the other to the south, beyond the ranges of Judæan hills; now came about twelve miles of undulating ground, like park-land at home, bright, glassy, flowery lawns, studded with oaks of various kinds, plane, terebinth, and caroub, with thick brushwood of lovely storax, and sometimes a wild olive-grove. Then, as we neared the south-eastern end of this long ridge, the plain of Esdraelon opened out before us, with Tabor, and Gilboa, and little Hermon, and the Basham mountains beyond Jordan: while, behind the hills to the north, beautiful Hermon appeared, looking so close to Tabor as to realise one of the Psalmist's expressions, "Tabor and Hermon shall rejoice in Thy Name." About an hour and a half after passing through the Druze village of Esfîyeh, we reached the easternmost termination of the ridge, and seated ourselves under a spreading oak to enjoy the wide-spread view. Somewhat to our right, on a little grassy plateau, below our position, but high above the plain, we saw the traditionary site of the memorable sacrifice, which still bears the name of "el Mahraka" (the burnt offering); it is wide enough to contain a large multitude of people, even if it was then, as now, half covered with trees and shrubs. Among these, concealed from us on the top, lies an ancient stone-built fountain, which probably supplied the twelve barrels of water which were poured over the altar and into the trench by Elijah's order. Meandering through the plain immediately below this was "that ancient river, the river Kishon," true to its name (*kishon*, twisted or winding), beside whose waters Elijah slew the 450 priests of Baal. Then, returning probably to the same spot where he had built the altar unto the Lord, the prophet "cast himself down upon the earth" in the earnestness of his supplication for the blessing of rain (now that the vengeance of God had been satisfied, and the pollution of Baal-worship removed); and up to this highest point, where we now sat, seven times over he bade his servant "go up, and look towards the sea:" until at last the little cloud arose on the horizon, foretelling the commencement of the autumn rains. It was easy to fancy one saw the chariot of Ahab hastening over the great plain of Esdraelon before us, stretching out eastwards from the foot of Carmel, and the prophet, with his loins girded like any one of the Arabs now around us, running before him all the way, even till he reached the entrance of his own royal palace at Jezreel,—there—on that green hill of Gilboa at the other side of the plain. And across that plain too, one also thought one could see the woman of that small village of Shunem, at the foot of Little Hermon yonder, riding on the ass, and, in the anguish of her heart, urging on her servant in driving it, that she might fall at the feet of the Prophet, and entreat him to save and restore to life the son which his prayers had obtained of God for her, refusing to leave him till he arose and followed her to the little home he had often hallowed by his presence. So the Scripture narrative acquired new life and reality as we read it here on the very spot, and all the natural features, only half expressed to the reader at home, unfolded themselves one by one to view, and seemed to deepen on the sacred page, like the landscapes drawn in sympathetic inks, developing their meaning in the living colours of Nature.

We returned to Hhaïffa by another lower road, passing large herds of cattle gathered under the shady trees, and descending to the banks of the Kishon, the windings of which we crossed several times before we reached the town. We carried away some pretty tortoises, but, torpid though they seemed, they would always escape from wherever they were put, in some wonderful way of their own; and we caught one of the huge locusts without wings, the marks on whose body are believed by the Fellaheen to be inscriptions written in the most ancient language used in the world.   This day's ride is worth any fatigue from its historical and natural interest; the character of the woodland and the scenery is much the same as that of the charming sides of Jebel Rihân in the Baruk range.

Another day we rode along the narrow plain between the sea-coast and the mountain, turning round the point of the headland, and southwards to the "Pilgrim's Castle" of the Crusaders, now called Athlît: a ride of nearly four hours from Hhaïffa, along an excellent smooth, soft road.   We came first to the outside end of a road of approach which was cut through the living rock, forming a pass, once closed by a gate, the places for the hinges and bolts of which are still perfect in the rock, as well as the foundations of a strong tower on each side that guarded the gate.   The rock-road itself is about eight feet wide, with ruts worn by the chariot-wheels passing over it: the rock at the sides is cut in regular banks or ledges one above another, probably *trottoirs* for the pedestrians going and coming.   It is supposed to be from this remarkable rock-cut road that the fortress was called "Petra Incisa."   Passing through this the place became more open, but we traced the road up to the outer gate of the city or castle, through which we went to look at the remains of an old church with gothic arches, string-courses, and some well-carved mouldings.   The citadel, which stands on a promontory of rock jutting out into the sea, must have been of very great strength from its situation and its enormously thick walls, formed of large well-hewn stones: the portions of wall still standing are fifteen feet thick and some thirty feet high; beyond these there was a very strong outer sea-wall connecting tower with tower, and protecting the semicircular piece of land between.   Here, close to the sea, are two large, grand halls, with pointed-arch groined roofs, and a huge, solidly-built cistern, while some fine, massive, granite columns lie on the ground beyond them.   There is a vast extent of ruin, most of which is believed to date several hundred years prior to the Crusaders; but the earliest notice on record of the place is of the twelfth century; it is a very fine place, very picturesque, and not a little interesting.   The people whose houses crowd, like the cells of a wasp's nest, the inside of the old ruins, have not a very good character, but they were hospitable and obliging to us, bringing us relays of hot coffee for luncheon.   We had a delightful ride back to Hhaïffa, lighted all the way by innumerable fire-flies, glancing and dancing round us as we went: they were small of their kind, but very bright and lovely.

A most suffocating sirocco blew the next day, so malignant that we found exertion impossible, until a little before sunset, when we managed to mount our horses, and follow the kindly guidance of our host to the mouth of the Kishon. Here he tied our steeds to the ghastly timbers of a wreck, one of four ships which had been driven up on the coast; two of these, both called "the Sisters Maria," had been built and launched together, had sailed on different tracks round the world, and then, by a strange romantic accident, had met here for the first time since their launch, only to be wrecked, and to lie there driven one into the other, hopelessly entangled in each other's arms! This bay is very dangerous in south-westerly gales, and many a hapless ship is driven ashore: but all looked peaceful and smiling enough this evening, as we hunted for shells on the sands and gathered handfuls of honeysuckle and oleander from the banks of the river; the mountains, however, were veiled in a dreamy, sad-looking sirocco fog, and even the bright blue sky was dimmed behind the thickened air. We forded the river with great success, but accidents are very frequent here from the rapid changes that take place in the banks at its mouth, and still more from the torrent of water which comes sweeping down with a sudden flood, carrying everything before it, after a day, or even half a day's rain; such was the end of many of the soldiers of Sisera. (Judg. v. 4, 19, 21.) Travellers fording the Kishon under the guidance of a dragoman instead of a native very commonly get into trouble.

The Austrian steamer came in at five the next morning, so, bidding good-bye to pretty, pleasant Hhaïffa, we went on board, and made a most agreeable voyage along the white cliffs and green banks of the coast up to Beyrout, which we reached in eight hours, and once more its lovely mountains delighted my eyes; but sad tidings greeted us of threatened disturbances in the Lebanon, and the very next passengers that came up from Hhaïffa watched the flames and smoke rising from our beloved Beit Miry.

The Archbishop Spaccapietra took us, on the following day, to see the Institution of the Sœurs de St. Vincent de Paul, which stands immediately behind the east gate of the town; it is now a very large establishment, built round two squares, and containing eight schools for different classes of girls, *all free* except the upper class of boarders, who are the daughters of native Consuls, merchants, &c.; these pay a small sum, and have their dormitory divided by curtains, into separate apartments: they numbered about fifty. There were sixty other boarders, forty day-scholars, and more than one hundred orphans and foundlings *: besides an upper school for training girls

---

* Another 100 have been added since the massacres in the mountains, and they are in hopes of soon having funds sufficient for the support of many more orphans.

as schoolmistresses : one of these assistant-teachers taught in every classroom under the direction of a Sister.   Every class was instructed in reading and writing, both in Arabic and French: plain work and various kinds of embroidery, arithmetic, music and singing; their writing struck us as marvellous : many little girls from eight to twelve years old, who had only been in the school two or three years, produced copybooks of admirable writing in both languages; every page was embellished with borders composed of flourishes, arabesques, flowers and leaves, of their own design as well as execution, and all spotlessly clean : many of the designs were excellent.   Their needlework was also very good, even to the Archbishop's satisfaction: we were extremely amused to hear him giving an elaborate lecture to his chaplain upon the qualities and characteristics of stitching, and explaining to him the proper finish of a well-made button-hole !   The schools are open to children of any creed : Christians, Mooslims, &c., all are taken in who wish to enter it, but of course no difference is made in the lessons they learn.

Attached to the schools is a Hospital, served by two of the Sisters : it is in the midst of a garden, the roses climbing pleasantly about the windows of the sick wards, each of which contains thirty beds ; the women's ward was quite full at the time of our visit ; the natives come from great distances to seek the assistance of the Sisters in the Dispensary, which is crowded for some hours every morning, and we heard of several rich people who thought so highly of their skill, that they came disguised as poor persons in order to obtain it; they have been very successful in their treatment of ophthalmia, the curse of hot countries : the patients frequently amount to three hundred and four hundred a day.

It was thirteen years since the Mother and a few of the Sisters arrived from France : they had but some half-a-dozen francs between them, and had much difficulty in getting enough to build a house : then came long nursing in the Cholera, followed by some other equally fearful epidemics, which put off the commencement of their schools : one young Sister died of the fever caught in attending prisoners in the Serai, and we heard some touching stories of the earnest, affectionate anxiety the men showed about her, and of their sorrow for her death ; her funeral was attended not only by all the Consuls in Beyrout, but the Pasha sent three of his officers to represent him at the ceremony.   The next Pasha also showed the greatest confidence in them, and once, when a criminal condemned to death was given up to them to nurse in a severe illness, and died in their hospital, the Superior sent to the Pasha to request he would have the body identified, as is usual in such cases, but he only answered that it was quite unnecessary, as he could trust to the word of a Sister better than to aught else. This was considered an extraordinary mark of confidence, but truth and earnestness in work are always appreciated by the Mooslims. All the buildings they now have, and they are really fine ones, have been erected from small subscriptions and alms, not without many difficulties and trials; there were nineteen Sisters at the time of our visit, but they were hoping soon to welcome more of them from France.

A few days after this, when tidings of horror were beginning to creep in from the mountains, and vague fears and anxieties were painting themselves on every face, we took advantage of the French steamer to carry us up to Latakia. We left Beyrout in the evening, and early the next morning went ashore to make our third visit to Tripoli, as the steamer was to remain there all day.

It is a pity that artists do not go to Tripoli, for no place is better worthy of their study for "street bits:" the costumes of Saïda and Hebron are as bright and fresh as those of Tripoli, but the streets themselves are built in a handsomer style both in the Marina and the inner town, the cafés on the river-side are more romantic, and the mosques more ornamental. Orange groves are very plentiful, and not only is the fruit piled up in every shop, but the windows are everywhere bowered in branches of the trees, with dozens of the golden fruit still hanging from them. The mountains rise so abruptly and grandly from immediately behind the town : the large gardens and fine old castles mingle so prettily with the rocks and sea, that altogether it is a charming spot. We passed a pleasant day, buying carpets and sketching, enjoying the delicious climate among the gardens on the sea-shore.

On arriving at Latakia, we immediately inquired for horses and mules, intending to pursue our way to Suédiyeh, across the mountains, a four days' journey : they did not, however, seem easy to be had ; at this season numbers of horses are sent down to the districts of Judæa on account of the pilgrims, and as all the tolerably good ones that remain are put out to grass, it is very difficult to obtain any. Unluckily it entered into our heads to go by sea, and we inquired about the boats, just now being made ready for the first days of the sponge fishing or gathering : and at last we decided upon hiring one for 150 piasters, a severe sirocco having filled our souls with suffocation when we thought of the four days' ride ; besides which we were assured that six hours of the clear, cool moonlight would carry us to Suédiyeh. A sail was rigged up, tent-fashion, over a hole, four feet by five, and everything that could be done to make us comfortable was arranged by our kind Consul. So we left

2 H

Latakia, with a favourable breeze and the moon shining gloriously over our heads, packing ourselves with our maid, like spoons in a row, into the small hole, with the awning about three feet above our heads. In about an hour the delightful breeze died away, the men turned sleepy and wouldn't pull: and, oh, horror of horrors! two whole days and nights we rocked and rolled in our flat-bottomed tub upon that hot and glaring sea! after twenty-four hours of it, we drew to land, and took to bathing in a shady nook, hoping that the salt water might prove a little distasteful to the myriads of wretches that had been making carnival on the strangers.

The worst of it was that, shut into our hole, broiled, baked, and qualmish, we could not look out enough to enjoy the scenery: we could only see that the coast was really pretty all along the foot of Mount Casius: the numerous little bays and creeks, the various ranges of hills dipping their rocky feet in the blue water, added to the very bright greens of the prickly oak, terebinth, and myrtle, with the gay flowers, all combine to make it very enjoyable—when one can see it. We crossed the bar of the Orontes near sunset on the second day, too late to get horses for our luggage, and only a strong breeze will carry a boat against the current of the river; so we had to sleep another night in our hole, dining on the shore by the light of the moon which shone down on the rocky defiles that form the amphitheatre of hills enclosing the rich little plain of Suédiyeh—the ancient Seleucia. The eagle who showed Seleucus where to place his city, was an eagle of taste as well as wisdom: but in these days the meek little silkworm reigns sole sovereign of the plain. Accustomed to the mountains clothed and terraced with mulberries throughout the Lebanon, the vivid greens of the gardens were not new to our eyes, but nowhere had we seen such mulberries as these: not sparingly planted as in the Lebanon, but closely crowded, with branches so loaded with leaves one wondered if there was space for one more: or how the small number of families in the place could gather half as many in the course of a silk season. The leaves, however, are used as fodder for the cows, especially when, as has been the case for several years, the worms partially fail, for a few hours of severe sirocco sometimes kill every silkworm in a district. These mulberry gardens are divided by well-made roads with a water-course on each side, and a high hedge of luxuriant pomegranates, tangled over with wild vines, while myrtle, apricots, peaches, plums, olives, and figs are seen everywhere. There is nothing prettier in Nature than a pomegranate hedge in summer: the trees grow so gracefully, and the peculiar dark yet bright glossy green of the leaf contrasts so well with the myriads of gorgeous scarlet blossoms.

We pitched our tents on a little olive-shaded hill, whence we could enjoy the lovely view of the gardens and their Swiss-looking cottages, the winding river, the sea, and the noble mountains. Right opposite to us was Mount Casius, 5318 feet high, rising abruptly from the water, with deep, narrow ravines and chasms, but all covered over with a green velvet mantle of underwood, and bright little sloping uplands: the apex, a cone of white limestone, alone deserving the Arab appellation of Okra—the Bald Mountain. The wood on this mountain is said to be beautiful: the myrtle covers its feet until replaced by lofty oaks, which are succeeded by pine forests: then, after 3500 feet above the sea, come glades of birch, pear, apple, and quince trees: while huge scarlet peonies, yellow asphodel, violets, and pansies flourish up to the very edge of the snow on the summit. The bay, which curves round at its foot, is varied by remarkably bright orange cliffs, cropping out here and there, while the successive lines of green corn, mulberries and fruit gardens, fill up the flat plain to the foot of the Pierian range on the northern side. These cliffs are the *heel* of the Amanus Mountains, which form the south-eastern side of the Gulf of Iskenderoon, and there join the great Taurus range: under the projecting promontory of these mountains—the Pig's Head, as it is called in Arabic—was the fine port, harbour, and fortress of Seleucia Pieria: built by Seleucus Nicator, the first king of Syria, B.C. 300, on the site of a more ancient fortress.

Half-an-hour after leaving the gardens of Suédiyeh, the road leads under fine bluffs of rocks, almost honeycombed with grottoes and excavated tombs, which extend up to the very back of the old town, and are now much inhabited by the peasants. After passing the remains of a large gateway, the city wall is distinctly to be traced the whole way to the shore, the ancient masonry rising in many places several feet above the ground: within these walls, about a quarter of a mile from the sea, is the basin or dock for the galleys, which occupies an area of 47 acres, and is now half filled up with mud. From this a passage between two thick walls, about 350 yards long, led out into the sea: the great gate which separated the passage from the basin, closed between two strong towers, the bases of which were cut from the living rock, and still seem loftily guarding the way. The harbour, which is now much sanded up, had formerly two strong jetties, curving towards each other, built of fine blocks of stone united by iron clamps: the greater part of one jetty remains and some of the other. The view hence is striking, as one looks back across the ancient walls and the rock-cut passage: through which one can fancy the Roman galleys gallantly passing in, with all their oars outspread; the mighty handiworks of ancient days contrasting with the split and tumbled-down rocks and walls, and the simple *chalets* of the silkworms and their tenders; behind them all stood the noble mountain covered with the rich green of the myrtles and oleanders and mulberries, and every here and there the darker spots of the squared or arched entrances to the ancient tombs.

But a greater work than basin or jetty yet remains to be seen: this is a cutting in the solid rock, nearly three quarters of a mile long, in some places 120 feet deep, and averaging twenty-four feet wide, mostly open to the air, but in many parts tunnelled through the rock; a little channel for a small stream of water runs nearly all the way along the side, keeping at a level height, while in one place a staircase is cut out and descends to within fourteen feet of the bottom, which was probably the usual level of the water. This magnificent work is believed to have been made to carry off the water (which might otherwise have injured both the city and the basin) from the ravine behind the town, where it collected from the hillsides and poured off into this tunnel; as even now, spite of fallen rocks and other obstacles, the water in winter still fills up the mighty excavation to the depth of fourteen or sixteen feet; and possibly another cutting, now much filled up and grown over, on the other side of a solid wall, which may have been a huge dam, was used to convey the stream occasionally into the basin or dock. For whatever purpose it was constructed, it was a very splendid work, and a triumph of labour, which must have cost many years, and very many hands to accomplish. We could discover no inscriptions or carvings, save one small tablet, about a foot square, at the eastern entrance, on which is very distinctly cut the oval of an eyelid, but without the eye itself.

The tombs in the rocks are well worth visiting: nearly all have but one entrance: to a few, however, there are two or three arches in front, divided by small columns: the principal Tomb—that "of the King," as the Arabs say—is very large; three arches give entrance to the outer chamber, the eight corners of which are ornamented with fan shells, and lead into a much larger chamber surrounded by arched niches, under which are tombs; some others are cut in the floor of the chamber; none of the lids remain, but the grooves upon which they were fastened are still visible. We counted about forty tombs in the one room or hall, two of which are very peculiar, standing in the centre of the chamber, they have been cut from the rock in isolated sarcophagi under a canopy supported at each corner by a column, looking much like an old-fashioned four-post bedstead:

the columns have rough capitals. Another room leads off from the right hand of the outer chamber, containing twelve or fourteen niches with handsome fan-shell ornaments, the same as those used in all the niches of the Temples of Baalbek, but roughly executed here: the entrance to this chamber is by a semicircular arch with six or seven mouldings. All the Tombs have been opened at some early date, but many Greek inscriptions have been found in later times: numbers of the sarcophagi are ornamented with garlands or wreaths, and contained small terra-cotta jars for the ashes of the dead.

A statue of large size, but headless, was dug up from a garden near the city wall, a year or two ago: it is of some river-god, perhaps Poseidon himself, habited in well-sculptured drapery, with a vase in one arm from which water is flowing: probably it was the personification of the Orontes.

The fire-flies danced round us as we rode back across the scented plain, and the great yellow moon illuminated even the colours of the pomegranates and oleanders, as we passed along the gardens up to our tents. More than commonly rich are the perfumes of this plain, for the late Mr. Barker*, who planted fully half of it, brought together into his own garden hundreds of trees and plants from far distant lands; Chinese, Persian, North and South American, and Indian flowers and fruits grow luxuriantly on the Syrian plain, and add their exotic beauties to the many lovely productions indigenous to the country. The garden is surrounded by trellises of Muscat vines, which bear abundantly, and the wine made from which was most delicious. The liquorice plant covers the whole of this country with its pretty lilac flowers, among which francolins, partridges, snipe, and quantities of other game hide themselves.

The bay of Suédiyeh supplies a very delicious little fish, called by the natives "Sultan Ibrahim:" it is a kind of red mullet, but very small, rich and delicate in flavour and of the prettiest bright colours.

But there is nothing so pretty about the plain of Suédiyeh as the women, whose large, lustrous, black eyes gleam from dark faces far more delicately and sweetly formed than those of any other Syrian women we had seen. The women of Nazareth and Bethlehem certainly are handsome, but they are cast in a rather clumsy, coarse mould, which is not particularly engaging; and though they have

* The late Mr. Barker settled at Suédiyeh about thirty years ago, devoting himself to the improvement of the land and of the peasantry. He was much beloved and respected by them all, and is one of the very few Christians of whom the Mooslims say, "he is *Merhoum*," *i.e.* blessed, and at rest with God.

been celebrated by so many travellers, I never could see as much to
admire in them, as in the sweet, smiling little mouth and white
teeth, the straight noses and slight figures of their charming sisters
of Northern Syria.   They wear an ugly costume of a coarse stuff,
drab coloured, without any relieving tints; however, their faces are,
fortunately, unveiled.   The men of Suédiyeh are chiefly Ansayreeh,
the curious sect about whose tenets and secret rites so little is
known: they have most pleasant, courteous manners, and are remarkably handsome and well-made men, with open, intelligent
countenances; they dress gaily in bright crimson and orange *abbahs*
and white shirts, and nearly all have red leather boots reaching to
the knees.   They call themselves simply Fellaheen, disliking to be
given the name of Ansayreeh, and are most friendly with the Christians, but very quarrelsome with the Mooslims: they never speak
of their own creed, and are too abstemious and sober ever to let out
the slightest allusion to their secrets; it is said that, if any person
should ever by accident approach them when they are holding a
sacred feast, his life would be in great danger, if he was not fortunate enough to steal away unobserved.   People say they worship
the Sun and Moon, but this is probably untrue: they appear to keep
some feasts relating to our Lord and His blessed Mother, as they
believe Him to have been one of the Incarnations of the Deity; the
virtues they seem to prize the most, are those of hospitality and
generosity among themselves; at their meetings for worship, which
are held near the Tomb of one of their Saints, a feast is always
made for the poorer brethren.   Like the Metouaalees and Druzes
they say that the archangel Gabriel made a mistake in bringing the
revelation of the true religion to Muhammad, as it was in reality
intended for his son-in-law 'Ali.

A very pretty ride is the road to Antioch from this Seleucian
plain, passing chiefly along the banks of the Orontes: we took the
road by the south bank, crossing and recrossing ever so many
streams, and were finally ferried over the wide and rapid current of
the muddy river in a rude boat, secured by stout vine tendrils, by
way of ropes, to each shore!   The road lay through fruit gardens
and miles of luxuriant shrubs and flowers with lofty trees: poplars,
lime, and maple, which, with the pretty mountain views, rejoiced
one's heart and eyes.   Along these shady lanes, 1800 years ago,
came the two Apostles Paul and Barnabas, weary, perhaps, in body,
but " strong in the Lord," when, having been " separated for the
work " at Antioch, they " departed unto Seleucia, and from thence
they sailed to Cyprus."   After nearly five hours' riding, we turned
up over a hill, where we saw curious cavern tombs, and the remains

of an underground aqueduct; and, after riding over a flat plain, arrived suddenly at the edge of a steep descent into a deep, close dell, between the plain and the foot of the mountain. The banks of the dell were thickly covered with shrubs and shady trees in tangled masses, through which a hundred streams were dashing in cascades of snowy foam, with loud and half deafening music: this beautiful spot was the famous grove of Daphne, where wild revels were annually held by the thousands of pilgrims who came to enjoy its deliciousness. Of the noble Temples, dedicated to Apollo, which long ago adorned the groves, whence the mysterious voice of the Oracle issued, not a trace now remains, except in the stones of a dozen corn-mills turned by the once sacred streams; these are still surrounded by the thickets of bay and aromatic shrubs sacred to the gay god. The sacred cypress has disappeared, and is replaced by mulberries and figs; the words of ancient wisdom are hushed, prophecy is no more, the Arcadia is withered, and naught remains to whisper legends of the "god of Love, and Light, and Poesy," but the perfumes of the groves he loved, and the echoes of the shepherd's pipe, which sound sweetly through the valley. But ere these changes had been quite effected, the unholy atmosphere of this "sensual paradise" had been purified or at least neutralised by the bones of St. Babylas, a martyred Bishop of Antioch: while, much to the disgust of the priests of Apollo, a Christian church was erected in the very heart of the sacred grove of Daphne. Julian the Apostate, however, made them happy by the removal of the episcopal remains, but on the very same night the Temple was set on fire, it was said by the lightnings of Heaven, and the statue of Apollo entirely consumed. Julian's reign was no sooner over than Daphne was resanctified by the restoration of the holy bones to their original resting-place, and the memory of the miracle became as dear to the hearts of the Christians as the oracles of Apollo had been to Pagan worshippers.

We rested for some time under the shade of a splendid lime-tree before we pursued our way along the pleasant lanes, passing through Ansayreeh villages, of neatly built houses, roofed with tiles, and with little gardens enclosed in 'osier woven fences; less than two hours took us to Antioch—proud old Antioch—spreading out in the broad, flat, fertile plain at the feet of the fantastic crags of Mount Silpius; the Orontes shining brightly in its numerous windings past the city, while on the other side of the valley many a fine peak or cone, in the rugged outline of the Amanus Mountains, lost themselves in little wreaths of light mist resting here and there on their summits. Our tents were pitched outside the town, and near the river, where gigantic *sakiyah* wheels are employed to raise water into the gardens, groaning loudly and distressfully at every turn. Not far off were two huge structures built by Ibrahim Pasha as a palace for himself and barracks for his troops; only the shells have ever been completed, and from these the roofing was taken by the English Consul, with the permission of the Government, for the barracks built for the Land Transport Corps at the time of the Crimean War: it is said that the walls are going to be pulled down now. These ill-fated buildings were raised from materials, taken by the Pasha, from the ancient walls and fortifications of the city.

Antioch retains its ancient name in the Arab appellation of Antâkie: its site like that of Seleucia, was chosen by Seleucus Nicator, from the alighting of an eagle after sacrifice on Mount Silpius, and named by its founder after his father Antiochus: it is royally well placed. During the 300 years which followed its foundation up to the Christian era, the kings of Syria delighted to add fresh beauties to their metropolis: temples, palaces, colonnades, and bridges adorned the streets: Pompey added new temples, baths, theatres, aqueducts, and a basilica. These, and the grand colonnade leading from the city gate along the Berœa or Aleppo road, must have been standing in undiminished glory when Barnabas the Apostle brought Paul from Tarsus to assist him in "opening the door of faith" to the Gentiles of Antioch: the first converts that called themselves by the name of Christians. The good seed sown by them grew and increased, and brought forth fruit abundantly, watered from time to time by the blood of martyrs, and sending out into the world fathers and confessors of the faith, and scholars of great renown, from whom she earned the name of "the Eye of the Christian Church," until about 600 years after Christ, when the Persians under Chosroes destroyed the whole city. Once more rebuilt by the Saracens, she saw the first onset of the Crusaders in Syria; they had already undergone great sufferings in crossing Asia Minor, and many a ghastly corpse had strewed the mountain passes of Cilicia; but the very terrible sufferings that afflicted them during the seven months' siege of Antioch were only equalled by the supreme valour which distinguished the army of Godfrey de Bouillon. The horrors of famine and pestilence had been brought on by their own improvidence and the shameless sensuality which pervaded the camp: jealousy of each other hampered every measure and protracted the duration of the siege: and only treachery at length enabled a small body of men to scale a distant postern, when nearly every man, woman, and child in the city was massacred by the Christian troops in June, 1098.

Much of the Roman fortifications are still standing, and can be descried from a great distance: as they are carried straight up the steep sides of the mountain, they are very fatiguing to examine: the finest portion, however, is within an easy walk along a good path. This part is the " Iron Gate "* which defended the eastern end of the city from the attack of an army stealing in through the narrow mountain pass on the southern side: the only road from whence they could be hidden from the citizens. The ravine, which is excessively narrow and lofty, turns with a sudden elbow round the end of Mount Silpius, and is filled up with a solid and immense wall of masonry (built with intervening lines of Roman red tiles), fitted to the rough natural sides of the gorge as if the walls had grown into the rocks: it stands across the ravine rising to about half the height of the mountain; from thence another wall ran up the dizzy height to the summit, where it met the many-towered wall that had come up from the western end of the town, and had passed frowning along the mountain top, looking down from this height and enclosing all one side of the city. Just at the summit are the remains of a church dedicated to St. Peter and St. Paul: and here the city wall was built in a row of arches, open on one side, easily distinguished from the city. The wall descended from the Iron Gate into the plain, passing below the ancient Church of St. John, lately purchased by the French with a piece of ground for a cemetery. This church is in fact a very ancient excavation from the living rock: two pillars have been left standing in front as a portico. In one corner, close beside the altar, is a small well, and the grotto seems to have been excavated some way further: the colours on the sides can still be traced: and the simple rude solemnity of the time-honoured spot seemed a fitting place for the streams of living eloquence poured forth to the scholars and disputers of the proud old city,

> " awed by truth divine
> Breathed through the golden lips of Chrysostom ! "

Some way above this, and only to be reached by a steep scramble up the cliff, there are some curious colossal figures sculptured on the face of the rock; one is a female head and figure down to the waist, the features are worn away, but the hair is still distinct, parted in the centre and rolled back: beside her stands a full-length male figure; the view over the beautiful plain from them is fine. The ancient Aleppo Gate, Bab Bulus—Gate of Paul—is still standing

* The " Iron Gates " of this Pass are usually confounded in descriptions of the sieges of Antioch with the bridge on the plain at the north side of the town : this bridge was closed at one end by iron gates,—hence the mistake.

a handsome archway shaded by a fine lime-tree : thence the wall may be traced through the plain half-way to the bank of the river, and at a short distance beyond it are some very remarkable and mysterious remains.   First, there is a series of thirteen masses of solid masonry shaped like buttresses ; the height of each is fourteen foet and the width fifteen feet : but as there is no trace of any wall which they had once supported, they must have been erected for some other object : nothing is now to be seen but the heavy masses of stone and cement.

At the distance of a hundred yards or more from these, are some massive, broad walls, built in two oblongs one within the other, with an opening on three sides : these walls are fourteen feet high and twelve feet thick, and are built of an extremely hard cement : at the northern end inside both is a detached mass of masonry of the same width and height as the wall, and at the same distance from the inner one as they are from each other.   It is difficult to imagine for what purpose these walls could have been originally constructed ; the only conjecture that seems in the least probable is that it was a theatre for sea-fights, the part between the walls being always kept full of water with gates to let it pass at pleasure into the inner court : the spectators may have been placed on the top of these thick walls, to which they mounted by exterior steps : the proximity of the spot to the river seems to favour this idea.   It has also been suggested that the buttresses supported an aqueduct bringing water to this theatre, but they do not appear to lie in connection with this building, nor to have any special adaptation to an aqueduct.   The walls of the city, in the plain, are still distinct : very fine walls they have been and marvellously massive : history tells that they were wide enongh for two chariots to drive abreast on them.

We were very much pleased with Antioch : there is great variety in the scenery : the mountain peaks are more sudden and varied than is usual in Syria, the plain is particularly rich, and the river is a very noble stream ; in its days of glory Antioch must indeed have been magnificent ; it was called the third city in the world. It is a remarkably healthy place : the strong breeze down the wide, open valleys blows away all miasma, so that fevers and epidemics are little known.   The people are somewhat fanatical, but thrifty and industrious.

We left Antioch after a few days' most pleasant sojourn in the hospitable house of our Consul, and wended our way along the rich, flat plain, fording many small streams and passing several ancient ruined bridges and aqueducts, around each and all of which were complete forests of oleander. After about five hours' slow riding we turned up one of the defiles of the Amanus Mountains, and reached a large ruined khan, where we expected to find our tents all ready: but our interesting Arab cook, a man we had engaged at Latakia, had piled up all the luggage in a heap, and was sitting quietly smoking beside it when we arrived, coolly remarking that he " couldn't think where to pitch them." It was then quite dark, and the pitching was slow work: we fell fast asleep on the grass while waiting, and were much astonished when at 11 P.M. we were wakened with the announcement that dinner was ready.

Our ride, on the following day, was a lovely one: we wound up the steep pass of Beylan, enjoying beautiful views of the plain of Aleppo and the great lake—Bahr-el-Abiad—stretching far away, while our path led among the most charming glades and glens clothed with thick forests of various kinds of oak and pine, filled up with judas-trees, laurustinus, and myrtle, while the pass became continually higher, grander, and more richly wooded. I am sure there is not anywhere in Syria so fine a pass: the scenery and foliage of the valley itself is worthy of the Mysian Mount Olympus: but the views from it are not equal to the magnificent surroundings of Broussa. Almost the whole way the old Roman road was invisible, but the broken remains were worse than the roughest natural ground: fortunately there is usually a narrow track beside it. Beylan is known in all history as the " Iron Gate of Syria:" it is the only entrance into the country from the Gulf of Issus—now called of Iskenderoon—and it is not easy to enumerate its various appearances in history. The armies of both the First and Second Crusade passed through the long defile, weary and wayworn, with but few remaining of the gallant thousands that had started from Europe: Alexander the Great, flushed with the utter defeat of the Persian army under Darius Codomanus, the last king of that great empire, triumphantly advanced through the " Iron Gates " for the conquest of Phœnicia, which ended in the capture and destruction of Tyre: and along here the " Son of Consolation," the Apostle Barnabas, went from Antioch to seek Saul, the zealous convert, at his home in Tarsus, and brought him back to teach much people at Antioch.

The caravans to Aleppo and Antioch all pass along this road, and we found it gay with passengers. In about three hours we came in sight of the town of Beylan, most picturesquely perched on ledges of the mountain, up both sides; the gorge is throughout excessively narrow, with only room for a powerful torrent at the bottom, but the depths are bridged in several places with fine aqueducts mounted on double arches, and its sides are richly ornamented with wood, from out of which a thousand foamy cataracts come tumbling down with marvellous beauty : it is a place for any kind of romance, there is such variety and grandeur in the scene at every step. Various Sultans have at different times enriched the town with mosques and other buildings, but there is nothing handsome about it now : it is but an enchanting combination of wild, savage, and fantastic rocks, luxuriant foliage, graceful cascades, and shelf after shelf of yellow-brown houses, each with its little dome and open verandah, clinging round the deep ravines of the great chasm. The men are a very fine-looking, well-dressed set, and bear a good character : the women, soft-eyed and handsome ; but they wear the most frightful dress—an *eezar* or cotton sheet enveloping the figure from the head to the feet in one great bundle, of a deep brickdust red !

We found a delightful garden just beyond the town where we encamped under the shade of fine pomegranate trees, then in full blossom : hence we could make excursions, on foot, among the rocks and gardens of the ravine, until it was time to go down to meet the steamer at Iskenderoon (or Alexandretta). Just beyond the town, the road has been cut through the promontory on the east side of the gorge to the depth of about forty feet—this was the " Iron Gate ;" here a handful of men could have kept a large army at bay for almost any length of time, so tremendously steep are the sides of the ravine. Passing round this projecting cliff, the sea burst upon our view : the vast Bay of Issus—with the beautiful snow-covered heights of the Taurus Mountains on the other side and Iskenderoon on the little plain by the shore ; our steamer was descried waiting there, even her colours visible in the clear air. We descended to the plain in two hours, winding through delightful woods all the time and enjoying the noble panorama. But after the fresh, sweet, healthy mountain air the stifling heat of the unwholesome marshy plain, reeking with fever, was most disagreeable : it is said that a very little drainage would render this plain perfectly healthy and productive ; the soil is very rich, but so deadly is the miasma that there are scarcely any inhabitants to cultivate it ; the town is a miserable collection of huts, mostly made of osiers and wattles, with the strange little sleeping-places mounted up on high poles, such as we had seen at Banias, to ensure the occupants from snakes, scorpions, &c. We did not linger longer in the town than to see the caravan for Baghdad starting on its long march, and another for Aleppo ; both carry on the passengers and merchandise brought by the steamers. The road from this to Baghdad is the easiest of all the land routes to that city, avoiding the great heat and fatigue of the Palmyra Desert, and passing through green meadow-land the whole way; the caravan marches to Mosul, and the passengers then descend the Tigris to Baghdad.

I had a raging headache, for the low fever then lurking in me was brought out instantly by exposure to the slightest miasma: and it was therefore with but half-opened eyes that I saw the shores of Syria receding from us as we pushed off in the little boat from Iskenderoon. One year and one week had elapsed since we had first touched the shores of Syria in this very spot, when the snowy mountains and the glowing oleanders had given us as sweet a welcome as they now bade us a kind good-bye: then, much as we anticipated and expected, we little knew the pleasure and happiness in store for us; now—the serene days of our dear little mountain home—the magnificent country rides—the glorious Desert and the wild Bedoueen—the long, long stay in the desolated but ever Holy and beloved City—bright and sunny hours with kind and valued friends—all rushed into my mind, and made my heart sink with the same feeling as that of parting from a long and tenderly loved companion, as my foot quitted that sandy shore.

Farewell, most Holy Land: Farewell, dear and beautiful Syria; already the blood of her massacred natives was crying out from the earth, and the flame and the smoke of her burning houses was rising into the unclouded sky; and yet we dare to hope and believe that the day will come when industry and enterprise will be spread throughout the country, and happy homesteads clothe the mountains and fill the pleasant valleys; when truth and justice and honesty will be found in every village, and honour in every heart; and, better than all, when Salvation by the Cross of Christ, Whose Blood was shed for us in that sacred country, will be proclaimed from north to south, from end to end, making " the Desert to blossom like the rose."

CHAPTER XXIV.

KNIGHTS OF THE PAST AND HEROES OF THE PRESENT.

We had written by the steamer of the previous fortnight to engage horses to be ready for us on landing at Mersina, and the English Consul obligingly sent a boat and kawass to bring us on shore early in the morning, as we were anxious to occupy the time of the steamer's stay at Mersina in visiting the fine ruins of Pompeiopolis or Soli—now called Mezetlu; it is about five miles from the town, the ride passing near the sea-shore, along a plain densely covered with thickets of myrtle, and a few oleanders: two streams are crossed, both pleasantly shaded by trees.

Soli was peopled by a colony from Rhodes, and is mentioned by Strabo as a city of renown: it was destroyed by Tigranes, king of Armenia, and rebuilt by Pompey, who gave it his own name.   The port was enclosed by two fine jetties with circular ends, constructed of large stones, secured by iron clamps, and filled in with rubble; much of these still remain, but at the time of our visit a Turkish boat was loading with the stones at the end of each jetty, to use in some other building: and perhaps by this time both have disappeared. Opposite the harbour, at a short distance from the shore, there once stood a noble portico, at the commencement of an avenue of 200 columns which led up to a temple further inland: forty of these columns are still standing on one side and four on the other, and the ground is strewed with their fallen drums. At the southern end some stones yet remain above the columns, enough to show that it was once vaulted over, so as to form a covered way: but it is remarkable that some two or three of the columns are shorter than the rest; most of them are about thirty feet high and plain, but some are fluted vertically, others spirally: all have acanthus capitals, amongst the leaves of which heads of Venus and Hercules also appear: the work of all is poor and not in good taste. They are now enclosed in deep groves of myrtle and laurustinus, &c.

Near this are the remains of a once fine theatre, now almost buried in the soil; it was built of white marble, and had a cornice running all round the top of wreaths, sculptured with tragic masks: some of the vomitories still remain; the figure of a Venus, life-size, sculptured in white marble, but broken, was found here. The city walls are also traceable, with the ruins of small forts all round them; and the tombs are said to be peculiar and very interesting, resembling the large and very curious mausoleums discovered at Tarsus.* This little expedition was very pleasant; full time is allowed for it by every French steamer, and horses of some kind are always procurable.

We found the town of Mersina perfectly full of Tartars, whom the Turks called Circassians (Tcherkesses): these poor creatures belonged to a tribe called Nogay, and of course became Russian subjects from the time of her conquest of the Caucasus: but, being Mooslims, and very much attached to their religion, they could not endure being under the yoke of Russia, and they, therefore, about two years ago, applied to the Sultan for his protection and assistance in emigrating from the hated empire. The Sultan acquiesced in their demands, and sent ships to Kertch and Poti to bring them off: at first, the Turkish Government allowed them three piasters a day per head, and promised each man a bullock and agricultural implements: but neither were ever forthcoming, and when the number of emigrants amounted to some thousands, the money could no longer be given; they came down in batches of from 800 to 1000 at a time, men, women, and children; fine, active fellows, and as we were told, excellent workmen, but there was nothing for them to do; and horrible as their sufferings were during the three weeks' or month's voyage, usually without food or covering, huddled on the decks †, yet they were scarcely more miserable than on arriving at their destination.

The Sultan gave them a small island in the Sea of Marmora and the great plain of Adana and Selefkeh, south of the Taurus: and on this they were turned out as soon as they reached Mersina; at the time of our visit they already numbered 20,000—13,000 having died between their homes and their destination! On arriving they fought, a whole day with an Arab tribe, that had attacked five of

---

* See a detailed account and plan of the Ruins in Admiral Sir Francis Beaufort's ' Karamania.'

† In one instance more than 1000 were shipped on board a steamer of 500 tons.

their number, who had been sent up some little distance to purchase cattle: the Tcherkesses gained the day; they had scarcely a
piaster between them, and who could blame them if they took to
highway robbery, simply to prevent starvation? The authorities
did what they could, but among such enormous numbers, with
12,000 more expected in a few weeks, what could be done? pestilence was already beginning among them, and during the summer
months would inevitably thin their numbers; in one year, the rich
and beautiful plain would amply repay cultivation and draining,
but how were they to find seed to sow, or tools to work with, even
if they could struggle through that one year?

They were a very fine set of tall, well-made men, though but few
were in the least handsome, the Mongolian type being too strongly
marked in their features; the high cheek-bones, still more prominent from starvation, the sloping eyes, and large, long teeth,
give a mingled impression of fierceness and cunning which is not
pleasing; we saw some rather pretty women among them, but their
costume is ungraceful in the extreme: a badly-made cotton gown
à l'Européenne and a handkerchief tightly tied over the head and
round the neck. The men wore long gowns of very thick brown
woollen stuffs, like the old Jews at Jerusalem, tied in at the waist
with leathern thongs, and six or eight cartouches sewed outside
these coats, looking like a couple of rude Pan's pipes on each
breast. Their head-gear is a huge, round muff of the coarsest sheepskin, with the long wool unshorn, dyed a dark brown, and looking
very droll over the unkempt black locks which hang down beneath
them.

We have spoken before of the exceeding beauty of the southern
coast of Asia Minor: it suffices now to say that, after all the
splendid country we had seen since we came along this coast in
the previous spring, it seemed quite as beautiful as before: since if
the fortnight later had melted some of the snow from the lovely
mountains, it had also brought out more and more of the foliage
and flowers. Alas! the foliage will not long add its delightful
charms to this coast, for it is fast disappearing, owing to the
horrible habit of the natives of setting fire to any tree they want to
use instead of cutting it down: of course the fire is communicated,
and a thousand trees are burned where one was needed; every year
the decrease of wood becomes more apparent, and often and often
those terrible fires are watched from Rhodes burning for two or
three days at a time, to utter waste and ruin.

We reached Rhodes early on the morning of the 18th of May,
and were glad to have a few days of rest in that pleasant climate

and the hospitable house of our Consul. The island was now looking pretty; the plane trees, for which Rhodes is celebrated, were fresh, but shady; the Judas trees in the hedges were in full blossom; the gardens bright and gay, while the air was laden with flowery perfumes, borne on the gentle sea-breezes, which keep the summer temperature of the island at a very agreeable coolness. The environs of the town are pretty; the varied outline of the little bays, as well as the beautiful coast of the mainland, Anatolia, opposite, add much to the beauty of the scene. The suburbs were full of the unfortunate Tcherkesses, some of whom had been dropped here instead of going on to Mersina: hungry and homeless, here as there, sitting chiefly in the cemeteries, waiting for employment, or to be sent on further.

We went on the following day with the Consul and his wife to call on the Colonel commanding the Turkish troops at Rhodes, Suleiman Bey: he speaks English well, having passed five years at Woolwich for his education. Under his care we were shown over the barracks, once the convent of the Knights, usually called the "Hospital," in memorial of the first building of any kind that the Christians were allowed to possess in the Holy Land, viz., a hospital for the reception of such pious pilgrims as fell sick at Jerusalem, for whose nursing and protection the Order of the Knights of St. John was instituted in 1048. It is built in the same shape and form as the Hospital in the Holy City, which the Knights so unwillingly quitted, but this building is larger: it is a square of four arches on each side, and of two stories, covering a wide corridor, into which the rooms open. One side was wholly taken up by a very fine hall — the ancient Refectory — with a ceiling of cypress* wood (a durable wood of a pretty red brown colour, with a pleasant perfume and the property of resisting the intrusion of any and all insects): the arches of the hall, ornamented with cable mouldings and leaves, are supported on very short columns, the capitals and bosses bearing the shields of the Knights. All this building the English-taught Colonel makes the soldiers keep beautifully clean and nice: they have also a small court containing twenty-four streams of water issuing from Saracenic mosaics in marble, for their ablutions. We went into the great kitchen, which was perfectly clean and tidy, and tasted the dinner of boiled rice, suet, and beans preparing for the soldiers; five times a week they have meat.

With all this seeming comfort there was yet discontent and

---

* This wood is frequently misnamed "Cyprus wood;" there is no wood peculiar to that Island.

2 I

misery among them, for these soldiers had been sponge-divers, or sailors, or artisans of various lucrative handicrafts, from which they earned enough to support their wives and families, besides serving as a sort of militia-men occasionally: now that their Government has seized them and made them soldiers perforce, they have but one piaster a day for their pay, and of course their wives and families are starving. These poor wives had come up in a body, only a few mornings before, to the English Consul, weeping and wringing their hands to entreat his interference, and could scarcely be persuaded that he could not settle it all, and make them comfortable by "one English word" to the Pasha.

Then we went up the famous street of the Knights' "Auberges" or Priories: it was here that, ten years after they took possession of the Island, they were divided into the eight "languages" of the Order: only five of the eight Priories still remain distinguishable. The first is that of England, bearing a shield with the arms of Peter d'Aubusson, the Grand Master, who won for the fortress the title of the "Buckler of Christianity" during the First Siege of Rhodes, —the date is 1483: then the Priory of Italy, bearing the arms of Fabrice de Carretto, the last Grand Master before the Second Siege, and the date 1519. Then comes the Priory of France, the best preserved of all, as it has received some little care and attention in modern days; the door has some elegant mouldings of the usual twisted cable—the Saracenic type—with small columns, and bands of the same mouldings between the floors; and the motto over the door " *De France le gn̄t* (grand) *prior F. Emery de Amboise* 1492 ;" the Cross of the Order and the three pales of Amboise: and two scutcheons leaning on lions rampant with three nails on each, the *canting* arms of Pierre Clouet the architect. There are two tablets bearing the arms of the Order and of Amboise with the legend " *De Amboise em gn̄t prior ;*" later tablets with the arms of Villiers de L'Isle Adam, and a scutcheon of the Royal arms of France dated 1495, with the legend " *Voluntas Dei* " underneath, Saint Louis at the sides, and " *Dieu* (ayde) *le pélerin* " above it; then the scutcheon of Amboise again, and the Cardinal's hat presented to Pierre d'Aubusson ; and after this his shield and that of the Order placed at the left-hand end on his death by his successor Emery (or Almeric) Amboise.

A little beyond is the Chapelle de France, bearing five shields set in a cross with the arms of France in the centre and the legend " *Capelle Francie,*" the arms of the Order and of the Grand Master Fabrice de Carretto : this building, finished in 1519, replaced another which had been destroyed in the First Siege as the inscription denotes by initials " R(everendus) D(ominus) F(rater) P(ierre) P(ape-fust) B(ases) R(estauravit) 1483. There is also a little preaching pulpit, stuck on the outer wall, such as one still sees in Italy, with a small staircase from the street.

Opposite to this is the Priory of Spain and Portugal, with the scutcheons of the two nations united, of the Order, of d'Amboise, and of two Commanders. And a little further on comes that of Toulouse or Auvergne: with the inscription " *P.S. Dñs F. Francis-cus Flota Prior Tholose construxit anno* 1518," engraved under the arms of France, the Order, de Carretto, and the Commander Flota.

All these, therefore, were built after the First Siege in 1480: but there is said to be still a house at the top of the Knights' Street which was built before the Siege, as it bears the arms of the Grand Master Roger (or Gerard) de Pins with the date 1356–1365; and another on the quay dated 1407: we did not, however, find these houses (which are described by M. le Comte de Vogüé), and I think they must have been destroyed in the explosion. I have been thus particular in giving the names to the scutcheons, as the knowledge of them adds greatly to the interest of seeing them, and most travellers, having but an hour or two to give to Rhodes, cannot linger long enough to decipher them easily for themselves.

Beyond the Knights' Street, the Turkish Colonel took us into the remains of the Grand Master's Palace, once a splendid building, but alas! completely demolished in the explosion of 1856, as it adjoined the Church; the walls of a few chambers, and the grand staircase are all that can be distinctly traced now, though the openings into twelve granaries under the courtyard still remain, and are used by the Turks. Opposite to the gate of the Palace are some richly ornamented windows belonging to the Church, and the tower is partly standing; the dial of its clock was found some time ago with the hands still pointing to the hour of the explosion which had so suddenly buried it in ruin!

A good idea of the old fortress is derived from a walk round the ramparts, to which the Turkish Colonel obligingly accompanied us: they afforded also some charming views of the Island and the lovely shore of the mainland: and it is pretty looking down into the town with its picturesque *bits*, remaining from the time of the Knights, its little domes and minarets, gardens and palm-trees: the handsomest part is in the Jews' quarter, although on this side the Siege was the hottest and fiercest. In one corner, on the eastern side of the fortress and precisely over the bazaar gate, originally called St. Catherine's gate, is a square tower, containing a tiny chapel, the interior of which has received three coatings of frescoes at various times, now nearly all alike destroyed. One figure remains, which is

2 ɪ 2

often called St. George, but which must have been commemorative
of the well-known story, sculptured on a marble tablet let into the
wall of the great bastion of Auvergne, on the eastern side of the
ramparts: viz. that of the young Knight Deodato de Gozon who,
disregarding the interdiction of the Grand Master Elyon de Villanova,
went out to fight and soon overcame some great monster, usually
called a crocodile by the old historians, who had devoured many
women and children in the island; and who was for his disobedience
stripped of his habit, by his stern and angry Superior, in spite of
the acclamations of gratitude of the islanders at the courage and
gallantry of their deliverer; having thus punished his rebellious son,
it is pleasant to add that Villanova afterwards restored him to the
Order and amply rewarded him.   Doubtless the details of this story
are fabrications and exaggerations, but some fact of the kind is,
almost as undoubtedly, true, since up to the time of the explosion
the inscription on the tomb of Deodato de Gozon (he was afterwards
Grand Master) remained legible, " *Ci git le vainqueur du Dragon.*"
This little tower is the more interesting as it is thought to be of an-
terior date to the time of the Knights, and to have been one of the
angular towers of the Byzantine fortification: an opinion confirmed
by the appearance of the frescoes where the second and third coatings have peeled off, which seem to be of a much earlier period than
the twelfth century.

The little gate by which the Turks, headed by Solyman the Magnificent, entered the city after the capitulation, has been long since
walled up, but on the ramparts above, there are still scores of witnesses of the sanguinary but gallantly-withstood Siege, in the shape
of balls and stone shot lying about, some of the latter thrown by
" basilisks," too huge to be carried far, but whose weight in falling
must have been crushing.   Many of the old guns remain also, some
of them prettily ornamented; one, from which a ball passed so inso-
lently close to Solyman the Magnificent as even to scorch his beard,
was afterwards punished by the Turks by being filled up and
covered externally with ugly heads of negroes stuck on in bronze !

We came back through the extensive cemeteries which almost
surround the town, and puzzled a long time over the stone altars,
as they seemed, which appeared every here and there, until it was
explained to us that the Turks bring the corpses of the dead to the
cemetery and lay them on these stone slabs to be washed before interment: a very horrid arrangement it appeared to me, to perform
this office in public, for these stone tables frequently stand in the
high road, close by the city gates.

But by far the most interesting part of our stay in Rhodes was spent in examining some antiques, beside which the remains of mediæval chivalry were dwarfed into trifles of yesterday : these were from an entire Necropolis of the time of the Phœnician-Greeks, which has been within the last two years discovered : they are among the very few undisturbed Phœnician tombs that have ever been found anywhere. They were discovered by M. A. Biliotti, son of the English Vice-Consul at Scio, who on seeing some traces of tombs cut in the rock began to dig there for same time in vain, till in the winter of 1858–59 a part of the hill slipped and exposed some vases to view, which M. Salzmann, a French antiquarian, pronounced to be Phœniko-Greek. Excavations were immediately recommenced, and M. Salzmann has been since commissioned by the British Museum to uncover and collect the antiquities. This Necropolis is situated about a mile from the village of Kalavarda, and is believed to be that of the ancient Camiros, the principal city of the three Dorian settlements in Rhodes, which were united, in days of unknown antiquity, with Cos, Cnidus, and Halicarnassus into the Dorian Hexapolis.*

The bodies appear to have been buried usually without a sarcophagus, as only a very few sarcophagi have been found ; they were probably surrounded with vases, &c., but the whole series of tombs have been so much disturbed by earthquakes (which are very frequent in Rhodes) and their contents, as it were, intermingled, the lighter articles generally pushed up nearest the surface, that it is impossible to judge in any way of the original arrangement of the sepulchres. Everything is found thickly encrusted with earth, which, if any damp has reached it, has eaten away the enamel : all this strongly adhering-earth has to be melted off with diluted aquafortis, and the cleaning of each, even of the smallest vases, is the work of many days with constant watching ; then the polish of the enamel is afterwards renewed by the friction of the naked hand. The vases are of all sizes, from about three feet in diameter down to a few inches, and of every conceivable form, each one more graceful than the last ; they are all covered, within and without, with figures, chiefly of allegorical animals and intricate patterns, generally on each the figure of Astarte in the form of a female face with the body of a bird. With but few exceptions they are in black and red, the latter in various shades : on one of the vases there were some portions of the figures—a bird, an ornament, and a part of a shield—in a brilliant pure white enamel ; but this is very rare. There were quantities of figures surmounting long bottles, or tubes, of alabaster or stone : and a vast number of small figures in porcelain, pierced, as if used

* Herodotus, book i. 144.

for amulets, charms, necklaces, &c., &c., some of them quite Egyptian, representing Pshent and other Egyptian gods; scarabei also, and a figure of the size and form of a scarabeus, but bearing on its back a well-cut human face with a quantity of hair carved round it. There were numbers of small buttons, with *cartouches* on them in what we were told were Phœnician characters: and some oval-pointed stones along with a great many pieces of lead of the same shape, marked over with Phœnician symbols; these are very heavy, and were probably used for their slings.

Among the metal ornaments there was one band of gold, gleaming bright after a little cleaning, with a rich pattern beaten in it: a gold bracelet with a lozenge pattern cut out from it: an olive crown where the leaves had been made in bronze and afterwards gilt, and the fruit added in porcelain: and one most delicately-made wreath of myrtle with the berries hanging down, all in gold—which made one fancy the fair head the pretty thing had probably once adorned. There is another golden ornament, so commonly found in the tombs that M. Salzmann conceives it must have been a Hieratic ornament which each corpse was obliged necessarily to wear, perhaps as a kind of passport of the soul, or credential of salvation and sanctity: it is an oblong plate, about two inches long, always bearing a figure of Astarte on it, and with little bells hanging from the lower end: sometimes two birds perched on the upper corners form the hooks by which the ornament was fastened on. There were a great many lamps, some of them very pretty in shape, and natural shells now commonly found in the Island: these, with many little boxes and odd things, are supposed to have been playthings placed in the tombs of children. Nothing remains of the dresses worn by the corpses, save numbers of tiny rings and beads in blue porcelain, with which they are supposed to have been embroidered; and only very few bones remain, but some have been found, curiously enough, pierced through by the roots of a tree! and one skull, that of a woman, of the Circassian type, not Semitic: but from this no inference can be drawn, as it might have been the skull of a slave.

Some writers have thought that the word Rhodes was derived from the Phœnician for a serpent, but it seems more natural that the *riante* and fertile island should have so been named by the Greeks from the abundance of roses which blossom there; a specimen of which was stamped on one side of the ancient coins of the country in her days of proud independence.

We left Rhodes at mid-day on the 23rd of May in the Austrian steamer *Elleno*, about the very dirtiest old tub that I should think the paternal government could possibly keep for the unhappy passengers whom they convey. Our companions were numerous, but the *human* ones were pleasant; the weather, however, was stormy, and conversation was not much in fashion that day; I sat on deck watching the islands, as we rolled past them, looking all the prettier for the heavy broken clouds and sudden lights of the changing sky. We had now entered the " White Sea," as the Turks and Greeks call the Ægean, and were among the Sporades: a number of apparently barren rocks, within whose little valleys and tiny plains generations of men have been born whose names will be written in some of the brightest pages of the history of Heroism that the world has ever known. The Sporades, with the exception of about half-a-dozen islands that lie close to the Thessalian coast, belong to Turkey, and are nominally under the government of the Pasha of Rhodes; but the inhabitants are a thoroughly independent people, and more frequently hoist the Greek flag than the Turkish on their ships.

We had thought of making a little tour among the splendid scenery of Crete, but the summer was too far advanced, even if the unsettled state of the Cretan peasantry would have permitted us to do so in safety. I can, however, imagine nothing pleasanter than spending a year or two among the Archipelago islands, gliding over the exquisitely blue sea, examining the thousand differences that exist between one island and another, instead of the somewhat monotonous likeness they bear to each other at a distance: extracting little treasures of antiques from their classic soils, and listening to the thrilling tales of their heroic wars. Great numbers of pretty things are constantly found in the islands, and they would probably repay a more careful search: ancient Greek tombs abound in Scarpanto, Nisyros, Kalymnos, and Stampalia, and in these, gold and silver ornaments are constantly found; Greek vases, cups, and statuettes, are often picked up, especially in the two latter. These researches would be the pleasantest in Stampalia, in which, for some unknown reason (which is, however, a fact), no serpent or venomous reptile will live: if such are imported, as they sometimes are in firewood from the mainland, they die almost immediately.

Most of these islands subsist now upon the products of the sponge-fishery; the young men are the divers for gathering them, while the elderly men form the robust and hardy seamen. A good diver can make from eight to ten dives in a day; the constitution is, however, soon impaired by the laborious life if carried on too long; but in olden times, and perhaps still, no youth was considered by the island maidens eligible for a husband, until he could remain a certain time, fixed by law, under the water. Accustomed as we are to the pretty sand-coloured articles we buy, we should be a little surprised at being offered the sponge in its native state; when freshly torn off from the rocks it is covered with a thin but tough black case, inside of which is the sponge growing in a lake of white liquid like milk. The sponge-gathering is a very lucrative business, extending over a vast area of sea; the annual value of the sponges taken in Kalymnos alone amounts to about 25,000*l.* sterling. This island has 260 boats, and employs about 1650 men and boys; the average depth of the finest sponges is 30 fathoms, those of an inferior quality are gathered at lesser depths: the finest are sent to Great Britain: they cost in Smyrna about three-quarters of the price that they are in England, but on the coast of Syria we got very good sponges, well-sized and fine, for one or two shillings each.

Some fine mediæval castles ornament these islands, especially in Stampalia, Cos, Leros, and Patmos: many standing columns still remain, capitals, and bits of sculpture that have survived from the ruins of ancient Greek Temples. At Leros, an ancient granary was lately discovered, which on being opened was found to be full of Indian corn, which must have been there since the beginning of the 16th century at least, when the Knights gave up Rhodes and all the small dependencies round them. On Cos (then called Lango, from which perhaps it derives its present name of Stanco), they erected a large castle, embedding in its walls some fine slabs of classic sculpture; and around this island they many a time gallantly repulsed the attacks of the Turks, the eccentricities of the coast, which runs out into peninsulas as if it was playing at hide-and-seek with the islands, enabling them to perform some amusing tricks of war. On one occasion the commandant of the fortress, contriving to cut off the two foremost of the galleys, hastily landed the Turks they had contained, and sailed back among the enemy's fleet in their own vessels, filled, however, with Christian sailors, when to their astonishment their seeming brothers opened a broadside upon them, and speedily carried the nine vessels and their crews triumphantly into port!

At Lemnos the remains of the famous Labyrinthus, the columns still erect, are as yet unexplored: while on Patmos there still exists part of a very fine acropolis on the top of the mountain, the lower parts of the walls being cyclopean. Patmos is famous for its beautiful women, and learned professors; the monks pretend to be poor, but they are enormously rich: it seems to be a very interesting island to visit.

But the islands which possess the most living interest at present are Cassos (or Caxo) and 'Psarà: the sound of their names alone suffices to thrill many a heart with admiration and sympathy. Cassos we had passed in coming from Egypt, but we were then too sea-sick even to look at the picturesque and world-famous rock. When, in 1821, the news came that the Greeks had borne their yoke long enough, and had risen to arms under Alexander Ypsilanti, the bold hearts of Cassos fitted out several small vessels—all they had—well armed and manned, and proceeded to the coasts of Syria and Egypt, where they captured a great number of vessels, much larger than their own, with valuable cargoes on board. They next made a descent upon the island of Rhodes, and managed to drive the Turks out of the villages into the fortress. With a portion of the proceeds of the booty they had thus obtained, they brought 120 guns of heavy calibre, with some of which they fortified their own little island; with the remainder they armed eight vessels, and with this squadron they hastened to the succour of their brethren in Candia, affording them most timely relief.

Elated by all this success, the little squadron in the following year appeared off Alexandria, and after a very sharp engagement, four of their vessels captured a large Egyptian man-of-war, in the very sight of the port: while the other four vessels ran into the port of Damietta, and made prizes of twenty ships lying there laden with corn, ready to start with their provisions for the Turkish fleet. They then sailed back to Crete and blockaded the Mahommedan towns in that island. Naturally enraged at all the damage which this little body of hardy and courageous men had inflicted on his Turks, Muhammad 'Ali, Pasha of Egypt, made several energetic attempts to get possession of the tiny island; but he failed in them all, and was finally obliged to recall his ships. However, in the summer of 1824, he sent a Turkish fleet of forty-five vessels, and surrounded the island with them; after repeated efforts to effect a landing, in all of which they were still disappointed, the Turkish Admiral was on the point of raising the blockade, when a Rhodiote pilot on board his ship offered to land a body of men. Forty gun-boats were accordingly placed under his orders, with which he appeared off a place called San Giovanni di Maritza, and then, to deceive the Cassiotes, he stood out into the offing in the direction of Crete. When it became dark, however, he returned, and hid his gunboats among the deep caverns and creeks running in from the sea and under a steep mountain. The next night he landed with all his men, they jumping on shore from the yards of the gun-boats on to the extraordinary rocks which had so well hidden them. The poor Cassiotes fought long and gallantly for some days, and would probably have driven back their enemies, had not reinforcements arrived from the Turkish fleet: then the island was taken, but not before the greater number of those who could bear arms had fallen. Old men, women and children were massacred in cold blood by the Turks; and about 2000 women and children were taken away and sold as slaves; so that the population, which had been in 1820 about 13,000 souls, was reduced to 3000. The island is now beginning to recover from its losses.

'Psarà we passed in the middle of the night about a month later, and I greatly regretted not having seen the birthplace of so many bold hearts and sturdy frames; this island has an area of scarcely ten geographical miles, and the people depend wholly on commerce for their subsistence, as the island itself can produce but food enough for three months' consumption: yet they have some really good schools, and the 'Psariote men, though almost always at sea, keep their families comfortably supported by their gains. During the war the 'Psariote marine obtained complete mastery over the immensely superior number of Turkish vessels, chasing the enemy even into the Dardanelles, under the brave leader Canaris and some others; the Sultan at last, in July 1824, sent down the Captain Pasha himself with 200 ships and an enormous number of troops on board; they surrounded the island, the inhabitants of which had been increased by about 5000 refugees and soldiers from various parts of Greece. Attacked on all sides, the unhappy islanders were butchered, the town was burnt and utterly destroyed, and hardly 2000 managed to escape from the island; the few who remained alive assembled over the powder magazine, to which, just as the Turks were scaling the walls, they set fire and perished all together in one grave under the tremendous explosion! A month after the 'Psariotes retook their island from the Turks, and the peasants mostly returned to it, but the richer men settled at Syra. Before this destruction of the island the 'Psariotes were the best shipwrights and seamen in the Levant, and their ships were models of naval architecture; now the island possesses only 60 trading boats and no vessels of its own; but there are 40 large vessels, built at Syra, of about 8000 tons in all, which make voyages all over the world under the Hellenic flag, and are manned and navigated by 'Psariote seamen.

The next day beamed more brightly upon us, and pretty and green were the coasts of Khios (or Scio) and the mainland as we turned into the lovely Gulf of Smyrna: the sunset lighting up the bright little meadows and the richly wooded hills and lofty rocks, as we glided along through shoals of jolly porpoises tumbling about in the water: then it faded off from the white houses and red roofs of the city, and left us in darkness as we came to anchor to our great disgust too late for *pratique* that night. Down in the dirty steamy cabin we had to sleep another night, where our condition was not improved by the perfumes of the water around us; the darkness therefore was scarcely dispelled before we exchanged the marine fleas for their terrestrial cousins, and took up our old quarters in " les deux Augustes."

The bazaars, no longer very Oriental or new in our eyes, were all we had to amuse us while waiting five days for a steamer to Athens; we might have made some pretty excursions, for the neighbourhood of Smyrna is interesting in every way, but the low fever from which I was suffering clung to me, and the weather was too hot for any exertions. We could not, however, omit seeing the view from the Castle again: and, having admired it so much at sunset last year, we took it this time at sunrise, and thought the prospect still more beautiful than before; the cypresses too are certainly finer than any we have seen elsewhere, even at Constantinople. The eighteen miles then completed of the Aïdîn Railway appeared to pass through lovely country, and the summer residences of the Smyrniote gentry looked most inviting; the neighbourhood of Smyrna is indeed very charming, and it is no wonder it is so universally admired.

We were by this time tolerably well acquainted with the long Gulf, but it would be difficult to weary of its beauty, which we again enjoyed, as, for the *fifth* time, we steamed along its waters on the afternoon of the 29th of May: coming, however, suddenly to a full stop near the mouth. A screw had fallen out from the piston of our engine, and we lay for twelve hours in the same spot, thereby arriving at Syra at twelve o'clock of the following night, and missing the curious view of the island which we had much wished to see.

There are two towns in the island of Syra: the old one mounted upon the top of a steep cone out of the way of the pirates that then infested the Archipelago, and the new one down on the beach, where quays and lighthouses and stately buildings of white marble find easy communication with the vast number of ships and steamers that are always entering or leaving the harbour. The double town is picturesque, and the mountain curves prettily round the bay.

Soon after sunrise we were on deck, gliding past the islands of Gioura, Thermia, Zea, St. George, and Makris: the fine cliffs of which, though wanting in vegetation, are beautiful in outline, and were then finely coloured in the morning sun. Shortly after 10 A.M. the square rock of the Acropolis—recognised in a moment by its well-known portraits—became very distinct, and in another half-hour we landed at the Piræus. The wide quays, the bright European-built houses, the pretty pleasure-gardens so completely Western, and the active, working look of the people, seemed very gay and modern to our eyes, so long used to the inactivity of the East: but far more surprising and very delightful did it seem, to be whirled along the excellent road in an easy open carriage, such as we had not seen since we left Egypt. Our enjoyment of it was, however, soon quenched under the thick and heavy clouds of dust, that nearly overwhelmed us in the hour's drive, and which had whitened the fields of low vines into dull masses, and weighed down the olives, acacias, and plane-trees bordering the roads, which are as straight and formal as the famous "Long Walls" connecting the Piræus with the Fair City.

The view of Athens from the sea, and the approach from the Piræus, is, I think, the least pretty of all: for myself, I was so immensely struck with the arid dreariness of the whole view, that half of my imagination of the romantic beauty of "divine Greece" vanished: my eyes and memory were so full of the rich luxuriance of colour and the endless shades of verdure and fertility in Syria and Asia Minor, that Greece appeared to me far more stern than sad, more dreary than lonely. And this, I fancy, is the first feeling of most strangers; you must wait till the morning and the evening, the sunrise and the sunset, have thrown their "bright investiture and sweet warmth" across your eyes: till the purple and the crimson sheen of evening have mantled on the mountains: till you have watched the shadows stealing in dim haziness, scarcely veiling the dazzling marbles of the exquisite buildings, and till the turquoise blue of the calm, clear ocean has deepened into sapphire, before the mind can really take in the perfection of beauty in Athens—

> " Fairest of all ! oh Queen of Cities !
> Lying beneath a lovely sky."

And, to be struck with Greece, one should come to it first from the West: after the chill north and the west, it would seem half Oriental: while to the eyes of the Eastern traveller Greece has lost the golden halo and the glorious luxuriance of the East, without gaining (what one *then* thinks of as the greatest charm of all) the cool shadiness of the West. No place is as pretty at midday as at any other time, and Athens loses more than most cities do : the sun too was so scorchingly hot, through the suffocating dust, that we were glad to be housed at once in the Hôtel d'Angleterre, where we found kind friends to welcome us ; it seemed luxuriously delightful after the rudely simple, or uncivilized dirtiness of most of the inns of the East.

CHAPTER XXV.

THE PARTHENON AND PARNASSUS.

" Have ye left the mountain places,
   Oreads wild, for other trysts?
Shall we see no sudden faces
   Strike a glory through the mist?
Not a sound the silence thrills
   Of the everlasting hills.
       Pan, Pan is dead."
           E. B. BROWNING.

NEARLY the whole of our first three days in Athens were devoted to the Acropolis, viewing it by the earliest morning, by the sunset, and by the light of the full moon: each portion of the day throws its own perfection on the view, and the Acropolis has not been really seen unless by all three lights. Fortunately the buildings united there need no description from my feeble pen, as drawings, paintings, and photographs of them abound; the latter, however, give no idea of anything but the architectural detail and the general proportion, and Athens is sadly travestied in a sepia-brown representation of its marbles. The remarkable beauty of the sparkling material has, perhaps, a still larger share in the perfection of these structures than we are apt to think of: but one has to only contemplate the difference between the impenetrable black darkness, the heavy shadows, and the great masses of St. Ouen or of one of our own Northern Cathedrals, with the fanciful building up of snow, changed by fairy hands into stone, of the pinnacles and towers of Milan Cathedral, which gives such an indescribable feeling of embodied spirituality to the upper part of the building, and blends in so much harmony with the snowy mountains in the distance,—in order to fancy the wonderful charm of Pentelican marble in pure Doric, under a Grecian sky.

I had this feeling of almost tangible spirituality in my mind whenever I looked closely at the Parthenon ; well may she be called " Athena Parthenos " (the Virgin), for truly she is the invincible, matchless Jungfrau of Athenian monuments, standing on the proud summit of her noble pedestal, elevated, uplifted above all others ; and it is no wonder that the Athenians, who knew not that " God dwelleth not in temples made with hands," should believe that the circumambient atmosphere around her Temple was fairer and purer than anywhere else, and that a " crown of light " hung eternally over the head of the virgin citadel. Strange fitness, indeed, that after various vicissitudes of paganism, the " Virgin's chamber " became a church dedicated to the Virgin Mother, and the Life of Love revealed to us in her Divine Son was there proclaimed in its full perfection and completeness, such as Plato had shadowed out in his grand ideas and words as the only happy and satisfying life : that Life which *he* could only know as a still hidden problem, not an actual, finished fact. Pity that a few hundred years later the mantle of darkness should have again dimmed its lustre, and the fair building have been perverted into a mosque : after which it fell into complete ruin : ruined, indeed, yet glorious and beautiful still, like some noble matron who has borne her part through all the prime of life, now fading into the silvery tresses, and bending stoop, and the lingering step of age, yet in whom, although the loveliness of youth has vanished, the soul shines forth in pure and holy spiritual beauty, while she " walks with inward glory crowned." *

> " And how . . . describe
> Thy Perfectness, when such thy Ruins are ! "

One of the spots in the Acropolis where thoughts of the past crowd most rapidly on the mind, is when standing below the steps of the Propylæa—the giant portal, the barrier-gate, the triumphal arch which led into the Fortress and up to the Sacred Altar of Athena—completed more than three hundred years before Christ, yet still erect in proud stern majesty : the mind rapidly peoples the pavement with the solemn pageants that passed up the very steps on which one stands, while the mark of the chariot wheels, and the groove scooped by the heavy doors moving over the marble floor, still distinctly visible, seem to bridge over the two thousand years since Greece became a Roman province. Delicately glowing with the minute detail of bright colours still traceable on the friezes and mouldings, which made the lustre of the snowy marble shine still more brightly, the Propylæa with its five lofty gates, formed the magnificent object of that view ; in the foreground on the left, stood

* Shelley.

the equestrian statues of the sons of Xenophon, and on the right the
small but lovely Temple of Nike Apteros : while, seen through the
open gates and directly opposite to the centre of them, was the
splendid statue of Athena Polias, in bronze, whose helmet and spear
were discernible from the sea beyond Sunium : then mounting the
steps, the Parthenon and the Erechtheum—objects dear to all
Athenian hearts—were obliquely seen within the Sacred Enclosure.
Now, the Propylæa forms a great hospital of its own sick and
wounded ; the scattered fragments, a thousand statues, urns, vases,
mouldings, friezes, ranged upon shelves, or embedded in square
frames filled up with clay, are here carefully preserved ; it is delightful to see them so well cared for : but the scores of arms, legs,
noseless heads, broken fingers, bits of rounded shoulders, sorted
under their respective denominations, always reminded me of
" Tate and Brady's versification of the Psalms of David with the
poetry extracted."

The small Ionic temple of Nike Apteros was for two hundred
years completely lost : at last some fragments were accidentally discovered *in situ*, and the whole was built up again from its own
ruins, and now stands in wonderful perfection in its own place ;
many of its friezes are intact, but copies of those taken away by
Lord Elgin ought to be sent out to replace the hiatus of others.
The Nike Apteros, or Wingless Victory, expressed the proud determination of the Athenians that Victory should never be absent from
their arms ; they therefore represented her without wings lest she
should use them in flying over to their enemies. It was from here
that old Ægeus threw himself down to end the life that became intolerably bitter to him, when deprived of his beloved son Theseus,
who thus received, in the death of his father, his punishment of
sorrow for the desertion of the beautiful Ariadne in the island of
Naxos.

Passing through the Propylæa you are in the presence of the
ghosts of the three Athenes of the Acropolis : the bronze statue of
Athene Promachus, which stood on a pedestal, in the great enclosure, alone in her glory : the chryselephantine statue of Athene
Parthenos, also by Phidias, which was placed within the sanctuary :
and the original olive-wood statue of Athene Polias, said to have
come down from heaven, which was mysteriously concealed from
vulgar view within the inner chamber of the Erechtheum.

The interior of the Parthenon was completely destroyed by the
shells of the Venetians in 1687, and the central columns, six on one
side and eight on the other, of the noble peristyle were thrown
down : but the rest of the columns, with the beautiful porticos at

the eastern and western ends, remain to delight the eyes of the world. It is sad to pass from under the rich sculptures and many columns of the exterior into the empty space and ruin within; some beautiful fragments are treasured there, but all broken and defaced like the walls that shelter them: and the only way to fancy the Parthenon less a ruin than she is, is to stand without, where naught but the rich tomb raised upon the marble bier can be seen, from whence even the fair form of the dead maiden has been rudely torn away.

The eastern half of the Erechtheum was dedicated to Athene Polias: all the columns of the Ionic portico but one are still standing, and they look very fine in the morning sunlight. The western end had no direct entrance, but a splendid and still beautiful portico on the northern side led into the Temple, and through it to the famous Caryatide-supported portico, the Cecropium, as well as to the Pandroseum Proper. All is sadly ruined within, but outside it appears little changed, as much that had fallen has been replaced: the fragments strewn around are of exquisite workmanship. Erechtheus was supposed to have been born of Atthis or Attica, and adopted by the goddess Athene; Poseidon and Minerva, having contended for the possession of the city, the prize was adjudged to Minerva as the provider of the best gift, the olive-tree, while Poseidon had only given the horse (of which the salt spring was a symbol): they were therefore reconciled and united within the walls of the Erechtheum, which was thus made a type of the future glory of the Athenian arms by sea as well as by land. To this union, doubtless, Themistocles and Pericles frequently referred in their exhortation to the people to make Athens a maritime power: the altar of Poseidon was placed within the sanctuary of Athene Polias, the guardian of the city, and their respective emblems of the salt well and the olive-tree were enshrined within the Pandroseum. The miraculous olive-tree has withered away since that Morning Sun brightened over Bethlehem which caused the death of Pan; but the marks of the trident of Poseidon are still shown in the living rock! The southern (Caryatide) portico has no entrance from the outside, and was chiefly an external ornament commemorating the sepulchre of Cecrops: it has been completely restored, the new pieces contrasting rather glaringly with the old, the workmanship of which they do not rival.

One lingers long on the western steps of the Parthenon to gaze at the view spread out before one's eyes: but this is still better enjoyed from the monument of Philopappos erected on the summit of a conical hill some little distance to the south-west of the Acropolis.

2 K

Many a sunset found us there during our short stay in Athens, and my pulse quickens as I recall the indescribable loveliness of that view, dyed in hues that no paint-box can imitate. The great plain of Attica lies at one's feet, covered with the gardens that surround the city, and the olive woods which are now, in the slanting rays of the sun, of a deep, dark myrtle-green: the calm sea, like a turquoise mirror, stretches out beyond, the white lines of the Piræus brightly marked on the shore and the pretty bay of Phalerum curving round with the ancient port of Munychia at one side; the two lovely islands of Ægina and Salamis, dyed in deep lustrous purple, seem to lie floating on the bosom of the sea: the mountains of the Peloponnesus, in clear forget-me-not blue, range behind its distant shore, where stand Epidaurus, Methana, and Trœzen: while, to the left, the sun sinks in floods of orange behind beautiful Geranea and the other mountains on the isthmus of Corinth, all bathed in a dark, mysterious violet, the summit of Kithæron coming in behind the sloping foot of Mount Parnes, which formed the boundary wall of Attica. Gaze upon this till every lovely line is imprinted for ever on your mind: then turn in haste, and catch the last rosy glow on the Acropolis with the Parthenon exalted in lofty majesty above all: their ruin and decay veiled over by the kindly distance, and the ancient splendour almost restored in the loveliness of the golden hue spread over the noble marble fronts; mark the crimson tint on the barren rock beneath, and the " wine-empurpled " violet of wild, stern Lycabettus and beautiful Hymettus behind them; do not shun a hasty glance at modern Athens which then, and then only, comes out in a thousand nameless tints of delicate colours, softening the staring, upstart modernism it wears by day : and acknowledge that the whole scene is transcendently lovely ! Then wait, only a few moments, till the full moon, such a moon as the clear atmosphere of Greece alone can show, has slowly risen above the summit of Hymettus, silvering the purple of the mountain and gleaming on the side of the Parthenon ere yet the golden glow of the sunset has completely faded from the snowy marble, and look upon it unmoved—if you can!

Then you must go up to the Acropolis itself: watch the grand and solemn masses of the Propylæa with the shadows of the front columns falling across the western wing, and the dazzling brightness of the little Wingless Victory shining out from the deep shadow at its base. Go on to the Parthenon and look at the exquisite line of the imperceptibly curved steps illumined with the silvery hue, and at the shadows of the columns and of the marble roof-beams falling athwart the ground and the cella wall : mark the background slopes of Hymettus and the rich, clear darkness of colour they assume under such a moonlight,—peculiarly and sadly sweet; and, lastly, go and stand beneath the Caryatides that still guard the memories of the daughters of Cecrops, and look at the calm, serene smile which Diana lays with her cold finger upon each marble maiden face and each stately figure. You need not despise the twinkling lights of the little town in the distance below; and pray earnestly the day may come when native hands and heads will be found to make Greece a great country as well as a free one! Alas! the day seems yet a very long way off.

Modern Athens has been wise in refraining from any interference with the ancient: had she in any way endeavoured to imitate the old model, or forced a contrast of even the finest examples of other styles with the unique perfection she glories in, the failure would have been glaring and painful; as it is, the huge, white, unornamented pile of the Bavarian Palace—like a vast white mass with rows of black dots upon it—interferes with nothing; it is simply a very large receptacle for a very large household, and one can turn to it from the Temples and the Monuments without any kind of jar in the mind. The Venetian tower, built when the Acropolis was refortified by the Republic of Venice, carries its own mark of venerable respectability, and produces no discord in the mind. The very interesting and beautiful old Byzantine Cathedral of Athens would be more beautiful anywhere else; and one is half ashamed in descending from the Parthenon, and entering the new Cathedral, to feel oneself admiring the light arcades, the groups of daintily-carved columns, the upspringing domes, and the delicate poetry-in-stone of this fine specimen of the Byzantine grand-daughter of the ancient Doric.

The houses of the citizens are solid, substantial and neat, with a certain degree of handsomeness about them derived from the good stone employed in their building; they are plainly ornamented, but are rather staring; there is a great fashion for gardens in the squares, and avenues of trees in the streets, but they are always so laden with dust, that it seems a waste and a cruelty to plant them. For the dust at Athens is something indescribable—stifling—and intolerable; on a calm day it lies thickly upon one's tables and chairs, and penetrates even into one's bed—when there is a breeze it filters through the closed windows and fills one's hands, one's mouth, and one's hair, till one feels half suffocated. The fragile pepper trees best resist its disfiguring appearance, but the unfortunate oleanders, of stiffer growth, are really transmogrified into white and grey heaps which look most melancholy.

The Temple of Theseus, which stands on a slight rise at the foot of the Acropolis, is singularly graceful and beautiful; thanks to St. George (who was made to serve during the time of its occupation as a Christian Church for Hercules and Theseus, in the commemorative friezes that surround it), it has been preserved nearly in perfection; it is low and small, but in beautiful proportion and finely finished. Its contents are still more beautiful than its exterior, for it is now the Museum containing all the noblest and loveliest of the works of Art yet remaining in Athens: some statues of Apollo, an exquisite Achilles, a Mars, a Pan, and some female figures of almost unrivalled beauty. Among them also is the famous bas-relief of the Persian warrior found under the modern soil of Marathon; while on the platform outside are a number of venerable stone seats, brought down from the Areopagus, which were once the chairs of the judges of the Senate—the solemn Council who sat on " Mars' Hill."

One of these simple stone seats was one day occupied by an Elder of the Senate, who took his accustomed place when a dispute had to be heard upon the Areopagus, and began to listen with weariness of mind to the " new thing" the stranger had to tell, when lo! the Spirit of God stirred within his breast: he had " felt after Him and found Him "—Him, the Christ, the Incarnate Son of God, the pure, the lowly, the all-merciful, the loving; he saw Him in contrast with the abstract principles to which a thousand altars stood erected all around: the shadows he had been groping after in deep darkness vanished before the firm reality and simple loveliness of Light and Truth: and casting away at once those gods who could not save any one of the multitudes who worshipped them from suffering or from sin, because their religion was selfish and self-reliant—he lifted up his heart in the Righteousness of Christ, and accepted with humble gladness the good tidings of great joy which proclaimed peace of heart and salvation to all the world. This Elder's name was Dionysius, and the messenger who set forth the " strange thing" was Paul the Apostle. The traces of a small church dedicated to the memory of Dionysius, who afterwards became Bishop of Athens, are still visible on the summit of the Areopagus.

No picture, however gloriously painted, can adequately portray the scene of St. Paul's discourse: to enter into its spirit and to realise its hold upon the minds of his hearers, one must behold that " worship of men's hands," " the gold, the silver, and the stone, graven by art and man's device," and embody that atmosphere of idolatry and ignorance which pervaded " all the nations of men on the face of the earth" assembled in this crowd; one must see the

innumerable altars raised to the comprehended and uncompre-
hended attributes of the Divine Nature, or for the propitiation of
gods whom they knew not, and to whom they could not even apply
a name : one must feel that religious yearning which was a part of
the very being of these high-hearted and excitable citizens, which
vented itself in such a prodigality of material worship that Athens
was called *a city of gods*,—without remembering all this, the
peculiar mark and character of that singularly beautiful address
are lost. Unseen, but felt, in the bosoms of the superstitious
Athenians, was the immediate vicinity of the dark and awful
fissure, part of which runs under the very seats of the Judges, the
sanctuary of the Eumenides or Furies; probably the inner recess
of the chasm and the black pool of water were then completely
concealed in the Temple which once stood at the entrance: now
one can look down into the very heart of the black darkness of the
gloomy and once awful cavern, of which the rocks are thought to
have been split further open by more recent earthquakes. They
felt that it was deliverance from the dreaded punishments they
believed to be inflicted, both here and hereafter, by these terrible
serpent-covered maidens, that St. Paul proclaimed there on that
rocky hill by the doctrine of Repentance from their sins, along with
the welcome assurance of the Resurrection from the dead. The
steps up to the summit from the valley below, the stones on which
the accuser and the defendant stood, and a rude bench all cut in
the living rock, still remain perfect: it is to the Christian the most
impressive spot in Greece.

On the south-western side of the Acropolis stands the picturesque
Theatre or Odeum of Herodes; it is but little destroyed, and late in
the afternoon, when the sun lights up the ruddy stone and brick of
the arches, and shows out the graceful curve of the seats, this
building is a beautiful object. The Greek plays, so full, in every
line, of natural imagery and allusion to the surrounding scene,
would be read with thousandfold pleasure, seated on one of those
old seats, under the blue sky, and breathing the sweet " pellucid
air " which happily can never change.

From this, passing over the remains of the Dionysiac Theatre,
one of the largest and grandest ever made, the eye naturally travels
round to the splendid Temple of Jupiter Olympius, which became,
from the length of time that passed between its commencement and
its completion—seven centuries—a byword and a proverb among
the Athenians, who after all left the Romans to finish it. It is
hardly possible now to imagine how very magnificent and glorious
it must have been, as, of the 120 columns which once adorned the

exterior, only fifteen now remain. A double row of columns surrounded the cella, doubled again at each end, each column 58 feet
in height and fluted, surmounted by a capital of the most elegant
and bold though delicate Corinthian acanthus. No other Temple
could have rivalled this one unless it be that of the Sun at Baalbek,
which in the general design and the richness of the detail will well
bear comparison with its Athenian brother, but the situations of
the two are different. The Temple of Baalbek stands, with its
brother Temple, upon a hill overlooking a vast plain and opposite
to the loftiest portion of the wooded and snow-capped Lebanon
mountains: there could not be found a finer site in itself for the
noble group, standing thus alone, for no other object attracts the
eye: the Temple of Jupiter Olympius is placed on the level plain,
commanding no distance, and backed by low and barren hills, but
near to the foot of that rock which rears up aloft for the admiration
of all generations one of the most exquisitely lovely of all the
buildings in the world, and the glory of Greece.

The view of the Acropolis from the neighbourhood of this
Temple is one of the finest that can be had: from this the abrupt
rising of the rocky hill from the plain, and the steepness of its
sides, are better seen than from elsewhere; while, shining in its
whiteness, the Parthenon appears on the summit of her noble
pedestal. The situation of Tadmor is, in my opinion, finer and
grander than that of any of these temples—Jupiter Olympius,
Baalbek, and even than the Parthenon; but Palmyra lacks the
memory enshrined in every heart, of those centuries of Poetry and
Heroism, which form the real " crown of light " fixed for ever in the
sky above the Acropolis.

Bending round the eastern end of this world-famed rock a small
street anciently ran: a street of monuments raised to commemorate
the victory of such-and-such a chorus in the Dramatic contests.
One specimen only of the monuments is still standing, but this one
is nearly perfect: it is a very small circular structure, surrounded
by six Corinthian columns, and standing on a plain square base; a
rich frieze and a highly ornamented roof support a beautiful
pedestal on which the Tripod—the prize of the successful candidate
—was placed: the name of the Chorus, in this case of Lysicrates,
was engraved on the architrave. If all the monuments were as
pretty as this one, the street must have been beautiful indeed.

A larger building, but not nearly so pretty, called the Temple of
the Winds, stands further to the north: on its eight sides are sculptured the winds of each season with their respective characteristics
from the lighted charcoal and thick garments of Winter to the

flowers and fruits of Summer and the rains of Autumn ; the beautiful capital of the doorway, uniting the Egyptian water-leaf with the Grecian acanthus, has disappeared. The most picturesque among the other ruins is the Portico of the New Agora, erected by Julius Cæsar : it stands alone, looking very majestic, but very lonely and sorrowful in the midst of the shops and booths that surround it.

We drove very early one hot morning to the cool " groves of Academe :" the " olives " are outside the walled garden, in which there are some fine oriental planes (the descendants of course of those which formed " Plato's retirement "), with acacias, flowering shrubs, and vines; but " the Attic bird " refused to " trill her thick-warbled notes "[*] for the stranger, and we were only consoled by the pretty view of the Acropolis from between the trees, which is, however, a good deal prettier in the evening. The Kephissus, in summer a very poor and feeble stream, just as it was in ancient times, runs in green ditches along the Academy groves, but she had just then found the road more to her taste, and we drove through pools of water, and tumbled in and out of deep holes [in the most alarming manner, until we were quite tired with the unusual exercise. The roads were lined with mud walls, built in thick slabs, topped with brushwood.

Having thus had enough of the Kephissus, we walked out in the afternoon one day to the Ilissus, which we crossed, stepping on pebbles over the shallow stream, and ascended into the Stadium, the traces of which are yet very perfect : a fine bridge once spanned the river, in winter a copious stream, and must have made a grand approach to the spacious semicircle, when the hill side was lined with the ranges of white marble seats. There is something touching now in the utter loneliness and silence of the grass-grown hollow, when one thinks of the gay and excited multitude that thronged its banks to witness the races, holding in their hands the wreaths and bouquets of flowers to be showered down upon the fortunate victor; Time has clothed the little plain with " the peacefulness of grass :" and not a flower was to be seen on the banks of the river that went lazily murmuring by, save the lavender spray of the fragrant agnus-castus, a humble substitute for the delicate heliotrope that once grew wild there, a plant consecrated to Plato, as the only flower mentioned by him. Under some tall bushes of this shrub, for not a tree remains on the bare banks of the Ilissus, we sat down to read Socrates' invitation to Phædrus to rest awhile with him under the shadow of the plane-trees there : the ruined heaps of the bridge-piers were opposite to us, and a little further down was the site of

[*] Milton.

the Temple of Artemis (since a church); but alas! we had stumbled upon the steaming carcase of a dead horse, and other abominations, and we were obliged to beat a hasty retreat.   So we went on to the Fountain of Callirrhoë (the Nine Springs), where the Athenian women have washed their clothes ever since the days of Pisistratus, and were still washing (probably not the same clothes) when we passed by, and listened to the babble of tongues joining in loud duets with the gushing noise of the pipe-led stream.

Such was the suffocating heat of Athens at this time that the sound or sight of water was absolutely a relief: we found we could attempt nothing in the way of sight-seeing between the hours of ten and five, which did not leave much daylight at our disposal: the most luxurious enjoyment was to go and sit for two or three hours before sunset in the gardens of the Palace, which are thrown open with great liberality to the public, and which contain, besides some interesting Roman remains, a great variety of fine trees and flowering shrubs; they are laid out with much taste and ingenuity.

The Queen has also a large farm with a *maisonnette de plaisir* at a few miles' distance from the city, reached by an excellent road lying between gardens hedged with oleanders; there is a lovely view from the top of the small tower, and very pleasant are the avenues of white and yellow roses, the innumerable clover beds which perfume the air, and the fine trees of this carefully kept garden.   The cowhouse, containing about sixty cows, was worth seeing for its good order and arrangements, besides some gentle and very tame giraffes lately arrived from Egypt.   This is a very pleasant drive from Athens: we went back slowly, enjoying the sight of the full moon, with Venus, a little world of glowing silver, triumphing in radiant beauty over Jupiter; while every mountain height —Hymettus, Pentelicus, Lycabettus— was crowned with immense bonfires to celebrate King Otho's birthday. It was most strange and weird to see the Acropolis lighted up with the brilliant, fiery glare which revealed every temple and column in a strange, uncanny fashion.   The town had been very gay and noisy all day, the German soldiers filling the streets; and when we re-entered it, the pavements outside the *cafés* were crowded with gentlemen and ladies, many of the former and nearly all the latter in the national costume, certainly the most picturesque man's dress possible.   Everybody knows, from pictures, the bright waistcoat, hanging jacket, tight cloth buskins, and full white kilt or petticoat (most ingeniously made) of the Greek, which become their sharp faces and lithe figures so well.   The only peculiarity of the ladies' costume is a richly embroidered jacket and a falling scarlet cap, with a long gold tassel:

it is a graceful and pretty dress ; the cap is arranged with immense care and art.

As we were curious to see the very varied costumes of the Greek peasants, we were pleased to hear of a great annual fête to be held on Mount Pentelicus on the 4th of June, the Feast of the Holy Trinity, and gladly agreed to accompany some friends thither. We started at 8 A.M. in a covered carriage, leaving the town by the north-east. The road crossed an apparently very long subterranean aqueduct, with openings to the air, covered with iron lids, at every few yards : and then lay over an open, heathy country, for about an hour, after which we passed through a grove of really noble old olives and some vineyards, before we came to the pretty stream of the Kephissus. We then began to ascend the hill through thick brushwood of agnuscastus, lentisk, and prickly oak, with arbutus, judas-tree, and abundance of yellow broom ; and arrived on a grassy plateau, shaded by a thick wood of lofty silver-poplars, covered with crowds of carriages, carts, unharnessed horses, and parties of people, all busy upon wine, lemonade, coffee, and more substantial viands. We went first, as in duty bound, to the little chapel, which is ornamented with Byzantine frescoes, representing all kinds of martyrdoms of a horrible and lugubrious nature : and then sat down to watch the dancers, and to examine the endless variety of costume, which is really worth seeing. The fair faces of the Greek peasant-women look very delicate and refined after the coarse Syrian and the ugly Egyptian women ; but we saw very little real beauty among them ; good eyes and eyebrows are their best feature, and their figures are as beautiful as their movements are graceful. The dancing was all very slow and monotonous, seemingly without any particular rule : the couples went hand in hand, or followed each other, sometimes with a handkerchief twisted about between them, and the women's eyes were invariably bent on the ground. I began to sketch two or three of the prettiest women, but a great crowd gathered around me, and made merry with so many jokes and witticisms, that the husbands always snatched away my victims before I had made any progress in their portraits. At last we were invited into a little room in the monastery, where a handsome young woman, the sister of one of the priests, was induced to sit to me : but nothing could make the blue-satin-robed priests understand that I wanted light and elbow-room, and that I did not like their leaning over my shoulders ; and the girl was so shy and modest that the picture-taking was an unpleasant proceeding on both sides and succeeded very ill : it was, however, considered very splendid by the monks and peasants, and the poor thing was allowed to escape before her blushes had quite burnt through her cheeks.

Her dress was truly magnificent, though how she carried the weight of it, that hot day, I could'not understand ; and it was so stiff with its great thickness that it hid all beauty of figure. Her gown was of very thick white cloth, reaching almost to the ground, and nearly tight round her, embroidered, to the depth of two feet from the bottom, in coarse worsted and silk, chiefly dark green and orange, so as entirely to hide the material : it was open on the bosom, showing a white gauze shirt, and was bound round with a girdle of very thick crimson woollen stuff, finished with tassels : every girl embroiders such a dress for herself before her marriage. Over this gown and the white apron trimmed with lace, comes a long shapeless coat, reaching to below the knees, of double crimson cloth, the under cloth an inch or two larger than the upper, embroidered all over with gold and a little coloured silk until it is as stiff as a board : it is excessively rich and ungraceful : the sleeves are long and the dress very open on the bosom, which was entirely covered with seven or eight gold chains, strung with gold coins, very tastefully arranged with Greek crosses stuck with jewels : and a necklace of a dozen strings of pearls was round her throat. The red cap was bound upon her head by a coloured gauze handkerchief, and edged with two rows of gold coins ; her nice brown hair was plaited in two long braids with thick red silk cords, and enormous tassels reaching down to the ground, topped with gold and silver— a huge bunch to each braid, of which the weight was quite fearful. Over all this was a beautiful white gauze veil, richly and elegantly embroidered with gold, not hanging over the face, but swathed round the neck under the chin, and hanging down behind. Such a dress, without including the coins, which seemed to be chiefly foreign moneys, or the pearls, costs from 60*l.* to 80*l.* The dress of the unmarried girls is simpler, but also much embroidered.

From the little chapel above the monastery there is a lovely view of Attica and the islands with the Peloponnesian mountains; Corinth is very distinctly seen; and close by we found delicious cool shade beside a clear fountain, where we ate bread and oranges in preference to the sour lemonade, and bitter acrid wine (like a *tisane* of resin and vinegar), with which our neighbours were refreshing themselves. All seemed bright and happy, and we saw not the slightest sign of drunkenness, nor even heard any loud, vulgar shoutings: the road was covered with returning parties as we drove back to Athens, riding on donkeys, or packed into rough carts.

We had intended to make a rather extensive tour in Greece, and on arriving in Athens we had at once commenced our preparations: but, to our great disappointment, we were met on all sides with the most complete discouragement: the people seemed to think us more than half crazy for the very idea of travelling in Greece in the month of June. At first we assured them we had come from a hotter country, and were well inured to the sun, but when we found the very dragomans who offered their services refused to engage for excursions in the country, we began to think there "must be something in it," and we very soon learned by our own experience that the Grecian sun was not to be defied; moreover, that the air of Greece has such an effect upon the nerves, that the heat is more irritating and injurious there than in Syria, from the body being in a less healthy condition. On first arriving in Greece, the stranger feels exhilarated and buoyant: he realises that he is "lightly tripping through an atmosphere of surpassing brightness;" * he feels so strong and well and happy that he is delighted with himself and with everything around him: but in this very charm lies a sweet poison; the nerves, which have rejoiced in their sudden tension, are in a day or two (or more, according to the power of the sun and the constitution of the individual) strung to a pitch beyond endurance, and the result is either fever, or some form of neuralgia. The extraordinary prevalence of the latter complaint, among all classes and both sexes, must unquestionably be produced by the climate, and it seemed fully to deserve the name we heard given to it—"the curse of Attica." The stranger, after a few days, finds his new strength has unaccountably disappeared; a feeling of intense fatigue and heavy limbs overpowers his energies, and the hot, suffocating nights bring him neither rest nor sleep. If the mosquitos will let you venture out of your curtains, you roam from room to room, or from bed to sofa and sofa to bed: but you always arrive at the conviction that there was more air in the place you have just left than in the one you have just got to. Your temples seem bound up with cords and your head feels bursting: and then, if you stay another month in Athens you are pretty sure to have some attack of *tic*, which will fill you full of sympathy for those Athenians who cannot leave Athens during the heat of summer.

We knew, however, that refreshing air would be found upon the mountains, and so in spite of all fears we engaged a very highly recommended dragoman, Spiro Adamopulos, to arrange a six days' excursion for us, parting at the same time with our good Syrian

* Euripides.

Habeeb Soma, who had accompanied us thus far. We were anxious to travel in the same manner as we had done in Syria, but alas! we yielded reluctantly to the dissuasive eloquence of our new attendant, and included only beds and provisions in our engagement with him. I strongly advise no one else to listen to such dissuasions; a tent adds but one mule to the troop, and besides enabling you to stop where and when you please, it affords you peace, quiet, and a sound refreshing sleep: the dragomans are only unwilling to take it because of course it adds as much to their trouble as to your comfort.

General Sir Richard Church—one of the heroes of the Greek War of Independence, whose kindness to us was untiring and whose advice proved most useful—provided us with letters of introduction to various gentlemen's houses, for in Greece, private hospitality still supplies the place of public accommodation: a government order, called a *Bouyourouldi*, was procured for us, which was to insure us lodging and attention wherever we demanded them. Our baggage mules and horses had been sent on the night before, as, in order to lessen our fatigues, we had engaged a carriage to take us as far as the road was then completed: a seven hours' drive. We arranged to set off at 6 A.M., but, not being ready till half an hour later, we were rather surprised at receiving a message from the coachman to say that he would not go at all if we delayed another moment, as he considered that a few minutes later it would be too hot to set out! the hotel people wished us good-bye in a melancholy manner, as if they thought we were going to perdition, and altogether we became very much impressed with the possible imprudence of our proceedings. It was, however, too late to draw back, and our peace of mind was soon restored by the luxurious enjoyment of the easy, comfortable, covered britschka, rolling along the excellent road with four horses, at a speed that tempered the heat by the pleasant breeze. After leaving the plain the road runs through the pass of Daphne, a narrow and pretty valley (not half as charming as its romantic Syrian namesake), from whence there is a most beautiful view of Mount Geranea and the Bay of Eleusis, looking like a lake—so completely does it appear enclosed by the famed island of Salamis: one could scarcely even *fancy* its tranquil loveliness disturbed by the noise and strife of such a victory as that of Salamis: without a single boat, or human being, or any sign of life, the landscape seemed like a most exquisite picture; and yet one's heart thrilled in only thinking of the two-thousand-year-old memory! Skirting the edge of the bay, we drove round to the village of Eleusis, where we alighted for a few moments to examine some excavations commenced about six weeks previously by a M. Le Norman: the French Government had purchased some houses which were believed to cover the site of the Temple where the Eleusinian Mysteries were practised, and the workmen were then engaged in laying bare its foundations, and were daily discovering capitals, drums and bases of columns, and broken bits of very beautiful sculpture, heaps of which were already collected in a little house hard by. We saw capitals of each of the three orders of architecture, one very large Corinthian capital, with richly and finely cut acanthus leaves, was being then uncovered; and the pedestal of a statue, with two torches crossed on the front. There was also an enormous medallion containing the bust of an Emperor. We walked on a little way to the site of the Temple of Ceres, from which one can see the extreme narrowness of *the* straits where the battle was fought, and the rocky seat on the brow of Ægaleos whence Xerxes sprang up in an agony of grief and rage at his effeminate generals.

After leaving the Bay, we struck to the right, and followed a very pretty and wild road, marvellously winding, for

> "the upland paths
> Of Kithæron's glades are steep,"

through rocks and low woods, till we came to a little Khan, called Casae, where we reluctantly left our carriage. The house had only one room above and two below: we mounted to the upper one, which was unfurnished, and lay down on the bare floor wrapped in our cloaks for an hour, but it was very hot, and we were glad to leave it at 3.30 P.M. to ride up the pretty wooded gorge, and look back at the fine and picturesque Gipsy Castle, as it is now called, the site of the ancient Œnoe (Col. Leake). A cool breeze greeted us on the brow o the defile, refreshing us enough to enjoy a glorious view, when for the first time our eyes beheld Mount Parnassus. On the right, the lofty snow-covered peak of Mount Delphos in Eubœa, with range behind range of mountain and hill: then the fertile Bœotian Plain of Thebes and Platæa: and to the left, the hill of the Sphinx stretching out its length, like fore-paws folded, below the rugged heights of Helicon and the snowy peaks of Parnassus. The light was shining upon the white houses of Thebes—and one could not help fancying how splendid a point in the fine landscape it must have been, when the music-built walls of the ancient Acropolis yet crowned the hill on which its humble descendant now stands.

We now descended the other side of "Kithæron's wooded glades," riding among some scores of men employed in constructing the road; in the fields we observed here, and everywhere else in this expedition, little sheds or tents stuck up on a few sticks to shade even the poorest peasant during his field-labours; it seemed strange, coming from much hotter countries, such as Egypt and Syria, to find so many more precautions taken against the sun; yet on the other hand the peasants wear only a thin straw hat! so poor a protection from an Eastern sun would be almost fatal to a Syrian.

We reached Thebes about sunset: the approach to the town is remarkably pretty, and the principal street is substantially built; we alighted at the house of a Greek gentleman, M. Theagene, whose hospitality, already bespoken for us, was most kindly given; but we enjoyed only a very short sleep, for warned by the heat and fatigues of our first day, we left Thebes before 5 A.M., descending the pretty hill on which the town is built, into the plain, which we were three hours in crossing; the whole plain was covered with water from the Asopus, and we splashed and waded through the rushes, the water frequently reaching to the horses' middles. Crossing a little ridge, we entered the Plain of Leuctra, the scene of Epaminondas's victory over the Spartans; and passing by the ruins which mark the site of the ancient city, we stopped about 9 A.M. at a small khan. Here our beds were put up in an empty room, and we lay down to cool and rest, for the heat was already too great to admit of further exposure to the sun: repose in such houses, however, is not very easy to obtain; for the large apertures left in the floor of the upper rooms, to facilitate communication with the *cabaret* below, give free access to the noise and chatter which the peasants love to prolong over their sour wine. We left the house at 4 P.M., passing over the richly cultivated and charming plain—one of the prettiest rides possible—winding along the foot of Helicon, whose jagged, craggy peaks towered up above us; we passed the sites and ruins of several ancient cities, among them Coronea, where ruins of a theatre, Agora, and Temple of Hera may still be seen: and then we wound close under a noble perpendicular cliff, called Petra, which the Greeks fortified and held for a long time successfully against the Turks, in the War of Independence. Down from Helicon's sacred sides, danced a hundred little rills of clear, cool water; no wonder the nymphs that lived among them were inspired with poetic thoughts and sweet songs; and the way was bright and fragrant with flowers and shrubs, under which the ground was actually swarming with tortoises, some of them very large and beautifully stained: the path was also marked with innumerable serpent trails.

The previous afternoon, as we descended the side of Kithæron, one of our men killed a huge snake: it was certainly little under five feet long, and thicker than my arm: the skin was of a pale blue-green, very bright and pretty, with yellow underneath: our servants said it was of a very venomous kind. A few minutes after, we passed another of the same size, and here at the foot of Helicon we saw two more: they were much larger than any we had seen in the east. It is curious that Helicon and Kithæron, the time-honoured haunts of the gentle Muses, the sacred pleasure-grounds of the sport-loving Artemis, every rock, glen, grotto and spring of which were peopled with their own sweet nymphs, should now be infested with serpents and snakes, more, it is said, than any other spot in Greece. Were the serpents that entwined the tresses of the wild Bacchanal maidens, who tore poor Pentheus to pieces merely because he was too prosaic and sober, the only beings that survived the evaporation of all the spirits on these sacred mountains? or is it a nineteenth-century parody of Nature on the noble old allegories and poetry of ancient Greece, that has translated the Nymphs and Oreads of old into snakes and serpents, spotted frogs and tiny newts?.

Moreover, as we looked onwards upon the snowy heights of Parnassus, the rosy glow of sunset suddenly illuminated his "horned head" and we were free, despite all modern "common sense," to believe with the delightful old creeds of yore, if we pleased, that the crimsoning of the snow announced the arrival in person of the youthful god upon the summit of his favourite vine-clad mountain. But when the sun had sunk, and the golden haze had gone—when dead silence had fallen on the woods, and even the murmuring rills seemed hushed into half-tones, and the leaves were whispering their hopes and fears to each other under cover of the darkness, and only the stars shone down in quiet radiance,—I looked and looked among the woods, and fondly hoped I night catch a glimpse of an ivy crown, or a white arm, or the wild eyes of an Oread, or a Bacchanal's thyrsus; but alas for the golden dreams of the Past! some cruelly modern breath must have passed over my soul and veiled my eyes, for the fierce and fatal maidens hid themselves and would not appear: and all I could obtain to cheer me on my path were a few glow-worms, shining meekly on the grass.

In spite of the pleasantness of the ride, we were excessively tired before we reached Levadea, the lights of which had long twinkled most invitingly from the wooded heights on which the town is built, as we groped our way through the luxuriant meadows. We stopped at a filthy khan where our cook had already prepared our dinner, declaring that it was impossible to find better quarters at Levadea, while to us it seemed equally impossible to remain for the night among the fleas and fowls which pervaded every room; we had, however, disconsolately alighted, when a venerable white-bearded priest came to announce that a gentleman had prepared his guest-room for us, and was expecting us: so we went on most thankfully to a clean-looking house, where, nevertheless, our hopes of an undisturbed sleep were wofully disappointed.

Levadea is a most picturesque, charming town, and though small, seems lively enough, with gay little shops, which were already open at 5 A.M., as we rode up to the ancient Sanctuary of Trophonius, a natural cave in a narrow mountain gorge, which it is considered very unlucky to enter; outside the cavern there are several niches and tablets cut in the face of the rock, and from it a small stream issues into a weedy basin: while further on, from under the noble rocks of the gorge, a copious mountain torrent—the Hercyma—wells out, tossing, tumbling, and foaming down the rocks into the valley beneath. On the heights above is a well-placed modern castle, in ruins. We had quitted the town by five o'clock, and after fording a river we mounted a low hill, whence snowy Parnassus looked splendidly beautiful. Two hours brought us to Chæronea, where we stopped to see the broken marble lion which has for twenty-one centuries marked the spot where the Thebans fell—broken, but not bent—in the battle which made Philip of Macedon master of Greece, and in which Alexander the Great first gave promise of his future fame. It was a fine thought to render the memory of the nobility and courage of these unfortunate patriots undying by an almost imperishable emblem, but we failed to discern the wonderful depths of mixed expression said to exist in the features of the lion's face; with which in fact we were very much disappointed.

We were more interested with the very curious little old Church of the Panagia in the village, which contains two Doric and two Ionic columns, some ancient frescoes, a stone chair from which it is said Plutarch was wont to teach, and a number of strange inscriptions outside the building which tell of the worship of Osiris of Egypt, according to the Greek and Roman knowledge of him. The Mayor of the village, advised of our coming, came out to meet us, and offer his assistance: but we could invent no cause for his services, and could therefore only thank him. We rode on to the remains of the Theatre, partly cut in the rock, on the side of the hill: the semicircles of seats are so distinctly visible that it is worth seeing, although their marble coverings have disappeared; towering perpendicularly above the theatre are the remains of the ancient Acropolis of Chæronea; and below are the ruins of an aqueduct and of a beautiful five-mouthed fountain well deserving of imitation elsewhere.

It was now eight o'clock and broiling hot; a scorching sun was shining on the Plain of Davlia, the old Daulis, which it cost us two hours to cross, and which seemed all the hotter for the very beautiful view of the stern, grey rocks and sparkling snows on Parnassus before us and the glacier which we fancied we could distinguish between the summits. At length we began to mount the steep hill, the foot of Parnassus, and to approach the thick pomegranate groves, laden with flowers, in which the little houses of Davlia are hidden. All the nightingales in the world are descended from the birds of these groves, for here it was that poor Philomela became the first specimen of those small singers. We got into a cool, airy room in one of the Davlian houses, and lay down to rest, till two o'clock. Nothing could be more charming than the rest of our ride that day: and this consoled us for not being able to ascend Parnassus from Davlia, descending upon Aráchova, as we had wished to do, but the intense heat and the want of sleep had deprived us of so much strength that we were really afraid to attempt so fatiguing an undertaking, especially as we had no tents, in which to take a night's rest *en route*. From Davlia the path mounts up and up, cooled with refreshing mountain breezes, the views changing at every step: now among narrow, winding passes: then over bold mountain brows: barren rocks and lofty cliffs contrasting with green little meadows and luxuriant brushwood; and after passing an isolated rock called the Brigand's Tower, where twenty-five of these gentry were taken last year, after many unsuccessful attempts, by surrounding their stronghold, we turned suddenly to the west, and pursued a long narrow and steep gorge, which was very grand and beautiful: Mount Parnassus, on the right, rising up sheer to the summit, with quantities of snow on the side, the frowning rock looking very cold and Alpine, and, on the left, the steep sides of Mount Elemon clothed with a thick wood of lofty pines and other trees: while, deep down in the bottom, rushed a stream. This is the Pass of Schiste, and just at its commencement is the narrow place where Œdipus met and murdered his father Laïus; I fear from what we heard he only set the example for a great many murders that have been committed there since that unhappy day.

As we went on, the views became still more rich and varied.

2 L

Wherever human foot could stand vines were planted, the finest plants and the most neatly tended we had seen in Greece: each vineyard had its own stone vine-press, but the grapes are pressed a second time in the peasants' houses. The road wound along steep and narrow ledges rather giddily, and the rocks seemed wonderfully split and broken at the edges by earthquakes, which are said to be of not uncommon occurrence here: the air was deliciously laden with the perfume of the yellow and white broom and the abundant honeysuckle clambering everywhere. As we mounted the last ridge such a magnificent panorama opened upon us, looking down over the whole gorge with the Gulf of Corinth and the Peloponnesus beyond, that we regretted greatly not having arrived five minutes sooner to catch the full daylight upon the scene: as it was, the light lingered upon the mountain tops gloriously, and crimsoned the snow on the five lovely peaks of Pentebro and the other mountains of the Morea, in perfect beauty. Arāchova was immediately before us, *se crum-ponnant* on the very steep side of Parnassus in an apparently wonderful way, and we were very glad to get through the crabbed lanes of the place before it was quite dark. The people were all out, enjoying the evening after their day's work, and excessively gay and picturesque it was: the men with bright-coloured clothes about them, smoking and chattering: the women, every one with a strong scarlet and yellow woollen apron fastened down upon the hips, and plenty of silver ornaments on their heads, with their spinning distaffs in their hands; and what a noise the pretty, buxom creatures did make with their voluble tongues and high-pitched voices! Our dragoman took us to a nice room in a large house belonging to a friend of his own, where about fifteen women and children, some of them very pretty, surrounded us for the next two hours to examine and shake hands with the interesting strangers; our riding-habits and hats exciting immense astonishment.

The best wine in Greece, we were told, was made here, and we were therefore anxious to taste it, but we found it excessively un-palatable, so saturated with resin and vinegar that none of us could take a second sip. The Arāchovians are famous for another manufacture which is really good and pretty, a thick strongly-woven tweed, used for carpets and cushions and sofa covers: it is warm, of colours tastefully arranged in patterns, and closely resembles the Spanish peasant's *manta* or woollen scarf, which is, however, of much brighter colours.

The women fed us in the morning with their finest wheaten bread, made only as an offering to the priest, and marked with sacred symbols: and we left them at eight o'clock following a beautiful path along the mountain-side, looking down into the great valley below, and bowered thickly over with wild roses, honeysuckle, prickly oak, and zakkhoum, till after two hours' ride we turned a corner and came upon Delphi, one of the most sacred spots in all Greece, the oracle of which was revered till a comparatively late period, by the Grecians and their colonies. The mountain here recedes from the valley in a sloping semicircle, round which, like the seats of a theatre, were the terraces on which the city of Delphi was anciently placed; portions of the Pelasgic masonry which supported these terraces are still very evident under the modern houses. Doubtless the appearance of this finely-placed city, adorned with rich buildings and commanding such beautiful views, must have been very splendid. In the deepest portion of the semicircle, the rock is split into a chasm or fissure, down which the stream of the Pleistus used to tumble: it is dry now, and the cliffs are of no great height, but it must have made a fine background to the Temple, built of Parian marble, which once covered over the small basin in which the Priestess bathed when about to deliver her oracle. The steps by which she descended into the Castalain fountain still remain, but the basin itself is now overgrown with weeds and contains only a half-dry puddle; behind it, in the face of the rock, are a variety of niches, large and small, one of which has been converted into the very tiniest chapel possible, dedicated to St. John; and there is also a channel, cut in the rock, which conducted the stream beyond the Temple; this too seemed dry. The spring seemed to fill a few yards lower down, where several women were washing clothes, with the aid of men and boys; and altogether, with the extreme filth and neglect of the whole place, it is now singularly unromantic and unattractive. We went down to the monastery built on the site of a large temple, and found some fine fragments of sculpture scattered about, with some Doric columns and other remains; and the view from under the noble old olives, some of them perhaps a thousand years old, was most beautiful.

While we were looking about a sergeant and a private in uniform came up with a salute, and announced that they had been sent from Scala, in obedience to a letter from the "Home Office" of Athens, to attend our orders and to accompany us down to Scala. They had come up the night before, and had prepared a house for us to sleep or breakfast in; but of this our dragoman thought proper not to inform us till after they were gone; he chose only to say that, happening to be there they politely offered us their services if we wanted anything, and he suggested that we should give them a *pourboire* and send them away. They refused the money, but shortly after went away, leaving us to breakfast, very uncomfortably in the sunshine, by the spring: we had asked for some house, but the dragoman assured us there was none in the village fit for us to go into, and that we had better breakfast in the open air. It was so hot in this shadeless place that we were glad to ride on as soon as possible, though we had contemplated remaining at Delphi some hours, to enjoy the view, which is, both to the north and to the south, magnificent: so, only taking a hasty glance at the Stadium, which is worth examining, and at a rock-hewn tomb by the roadside, we continued our route, our dragoman having sent on the baggage mules ten minutes in advance of us. The road was tolerably rough, but wide, and well protected from the precipice on the outer side; in a quarter of an hour, however, we heard a great shouting, " Spiro! Spiro!" to which our dragoman for some time gave no heed: at last we asked him why he did not attend; he then announced that the muleteers had taken a wrong road, or rather that they had turned off from the only road, that one of the mules had been on the point of falling over the edge of the precipice, when to save it, the cords securing our luggage had been obliged to be cut, that his own canteen, &c., which was fastened to the same mule was quite safe, having been placed on the inner side, but that all *our* things which had been tied on the outside had gone to the bottom of the valley! He recommended that we should go on to Chrisso, an hour and a half further, and await the arrival of the muleteers, who were trying to recover the scattered goods. The heat was now intense and we could do nothing better, so seeing a nice, clean house in the village, we asked permission to enter, and receiving a hearty welcome, were soon installed in a large, airy room with mattresses laid for us to rest on.

After waiting a weary hour we insisted upon Spiro sending down after the soldiers who had come to meet us at Delphi, and on his going himself to look after the luggage; he returned, in another hour, with a bundle tied up in one of our garments containing a few books, clothes, &c., all things of no use to the finders, some circular notes, of which happily they did not know the value, but of course not a single halfpenny of some 50*l.* in coin, or of a bag of gems, turquoises, and Syrian antiques, which will probably be offered for sale to travellers in Greece for the next five years. That the box had tumbled down the precipice was probably true, for it was completely crushed, the clothes were torn and the books spoiled,—but whether its descent was accidental or pre-arranged, we shall never be quite certain: why our guards should have been carefully sent away, or why the mules should have been taken off a very well-known road, or why letters, placed with the money in a leather bag so stout and thick that no tumble could possibly have torn it open or burst the lock, should have been taken out and restored to us *uncrumpled*, while all the rest of the valuable contents of the bag were *nowhere*— are questions which will probably never receive a more definite answer than "it is just what you may expect in Greece;" the poor consolation which was afterwards bestowed on us from many quarters.

We sent for the Mayor of Chrisso, who held a regular court of justice in our resting-place, taking down our depositions (to which my sister was required to swear on a splendid copy of the Gospels, cased in embossed silver); they asked about a hundred and fifty irrelevant questions which would have amused an English court very much, touching her birth and parentage, confession of faith and education, whether she had been at school or not, &c., in short, writing a brief biographical memoir of her which must no doubt be an interesting item in the archives of Chrisso. It was sunset before we escaped, and we had a rough descent to make in the dark to Scala: it was slippery and very disagreeable, but we were a large party, half a dozen soldiers accompanying us in order to hold the door shut after the horse had gone; we were not in the most comfortable frame of mind: the air was very hot and close, but sweet, and the fire-flies danced around us. We reached the steamer at eleven in the evening, a very small Greek boat from Patras: there were ten ladies on board and only three berths appropriated to them, and these were in the general saloon: so we lay down on the deck and enjoyed the fresh sea air and the early dawn on the grand and lovely mountains that surround the Gulf of Corinth, reaching Lutraki at four in the morning.

Here we stayed till eleven, letting the other passengers go on, and waiting for a return carriage to convey us across the Isthmus (for which they ask any price they fancy at the moment); and we spent our Sunday morning in the shade on the deck of the steamer looking at beautiful Corinth. It is a noble situation: the white town of New Corinth on the water's edge with gardens all round, the lofty Acropolis of ancient Corinth, towering grandly behind it, standing out from the surrounding mountains, and looking over the calm and lovely blue gulf at its feet. We wished to drive to the Seven Columns, but there was no carriage to be had except for the drive straight across the Isthmus to Kalamaki. There are pretty views all along this well-made road: Mount Geranea, the real key of the Morea, on the left, and the Oncan Mountains on the right; corn-fields and vineyards border the road, but the Isthmus is chiefly clothed with the fresh bright green of the Isthmian pine, from whose branches were woven the simple crowns of the chivalry of ancient Greece—crowns that were soon withered and valueless in themselves, but which remained wreaths of unfading virtue in the memories of the people.

We made the best toilette at Kalamaki that we could with the remains of our garments and the ruins of our dressing apparatus in the hospitable house of a currant merchant: after which a very slow, dirty steamer took us on to the Piræus in six hours: nothing can exceed the beauty of the sail across the Saronic Gulf and round the island of Salamis; every island is of a different colour and form, seeming to recede and advance in the clear atmosphere as we passed by. We reached Athens at eleven o'clock very much in need of rest and sleep.

It was some days before we recovered strength enough to make any more expeditions: the far-famed Ægina, however, was not to be resisted, and we made an effort to accompany a friend to that pleasant, pretty island. Our dragoman had engaged an open fishing-boat to carry us across the gulf, and we drove down early to the Piræus, getting on board by 7 A.M.; they had promised to run us over to the island in forty-five minutes, but it was ten o'clock before we reached the shore, and the sun was excessively hot, as of course the little boat afforded no shelter whatever. We had then a roasting walk before we found an umbrageous fig-tree under which to rest and breakfast; fortunately from this fortress of comfort we espied three donkeys whom we captured and mounted, sitting somehow on the wooden pack-saddle: an hour, through charming varieties of wood and rock, shrub and flower, myrtle, arbutus, laurel, and pine, carried us up to the beautiful ruin of the Temple dedicated to Minerva by the Athenians, who built it on the north-eastern corner of the island, in the idea of the goddess ever regarding, and being seen from Athens. It is magnificently placed, facing Attica, Salamis, and Sunium, with Kithæron, Pentelicus, and Hymettus: the eye sweeping round the mouth of the Saronic Gulf and the beautiful islands of St. George and Hydra, and across its own lovely curving bays to the Hieron mountains behind Epidaurus and Methana. In the opposite corner of the island rises a cone-shaped mountain, on which a Temple to Jupiter once stood; it was built by Æacus, the king of Ægina, and long afterwards dedicated to Elias the Prophet, in order to take up the thread, as it were, and thus translate into Christianity, the legend of the king's prayers for rain having been answered by Jove in a plentiful and immediate shower.

The Temple of Minerva was built, probably, six hundred years before Christ; it is of a soft stone, which has become a venerable grey colour: the sculptures have all been carried off to Munich, but twenty-two beautiful Doric fluted columns remain *in situ*, the fluting carried up to the abacus, and ending in a row of beads surrounding the column. It is said that the vermilion-coloured stucco which covered the pavement, and the azure ground against which the sculptures of the tympanum rested, could till lately be distinguished, but the whole of the architrave has now fallen, and we could not discover a trace of colour anywhere. But it is still a very grand and very beautiful ruin, with a simple, noble grace peculiarly its own.

The sailors insisted on our going on board again by one o'clock, declaring that the wind would be unfavourable by three: but it was even then dead against us, and we did not reach the Piræus till past six o'clock, after five hours of a roasting which fully realised one's ideas of purgatory, the whole party being really ill from the fearful heat on the head and the glare of the water. We found the next day that the King's cutter had been kindly placed at our disposal for Ægina, but unfortunately we had gone before the offer had reached us.

Our last expedition was a long ride up to the summit of Pentelicus, an expedition that no traveller should omit: it is not a fatiguing ride with good horses. We passed on the side of the mountain a very pretty little turn, embowered in trees, and then followed a wild and steep path up through flowery woods, and past the quarry whence the marble used for the Parthenon was taken; past the great grotto, which contains some very white stalactites, and then winding round some narrow dizzy bits among the low woods emerged at the foot of the bare cone. Here we dismounted and walked up to the summit; the view is extensive and very beautiful, including the islands, lovely Eubœa with all its bays and mountains, all the Cyclades, and on a clear day Mitylene, and Khios, with the Negropontine strait up to Volo, the whole of Attica and part of Bœotia: while directly under the foot of the mountain lies the ever famous Plain of Marathon. Nothing struck me more in this magnificent panorama than the extreme *petiteness* of the country which composed it: one began to comprehend the reality of all the different peoples of the Greeks belonging to cities, not states: and the impossibility of real union among such a number of very small independencies, each contained within its own walls, and jealous of its own exclusive honour, which eventually caused the fall of Greece; but one marvelled all the more at the seemingly inexhaustible number of these very citizens, when one remembered the armies engaged at Platæa and Miletus on the same day, and a hundred other similar instances. Truly the Athenians deserved the name of the "Immortals," when one thought of the almost immeasurable Persian Empire, and looked on the little Attica at one's feet!

So ended our Grecian excursions, for the rest of our stay was unpleasantly occupied by illness, and all the other expeditions we had planned we were compelled to give up; the hot, dry climate had by this time so seriously affected both ourselves and our servants, that we were glad to leave the beautiful country, in spite of the deep interest and delight we had in all the memorials of ancient Greece, and the great pleasure which the kindness we met with at Athens afforded us. We left the city reluctantly enough, in a suffocating sirocco to go on board the *Neva* (one of the finest steamers of the Messageries Impériales); and the last object we saw in Greece was the Doric Temple of Sunium, dedicated to Minerva as the Providence of all Athenians. It stands on the very brow of a dizzy cliff, and thence the Grecian exile, or mariner, snatched the last blessing of the goddess of virtue and wisdom, whose sweet and strong lesson he bore away in his heart to other lands, where, whatever happened to his person, his heart was still Greek; thence again, on returning, he received his first bright welcome back to the country of his birth, his love for which aroused all that was noblest and highest in his soul. Twelve fluted columns* still stand, riveting the eye by their lonely, desolate beauty: to us they appeared in singular loveliness, for the white marble was glowing in the sunset as we glided beneath the cliff, and in another moment, the young moon appeared just above the columns, like Dian's kiss resting there: and long after all else around us had sunk into dark masses, they shone out in silvery splendour against the sky, casting down a long line of bright reflection on the trembling waters at their feet. I thought, as the fair scene faded away, how many a Greek sailing past them had said in his heart,

"   .   .   .   Better
Be ashes *here* than aught that lives elsewhere!"

---

* Whence the modern name of Cape Colonna.

CHAPTER XXVI.

PARADISE ON MOUNT OLYMPUS.

DAY broke as the Sea of Marmora contracted to the entrance of the Bosphorus, and the red lines of the coming fire appeared above the horizon among the deep blue crowds of Night, as we glided in through crowds of Turkish ships and foreign steamers. We had been on deck for an hour before, but the view was scarcely striking, nor even very pretty until the sun came lightly flecking the Palace on Seraglio Point, and lighting up the dark masses of the cypress trees among the buildings.

Being too ill to walk, I was carried up in a sedan-chair to the hotel, where I remained for a week in bed, all unheeding the far-famed beauties of Stamboul, until one evening when I was able to enjoy a really lovely view from our window in Missiri's pleasant hotel. Some heavy showers the night before had cooled and cleared the air, and the colouring, misty and tame by day, came out well under the sunset hues: looking over the piled-up confused mass of roofs below us, the eye rested on the mouth of the Golden Horn filled with ships and steamers, between which scores of caïques were lightly skimming the water. Then came the white buildings, palaces, and government houses, of Seraglio Point, mounting one above the other, with the lofty cypresses between them. The height, indeed, is not great, but the domes and minarets of the great mosques, Santa Sophia, Suleymanyeh, and others, rise behind them as crowning points above the general mass. On the other side of the water is Skutari, green and white like Stamboul, with the quaint-looking Maiden Tower,* as redolent of legends as any Rhenish Castle, standing in the sea before the point: while stretching away in the distance came the pretty outlines of the Prince's

---

* Absurdly called by Europeans " Leander's Tower."

Islands, in front of the blue wall of the Asia Minor mountains, from which for an hour or two, the beautiful snowy heights of Olympus, shone out with majestic grace against the clear blue sky. This was just for the time a really fine view. The climate is also delightfully refreshing, even in the city, after Greece; and on the Bosphorus the air is still more enchanting.

We were anxious to get out, but here was a difficulty for I was not strong enough to walk: or to ride, and we had, besides, left our saddles in Greece: donkeys are not used at Constantinople for carrying human burdens, and the caïques were too far off. So we sent for a *telega*, and the article was soon at the door: imagine an oval pill-box warranted to contain four people when packed like figs in a drum, painted a brilliant rose colour, covered with carving and gilding like a juvenile Lord-Mayor's coach, and with windows all round, mounted on huge wooden and leather springs of the most primitive construction. The horse was driven by a man who walked beside the vehicle (which is called an *araba* when oxen are harnessed to it): but sometimes he sat on a little seat considerably below the level of his horse's back: the furious jolting is quite indescribable, and until we had left the streets of Pera, very far from agreeable, save as a means of taking involuntary exercise.

The brown hills behind Pera are entirely ugly, as are also the mean wooden houses of the suburbs of the town, too ordinary looking to be in the least picturesque: but before we reached the country, we passed the Sultan's Palace, a fine object from the water, close to which it stands. It is of dazzling whiteness, covered over with wreaths and ornaments of the same white stucco as the walls, so as to resemble a bride-cake ; it is surrounded by huge walls with gates of much gilt bronze, and a small garden. The Sultan's Theatre is close at hand, which, as well as his kiosk, a pleasure building in a little wooded dell close by, is in the same style of ornament and as dazzlingly white.

After an hour's drive, we descended a steep road into a delicious little narrow valley with a winding stream and a forest of park-like and lofty trees, perhaps two miles in length: this is the Sweet Waters of Europe, where the Turkish women congregate to smoke, laugh, eat, chatter, and flirt. An ornamental weir has been made beside a pretty kiosk, and the place is really charming. It was too late in the season for seeing the fair visitors: in the summer they frequent the Sweet Waters of Asia, but we found the more natural beauties pleasant enough to reward us even for the abominable jolting of the *trajet* there and back. It is much pleasanter to go there on horseback and to return by caïque along the Golden Horn.

Another morning we started early, in a caïque, to see the far-famed beauties of the Bosphorus. Perhaps they are better seen from the decks of the steamers, but the caïque is pleasanter, and you have more time to contemplate the views. I do not know what will be thought of my confession, but I fear I must record my humble opinion that Constantinople and the Bosphorus do not deserve the immense amount of praise and admiration with which they have been bepainted and besung over and over again. If the City were a less confused mass than it is of very poor houses with some few splendid palaces and a great many lovely mosques, and had hills rising above and behind it, it would be much more imposing. It is the same with the Bosphorus, the windings of which are very graceful: but the hills which border it, though picturesque and well wooded, are too low for its width and very monotonous: call the view very pretty, and then you have said all that you can (I think) justly or reasonably say about it. The greater part of the Straits at least, on both sides, are lined with houses, with gardens or woods behind them: about the middle and at a pretty bend the two Castles of Anadol (Asia) and Roumelia (Europe) are picturesque enough: and there are half-a-dozen little wooded meadows and valleys, either between or behind the towns, which are extremely pleasant and make most refreshing *séjours* for the Perotes in the summer. As you leave Constantinople to ascend the Bosphorus, with the morning sun shining on Pera, it looks well: the Russian Embassy Palace, the Barracks, the great Arsenal, the beautiful Mosque of the Valideh (Sultan's Mother), and the Sultan's Palace look really imposing, and here and there the Palaces of the Sultan's sons-in-law, of his sisters, or of his Ministers are also handsome enough: but in general the effect of the wooden houses everywhere, always more or less tumble down, is poor; the Embassies at Theràpia are the only wooden houses which look well, and here the Bosphorus is really pretty. Standing among the gardens and flowers of Theràpia, one looks across the water at the largest Kiosk of the Sultan (built and presented to him by Muhammad 'Ali), and at the well-shaped hill called the Giant's Mountain further on, while on the European side the bay sweeps gracefully round, richly wooded above, and fringed below with the gaily-painted houses of Buyùkderè. This, with the fine opening of the Black Sea, and the delicious air blowing in on your face, is indeed a pretty view, and one to be remembered; while looking back at Theràpia from the Cyanean Rocks, or Symplegades, is a still finer view and the most beautiful of all on the Bosphorus: this indeed is the only spot from which, in my opinion, the Bosphorus can be called really very beautiful.

Buyùkderè is charming; but the country behind it is much more so: we disembarked ourselves from our gliding caïque, at the hotel, and got into a t lega to drive to the Forest of Belgrad. And *such* a drive as we had after the gentle motion of the caïque! along a narrow road, roughly paved and full of holes, over which we jogged and jolted to that degree that we came back with our shoulders sore from bruises, and the vertebræ of our necks aching with the unusual effort of keeping heads on, while they seemed continually on the point of coming off! Nothing could be more fatiguing by way of a three hours' drive, but we were well repaid for our sufferings. First came English-looking hedges of luxuriant hawthorn, elder, blackberry and nuts, tangled over with nightshade and wild un-English vines, behind which were fields of graceful dhourra; further on, after wonderfully steep bits and turns, we passed under the double tier of arches of the Aqueduct built by the father of the present Sultan, and mounting the hill caught a beautiful view of Buyùkderè and the "gates" of the Black Sea; and then we went deep down into the Forest under fine plane-trees, English oaks, chestnuts, poplars, beech, and a few pines in dark delicious shades and winding paths, through a brushwood of ilex, arbutus, and elder. Not a branch is allowed to be cut in the Forest, except by the Verderers of the Sultan, for it is all Royal property, though open to every Constantinopolitan to take his *kef* under its "care-dispelling" shades, and to sleep in the pretty kiosks built beside the Bends (or Reservoirs) which the forest contains. The water, in fine wide streams, is carried by the aqueducts into Constantinople: there are seven of them, with a huge reservoir to each; and altogether it is a noble work.

Belgrad was the favourite abode of Lady Mary W. Montagu, and her house is still shown in the little village.

A party having been formed at the hôtel to share in the use of a Firmân for seeing the sights of Stamboul, we joined it, and started early in the morning in a t-lega to save fatigue, commencing our round with the Seraglio—a large palace of rather low rooms, built by Sultan Mahmoud II., altered and added to since then, and last used by the present Sultan's father; it is built, I believe, over the remains of the Baths of the Greek Emperors. The palace is furnished in a very heavy style of painting and gilding, in bad taste and now quite dingy: all except some marble baths, and a little octagonal room lined with Damascene mosaic of tortoise-shell and mother-of-pearl, with an enormous fireplace covered with plates of brass. Then we came to the well-kept and pretty garden, where we gathered great bouquets of flowers; and then to a beautiful kiosk beyond it, all gilding and inlay and delicate tracery of fine marbles; inside is the Divan (like a four-post bed), on which the Sultan comes to repose himself for an hour after performing his devotions in the Mosque of Achmet on the day of the Kourban Bairâm: this little room is full of pretty things. From the window of this kiosk, all the Sultan's answers to foreign Ambassadors were given up to a few years ago: no foreigner being then ever admitted to his Sublime Majesty's presence. This kiosk is a perfect gem of architecture. Then we passed the hall where the Sacred Banners and some sacred arms are kept; but no infidel, even of Royal or Imperial rank, has ever been allowed to enter the hallowed precincts. The most sacred of the Banners is carefully concealed from vulgar gaze, except on the occasion of a religious war, when it is exhibited by the Sultan himself in order to stir up the hearts of the faithful. The Banner is said to be made of a robe worn by the Prophet.

After this we saw a large collection of the ancient costumes of the Court displayed upon very well made waxen figures of life-size; they are very dirty, but curious, and rather interesting in showing the various costumes worn by the officers of state, dignitaries, and heads of trades in past days: some of the faces are excellent.

Then we drove on to a side door of the great Mosque of Santa Sophia, entering by a winding staircase and coming out at the west end into the clerestory gallery now appropriated to the Mooslim women. This *coup d'œil* of the interior is the most interesting, as you can thence examine the details of the workmanship, but from below, the building is indeed surpassingly beautiful. The ground plan is divided into three parts, a square with a semicircle at each end, the whole surrounded by a wide aisle. The centre dome is surrounded by two domes and seven half domes, to which the eye is carried up far above the real height by the tiers of columns and galleries: forty columns on the ground and sixty smaller ones above them, and so on till it reaches the dome, which is low (and therefore appears all the wider in span), pierced with forty-eight windows; while, looking beyond the central part itself, the eye is lost in the perspectives of the slender columns and galleries in endless but tasteful sub-divisions of the surrounding aisles, covered in by their own domes and half domes. The insides of these domes are all of gilt mosaic; the columns are everywhere of porphyry or serpentine; and the capitals are of white marble wrought, as are also the spandrils of the arches they uphold, in such exquisite incised tracery as to look like petrified lace, the classic forms flattened down into harmony with the mosaics which line the whole church, and the severe Corinthian original is almost forgotten in the luxuriant richness which has broken out into what one might call a hot-house Grecian order—a Romanesque Classic—or a free Oriental translation of the Western text.   Each capital bears the monogram of the Emperor Justinian who built the church, and these the Mooslims have spared, but the faces of all the Seraphim that support the corners under the dome, the figure of Christ the Saviour in the act of blessing, which once filled up the western dome, and every cross in the whole building have been carefully effaced.   Of the great columns, eight were brought from the Temple of Diana at Ephesus, and eight from the Temple of the Sun at Baalbek: those of porphyry are banded round with iron.   On one side is the Sultan's gallery enclosed in a network of gilt tracery, to conceal his Majesty from common eyes, should he ever visit the mosque; and opposite to it another small gallery is kept for the descendants of the Prophet to pray in: above this the carpet on which Muhammad knelt at Mecca is suspended against the marble-encrusted wall: while near it is the rude picture of a hand—the hand of the Prophet: and without this no mosque is legally acredited.

The marble floor, unconcealed by pews or any such like obstructions, had some picturesque groups of kneeling or seated Mooslims on it, collected round an old Moollah, who was energetically and solemnly preaching to them on " the sixty religions in the world ;" their bright dresses and turbans, and the venerable figure of the old Moollah, with his fine face and long white beard made a good picture and an interesting one ; but suddenly a wild but harmonious chant broke from the lips of a set of Mooslims at prayer in the side aisle, and flung back one's thoughts to the time when here

> "The Faith was led in triumph home,
> Like some high bride, with banner and bright sign
> And melody and flowers ———"

and one's heart yearned for the time when the Ottoman prophecy shall be fulfilled, and Santa Sophia shall be Christian once more! One almost fancied one already heard the glad praises of the Te Deum resounding through the aisles, and saw borne aloft the Red Cross Banner of our Eternal Hope and of our Faith, before which, even in this land, so much of the best blood of Christendom has been joyfully spilt!

The outside of the mosque is excessively ugly; but its form may once have been forgotten under mosaics and colours: such a lovely interior ought to have been cased in the porcelain tiles from the old potteries at Kutayia in Asia Minor: one could forget or forgive any form in looking at their beautiful colours and patterns. There is a very fine Fountain in the Court.

But I am not going to act guide-book through all the other scenes and sights of Contantinople; not even into the Mosque of Sultan Achmet, where the huge disproportioned columns look as if they had the dropsy: nor yet to the Mausoleum of the last Sultan, though I might well linger there over the exquisite illuminations of many Korāns that stand on inlaid desks placed round the group of tombs in the circular hall—superbly delicate and highly finished, and of a variety of patterns both in flowers and arabesques superior to many of what we consider our finest specimens of mediæval work:—nor even shall I linger in the Bazaars of Stamboul; for although they are unquestionably very fine from their great extent and evident prosperity, they are so infinitely less Oriental and picturesque than those of Cairo and Damascus, that our Easterned eyes were quite disappointed. These Bazaars are built of no particular architecture; they have regular skylights, and are painted and whitewashed: in the other cities they are mostly rough constructions of wood and matting, all in tumble-down confusion, producing dark shades, and sudden strong lights, and making a new and striking picture at every yard: or if regularly built, they are always handsome and imposing stone structures of Saracenic architecture, suggesting both power and grace. Then in Constantinople, numbers of them are regular shops with counters in them, and you hear French, Italian and English on every side; besides that fully half the men in the bazaars are in European dress. There are some fine and purely Oriental things in them, nevertheless: old arms, Persian objects of all kinds of beauty, especially silk stuffs and enamels, and saddle-cloths covered with splendid gold embroidery; the slipper bazaar with its shelves of bright colours and silver threads, like shows of cut flowers; and the drugs, in a solemn, dark, really Oriental-looking place, full of such mystery as befits the kill-if-not-cure destination of its wares. After all, I think seeing Preziosi's beautiful drawings is quite as good as looking at the Bazaars themselves: they have all the life itself transfixed by his magic brush, without the noise, confusion, dirt and dogs of the originals.

The gayest sight we saw was the Sweet Waters of Asia, to which Lady Bulwer kindly took us, on the great feast-day of the year—the Friday after Kourban Bairâm. This is the summer Hyde Park of Constantinople, the Sweet Waters of Europe being only in fashion

during the winter season; there is no beauty in the spot save that
of a few fine trees beneath whose shade the women sit the whole day.
The place was excessively crowded, and one could not have a better
opportunity of studying Turkish women : the gay flaunting flowers
of the Bosphorine hareems were sitting in a closely-packed mass
upon the green sward, under the shade of the oak and the elm, the
colours jumbled into each other, like the pattern of a brilliant
Parisian carpet, thrown up upon a groundwork of their white veils,
almost dazzling in its confused brightness, while the harsh, bird-
like, ceaseless chatter of the ladies' tongues was almost *relieved* by
the occasional cry of a spoilt child or the squeak of a swaddled
baby.   Each group of two or three women had their own mattress,
goolleh (clay jar) of water, and an embroidered handkerchief containing their eatables for the day, chiefly raw cucumbers, of which
they eat from morning till night, and most of them were smoking
nargilehs.   The richer ladies were driving round and round the
small meadow seated in gilded and painted *telegas*, something like
our Royal state coach, only two or three of which had curtains
drawn to conceal the inmates.   Some of the Sultan's family were
there, each lady with a couple of slaves on the back seat of the
carriage, dressed as gaily, if not as richly, as herself; many of the
slaves are petted almost as much as their mistresses, and their
slavedom is sometimes the extreme of luxury.   Since the last few
years, the yashmak has ceased to be a "snare," and has become only
a "delusion;" once it concealed the features of its wearer: now it
only sets off and enhances their beauty—

> " Like the indistinct, golden, and vaporous fleece
>   Which surrounded and hid the celestials in Greece,
>   From the glances of men :"

the single fold of gossamer gauze across the mouth and chin acting
far less jealously on the fair faces of the Constantinople ladies than
the veils of the ladies of our own country.   There were a few beauties
among them, and some of those more remarkable for intelligence
than the others, reminded me of sweet gentle faces at home: but
these were exceptions, for, in general, they look sadly inane.   And
yet we were assured on the best authority that they do not now,
by any means, lead the entirely vacant lives we are accustomed to
believe; there is scarcely a hareem belonging to a tolerably rich
person, where the ladies do not read French and play on the piano-
forte, besides occupying themselves with many kinds of embroidery,
and some even sing and draw.

We walked for some time among the noisy crowd under the trees, listening to gipsies under the hedge at one side of the meadow, who were singing badly enough, and playing on various instruments, of which a kind of guitar was the prettiest. Their swarthy, coarse, Spanish-looking faces contrasted strongly with the dead-white, waxy complexions of the Turkish ladies: but the greatest contrast of all happened to be the young Count de Paris, sitting quietly smoking and looking on at the motley crowd, with his fresh fair young face, his shining French hat, and his unimpeachable boots and gloves.

There are several pretty meadows and pleasant little valleys along the banks of the Bosphorus, especially on the Asian side: the " Sultan's Valley " is a charming shady grove of fine elm-trees and oaks, under the lee of the Giant's Mountain: the meadow north of Kandilli is another: to this the legend is attached that it is the meadow where Jupiter found Europa playing with her maidens, whence she made a most unpleasantly long voyage, all the way to Crete, mounted on the plunging bull. There are many others which we had not time to visit.

We had but a short time to remain in Constantinople, but fortunately the grandest fête in the year—the Sultan's Reception during the Kourban Bairâm took place while we were still there, and my sister was kindly sent a ticket to see the ceremony. Leaving the hotel immediately after sunrise she crossed over from Pera to Seraglio Point in a caïque, and waited for an hour or two, while the party she accompanied were collecting, watching the early light shining on the city, and the dancing caïques bearing richly dressed Pashas to meet the Sultan. When all were assembled they were admitted into the inner court of the Seraglio Palace, passing by the great plane-tree on which the Janissaries were hung, and which flourishes greenly still, however great its own disgust at its temporary degradation. Within the court they found the Sultan's seven riding horses: beautiful animals splendidly caparisoned, each with an aigrette of white and coloured plumes on his head, and a splendid saddle cloth with harness to match—three embroidered in gold and coral on dark-blue cloth—one in pearls and rubies—another in pearls and emeralds—another in gold and silver, with jewelled and enamelled ornaments hung over their faces and chests: all his favourite riding horses are brought, as he chooses at the moment which one he will mount. After a short time my sister and her companions seated themselves on some raised seats under the shade of an old tree close to the great doorway of the Seraglio, whence the Sultan, announced by cannons, issued on horseback, preceded by his guard of honour, and all his Court on foot. His spirited horse seemed to bear only a dead burden, for with his head

2 M

stooping, his face ghastly, lividly pale and expressing only the deepest dejection, the Sultan passed on, with a rigid, fixed stare on the ground before him, without appearing to see or even to be aware of the brilliant scene around him. He was now on his road to the Mosque of Suleymanyeh, to perform the most solemn of all the Mooslim ceremonies, viz., the sacrifice of a lamb to Allah, which he is supposed to slaughter with his own hands; and the annual renewal of his Coronation vow. The Sultan returned from the mosque in three quarters of an hour, looking like a man walking into his grave, and retired into the Seraglio to rest in the beautiful kiosk I have mentioned before. Meantime carpets, embroidered in gold, and a gilt *fauteuil* were placed before the gateway: the chair was covered with a light gold tissue lest any profane dust should precede the Sultan on the sacred seat; and the scarlet-and-gold guards, and 200 or 300 splendidly attired Pashas, arranged themselves around it in a semicircle, every now and then relieving themselves for a moment from the heavy state helmet, which bears a huge fan of large feathers bending over the crown of the head. Others had smaller feathers made into bouquets or flowers in white and green.

When the Sultan had seated himself he was presented with a large scarf of red silk squared and fringed with gold, one end of which he held in his hand: while the ministers and officers came up with salaams that were almost prostrations, and touched the other end of the scarf with forehead and lips—the nearest approach permissible to the Sultan's hand. After a certain number had kissed the sacred scarf on the right side of the Sultan, this end was folded up, and the other unfolded for a much more numerous set of kisses and salaams, on the left side. Once or twice an Ulema came up, and then instead of kissing the scarf, he prostrated himself before the Sultan and kissed the hem of his robe: this is the ecclesiastical privilege: the Sultan sitting utterly impassive, and apparently quite unconscious of the obeisances made to him: in fact the scarf was so placed over the arm of the chair that they were made almost behind him; once he called to an officer in the circle and spoke to him for a few minutes, and, at the end, when a body of Sheikhs and Ulemas approached, he rose up and received their prostrations standing. These priests were most gaily dressed in bright-coloured gold-embroidered robes. After them came the Sheikh of Mecca in a green cloak: he has a fine face and long white beard; approaching within a few yards of the Sultan, he raised his hands and pronounced a prayer or blessing on his majesty, while every officer and Pasha present, drooping their faces between their hands at the end for a moment, seemed to be joining in the prayer for their Sovereign's welfare. They care not a rush for Abdoul Medjid individually, but for his office they care most lovingly and reverentially, and would readily give their lives for whomever fills it. This ended the ceremony, and the Sultan forthwith disappeared. The whole affair is the coldest thing imaginable; Eastern etiquette forbidding any animation on the faces of the soldiers and courtiers, and the reception, so brilliant to the eye, would have been conducted in unbroken silence, save for the performance at regular intervals of the short tune, the "God save the king" of the Turks, which concluded with a formal, measured, unhearty cheer given by a few selected men. This silence and stillness in such a brilliant scene was most oppressive: civilisation, however, like everything else, has its own dullnesses, and one cannot return to those much more amusing ancient days when the Byzantine Emperors, in this very city, received distinguished foreigners seated on a throne surrounded by lions of gold and silver, which, at every salaam of the guests, opened their mouths and *roared!* while birds sat on branches of gold and silver trees singing long songs: but these sounds must have been meant as very broad hints, for the history says that as soon as the persons introduced had presented their offerings to the Emperor, the lions left off roaring, and the birds ceased to sing!

The time had unhappily come for us to return to Europe, and we had calculated upon leaving the Bosphorus this week, but we had been very desirous of seeing Broussa, and the temptation of lingering a little longer under a real blue sky and a warm sun was too strong for us: so on July 7 we started in the steamer for Jemblik. It is a pretty run, across the end of the Sea of Marmora and into the Bay of Moudhania, of about five hours, but we had to include an hour's delay in landing about fifty heavy bags of specie for paying the troops encamped near Moudhania : we heard that their pay had then been about two years in arrear, and, though nothing ever is true that one hears in the Levant, there is every probability that this was a fact. There were plenty of horses to be hired at Moudhania, the nearest port to Broussa, but we had no saddles with us, and were obliged to go on to Jemblik to find a *telega*, a vehicle of a very much more primitive construction than even those to which we had become accustomed in Constantinople; it was shaped exactly like the half of an egg-shell cut lengthways, each end sloping backwards: we packed closely in, four of us, with cloaks and shawls, acting as wedges to each other against the fearful jolts which ensued. The road is excellent for about one-third of the distance, the rest of it is in a state of nature, and the drive was dreadfully fatiguing. The views at first repaid one well, looking back over the lovely little bay and the hills on the other side of the Sea of Marmora : and they became glorious as we at last reached the crest of the coast hills before descending into the Plain of Broussa : the immense plain in all its richness, dyed in deep browns and shady greens, enclosed in mountains of every variety of form in brown and rich violet, deep blue and lilac, while towering over the opposite side stood Olympus, in unclouded majesty, its naked peaks shining against the deepening sky in a mantle of rose-coloured snow : while behind us, between the defiles and woods, came one blue corner of the little bay. It was very beautiful indeed, but alas ! the sun went down as we stood here instead of our reaching Broussa in time for a seven o'clock dinner as we had been promised, and moreover there was to be no moon till nearly morning. We had been told the roads were usually safe, but we entirely appreciated the apparently endless and utterly dark woods of that plain, and the enormous length of the town as we jolted through one half of it : for it was half an hour after midnight before we reached the clean little German hotel at one end of Broussa. The effects of the eight hours' jolting, to say nothing of the starvation, lasted through the next day, and we were not in the most easily-to-be-pleased humour when we made our first inspection of the town that evening.

There was, however, little danger of discontent : for the eyes must be dull indeed and the heart cold that could fail to be delighted with the enchanting loveliness of Broussa. My mind was full of Damascus and Beyrout, Antioch and Smyrna, and the golden halo of Greece was shining fresh and strong in my memory : but they vanished from my thoughts as the rare beauties of Broussa unfolded themselves one by one to my view : truly, I thought, we have kept the best till the last. One vast, gloriously fertile plain, covered with little streams of water, and meadows, and orchards and woods —not brushwood, but fine lofty groves of trees : while the town lay curling round the feet of the noble mountain, running up the small ravines and hiding itself in the rich deep woods, with hundreds of fine domes of bright colours and quaint buildings, rising from its bosom : while more than one range of mountains of most varied shape and colour, some of which were snow-capped, bordered the plain. It sounds no finer than many another place in description, but it is the wonderful combination of beauty which makes Broussa so romantically delightful ; still more, that however much charmed one may be with the *tout-ensemble*, each feature in it is still lovelier when seen in detail. As for the town it is the most picturesque town I have ever seen in any country : the streets wind in the most curious way up and down very steep slopes, so well watered that the sound of rushing water never ceases in any part'of the town, and they are all kept perfectly clean, while they are so narrow that the houses, being all built with projecting upper stories, nearly meet overhead, giving those heavy black shadows down each side, under the projection, which add so much to the picturesqueness of the effect. All the houses are of wooden framework, with high-peaked gables, so that one might fancy oneself in a quaint Flemish or Swiss town, were it not that each house is painted bright sky-blue, pink, or red, and that every street is filled with rich and gay Oriental costumes, while the overhanging mountain is clothed with an Eastern vegetation and luxuriance : besides that wherever the eye looks it is met by many-domed baths or by one of the 360 mosques which adorn or have adorned the town. Great numbers of *filatures* the *fabriques* for reeling the silk for which Broussa is so famous, are scattered about the town : these are principally French, and are gay, handsome-looking buildings : they lie chiefly towards the outskirts of the town. Within the town are the Bazaars, which are remarkably amusing and picturesque : they are very extensive, and are richly stocked with European as well as Oriental goods, Manchester prints and German hardware, besides Broussa silks and cottons, and embroideries of the finest kinds : the Constantinople bazaars are supplied with these articles from Broussa, and many merchants have shops in both places. Broussa is famous for its cotton towels and bathing dresses, made of a peculiar fluffy texture, for its rich silks, cloths made of camel's and goat's hair, and for its elegant silk gauzes : these latter are chiefly woven by the Greeks and Armenians : each has a loom, or several looms in his own house : nothing can be finer, or more delicate than the fabric or brighter than the colours woven into them. The embroidery of gold upon cloth for saddles is most splendid of its kind, and that upon camel's-hair cloth for the *sejjadehs*, or praying-carpets, was the best we had seen anywhere. At every three or four yards there is a cooking, or sweetmeat shop, containing messes of all the colours of the rainbow, and every two minutes you meet a man with hot bread and cakes on his head, or with pails of cherry and lemon ice on his arm. The Bazaars are full of dogs, fiercer than any we had met even in Constantinople : one day riding through the town on a donkey with my dog in my arms, the brutes spied the little stranger, and I was obliged to give him to one of the dragomans to carry, they leaped up so fiercely to tear him from me : every turning added to the troop, and, despite two strong kourbashes with which they were plentifully belaboured, it was difficult to get quit of them, and the din of their yells and howls was so horrible that we were too glad to escape from the Inferno.

Our hôtel stood at the west end of the town, with a fine view of the plain and the opposite mountains, but nestled too closely under Olympus to show much of his noble old head: we had the early morning sun, and cool rooms all day, a rather important point in July, as Broussa is of course hotter than Constantinople: a delightful draught of wind comes down the broad plain nearly every' day, but it has not the fresh feeling of the breeze off the Bosphorus, and Broussa is, occasionally, too hot. In the winter there is much snow on the sides of the mountain, and the air is sometimes keen, but we were told that with a good woollen dress one is never really cold, and that scarcely any one uses a *mangal* (or pan of charcoal). The Perotes say that Broussa is liable to fever, but we were assured that the report is untrue: the English Consul who has resided in Broussa for twenty years informed us that no member of his family had ever been attacked by it, and that he did not believe any one but the very poor or very imprudent ever suffered from it. The Turks clothe warmly, in silk and cloth frequently lined or trimmed with fur, in order to avoid a chill on perspiration, and they live on proper food: the poor work in sun and shade only half clothed, and feed entirely on raw and unripe vegetables; they eat raw cucumbers, vegetable marrows, and green tomatos all day long, and of course fever is the consequence; but it is impossible to persuade the common people to wait till fruit or vegetables are ripe, they delight so much in the sharp acid of the green fruit. The town is well supplied with both, as well as with excellent meat and milk: from the latter, quantities of *kaimak* and *yaourt* * (clotted, and curdled milk) are made daily, and are most refreshing and wholesome food. There is also good fish of various kinds from the mountain streams, and game .in abundance.

But the glory of Broussa is in its mosques: whether the numbers given are correct or not, I know not: but as the city is more than three miles long, containing about 75,000 inhabitants, and as a mosque or the ruins of one is seen literally at every twenty yards throughout the town, it is not unlikely that the reputed 360 may be counted. They are continually destroyed by the earthquakes, and as neither the rents in the walls are repaired, nor is it considered right to remove the ruins of a mosque, but a new one is immediately built up to replace the fallen one, they increase in number very rapidly, and a marked feature in the characteristics of the place is

* In Arabic—*leben.*

this contrast of gay, brightly-painted houses, brilliant and gaudy bazaars, and handsome, finely-ornamented mosques and baths, with the masses of ruin and tatteredness intervening at every step. It was something quite new, an innovation on hitherto invariable custom, that the most ancient of all the mosques had just been restored: this was the Ulu Jami: the dome had fallen in, though the minaret, which is very pretty, had not been touched: every arch and ponderous square column was just cased in fresh whitewash, and ornamented with coarsely-painted wreaths and arabesques: the style of the building was too heavy to be beautiful, but the space, height, and proportions were really good.

Beyond the town there is one mosque beautiful above all the others: it is called the Mosque of Tchelabi Sultan;* it stands alone with its fountain, on a projection of the mountain, shaded by a grove of splendid plane-trees and cypresses; it is built of well-hewn blocks of rose-coloured limestone, the doorways and windows placed in square-headed recesses, with niches and bands filled up with elegant patterns; the spandrils of each arch, the sides of the great door and the recesses everywhere enriched with the most exquisite Saracenic tracery; it has a large and gracefully-shaped dome, and a projecting roof over the terrace most beautifully painted in Damascene style: while inside, the walls, niches, and Sultan's gallery were all adorned with the richest porcelain tiles and mosaics. This mosque is very ancient and very beautiful; there is one thing, however, still more beautiful—as perfect a gem as one could find anywhere: it is a tomb or mausoleum called " Yeshil Jami," which has been used as a mosque, but is now so much shattered by earthquakes that it is unsafe to enter, and is kept locked: perhaps in another year the whole of the graceful fabric may be a heap of ruin. The mosque is very small, an octagon of ten or twelve feet on each side, surmounted by a dome; the whole of the walls cased in enamelled porcelain of the most perfect turquoise blue, with bands of darker enamel, and medallions in pale green arranged in patterns in the upper part: each side is broken by a window closed with lattices of open iron-work, and ornamented with coloured patterns, as are also the niches beside the entrance door: all so beatifully blended and harmonized that at a few yards' distance one could fancy the mosque was literally carved out of one huge turquoise! Alas! the grass all round was covered with the fragments, a rent yawned in each wall, and we longed to carry away the whole thing and build it up again, before another earthquake should have wholly destroyed it, however cruel it would have been to place such a piece of delicate

* *Tchelabi* means handsome, noble, grand: the same as *shellabee* in Arabic.

colouring under the grey skies, and damp ill-humoured-looking clouds of England. We brought away a few specimens of the porcelain, as well as another piece of still more ancient enamel from the tomb of Emir Sultan: the colours of this are remarkably brilliant, and the pattern is an imitation of natural flowers. All these porcelain enamels were made at Kutayia, a town to the south-east of Broussa: the manufacture still flourishes, but, I believe, the porcelains are not by any means as fine as the ancient ones: nothing of the kind can be more beautiful than the really old ones, both in the delicate texture of the material, and in the rich full colours.

There are a great many other mosques worth visiting, but none equal to these; the very modern ones are ordinary-looking buildings, so gaudily and staringly painted over in red, blue, and green, that they look only like cafés or baths; but it is not very encouraging to build anything in a place so cursed with earthquakes as Broussa is: we were told that six weeks seldom pass without one, and that in the summer they frequently occur every week or fortnight; except for this one drawback, Broussa would be a paradise indeed.

The city was anciently fortified, and the remains of the Castle crowning a great rock in the centre, as well as much of the walls, are still to be seen; besides some strange old Byzantine gateways, built in an odd jumble of Roman and Saracenic styles, the arches formed and ornamented with red bricks placed edgeways and shaped like wedges. In 1856 a most fearful earthquake occurred at Broussa, and threw down a large portion of this Castle wall, with the rock on which it had been built, the whole mass detached itself from the mountain-side and fell, chiefly upon a *fabrique* in the town below, crushing fifty of the poor girls at work there. The ruins remain in heaps still as they fell, and the natives declare that the ghosts of the unfortunate girls are heard to shriek there on the anniversary of their deaths. This earthquake shattered half the buildings in the town, and at the same time a fire broke out at the other end of it, the ravages of which were most terrible, and are still to be seen in the blackened and charred heaps of ruin.

A little beyond the town, at the west end, and after passing a beautiful mosque, there are a number of very handsome royal tombs in a garden, or rather in several gardens filled with roses and mignonnette, under lofty plane-trees: each tomb, or set of tombs, stood in its own domed mosque or mausoleum, the grave itself usually covered with a stone trough full of grass and roses. These buildings are all of brick, ornamented in the Byzantine style with borders and lines of red brick bedded in white cement: inside they are enriched with the same beautiful enamelled porcelains as the handsomer mosques. They are all remarkably picturesque, and would make fine subjects for drawing, with their overhanging trees, and the storks, balancing themselves on the domes round which they build ther nests in undisturbed freedom. Among these tombs is that of Sultan Orchan, the son of Othman, who conquered Broussa in 1326.

As to the Baths, they are innumerable; the best are at the west end of the city, some way beyond it; there are two sets of handsome buildings, containing very extensive and well-arranged baths and swimming pools, which are handsomely ornamented inside with coloured marbles and mosaics: these are called the Kalputcha Hammâm; the spring is chalybeate, of 180° of Fahrenheit.

Broussa is one of the best places in which to study Oriental manners and customs, being far more Asiatic than Constantinople; and although intensely Mooslim * so that the lower classes are very fanatical, yet strangers are occasionally admitted into the higher society, such as it is. Among the Turkish women education is making progress along with the French style of dress, for which their own costume is becoming completely discarded: they spend enormous sums on their dress, as they have no other expenses, and nothing else to think about. Expensive furniture is not very common among them, but is sometimes given with a dowry; when really handsome, such as gold-embroidered velvet, it is used on the occasion of a marriage or some grand ceremonial in the family, and is handed down from mother to daughter. They have much freedom of life, going out in the streets as much as they will, but of course veiled, and receiving visitors at home: even the very poorest have separate rooms, and if the wife's visitors leave their yellow *babouches* (slippers) outside the door of the room, no husband dare enter it, though he may send to desire her visitors to go away. They have no regular meal-times, and never eat together; the husband eats when he is hungry, waited on by his wife: she by herself in her own apartment; at this time of year (summer) they live entirely on melons, perhaps as many as ten in a day, as well as raw cucumbers, without even bread; and three or four huge bowls of *yaourt* or sour milk: they rarely eat meat, but if they do, it is generally the heads of sheep, roasted.

Of course we heard much of the silk crop, as this was the season of the " harvest," and the French merchants were searching the country for the best. The silk was this year very scarce, in

* The Christian population of Broussa does not amount to a quarter of the whole.

consequence of the terrible distemper that has lately prevailed among
the worms both here and in Europe, by which the old species have
become almost extinct; new seed had been imported from Bengal
and China, but it seemed to have failed generally.   The silk of the
Lebanon and of Broussa is considered of equal value, and far superior
to that of Persia or China, which sells for from 60 to 80 francs the
kilogramme, while that of the Lebanon fetches 100 francs.   We
saw some of the very best quality known, which comes from a small
village between Broussa and Jemblik: most exquisite stuff it was,
so perfectly fine, white, and elastic: it is the two latter qualities
which render it most valuable; the superiority arises, it is believed,
from the purity of the water through which the cocoon is reeled:
the Broussa water, being all slightly mineral, impairs the pure
whiteness of the silk.   We learned that the Turkish women were
found to be more diligent workers in the *filatures* than the
Greeks and Armenians: it was amusing to see them holding their
eezars, or white veils, in their teeth while both hands were employed
in the basins before them; but when we did see them we thought
the Christian girls were generally the prettiest; the usual hours of
work are from 4 A.M. to 7 P.M., with three intervals allowed for
meals in the day, of three-quarters of an hour each.   The merchants
whom we met with all agreed in bearing testimony to the honour
and honesty of the Turks here; the word or promise of a Turk,
they said, was always to be depended upon: that of a Greek,
never, if it suited him to break it; and they spoke much of the
perfect safety of travelling now all over this half of Asia Minor
without incurring any risk of robbers, even in the unfrequented
parts where their business led them.

   The Pasha of Broussa is a very active and intelligent governor,
applying himself for several hours of every day to his Pashalik
business; always reading his despatches himself, and insisting on
everything passing through his own hands.   We went to meet him
at dinner at the English Consul's house, for whom the Pasha has the
utmost respect, consulting him on all affairs of importance, and
almost always following his advice.   He expressed his horror at the
Syrian affairs, and told us how *he* would have acted in stopping the
fanatics and miscreants of Damascus, recounting also how he had
succeeded in quelling an insurrection in European Turkey, so
quickly and completely, that he was at once rewarded with the
Pashalik of Broussa, one of the highest in the Sultan's dominions.
The Pasha wore a plain Turkish frock-coat when we met him in
the morning, but at dinner he was attired in a splendid robe of
cranberry-coloured silk, while the Sheikh of Islam wore a pale

salmon-coloured silk dress and white turban: this latter was described to us as a man of great talent—"the brains of all Broussa"—and of the highest character: as truthful and straight-forward as an Englishman.

We were advised to take the opportunity of seeing the Dancing Dervishes on the last Friday of our stay, as this exhibition is said to be better conducted at Broussa than elsewhere: so we started early one afternoon, crossing the Bournabashi, or "Sweet Waters," where the ladies of the town were disporting themselves on the grass, eating cucumbers and ice, and arrived at the Dervishes' College, a large pink building surrounded with gardens, in which were several tombs of departed Dervish Sheikhs and Saints. In the centre of the garden there is a square building: one large hall with a circle of columns dividing off the corners and supporting a gallery; the floor under the gallery was raised above the circular centre, and on this raised part the spectators were placed. The Dervishes came in one by one, leaving their shoes in a cupboard at the door, each wearing a high round, unbrimmed cap of camel's-hair cloth, and a cloak of camlet, black, brown, green, &c., com-pletely enveloping the body. Each made a deep obeisance to the name of Allah, which was written in large letters over the Sheikh's place, and took up his position leaning against a column: last of all came the Sheikh, a handsome but very small man, dressed in a black cloak, with a white turban, and high black leather boots, which he never took off. The Sheikh offered several prayers, holding up his two palms before him, and fixing his eyes on them as if he was reading from them; and, after some recitations, they all commenced a sweet, harmonious chant, accompanied by some wind instruments, making prostrations every now and then when the name of Allah occurred, with most solemn gestures. Presently they all arose and followed the Sheikh in a slow walk round and round the circle; each one as he approached the unoccupied carpet of the Sheikh bowed down to the ground and swept round in the most peculiar fashion, so as not to turn his back to the spot. Having returned to their columns, each one suddenly undid some string, and down fell a long petticoat over his feet: then laying aside his cloak, which he reverently kissed, they all stood prepared for the dance: their costume now was pretty, the short jacket buttoned to the throat, long loose sleeves, and the wide skirt, wadded round the hem, and made with such a number of gores as to form a perfectly smooth wine-glass shape: most of them were white, some were green, and some fawn-coloured. Three times they slowly paced round the circle, bowing to the Sheikh as they passed, their arms folded on the breast with a hand on each shoulder: then, as each completed his third circle and bow, he began to turn slowly round and round—the eyes apparently quite closed, the arms extended, one towards heaven, the other towards earth, without the slightest possible change of expression upon the rapt, absorbed countenance: the long full dress expanded to its fullest width, which neither lessened nor fell in the perfectly steady, sailing movement which never seemed for a single instant to hesitate or falter, and which had something in it most singularly graceful and pleasing; the feet were twisted rapidly over each other in a very peculiar manner, but the turning was very slow and almost solemn. One old man amongst them seemed master of the ceremonies, as it were, setting each off, and standing a few seconds first by one, then another, sometimes stamping with his foot as if to give the time or regulate the movements. After three rounds of the hall they rested, the singing continuing through the whole, and when they recommenced the Sheikh, still keeping on his black cloak, rose and joined them; but he wore no long skirt as the others did, and the twisting of his thick, heavy leather boots one over the other, looked very odd and awkward; then the singing ceased, the cloaks were resumed, a few more prayers recited, and they all disappeared. We had expected to find the scene absurd or disgusting, but it was neither the one nor the other: the whole thing was so solemn, and they appeared to be so completely absorbed in what they were doing, that a certain air of devotion and reverence reached even the mind of the spectators, and made one fancy, that however extraordinary the distortion of ideas which led to such an exercise as an expression of religious worship, there was still something higher and better than fanatic folly or hypocrisy in the mind of the actor.

From this graceful exhibition we went to a very different scene— the Mosque of the "Howling Dervishes;" this mosque was but a plain square lofty room, with a small gallery at one end, in which we sat; in the place of honour a venerable old Shiekh with a white beard was seated with two tiny children, a boy and a girl, at one side of him: opposite to him sat about twenty men on lambskins, all repeating the "Fatha" as fast as possible: presently they stood up, and the lambskin mats were arranged in the middle of the mosque for some men to sit on, who played on flutes. Then the performers, standing close together in a row, joined their hands and commenced repeating the "La ilāha illa llāh" as fast as possible, throwing out the words with a violent jerk of the body, thrown forward with the head and heels jerked first to one side and then the other, the jerks and the words gradually coming louder and louder, faster and faster, till they had lost all likeness to human beings and seemed to become only mad animals or machines. The old Sheikh and the little children kept time gently, the fair pretty faces of the latter contrasting sadly with the frenzied faces near them. Twice they all came to a rest, while the zikkrs wiped the perspiration from their streaming heads and necks; the first pause was occupied by two attendants dressing themselves in green scarfs which were put on with some ceremony before the mihrab: the second by a long recitation of something by the old Sheikh sitting with his hand pressed upon the heart of a Turkish officer who knelt before him; we supposed that the Sheikh was healing him of some disease, or charming away some misfortune.

After this the zikkrs recommenced their furious jerks and grunts to the accompaniment of huge coarse tambourines, one of which was given to each zikkr, and a pair of cymbals to the little children: with all these instruments the excitement became quite maddening and the din deafening; in the midst of it, an iron instrument—a large spike about a foot long, with a bunch of short chains hung to the head of the spike—was given to each of two selected performers, who immediately commenced leaping with opera-dancer bounds about the mosque, evidently according to rule and figure, throwing up the spikes in the air with a circling motion, and catching them as they fell: the third or fourth time they fell the points were received in the cheek of one man, and in the neck of the other, and twirled rapidly round as if entering deeply into the flesh. This was repeated several times, until one of the performers became "melboos" or *possessed*: his arms dropped at his sides, his head fell forward, and he seemed suddenly stiffened into the rigidity of a dead body; a bystander caught him as he fell down, dragged him to the side of the room, and propped him up against the wall, where he stood like a statue, as if pinned to it: and I saw the blood slowly trickle down from the wound made by the iron spike in his neck. These spikes are said to have a small ring round the point, which hinders them from entering into the flesh: the other performer seemed unhurt, but this one was really wounded. The shouts, yells, and grunts then suddenly ceased, and the performance was over: as we came away we saw the poor " possessed " wretch was coming to life again, looking livid and ghastly. Altogether it was the most disgusting and unedifying sight I have ever witnessed, especially by way of a religious exercise, and I should be sorry to see such another: it had that strange effect upon one that, although feeling it too horrible to look at, one could not look away from the scene.

We had intended to remain but three or four days at Broussa, but the place was so enchanting and the air so delightful that we stayed on and on till more than a fortnight had elapsed, and we were yet most unwilling to go: we half thought of taking a house and staying till the winter, but the horrible news from the Lebanon had so much alarmed the European world on the Bosphorus, that, though we had no particular fears ourselves of the ill-feeling shown in Syria spreading over Turkey, we were so strongly advised not to linger alone and unprotected in the country, that we determined to go on into Europe. Before quitting Broussa, however, we were quite resolved to ascend Mount Olympus, but the summer heats and mists are so bad for extensive views that we had delayed from day to day in hopes of better weather; and, in the end, of course we selected the worst day of our whole stay.

The ascent of the Mysian Olympus is nowhere so steep and difficult as the greater part of Hermon: but it is a very long expedition, and we made it, alas! a work of seventeen hours, the last five of which, owing to our having started late in the morning, were in total darkness. The woods of the mountain came down quite to the streets of the city, and the path led along the edges of grand and romantic ravines, among which we had glimpses of beautiful views, between the mist-wreaths which rested clinging to the steep sides of the valleys: in these ravines, several of them at less than half an hour's distance from the bazaars of the town, the scenery is as wild, rich and lovely as the finest bits of Switzerland or the Tyrol, and more varied.

We were soon in the depths of the glorious forest that clothes the sides of the mountain, riding through delicious fern-brakes under the lofty trees, chiefly pines, oaks, chestnuts, beech, and plane trees, while among the bluebells and harebells and a hundred other gay wild flowers, multitudes of ripe Alpine strawberries begged of us, by their bright colour, to stop and eat them as we passed by. Higher up we came to an open common, with several pools in which herds of buffaloes were splashing and cooling themselves, and in which were many wide and somewhat treacherous morasses; and from this we saw large groves of dead fir-trees killed by the white moss, *baumhaar*, which clings to and eats the life out of every branch, leaving only the grey ghost of what was till lately a living tree: most sadly weird and melancholy they looked. It was mid-day before we reached a lone shepherd's hut at the foot of a snow-covered summit where we breakfasted and rested after our five hours' ride; and then commenced the last ascent on foot. The snow here lay in great masses, and the bare crags and chasm rock (in one of which was a small glacier) were very wild and savage: the slope was covered with small loose stones, but between them, the ground was thickly spread over with large yellow pansies, blue gentian, pink hyacinths, and a little pink heath: and the air was quite perfumed with the pansies. The last part of the ascent was very steep, but nothing difficult, and we hoped to be rewarded by the magnificent view which extends from Smyrna to Constantinople, and is justly famed for including one of the most lovely panoramas in the world: and we had indeed a most extensive view from the summit—but it was entirely of——clouds! mass after mass rolled by, varying from an inky grey up to brightly shining silver and snow; and during the half-hour we braved the cold on the summit, wrapped up in cloaks, we only got one pretty glimpse to the south, and two or three broken hasty views of the sea of Marmora with the mountains beyond Constantinople and Ismid: we only saw enough to be quite sure of the immense beauty and grandeur there must be in the view when clear, and I envy the traveller who ascends there on a clear day at the end of the autumn.

We did not leave the shepherd's hut till six o'clock, and the pitch darkness under the thick, lofty forest in the descent was very trying, and the *horror umbrarum* seized me pretty strongly, as, though a tolerably good path by daylight, there were plenty of jutting crags and deep holes in the narrow paths, where a false step would have been destruction; the branches were continually threatening to sweep one out of one's saddle, so we had good reason to say "El hamdu illáh!" (praise be to God), when, to the great astonishment of the dogs, we reached the hôtel exactly at midnight.

Almost more, even, we enjoyed the ride to Moudhania, when we at last succeeded in tearing ourselves away from ever-lovely Broussa: we descended into the plain at 4 P.M., and rode over the park-like ground and grassy meadows, studded with clumps of fine trees, and now and then a thicket of hawthorn or elder, covered over with honeysuckle: every moment looking back to the glorious mountain, with the long, picturesque town clinging round its feet, the deep green woods veiling all the sides, the romantic ravines and gorges, the barren wild crags, and above all the beautiful head, covered with its mantle of snow, now blushing rosy red in the sunset glow. How lovely it was! more richly, luxuriantly beautiful than almost any other view I remember. It faded in the deepening twilight (for we were now coming nearly into the latitudes of twilight), and we turned into the green wooded valleys of the low mountains which border the Sea of Marmora, with very sad hearts at bidding good   such a   as Mount Olympus. It was soon dark, and we lost the pretty views of the sea which had pleased us so much in coming from Jemblik, but the glow-worms and fire-flies tried to console us, and gave us pleasanter meditations than the howling of a pack of wolves in some valley close to us: there were plenty of jackals besides, but the deep voices of the wolves are far more sonorous.

A room had been provided for us in the large village of Moudhania, but it was so dirty and so swarming with vermin, that we could not rest in it for a single moment: and we gladly sallied out to refresh ourselves in the streets at half-past three in the morning. After some time we found a caïque to rest in until the steamer which was to take us to Constantinople came up, upon the dirty deck of which we could not even get standing room, it was so much crowded.

As this was to be our last day in Constantinople, we mounted the Fire-tower of Galata, to take a farewell view of Stamboul and its environs: a beautiful view it is: the positions of the various parts of the city are so well seen with the opposite shores and the mountains beyond, the Golden Horn and the Bosphorus winding along deep below one's feet like a living picture, thickly covered with vessels, some of them shrouded in smoke, others, including the hundreds of caïques, gay with costume of flags of bright colours; the shining white palaces and mosques of Stamboul standing among the Cypresses were so brightly coloured in the sunset that for a few moments they looked like opals set in an enamel of dark green.

The Bosphorus grows upon one; as perhaps is the case with all very beautiful scenes of which so much has been heard beforehand, that at the first moment one feels disappointed: certainly the Oxford of the East never appeared to me so lovely as when, after a very busy and fatiguing morning in Pera, we went gliding along its sunlit waters in the cool refreshment of evening, resting in a graceful caïque (which by-the-bye it is the fashion to abuse and to designate as " miserably uncomfortable and cramping," &c. &c. I wonder how lovingly any one would think of a caïque after the same number of hours in an old cab or a malle-poste!) under the shadows of Therapia. And then that evening, sitting in the balcony of the English Embassy, enjoying the deliciously cool breeze among the trees and flowers, listening to the ripple of the water against the quay below us, the young moonlight playing on the calm sea, and the stillness only broken by the gentle plashing of the oars as a caïque now and then silently glided by, and by the faint echo of the band which was playing at Buyúkderé coming stealing across the bay—a musical stillness, all perfumed and sweet! That was an evening to be remembered: and I was beginning to think that civilised life in a luxurious drawing-room, with pleasant conversations and kind friends, decidedly had its advantages, when my enjoyment was suddenly cut short by the appearance of the Austrian Lloyds' steamer *Mercur* stopping for us opposite the Embassy and demanding our company, baggage and all, to be conveyed back to Europe once more.

It was a lovely afternoon, and the big vessel sheered off, slowly passing each pleasant house and garden in Buyúkderé: then under the pretty Giant's Mountain, and between the two frowning batteries: past one wooded and vine-clad hill after another, till we looked back through a most lovely vista on the winding Bosphorus. Just at its loveliest and tenderest beauty, the stern rocks rush in and close together, and we shot out into the wide Black Sea, while the beauties that a thousand ages of poets have sung vanished, probably for ever, from our eyes. The "inhospitable" Axine, however, seeing our sorrowful regrets, behaved with the most hospitable kindness by the way of consolation to the home-returning wanderers on its bosom: not a breath ruffled the waters, not a cloud flecked the glowing sky, and only rosy hues were thrown over the retreating landscape of blue mountains. The southern coast faded out of sight as darkness gradually covered the sky, and spread a stern, thick veil between me and all the sunshiny dreams of my "Wonderland,"—Asia and Africa, the East and the South; one by one all the memories of the two years I had spent in them rose up like picture-visions across my mind,—the silver splendour of the mornings—the fierce sunshine and cool shades of the days— the golden glories of the sunsets—the indescribable deliciousness of the nights—the boundless loveliness of the Desert—the magni- ficence of the snow-capped mountains and the stern rocky hills— the rushing streams—the cloudless skies—the olive, the fig, and the vine—the unhackneyed people and the bright colours—the free, wild, airy life—the kind hearts and true friends we had met and made,—all combined in one sad memory with the days that are gone to come back no more, and had faded one by one from the Present as the misty distance was now dying away beneath the last soft, rosy ray of the dying Sun.

> " The rugged steersman at the wheel
> Comes back again to vision. The hoarse sea
> Speaketh from its great heart of discontent,
> And in the misty distance dies away
> The wonderland ! 'Tis past and gone."

And so I took my last sad look of Asia and the Eastern world.

" I used to think," said Frederika Bremer, one day during her late travels in Syria, " in my childish days I used to think what supreme happiness it would be to be Queen of a thousand countries: not only to reign over them but to possess them for my very own; I little thought then, or for many a long year afterwards, how nearly my brightest dreams would one day be realised. I have travelled over country after country in all the wide world, and *I have made them mine:* the sights and scenes, the people, the mountains and the trees, the earth, air, and sky, each live in my mind and memory, with a vividness and, so to speak, a tangibleness that gives them to me as my own possession, and makes them belong to me with an untangibleness that no one can interfere with, and that nothing can take away from me. My memory makes me Queen of all I have passed through!"

Such is the feeling, I believe, more or less of all travellers: such is the store of treasure accumulated day by day as one wanders on through land after land: such is the honey gathered from the far-off flowers: and such is the fruit which, Reader, I would fain share with you: to reproduce something of it by pen and pencil has been my pleasure and my task—I hope not wholly in vain.

THE END.

LONDON: PRINTED BY WILLIAM CLOWES AND SONS, STAMFORD STREET, AND CHARING CROSS.

BOOKS OF TRAVEL, &c.

ISMAILÏA: a Narrative of the Expedition to Central
Africa for the Suppression of the Slave Trade, organised by Ismail,
Khedive of Egypt. By Sir SAMUEL W. BAKER, Pasha. With Portraits,
Maps, and Fifty Full-page Illustrations by ZWECKER and DURAND.
Two vols., 8vo., cloth extra. 36s.

THE NILE TRIBUTARIES OF ABYSSINIA,
And the Sword Hunters of the Hamran Arabs. By Sir SAMUEL WHITE
BAKER, M.A., F.R.G.S. With Maps and Illustrations. Fifth Edition.
Crown 8vo. 6s.

**THE ALBERT N'YANZA GREAT BASIN OF THE
NILE,**
And Exploration of the Nile Sources. By Sir SAMUEL W. BAKER.
Maps and Illustrations. Fourth Edition. Crown 8vo. 6s.

**A NARRATIVE of a YEAR'S JOURNEY THROUGH
CENTRAL and EASTERN ARABIA.**
By W. GIFFORD PALGRAVE. With Map and Plans. Sixth and Cheaper
Edition. Crown 8vo. 6s.

GREATER BRITAIN.
A Record of Travel in English-speaking Countries during 1866–67
(America, India, Australia). By Sir CHARLES WENTWORTH DILKE, M.P.
Illustrated. Sixth Edition. Crown 8vo. 6s.

AT LAST. A Christmas in the West Indies.
By the Rev. CHARLES KINGSLEY, M.A., Canon of Westminster. Illustrated. Fourth Edition. Crown 8vo. 6s.

THE MALAY ARCHIPELAGO.
The Land of the Orang Utan and the Bird of Paradise. By ALFRED
RUSSEL WALLACE, F.R.S. With Maps and Illustrations. Third Edition.
Crown 8vo. 7s. 6d.

**LADY DUFF GORDON'S LAST LETTERS FROM
EGYPT,**
To which are added Letters from the Cape. With a Memoir by her
DAUGHTER, and Portrait engraved by JEENS. Crown 8vo. 9s.

MACMILLAN & CO., LONDON.

BOOKS OF TRAVEL, &c.

THE RUSSIAN POWER.

By ASHTON W. DILKE. With Maps and numerous Illustrations. Two vols., 8vo. 32s.

A RAMBLE ROUND THE WORLD, 1871.

By M. LE BARON DE HUBNER, formerly Ambassador and Minister. Translated by Lady HERBERT. Two vols., 8vo. 25s.

TALES OF OLD JAPAN.

By A. B. MITFORD, Second Secretary to the British Legation in Japan. With Illustrations drawn and cut on Wood by Japanese Artists. New and Cheaper Edition. Crown 8vo. 6s.

SIX WEEKS IN THE SADDLE:

A Painter's Journal in Iceland. By S. E. WALLER. With Illustrations by the Author. Crown 8vo. 6s.

BY SEA AND BY LAND:

A Trip through Egypt, India, Ceylon, Australia, New Zealand, America —All Round the World. By HENRY A. MEREWETHER, one of Her Majesty's Counsel. Crown 8vo. 8s. 6d.

HOLIDAYS ON HIGH LANDS;

Or, Rambles and Incidents in Search of Alpine Plants. By the Rev. HUGH MACMILLAN. Second Edition, revised and enlarged. Globe 8vo. 6s.

MR. PISISTRATUS BROWN, M.P., IN THE HIGH-LANDS.

Reprinted, with additions, from the *Daily News*. With Illustrations. New Edition. Crown 8vo. 3s. 6d.

STATION LIFE IN NEW ZEALAND.

By Lady BARKER. Third and Cheaper Edition. Globe 8vo. 3s. 6d.

MACMILLAN & CO., LONDON.

Lightning Source UK Ltd.
Milton Keynes UK
UKHW030649150219
337397UK00005B/461/P